THE GREAT NOVA SCOTIA COOKBOOK

TRADITIONAL TRENDY BEST

PAULINE CARTER

NIMBUS
PUBLISHING LTD

Nimbus Publishing Limited
PO Box 9166
Halifax, NS   B3K 5M8
(902) 455-4286

Printed and bound in Canada

Canadian Cataloguing in Publication Data

Carter, Pauline, 1923-
        The great Nova Scotia cookbook: traditional,
        trendy and best recipes
        Includes index.

        ISBN 1-55109-346-4
1. Cookery, Canadian—Nova Scotia style. 2. Cookery—
Nova Scotia. I. Title.
TX715.6.C372 2001   641.59716   C2001-900487-7

We acknowledge the financial support of the Government of Canada
through the Book Publishing Industry Development Program (BPIDP)
and the Canada Council for our publishing activities.

To my mother, Gertrude Marion (Carmichael) Foster
(1891-1975), whose enthusiasm and love of cooking,
entertaining and recipe collecting planted
the seed for this book.

Acknowledgements

Our effort here is the work of a great many people…in fact some may not have fully realized their contributions at the time. And I want to say that I appreciate and value their help.

First, thanks to those cooks whose assistance and ideas as well as recipes went a long way to making *The Great Nova Scotia Cookbook* the fine piece of work it is:

Cathryn Biddulph
Dorothy Blythe
Christine Carter
Judy Kelly Carter
Lorraine Carter
Rose Carter
Sylvia Carter
Norma Collins
Jean Curtis

Elda Foster
Lilla Gilroy
Ruby Hatfield
Anne Hennigar
Beatrice Kennedy
Andrea Kolstee
Jean Kolstee
Diane McRae
Tara McRae

Margaret Matheson
Helene Maynard
Denise Mayo
Marion Melanson
Alana Murphy
Jean Taggart
Hilda Visser
Phyllis Ward
Florence Yuill

Finally, thanks to my family and Dorothy Blythe, Publisher and her staff at Nimbus Publishing Ltd., for their encouragement and patience as we worked to invent this book.

Contents

Introduction

Recipes are like stories—they change as they pass from hand to hand, generation to generation. The culinary trends of each new generation are influenced by various social and cultural factors: ethnic background, locale, personal style, family, community, and economics. But each generation also influences culinary trends in turn by adding its own tastes and favourite ingredients. For generations Nova Scotia cooking has involved a delicate balance between the traditional and the new, and from this approach have evolved recipes that are simply the best.

From the early days of European settlement to the present, immigrants have shaped Nova Scotia's culinary tradition. As early European settlers gained knowledge from the Mi'kmaq, plants and wild game native to the province became readily accepted as standard fare. Historically the majority of Nova Scotia's population followed the cooking traditions of England, Scotland, Ireland, and English-speaking North American colonies, particularly New England. In the 1770s and 1780s the American colonial influences became even stronger as the large influx of British Loyalists, which also included a large group of Black immigrants, sought refuge and became permanently established in the province as a result of the American Revolution. The original German, Swiss, and French colonists of Nova Scotia's South Shore contributed many of their own ethnic trends to the cuisine. And the French-speaking Acadian people of Nova Scotia managed to retain their own distinct cooking style despite living in a predominantly English-speaking culture. For those seeking a sourcebook of heritage recipes, *Out of Old Nova Scotia Kitchens* by Marie Nightingale provides a varied collection of traditional recipes together with descriptive narratives of the founding peoples of the province.

Apart from the various cultural influences shaping Nova Scotian cooking, there were geographical and economic factors as well. Although it covers a relatively small physical area, Nova Scotia possesses a varied landscape that has had an impact on regional eating habits. In the past, fresh fish from the Atlantic Ocean was common fare in coastal regions, and fresh lake and river species of fish were more the norm in the interior. Salted, dried, pickled, and smoked fish were common in all areas of the province. The quality of agricultural land and climactic conditions have shaped food preparation in Nova Scotia as well. The extended growing season in the bountiful and fertile Annapolis Valley has always supplied a much wider array of produce than other areas of the province. Generally, the northern and central areas of the province were largely agricultural, whereas the South Shore and many coastal areas were far more dependent on the fisheries or a mixture of farming and fishing.

Economic conditions in Nova Scotia have also been a major factor in the shaping of local cuisine. Nova Scotians have enjoyed periods of prosperity as well as years of financial hardship. Local cooks learned the art of dealing with adversities quickly—as long as there were a few food staples in the house, thrifty Nova Scotians could make a hearty and delicious meal. Many recipes using the simplest ingredients have become our most cherished.

Both my grandmother and mother witnessed bountiful meals that signalled times that were, for the most part, prosperous. Living most of their lives in the country, they were part of self-sufficient communities, where families, friends, and strangers gathered to share baskets of food brought to mark a special event. Whether it was a ship launching, church fair, or school picnic, food often competed with the social aspects of the gathering as the focus of attention. Early in her life, my paternal grandmother experienced Nova Scotia's celebrated golden age—the industrious late-nineteenth, early twentieth century era of shipping and shipbuilding. Indeed much of the developed world revolved around these industries and Nova Scotia was a major player in them. Together with its two maritime neighbours, New Brunswick and Prince Edward Island, Nova Scotia owned the fourth largest sailing fleet in the world. From Nova Scotia's early sea-going days, non-perishables like dried fruit, spices, rum, cocoa, coffee, sugar, and molasses, mostly from the warmer climates of the United States and the Caribbean Islands, supplemented the food produced in-province. A brisk trade carried out largely by Nova Scotian import businesses supplied these exotic delights in exchange for dried salted fish and local produce and products.

Tea, coffee, cocoa, spices and other commodities were imported from many parts of the world. John Tobin & Company of Halifax was one such importer and wholesale grocer. Among the array of commodities offered for sale were evaporated and dried fruits from South Africa; canned peaches and pears from Australia; marmalade, jams, and other manufactured goods from Great Britain; onions from Egypt; pineapples from Hawaii; coffee from Brazil, Java, and Arabia; cloves and spices from Singapore; figs from Turkey; rice from China and Siam; teas from India, Ceylon, and Formosa; raisins from Australia; caviar from Russia; sardines from Norway and France; nuts from Brazil, Sicily, Spain, and Italy; cheese from Holland; cream of tartar and fine table specialities from France. In the late nineteenth and early twentieth centuries, these imported commodities remained, to a great extent, the only foreign influence directly affecting the province's cuisine. The perishable nature of many foods (especially fresh tropical fruits) had much to do with this fact—the technology to refrigerate and ship large quantities of perishable fresh foreign produce to local markets was simply lacking. Improved preservation methods and more efficient shipping would add some new food choices.

In the 1940s Halifax could boast a number of Chinese restaurants, but the ethnic Chinese selections on the menus were limited to only a few items. Within several decades the resistance to foreign fare dissipated, giving rise to the popularity of Chinese and other oriental cuisines. In the 1950s and 1960s, a significant population of Dutch and German farmers immigrated to Nova Scotia and their influence can be seen on the local culinary landscape—German-style prepared meats, Dutch Gouda cheese and rye breads, for example.

Cooking schools and even home science courses were unknown luxuries for many rural Nova Scotians until the 1950s unless they attended special schools in the towns and cities. It was urban areas such as Halifax and Truro that could boast schools of domestic science in the early 1900s. The Halifax school produced a small cookbook featuring a variety of recipes typical of the era. The Truro School of Domestic Science had an enrollment of four hundred students in 1902. During the nineteenth and early twentieth centuries, Nova Scotian publishers produced several cookbooks, all of which had an impact on local cuisine.

In addition to cookbooks, newspapers and magazines of the Victorian and Edwardian eras provided additional inspiration for local cooks. American magazines were widely available, as were British and Canadian editions. However, the recipes and methods of food preparation featured in these publications seldom ventured far from the norms of the British and American cooking styles of those eras. Occasionally a hint of French-style cooking would be featured, but that was usually the extent of the adventurousness.

In more recent decades, Nova Scotians have embraced an even more varied range of things to eat, adopting many kinds of food into their daily diets. Garlic, curry, pasta, oriental noodles, eggrolls, burritos, tacos, along with a variety of exotic fruits and vegetables, oils, and sauces can now be found in the larder beside locally grown fruits, vegetables, bread, butter, fish, eggs, and dairy products.

Today, the array of ethnic-style restaurants, speciality food stores and delicatessens in Halifax is a testament to the growing interest in foreign foods. Chinese, Japanese, Korean, Vietnamese, African, Italian, East Indian, West Indian, Mexican, Cajun, Turkish, Greek, Lebanese, Scandinavian, French, Dutch, and German food have tempted our palates in recent years.

For some time now we have had a tendency to malign some of our traditional foods in favour of food that is more trendy, exotic, or easier to prepare. Much of this problem stems from the cooking methods as opposed to types of food used. The unhealthy fashion of frying foods in saturated (animal) fats was all too common in days gone by. Our methods of food preparation have changed dramatically—as informed cooks, we can now prepare traditional foods in a healthier way.

Several individuals have contributed to my keen interest in and knowledge of cooking. As a child, I didn't have to pull a lot of apron strings to persuade my mother to allow me to help in preparing whatever recipe she had on the go. She eagerly responded to my interest by frequently allowing me to be involved in her cooking tasks—especially baking. I recall with great delight making cookies and arranging them on a pan and my mother placing the pan in the oven of the monstrous black and chrome Home Comfort range. The wonderful mixture of wood fire and the aroma of baking remains a vivid memory.

My childhood home was in Princeport, a tiny community on the eastern side of the Shubenacadie River in Colchester County, Nova Scotia. My mother was an exceptionally good cook and undoubtedly many of her culinary skills, her resourcefulness, and her passion for cooking have been passed down to me. In fact, many traditional-style recipes in this book were my mother's favourites. Her approach to cooking was by all accounts typical of Nova Scotians for the time.

My mother, Gertrude (Carmicheal) Foster, was born in Margaree, Inverness County, Cape Breton. When she was ten years old her mother passed away, cutting short her childhood and changing her life completely. In the short time that she shared with her mother she had learned the art of making bread. She also learned, with the aid of her older sisters, to prepare special healing food for her ailing mother. She cherished the memories of going to the mountainside to pick berries and of her mother preparing salmon caught by her father in the nearby Margaree River. After her mother's death, the family left the pastoral setting of the Margaree Valley and relocated to Glace Bay, Cape Breton. The region was then in its industrial heyday—a thriving centre for coal mining, steel making, and trans-Atlantic communications. Her father worked as a salesman for a cutlery firm and was also employed as a railcar inspector for the coal company. To supplement the family's income, they took boarders into their company-owned home. As the only child remaining at home, my mother was required to prepare the meals. This she did while going to school. Apparently she took this responsibility in stride for never once did I hear her complain about it. From my mother's perspective—even at a young age—cooking was an art to be enjoyed rather than an arduous chore. After working in a bookstore for some time, she left Cape Breton for the "Boston states." While in Boston she lived with an aunt who introduced her to an affluent world full of new and more sophisticated foods and presentation. There, she secured a job at the well-known Walter Baker Chocolate Factory. As much of her early life revolved around food, it is little wonder that she would later instill a special love for food in her family and friends.

My mother returned to Nova Scotia in 1912 to marry a handsome young man from Princeport, Colchester County. She would gain even further knowledge from a renowned local cook—her mother-in-law, Ellen (Phillips) Foster. The two women seldom saw eye to eye, but when it came to cooking, all knowledge was shared liberally. Such was the case with the Christmas plum pudding—my grandmother's recipe—as well as other culinary treasures that have remained in our family to this day. Upon starting married life, my mother entered a well-equipped kitchen and a well-stocked pantry. Unlike many rural homes in her community at that time, my mother's kitchen had both hot and cold running water and a large ice chest for refrigeration.

In those days, a farm, if not the mainstay of a family income, at least supplied a family with milk, fruit, vegetables, eggs, and meat. Each spring, gaspereaux, shad, bass, and salmon could be caught in the Shubenacadie River. Small rivers like the Stewiacke River where locals would gather for the annual "smelt-run" were popular for spring-time fishing. Lakes and small freshwater streams offered an abundant supply of trout. Maple trees on the property delivered pails of sap for maple syrup each spring. An orchard with many varieties of apples provided a constant supply of the flavourful fruit throughout the fall and winter. The fruits and vegetables of the autumn harvest were preserved by various methods for the long winters, and my father devised his own smoke system to cure delicious hams. This resourcefulness and near self-sufficiency was a way of life for many rural Nova Scotians. My mother accepted all of these blessings with great enthusiasm and settled into her new role. In time she became a mother of three children—two daughters and a son. A born entertainer, she and my quiet but affable father would host parties and dances in our home. My mother always reached an emotional high point when preparing for these occasions. Many women would be in a frantic state under similar circumstances, but my mother would remain calm, maintaining a total state of control while producing copious amounts of food for their guests.

My mother and grandmother both lived through two world wars and the great depression of the 1930s. As with all cooks of this era they learned to be more frugal—substitutions and the outright omission of ingredients were often the norm. The war years were particularly difficult; food rationing was legislated and inflation was high. I recall my mother relating an event following World War One. Having a low supply of her own farm eggs for Christmas baking, she went to a neighbour to buy eggs. She was shocked to find that the price of eggs had risen to $1.00 for a half-dozen, which in 1917 represented a great deal of money. Faced with having either to go without her Christmas goodies or pay dearly for the commodity, she opted for the latter. She said that she couldn't possibly celebrate Christmas without the baking. I also recall her telling me about the whole-grained flour that was the substitute for the banned white flour during World War One. The white flour was reserved for the troops overseas. The whole-grained blend made the loaves of bread very heavy, but as a healthy alternative it was perhaps a blessing in disguise. The depression years were very difficult in terms of food supply for many Nova Scotians. However, for those living on self-sufficient family farms, the food supply was less of a challenge. It is interesting to note that during this period, Nova Scotia, along with the two other Maritime provinces, displayed their generosity despite their own difficulties by sending supplies of fish and other foodstuffs to the drought-stricken West. The years of World War Two saw the government enforcement of food rationing. The sale of butter and sugar were under strict control, so molasses was commonly substituted for sugar. The War Cake recipe gained popularity during that time.

During the early years of my mother and father's marriage, my father was a highway foreman. Occasionally when the distance was too far or difficult to travel by either horse and buggy or the Model T on a daily basis, my father would find accommodation at Mary Sandeson's boarding house in Truro. He always enjoyed her supper dish of potato scallop. He learned that the dish was made from cold, sliced, pre-cooked potatoes, onion, breadcrumbs, and milk. My mother immediately adopted the recipe, naming it "Mary Sandeson" and following this, we often had "Mary Sandeson" for supper. In the 1920s my father worked as a carpenter at the Mersey Paper Mill in Liverpool, Queens County. My father was introduced to a popular South Shore recipe called "House Bankin" by the locals or as "Dutch Mess" by people outside the area. My mother couldn't rest until my father brought back the recipe, which was a simple one: salt cod, potatoes, pork scraps, onion, and a lot of butter.

While my father was still working in Liverpool in the late 1920s he decided to send a cooked lobster to our home in Princeport. He asked a friend who happened to be returning home to deliver the neatly wrapped delicacy. Being quite young, and "an in-lander," I had never seen such a creature, let alone sampled one. Being completely unaware, my mother picked up the mail and became quite excited when she saw the unexpected package. With tingling fingers she hastily removed the layers of wrapping paper and a portion of the red, leggy creature came into view. Not fully realizing the contents, she screamed in horror. We were all startled and speechless. Eventually she regained her composure and bravely examined the contents of the package more closely, finally realizing what it was. We all ate the lobster with great delight.

In the 1930s my mother became acquainted with a kind and neighbourly Scottish lady who worked at the nearby Beach Hill Farm. Their common interest in cooking and sharing recipes developed into a friendship. Being of Scottish descent and a having a sweet tooth, my mother was delighted to receive Mrs. Wilson's shortcake recipe (shortbread). Following the recipe closely, my mother packed the dough in a pan and then cut it in squares. The same recipe appears in this book.

Mom was the "mad recipe collector"—she collected cookbooks, robbed all magazines of their cooking sections, collected recipes from friends and neighbours near and far, often reinventing and adapting them to her own tastes. Once a recipe was perfected, she would share it in turn with her friends. The process of housing this collection became challenging as the years rolled on. Thankfully she had a large pantry. Once the drawers and shelves were overridden with her culinary treasures, extra hooks were placed on the walls to hold the bulging files. The more ancient material found a safe haven in the attic. My mother's vast recipe collection posed absolutely no access or retrieval problem to her. No need for library classification or indexing—she could lay her finger on any one of her recipes at any given time.

I can recall one shopping trip to Truro, where she met a salesman for Egg-O Baking Powder at the L.A. Ryan Grocery Store on Inglis Street. It was highly unlikely that the salesman had to apply any high-pressure sales techniques to a would-be customer like my mother, for she was always eager to try new products. She returned home not only with the baking powder, but also with a complimentary recipe for chocolate cake. The following day, to no one's surprise, she was in the pantry beating a batter vigorously—lovingly placing the batter in a large pan (she had doubled the recipe). That evening she proudly presented her latest creative confection, beautifully frosted, light textured, rich in colour—a delight to the eye as well as the taste buds. The recipe unfortunately did not survive and I often wonder what happened to Egg-O Baking Powder.

Years would pass by and things changed for my mother. Her children reached maturity and left home and my dear father died suddenly. Eventually my mother sold the farm and came to live with me—by this time I was married with a family. Along with my mother came the collection of recipes. Reluctantly the collection was stored in boxes and packages and removed from the old farmhouse. In the process of moving, my mother lost interest in the collection, its purpose turning to a faded memory.

At some point after moving she apparently decided that she could not deal with the extra baggage, especially while living in someone else's house. With tears in her eyes, I saw her with a bundle of papers in her arms feeding pages into the open flames of the wood-fired range. I realised much too late what she was doing—she had burned much of her collection of recipes. Saddened by this event I could only ask, why? Much of a lifetime of collecting recipes had been lost, for reasons I would never fully understand.

My mother passed away many years ago. Luckily her collection was not lost entirely. Together with my memories of her, the surviving recipes provided a major source of inspiration for this book. The fondest thoughts of my mother and those bygone years return quickly when I remove a pan of date-filled cookies from the oven or when a dab of hard sauce is served with the ancient Christmas pudding, just as my grandmother served it so many years ago. Like my dear mother, I too became an avid recipe collector. Lacking my mother's organizational skills, however, my collection has ended up in boxes or canisters—a chaotic jumble of recipes successful, failed, and untried.

Another among the contributors to this book and an influence on my approach to cooking is my late mother-in-law Eleanor (Nellie) Carter. Anyone who knew this lady will confirm that she never used a written recipe. An innate knowledge of cooking and a hand that seemed to have invisible if not magical measuring powers were her tools. Her hand shaped in a certain manner held a cup or other units of measure. Her thumb and finger possessed the same ability: a large pinch of this and a small pinch of that. Liquid measures were a cinch—she just held the pitcher over the mixing bowl and let the exact amount flow in. Only if a drop or two were needed did she become a little bit more cautious.

For the greater part of her life Nellie enjoyed baking with a wood-fired Enterprise range. To make biscuits she would pack an armful of wood into the firebox, all air drafts fully opened, the already hot coals turning the wood to flames. Quite often, the intense heat would cause the stove top to glow a fiery red. A concerned family member or guest would often draw this to Nellie's attention. With her face glowing from the heat, she would exclaim, "You know, I'm making biscuits!" Within moments she would appear from the pantry with a huge pan of neatly arranged rounds of dough. After the biscuits had baked she would take them to the kitchen table where she turned them out on a cloth. Like clockwork she would return to the pantry, quickly place another pan in the oven, and add more wood to the still-raging fire. Her hungry family and any number of frequent guests were always happy to partake. Nellie Carter's cooking ability also extended to baking muffins, pies, cakes, and cookies. She was unequalled in the preparation of venison and fish. Cooking was indeed her special art. To learn a recipe from Nellie Carter you would have to be a very close observer and a skilled note taker. Unfortunately none of her recipes were ever recorded. What I would give today to know the recipe for her renowned biscuits!

Another person who has greatly influenced my cooking interests was my sister, Ruby (Foster-Drake) Hatfield. Ten years my senior, her cooking skills were well developed by the time I reached my teen years. When I was a child, her fudge-making ability occasionally warranted some amount of bribery for a taste. Living with my sister and her family while attending high school and the Normal College in Truro, I learned much from her mastery of cooking. Her first husband Barry Drake operated a wholesale fruit and vegetable business and his top-quality produce provided feasts fit for royalty. He too took special delight in preparing a meal. Ruby's baked goods, especially the doughnuts, were simply the best I have ever tasted. I will never forget the surprise bridal shower she held for me when I was married. The baking and the presentation for the occasion were unbelievable and accomplished all on her own. As a mother of four, her patience was more than occasionally tested. I remember one Christmas when the Christmas tree was upset three times all while she managed to complete the holiday baking. She set a wonderful example for me, indeed.

One special experience with which many country folks of my generation are familiar is that of the cookhouses and the large farmhouse kitchens that served hungry crews employed in farming and lumbering. One such person having that particular experience is my sister-in-law Elda (Sandeson) Foster. As a cook she was required to prepare food for large work crews. A full range of cooking and baking was required daily—a routine that she took in stride. Eventually she and my brother moved to the Annapolis Valley, where she honed her skills in canning and preserving fruits and vegetables. A large number of her pickle recipes appear in this book.

In the early thirties, Nova Scotians were treated to their first locally produced fast-rising yeast. Older folk may remember the Liverpool-made "Best Yeast," a by-product of the Mersey Paper Mill in the Queens County town. This new product was accepted with great enthusiasm—it meant that the cooks would no longer have to mix their bread at night or, as some were accustomed, to make a "sponge" on the evening prior to bread-making day My aunt Mable MacKenzie was quite possibly the first person in Princeport to try the new product, which was advertised as being quick—instant in fact. One morning after her children left for school, she started her first batch of bread using the "Best Yeast." Feeling a little leery of the yeast, which was a soft and pasty substance, foil- wrapped in one-inch cubes, she followed the directions, carefully crumbling it into a dish containing slightly sweetened warm water. She placed it on the warming oven of her Enterprise wood range. While the yeast was dissolving, she attended to some housekeeping duties upstairs. These tasks she accomplished quickly, knowing that the yeast was fast. She no doubt wore a happy smile knowing that she was about to be blessed with this latest advance of science. The task of preparing bread the night before was to become a thing of the past. When my aunt descended the old creaky stairway and entered the kitchen she saw a sight that was almost unbelievable. The advertising was true to its word—the new product had risen quickly, so quickly that the bubbling creamy-white substance was running down over the warming oven, oozing onto the top and front of the stove and finally cascading onto a mat on the floor. She watched in disbelief as the bubbling mass grew and burst, and burst again and again. The family cat, suddenly surprised by the event, quickly turned the catastrophe into a golden opportunity by feasting on this scientific breakthrough. Needless to say, Mable spent the rest of the morning cleaning, something she hadn't planned to do. There would be no more time to make bread that morning. The joyous little bread-making chore turned out to be neither quick nor easy. After regaining her composure my aunt went to the old crank telephone and "rang-up" my mother, who enjoyed one of the greatest laughs of her lifetime.

And so history was made that morning. The old dry yeast cakes became a thing of the past and the quick yeast eventually took its place—not without problems, however. This new invention had to be refrigerated at the time when most country folk did not have refrigerators. As electricity came our way, the new yeast cakes found a cool place to await the cook's next batch of bread. Later we would be treated to another type of yeast—fast dry yeast. Only this time we were prepared—fast means fast!

The Great Nova Scotia Cookbook is a collection of favourite family recipes combined with contributions from individuals throughout the province. This book is not intended as a cursory approach to cooking nor is it an examination or a total representation of the cooking styles of Nova Scotia's diverse population. It is a sampling of at least four generations of good, basic, Nova Scotian cooking. You won't find an extravaganza of haute cuisine in this cookbook. You will find recipes that represent traditional favourites and newer additions together with some of the best Nova Scotia has to offer. *The Great Nova Scotia Cookbook* is a tribute to the many good Nova Scotian cooks who, over time, have helped to shape the course of the province's cooking. Celebrating Nova Scotian cooking, both old and new, and perpetuating the ritual of sharing recipes were the key concepts I had in mind when I took on the challenge of writing this book. I could see great value in sharing this culinary legacy with others to preserve a valuable part of our Nova Scotian heritage.

Pauline Carter
Pleasant Valley
April, 2001

The following designations have been assigned to all recipes in the book with the exception of the "Recipes for Kids" section. Recipes designated traditional refer to time-honoured favourites, while those in the trendy category are those that have become popular recently. In the case of the best category, the recipes have come highly recommended by an experienced cook.

The Great Nova Scotia Cookbook

• APPETIZERS •

• Best •

• Traditional •

• Trendy •

Mushroom Appetizer
Turnovers

For a special occasion.

1 8-oz pkg	cream cheese	250 g		½ tsp	salt	2 ml
				pinch	thyme	
⅓ cup	butter	75 ml		2 tbsp	flour	30 ml
1 cup	flour	250 ml		¼ cup	sour cream	50 ml
2 tbsp	margarine	30 ml		1	egg, beaten	1
1	medium onion, minced	1				
½ lb	fresh mushrooms chopped coarsely	225 g				

To make pastry, cream the cheese and butter together. Add flour and mix until smooth. Wrap pastry in waxed paper; chill for 1 hour. Sauté onions in margarine until translucent. Add mushrooms and cook until tender. Stir in salt, thyme, flour and sour cream. Cook until thickened. Cool completely.

Divide pastry in half and roll out on a floured board to ⅛-inch thickness. Cut into rounds with a 2¾-inch (7 cm) cookie cutter. Drop a small teaspoon of filling in the middle of each round. Brush edges with beaten egg, fold and seal. Cut slits on top to allow steam to escape during baking. Bake at 450F (230C) for 10-12 minutes. These turnovers freeze well. Makes 3½ dozen small turnovers.

Vegetable Pizza

1	large Pillsbury crescent roll	1		broccoli, finely chopped	
				cauliflower, finely chopped	
1 8-oz pkg	cream cheese	250 g		carrot, grated	
				green onion, finely chopped	
½ cup	Miracle Whip	125 ml		old Cheddar cheese, grated	
1 tsp	garlic powder	5 ml			
1 tsp	onion powder	5 ml			
½ tsp	dillweed	2 ml			

Unroll crescent roll onto a cookie sheet, flatten, and press seams together. Bake at 350F (180C) for 8-10 minutes and let cool. Mix next 5 ingredients together in food processor, then spread over baked crescent roll. Sprinkle with a mixture of vegetables and top with grated cheese. Press topping into cream cheese mixture.

Crabmeat Pizza

1 8-oz pkg	cream cheese	250 g	1 8-oz can	crabmeat	250 g
	garlic, to taste			seafood or chili sauce	
	Tabasco sauce, to taste			parsley, fresh or dried	
	lemon juice, to taste				

Place cream cheese, garlic, Tabasco sauce and lemon juice in food processor and blend. Spread mixture on plate, to resemble pizza dough. Spread seafood sauce or chili sauce over top. Arrange well-drained crabmeat on top, and sprinkle with fresh or dried parsley.

Grilled Hoisin Shrimp Appetizer

1 lb	extra large, shrimp, peeled and deveined	500 g

Dipping Sauce:

¼ cup	Hoisin sauce	50 ml	1 tbsp	garlic, minced	15 ml
2 tbsp	fresh coriander, chopped	30 ml	2 tsp	wine vinegar	10 ml
			¼ tsp	hot pepper sauce	1 ml
1 tbsp	ginger, minced	15 ml			

Place shrimp on greased grill over medium heat; cook for 3-5 minutes or until opaque. They may also be placed on broiler pan 4-6 inches (10-15 cm) from heat and broiled for 3-5 minutes. Mix all sauce ingredients in a bowl, and serve with hot shrimp. Makes 30-40 appetizers.

Mussel Appetizers

Don't throw away all the shells!

2 lb	mussels	1 kg	2 tbsp	lemon juice	30 ml
⅔ cup	sweet red pepper, diced	150 g	1 tbsp	olive oil	15 ml
			1 tbsp	ginger, minced	15 ml
¼ cup	green onion, minced	50 ml		salt and pepper	
2 cloves	garlic, minced	2	dash	hot pepper sauce	
4 tbsp	parsley	60 ml			

Scrub mussels and remove any beards; discard mussels that do not close when tapped. Place in a large heavy pot over medium heat; pour in ½ cup (125 ml) water, cover and cook, shaking pan occasionally to redistribute, for about 5 minutes until mussels open. Drain and cool. Discard any mussels that have not opened. Remove mussels from shells, reserving half the shells. In a bowl, stir together red pepper, onion, garlic, parsley, lemon juice, ginger, oil, salt, pepper and hot pepper sauce. Add mussels and toss to coat. Refrigerate for 30 minutes or longer. Arrange reserved shells on platter; fill each with mussels and some of the marinade. Makes 50 or 60 appetizers.

Stuffed Mushrooms

Tasty little morsels.

1 ½ lb	mushrooms, with 1-inch caps	750g		1 tsp	sugar	5 ml
				dash	Tabasco sauce	
1 lb	fresh Italian sausage	500 g		1 cup	bread crumbs, fine and dry	250 ml
1	onion, minced	1				
3 lg	garlic cloves, minced	3			enough sherry, white wine or chicken stock to make a paste	
½ tsp	fennel seed, crushed	2 ml				
2 tsp	red chili powder	10 ml				
1 tsp	salt	5 ml				

Remove and chop stalks from the mushrooms. Reserve the caps. Sauté the stalks in a few tablespoons of butter until tender. Set aside. In a heavy frying pan, gently brown sausage, then sauté next 7 ingredients until onion is transparent. Blend in bread crumbs, chopped mushroom stalks, and sherry. Fill the reserved mushroom caps with stuffing. Dip the stuffed mushrooms quickly in hot, melted butter and drain. Refrigerate until ready to serve. Let them come to room temperature, then put them in a hot oven for a couple of minutes until they begin to sizzle. Serve immediately.

Easy Stuffed Mushrooms

30-36	medium-size mushrooms, caps removed and stems chopped	30-36		1 cup	onion, minced	250 ml
				1 cup	Parmesan cheese, grated	250 ml
1 lb	fresh sausage (hot or sweet), chopped	500 g			kale greens, for garnish	
¾ cup	breadcrumbs	175 ml				

Place caps bottom-side-up on a baking pan. Mix remaining ingredients together, including the chopped stems. Place mound of sausage mixture in each cap. These can be prepared a day in advance and refrigerated. Just prior to serving, bake at 350F (175C) for 30-40 minutes. Place caps on a tray or platter garnished with kale greens.

Mini Sausage Appetizers

2 lb	lean ground pork	1.4 kg		1 cup	breadcrumbs	250 ml
2 tbsp	butter	30 ml		½ tsp each	lemon thyme, sage, ginger, salt, pepper and dry mustard	2 ml
1 cup	onion, finely chopped	250 ml				
½ cup	parsley, finely chopped	125 ml		¼ cup	chicken stock	50 ml

Melt butter in fry pan; add onion and parsley. Cook until onion is transparent. Remove from heat, stir in breadcrumbs and seasonings. Place pork in food processor. Process until pork is finely ground. Add breadcrumb mixture and chicken stock. Mix well.

Roll into balls. Allow to stand for 30 minutes. Place on greased baking sheet and bake until nicely browned and cooked through. Serve with honey mustard.

These may be frozen before cooking. If so, roll each ball in flour and store in single layers in shallow, covered dishes.

Deviled Eggs

An old favourite!

12	eggs, at room temperature		½ tsp	ground white pepper	2 ml
1 tbsp	onion, minced	15 ml	dash	salt to taste	
1 tbsp	celery, minced, or celery salt (½ tsp, or 2 ml)	15 ml	dash	Tabasco sauce	
¼ cup	mayonnaise or sour cream	50 ml			

Gently lower eggs into a pot of boiling water. Return to boil and boil gently for 12-15 minutes. Drain and immediately cover with cold water. When eggs are cool, peel, cut in half lengthwise with a very sharp knife and remove yolks. Reserve whites. Put yolks in a small bowl and add all remaining ingredients, mixing well. Fill reserved whites with this mixture. Garnish with a few specks of paprika, or one of the following: chopped capers, a few drops of hot chili sauce, a small bit of caviar, chopped black olives, chopped red pimento, grind of black pepper or slice of pickled green chili pepper. Chill well and serve.

Smoked Salmon Tartar

6 oz	smoked salmon, finely diced	168 g	1 tbsp	parsley, chopped	15 ml
			1	egg, hard-boiled	1
4 tbsp	gherkins in vinegar, minced	60 ml	2 tbsp	vinaigrette	30 ml
				salt and fresh ground pepper	
¼ cup	red onion, minced	50 ml	4 slices	whole grain bread	4

Combine salmon, gherkins, red onion and parsley in mixing bowl. Sieve hard-boiled egg through a strainer into the bowl. Toss all with vinaigrette and season with salt and pepper. Toast bread, and divide salmon tartar among the four slices. Trim crusts off bread and cut slices diagonally from point to point. Serve at room temperature, or chill until serving time.

Stuffed Clams

	rock salt	
1½ cup	clams, chopped, fresh or canned	375 ml
1 cup	breadcrumbs	250 ml
⅓ cup	parsley, minced	75 ml
½ tsp	dried oregano, crumbled	2 ml

2 cloves	garlic, minced	2
2 tbsp	olive oil	30 ml
½ cup	Parmesan cheese, finely grated	125 ml
	salt, to taste	

Preheat oven to 400F (205C). Put 1 inch of rock salt in a shallow pan large enough to hold the clam shells, which have been washed and dried. Set pan in oven to warm. If using canned clams, drain them and reserve juice. Combine clams, 2 tbsp (30 ml) reserved clam juice (if available), ¾ cup (175 ml) breadcrumbs, 3 tbsp (45 ml) parsley, oregano, garlic, olive oil, salt and 5 tbsp (75 ml) cheese. Toss together lightly, and spoon a small amount of the mixture into each shell.

Mix the remaining 2 tbsp (30 ml) of parsley, 3 tbsp (45 ml) of cheese, and remaining breadcrumbs and sprinkle a little on each shell. Set the shells on the bed of rock salt or crumpled foil and bake for 6-7 minutes until the crumbs are lightly browned.

Oysters in Bacon

24	oysters, shucked and patted dry	24

12 slices	bacon, cut in half	12

Preheat oven to 425F (220C). Wrap each oyster in a piece of bacon. Arrange the wrapped oysters, with bacon ends down, on a rack in a shallow pan. Bake only until bacon is slightly browned. Drain on paper towels.

Roll-Ups

Trim crust from 24 slices of bread. Flatten with rolling pin to ¼ inch (0.5 cm) thickness. Place 1 heaping tbsp (15 ml) filling along one end of bread. Roll up, cut in half, and place on baking sheet. Brush with butter; sprinkle with minced parsley before baking. Bake at 350F (180C) for 15 minutes until golden. Serve warm.

Bacon and almond filling:
Mix 6 cooked bacon strips, crumbled, and ⅓ cup (75 ml) each Miracle Whip salad dressing, slivered toasted almonds and finely grated Swiss cheese. Add 1 chopped green onion. Makes 48.

Salmon and dill filling:
Mix together one 7½-oz can (235 g) of sockeye salmon, drained and mashed, ¼ cup (50 ml) Miracle Whip salad dressing, 1 tbsp (15 ml) each fresh dillweed and lemon juice. Makes 48.

Dilled Smoked Salmon Appetizers

A great way to serve smoked salmon.

4 slices	smoked salmon	4	⅓ cup	Renee's Gourmet Cucumber Dill Dressing	75 ml
8 slices	cucumber, thin	8			
8 slices	pumpernickel bread, cut in cocktail size pieces	8	8	dill sprigs, fresh	8

Cut salmon slices in half and roll up like a jelly roll. Place a slice of cucumber on top of each slice of pumpernickel bread. Top with cucumber-dill dressing, and tiny pieces of rolled salmon. Decorate with sprigs of dill.

Smoked Salmon Canapés

As tasty as they are simple.

Serve thin slices of smoked salmon on dark bread, toast, or crackers; dust with freshly ground pepper and lemon juice, and garnish with any combination of hard-boiled egg, chopped onion, parsley, lemon or capers.

Curried Seafood Filling

1 7-oz can	crab or shrimp	220 g	3 tbsp	green onion, chopped	45 ml
⅓ cup	mayonnaise	75 ml	12 small	cream puff shells	12
½ tsp	curry powder	2 ml			

Mix all ingredients together. Fill cream puff shells that have been cut in half. Replace tops. Heat before serving.

Spinach and Ricotta Filling

1 cup	spinach, cooked and drained	250 ml		salt, to taste	
				pepper, to taste	
½ cup	ricotta cheese	125 ml	⅛ tsp	nutmeg, if desired	0.5 ml
2	eggs	2	24	tarts shells	24
1	egg yolk, lightly beaten	1			

Mix all ingredients and pour into tart shells. Bake 20 minutes at 350F (175C). Makes 24.

Ham and Cheese Filling

2 tsp	prepared mustard, sharp	10 ml		½ cup	milk or cream	125 ml
				2	eggs, slightly beaten	2
2 oz	ham, chopped	60 g			salt and pepper	
¾ cup	Swiss cheese, grated	175 ml		24	tarts shells	24

Brush the inside bottoms of tart shells with mustard and divide the ham among them. Mix remaining ingredients, pour into shells, and bake 20 minutes at 350F (175C). Makes 24.

Roasted Potato Wedges

2 lb	new russet potatoes	1 kg		2 cloves	garlic, minced	2
					salt and pepper	
3 tbsp	olive oil	45 ml				

Cut potatoes into halves or wedges. Toss with olive oil, garlic, salt and pepper. Place on baking sheet and bake at 350F (175C) for 20-30 minutes. They should be very crispy on the outside and soft on the inside. These are great with sour cream dips, and ranch or blue cheese dressings.

Rosemary, Lemon &
Garlic Buffalo Wings

These fit that old phrase, "finger-lickin' good."

3-4	chicken wings per person	3-4		1 tsp	salt	5 ml
				1 tsp	pepper	5 ml
For each lb of chicken:				3 tbsp	oil	45 ml
2 tbsp	fresh rosemary	30 ml			rosemary sprigs and lemon wedges, for garnish, barbecue sauce and ranch dressing	
1 clove	garlic, minced	1				
2 tbsp	lemon zest	30 ml				

Toss all ingredients together and place on baking sheet. Bake for 30-35 minutes at 350F (175C) until crispy and golden. Garnish with sprigs of rosemary and lemon wedges. Serve plain or with a barbecue sauce or ranch dressing.

Cheese Ball

This will disappear in a jiffy.

1 8-oz pkg	cream cheese	250 ml		2 tbsp	mayonnaise	30 ml
				1 tsp	Worcestershire sauce	5 ml
1½ cups	sharp cheese, grated	375 ml		½ cup	walnuts, finely chopped	125 ml
½ cup	dill pickle, chopped	125 ml		2 tbsp	parsley, chopped	30 ml
¼ cup	green onion, chopped	50 ml				

Mix all ingredients except walnuts and parsley. Cover mixture and chill in fridge overnight. Shape into ball and roll in a mixture of walnuts and parsley. Serve with a variety of crackers.

Chicken and Cheese Ball

1 8-oz pkg	cream cheese	250 g	1 6½-oz can	turkey or chicken, flaked	200 g
3 cups	Cheddar cheese, grated	750 g	dash	Worcestershire sauce	
¼ cup	sour cream	50 ml	dash	Tabasco sauce	
¼ cup	green onion, chopped	50 ml	1 tsp	garlic	5 ml
				parsley or nuts, chopped	

Blend all ingredients except nuts and parsley in food processor. Form into a ball. Roll in finely chopped nuts or parsley. Serve with a variety of crackers.

Ham and Cheese Ball

1 8-oz pkg	cream cheese	250 g	1 6½-oz can	Flakes of Ham	200 g
1½ cups	Cheddar cheese, shredded	375 ml	dash	Worcestershire sauce	
			dash	Tabasco sauce	
¼ cup	mayonnaise	50 ml	¼ tsp	dry mustard	1 ml
1 tbsp	onion, chopped	15 ml		parsley or nuts, chopped	

Combine ingredients in blender until smooth. Form into a ball, and roll in finely chopped nuts or parsley. Serve with a variety of crackers.

Coconut Fruit Dip

1 8-oz can	crushed pineapple, undrained	227 g	½ cup	non-fat sour cream	125 ml
¾ cup	skim milk	175 ml	1 3-oz pkg	instant coconut cream pudding mix	90 g

Combine all ingredients in blender. Cover and blend for 1 minute or until smooth. Serve with fruit such as: melon slices, strawberries, grapes, fresh pineapple, etc.

Fresh Fruit Dip

2 cups	whipped topping, frozen	500 ml	4 tbsp	sugar	60 ml
			3 oz	pecans, chopped	90 g
1 8-oz pkg	cream cheese	250 g	3 tbsp	crushed pineapple, drained (optional)	45 ml
4 tbsp	mayonnaise	60 ml			
2 tbsp	lemon juice	30 ml			

Combine all ingredients in blender until smooth. Serve chilled with an assortment of fresh fruit.

Nutty Cheese Spread

1 cup	old Cheddar cheese, grated	250 g	2 tsp	parsley flakes	10 ml
			2 tsp	onion flakes	10 ml
⅔ cup	walnuts, chopped	150 ml	½ cup	mayonnaise	125 ml

Combine all ingredients in blender until smooth. Serve with an assortment of crackers.

The Great Nova Scotia Cookbook

Cuisine Log

1 8-oz pkg	cream cheese, softened	250 g	1	green onion, finely sliced	1
½ lb	variety deli meat or grated sausage	250 g		freshly ground pepper	
				parsley, chopped	
1 tsp	horseradish	5 ml		ground nuts	
1 tbsp	lemon juice	15 ml			

Combine first six ingredients. Shape into a log. Wrap in plastic wrap and refrigerate. Before serving, roll in chopped parsley and/or nuts. Serve with an assortment of crackers.

Salmon Pâté

Salmon lovers, this one's for you!

½ cup	butter	125 ml	3 tbsp	Hellman's mayonnaise	45 ml
2 6½-oz cans	sockeye salmon, drained	2	½ tsp	prepared mustard	2 ml
2 tsp	lemon juice	10 ml	1 8-oz pkg	cream cheese	250 g
pinch	dillweed				
1 tbsp	chives, chopped	15 ml		salt, if desired	

Melt butter. Remove skin and bones from salmon. Place butter, salmon, lemon juice, chives, cream cheese (cut in pieces), mayonnaise, mustard and dill in blender. Process until smooth. Pour into a bowl and chill. Serve with assorted crackers or squares of dark bread.

Guacamole (Avocado Spread)

Here is a good, basic recipe for guacamole; experiment to develop your own version.

In a glass or stainless steel bowl, mix together:

2-3 cups	avocado	500-750 ml	juice	of one lemon or two limes	
⅓ cup	chili sauce	75 ml			
3 cloves	garlic, minced	3	3 tsp	dry leaf oregano	15 ml
½ cup	medium onion, finely chopped	125 ml	1 tsp	cumin seed, freshly crushed	5 ml
				salt and pepper	

Mix all ingredients together until smooth. Sprinkle a little more lemon or lime juice over the top to keep mixture from darkening, and let mellow for an hour or two. Serve with corn chips.

Smoked Mackerel Dip

The distinctive flavour of smoked fish makes a sharp, tasty dip.

2	medium smoked mackerel fillets	2	juice	of ½ lemon	
				black pepper	
5 oz	sour cream	150 g	dash	Tabasco sauce	
4 oz	cottage cheese	125 g			

Skin the mackerel and break into pieces. Blend all ingredients until smooth. Spoon the mixture into a bowl and refrigerate for a few hours. Garnish with sliced black olives, lemon wedges and parsley. Serve with crackers or toast.

Homemade Melba Toast

An old-fashioned way to use leftover bread.

Slice bread very thinly—about ⅛-inch (0.5 cm). Crusts may be removed if desired. Spread bread out on a cookie sheet and place in very slow oven 250-300F (120-150C) until bread is very dry and crisp. Toast should be light brown. Serve with butter, cheese or most dips. If desired, rounds can be cut out of bread slices. Use a sharp cookie cutter. Round shapes do not crack or break up quite as easily as square shapes.

Melbas and Crabmeat Dip

1 8-oz pkg	cream cheese	250 g	2 cups	Mozzarella cheese, shredded	500 ml
½ cup	Hellman's cucumber or garlic mayonnaise	125 ml	1	green pepper, chopped	1
¼ cup	yogurt	50 ml	1	tomato, chopped	1
1 cup	seafood cocktail sauce	250 ml	3	green onions, chopped	3
1 8-oz can	crabmeat	250 g		melba toast squares or rounds	

Mix cream cheese, mayonnaise and yogurt together until smooth. Spread over a 12-inch (30 cm) plate. Top with seafood sauce and a layer of Mozzarella cheese. Crumble crabmeat over cheese. Combine pepper, tomato and green onions and arrange attractively over all. Cover and chill until ready to serve. Serve with melba toast.

Green Goddess Dip

This is a great vegetable dip.

1	ripe avocado	1	½ tsp	salt	2 ml
1 cup	sour cream	250 ml	½ tsp	seasoning salt	2 ml
½ cup	parsley, finely chopped	125 ml	¼ cup	mayonnaise	50 ml
⅓ cup	green onions, finely chopped	75 ml			

Mash avocado. Add sour cream, mayonnaise, salt and seasoning salt. Mix well, then fold in parsley and green onions.

Garlic Lover's Hummus

2½ cups	chick peas, cooked in water	625 ml	¼ tsp	oregano	1 ml
			1 tbsp	olive oil	15 ml
3 cloves	garlic, crushed	3		salt and pepper	
3 tbsp	tahini	45 ml			
juice	of 1 lemon				

Mash the chick peas and put all ingredients in a food processor to make a paste. Place mixture into a bowl and decorate with finely chopped onions, parsley or cilantro. Drizzle olive oil on top.

Spinach Dip in a Basket

1 cup	sour cream	250 ml	1 pkg	Knorr vegetable soup	1
1 cup	Miracle Whip	250 ml			
1 10-oz pkg	frozen spinach, thawed and very well drained	285 g	2 loaves	pumpernickel round, or 1 loaf pumpernickel and 1 round white bread	2
1 10-oz can	water chestnuts	285 ml			

Chop spinach until fine. Combine sour cream, Miracle Whip, spinach, water chestnuts and Knorr vegetable soup. Mix well. Let sit overnight. Before serving, cut the top off pumpernickel bread and hollow out the inside. Pour dip into the hollowed-out bread. Cube bread for dipping, using the inside of the pumpernickel and the white bread.

Dill Dip

½ cup	mayonnaise	125 ml	1 tbsp	parsley, chopped	15 ml
1 cup	sour cream	250 ml	½ tsp	salt (or less)	3 ml
2 tbsp	horseradish	30 ml	1 tsp	dillweed	5 ml
1 tbsp	green onion, chopped	15 ml			

Combine all ingredients and refrigerate. Serve with raw vegetables.

Taco Dip

This hearty recipe is easily doubled. Adjust spices to taste.

1 lb	ground beef	250 g		2 dashes	Tabasco sauce	2
1 tbsp	chili powder	15 ml		½ cup	salsa sauce, chunky style	125 ml
1 tbsp	chili peppers, ground	15 ml		1	small onion, finely chopped	1
1 tsp	salt	5 ml				

Brown ground beef in a saucepan. Add remaining ingredients and cook until onion is translucent. Remove mixture to an ovenproof casserole dish. Top with one layer of each of the following ingredients:

½ cup	sour cream	125 ml
1	medium tomato, finely chopped	1
½-1 cup	old Cheddar cheese, grated	125-250 g
1	green onion, chopped, for garnish	1

Before serving, bake at 350F (180C) until bubbling. Serve hot with tortilla chips.

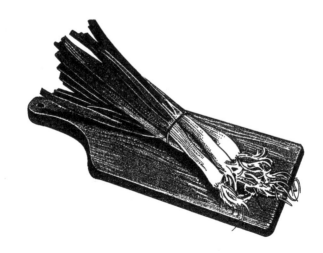

• SALADS •

• Best •

• Traditional •

• Trendy •

Green Salad with Bacon, Croutons & Mustard Dressing

				Dressing:		
4 slices	bacon, cut into pieces	4		3 tbsp	red wine vinegar	45 ml
1 tbsp	oil	15 ml		2 tsp	Dijon mustard	10 ml
4 slices	French bread, for croutons	4		½ tsp	pepper	2 ml
				1 clove	garlic, crushed and minced	1
12 cups	mixed salad greens, torn	3 L		¼ tsp	salt	1 ml
½ cup	walnuts, toasted	125 ml		⅓ cup	olive oil	75 ml

Cook bacon until crisp. Drain on paper towel. Brush oil over sides of bread; cut into cubes. Spread on a baking sheet. Bake at 400F (200C) for 5-10 minutes until golden. In a small bowl for dressing, whisk together vinegar, mustard, pepper, garlic and salt. Whisk in oil. In a salad bowl, toss greens, walnuts, bacon, croutons and dressing, until greens are well coated. Serves 6.

Romano Salad

5	celery stalks, finely sliced	5		¼ cup	Romano or Parmesan cheese, freshly grated	50 ml
½ lb	mushrooms, finely sliced	250 g			vinaigrette dressing	

Mix all ingredients in a salad bowl, chill well, and toss lightly with a bit of vinaigrette dressing when ready to serve. Garnish bowl with some chopped parsley and a light dusting of paprika. Serves 6.

Caesar Salad

This is probably the recipe that made this salad famous.

1 head	romaine lettuce, cut into 1-inch pieces	1	1 tsp	fresh ground pepper	5 ml	
1 cup	olive oil, divided	250 ml	1 tsp	kosher salt or other coarse ground salt	5 ml	
2 cloves	garlic	2	2	large egg yolks (or egg substitute)	2	
8	anchovy fillets	8				
1 tsp	Worcestershire sauce	5 ml	½ cup	Parmesan cheese, grated	125 ml	
1 tsp	dry mustard or 2 tsp (10 ml) prepared Dijon mustard	5 ml	¼ cup	Parmesan cheese, shredded or shaved	50 ml	
1 tbsp	lemon juice	15 ml	4	slices bread, cubed	4	
1 tsp	white vinegar	5 ml				

Trim the romaine lettuce of bruised or browned leaves, then cut into pieces. Wash and drain the lettuce, pat it dry and refrigerate for 30 minutes to crisp the leaves. To make the croutons, heat ½ cup (125 ml) olive oil in a sauté pan over medium-high heat. Fry the bread cubes in the oil, tossing frequently, until crisp. Drain croutons on paper towel. Put the garlic cloves in a large wooden salad bowl. Mash the garlic cloves against the sides of the bowl with the back of a wooden spoon. Rub the pieces against the bowl until they begin to disintegrate. Remove most of the garlic from the bowl and discard. Add the anchovies and repeat the procedure, but leave the anchovy pieces in the bowl. Add the dry mustard, Worcestershire sauce, lemon juice, white vinegar, pepper, and egg yolks, and blend well (these days, it is not advisable to use raw eggs, so egg substitute may be used). Slowly drizzle in 8 tbsp (125 ml) of olive oil whisking until a creamy mayonnaise-type dressing forms. Add the lettuce, croutons, Parmesan cheese, and salt. Toss and serve directly from the salad bowl. Serves 6.

Simple Caesar Salad

2 heads	romaine lettuce	2		1 tsp	parsley, chopped	5 ml
6 tbsp	vegetable oil	90 ml		1 tsp	garlic, chopped	5 ml
2 tbsp	vinegar	30 ml		1	raw egg (or egg substitute)	
1 tbsp	olive oil	15 ml				
1 tbsp	lemon juice	15 ml			bacon bits, croutons, parsley and Parmesan cheese, as desired	
1 tsp	salt	5 ml				
pinch each	sugar, pepper, dry mustard, and tarragon					
dash each	Tabasco and Worcestershire sauce					

Wash and dry lettuce. Mix dressing ingredients well, and toss all together. Serves 12.

Crunchy Tossed Salad

The noodles top it off.

½ cup	vegetable oil	125 ml		6 slices	bacon, cooked and crumbled	6
¼ cup	sugar	50 ml		⅓ cup	sliced almonds, toasted	75 ml
2 tbsp	vinegar	30 ml				
1 tsp	salt	5 ml		¼ cup	sesame seeds, toasted	50 ml
¼ tsp	pepper	1 ml		4	green onions, sliced	4
1	large iceberg lettuce, sliced	1		¾ cup	chow mein noodles	175 ml

In a jar with a tight cover, combine oil, sugar, vinegar, salt and pepper, and shake well. Chill for 1 hour. Just before serving, combine lettuce, bacon, almonds, sesame seeds and onions in a large bowl; add dressing and toss. Top with chow mein noodles. Serves 6.

The Great Nova Scotia Cookbook

Dandelion Salad

Dandelion greens are delicious and they're free! Dig up young plants. Cut off roots and stalks. Separate the outside and inside leaves into two piles. Use the tender inside leaves for salads and the outside leaves for cooking.

Wash in warm water, lifting out each leaf to clean thoroughly. Drain well and store in a plastic bag in crisper until ready to use.

For the salad:

Break the tender dandelion leaves in a bowl and keep well chilled until serving time. Add some broken lettuce if you wish. The traditional dressing is buttermilk, sweetened and flavoured with sugar and salt, or serve with your favourite dressing.

BLT Salad

This recipe is reminiscent of the classic bacon, lettuce, and tomato sandwich.

1 lb	bacon	500 g		salt	
¾ cup	mayonnaise	175 ml	1 head	iceberg or Romaine lettuce, shredded	1
¼ cup	milk	50 ml			
1 tsp	garlic powder	5 ml	2	large tomatoes, chopped	2
⅛ tsp	black pepper, ground	0.8 ml			
			2 cups	seasoned croutons	500 ml

Place bacon in a large, deep skillet. Cook over medium-high heat, turning frequently, until evenly browned. Crumble, and set aside. In a blender, blend mayonnaise, milk, garlic powder and ground pepper. Season with salt to taste. Place lettuce in a large salad bowl. Layer tomatoes, crumbled bacon and croutons over the lettuce. Toss with dressing and serve immediately. Serves 6.

Crunchy Vegetable Salad

¼ head	purple cabbage, finely sliced	¼
¼ head	cauliflower, broken into bite-size pieces	¼
1	broccoli stalk, broken into bite size pieces	1
2	small carrots, sliced diagonally	2
⅓ cup	fresh peas, raw	75 ml
2-3	radishes, sliced	2-3

Dressing:

¼ cup	plain yogurt	50 ml
¼ cup	mayonnaise	50 ml
1½ tsp	lemon juice	7 ml
⅛ tsp	onion powder	0.5 ml
dash	garlic powder	
	salt and pepper, to taste	
1½ tsp	brown sugar	7 ml
1 tbsp	parsley	15 ml

Mix all vegetables in a large bowl. Combine dressing ingredients and mix well. Pour over vegetables and toss. Chill until serving time. Serves 4-6.

Seven-Layer Salad

¼ head	iceberg lettuce, washed	¼
½ cup	real bacon bits	125 ml
½	medium green bell pepper, seeded and chopped	½
½	small onion, chopped	½
½ cup	frozen peas	125 ml

2	celery ribs, chopped	2
1	carrot, peeled and shredded	1
½ cup	Cheddar cheese, shredded	125 ml
¾ cup	mayonnaise	175 ml
2 tbsp	sugar	30 ml
½ cup	croutons	125 ml

Prepare one day before serving. Arrange lettuce in the bottom of a deep baking dish or plastic container with a cover. Sprinkle with bacon pieces. Layer with remaining vegetables and sprinkle with cheese. Combine mayonnaise and sugar in a bowl. Spread over top of salad. Cover and refrigerate until serving time. Just before serving, toss and add croutons, if desired. Serves 6.

Real Crunch Salad

1 bunch	broccoli, chopped	1	½ cup	raisins	125 ml
1	small onion, chopped	1	½ cup	mayonnaise	125 ml
12 slices	bacon, crumbled	12	½ cup	sugar	125 ml
1 cup	sunflower seeds, roasted	250 ml	2 tbsp	vinegar	30 ml

Prepare the dressing by combining mayonnaise, sugar and vinegar. Add dressing to other ingredients just before serving. Serves 6.

Mushroom and Spinach Salad

2	large hard-boiled eggs	2	6 tbsp	extra-virgin olive oil	90 ml
½ lb	fresh spinach	250 g	3 tbsp	minced shallots (about 2)	45 ml
10 oz	fresh mushrooms	280 g			
3 tbsp	tarragon white wine vinegar	45 ml	2 tbsp	fresh tarragon leaves, finely chopped	30 ml
1 tbsp	Dijon mustard	15 ml			

Mash egg yolks and chop whites finely. Set aside. Wash spinach well, discard coarse stems, dry and thinly slice. Thinly slice mushrooms. Mix together remaining ingredients for dressing. Spread spinach leaves on a platter, and mound mushrooms in centre. Sprinkle with egg yolks and whites. Drizzle dressing over all. Serves 6.

Broccoli Salad

Dressing:

¾ cup	mayonnaise	175 ml		4 tbsp	white vinegar	60 ml
½ cup	white sugar	125 ml				

Salad ingredients:

2	broccoli stalks, cut into bite-size pieces	2		1 cup	Mozzarella cheese, grated	250 ml
½ cup	red onion, thinly sliced	125 ml		½ cup	bacon bits	125 ml

Break broccoli into bite-size pieces. One hour before serving, pour dressing on broccoli and onion. Top with Mozzarella cheese and bacon bits. Serves 4.

Zucchini Salad

5	small zucchini, trimmed	5		Dressing:		
1	small red pepper, seeded and chopped	1		2 tbsp	vegetable oil	30 ml
				1 tbsp	lemon juice	15 ml
2 tbsp	drained capers	30 ml		pinch	sugar	
1 tbsp	fresh parsley, finely chopped	15 ml		pinch	dry mustard	
					salt and pepper	
1 head	lettuce, leaves separated	1				

Quarter the zucchini lengthwise, then cut in ½-inch (1.3 cm) slices. Mix the slices in a bowl with the red peppers, capers and parsley. Put the dressing ingredients in a small bowl with seasoning to taste, and beat together with a fork. Pour the dressing over zucchini mixture and stir with a spoon. To serve, line 4 salad bowls with lettuce leaves, then pile zucchini mixture into the centre of each bowl just before serving. Serves 4.

Greek Salad

4	tomatoes	4
½	cucumber	½
1	small green pepper, seeded	1
1	small onion	1
6 oz	pitted black olives	168 g
¼ lb	feta cheese, cubed	125 g

Dressing:

¼ cup	olive oil	50 ml
juice	of 1 lemon	1
½ tsp	dried oregano	2 ml
	salt and pepper	

To make dressing, put the oil in a small bowl with lemon juice, oregano and seasoning to taste. Mix well with a fork.

Cut each tomato into 8 wedges, and slice the cucumber thinly. Cut the pepper and onion into thin rings. Divide the tomato, cucumber, pepper and onion among 4 small salad bowls. Place a few olives and cheese cubes on top. Pour dressing over each bowl, and serve.

Note: Do not use canned olives.

Italian Tomato and Veggie Salad

2 cups	cauliflower florets	500 ml
2 cups	sliced green beans, fresh or frozen	500 ml
1 cup	cherry tomatoes, halved	250 ml
1 cup	canned chick peas, drained	250 ml

1 cup	stuffed olives, thinly sliced	250 ml
	oregano-flavoured prepared dressing	
	sundried tomatoes, as desired	

Steam cauliflower and green beans. Add tomatoes, chickpeas and olives. Toss with an oregano-flavoured prepared dressing. Add sundried tomatoes. Toss well and chill. Serves 6.

Miracle-Dill Cabbage

1 head	red cabbage, finely shredded	1	¼ cup	fresh dillweed, chopped	50 ml
1	each red pepper and red onion, sliced	1	1 tbsp	fresh lemon juice	15 ml
½ cup	Miracle Whip	125 ml		salt and pepper, to taste	

Mix vegetables in a large bowl. Stir remaining ingredients together until smooth; add to vegetables, tossing lightly to coat. Refrigerate until ready to serve. Makes six ½-cup servings.

Cucumber Salad

1	large English cucumber	1	¼ tsp	white pepper	1 ml
¾ tsp	salt	3 ml	½ cup	white sugar	125 ml
½ cup	water	125 ml	1 tbsp	snipped parsley	15 ml
½ cup	white vinegar	125 ml			

Cut cucumber into paper-thin slices. Place in medium-size bowl. Rub in salt with fingers. Allow to sit for 10-15 minutes. Squeeze and pour off excess liquid. Mix in water, vinegar, pepper and sugar. Refrigerate at least 4-6 hours. Garnish with parsley. Serves 4.

Cucumbers in Sour Cream

2	medium cucumbers, thinly sliced	2	½ cup	sour cream	125 ml
			1 tbsp	sugar	15 ml
1	medium onion, thinly sliced	1	1 tbsp	vinegar	15 ml
			½ tsp	salt	2 ml

Slice cucumbers and onions to a uniform size. Stir together sour cream, sugar, vinegar and salt. Toss sauce with cucumbers and onions. Cover and chill, stirring occasionally. Serves 6.

Tangy Cucumber Salad

Refreshing!

2	small cucumbers, thinly sliced	2	1 tbsp	honey	15 ml
1 tsp	salt, divided	5 ml	½ tsp	dried basil	2 ml
2	medium tomatoes, chopped	2	½ tsp	celery seed	2 ml
			½ tsp	ground, dry mustard	2 ml
1	medium onion, chopped	1	¼ tsp	garlic powder	1 ml
¼ cup	cider vinegar	50 ml	¼ tsp	dried oregano	1 ml
2 tbsp	vegetable oil	30 ml	dash	cayenne pepper	

Place cucumber in a strainer; sprinkle with ½ tsp salt and toss. Let stand for 30 minutes. Rinse and drain well. Place in a large bowl and add tomatoes and onion. In a small bowl, whisk together the remaining ingredients; pour over cucumber mixture and toss. Cover and refrigerate for several hours. Serve with a slotted spoon. Serves 6.

Hot Five-Bean Salad

8 slices	bacon, diced	8	1 16-oz can	lima beans, rinsed and drained	455 ml
⅔ cup	sugar	150 ml			
2 tbsp	cornstarch	30 ml	1 16-oz can	garbanzo beans, rinsed and drained	455 ml
1½ tsp	salt	7 ml			
pinch	pepper		1 16-oz can	green beans rinsed and drained	455 ml
¾ cup	vinegar	175 ml			
½ cup	water	125 ml	1 16-oz can	wax beans rinsed and drained	455 ml
1 19-oz can	kidney beans, rinsed and drained	455 ml			

In a skillet, cook bacon until crisp, reserving 2 tbsp (30 ml) of drippings. Set the bacon aside. Add sugar, cornstarch, salt and pepper to the drippings. Stir in vinegar and water; bring to a boil, stirring constantly for 2 minutes. Add the beans; reduce heat. Cover and simmer for 15 minutes or until beans are heated through. Place in serving bowl; top with bacon. Serves 10-12.

Calico Bean Salad

Tangy and colourful.

1 19-oz can	green beans	540 ml
1 12-oz can	whole kernel corn	341 ml
2 cups	carrots, sliced, cooked until just tender	500 ml
2 tbsp	raw onions, sliced	30 ml
	celery-seed dressing	
	salad greens	

For Celery-Seed Dressing, combine:

½ cup	brown sugar	125 ml
⅓ cup	cider vinegar	75 ml
1 tsp	salt	5 ml
2 tsp	celery seed	10 ml
¼ tsp	turmeric	1 ml
dash	pepper	

Combine vegetables. Toss with celery-seed dressing. Chill in a covered container overnight. Serve on salad greens. Serves 6.

Fresh Mushroom Salad

2 lb	fresh mushrooms, sliced	1 kg
2 oz	salad oil	60 ml
2 oz	white vinegar	60 ml
½ tsp	dry mustard	2 ml
½ cup	heavy cream	125 ml

1 tbsp	lemon juice	15 ml
½ tsp	salt	2 ml
pinch	fresh ground black pepper	
1 head	lettuce	1
pinch	chives	

Mix oil, vinegar and dry mustard. Stir in cream, lemon juice, salt and pepper. Line salad plates with lettuce leaves. Toss mushrooms with dressing, and serve on lettuce. Sprinkle with chives. Serves 6.

Colourful Corn Salad

The title says it all.

4 cups	frozen corn	1 L	2 tsp	ground cumin	10 ml
2 cups	green pepper, diced	500 ml	1½ tsp	salt	7 ml
2 cups	red pepper, diced	500 ml	¾ tsp	pepper	3 ml
2 cups	celery, diced	500 ml	½ tsp	hot pepper sauce	2 ml
1 cup	parsley, minced	250 ml	⅛ tsp	cayenne pepper	0.5 ml
1 cup	green onions, chopped	250 ml	3 tbsp	olive or vegetable oil	45 ml
½ cup	Parmesan cheese, shredded	125 ml	2 cloves	garlic, crushed and minced	2
			6 tbsp	lime juice	90 ml

In a large bowl, combine the first 12 ingredients. In a microwave-safe dish, combine garlic and oil. Microwave uncovered on high for 1 minute. Cool. Whisk in lime juice. Pour over corn mixture and toss to coat. Cover and refrigerate until serving time. Serves 16-18.

Bacon and Potato Salad

A newer version of the old standby.

8	medium potatoes, cooked and diced	8	10 slices	bacon, cooked crisp and cut into 1-inch (2.5 cm) pieces	10
2	eggs, hard boiled, peeled and sliced	2	1 tsp	dry mustard	5 ml
3	green onions, cut into thin slices	3	2 tbsp	red wine vinegar	30 ml
			½ cup	vegetable oil	125 ml

Combine potatoes and eggs in a large salad bowl. Whisk together mustard, vinegar and oil. Pour over potatoes and toss lightly. Add bacon and green onions. Season to taste. Serve on crisp lettuce leaves. Serves 6.

German Potato Salad

4	medium potatoes	4	¼ cup	white wine vinegar	50 ml
4 slices	bacon	4	½ cup	green onions, chopped	125 ml
1 tbsp	all-purpose flour	15 ml			
2 tbsp	white sugar	30 ml		salt and pepper, to taste	
⅓ cup	water	75 ml			

Bring a large pot of salted water to a boil. Add potatoes; cook until tender but still firm (about 15 minutes). Drain, cool and chop. Place bacon in a large, deep skillet. Cook over medium-high heat until crisp. Drain, crumble and set aside. Reserve some bacon fat in skillet and add flour, sugar, water, vinegar, salt and pepper. Cook and stir until smooth. Pour over potatoes. Top with bacon and green onions. Serve warm. Serves 2-4.

Microwave German Potato Salad

This is a traditional recipe, but microwave preparation makes it trendy.

2 lb	red potatoes, cooked and sliced	1 kg	2 tbsp	sugar	30 ml
			4 tsp	flour	20 ml
3	hard-boiled eggs, chopped	3	2 tbsp	vinegar	30 ml
			½ tsp	salt	2 ml
½ cup	onion, chopped	125 ml	⅛ tsp	pepper	0.5 ml
½ cup	celery, chopped	125 ml	¾ cup	milk	175 ml
6 slices	bacon, diced	6			

In a large bowl, combine potatoes, eggs, onion and celery; set aside. Place bacon in a microwave-safe bowl; cover with a paper towel and microwave on high for 2 minutes. Stir. Microwave 3-4 minutes longer or until the bacon is crisp, stirring after each minute. Remove bacon to paper towel to drain, reserving 2 tbsp (30 ml) drippings. Stir sugar, flour, vinegar, salt and pepper into drippings until smooth; gradually add milk. Microwave on high for 5-6 minutes, stirring every 2 minutes until thickened. Pour over potato mixture; toss. Top with bacon. Serve immediately. Serves 2-4.

Potato Salad

This was always served at church suppers, and there were never any leftovers.

5-7	medium potatoes	5-7	1 tbsp	dried minced onions, softened	15 ml	
1 cup	mayonnaise	250 ml	⅓ cup	sweet pickle relish (optional)	75 ml	
1 tbsp	vinegar	15 ml				
1 tsp	salt	5 ml	1 small	jar pimentos (optional)	1	
¼ tsp	pepper	1 ml				
1 cup	celery, diced (about 2 medium-size stalks)	250 ml	5	hard-boiled eggs, peeled and chopped	5	

Boil potatoes with skins on until cooked. Peel skins off and dice potatoes while still warm. Mix mayonnaise, vinegar, salt and pepper, then add celery, onions, pickle relish, pimentos and eggs. Mix in potatoes. Cover and refrigerate at least 4 hours. Serves 6.

Party Potato Salad

6 cups	potatoes, cooked and cubed	1.5 L	**Dressing:**		
			1 cup	sour cream	250 ml
1	cucumber, unpeeled and cubed	1	½ cup	Miracle Whip	125 ml
			½ tsp	salt	2 ml
1 cup	raw carrots, shredded	250 ml	½ tsp	dillweed	2 ml
			1 tsp	prepared mustard	5 ml
2 tbsp	chives, finely chopped	30 ml	dash	pepper	

Place salad ingredients in a bowl. Set aside. In a small bowl, combine dressing ingredients and mix well. Pour dressing over salad and toss lightly. Chill and serve. Serves 6.

Potato, Bacon and Bean Salad

Stick-to-the-ribs goodness.

1 lb	bacon	500 g
3 lb	small red potatoes, unpeeled, cut into chunks	1.5 kg
1 lb	green beans, cut in 1-inch pieces	500 g

Dressing:

½ cup	olive or salad oil	125 ml
¼ cup	fresh parsley	50 ml
¼ cup	tarragon vinegar	50 ml
½ tsp	salt	2 ml
½ cup	green onions, chopped	125 ml
1 clove	garlic, crushed and minced	1
1 tsp	dry mustard	5 ml
dash	pepper	

Cut bacon in 1½-inch (4 cm) pieces (no need to separate pieces—they will come apart when cooking). In a large skillet, cook bacon and drain on paper towels. Discard drippings. Place potatoes in salted boiling water. Cook until tender. Drain, saving water. Boil beans in potato water until tender. Place potatoes and beans in large bowl. Combine all dressing ingredients, stirring well. Pour over warm vegetables. Add bacon and toss lightly. Serve immediately, or cover and let "set" at room temperature for an hour or two. Serves 8.

Apple and Celery Salad

1½ cups apples, finely chopped	375 ml	mayonnaise	
		lettuce leaves	
1½ cups celery, chopped	375 ml	pimento, cut in strips	

Mix apples, celery and mayonnaise, to taste. Serve, chilled, on lettuce leaves garnished with strips of pimento. Serves 3-4.

Spinach-Orange Tossed Salad

4 cups	fresh spinach or romaine lettuce, torn	1 L
½ tsp	orange peel, finely shredded	2 ml
2	oranges, peeled and sectioned	2
¾ cup	fresh mushrooms, sliced	175 ml

⅓ cup	blue cheese, crumbled	75 ml
3 tbsp	salad oil	45 ml
1 tbsp	lemon juice	15 ml
¼ tsp	grated ginger	1 ml
¼ cup	slivered almonds, toasted	50 ml

Place torn greens in a large salad bowl. Add orange sections, sliced fresh mushrooms and blue cheese. Toss lightly.

In a screw-top jar, combine salad oil, lemon juice, ginger and orange peel. Cover and shake well. Pour dressing over salad. Toss to coat. Sprinkle toasted almonds over salad. Serve immediately. Serves 6.

Strawberry Poppyseed Salad

1	romaine lettuce, torn	1
1	red onion, sliced	1
2 cups	strawberries	500 ml
Dressing:		
⅓ cup	white sugar	75 ml
¼ cup	white vinegar	50 ml

2 tsp	poppy seeds	10 ml
½ tsp	Worcestershire sauce	2 ml
½ cup	cooking oil	125 ml
2 tsp	sesame seeds	10 ml
⅛ tsp	paprika	0.5 ml
¼ cup	plain yogurt	50 ml

Place torn greens, sliced onions and strawberries in a salad bowl. Blend dressing ingredients well. Prior to serving, pour dressing over salad and toss to coat. Serves 6.

Arugula, Walnut and Orange Salad

An interesting combination of greens with a bite that makes a light accompaniment to a hearty brunch.

				Dressing:		
4 cups each	romaine and arugula	1 L each		1/4 cup	orange juice	50 ml
2 cups	radicchio	500 ml		2 tbsp	lemon juice	30 ml
1 bunch	watercress, coarse stems discarded	1		1 tsp	Dijon mustard	5 ml
				1/2 cup	olive oil	125 ml
1 cup	toasted walnuts, chopped	250 ml			salt and freshly ground pepper, to taste	
2	oranges	2				

To toast walnuts, bake at 350F (175C) for 7-10 minutes or until browned. Combine romaine, arugula, radicchio, watercress and walnuts. Peel oranges, removing all white pith. Divide into sections and toss with lettuces. In a bowl whisk together the orange and lemon juices and the mustard. Slowly whisk in the olive oil. Season with salt and pepper to taste. Toss with salad just before serving. Serves 6.

Waldorf Salad

1 cup	apple, peeled and diced	250 ml		1/4 cup	mayonnaise	50 ml
				2 tbsp	lemon juice	15 ml
1 cup	celery, chopped	250 ml				
1/2 cup	walnuts, chopped	125 ml				

Mix apple, celery, and walnuts with mayonnaise. Add lemon juice to prevent apple from turning brown. Serve immediately. Serves 2-3.

Spinach Salad with Mandarin Oranges

This colourful salad is a wonderful addition to any meal, or can be a meal in itself when topped with two to three ounces of grilled chicken breast. Other fruit can be substituted.

1 head	red or green leaf lettuce, torn into bite-size pieces	1
4 cups	fresh spinach leaves, torn into bite-size pieces	1 L
1	medium red onion, thinly sliced	1
2 10-oz cans	mandarin oranges, drained	2 x 284 ml

Dressing:		
¼ cup	sugar	50 ml
½ tsp	dry mustard, or 1 tsp (5 ml) Dijon	2 ml
½ tsp	paprika	2 ml
½ tsp	celery salt	2 ml
¼ cup	canola oil	50 ml
½ cup	cider vinegar	125 ml

Mix lettuce and spinach with onion and oranges in a large salad bowl, reserving several onion slices and mandarin oranges for garnish. Combine salad dressing ingredients in a blender or shaker jar; blend or shake well. Add half the dressing about ten minutes before serving. To serve, toss well with remaining dressing and garnish with reserved mandarin oranges and red onion slices. Makes 14 cups (3.5 L).

Five Cup Salad

1 cup	mandarin oranges	250 ml
1 cup	sour cream	250 ml
1 cup	pineapple	250 ml

1 cup	angel flake coconut	250 ml
1 cup	marshmallows (miniature)	250 ml

Mix all ingredients together and chill. Serves 5.

Jellied Lime Salad

1 3-oz pkg	lime Jell-O	90 g	1½ cups	cottage cheese, creamed or dry	375 ml
½ cup	hot water	125 ml	½ cup	pineapple, drained	125 ml
½ cup	green onions	125 ml	½ cup	salad dressing	125 ml
1 cup	celery	250 ml			

Dissolve Jell-O in water. Chop green onion and celery in small pieces and add to Jell-O mixture. Add cottage cheese, pineapple and salad dressing. Mix. Chill in refrigerator. Serves 6.

Chinese-Style Pasta Salad

The Chinese five-spice powder called for here is sold in most supermarkets and specialty stores. Originally a blend of star anise, cinnamon, chives, fennel, and Szechwan pepper, some versions of the powder also include ginger and licorice.

8 oz	rotini spirals	250 g	⅓ cup	walnuts, coarsely chopped	75 ml
2 tbsp	margarine	30 ml			
1½ tsp	hot chili oil	7 ml	¼ tsp	Chinese five-spice powder	1 ml
2 cups	sugar snap pea pods, tips and strings removed	500 g			

Prepare rotini following package instructions. Meanwhile, in a large, non-stick skillet, heat margarine and oil over medium heat. Add peas and cook, stirring, until peas are brightly coloured and tender. Stir in walnuts and five-spice powder, and cook until walnuts are lightly toasted—about 2 minutes. Toss pea mixture with cooked, drained pasta. Serve immediately. Serves 6.

Pasta Salad

2 cups	broccoli florets	500 ml	1 small jar	olives, sliced	1
2 cups	cauliflower florets	500 ml			
2 cups	fresh mushrooms, sliced	500 ml	12 oz	spiral macaroni	375 g
1 16-oz jar	artichoke hearts, rinsed and chopped	500 ml			

Cook macaroni *al dente* and rinse in cold water. Mix in vegetables.

Dressing:

1 cup	vegetable oil	250 ml	1 tsp	pepper	5 ml
½ cup	vinegar	125 ml	4 tbsp	Parmesan cheese	60 ml
2 tbsp	Dijon mustard	30 ml	6	fresh garlic cloves, minced and crushed	6
2 tsp	sugar	10 ml			

Mix all ingredients together. Toss with salad. Chill at least 2 hours before serving. Serves 6.

Sauerkraut Apple Salad

Good with baked beans.

27 oz	sauerkraut, rinsed and drained	796 ml	3 tbsp	lemon juice	45 ml
			1 tbsp	sugar	15 ml
1	medium tart apple, peeled and chopped	1	1 tbsp	dried basil	15 ml
			1 tbsp	dried parsley flakes	15 ml
1	small onion, chopped	1	½ tsp	salt	2 ml
¾ cup	dill pickle, chopped	175 ml	¼ cup	vegetable oil	50 ml

Combine first 9 ingredients in a bowl. Drizzle on oil and toss to coat. Cover and refrigerate for 2 hours before serving. Serves 8.

Antipasto Pasta Salad

A delicious pasta, meat and cheese combination with a homemade dressing. It serves a crowd and is great for a picnic.

1 lb	shell, bowtie or elbow macaroni pasta	500 g	3	ripe tomatoes, chopped	3
¼ lb	salami, chopped	125 g	¾ cup	extra virgin olive oil	175 ml
¼ lb	pepperoni, chopped	125 g	¼ cup	balsamic vinegar	50 ml
½ lb	sharp cheese, diced	250 g	1 tbsp	dried oregano	15 ml
1 6-oz can	black olives, drained and chopped	168 g	1 tbsp	dried parsley	15 ml
			1 tsp	Italian seasoning	5 ml
1	red bell pepper, diced	1	1 tbsp	Parmesan cheese, grated	15 ml
1	green bell pepper, diced	1		salt	
				ground pepper	

Cook the pasta in a large pot of salted boiling water until *al dente*. Drain and cool under cold water. In a large bowl, combine the pasta, salami, pepperoni, cheese, black olives, bell peppers and tomatoes.

To prepare the dressing, whisk together the olive oil, balsamic vinegar, oregano, parsley, Italian seasoning, Parmesan cheese, salt and pepper. Just before serving, pour dressing over salad and mix well. Serves 12.

Chicken Waldorf Salad

⅔ cup	mayonnaise	150 ml	4 cups	red apples, unpeeled and diced	1 L
4 tsp	sugar	20 ml			
¼ tsp	dry mustard	1 ml	½ cup	walnuts, coarsely chopped	125 ml
¼ tsp	salt	1 ml			
2 tsp	lemon juice	10 ml	1 10-oz can	white chicken or turkey, drained	280 ml
½ cup	celery, diced	125 ml			

Blend mayonnaise, sugar, mustard, salt and lemon juice. Add remaining ingredients. Toss gently to coat. Serve on bed of lettuce or mixed greens, or simply serve as is.

Tortellini Salad

This is a Greek-style salad hearty enough to serve as a main course.

1 16-oz bag	frozen cheese tortellini	450 g	½ cup	feta cheese, crumbled	125 ml
1	green bell pepper, seeded and julienned	1	8 oz	chicken breast, cooked and sliced into strips	225 g
1	red bell pepper, seeded and julienned	1	¼ cup	olive oil	50 ml
1	small red onion, julienned	1	2 tsp	minced lemon zest	10 ml
			¼ cup	lemon juice	50 ml
½ cup	black olives, sliced	125 ml	2 tbsp	ground walnuts	30 ml
			1 tbsp	honey	15 ml

Cook pasta in a large pot of boiling water until *al dente*. Drain and cool under cold water. Refrigerate until chilled. Prepare the dressing in a small bowl by whisking together the olive oil, lemon zest, lemon juice, walnuts and honey. Refrigerate until chilled. In a salad bowl, combine pasta, peppers, red onion, olives and chicken. Add lemon dressing and feta cheese, toss and serve. Serves 6.

Chicken Salad

½ cup	mayonnaise	125 ml	⅓ cup	almonds, toasted slivered	75 ml
1 tbsp	lemon juice	15 ml			
½ tsp	salt	2 ml	2	medium celery, stalks, sliced (1 cup)	250 ml
¼ tsp	pepper	1 ml			
2 cups	chicken, cooked and diced	500 ml	4 slices	bacon, cooked and crumbled	4

Mix mayonnaise, lemon juice, salt and pepper; toss with chicken, almonds and celery. Cover and refrigerate at least 3 hours. Add bacon to salad just before serving.

Tabbouleh

A Middle-Eastern salad that caught on.

¾ cup	bulgur wheat	175 ml	1	small onion, finely chopped	1
2 large bunches	parsley, finely chopped	2	⅛ tsp	cinnamon	0.5 ml
1 cup	fresh mint, finely chopped (optional)	250 ml	1 tsp	salt	5 ml
				pepper to taste	
⅓ cup	dried mint (optional)	75 ml	½-⅔ cup	fresh lemon juice	125-150 ml
½ bunch	green onion, with green ends finely chopped	½	½ cup	olive oil or vegetable oil	125 ml
1-2 large	tomatoes, finely chopped	1-2			

In a large mixing bowl, soak bulgur in water for 2 minutes, drain well and set aside. Wash parsley, drain well, then chop. Add parsley and mint to bulgur. Just before serving, add remaining ingredients. Serve with romaine lettuce and pita bread. Serves 4-6.

Curried Chicken Salad·

This is a wonderfully flavourful chicken salad. In typical curry fashion, sweet fruit is combined with meat in a savoury sauce.

6 slices	bacon, uncooked	6	2 tbsp	red onion, minced	30 ml
3 cups	chicken breast meat, cooked and diced	750 ml	1 tsp	lemon juice	5 ml
			½ tsp	Worcestershire sauce	2 ml
½ cup	celery, chopped	125 ml	½ tsp	curry powder	2 ml
1 cup	mayonnaise	250 ml		salt and pepper, to taste	
1 cup	seedless red grapes, whole or halved	250 ml			

Place bacon in a large, deep skillet. Cook over medium-high heat until brown. Crumble and set aside. In a large bowl, combine bacon, chicken, celery, and grapes.

Prepare the dressing in a small bowl by whisking together the mayonnaise, onion, lemon juice, Worcestershire sauce, curry and salt and pepper. Pour over salad and toss well. Serves 6.

Layered Chicken Salad

4-5 cups	iceberg lettuce, shredded	1-1.25 L	4 cups	cooked chicken, cut in strips	1 L
¼ lb	bean sprouts	125 g	2 cups	mayonnaise	500 g
1 8-oz can	water chestnuts, sliced	227 g	1 tbsp	curry powder	15 ml
			½ tsp	ground ginger	2 ml
1	cucumber, thinly sliced	1	1 tbsp	sugar	15 ml
½ cup	green onions, thinly sliced	125 ml	10-12	cherry tomatoes, halved	10-12
8 oz	fresh pea pods	250 g			

Spread lettuce as evenly as possible in 4-quart (4 L) glass bowl. Top with layers of sprouts, water chestnuts, cucumber, onions, pea pods and chicken, making sure pea pods are dry. In a separate bowl, stir together the mayonnaise, curry, ginger and sugar. Spread evenly over salad. Decorate with tomatoes. Refrigerate until ready to serve. Serves 6-8.

Crunchy Chicken Salad

8	chicken breast halves, boneless, skinless, cooked and cubed	8	¾ cup	mayonnaise	175 ml
			½ cup	sour cream	125 ml
			1 tbsp	white wine vinegar	15 ml
2 cups	seedless red grapes, halved	500 ml		lettuce leaves	
2 cups	salted cashew halves	500 ml			
2	celery stalks	2			

In a large bowl, combine chicken, grapes, cashews and celery; set aside. In a small bowl combine mayonnaise, sour cream and vinegar; mix well. Pour over chicken mixture, tossing to coat. Cover and refrigerate for at least 1 hour. Serve in a lettuce-lined bowl. Serves 8.

Mandarin Chicken Salad

A mix of good flavours and pleasing textures.

4 cups	cooked chicken, cubed	1 L	½ cup	sliced ripe olive	125 ml
1 19-oz can	pineapple tidbits, drained	540 ml	½ cup	green pepper, chopped	125 ml
1 10-oz can	mandarin oranges drained	284 ml	2 tbsp	onion, grated	30 ml
			1 tbsp	prepared mustard	15 ml
1 cup	celery, chopped	250 ml	¼ tsp	salt	1 ml
1 cup	mayonnaise or salad dressing	250 ml	⅛ tsp	pepper	0.5 ml
			1 5-oz can	chow mein noodles	140 g
				lettuce (optional)	

In a large bowl, combine the first 11 ingredients. Refrigerate until serving time. Serve on lettuce, if desired. Sprinkle with chow mein noodles. Serves 8.

Turkey Salad

This one will take care of leftovers.

4 cups	cooked turkey, diced	1 L	½ cup	mayonnaise	125 ml
4	celery stalks, sliced	4	1 tbsp	lemon juice	15 ml
4	green onions, sliced	4	¼ tsp	dillweed	1 ml
½ cup	pecans, chopped and toasted	125 ml	¼ tsp	salt	1.5 ml
			⅛ tsp	pepper	0.5 ml
½ cup	sweet red pepper, chopped	125 ml		lettuce leaves	

In a large bowl, combine turkey, celery, onions, pecans and pepper. Combine mayonnaise, lemon juice, dillweed, salt and pepper. Stir mixtures together. Refrigerate until serving time. Serve on lettuce. Serves 4.

Hawaiian Salad

This tasty salad will disappear quickly!

3 cups	turkey, diced	375 ml	¼ cup	flaked coconut	50 ml
1 cup	celery, diced	250 ml	½ tsp	salt	2 ml
1 cup	pineapple, diced (drain, if canned)	250 ml	½ cup	salad dressing	125 ml

Toss all ingredients together. Keep refrigerated. Serves 6.

Crunchy Pork Salad

A meal and a salad!

1 cup	fresh mushrooms, chopped	250 ml	2	medium-size apples, diced	2
2 tbsp	butter	30 ml	½ tsp	salt	2 ml
3 cup	cooked pork, diced	750 ml	⅛ tsp	pepper	0.5 ml
1½ cups	celery, diced	375 ml	½ cup	salad dressing or mayonnaise	125 ml
¼ cup	green pepper, diced	50 ml			

Sauté mushrooms in butter. Cool. Combine pork, celery, pepper, apples and seasonings. Add mayonnaise just before serving. Keep refrigerated. The diced apples will not turn dark if sprinkled with lemon juice. Stir to coat the apple pieces. Serves 6.

Curried Pork Salad

With just a hint of curry, this is a delicious, crunchy addition to a lunch.

2½ cups	roast pork, cut into bite-size cubes	625 ml		½ cup	salted peanuts	125 ml
				⅔ cup	mayonnaise	150 ml
1 14-oz can	pineapple bits	392 g		3 tbsp	chutney	45 ml
				2 tbsp	lime juice	30 ml
2	small carrots, coarsely grated	2		½ tsp	curry powder lettuce	2 ml
1 cup	celery, sliced diagonally	250 ml				
⅔ cup	green onion, sliced	150 ml				

Toss together pork cubes, pineapple, carrot, celery, green onion and peanuts in a bowl. Combine mayonnaise, chutney, lime juice, and curry. Stir into pork mixture. Chill. Serve on crisp salad greens. Serves 6.

Salmon Fruit Salad

Who would have thought this would work—but it does!

1 large can	salmon, skin and bones removed	1		1	red apple, unpeeled and diced	1
⅓ cup	almonds, sliced	75 ml		3 cups	lettuce leaves, cut up or shredded	750 ml
⅔ cup	fresh oranges, cut into bite-size pieces	150 ml			homemade mayonnaise or salad dressing (see Salad Dressings)	
1	banana, sliced	1				
1	green apple, unpeeled and diced	1				

Break up salmon. Toast almonds in moderate oven for 5 minutes. Place salmon and almonds in a large bowl, and toss together. Add oranges, banana, apples and lettuce. Toss with your favourite mayonnaise. Serves 6.

Smoked Salmon Salad

A meal in itself!

1½ cups	smoked salmon strips	375 ml	1 tsp each	olive oil and balsamic vinegar	15 ml each
¼ cup	green beans, sliced lengthwise	50 ml			
1 small head	red leaf lettuce	1	Dressing:		
1 small head	leaf lettuce	1	1 tbsp	Dijon mustard	15 ml
			2 tbsp	olive oil	30 ml
¼ cup	blueberries	50 ml	1 tbsp	chopped sweet tarragon	15 ml
¼ cup	mushrooms and avocado, mixed	50 ml	5 tbsp	good quality salad oil	75 ml
			4 tbsp	good quality vinegar	60 ml

To make dressing, mix mustard with oil, and slowly add vinegar. Add tarragon last. Toss salmon, lettuce and vegetables gently in some of the dressing. Shake berries, olive oil and balsamic vinegar into a hot skillet and sprinkle on top. Drizzle on a little more dressing, and serve. Serves 6.

Lobster Salad

2 5-oz cans	lobster meat, drained and broken up	2x150 ml	5	lettuce leaves, shredded	5
			1-2 cups	alfalfa sprouts	250-500 ml
1 cup	celery, sliced	250 ml		homemade salad dressing (see Salad Dressings)	
2	eggs, hard-boiled and chopped	2			
3	olives with pimento, sliced	3			

Toss lobster, celery, eggs and olives together in salad bowl. Place portions of lobster mix on top of lettuce and alfalfa sprouts. Spoon dressing over top. Lemon wedges served at the side make an attractive salad plate. Serves 6.

Shrimp Salad

1 4-oz can	shrimp, rinsed, drained and chopped	125 g			lettuce leaves	
			⅔ cup	mayonnaise		150 ml
1 cup	cauliflower, bite-size pieces	250 ml	1 cup	long grain rice		250 ml
			2 cups	boiling water		500 ml
1 tbsp	lemon juice	15 ml	½ tsp	salt		2 ml
1 tbsp	onion, chopped	15 ml		paprika		
1	green onion, chopped	1				

Boil water with salt in saucepan. Add rice. Reduce heat and simmer for about 15 minutes or until tender. Cool. Add first 5 ingredients to cooked rice and stir. Place on crisp lettuce leaves on salad plates. Top with mayonnaise and a sprinkle of paprika. Serves 6.

Crab and Radish Salad with Lemon Vinaigrette

If fresh crab is not available, you can substitute lobster or grilled salmon.

1 lb	fresh crabmeat	500 g	**Vinaigrette:**		
1 lb	radishes	500 g	½ cup	olive oil	125 ml
3	carrots	3	3 tbsp	fresh lemon juice	45 ml
3	celery stalks, cut into matchsticks	3	1 tbsp	shallots, minced	15 ml
			1½ tsp	Dijon mustard	7 ml
2	cucumbers, peeled, seeded and cut into matchsticks	2	½ tsp	lemon peel, grated	2 ml
			½ tsp	sugar	2 ml
	mixed salad greens				

To make the vinaigrette: whisk together all ingredients until emulsified. Using a vegetable peeler cut carrots and radishes into 3-inch long ribbons. Toss with crab, celery, cucumber and vinaigrette. Serve on a bed of mixed salad greens. Serves 6.

The Great Nova Scotia Cookbook

Buttermilk Dressing

Melt 2 tbsp (30 ml) bacon fat or butter in the top of a double boiler and stir in 2 tbsp (30 ml) flour, 2 tbsp (30 ml) sugar and 1 tsp (5 ml) dry mustard. When smooth, slowly add 1 cup (8 oz) buttermilk, and set over boiling water. Cook and stir until thickened and smooth, then add 1 tsp (5 ml) salt. Remove from heat and stir in 3-4 tbsp (45-60 ml) vinegar and 1 tsp (5 ml) grated onion. Chill thoroughly before using. Makes 1 cup.

Balsamic Vinaigrette

This is a tangy vinaigrette—wonderful on mixed greens, tomato, onion and cucumber salads. It's also good if used sparingly over steamed veggies or stir-frys.

½ cup	extra virgin olive oil	125 ml	pinch	salt	
				ground black pepper	
½ cup	white balsamic vinegar	125 ml	1 tsp	minced fresh herbs, optional	5 ml
1	clove garlic, crushed	1			
1 tsp	mustard powder	5 ml			

In a small bowl, whisk together olive oil, white balsamic vinegar, garlic and mustard powder. Season to taste with salt and black pepper. Stir in minced fresh herbs if desired. Makes 1 cup.

Mustard Dill Dressing

This is an excellent dressing for salads or as a flavouring for other recipes. It stores well. Marjoram, tarragon, basil and/or black pepper may be added or substituted.

½ cup	prepared mustard	125 ml	2 tbsp	Parmesan cheese, grated	30 ml
½ cup	white wine vinegar	125 ml			
1 tsp	dried thyme	5 ml	2 tbsp	evaporated nonfat milk	30 ml
1½ tsp	dried dill	7 ml			
1 cup	canola or olive oil	250 ml			

In a medium-size bowl, combine the mustard, vinegar, thyme and dill. Let stand for 10 minutes. Add oil in a slow, steady stream, whisking constantly until thickened and smooth. Blend in Parmesan and milk. Transfer to a sterile jar with tight-fitting lid, and refrigerate until ready to use. Makes 2 cups.

Sour Cream Dressing

When a creamy dressing is required, try this.

1 cup	olive oil	250 ml	2 tsp	fresh parsley, chopped	10 ml
5 tbsp	red wine vinegar	75 ml			
¼ cup	sour cream	50 ml	1	clove garlic, minced	1
1½ tsp	salt	7 ml	dash	pepper	
½ tsp	dry mustard	2 ml			
¼ cup	white sugar	50 ml			

Whisk together all ingredients. Refrigerate at least 6 hours before serving. Makes 1½ cups.

Homemade Mustard
Salad Dressing

These ingredients are already in most kitchen cupboards.

½ cup	white sugar	125 ml	¼ cup	white wine vinegar	50 ml
2 tbsp	all-purpose flour	30 ml	¼ cup	water	50 ml
1 tsp	prepared mustard	5 ml	1	egg, beaten	1
½ tsp	salt	2 ml			

Whisk together all ingredients. Cook in a double boiler until thick; allow to cool. For potato salad, mix with equal parts mayonnaise. Makes 1 cup.

Orange Vinaigrette

A low-fat vinaigrette recipe.

¼ cup	orange juice	50 ml	2 tsp	honey	10 ml
2 tbsp	balsamic vinegar	30 ml	⅛ tsp	black pepper, cracked	0.8 ml
1 tbsp	Dijon-style mustard	15 ml			

In a small jar with a tight-fitting lid, combine the orange juice, vinegar, mustard, honey and pepper. Cover and shake until combined. Refrigerate for up to 1 week. Shake well before serving. Makes ½ cup.

Blue Cheese Dressing

Use on salads as well as on chicken wings, especially the hot and spicy ones.

1 cup	mayonnaise	250 ml		1 tsp	garlic powder	5 ml
1 cup	sour cream	250 ml		1 tbsp	Worcestershire sauce	15 ml
1 cup	buttermilk	250 ml		2 tbsp	Parmesan cheese, grated	30 ml
4 oz	blue cheese, crumbled	125 g		1 tbsp	parsley flakes	15 ml
1 tbsp	hot sauce	15 ml				

Whisk together the mayonnaise, sour cream, buttermilk, hot sauce, garlic powder, Worcestershire sauce, Parmesan cheese and parsley flakes. Add blue cheese, mix and refrigerate until chilled. Makes 3½ cups.

Poppy Seed Dressing

This dressing is wonderful over fresh fruit or shredded cabbage and halved grapes.

¾ cup	white sugar	175 ml		1 tbsp	onion juice	15 ml
1 tsp	dry mustard	5 ml		1 cup	vegetable oil	250 ml
1 tsp	salt	5 ml		1½ tbsp	poppy seeds	23 ml
⅓ cup	apple cider vinegar	75 ml				

Grate onion for juice. Whisk together all ingredients. Cover and refrigerate until ready to serve. Makes 2 cups.

Spinach Salad Dressing

1 clove	garlic, minced	1	1 tsp	dry mustard	5 ml
2 tbsp	red wine vinegar	30 ml	½ tsp	pepper	2 ml
1 tsp	sugar	5 ml	6 tbsp	salad or olive oil	90 ml
1 tsp	salt	5 ml			

Mix ingredients together and shake. Refrigerate. Makes 1 cup.

Salad Dressing with Condensed Milk

A sweet dressing.

2	eggs, beaten or egg substitute	2	1 10-oz can	condensed milk	300 ml
1 tsp	salt	5 ml	¾-1 cup	vinegar	180-250 ml
1 tsp	mustard	5 ml	juice	of 1 lemon	

Beat all together. Nice with potato salad. Makes 3 cups.

Maple Salad Dressing

1 cup	maple syrup	250 ml	¼ tsp	celery seed	1 ml
2 tbsp	vegetable oil	30 ml	¼ tsp	salt	1 ml
1 tbsp	lemon juice	15 ml	¼ tsp	onion salt	1 ml
½ tsp	paprika	2 ml	¼ tsp	dry mustard	1 ml

Combine all ingredients in a jar with tight-fitting lid; shake well. Serve over salad greens. Makes 1½ cups.

Quick Salad Dressing

1½ tsp	salt	7 ml	½ cup	evaporated milk, undiluted	125 ml
1½ tsp	dry mustard	7 ml	1½ cups	salad oil	375 ml
¼ cup	sugar	50 ml	⅔ cup	vinegar	150 ml

Combine salt, mustard and sugar in deep bowl. Add milk slowly. Beat well. Add oil, a quarter cup at a time, and beat after each addition until mixture is smooth. Add vinegar all at once. Beat until mixture thickens. Store in refrigerator in covered jar. For variations add ¼ cup (50 ml) chopped parsley. Makes 2½ cups.

Simple French Dressing

1 cup	salad oil	250 ml	1½ tsp	salt	7 ml
⅓ cup	vinegar	75 ml	½ tsp	paprika	2 ml
1 tbsp	sugar	15 ml	½ tsp	dry mustard	2 ml

Combine all ingredients in a bottle. Cover tightly and shake well. Chill several hours. Shake well before using. Makes 1½ cups.

Sweet and Sour French Dressing

1 cup	oil	250 ml	1 tsp	salt	5 ml
½ cup	vinegar	125 ml	¼ tsp	pepper	1 ml
1 cup	ketchup	250 ml	¼ tsp	garlic powder	1 ml
½ cup	sugar	125 ml	¼ tsp	celery seed	1 ml
2 tsp	paprika	10 ml			

Combine all ingredients. Beat or shake until well blended. Chill several hours to blend flavours. Makes 3 cups.

Snappy French Dressing

1 cup	vegetable oil	250 ml	1 tsp	dry mustard	5 ml
⅔ cup	ketchup	150 ml	1 tsp	paprika	5 ml
½ cup	cider vinegar	125 ml	¼ tsp	garlic powder	1 ml
½ cup	sugar	125 ml	dash	pepper	
½	onion, small	½	dash	salt	
1 tbsp	lemon juice	15 ml			

Put all ingredients in a blender. Cover and process. Makes 2 cups.

Tomato Soup Dressing

1 10-oz can	cream of tomato soup	284 ml	2 tbsp	sugar	30 ml
			1 tsp	dry mustard	5 ml
½ cup	salad oil	125 ml	1 tsp	paprika	5 ml
⅓ cup	cider vinegar	75 ml	1 tsp	salt	5 ml
1 tsp	Worcestershire sauce	5 ml			

Put ingredients in a bottle in order given. Cover tightly and shake well. Chill. Shake well again before using. Makes 2 cups.

Thousand Island Dressing

1 cup	mayonnaise	250 ml	1 tbsp	chopped sweet pickle	15 ml
½ cup	chili sauce or ketchup	125 ml	1 tbsp	olives, chopped finely	15 ml

Combine all ingredients and mix thoroughly. Makes 1½ cups.

No-Cook
Mayonnaise Dressing

2 tsp	sugar	10 ml	1 tbsp	lemon juice	15 ml
1 tsp	dry mustard	5 ml	1 tbsp	vinegar	15 ml
1 tsp	salt	5 ml	1½ cups	salad oil	375 ml
¼ cup	egg substitute	50 ml	1 tsp	boiling water	5 ml
dash	cayenne				

Mix dry ingredients; add egg substitute and beat well. Add part of vinegar, beat, then add ½ cup (125 ml) salad oil—drop by drop. Continue to add acids and oil, alternating between the two, until all is used, beating constantly until dressing is well thickened. Last of all, add the boiling water to prevent separation. Makes 1½ cups.

Mayonnaise Dressing

1 cup	milk	250 ml	2 tbsp	butter, softened	30 ml
3	eggs, beaten	3	6 tbsp	sugar	90 ml
¾ cup	vinegar	175 ml	¾ tsp	mustard	3 ml
2 tbsp	flour	30 ml			

Place milk in top of a double boiler, over hot water. Add beaten eggs. Heat vinegar in a saucepan. Mix dry ingredients with butter in a small bowl. Add a little milk to make a thin paste. Add this mixture to hot milk and eggs in double boiler. Cook until thick. Add heated vinegar. Stir together and remove from heat. Cool and store in a glass jar in refrigerator. Makes 2 cups.

Sweet Mayonnaise

Combine:

1 cup	vinegar	250 ml		1 tsp	salt	5 ml
1 cup	sugar	250 ml		1 tbsp	butter	15 ml
3	eggs	3		4 tsp	cornstarch	20 ml
1 tsp	mustard	5 ml				

Beat all together and cook in a double boiler. Makes 2½ cups.

No-Fat Mayonnaise

1 cup	yogurt, fat free	250 ml		1 cup	cottage cheese, fat free	250 ml

Use a blender to mix the ingredients to a smooth sauce. Season as desired with salt, pepper, garlic, mustard, herbs, spices, sugar, vanilla, or other flavouring.

Holland Dressing for Green Salads

2	hard-boiled eggs, grated	2		2 tsp	sugar	10 ml
				½ tsp	salt	2 ml
½ cup	Swiss cheese, shredded	125 ml		¼ cup	French dressing	50 ml
				⅛ tsp	garlic powder	0.5 ml
2 tbsp	vinegar	30 ml		dash	cayenne	
2 tbsp	oil	30 ml		½ tsp	dry mustard	2 ml

Mix all together in a screw-top jar. Shake well to mix. Shake again before using. Refrigerate. Makes 1½ cups.

Old-fashioned Cooked Dressing

1¼ cups	milk	310 ml		½ cup	vinegar	125 ml
⅓ cup	sugar	75 ml		2	egg yolks, slightly beaten	2
3 tbsp	flour	45 ml				
1¼ tsp	salt	6 ml		2 tbsp	butter	30 ml
2 tsp	dry mustard	10 ml				

Scald milk in top of double boiler. Mix sugar, flour, salt and mustard together in a small bowl, then stir in vinegar and egg yolks. When smooth, stir into scalded milk; whisk and cook until thick and smooth. Remove from heat and stir in the butter. Cover to prevent film from forming. Cool. Makes 2 cups.

Boiled Dressing

Nice with chicken salad.

4	beaten eggs	4		2 tsp	mustard	10 ml
2 cups	warm water	500 ml		1 tsp	salt	5 ml
4 tbsp	butter	60 ml		dash	paprika	
6 tbsp	flour	90 ml		1 cup	vinegar	250 ml
6 tbsp	sugar	90 ml				

In the top of a double boiler, cook first 3 ingredients over hot water, stirring until hot. Add next 5 ingredients, which have been blended together. Stir quickly to combine and continue to cook until thick. Add vinegar and continue to cook, stirring until thickened and blended. Thin with cream when cold. Store in refrigerator, in a glass jar. Makes 4 cups.

Tarragon Dressing

3 tbsp	balsamic vinegar	45 ml		2 tbsp	onion, finely chopped	30 ml
3 tbsp	lemon juice	45 ml				
2 tbsp	chopped tarragon, fresh	30 ml		1	clove garlic, minced	1
				⅔ cup	olive oil	170 ml
1 tbsp	honey	15 ml			salt and pepper	

Combine all ingredients except oil, in a bowl. Gradually whisk in oil.

Basic Vinaigrette

8 oz	Dijon mustard	224 g		2 tbsp	sugar	30 ml
1¼ cups	cider vinegar	300 ml		1 tbsp	salt	15 ml
¼ cup	cold water	50 ml		1 quart	Italian olive oil	1 L

Blend the first 5 ingredients, then slowly whisk in the olive oil using a wire whisk, food processor or blender. Store in an airtight container. May be kept in or out of the refrigerator. Use within 4 days for the freshest taste. Makes 7 cups.

Vinaigrette

¾ cup	extra virgin olive oil	175 ml		1 tsp	fresh basil, minced	5 ml
¼ cup	wine vinegar	50 ml		1 clove	garlic, minced (optional)	1
1	medium shallot	1			salt and pepper, to taste	
1 tbsp	fresh Italian parsley, diced	15 ml		dash	Dijon mustard	

Whisk together the olive oil, wine vinegar, shallot, parsley, basil, garlic, salt and pepper, and Dijon mustard. Allow to refrigerate overnight. Remove from refrigerator and serve at room temperature. Makes 1 cup.

Cumberland Dressing

2 tbsp	vinegar	30 ml		1 tbsp	heavy cream	15 ml
½ tsp	salt	2 ml		1 tbsp	currant jelly	15 ml
¼ tsp	pepper	1 ml		¼ tsp	lemon rind, grated	1 ml
½ cup	olive or salad oil	125 ml				

In a salad bowl, mix vinegar and salt. Let stand a few minutes. Add pepper and whisk in oil. If not acidic enough add more vinegar, to taste. Add cream, jelly and lemon rind. Stir to combine. Store in a jar with a tight cover, and shake well before using. Makes 1 cup.

Italian Salad Dressing

1 tsp	carrot, grated and chopped	5 ml		⅛ tsp	dried parsley flakes	0.8 ml
1 tsp	red bell pepper, finely chopped	5 ml		1 tsp	salt	5 ml
¼ cup	vinegar	50 ml		¼ tsp	garlic powder	1 ml
3 tbsp	water	45 ml		⅛ tsp	onion powder	0.5 ml
½ cup	oil	125 ml		2 tsp	sugar	10 ml
I tsp	lemon pepper	3 ml		⅛ tsp	pepper	0.5 ml
				2 tsp	Certo crystals	10 ml
				pinch	ground oregano	

Bake carrot and bell pepper at 250F (120C) for 45-60 minutes, or until all small pieces are completely dry but not browned. Combine the carrot and bell pepper with the vinegar in a cruet or jar. Add water, then add dry ingredients. Seal and shake vigorously. Add oil and shake until well blended.

If you would like to make the dressing with less oil, substitute with ¼ cup (50 ml) of water and ¼ cup (50 ml) of oil.

Caesar Salad Dressing

Don't leave out the anchovies! They provide the "tang."

2-3	garlic cloves	2-3	1 tsp	Dijon mustard	5 ml
2	green onions	2	3 tbsp	red wine vinegar	45 ml
1 3-oz can	anchovies	85 g	2 tbsp	lemon juice	30 ml
			1 cup	oil	250 ml
¼ cup	egg substitute	50 ml		salt and pepper	
1 tsp	Worcestershire sauce	5 ml	3 tbsp	Parmesan cheese	45 ml

Mix garlic, onions and anchovies in food processor. Add egg substitute, Worcestershire sauce and mustard. Mix for 1 minute. Add vinegar and lemon juice. Mix. Add oil, salt, pepper and Parmesan cheese. Makes 1½ cups.

Quick Caesar Dressing

1 cup	mayonnaise	250 ml	1 tbsp	anchovy paste	15 ml
¼ cup	egg substitute	50 ml	2 cloves	garlic, pressed	2
¼ cup	Parmesan cheese, grated	50 ml	2 tsp	sugar	10 ml
			½ tsp	coarse ground pepper	2 ml
2 tbsp	water	30 ml	¼ tsp	salt	1 ml
2 tbsp	olive oil	30 ml	¼ tsp	dried parsley flakes, crushed fine	1 ml
1½ tbsp	lemon juice	23 ml			

Combine all ingredients in a medium-size bowl. Use an electric mixer to beat ingredients for about 1 minute. Cover bowl and chill for several hours so that flavours can develop. Makes about 2 cups.

The Great Nova Scotia Cookbook

• SOUPS •

• Best •

• Traditional •

• Trendy •

Chicken Soup

Homemade soup is economical and easy to prepare. It starts with a good stock, made by simmering meat, bones and small amounts of vegetables and seasonings in water until the flavour in the solids is extracted and the liquid boiled down by a quarter of its original quantity. It is then ready to be strained and used as a base for soup.

For a most flavourful soup, use the carcass from a roasted, stuffed bird. The bones are deliciously flavoured with savoury stuffing. Remove all the meat from the bones as well as the small pieces left in the roaster or on the serving platter and place in refrigerator for later use in the soup.

Save and freeze the water used for cooking vegetables, and use later in other soups and gravies. Place bones and any vegetable water you have in a large soup kettle. Place kettle on heat. Add enough water to cover. Add a little salt to draw out the flavour of the ingredients. Add to the pot: celery tops, outside lettuce leaves, carrot peelings, mushroom stems, leftover chicken gravy, giblets and seasonings such as parsley or peppercorns, and anything "interesting" you may have on hand.

Bring all ingredients to a boil. Skim off any scum that forms on top. Reduce heat and simmer from 3-5 hours. Remove kettle from heat and strain through a sieve into a bowl. Cool and place uncovered, in the refrigerator. Remove fat, which will collect on surface. Measure the amount of stock.

Pour stock into soup kettle and place on heat. Add more liquid if desired. Bring to boil. Add about 1½ tbsp (22 ml) of rice to each 2 cups (500 ml) of stock. Continue to boil gently and add generous amounts of your favourite vegetables, either sliced or grated, which should include onion, green onion, celery, carrots, potato and peas plus chicken gravy and any seasonings you enjoy. Shortly before serving, add leftover chicken meat. Serve piping hot with crackers or crispy rolls.

Vegetable Stock

½ cup	onions, finely chopped	125 ml		2 cups	celery with leaves, diced	500 ml
dash	white pepper			1 cup	green lettuce, shredded	250 ml
dash	black pepper					
dash	cayenne			1 cup	mushrooms, chopped	250 ml
½ tsp	salt	2 ml				
½ cup	carrots, chopped	125 ml		1 cup	ripe tomatoes, sliced	250 ml
½ cup	turnip, chopped (optional)	125 ml				
				1 tsp	sugar	5 ml
½ cup	parsnips, chopped	125 ml				

In a heavy pot sauté onion in vegetable oil, add all other ingredients. Simmer for an hour and a half, or a little longer, in enough water to cover. Remove from heat; strain and chill. This stock may be frozen. Vegetables such as leeks, watercress and asparagus may also be used. Care must be taken, depending on how the stock is being used. Some vegetables such as peas, pea pods, cauliflower, broccoli, cabbage and some varieties of turnip are good for some recipes but too strong for others. Be aware that carrots and parsnips will sweeten the stock. If darker stock is required, try caramelizing the sugar.

Clam Broth

4 cups	clams in shell	1 L		1 cup	water	250 ml
1	celery stalk	1			salt (if desired)	
1	small bay leaf	1			pepper	

Wash clams in shell making sure all sand is removed. Change water several times. Place clams (in shell) in a large pot along with celery and seasonings. Add water. Cover and bring to boil. Simmer until shells open. Remove clams from broth. Strain broth and use as desired. Be careful when adding salt; clams can be quite salty. Clams are delicious served with melted butter or chopped and used in chowders.

Chicken Stock

Four pound (2 kg) chicken bones: legs, backs, wings, necks, and giblets or livers. Break apart as many bones as possible, so as to get the most flavour. Older birds are better than younger birds. Leftover chicken carcasses can be used with excess fat removed. Place meat and bones in a large, heavy stock pot. Cover with cold water to extract as many juices from the bones as possible. Use at least 4 quarts (4 L) of cold water. Add to the stock pot:

8	white peppercorns	8	6	parsley stems	6
1	bay leaf	1	1	medium onion, diced	1
1 tsp	thyme	5 ml	3	celery stalks, diced	3
1 tsp	savory	5 ml	1	medium carrot, diced	1

Bring all to a boil. Reduce heat and simmer for 2-3 hours or until stock is reduced by one-half. Remove from heat. Strain and chill. Before using, skim all fat off top. The stock may be frozen.

Turkey Soup

12 lb	turkey bones	6 kg	1 28-oz can	tomatoes (optional)	796 ml
3 quarts	water	3 L			
1 cup	celery, chopped	250 ml	¾ cup	peas	175 ml
2	large carrots, shredded	2	¾ cup	long grain rice	175 ml
			2 tsp	salt	10 ml
1	large onion	1	¾ tsp	pepper	3 ml
4	chicken bouillon cubes	4	½ tsp	marjoram (optional)	2 ml
			½ tsp	thyme	2 ml

Place turkey bones in a large kettle with water and salt. Bring to boil and simmer for 1-2 hours. Turn bones occasionally. Remove from heat and strain in colander. Return broth to kettle. Remove meat from bones and cut into bite-size pieces. Set aside. Add carrots, celery, onion, and bouillon to broth in kettle. Bring to a boil. Reduce heat and simmer for about a half-hour. Add tomatoes and peas. If necessary, add more salt. Also add rice, pepper, marjoram, thyme and reserved turkey meat. Return to boil. Cook until rice is tender.

Scotch Broth

1-2 lb	stewing lamb	500 g-1 kg	1-2	leeks	1-2
⅓ cup	pearl barley	75 ml	2-3	carrots	2-3
½ cup	dried green peas	125 ml	1 cup	turnip	250 ml
1 tsp	salt	5 ml		black pepper, to taste	
6 cups	water	1.5 L	1 tsp	parsley (more if fresh)	5 ml
1	medium onion	1			

Soak dried peas in water overnight or 6-8 hours. Dice the meat, removing any fat. Bring meat, barley, peas, any bones, salt and water to a boil and simmer for two hours. Prepare vegetables and cut into ½-inch (1.3 cm) cubes; add to broth and simmer another hour. Add pepper and more water, if needed. Remove bones from pot. Add extra seasoning if you wish. Skim fat from top. Add chopped parsley and serve.

Beef and Barley Soup

3 lb	cross-cut beef shank, meaty	1.5 kg	½ cup	parsley, chopped	125 ml
¼ cup	flour	50 ml	2 tsp	salt	10 ml
¾ cup	pearl barley	175 ml	½ tsp	pepper	2 ml
2	carrots	2	4 cups	water	1 L
2	medium onions, thinly sliced	2			

Dredge meat with flour. Sear on all sides in a little oil in a large kettle. Add water and cook on low heat for about 2 hours. Keep adding water as the broth boils down.

Remove meat. Discard bones and skin, and cut meat into small pieces. Return meat to pot, adding the barley, carrots, onion, parsley and salt and pepper. Boil until all ingredients are tender. Remove from stove and serve.

Goulash Soup

2 tbsp	vegetable oil	30 ml		1 tsp	thyme	5 ml
2	large carrots, peeled and chopped	2		1½ lb	lean ground beef	750 g
				1 cup	tomato paste	250 ml
2	celery stalks, chopped	2		1 tsp	paprika	5 ml
1	onion, chopped	1		6 cups	beef stock	1.5 L
1 cup	turnip, chopped	250 ml		3	medium potatoes, peeled and chopped	3
1 clove	garlic	1				
1 tsp	oregano	5 ml		1 tbsp	vinegar	15 ml
1 tsp	basil	5 ml				

In a large, heavy saucepan, heat oil. Cook carrots, celery, onion, turnip, garlic, oregano, basil and thyme, stirring occasionally, until soft. Add beef and cook. Most liquid should be evaporated. Stir in tomato paste and paprika. Add stock, potatoes and vinegar. Bring to boil. Reduce heat and simmer until potatoes are tender. Serve in heated bowls.

Mushroom Barley Soup

1½ lb	boneless beef chuck, cut in ¾-inch cubes	750 g		2 cloves	garlic	2
				7 cups	chicken or beef broth, bouillon will do	1.75 L
1 tbsp	vegetable oil	15 ml				
2 cups	onion, finely chopped	500 ml		2 cups	water	500 ml
				½ cup	pearl barley	125 ml
1 cup	carrots, diced	250 ml			salt and pepper, to taste	
½ cup	celery, sliced	125 ml				
1 lb	fresh mushrooms, sliced	500 g		3 tbsp	parsley	45 ml

In a soup kettle, brown meat in oil. Remove meat from kettle with a slotted spoon and set aside. Use drippings to sauté onion, carrots, and celery, over medium heat until tender, about 5 minutes. Add mushrooms, garlic and thyme; cook and stir for 3 minutes. Add broth, water, barley, salt and pepper. Return meat to kettle, bring to boil. Reduce heat, cover and simmer for 1½-2 hours, making sure barley and meat are tender. Add parsley.

Bean Soup

¼ cup each	dry yellow split peas, lentils, black beans, great northern beans, pinto beans, baby lima beans and kidney beans	50 ml each		1 tsp	thyme	5 ml
				1 tsp	rosemary, crushed	5 ml
				1 tsp	garlic powder	5 ml
				½ tsp	celery seed	2 ml
				½ tsp	basil	2 ml
½ cup each	dry green split peas, black-eyed peas and navy beans	125 ml each		¼ tsp	red pepper flakes crushed	1 ml
				½ tsp	dry mustard	2 ml
2 quarts	water	1.75 L		1 28-oz can	crushed tomatoes	796 ml
⅓ cup	onion, dried and minced	75 ml				
1 tbsp	salt	15 ml				

Place peas and beans in a Dutch oven; add enough water to cover. Bring to boil; boil for 2 minutes. Remove from heat let stand for 1 hour. Drain and discard water. Add 2 quarts (2 L) of fresh water and seasonings; bring to a boil. Reduce heat and simmer for 2 hours, or until beans are just tender. Stir in tomatoes. Increase heat to medium. Cook uncovered for 15-30 minutes. Serve.

Garden Tomato Soup

8 cups	ripe tomatoes, coarsely chopped	2 L		1½ cup	onions, chopped	375 ml
				¾ cup	celery, chopped	175 ml
2 tbsp	parsley, chopped	30 ml		1 tsp	salt	5 ml
4 cups	chicken broth	1 L		½ tsp	pepper	2 ml
½ cup	butter	125 ml		2 tsp	sugar	10 ml

Heat butter in a skillet, add onions and celery. Place tomatoes and parsley in a large saucepan; add chicken broth, sugar, salt and pepper. Add sautéed onions, celery and butter. Simmer for 1 hour or more. If desired, more spices—garlic, oregano or thyme—may be added. Sprinkle a few croutons on top when served.

Four-Onion Soup

The onion flavour is unmistakable.

5	green onions, with tops	5	3 tbsp	butter	45 ml
			3 cups	beef broth	750 ml
1	medium red onion	1	1 tsp	Worcestershire sauce	5 ml
1	medium yellow onion	1	1 cup	Swiss cheese, shredded	250 ml
1	medium leek, white portion only	1	6 slices	French bread, toasted	6
1	garlic clove, crushed and minced	1		Parmesan cheese, grated, if desired	6

Coarsely slice onions and sauté in butter in a large saucepan until tender. Add broth and Worcestershire sauce. Bring to boil. Reduce heat and simmer for a half-hour.

Sprinkle 1 tbsp (15 ml) Swiss cheese in the bottom of six warm soup bowls. Ladle soup into bowls. Top each with a slice of bread. Sprinkle each with remaining Swiss cheese (and Parmesan, if desired). Broil until cheese melts. Serve immediately. Note: Make sure soup bowls are ovenproof.

Tomato Vegetable Soup

1 tbsp	butter	15 ml	1 tbsp	soy sauce, less if desired	15 ml
3	green onions, cut into 1-inch pieces	3	¼ tsp	salt (optional)	1 ml
2	medium carrots	2	2 cups	broccoli florets	500 ml
1½ cups	mushrooms, sliced	375 ml	2 cups	spinach, chopped	500 ml
2 cups	chicken broth	500 ml			
1 28-oz can	tomatoes	796 g			

Melt butter in large saucepan. Sauté onions, carrots and mushrooms over medium heat for 2 minutes. Add broth, tomatoes (breaking apart with a fork), soy sauce and salt. Bring to a boil. Stir in broccoli florets. Cover and simmer for 5 minutes. Add spinach and cook 2 minutes longer.

Minestrone Soup

1	large beef soup bone	1	1 cup	carrots, diced	250 ml
½ cup	dried white beans	125 ml	1	large potato, cubed	1
10 cups	water	2.5 L	2 tbsp	parsley	30 ml
1 tbsp	salt	15 ml	½ lb	ground beef	250 g
¼ tsp	pepper	1 ml	¾ cup	parsnip, sliced	175 ml
¾ cup	celery, chopped	175 ml	½ cup	green beans, frozen	125 ml
1 cup	cabbage, shredded	250 ml	¾ cup	dry spaghetti, broken-up	175 ml
1	onion, chopped	1			
½ tsp	minced garlic, dried	2 ml			

Put the beef bone, beans, water, salt and pepper into a large covered kettle and simmer for a few hours. Remove from stove. Remove soup bone from mixture. Add onions, garlic, celery, cabbage, carrots, potato and parsley to pot. Brown ground beef in a little oil and add to soup pot. Cover and simmer. Add parsnips and green beans. Simmer until vegetables are nearly done, then add spaghetti and cook until *al dente*. Serve with a sprinkling of Parmesan cheese. Good with triangles of toast, crusty rolls or crackers.

Mulligatawny Soup

Boil a large beef bone in enough water to make 3 quarts, or over a litre, of beef stock. Pour stock into a large kettle and prepare the following ingredients:

½ cup	butter	175 ml	2-3 lb	fresh, ripe tomatoes	1-1.5 kg
1 cup	onions, diced	250 ml		or	
1 cup	celery, diced	250 ml	1 28-oz can	tomatoes, drained	796 ml
2 tbsp	curry powder	30 ml			
1 tbsp	flour	15 ml	2-3 cups	chicken, cooked and de-boned	500-750 ml
	salt and pepper, to taste				

Melt butter in frying pan on low heat. Sauté onions and celery. Stir in curry powder and flour. Cook for 1 minute. Add to beef stock in pot along with tomatoes. Simmer, uncovered, over medium heat until thickened, stirring frequently. Season with salt and pepper. Add chicken and serve.

Pea Soup and Dumplings

Unusual and delicious.

1 lb	salt beef or a 2 lb (1 kg) ham bone	500 g	3	parsnips, cubed	3
			3	onions	3
1 lb	yellow split peas	500 g	1-2 cups	turnip, cubed	250-500 ml
2 quarts	water	2 L		salt and pepper to taste	
3	carrots, cubed	3	¼ lb	butter	125 g

If using salt beef, soak overnight. Soak peas overnight. In the morning put meat, peas and water in soup kettle. Simmer for 1-2 hours. Uncooked vegetables may be added to the broth, or they may be fried in the butter until soft and golden and added to the broth—about an hour before serving. If desired, dumplings may be made and added about 10 minutes before serving.

Dumplings:

2 cups	flour	500 ml
1 tsp	salt	5 ml
1 tbsp	shortening	15 ml
4 tsp	baking powder	20 ml
	cold water	

Sift dry ingredients into bowl. Work in shortening and mix in enough water to form firm dough. Spoon balls of dough into soup one by one. Cook covered about 10 minutes.

The Great Nova Scotia Cookbook

Country Mushroom Soup

The chicken broth enhances the flavour.

2 cups	chicken broth	500 ml		¼ cup	onion, finely chopped	50 ml
¼ cup	butter	50 ml		3 tbsp	vegetable oil	45 ml
¼ cup	flour	50 ml		1 lb	mushrooms, sliced	500 g
½ tsp	salt	2 ml		⅔ cup	evaporated milk	150 ml
¼ tsp	pepper	1 ml				
⅔ cup	celery, chopped	150 ml				

In a large saucepan, melt butter. Stir in flour until well blended. Gradually stir in broth. Mix well. Add salt and pepper. Simmer for 20 minutes. In a skillet, sauté celery and onion in oil until tender. Add mushrooms. Cook and stir until tender. Add to broth mixture, and bring to boil. Reduce heat, and simmer for 20 minutes. Add milk, heat and serve.

Mushroom Soup

An old standby.

3 tbsp	butter	45 ml		3 cups	milk	750 ml
3 tbsp	onion, chopped	45 ml		3 tbsp	flour	45 ml
1½ cups	mushrooms, sliced	375 ml		½ tsp	salt	2 ml
⅓ cup	celery	75 ml		dash	pepper	

Heat butter in skillet. Add onions, celery and mushrooms. Sauté until tender. Mix flour, salt and pepper into a small amount of the milk. Stir to blend well. Place remaining milk in a saucepan, heat but do not boil, then add flour mixture, stirring constantly until mixture thickens. Add sautéed vegetables and heat; Do not boil. Pour into heated bowls; add a sprig of parsley, and serve with crackers.

Cream of Turnip Soup

For those turnip lovers!

3 lb	white turnips	1.5 kg	4 cups	rich chicken broth	1 L
2	large potatoes	2		salt, to taste	
5 tbsp	butter	75 ml		freshly ground pepper, to taste	
1½ cups	onions, coarsely chopped	375 ml	1 cup	heavy cream	250 ml
4 cups	water	1 L	¼ tsp	Tabasco sauce	1 ml

Peel turnips and cut them into 1-inch (2.5 cm) cubes. There should be about 8 cups (2 L). Set aside.

Peel the potatoes and cut them into 1-inch (2.5 cm) cubes. There should be about 2½ cups (625 ml). Heat 2 tbsp (30ml) of the butter in a kettle and add the onions. Cook. Add turnips, potatoes, water, broth, salt and pepper. Bring to a boil and cover. Cook 30 minutes. Drain the turnip and potato mixture. Reserve solids and liquids. Blend the solids in a food processor or electric blender, adding enough of the reserved cooking liquid to make a smooth purée. Combine the purée with the remaining liquid. Strain the mixture through a fine sieve into a clean kettle, pressing to extract as much liquid as possible from the solids that remain in the sieve. Bring to a boil and stir in the cream, the remaining butter and the Tabasco sauce. Serve. Makes 8 or more servings.

Creamed Corn Chowder

An old recipe that's still popular.

2 cups	potatoes, cut in small cubes	500 ml	1 cup	evaporated milk (undiluted)	250 ml
2 cups	water	500 ml	1 tbsp	butter	15 ml
2½ cups	creamed corn	625 ml		salt and pepper	

Cook potatoes in water until tender. Do not drain. Add milk, corn, butter, salt and pepper. Heat to just boiling. Turn off heat and simmer. Ladle into heated bowls and add a small piece of butter to each bowl. Serve with crackers.

Raspberry-Cranberry Soup

Served hot or cold, it's a beautiful, tangy soup.

2 cups	fresh or frozen cranberries	500 ml		1 tbsp	lemon juice	15 ml
				¼ tsp	cinnamon	1 ml
2 cups	apple juice	500 ml		2 cups	light cream, divided	500 ml
1 cup	fresh or frozen raspberries	250 ml		1 tsp	cornstarch	15 ml
½-1 cup	sugar	125-250 ml			whipped cream	

In a 3-quart (3 L) saucepan, bring cranberries and apple juice to a boil. Reduce heat and simmer uncovered for 10 minutes. Press through sieve; return to the pan. Press raspberries through the sieve; discard seeds, and add to the cranberry mixture; bring to a boil. Add sugar, lemon juice and cinnamon; remove from heat. Cool 4 minutes. Stir 1 cup (250 ml) of the cranberry mixture into 1½ cups (375 ml) of cream. Return to pan. Bring to a gentle boil. Mix cornstarch with remaining cream; stir into soup. Cook and stir for 2 minutes. Serve hot or chilled. Garnish with whipped cream and a few raspberries, if desired. Serves 6.

Corn Chowder

Here is a traditional recipe with an un-traditional convenience: frozen corn.

3 slices	bacon	3		1½ cups	milk	375 ml
¼ cup	onion, finely chopped	50 ml		2 tsp	parsley	10 ml
				¼ tsp	salt	1 ml
2 tbsp	flour	30 ml		¼ tsp	pepper	1 ml
1-2 cups	corn kernels	250-500 ml		1 cup	water	250 ml

Fry bacon until crisp; drain and chop. Drain off fat from skillet and add onion. Fry onion just until soft. Remove from pan. Add water and corn. Bring to boil for 3-4 minutes. Pour milk into saucepan on medium heat. Mix flour, salt and pepper with a little of the milk to make a smooth paste. Add to milk in saucepan and heat; stirring until slightly thickened. Add bacon, onion, corn, parsley, salt and pepper. Simmer, then serve in heated bowls. Serves 2.

Baked Potato Chowder

Baking the potatoes adds a rich touch to a hearty meal.

2	large potatoes, baked	2	1 tsp	salt	5 ml
3 tbsp	butter	45 ml	¾ tsp	pepper	3 ml
1 cup	onion, diced	250 ml	½ tsp	thyme	2 ml
2 tbsp	flour	30 ml	1 cup	rich milk	250 ml
4 cups	chicken broth	1 L	½ cup	Cheddar cheese, shredded	125 ml
2 cups	water	500 ml			
¼ cup	cornstarch	50 ml	¼ cup	bacon, cooked and crumbled	50 ml
1½ cups	instant mashed potatoes	375 ml			
			2	green onions, chopped	2

Cut cooled baked potatoes in half and remove contents with a dessert spoon. Chop into about ½-inch (1.3 cm) pieces. Melt butter in a large saucepan. Sauté onion until lightly browned. Add flour to onions and stir well. Add broth, water, cornstarch, instant potatoes and spices to the pot, and bring to boil. Reduce heat and simmer for a few minutes. Add chopped potato and milk to the saucepan. Bring soup to boil and then reduce heat and simmer for about 15 minutes or until thick. Spoon into soup bowls and top each with a tablespoon of Cheddar cheese and bacon and a teaspoon of chopped green onion. Serves 6.

Golden Squash Soup

5 tbsp	butter	75 ml	1 tsp	salt	5 ml
4 med.	carrots, chopped	4	½ tsp	thyme	2 ml
3 sliced	leeks (white part only)	3	¼ tsp	pepper	1 ml
3 lb	butternut squash, peeled and cubed	1.5 kg	1 cup	evaporated milk	250 ml
			½ cup	water	125 ml
6 cups	chicken broth	1.5 L		chives for garnish 3-4 inch lengths	
3 small	zucchini, peeled & sliced	3			

Sauté leeks and carrots in butter in large saucepan over medium heat. Add squash, zucchini, broth, salt, thyme and pepper; bring to a boil. Reduce heat, cover and simmer until vegetables are tender. Cool until lukewarm. In a blender, purée soup in small batches until smooth. Return to saucepan. Add milk and water. Mix well and heat; do not boil. Garnish with 2 or 3 chives in each bowl. Serves 6.

Clam Chowder

A meal in a bowl!

3 cups	chicken broth	750 ml		½ cup	parsley, chopped	125 ml
2 small cans	minced clams (or use fresh clams)	2		⅓ cup	celery, chopped	75 ml
				1	small onion, chopped	1
2	medium carrots, peeled and diced small	2		¼ cup	butter	50 ml
				2 tbsp	flour	30 ml
2 cups	potatoes, peeled and diced	500 ml		1 cup	evaporated milk	250 ml
					salt and pepper, to taste	

In a large saucepan, combine chicken broth, clams, carrots, potatoes, parsley, celery and onion. Bring to a boil. Simmer for 30 minutes on medium heat. Combine butter and flour in a small saucepan; blend well. Gradually add milk, stirring until well blended. Stir constantly over low heat until smooth and thickened. Add sauce to cooked vegetables and clams. Stir to combine and add salt and pepper to taste. Serve piping hot. Serves 6.

Crab Bisque

½ cup	margarine or butter	125 ml		½ lb	shrimp, cooked and cut up (optional)	250 g
¼ cup	green onions, chopped	50 ml		6 cups	milk	1.5 L
2 tbsp	flour	30 ml		1 cup	cream	250 ml
¼ tsp	curry powder	1.5 ml		1 tbsp	parsley flakes	15 ml
2 19-oz cans	kernel corn, drained	2x540 ml		1½ tsp	salt	7 ml
4 8-oz cans	white crabmeat, drained	4x250 g		¼ tsp	pepper	1 ml

In a Dutch oven, melt margarine and sauté onion until tender. Blend in flour and stir until smooth. Add milk gradually and stir until well blended. Stir in cream. Add remaining ingredients and heat. Do not boil.

Note: Check crabmeat for pieces of shell.

Sweet Corn Chowder with Crab

3 slices	bacon	3	1½ cups	water		375 ml
½ cup	onion, chopped	125 ml	1 cup	2% milk		250 ml
1	bay leaf	1	1 cup	whole milk		250 ml
½ tsp	thyme	2 ml	¾ lb	crabmeat, cooked and cleaned		375 g
2	medium potatoes, peeled and diced	2	2 tbsp	dry sherry or cooking wine		30 ml
2 cups	corn, fresh or frozen	500ml		salt and pepper, to taste		

Cook bacon in heavy saucepan until nicely browned and crisp; crumble and set aside for garnish. Cook onion in bacon fat over medium heat until translucent but not brown. Add bay leaf, thyme, potatoes and water and bring to simmer over medium heat. Add corn, milk and sherry. Simmer over low heat until potatoes are tender. Allow the chowder to stand overnight. If the chowder is simmered uncovered and stirred occasionally for several hours over very low heat, the flavours will blend beautifully. Add crabmeat and simmer a few minutes until crabmeat is completely warm. Serve hot in individual bowls. Garnish with chopped bacon.

Creamed Spinach and Fish Soup

1 12-oz pkg	frozen fish fillets, any variety, partially thawed	400 g	½ cup	onion, chopped	125 ml
			¼ cup	butter	50 ml
			⅓ cup	all-purpose flour	75 ml
1 10-oz pkg	frozen spinach, chopped	300 g	2 cups	light cream	500 ml
				salt and pepper	
4 cups	chicken broth	1 L			

Cut fish fillets into ¾-inch (2 cm) pieces. Simmer fish and spinach in broth for about 10 minutes or until fish is cooked. Sauté onion in butter in a large saucepan until tender. Stir in flour. Gradually add fish mixture, stirring until smooth. Cook, stirring constantly, just until thickened. Stir in cream and heat through. Season to taste with salt and pepper. Makes about 8 servings.

Basic Fish Chowder

2 lb	haddock	1 kg		1 quart	milk	1 L
8	potatoes, cut in small pieces	8		1 cup	cream or undiluted evaporated milk	250 ml
4	celery stalks, chopped	4		1 tsp	cornstarch	5 ml
1	small onion, chopped	1		2 tbsp	butter	15 ml

Poach haddock in salted water until it flakes. Remove fish from cooking pot. Reserve liquid. Check fish for bones. Set aside. Cook the potatoes, celery and onion in water left from the haddock, and drain. Potatoes may be put through a potato ricer, to give the base an added creamy texture. Put vegetables back in pot, add milk and butter. Mix cornstarch into a little water, mix with cream and stir into pot. Add haddock. Cook until slightly thickened. Do not boil. Stir frequently. This can be served as is, or carrots, chives and green onions may be added.

Cod Bisque

There is nothing better than hot soup on a cold day. Relax and enjoy this low-fat meal in a bowl.

2 tbsp	olive oil	30 ml		2 tbsp	flour	30 ml
1	small onion, diced	1		2 cups	evaporated skim milk	500 ml
1	carrot, sliced	1				
1	celery stalk, sliced	1		½ tsp	paprika	2 ml
12 oz	cod, thawed and cut into small pieces	336 g		¼ cup	scallion tops, finely chopped	50 ml
1 10-oz can	chicken broth	360 ml				

Heat oil in a heavy, 3-quart saucepan. Add onion, carrot and celery and cook for 5 minutes. Stir in cod and chicken broth. Simmer for 15 minutes until cod is white and flaky. Combine evaporated skim milk and flour in a shaker container, then slowly whisk into heated mixture. Bring to a boil, then reduce heat and simmer for 3 minutes, stirring continuously. Ladle bisque into serving bowls and sprinkle with paprika and scallion tops.

Seafood Chowder

A family favourite. Good for home or parties.

¼ cup	butter	50 ml
½ cup	onion, chopped	125 ml
2	bouillon cubes	2
2 cups	hot water	500 ml
1 cup	celery, chopped	250 ml
3	carrots, cut into small pieces	3
2 cups	potatoes, cut into cubes	500 ml
⅛ tsp	pepper	0.5 ml

1½ lb	haddock fillets	750 g
2⅓ cups	evaporated milk	575 ml
⅓ cup	flour	75 ml
1 8-oz can	crabmeat	250 g
1 8-oz can	lobster meat	250 g
2-3	bay leaves	2-3
	parsley	

Cook haddock in 2 cups hot water or enough water to cover. Remove from heat. Drain water and save. Check fish for bones.

Melt butter in a large, heavy pot. Sauté onion, add bouillon cubes dissolved in 2 cups (500 ml) of the haddock water. Add celery, carrots, potatoes, pepper and bay leaves. Simmer until just tender. Add haddock. To 1 cup (250 ml) of the milk add flour to make smooth paste. Add to above ingredients, stirring constantly. Add remaining milk and cook until mixture thickens. Remove bay leaves. Stir in crab and lobster with juice. Garnish with parsley. Make sure this mixture doesn't boil! Add salt if necessary (bouillon cubes are salty).

Recipe may be doubled or tripled, but be sure to make plenty. Demands for seconds and thirds can be expected.

Chicken Corn Chowder

Quick and spicy.

1½ lb	chicken breasts, boneless, skinless	750 g	2 cups	Monterey Jack cheese	500 ml
½ cup	onion, chopped	125 ml	1 19-oz can	cream-style corn	540 ml
1 clove	garlic, crushed and sliced	1	1 4-oz can	chopped green chilies, undrained	112 g
3 tbsp	butter	45 ml	¼ tsp	hot pepper sauce	1 ml
2	chicken bouillon cubes	2	1	medium tomato, chopped	1
1 cup	hot water	250 ml		parsley	
2 cups	milk	500 ml			

Cut chicken into bite-sized pieces. In a large saucepan, brown chicken, onion, and garlic in butter, until chicken is no longer pink. Dissolve bouillon in water and add to the pan; bring to boil. Reduce heat and let simmer for 5 minutes. Add milk, cheese, corn, chilies and pepper sauce. Cook and stir until cheese melts. Stir in tomato. Serve immediately. Garnish with parsley. Serves 6.

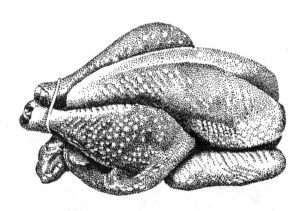

Asparagus Chicken Chowder

3-3½ lb	chicken	1½-2 kg		2 cups	potatoes, peeled and cubed	500 ml
3½ quarts	water	4-5 L		1 tsp	salt	5 ml
				1½ tsp	thyme	7 ml
2 tsp	chicken bouillon granules	10 ml		½ tsp	pepper	2 ml
				½ cup	flour	125 ml
5 slices	bacon, diced	5		1½ cups	cream or evaporated milk	375 ml
2	medium carrots	2				
1	medium onion, chopped	1			parsley	
½ lb	asparagus, fresh or frozen, cut in ½-inch pieces	250 g				

Place chicken, water and bouillon in a soup kettle. Cover and bring to a boil. Reduce heat and simmer for 1½ hours or until chicken is tender. Remove chicken and cool. Strain chicken stock to remove any skin or bone. Return stock to kettle, reserving 1 cup (250 ml). In a skillet, over medium heat, cook bacon until crisp. Remove bacon; drain on paper towels. Leave about 2 tbsp (30 ml) drippings in skillet. Sauté carrots, onion and asparagus in drippings, until tender crisp. Add to kettle along with potatoes, salt, thyme and pepper; bring to boil. Reduce heat; cover and simmer for 20 minutes or until potatoes are tender. Combine flour and reserved broth. Stir into soup. Bring to boil, cook and stir for 2 minutes. De-bone chicken and cut in strips. Add to soup along with milk and parsley. Heat, but do not boil. Serve in heated soup bowls. Sprinkle with bacon. Serves 12.

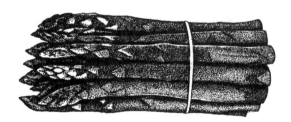

· MAIN COURSES ·

· Best ·

· Traditional ·

· Trendy ·

Roast Chicken with Stuffing

The traditional Sunday dinner.

Chicken:

Take a nice, plump roasting or frying chicken, remove the giblets and the fat pads and wash well. Be careful not to cut or tear the skin, since it will contain the stuffing. Drain the chicken and pat dry with a paper towel. Place the giblets in a small saucepan with 1 cup (250 ml) of water, a couple celery tops and a grind of black pepper, and simmer for a while to make stock. Add a chicken bouillon cube if desired.

Stuffing:

4 cups	bread, slightly dried out, cut or broken up in ½-inch (1.5 cm) cubes	1 L	pinch	thyme	
				black pepper and salt	
2 tbsp	butter	30 ml		summer savoury, as desired	
2	medium onions, chopped	2			
2	celery stalks with a few leaves, chopped	2	1	small apple, grated	1

In a large frying pan, sauté onion, celery, spices and apple until the onion and celery are limp. Add bread and toss together. Moisten with the chicken stock; the stuffing should be damp, but not so wet that it sticks together or turns to mush. The recipe may be doubled.

Stuff the chicken:

First, loosen the skin of the chicken (except for wings, thighs and legs). Carefully push your thumbs around between the skin and the meat. Use a small sharp knife to cut anything that doesn't loosen easily, like where the breast bone meets the skin.

Take about half of the stuffing and work it gently into the space between the skin and the meat of the chicken in an even plump layer. Stuff the main cavity and the front cavity with the rest of the stuffing. Sew up the skin, using a big needle and light cotton string, or fasten skin with toothpicks or skewers. When fastened, press to even out the shape of the bird. Put the chicken on a rack in a roasting pan; put a few pats of butter on top. Season with salt and pepper.

Roast the chicken at 325F (165C), basting with pan juices occasionally, until the skin is nicely browned and the juices run clear when the thickest parts of the thigh are deeply pierced. Make gravy from the pan juices.

Some cooks prefer stuffing made from potato or a mixture of potato and bread. Summer savoury is preferred by some, while others choose sage or poultry seasoning. Many cooks do not stuff birds, preferring instead to cook the stuffing in a dish. Let family preferences be your guide. Serves 6-8.

Maple-Baked Chicken Breasts

4	chicken breasts	4	1½ tsp	savoury, dried	7 ml
½ cup	all-purpose flour	125 ml	1 tsp	thyme, dried	5 ml
	salt and freshly ground		1 tsp	sage, dried (optional)	5 ml
	black pepper, to taste		1	onion, sliced	1
2 tbsp	butter	30 ml	½ cup	water	125 ml
½ cup	maple syrup	125 ml			

Dredge chicken in flour seasoned with salt and pepper. In a heavy, flame-proof casserole dish, heat butter until bubbling and brown chicken pieces quickly on both sides. Pour maple syrup over chicken. Sprinkle with savoury, thyme and sage. Pour water into the bottom of casserole. Bake, uncovered in a 350F (175C) oven for 50-60 minutes or until tender, basting chicken occasionally with pan juices. Serves 4

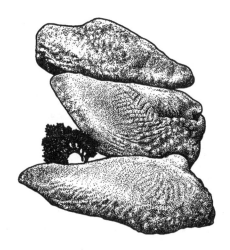

Grilled Chicken Burgers

1 lb	chicken, ground	500 g		½ cup	onion, minced	125 ml
1 cup	Mozzarella cheese, shredded	250 ml		½ cup	salad dressing	125 ml
				1 tbsp	barbecue sauce	15 ml
¾ cup	soft breadcrumbs	175 ml		1	egg, beaten	1

Mix all ingredients in a bowl. Form into patties. Grill over medium coals for at least 10 minutes per side, until juices run clear. Serve on toasted buns with lettuce, sliced tomato and salad dressing. Serves 4.

Chicken and Potatoes

½ cup	sour cream	125 ml		1 cup	chicken, cooked and cubed	250 ml
¾ cup	Cheddar cheese, grated	175 ml				
				1 cup	frozen mixed vegetables, cooked	250 ml
½ tsp	basil leaves	2 ml				
¼ tsp	salt	1.5 ml		2	large baking potatoes, baked	2
⅛ tsp	pepper	0.5 ml				

In a medium-sized saucepan, combine sour cream, ½ cup (125 ml) cheese, basil, salt and pepper. Add half remaining cheese, mixed vegetables and chicken. Heat gently until cheese is melted.

Cut potatoes in half. Spoon chicken mixture over potatoes and top with remaining cheese. Broil until cheese melts. Serves 2.

Chicken with Pastry

Chicken:

2-3 lb	chicken	1-1.5 kg
1	large onion	1
1	celery stalk	1
1 tsp	salt	5 ml
¼ cup	all-purpose flour	50 ml
¼ cup	water	50 ml
	salt and pepper, to taste	

Pastry:

2 cups	all-purpose flour	500 ml
1 tsp	salt	5 ml
¾ cup	shortening or lard	175 ml
¼ cup	cold water	50 ml

Place chicken, onion, celery and salt in a large pot. Add enough water to completely cover the chicken. Bring to a boil; reduce heat and simmer until chicken is tender and cooked through, about 1 hour. Remove chicken from broth, and let sit until cool enough to handle. Pick chicken off the bones and discard bones. Grease 9x13-inch (23x33 cm) baking dish. Place bite size pieces of chicken in baking dish. Strain broth and return 3 cups (750 ml) to the pot. In a small bowl, blend flour with water to make a smooth paste. Stir into hot broth. Cook 5-10 minutes or until broth is thickened. Season with salt and pepper. Pour over chicken.

To make pastry: In a large bowl, combine flour and salt. Cut in shortening with a pastry blender or two knives until mixture forms coarse crumbs. Sprinkle with cold water and mix until dough holds together and will form a ball. Roll out on a floured board or pastry cloth to about ¼-inch (5mm) thickness. Cut into strips and place over the chicken. Bake at 375F (190C) until the pastry is golden brown. Serves 6.

Southern Fried Chicken

1	frying chicken	1		1 tsp	pepper	5 ml
2	eggs	2		1½ cups	flour	375 ml
1 cup	milk	250 ml		3 cups	lard	750 ml
1½ tsp	salt	7 ml				

In a shallow bowl, beat eggs and stir in milk, salt and pepper. Cut chicken into pieces. Soak chicken in milk mixture for about 5 minutes. Roll each piece in flour. Set aside to dry. In a large, cast-iron skillet, heat the lard over medium-high heat. When the fat is very hot, add the thighs and legs and cook for several minutes. Add the other pieces, being careful not to overcrowd the skillet. Cook until chicken is golden brown on one side, about 5 minutes. Turn and brown on the other side. Reduce heat to medium low. Cover and cook 30 minutes, turning pieces after 15 minutes. Uncover the last 5 minutes so that the crust will be crisp. Serves 4.

Japanese Chicken Wings

3 lb	chicken wings	1.5 kg		For sauce combine:		
1	egg, beaten	1		3 tbsp	soy sauce	45 ml
1 cup	flour	250 ml		3 tbsp	water	45 ml
1 cup	butter	250 ml		1 cup	white sugar	250 ml
				½ cup	vinegar	125 ml
				½ tsp	salt	2 ml

Cut tips from wings. Dip wings into beaten egg and then flour. Fry in butter until deep brown and crisp. Place in shallow roaster and pour sauce over wings. Bake at 350F (175C) for 30 minutes. Baste frequently during baking. Serves 6.

Sweet and Sour Chicken

3 lb	broiler chicken	1.5 kg		¼ tsp	pepper	1.5 ml
½ cup	cornstarch	125 ml		⅓ cup	corn oil	75 ml
1 tsp	salt	5 ml				

Cut chicken into serving pieces. Cover chicken with cornstarch and spices. Brown on all sides in heated corn oil.

Sauce:

1 14-oz can	pineapple chunks	398 ml		¼ tsp	soy sauce	1.5 ml
				¼ tsp	ginger	1.5 ml
1 cup	sugar	250 ml		1	chicken bouillon cube	1
2 tbsp	cornstarch	30 ml		1	large green pepper	1
¾ cup	vinegar	175 ml				

Drain pineapple. Pour juice into 2 cup (500 ml) measuring cup and add water to make 1¼ cups (310 ml). In saucepan combine sugar and cornstarch. Stir in pineapple juice, vinegar, soy sauce, ginger and bouillon cube. Cook over medium heat until mixture has thickened and comes to a boil. Simmer for 2 minutes. Remove from heat. Place chicken in dish and cover with sauce. Bake uncovered at 350F (175C) for 30 minutes. Baste with sauce. Add pineapple cubes and green pepper. Bake for another 30 minutes. Serves 6.

Chicken and Mushroom Casserole

2½ lb	chicken pieces	1.25 kg		2 tbsp	flour	30 ml
½ cup	milk	125 ml		1 cup	mushrooms, fresh or canned	250 ml
⅔ cup	flour	150 ml				
2 tsp	salt	10 ml		2 cups	whole milk or evaporated milk	500 ml
½ tsp	pepper	2 ml				
¼ cup	oil	50 ml		¼ tsp	paprika	1.5 ml

Dip chicken pieces in milk. Shake in paper bag with salt, pepper and ⅔ cup flour. Heat oil in frying pan. Brown chicken on all sides. Transfer the chicken to a well-greased casserole. Pour off most of the fat from the skillet. Sauté mushrooms in frying pan for 5 minutes. Add 2 tablespoons of flour and mix well with drippings in pan. Add milk, scraping all browned particles in pan. Bring to a boil and pour over chicken. Add paprika and seasonings. Bake covered at 325F (175C) until chicken is tender. Serves 4.

Chicken Pot Pies

6	small carrots	6			salt and pepper	
6	small potatoes	6				
½ cup	celery, diced	125 ml		Pastry:		
12	tiny onions	12		1½ cups	flour	375 ml
3 cups	chicken, cooked and chopped	750 ml		½ tsp	salt	2 ml
				½ cup	shortening	125 ml
2 cups	chicken gravy	500 ml		4-5 tbsp	water	60-75 ml

Cook vegetables until nearly tender. Distribute with chicken in 6 individual casseroles or one large, shallow casserole. Season with salt and pepper. Pour chicken gravy over mixture. Make pastry by sifting flour and salt. Cut in shortening. Sprinkle water over flour mixture. Toss to moisten. Roll and cut to fit over casseroles. Fold edges under, and slit for steam vents. Sprinkle water over top. Bake at 425F (220C) until pastry browns and filling is bubbling. This recipe works equally well with turkey. Serves 4.

The Great Nova Scotia Cookbook

Honey-Mustard Chicken

A little different and very tasty.

⅓ cup	Dijon mustard	75 ml		½ tsp	grated orange rind	2 ml
⅓ cup	honey	75 ml		1 lb	chicken parts	500 g
2 tbsp	fresh dill, chopped	30 ml			(breasts or legs)	
	or					
1 tbsp	dried dill	15 ml				

Combine mustard, honey, dill and orange rind, and keep refrigerated in airtight container. Will keep up to 1 week.

Prepare chicken. Remove skin, if desired. Preheat oven to 400F (200C). Line a baking sheet with foil. Place chicken, skin side down, on prepared pan. Brush sauce over chicken, coating well. Turn chicken over and pull back skin and brush sauce on and under skin. Pull skin back over sauce. Bake until juices run clear when thickest parts are pierced with fork. Nice served with buttered beans and baked potato and orange wedges. Serves 4.

Rolled Chicken Sandwich

A good way to use leftover chicken.

3 cups	chicken, cooked and sliced or chopped	750 ml		½ cup	carrots, coarsely shredded	125 ml
⅓ cup	light sour cream	75 ml		⅓ cup	cucumber, cut into thin strips	75 ml
2 tbsp	lime juice	30 ml				
¼-½ tsp	hot pepper sauce	1-2 ml		2 cups	romaine lettuce, shredded	500 ml
2	soft tortillas: 10-inch (25 cm)	2				

Combine sour cream, lime juice and pepper sauce. Spread half the mixture on each tortilla. Divide chicken, carrot, cucumber and lettuce between tortillas. Roll up. Cut each rolled tortilla in half. Serves 4.

Coating for Oven-Fried Chicken

Try it on fish too!

3 cups	breadcrumbs, dry	750 ml	1 tsp	onion powder	5 ml
2 tsp	paprika	10 ml	1 tsp	celery seed	5 ml
½ tsp	salt	2 ml	1 tsp	poultry seasoning	5 ml
1 tsp	garlic powder	5 ml		pepper, to taste	

Combine all ingredients until well mixed. Keep in covered container until ready for use. Just before using place ingredients in a plastic or paper bag. Moisten chicken in milk and shake in bag of coating, one piece at a time. Discard bag and coating. Preheat oven to 350F (175C). Bake chicken in oil-coated pan, skin side up for 1 hour or until tender.

Chicken Enchiladas

12	small flour tortillas	12	1 10-oz can	cream of mushroom soup	284 ml
3 cups	chicken, cooked and diced	750 ml	¼ cup	green chilies, chopped	50 ml
½ cup	onion, finely chopped	125 ml	2 cups	Cheddar cheese, grated	500 ml
1 12-oz can	evaporated milk	385 ml			

Place chicken and onion in centre of each tortilla and roll up. Place side by side in greased 7x11-inch (18x27.5 cm) baking pan. Combine milk, soup and chilies; pour over tortillas. Sprinkle cheese on top, and bake at 350F (175C) for 30 minutes. Serves 6.

Note: Ground beef or turkey may be used as an alternative.

Chicken Cacciatore

½ cup	oil	125 ml	½ cup	onion, chopped	125 ml
5 lb	chicken, cut into serving pieces	2.25 kg	⅓ cup	carrot, chopped	75 ml
			2 tbsp	parsley, chopped	30 ml
⅔ cup	flour	150 ml	1 28-oz can	tomatoes	796 ml
1 tsp	salt	5 ml			
1 clove	garlic, crushed and sliced	1	1 tsp	salt	5 ml
			¼ tsp	pepper	1.5 ml

Dredge chicken in flour. Sprinkle with salt and fry in oil until golden brown on both sides. Place in covered dish and set aside. Brown onion, garlic, carrot and parsley in the skillet. Drain tomatoes, reserving 2 cups (500 ml) of pulp. Add pulp to browned vegetables in skillet. Add salt and pepper and bring to a boil. Add chicken and simmer 30 minutes or until chicken is tender. Serve with thick slices of fresh crusty bread. Serves 8.

Zesty Chicken Tortillas

⅔ cup	Miracle Whip (light, if preferred)	150 ml	6	chicken or turkey breasts, boneless, cooked and cubed	6
¼ cup	flour	50 ml			
2 cups	milk	500 ml	¼ cup	salsa, or to taste	50 ml
2 cups	Cheddar cheese, grated	500 ml	¼ cup	parsley	50 ml
			12	flour tortillas, 6-inch (15 cm)	12

Blend flour and salad dressing in saucepan. Stir in milk over medium heat, until thickened. Add 1½ cups (375 ml) cheese and stir. Remove 1 cup (250 ml) of sauce.

Add chicken, salsa and parsley to remaining sauce. Spoon about ⅓ cup (75 ml) of the mixture into each tortilla. Wrap tortilla around filling. Place tortillas, seam side up, in two rows, in 9x13 inch (23x33 cm) casserole. Spoon reserved sauce across centre of the tortilla. Top with remaining cheese and sprinkle with parsley for garnish. Bake at 375F (190C) for 30 minutes. Serves 6.

Note: Leftover chicken or turkey may be used.

Moroccan Crepes

Crepe skins:

1 cup + 1 tbsp	flour	265 ml		¼ tsp	salt	1.5 ml
				⅛ tsp	pepper	0.5 ml
3	eggs	3		3 tbsp	vegetable oil	45 ml
1½ cups	milk	375 ml				

Add all the ingredients to a mixing bowl and whisk well. Let sit for 30 minutes before using. Heat a nonstick skillet over medium heat, and add about 4 tbsp (60 ml) batter to skillet. Rotate skillet to cover completely. Let edges of crepe brown, remove from pan and continue until batter is used up. Place crepes between sheets of wax paper until ready to use.

Filling:

1 lb	chicken breasts, diced	500 g		2	celery stalks, chopped fine	2
¼ lb	raisins	125 g		1½ cups	mayonnaise	375 ml
¼ lb	water chestnuts, drained	125 g		¼ cup	butter	50 ml
½ cup	mushrooms, sliced	125 ml		¼ cup	sherry	50 ml

Sauté chicken, mushrooms, celery and water chestnuts in butter on medium heat, until chicken is cooked. Set aside in bowl. Mix together mayonnaise and sherry. Add chicken mixture, mixing thoroughly. Roll into crepe skins; cover with sauce and garnish.

Sauce:

1 cup	chicken stock	250 ml
2 tbsp	butter	30 ml
2 tbsp	flour	30 ml

Melt butter in a medium-sized saucepan and add flour. Mix thoroughly to make a roux. Add chicken stock and simmer until sauce thickens. Remove from heat. Pour over crepes. Serve with steamed rice and fresh broccoli. Garnish with mandarin orange segments, raisins and almonds.

Sticky Chicken

4 lb	chicken pieces	2 kg		½ tsp	garlic powder	2 ml
	salt and pepper			1 tsp	dry mustard	5 ml
1 tsp	paprika	5 ml				

Rub chicken pieces well with seasonings. Place in roaster, uncovered, skin side down. Do not add water. Roast at 400F (200C) for 30 minutes. Turn skin side up and roast 15 minutes longer.

Sauce:

2 cloves	garlic, crushed	2		½ tsp	ginger	2 ml
½ cup	soy sauce	125 ml		1 tbsp	cornstarch	15 ml
½ cup	honey or corn syrup	125 ml		2 tbsp	cold water	30 ml
2 tbsp	lemon juice	30 ml				

Remove roaster from oven. Pour mixture of garlic, soy sauce, honey or syrup, lemon juice, and ginger, which has been well blended, over chicken pieces. Reduce heat to 350F (175C). Cook another 30 minutes uncovered, basting occasionally. Dissolve cornstarch in water and add to hot sauce in pan. Return chicken to oven and cook another 3-4 minutes. Sprinkle with sesame seeds. Serve hot; or cool before freezing. Serves 6.

Dijon Chicken Salad Sandwich

4 cups	chicken, cooked and diced	1 L	2 tbsp	lemon juice	30 ml
				pepper	
1¼ cups	celery, diced	300 ml	8	lettuce leaves	8
2 tbsp	Dijon mustard	30 ml	16 slices	wholewheat bread	16
½ cup	mayonnaise	125 ml			

Mix chicken, celery, mustard, mayonnaise, lemon juice and pepper in bowl. Chill until serving time. Arrange lettuce leaves on 8 slices of bread. Top with chicken salad and remaining bread slices. Cut in half diagonally or as desired. Serves 8.

Chicken à la King

3½ cups	chicken, cooked and diced	875 ml	1½ cups	milk	375 ml
			1 tsp	salt	5 ml
2 tsp	lemon juice	10 ml	1 tsp	pepper	5 ml
1 10-oz can	mushrooms	284 ml	⅓ cup	peas, cooked and drained	75 ml
3 tbsp	butter, divided	45 ml	1-2 tbsp	pimentos, chopped	15-30 ml
3 tbsp	flour	45 ml			

Melt 2 tbsp (30 ml) butter in top of double boiler. Sauté mushrooms in the remaining 1 tbsp (15 ml) butter in fry pan. Blend milk into flour gradually and add to top of double boiler; stir constantly, until thickened. Add peas, mushrooms, pimentos, salt, pepper, diced chicken and lemon juice. Heat. Serve on hot toast points or in pastry shells. Serves 6.

Lemon Chicken with Broccoli and Red Pepper Stir-Fry

1 lb	chicken, skinless, boneless and cut into thin strips	500 g	1 clove	garlic, crushed and minced	1
4 tbsp	lemon juice	60 ml			

In a small bowl, marinate the chicken in lemon juice and garlic for 15 minutes.

Sauce:

1 cup	water	250 ml	3 tbsp	corn syrup, more or less, as desired	45 ml
2 tbsp	cornstarch	30 ml			
2 pkg	chicken bouillon mix, low-sodium	2	1 tsp	lemon rind, grated	5 ml

Mix sauce ingredients together and set aside.

Stir-fry:

2 tbsp	vegetable oil	30 ml	1	red pepper, cut in strips	1
3-4 cups	broccoli florets	750 ml-1 L			

Heat a large skillet or wok over moderate heat. Swirl oil around pan. Stir-fry chicken until no longer pink inside. Remove from pan. Add a little more oil if necessary, and cook broccoli and pepper for 3 minutes. Remove to heated serving bowl. Re-stir sauce mixture, pour in pan. Bring to boil, stirring constantly. Add chicken and boil for 1 minute to thicken. Arrange in a serving bowl with vegetables. Nice with cooked rice and egg rolls. Serves 6.

Honey Dijon Chicken

4	chicken breast halves, boneless, skinless	4	2 tbsp	lemon juice	30 ml	
			2 tbsp	light soy sauce	30 ml	
⅓ cup	honey	75 ml	2 tsp	Dijon mustard	10 ml	

Place chicken in an ungreased 11x7x2-inch (26x18x5 cm) baking dish. Combine honey, lemon juice, soy sauce and mustard. Pour over chicken. Bake, uncovered at 350F (175C) until juices run clear, turning and basting every 15 minutes. Serves 4.

Luncheon Chicken Tarts

½ cup	mayonnaise or salad dressing	125 ml	1 8-oz can	pineapple slices, drained and cut up	227 ml
½ cup	sour cream	125 ml	1 cup	celery, chopped	250 ml
2 tbsp	chutney	30 ml	¼ cup	slivered almonds, toasted	50 ml
½ tsp	curry powder	2 ml			
2 cups	chicken, cooked and chopped	500 ml		pastry for 6 tart shell	

Bake tart shells at 425F (220C). Remove from pan. Combine mayonnaise, sour cream, chutney and curry powder. Add the chicken, pineapple and celery. Toss lightly. Spoon chicken mixture into tart shells just before serving. Sprinkle almonds over top. Serve cold, immediately. Serves 6.

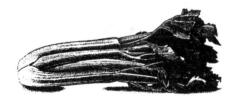

Judy's Chicken Tetrazzini

2 tbsp	butter	30 ml
1	medium onion, chopped	1
1 clove	garlic, minced	1
4	chicken breasts	4
1 10-oz can	cream of mushroom soup	284 ml
½ cup	milk	125 ml
1 tbsp	parsley, chopped	15 ml
½ lb	spaghetti	250 g
¼ cup	Parmesan cheese	50 ml

Sauté onion and garlic in butter until tender. Add chicken and brown on both sides. Stir in cream of mushroom soup, milk and parsley. Simmer for about 5 minutes. Place in oven and bake in a covered casserole for 30 minutes or until tender. Meanwhile cook spaghetti according to instructions. Drain and put in baking dish. Arrange chicken pieces on top, cover with sauce. Sprinkle with Parmesan cheese. Bake at 400F (200C) for about 20 minutes. Serves 4.

Broccoli & Chicken Casserole

2 10-oz pkgs	broccoli, frozen or	560 g
2	large broccoli bunches, freshly steamed	2
2 cups	chicken(or turkey), cooked	500 ml
2 10-oz cans	cream of chicken or cream of mushroom soup	2 x 284 ml
1 cup	mayonnaise	250 ml
1-2 tsp	curry powder, to taste	5-10 ml
1 tsp	lemon juice	5 ml
1 cup	grated cheese	250 ml
½ cup	breadcrumbs	125 ml
1 tbsp	margarine or butter	15 ml

Cook broccoli until tender and place in baking dish. Place chicken on top. Combine soup, mayonnaise, curry powder and lemon juice and pour over chicken. Sprinkle with cheese. Combine breadcrumbs and butter and place on top. Cook at 350F (175C) for 30-35 minutes. Serves 8.

Hoisin Sticky Wings

3 lb	chicken wings	1.5 kg	2 tsp	garlic, crushed and minced	10 ml
⅓ cup	Hoisin sauce	75 ml			
⅓ cup	soy sauce	75 ml	2 tsp	ginger, grated	10 ml
⅓ cup	liquid honey	75 ml	1 tsp	hot pepper sauce	5 ml

Cut off wing tops at joint (reserve for making stock). Cut remaining wings into two pieces at joint. Arrange wings in single layer on a large, rimmed baking sheet, sprayed or brushed with oil. Bake at 425F (220C) for 20 minutes. Meanwhile, combine remaining ingredients in small saucepan. Bring to boil for 3 minutes; set aside. Drain off any fat in baking pan. Turn wings over and drizzle with glaze mixture. Bake for 20-30 minutes longer, turning and basting wings several times with glaze as it thickens, until they are well-browned. Serve warm. May be made ahead and refrigerated for up to one day or frozen. Reheat in single layer on baking sheet in 350F (175C) oven for 15 minutes. Serves 6.

Sesame-Crusted Chicken Cutlets

1 lb	chicken cutlets	500 g	1 cup	breadcrumbs, fine and soft	250 ml
1	large egg	1			
1 tbsp	oil	15 ml	⅓ cup	sesame seeds	75 ml
1 tbsp	water	15 ml	2 tbsp	vegetable oil	30 ml
¾ tsp	salt	3 ml			

Pound cutlets to an even ¼-inch (5 mm) thickness. In a bowl, beat together egg, oil, water and salt. In a shallow bowl, combine breadcrumbs and sesame seeds. Dip cutlets in egg mixture, coat in breadcrumb mixture. In a skillet, heat half the oil on medium heat. Cook cutlets in batches, adding more oil. Cook 3-4 minutes on each side or until no longer pink inside. Serves 4.

Stuffed Chicken Breasts

4	sun-dried tomatoes, packed in oil or dried	4		2 tbsp	parsley, minced	30 ml
				⅛ tsp	salt, optional	0.5 ml
1 tsp	lemon zest, grated	5 ml		1 lb	chicken breast halves, boneless and skinless	500 g
1 tbsp + 1 tsp	butter, unsalted	20 ml				

If using oil-packed tomatoes, drain and chop finely. If using dried tomatoes, cover tomatoes with boiling water in a bowl. Let stand for 5 minutes. Drain and chop finely. Place 2 tbsp (30 ml) chopped tomatoes and half the lemon zest in small bowl. Add butter, parsley and salt. Mix thoroughly and set aside. Combine remaining tomatoes and zest in another bowl and mix thoroughly. Using a sharp knife, cut horizontally through the centre of each chicken breast to form a pocket. Do not cut all the way through. Divide tomato and lemon zest mixture into equal portions and spread in each pocket. Turn on broiler. Arrange chicken on a broiler pan and place 4 inches (10 cm) from heat source. Broil 5 minutes. Turn and broil another 4 minutes. Spread tomato and butter mixture over chicken breasts. Broil another 1-2 minutes or until chicken is opaque throughout. Serves 4.

Margaret's Chicken Casserole

1 cup	celery	250 ml		2 10-oz cans	cream of mushroom soup	2 x 284 ml
2	onions	2				
1	medium green pepper	1		2 cups	chicken, cut up	250 ml
1 tbsp	oil	15 ml			Chinese noodles	
1 10-oz can	mushrooms, drained	284 ml				

Fry celery, onions and green pepper in oil until limp. Add rest of ingredients.

Cover with Chinese noodles, and bake at 350F (175C) for 30 minutes. Serves 4.

Honey Mustard Turkey Meatballs

Low fat!

1½ lb	turkey, ground	750 g	¼ cup	green pepper	50 ml
1	egg	1	1½ cups	pineapple juice, unsweetened	375 ml
1 cup	crackers, crushed	250 ml	3 tbsp	honey	45 ml
⅔ cup	Mozzarella cheese, shredded	150 ml	2 tbsp	cornstarch	30 ml
⅓ cup	onion	75 ml	¼ tsp	onion powder	1.5 ml
½ tsp	ginger	2 ml			
½ cup	Dijon mustard	125 ml			

Combine turkey, egg, cracker crumbs, cheese, onion, ginger and ¼ cup (50 ml) of the mustard. Form into 1-inch (2.5 cm) balls. Bake uncovered at 350F (175C) in a greased 13x9x2-inch (33x23x5 cm) baking dish for about 30 minutes or until juices run clear. In a saucepan, combine pineapple juice, honey, onion powder, cornstarch and green pepper. Bring to a boil, stirring constantly for 2 minutes or more. Reduce heat and add remainder of mustard. Stir well. Brush meatballs with about ⅓ cup (75 ml) of sauce. Return meatballs to oven for about 10 minutes. Serve remaining sauce with meatballs. Serves 8.

Barbecued Turkey Burgers

1½ lb	ground turkey	750 g	½ cup	breadcrumbs	125 ml
½ cup	onion, chopped	125 ml	½ tsp	salt	2 ml
½ cup	barbecue sauce	125 ml		pepper	

Combine all ingredients in a large bowl. Mix thoroughly. Shape into 6 patties. Place on oiled grill. Grill over medium heat for 4-6 minutes per side or until no longer pink in centre. Baste with additional barbecue sauce if desired. Serves 6.

Turkey Tacos

1 cup	turkey, dark and white meat	250 ml		¼ cup	whole cranberry relish	50 ml
4	corn taco shells	4		1 tsp	chili powder	5 ml
1 cup	salad greens, chopped	250 ml		¼ cup	no-fat sour cream	50 ml
				1 tbsp	scallions, chopped	15 ml
½ cup	green beans, cooked and diced	125 ml		4 slices	avocado or	4
				4 tbsp	guacamole	60 ml
				¼ cup	low-fat cheese	50 ml

Cut the leftover turkey into strips. Mix the cranberry relish with chili powder. Slice the avocado. Warm the taco shells in an oven as directed on the package, then fill with salad greens, turkey and green beans. Top with sour cream, avocado slices or guacamole, seasoned cranberry relish, scallions and cheese. Good for a light dinner or a holiday evening snack! Serves 4.

Turkey Spaghetti Sauce

1 lb	ground turkey	500g		½ cup	water	125 ml
1 tbsp	vegetable oil	15 ml		1	medium carrot, chopped	1
1	medium onion, chopped	1				
				2	celery stalks, chopped	2
2 cloves	garlic, minced	2				
1 19-oz can	tomatoes, coarsely chopped	540 ml		1 tsp	oregano, dried	5 ml
				1 tsp	basil, dried	5 ml
1 5½-oz can	tomato paste	156 ml		½ tsp	Worcestershire sauce	2 ml

In a large saucepan, heat vegetable oil and sauté turkey with onion and garlic until onion is soft and turkey is no longer pink. Do not overcook. Add remaining ingredients and season with salt and pepper. Bring to a boil. Reduce heat, cover and simmer for 30 minutes. Serve over spaghetti. Serves 6.

Fruity Turkey Dressing

⅓ cup	butter	75 ml	3	large onions, chopped		3
2 cups	mixed dried fruit: apples, apricots, dried peaches or prunes, chopped	500 ml	½ tsp	pepper		2 ml
			1 tsp	salt		5 ml
			14 cups	breadcrumbs		3.5 L
5	celery stalks, finely chopped	5	1½ cups	chicken or vegetable stock		375 ml
4 cloves	garlic, crushed and minced	4	4 tsp	sage or savoury		20 ml

In a large skillet, melt half the butter over medium heat; cook fruit, celery, garlic, onions, sage, salt and pepper, stirring occasionally, for about 15 minutes or until softened. Place in a large bowl and toss with crumbs. Melt remainder of the butter with 1 cup (250 ml) stock. Drizzle over crumb mixture and toss to combine. Transfer to a 13x9-inch (33x23 cm) baking dish. Cover and bake at 350F (175C) for about 20 minutes. Stir in remaining stock. Bake uncovered for 10-15 minutes. Makes about 12 cups.

Grilled Turkey Scallopini with Dijon Sauce

1 lb	turkey scallopini	500 g	2 tbsp	lemon juice	30 ml
¼ cup	vegetable oil	50 ml	1 clove	garlic, minced	1
¼ cup	honey	50 ml	¼ tsp	thyme, dried	1.5 ml
2 tbsp	Dijon mustard	30 ml		salt and pepper	

Combine all ingredients except turkey. Brush mixture on turkey scallopini. Grill over medium heat, 2-4 minutes per side or until no longer pink in centre. As an alternative, the turkey can be pan-fried in 1 tbsp (15 ml) vegetable oil for approximately 2 minutes on each side.

If turkey scallopini is not available at your grocers, slice partially frozen turkey breast into slices and pound to ¼-inch (0.5 cm) thickness. Serves 4.

Crunchy Turkey Cutlets

4	turkey cutlets, steaks, or boneless breast slices	4	½ tsp	thyme, dried	2 ml
⅔ cup	breadcrumbs, fine	150 ml	½ tsp	tarragon, dried	2 ml
¼ cup	Parmesan cheese	50 ml	¼ cup	light mayonnaise	50 ml

Pound turkey to ¼-inch (0.5 cm) thickness. In a shallow dish combine breadcrumbs, Parmesan cheese, thyme, tarragon and salt and pepper, to taste. Brush both sides of cutlets with mayonnaise, then coat with crumb mixture. Cook cutlets in a frying pan with 1 tbsp (15 ml) vegetable oil for 4-5 minutes on each side over medium-high heat. You can substitute low-fat yogurt for mayonnaise. Serves 4.

Baked Seafood Rice

1 cup	cooked rice	250 ml	1 4½-oz can	shrimp, drained	1
1 cup	celery, chopped	250 ml	1 6½-oz can	crabmeat	1
½ cup	green peppers, finely sliced	125 ml	1 cup	mayonnaise	250 ml
3	green onions, chopped	3	¾ cup	tomato juice	175 ml
1 6½-oz can	water chestnuts	1		grated Parmesan	

Combine all ingredients except cheese. Place in shallow 2-quart (2L) casserole. Sprinkle with cheese. Bake at 350F(175C) for 30 minutes. Serves 6-8.

Cod Fish Cakes

These make a delicious supper dish with creamed peas and pickled beets.

1 lb	salt codfish	500 g		pepper
6	medium potatoes	6		butter
1	egg	1		

Soak fish overnight in saucepan. In morning, drain and add potatoes cut in halves. Add cold water to almost cover and cook until potatoes are done. Remove from heat. Drain off water. Remove fish and check for bones. Return fish to saucepan and add egg, butter and pepper. Beat all together with a fork until well mixed. Scoop out by the spoonful and pat into cakes. Keep refrigerated until ready to use. Fry in drippings or butter. When crusty brown on one side, turn over to brown on the other side. Serves 8.

Captain's Pie Supper Dish

An old stand-by that can be easily doubled when company comes.

2 tbsp	butter	30 ml		1 lb	haddock, fresh or frozen	500 g
1 cup	onion, chopped	250 ml				
1 cup	carrot, grated	250 ml		1 cup	peas	250 ml
2 tbsp	flour	30 ml		5-6	potatoes	5-6
1 tsp	bouillon powder	5 ml			milk, as needed	
	salt and pepper				butter, as desired	
1½ cups	milk	375 ml			paprika	

Cook potatoes in water until tender. Drain. Add milk and butter and mash until fluffy. Set aside but keep hot. Meanwhile, heat butter in fry pan. Add onion and carrot. Sauté. Add flour, bouillon powder, salt and pepper. Add milk. Let come to boil and thicken. Add fish and peas. Simmer covered until fish is tender and flakes easily. Pour into casserole dish 8-inch (20 cm) square. Spread hot, prepared potato mixture over fish. Brush butter over potato and sprinkle with paprika. Bake uncovered at 400F (200C) for about 20 minutes or until heated. Serves 8.

Oriental Halibut on the Grill

This recipe will become a favourite.

¾ cup	red plum jam	175 ml	⅛ tsp	garlic powder	0.5 ml
1 tbsp	vinegar	15 ml	4	halibut steaks, cut	4
½ tsp	ginger, grated	2 ml		1 inch (2.5 cm) thick	
½ tsp	red pepper, crushed	2 ml			

For glaze: combine jam, vinegar, ginger, red pepper and garlic powder. Bring to a boil, stirring frequently. Remove from heat. Brush grill rack with cooking oil. Place fish on rack. Lightly brush fish with cooking oil. Grill uncovered directly over medium hot coals for 5 minutes. Carefully turn fish over and lightly brush with more cooking oil. Grill for 3-7 minutes or until done; brush the fish with some of the glaze during the last 2 minutes. Serve with remaining glaze. Add a sprinkle of salt, as desired. Serves 4.

Baked Halibut with Mushrooms

An easy dish to prepare.

5	halibut (or haddock) steaks	5	2 cups	whole milk	500 ml
				salt and pepper	
¼ cup	butter	50 ml		flour	
¼ cup	onion, chopped	50 ml			
½ cup	mushrooms, chopped	250 ml			

Place butter in bottom of casserole dish. Dust steaks with flour and place on butter. Sprinkle with onions and mushrooms; add milk and sprinkle salt and pepper over all. Bake in moderate oven until fish flakes. Serve with lemon slices and sprigs of parsley. Serves 5.

Smoked Finnan Haddie

2 lb	smoked haddock	900 g	2 cups	milk	500 ml
5 tbsp	butter	75 ml		pepper, to taste	
3 tbsp	flour	45 ml			

Wash fish and drain well. Dust fish well on both sides with flour. Place in buttered baking pan. Pour the milk over the fish. Dot with butter. Bake in 350F (175C) oven until fish flakes easily and milk has thickened into a sauce. Buttered breadcrumbs may be sprinkled over top during the last 10 minutes of baking. Serves 6.

Baked Fish in Foil

It's so easy to clean up after this meal!

Lay heavy foil in baking pan. Grease well with butter. Place halibut or haddock fillets, whole haddock, shad or bass on foil. Spread fish with Miracle Whip salad dressing, salt and pepper, a little paprika and a dab of butter. Bring edges of foil up over fish to cover. Bake at 400F (200C) until fish flakes easily.

Broiled Almond Sole

1 pkg	fillet of sole, frozen	1	1 tbsp	lemon juice	15 ml
4 tbsp	butter (divided)	60 ml	¼ cup	almonds, blanched	50 ml
¼ tsp	salt	1.5 ml		parsley	
	paprika				

Place fillets in a single layer on a well-greased platter. Brush with 2 tbsp (30 ml) melted butter. Broil 4-inches from heat for 10 minutes or until fish flakes easily. Sprinkle with salt and paprika. While fillets cook, make sauce by melting remaining butter over low heat; add nuts and cook slowly until almonds are golden. Stir in lemon juice. Pour sauce over cooked fillets. Garnish with parsley. Serves 6.

Fried Flounder

A Bay of Fundy treat—simply delicious!

1½ lb	flounder fillets, fresh	750 g	1	egg, lightly beaten	1
3-4 tbsp	butter	45-60 ml	½ cup	milk	125 ml
1 cup	cracker crumbs, finely ground	250 ml		salt and pepper	

Cut fillets in portions. Place egg and milk in bowl and beat together. Place cracker crumbs in plate. Dip fillets in egg mixture and then in crumbs, one at a time. Season lightly with salt and pepper. Set aside. Melt butter in hot fry pan. Add fillets handling them carefully and leaving space to turn each piece. When slightly browned on one side, turn carefully. They will likely be cooked tender and flaky in 2-4 minutes. Transfer to warm platter and serve immediately. Serves 4.

Grilled Salmon

Sauce:

4 tbsp	unsalted butter, softened	60 ml	4	salmon steaks	4
1 tbsp	Dijon mustard	15 ml		salt and fresh ground pepper	
juice	of half a lemon			olive oil	
1 tbsp	parsley, finely chopped	15 ml			

Mix together ingredients for sauce and chill. Season salmon steaks with salt and pepper. Brush lightly with olive oil on both sides. Grill under hot broiler for about 7 minutes, turning once. Serve with sauce. Serves 4.

Maple-Grilled Salmon

This method of grilling salmon—without a barbecue—is exceptional! Grill the day before, if desired, and refrigerate. Remove from refrigerator an hour before serving.

4 lb	salmon fillets	2 kg		2 tbsp	vegetable oil	30 ml
¼ cup	maple syrup	50 ml		1 tbsp	black pepper, freshly ground	15 ml
¼ cup	cider vinegar	50 ml				
2 tbsp	rye whisky	30 ml				

Place salmon steaks in a large, flat dish. Combine maple syrup, vinegar, rye and oil. Pour over salmon. Dust with pepper. Leave to marinate for 2 hours, turning salmon occasionally.

Preheat cookie sheet under broiler for 5 minutes or until very hot. Place salmon steaks on cookie sheet and broil 6 inches (15 cm) from heat for 5-7 minutes, just until cooked. (It will continue to cook as it cools.)

Lemon Cucumber Sauce for Maple-Grilled Salmon

1	lemon, grated rind and juice	1		1 cup	yogurt	250 ml
1 cup	mayonnaise	250 ml		1	English cucumber, grated and drained	1

Place leftover marinade (see Maple-Grilled Salmon recipe) in a skillet. Add lemon rind and juice, and reduce on high heat until mixture thickens. Remove from heat and whisk into mayonnaise. Stir in yogurt and cucumber. Season with salt, pepper and extra lemon juice, if needed. Place cooled salmon on serving platter; you may garnish with cucumbers and watercress. Serve with sauce on side.

Mini Salmon Loaves
with Yogurt Dill Sauce

Although slightly higher in fat than some fish, salmon contains omega-3 fatty acids, which help reduce the risk of heart disease. Here is a quick and easy recipe to add this tasty fish to your diet.

2	egg whites, slightly beaten	2	1 15-oz can	salmon, drained, flaked, skin and bones removed	426 g
1 cup	soft, wholewheat breadcrumbs	250 ml	1 cup	plain, non-fat yogurt	250 ml
½ cup	Vidalia onion, finely chopped	125 ml	1 tbsp	dill	15 ml
2 tbsp	skim milk	30 ml	1 tbsp	Dijon mustard	15 ml
½ tsp	dill	2 ml	1 tsp	lemon juice	5 ml
			½ tsp	Tabasco sauce	2 ml

In a large mixing bowl, stir together egg whites, breadcrumbs, onion, milk and dill. Stir in salmon. Spray a shallow baking dish with nonstick cooking spray. Divide salmon mixture into 4 pieces. Shape each piece into a 4x2-inch loaf. Place loaves in baking dish. Bake uncovered at 350F (175C) for 20-25 minutes or until heated through and lightly browned. Meanwhile combine yogurt, dill, mustard, lemon juice and Tabasco. To serve, drizzle the yogurt sauce over each loaf. Serves 4.

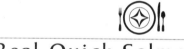

Real Quick Salmon Supper

1 1-lb can	salmon	about 440 g
1 cup	sour cream	250 ml

Drain salmon and spread into 9-inch (23 cm) pie plate. Top with sour cream. Sprinkle with salt and pepper. Bake about 20-30 minutes in 350F (175C) oven until sour cream is thick and dotted with brown patches. Serve with a lemon wedge and a green salad.

Basil-Buttered Salmon
or Halibut Steaks

4	halibut steaks, cut 1 inch (2.5 cm) thick	4	1 tbsp 1 tsp	fresh basil or dried basil	15 ml 5 ml
½ cup	butter	125 ml	1 tbsp	fresh parsley	15 ml
2 tsp	lemon juice	10 ml			

In a small bowl prepare sauce by combining butter, lemon juice, basil and parsley. Blend well. Lightly brush fish with sauce. Brush grill with cooking oil. Place fish on rack. Grill fish uncovered over medium-hot coals for 5 minutes. Carefully turn fish. Brush with more sauce and grill 3-7 minutes until fish is done. Pour remaining sauce over fish and serve. Serves 4.

Salmon Loaf

Generations of grandmothers have made this dish.

1 15-oz salmon can		426 g	2	eggs, beaten with a fork	2
1 cup	unsalted crackers, crushed	250 ml	2 tbsp	melted butter	30 ml
			1 tbsp	lemon juice	15 ml
1 cup	milk	250 ml		salt and pepper	

Preheat oven to 350F (175C). Remove bones and mash salmon. Mix in cracker crumbs. Add eggs, milk, lemon juice, salt and pepper. Pour into a greased casserole or pan. Make slits through the top to bottom and pour melted butter over all. Bake until firm. May be served hot or cold. Nice with potato salad on a crisp lettuce leaf. Serves 4.

Smoked Salmon and Eggs

eggs	butter or margarine
smoked salmon, sliced	English muffins
hollandaise sauce or crème fraîche	

Sauté slices of smoked salmon in butter or margarine until lightly browned. Place salmon on toasted and buttered English muffin. Cover with a poached egg and hollandaise sauce or crème fraîche. Add salt and pepper, to taste.

Salmon Patties

2	eggs	2	¼ tsp	salt		1.5 ml
1 cup	milk	250 ml	¼ tsp	pepper		1.5 ml
2 tbsp	lemon juice	30 ml	1 15-oz can	salmon, drained, bones and skins removed		426 ml
3 cups	crackers, crushed	750 ml				
2 tsp	onion, finely chopped	10 ml				

Dill Sauce:

2 tbsp	butter	30 ml	¼ tsp	salt	1.5 ml
2 tbsp	flour	30 ml	dash	pepper	
½ tsp	dillweed	2 ml	1½ cups	milk	375 ml

In a bowl beat eggs and add milk, lemon juice, crackers, onion, salt and pepper. Mix well. Add salmon. Mix together with fork. Shape into patties about 3-inches (7.5 cm) round. Place in greased baking pan. Bake at 350F (175C) until lightly browned, about 35 minutes. Meanwhile melt butter in saucepan. Stir in flour, dill, salt and pepper until smooth. Add milk gradually. Bring to boil. Cook and stir until thick and bubbly. Serve with patties, tossed salad and fresh rolls. Serves 4.

Planked Salmon

Clean and dress salmon. Fillet on both sides of backbone. Remove all bones using tweezers or pincers, if necessary. Place in refrigerator until ready to cook.

Prepare fire pit. Hardwood provides an excellent source of heat. Start your fire well in advance to establish a good bed of coals—a steady heat is important to the quality of the end product. A little smoke is fine as it produces more flavour.

Have ready hardwood boards or planks measuring about 3 inches (7.5 cm) thick, 8 inches (20 cm) wide and 36 inches (1 metre) long. Fish will not burn as easily if green planks are used. Wet planks well. Remove fish from refrigerator and brush all surfaces with melted butter. Do not remove skin. You may be able to place two or three fillets on each board, depending on size. Drive a number of common 1 inch (2.5 cm) nails about 2 inches (5 cm) apart into the board around the perimeter of the fish. Secure the fish to the planks with narrow gauge, non-coated brass wire by lacing wire around nails and over fish, back and forth from side to side.

Arrange the planked fish in front of fire pit and support the planks at a 70-80 degree angle about 2-3 feet (60-90 cm) away from the coals (determining the proper distance will depend on the intensity of the heat radiating from the coals). Turn the boards 180 degrees after 20-25 minutes. Baste the salmon with melted butter at 1-minute intervals for 15 minutes. Watch the salmon carefully and do not allow it to burn. Check for doneness as you apply the butter. Salmon is done when it flakes easily when pricked with a fork. Do not overcook. More wood may have to be added to the pit to maintain temperature. When done, remove salmon from planks and place on hot platter.

Note: Planks may be reused. Rinse planks. Clean and remove nails. Store in a cool place—not too dry. Soak planks in water for a few hours before using again.

Tuna Crunch

1 cup	celery, thinly sliced	250 ml		1 3-oz can	chow mien noodles	90 g
¼ cup	onion, finely chopped	50 ml		½ cup	cashew nuts, chopped	125 ml
2 tbsp	butter	30 ml				
1 7-oz can	tuna	198 g				
1 10-oz can	cream of mushroom soup	284 ml				

Combine celery, onion and butter in a 1-quart (1 L) casserole. Cook on stovetop until just tender. Drain tuna and flake with a fork. Add tuna, soup, ⅔ of the noodles and cashews to casserole. Top with remaining noodles. Bake in moderate oven until heated through and bubbly, about 30 minutes. Serves 4

Tuna-Pineapple Finger Rolls

Quick and easy.

1 7-oz can	tuna, solid	198 g		2 tsp	lime juice	10 ml
2 tbsp	almonds, chopped and toasted	30 ml		¼ tsp	salt, if necessary	1.5 ml
2 tbsp	crushed pineapple, drained	30 ml			salad dressing	
	lettuce			12	small finger rolls, split and buttered	12

Mix tuna, almonds, pineapple and lime juice together; add just enough salad dressing to moisten. Fill the split buttered rolls, and add a small ruffle of leaf lettuce to each.

Tuna-Chip Casserole

2 cups	evaporated milk	500 ml		3 cups	potato chips, slightly crushed	750 ml
⅛ tsp	pepper	0.5 ml		1¾ cups	asparagus or broccoli, cooked	430 ml
½ tsp	salt	2 ml		½ cup	ripe olives, chopped	125 ml
1 tbsp	prepared mustard	15 ml		½ cup	Cheddar cheese, grated	125 ml
¼ tsp	paprika	1.5 ml				
pinch	chili powder					
1 tbsp	lemon juice	15 ml				
1 7-oz can	tuna	198 g				

Combine salt, pepper, mustard, chili, paprika and milk. Slowly add lemon juice, stirring constantly to blend. Place 2 cups (500 ml) of the potato chips in a 2-quart (2 L) buttered casserole. Arrange the tuna, vegetables, olives and grated cheese in layers. Pour milk mixture over all. Top with remaining potato chips. Bake in moderate oven for 30 minutes. Serve immediately. Serves 6.

Noodle and Tuna Casserole

2 cups	noodles, cooked	500 ml		1 tbsp	onion, chopped	15 ml
1 10-oz can	mushroom soup	284 ml		¼ lb	sharp cheese	125 g
1 cup	milk	250 ml		1 7-oz can	tuna	198 g
2 tbsp	green pepper, chopped	30 ml			pepper, to taste	

Cook soup, milk, pepper, onion and cheese over low heat until cheese melts. Add noodles and drained tuna. Season to taste. Buttered crumbs may be placed on top. Bake at 350F (175C) until set. Serves 4.

Tuna with Cheese Rolls

¼ cup	butter	50 ml
1	small onion	1
½ cup	green pepper, diced	125 ml
⅔ cup	flour	150 ml

1 tsp	salt, or less	5 ml
3 cups	milk	750 ml
1 tbsp	lemon juice	15 ml
1 7-oz can	tuna	198 g

Melt butter; add pepper and onion. Cook until soft. Add flour and blend well over medium-to-low heat, stirring until thick and smooth. Boil 2 minutes. Add remaining ingredients. Put in a large baking dish. Cover with cheese rolls (see recipe below). Bake in a moderate oven for 30 minutes. Serves 6.

Cheese Rolls:

1½ cups	flour	375 ml
3 tsp	baking powder	15 ml
½ tsp	salt	2 ml
3 tbsp	shortening	45 ml
dash	cayenne	

1 cup	cheese, grated	250 ml
½ cup	milk	125 ml
2	pimentos, chopped	2

Sift together flour, baking powder, salt and cayenne. Cut in shortening and add milk. Roll into an 8x12-inch sheet (20x30 cm). Sprinkle with grated cheese and pimento. Roll up like a jelly roll. Cut into slices. Place slices on top of mixture in baking dish. Bake at 350F (175C) for 20 minutes.

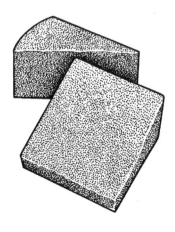

Gingery Scallops 'n Rice

1 cup	olive oil	250 ml	8 oz	mushrooms, sliced	225 g
2 tbsp	soy sauce	30 ml	4 oz	water chestnuts, thinly sliced	125 g
3 tbsp	red wine vinegar	45 ml			
¼ tsp	Tabasco sauce	1.5 ml	4 oz	red peppers, finely chopped	125 g
1 tsp	Dijon mustard	5 ml			
¼ tsp	ginger	1.5 ml	1 lb	sea scallops	500g
3 cups	white rice or clear noodles, cooked and cooled	750 ml	1 tbsp	parsley, chopped	15 ml
			1 tbsp	chives, chopped	15 ml

If scallops are thicker than ¾ inch (2 cm), slice in half. Blanch scallops in boiling water for 3-4 minutes or until firm, and cool immediately. Prepare a dressing with the oil, soy sauce, vinegar, Tabasco, mustard and ginger. Set aside the parsley and chives. Combine the remaining ingredients carefully so that the scallops do not become shredded, then mix with the dressing. Garnish with parsley and chives. Serve chilled. Serves 6.

Scallops in Garlic & Tomato

1 lb	scallops, floured	500 g	¼ cup	parsley, minced	50 ml
4 tbsp	butter	60 ml	1 tbsp	lemon juice	15 ml
2 cloves	garlic	2		salt and pepper, to taste	
1 cup	tomatoes, fresh, diced	250 ml		flour	

Cut scallops in half. Dry on paper towels, and then dust lightly with flour. Heat butter in a skillet, add garlic and mix. Add scallops and sauté until they are lightly brown. Stir in tomatoes, parsley and lemon juice. Season with salt and pepper. Serves 4.

Seafood Casserole I

Packed with flavour in a tangy sauce.

1 12-oz can	lobster	750 g	1 tbsp	dry mustard	15 ml
			½ tsp	salt	2 ml
1 4-oz can	shrimp	125 g	2 cups	milk	500 ml
			1 cup	sour cream	250 ml
1 5-oz can	crab	140 g	½ cup	white wine or apple juice	125 ml
½ lb	haddock	250 g	2 tbsp	butter	30 ml
½ lb	scallops	250 g	1 cup	breadcrumbs	250 ml
½ cup	butter	125 ml	½ cup	cheese, grated	125 ml
½ cup	flour	125 ml			

Place fish (except scallops) in a bowl. Break into bite-size pieces. Cover scallops in water in a medium-sized saucepan. Boil 5 minutes and drain. Cut scallops in half and add to bowl. Set aside. In the same saucepan, melt butter and stir in flour, mustard and salt. Add milk and cook, stirring the mixture until it boils. Add sour cream and juice. Pour over contents in bowl, stirring lightly. Pour into 2½ quart (3 L) casserole. Melt butter, add crumbs and cheese, and sprinkle over casserole. Bake at 350F (175C) for 20-30 minutes. Serves 8.

Seafood Casserole II

Delicious!

1	small onion, chopped	1	1½ cups	mayonnaise	375 ml
1 cup	celery, chopped	250 ml	½ tsp	salt	2 ml
1 cup	crabmeat	250 ml		pepper	
1 cup	shrimp	250 ml		Worcestershire sauce, to taste	
1½ cups	lobster	375 ml			
1 cup	tuna	250 ml	1 cup	buttered crumbs	250 ml

Toss first 10 ingredients together and place in buttered casserole. Top with buttered crumbs. Bake at 350F (175C) until heated through, about 20 minutes. Serves 6.

Grilled Trout

4 whole	trout, 10 oz (300 g) each	4		¾ cup	breadcrumbs, fresh	175 ml
				¼ cup	parsley, chopped	50 ml
½ cup	butter, melted and divided	125 ml			lemon slices	
					salt and pepper, to taste	

Heat broiler. Remove heads and centre bones to open fish flat. Arrange fish, skin sides down, in shallow pan and brush with half the butter. Sprinkle with salt and pepper. Broil 6 inches from heat for 3 minutes. Sprinkle fish with crumbs, drizzle with remaining butter, and broil 3 minutes until crumbs are crisp and fish opaque and cooked through.

Transfer to serving plate; sprinkle with parsley and garnish with lemon slices. Serves 4.

Trout with Roasted Pecan Crust

4	large rainbow trout fillets	4		1 2-3 tsp	egg, beaten with water	1 10-15 ml
1 cup	breadcrumbs, fresh	250 ml			flour	
1 cup	pecans, roasted and finely chopped	250 ml		1 tbsp	butter	15 ml
				1 tbsp	vegetable oil	15 ml
	salt and pepper, to taste				lemon juice	

Season fillets with salt, pepper and lemon juice. Let stand at room temperature 10-15 minutes. Combine breadcrumbs and pecans. Dredge fillets in flour; shake off excess. Dip in egg wash. Press fillets, skin side up, on crumb mixture. In a large skillet, heat the butter and oil over medium-high heat. Place fillets, skin side up, in skillet and cook until golden brown—3-4 minutes. Turn and cook 5-6 minutes on other side. Serves 4.

Lobster Luncheon Dish

¼ lb	butter	113 g	½ cup	whole milk	125 ml
3 cups	lobster, cut in pieces	750 ml	2 tbsp	sugar	30 ml
¼ cup	vinegar	50 ml		salt and pepper	

Melt butter in heavy skillet. When hot, add lobster and heat for 5 minutes. Reduce heat and add vinegar slowly, stirring constantly. Add milk and seasonings. Simmer for 10 minutes. Serve with hot, buttered toast points. Serves 4.

Broiled Basil Swordfish

3 tbsp	light mayonnaise	45 ml	1⅓-1½ lb	swordfish	670-750 g
1 tbsp	lemon juice	15 ml			
1 tsp	basil leaves, dried	5 ml		nonstick vegetable spray	
½ tsp	onion powder	2 ml			

Preheat broiler. With a wire whisk, thoroughly combine mayonnaise, lemon juice, basil and onion powder in a small bowl. Set aside. Place swordfish on broiler pan coated with nonstick spray. Blot the side of fish facing up with a paper towel to remove excess moisture. Spread evenly with half of mayonnaise mixture. Broil 6-8 inches from heating element for 5-6 minutes. Watch closely to keep the topping from turning black. Remove the fish from the oven; turn and blot again with a paper towel. Coat with remaining mayonnaise mixture. Broil for another 4-6 minutes, depending on the thickness of fish. Fresh tuna, whitefish, halibut, bluefish, mackerel and salmon may also be used. Serves 4.

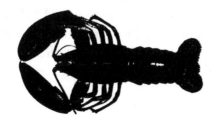

Boiled Lobster

Don't hesitate to use your fingers to get every morsel!

2	lobsters, 1½ lb (675 g) each	2	1 tbsp	salt

Bring enough water to boil to cover the lobsters when added. Add salt. Plunge the lobsters into the water and cover. Cook 12 minutes and drain. Serve hot or cold. To serve, cut the lobsters in half from head to tail. Remove and discard the tough sac inside the body near the eyes. Crack the claws. If served hot, serve with melted butter or a butter sauce. If served cold, serve with a plain mayonnaise-based sauce. Serves 2-4.

Grilled Mackerel

This is great served with fresh corn-on-the-cob and sliced tomatoes.

1⅓ lb	mackerel fillets	620 g	1 tsp	red pepper, preferably cayenne	5 ml
1 tbsp	sweet paprika	15 ml	¾ tsp	black pepper	3 ml
1½ tsp	salt	7 ml	½ tsp	thyme leaves, dried	2 ml
1 tsp	onion powder	5 ml	½ tsp	oregano leaves, dried	2 ml
1 tsp	garlic powder	5 ml			
¾ tsp	white pepper	3 ml			

Start a charcoal fire or preheat a gas grill. When the grill is ready, prepare the fillets by placing them side by side on a cookie sheet, skin side down. Combine the seasonings and evenly sprinkle over the fish. Place the fillets on a well-oiled preheated grill (you can top the grill with greased foil with holes), skin side down. Cook for about 4 minutes. Turn with care (don't worry if the skin sticks) and cook for another 2-3 minutes. When done, carefully remove from the grill and serve skin side down. (Take care with bones.) Serves 2.

Salting Mackerel, Shad or Salmon

For every 10 pounds (5 kg) of fish prepare:

1 cup	onions, sliced	250 ml	2	bay leaves	2
½ cup	olive oil	125 ml	½ tbsp	whole cloves	8 ml
1 tbsp	white pepper	15 ml	1 quart	vinegar	1 L
½ tbsp	black pepper	8 ml	1 quart	water	1 L
1 tbsp	mustard seeds	15 ml		salt	

Cut thoroughly cleaned fish into halves, quarters or smaller, depending on size of fish. Wash pieces in cold water, drain and dredge in salt. Place salted fish in refrigerator for at least 8 hours. Remove and wash in cold water. Cover fish with water and simmer for 10 minutes or until fish pierces easily with a fork. Strain and cool fish in the refrigerator. Sauté onion in olive oil, until golden and soft. Add remaining ingredients and simmer for 10 minutes. Cool sauce in refrigerator. Pour sauce over fish to cover. Refrigerate for 24 hours before using. Pack fish in sterile jars; cover with sauce; seal jars. Keep refrigerated.

Boiled Mackerel with Sauce

Sprinkle salt on fresh mackerel and let stand overnight. The following day, place mackerel in pot with cold water, bring to a boil, and simmer with a little onion until tender. Make a white sauce with 1 cup (250 ml) of the fish broth, 1 cup (250 ml) of milk, 1 tbsp (15 ml) butter, 2 tbsp flour (30 ml) and a sprinkle of pepper. Place boiled mackerel on a hot platter. Serve with the white sauce and vinegar.

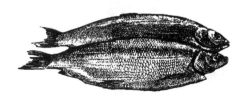

Salt Herring

Reserve enough time to pick out the bones.

Clean herring thoroughly, cut off heads and trim off belly flesh to the vent; wash, drain, and pack loosely in a large container. Prepare brine using 2 cups (500 ml) coarse salt, 4 cups (1 L) vinegar and 4 cups (1 L) water. Cover fish with brine and store in refrigerator. Leave fish in brine until the salt has penetrated the whole fish but remove before fish wrinkles and loses colour—3-7 days. When cure is complete, wash herring in cold running water to remove salt, and then proceed to make "Solomon Gundy."

Solomon Gundy

Still popular, after all these years!

6	salt herring	6	2 tbsp	pickling spice	30 ml
2-3	medium onions, sliced	2-3	½ cup	sugar	125 ml
2 cups	vinegar	500 ml			

Clean herring as described above. Cut flesh into 1-inch (2.5 cm) pieces. Allow to stand in refrigerator in bowl of cold water for 24 hours. Drain and squeeze fish gently to remove excess water. In sterile bottles, alternate layers of fish and onions. Mix vinegar, pickling spices and sugar in a saucepan; bring to a boil. Cool and pour over the herring. Refrigerate 4-6 days before serving. Keep refrigerated. Serve within a month.

The Great Nova Scotia Cookbook

Soused Mackerel

Clean, split open and cut fresh mackerel into serving pieces. Arrange in layers in baking dish with a few whole spices (cloves, allspice berries, peppercorns, or mustard seed) and a dash of pepper and salt. Cover with vinegar and dot top with 1 tbsp (15 ml) of butter. Bake about 30 minutes. Good hot or cold. Serve with boiled blue potatoes.

Cod or Clam Fritters

1 cup	cod or clams, cooked and flaked or minced	250 ml

Batter:

2	egg yolks	2
½ cup	milk	125 ml
1½ cups	sifted flour	375 ml
1 tbsp	baking powder	15 ml
¾ tsp	salt	3 ml
¼ tsp	white pepper	1.5 ml
2 tsp	Worcestershire sauce	10 ml
1 tbsp	Dijon mustard	15 ml
¼ tsp	paprika	1.5 ml

2 tbsp	parsley, chopped	30 ml
2 tbsp	onion, finely minced and cooked, or onion powder	30 ml
2 tbsp	green pepper, finely minced, cooked (optional)	30 ml
2	egg whites, stiffly beaten	2
	oil for frying	

Beat egg yolks until light. Add milk, Worcestershire sauce, Dijon mustard, parsley, onion, green pepper. Set aside. Fold in flaked cod or minced clams.

Refrigerate the mixture for 30 minutes. Deep fry, placing golf ball-size nuggets in 375F (190C) oil.

Scallop Casserole

Rich and elegant enough for a dinner party.

1 lb	scallops	500 g	1½ cups	whipping cream	375 ml
	milk		2	egg yolks, beaten	2
1 tbsp	butter	15 ml	2 tbsp	sherry	30 ml
1 tbsp	flour	15 ml	⅛ tsp	lemon pepper	0.5 ml
½ cup	Gruyère cheese, grated	125 ml	½ cup	breadcrumbs, buttered	125 ml

Prepare scallops by poaching in a small amount of milk—just until they turn opaque. Set aside. Melt butter in a large saucepan and add flour. Stir and cook over medium heat for 2-3 minutes. Add whipping cream to the butter-flour mixture. Stir in grated cheese. Whisk to combine and cook until thickened. Watch carefully to avoid lumping and scorching. Remove a small amount and mix well with egg yolks. Stir into cream mixture. Whisk constantly and heat very gently until hot. Mixture must not boil. Add scallops, sherry and lemon pepper. Heat again, just until hot. Pour into heated casserole dish. Top with buttered crumbs. Brown under the boiler. Serves 4-6.

Baked Scallops

1½ lb	scallops	750 g	½ tsp	salt	2 ml
1 cup	breadcrumbs, fine	250 ml	⅛ tsp	black pepper	0.5 ml
1	egg	1		cayenne pepper, a few grains	
2 tbsp	water	30 ml			
4 tbsp	butter, melted	60 ml			

Preheat oven to 450F (230C). In a small bowl toss breadcrumbs with salt, pepper and cayenne. In another bowl beat egg and water with fork. Dip each scallop in egg mixture and then in crumb mix. Place in baking dish and let stand for about a half-hour. This allows coating to set. Pour melted butter over all. Place in oven and bake for 30 minutes or until scallops are tender, browned and crisp on the outside. Serve with tartar sauce. Serves 6.

Smoked Scallops
in Cream Curry Sauce

4-6	smoked scallops per person, sliced in half	4-6	2 tsp	curry powder, mild	10 ml
2 tbsp	butter	30 ml	6 fl oz	medium cream (or 3 oz cream and 3 oz sour cream)	180 ml
2-3	medium green onions, tops included	2-3		egg noodles, as required	
1 tbsp	parsley, finely chopped	15 ml		flour, as required	

Melt the butter in a medium-hot pan and add the scallops. After a few seconds add the green onions and parsley. After another 30 seconds, add the mild curry powder and stir, letting the flavours blend. Lower the heat and carefully add the cream with a little flour to thicken if necessary. Reduce heat to low and prepare the noodles separately. Pour the scallops and sauce over the noodles. Garnish with a contrasting colour, such as red pepper or lemon.

Crab Cakes

2 lb	crabmeat	1 kg	2	egg whites, beaten	2
1 tsp	Dijon mustard	5 ml	1 cup	mayonnaise	250 ml
pinch	ground pepper		4 cups	breadcrumbs, fresh	1 L
2 tsp	Worcestershire sauce	10 ml	1 tsp	baking powder	5 ml
1 tbsp	parsley, chopped	15 ml	6 oz	clarified butter	180 ml

Clean shell fragments from crabmeat. Mix mustard, ground pepper, Worcestershire sauce, parsley and egg whites with mayonnaise; fold in crabmeat. Add breadcrumbs and baking powder, and blend well. Use a 3 oz (90 g) measure to scoop the correct amount of mixture, then form into cakes. Sauté in butter on flat grill, or in skillet over medium heat until golden brown on both sides. If desired, serve with coleslaw, corn relish, tartar sauce or mustard mayonnaise. Serves 6.

Crab Cakes with Roasted Red Pepper Sauce

1	leek, cleaned and chopped	1	1 tbsp	tarragon, dried	15 ml
			2 tbsp	chopped parsley	30 ml
½ cup	red pepper (or red/ yellow combination), finely diced	125 ml	½ tsp	hot sauce	2 ml
			½ tsp	salt	2 ml
			1 tsp	white wine Worcestershire sauce	5 ml
½ cup	scallions, chopped	125 ml			
1 lb	crabmeat	500 g	1 tsp	Dijon mustard	5 ml
½ cup	breadcrumbs	125 ml		breadcrumbs	
½ cup	mayonnaise	125 ml			

Sauté leeks and peppers until tender, add scallions. Combine with next 10 ingredients. Adjust seasonings, to taste. Form into patties 1 inch (2.5 cm) thick and coat with breadcrumbs. Chill until ready to cook. Sauté cakes in a nonstick pan with minimal amount of oil, approximately 3 minutes per side. Serve with a sauce of puréed, roasted red peppers with a dash of balsamic vinegar and cream, or with tartar sauce and lemon wedges. Serves 4.

Curried Scallops

Curry powder livens up this simple dish.

1 lb	scallops, fresh or frozen	500 g	1 tsp	salt	5 ml
			3 tbsp	butter	45 ml
⅓ cup	breadcrumbs, very fine	75 ml	1 tsp	curry powder	5 ml
			2 tsp	lemon juice	10 ml

Butter a large baking dish and preheat oven to 450F (230C). Rinse scallops under cold water. Dry well. Cut each scallop into two pieces and roll in breadcrumbs. Place one layer in baking dish and sprinkle with salt, if desired. Melt butter in small saucepan, add curry and cook gently for 2 minutes. Remove from heat and stir in lemon juice. Drizzle butter mixture over scallops. Bake 15-20 minutes, until scallops are tender. Serve immediately. Serves 4.

Oyster Stew

A family favourite back when oysters were plentiful and inexpensive.

2 tbsp	butter	30 ml	½ lb	bacon, cooked, drained and chopped	250 g
1½ cups	onion, diced	375 ml	24	oysters, shucked	24
3 cups	potatoes, peeled and diced	750 ml		salt	
1 cup	celery, diced	250 ml		fresh ground pepper	
½ cup	carrots, diced	125 ml	¼ cup	parsley, chopped	50 ml
2 cups	light cream	500 ml			
3 cups	fish stock or bottled clam juice	750 ml			

Melt butter in a large saucepan. Sauté onion over medium heat until transparent, about 15 minutes. Add vegetables and fish stock. Simmer over medium heat until vegetables are fork tender. With a slotted spoon remove 1½ cups of the cooked vegetables and reserve. Purée the remaining vegetables with the cream and stock, and reheat with reserved vegetables in the saucepan. Do not boil. Add bacon and oysters and simmer for 2 minutes. Add salt and pepper, to taste. Garnish with parsley. Serves 6.

Smoked Scallops Au Gratin

½ lb	smoked scallops, cut in small pieces	250 g	1 cup	Swiss cheese, grated	250 ml
5	medium potatoes	5	1½ cups	breadcrumbs	375 ml
2	onions	2		butter or margarine	

Thinly slice potatoes and onion. Layer potatoes, onions, and scallops in a buttered casserole dish ending with a layer of potatoes. Sprinkle with a layer of breadcrumbs and dot with butter. Cover and bake at 350F (175C) until potatoes are tender, about 1 hour. Uncover dish, top with grated Swiss cheese and broil until bubbly. Serves 4.

Poached Oysters

½ cup	unsalted butter	125 ml			seaweed	
½ cup	shallots, sliced	125 ml			salt	
½ cup	white wine	125 ml			white pepper	
½ cup	clam juice	125 ml		¼ cup	chives, chopped	50 ml
¾ cup	whipping cream	175 ml				
20	oysters, shucked (reserve lower half of shell)	20				

In a medium-sized saucepan, melt 2 tbsp butter over medium heat. Add shallots, cooking until tender, about 3 minutes. Add white wine and clam juice, cooking until reduced by half, about 5-10 minutes. Add cream, cooking until thick enough to coat a spoon, about 10 minutes. Heat shells on cookie sheet in oven at 300F (150C) for 5 minutes. Arrange shells on a seaweed-covered plate. Add oysters to sauce. Cook for 1-2 minutes until the edges just begin to curl. Place oysters in shells. Return sauce to boil, remove from heat and whisk in remaining softened butter. Adjust seasonings. Transfer to steel bowl and add chives. Whisk for ½ minute to stabilize. Spoon sauce over oysters and serve. Serves 4-6.

Baked Mussels

4 lb	mussels	2 kg			salt and pepper	
6 slices	bacon	6		½ cup	onion, finely chopped	125 ml
2 tbsp	lemon juice	30 ml				
1 cup	Cheddar cheese, grated	250 ml				

Remove beards from mussels and rinse well. In a large, covered saucepan, cook mussels in small amount of boiling water for 6-8 minutes or until shells open. Preheat oven to 375F (190C). Remove mussels from shells and place in a buttered 6-cup (1.5 L) baking dish or pan. Season with salt and pepper. Sprinkle with onion and lemon juice. Cover with chopped bacon and sprinkle with cheese. Bake at 375F (190C) for 15-20 minutes or until bacon is cooked.

Honey Citrus Pork

4	pork steaks, boneless 1-1½-inch (2.5-3.5 cm) thick	4

Marinade:

½ cup	soy sauce	125 ml
⅓ cup	chicken stock	75 ml
⅓ cup	lemon juice	75 ml
¼ cup	orange juice	50 ml
2 tsp	lemon rind, grated	10 ml
1 tsp	orange rind, grated	5 ml

1½ tsp	ginger, grated or	7 ml
½ tsp	powdered ginger	2 ml
1 clove	garlic, crushed and minced	1
⅓ cup	liquid honey	75 ml

Combine all marinade ingredients except honey. Pour over pork steaks in plastic bag. Close bag tightly. Marinate for 2 hours at room temperature or overnight in refrigerator. Barbecue steaks over medium heat, about 5-10 minutes on each side, brushing with marinade occasionally during last quarter of barbecuing time. Combine honey with marinade and heat to boiling for two to three minutes. Serve pork steaks with marinade. A high sugar content in marinade causes charring, drying out the meat. Serves 4.

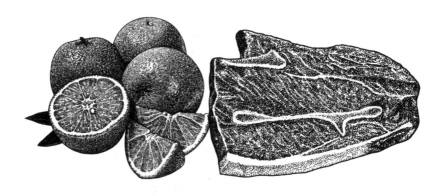

Maple Ribs

3 lb	pork ribs	1.5 kg	¼ tsp	salt	1.5 ml
1 cup	maple syrup	250 ml	¼ tsp	pepper	1.5 ml
½ cup	apple sauce	125 ml	¼ tsp	paprika	1.5 ml
¼ cup	ketchup	50 ml	¼ tsp	garlic powder	1.5 ml
3 tbsp	lemon juice	45 ml			

Place ribs in Dutch oven. Cover with water. Bring to a boil. Reduce heat and simmer for 10 minutes. Drain.

Place ribs in greased baking pan 9x13x2 inches (23x33x5 cm). Combine remaining ingredients; pour half over the ribs. Bake uncovered at 325F (165C) for 1½ hours or until the meat is tender, basting often with the sauce. Serves 6.

Barbecued Spare Ribs

3 lb	pork back or side ribs	1.5 kg	3 tbsp	lemon juice	45 ml
			½ tsp	cayenne pepper	2 ml
2 tbsp	butter	30 ml	1 cup	ketchup	250 ml
1	onion, finely chopped	1	3 tbsp	Worcestershire sauce	45 ml
			1½ tsp	dry mustard	7 ml
2 tbsp	vinegar	30 ml	1 tsp	celery salt or seeds	5 ml
¼ cup	brown sugar	50 ml			

Cut ribs into 2 or 3 rib portions. Place in a large pot, cover with salted water and bring to a boil. Reduce to simmer, cover and cook 60 minutes. Drain ribs; place in shallow baking dish. In saucepan, melt butter and brown sugar. Add remaining ingredients and simmer for 3 minutes, stirring constantly. Pour sauce over ribs and refrigerate for at least 1 hour, turning occasionally. Remove ribs from dish and barbecue over low heat about 10-15 minutes, turning occasionally until ribs are glazed. Serve ribs with remaining barbecue sauce, which has been reheated to a boil. Serves 6.

Famous Pork Ribs

2 lb	pork ribs, country-style lean	1 kg	12 oz	ketchup	330 ml
			½ cup	onion, grated	125 ml
½ tsp	red pepper flakes	2 ml		salt, to taste	

Cut the ribs into serving pieces. Place ribs in a large pot and cover with water. Cover the pot and simmer until ribs are tender, about 40 minutes. In a small saucepan prepare the sauce by combining the remaining ingredients. Bring to a boil, reduce the heat and simmer for 15 minutes. Place the ribs in a 3 quart (3 L) baking dish. Sprinkle with salt. Pour the sauce over the ribs. Bake at 350F (175C) for 30 minutes. Serves 4.

Pork Burgers

1 lb	lean ground pork	500 g	½ tsp	salt	2 ml
½ tsp	celery salt	2 ml	¼ tsp	pepper	1.5 ml

For flavour variations add one or more of the following ingredients:

1 tsp	dry mustard	5 ml	1 tsp	savoury	5 ml
1 tsp	garlic powder	5 ml	1 tsp	onion powder	5 ml
1 tsp	oregano	5 ml			

Combine ground pork and seasonings thoroughly. Shape into 4 patties and barbecue over medium heat for 5-10 minutes on each side. Place burger on a toasted hamburger bun and top with favourite condiments.

Ribs with Plum Sauce

5-6 lb	pork spareribs	2.5-3 kg	¾ cup	honey	175 ml
¾ cup	soy sauce	175 ml	2-3 cloves	garlic, crushed and minced	2-3
¾ cup	plum jam	175 ml			

Cut ribs into serving-size pieces; place with bone side down on a rack in a shallow roasting pan. Cover and bake at 350F (175C) for 1 hour or until ribs are tender; drain. Combine remaining ingredients; brush some of the sauce over ribs. Bake at 350F (175C) or grill over medium coals, uncovered for 30 minutes, brushing occasionally with sauce. Serves 6.

Teriyaki Pork Burgers

1 lb	ground pork, lean	500 g	¼ tsp	garlic powder	1.5 ml
¼ cup	breadcrumbs, fine and dry	50 ml	¼ tsp	pepper	1.5 ml
			1	egg	1
1 tsp	salt	5 ml	2 tbsp	onion, chopped	30 ml

Sauce:

2 tbsp	soy sauce	30 ml	¼ tsp	ginger	1.5 ml
¼ cup	orange juice concentrate	50 ml	1 tsp	brown sugar	5 ml
			1 tsp	cornstarch	5 ml
2	green onions, finely chopped	2	1 tbsp	water	15 ml

Combine ground pork, breadcrumbs, salt, garlic powder, pepper, egg and onion; blend well. Form into 4 patties. Barbecue over medium heat 5-10 minutes each side or until done. Meanwhile combine soy sauce, orange juice concentrate, green onion, ginger and brown sugar. Heat until bubbly.

Blend cornstarch and water. Add to sauce mixture. Heat and stir until thickened.

Serve patties on hamburger buns with a lettuce leaf, a slice of pineapple and a dollop of sauce. Serves 4.

Honey Garlic Steak on a Bun

6	pork steaks, boneless, well trimmed	6

Marinade:

½ cup	lemon juice	125 ml	4 cloves	garlic	4
½ cup	honey	125 ml	2 tbsp	parsley, finely chopped	30 ml
¼ cup	soy sauce	50 ml			
2 tbsp	white vinegar	30 ml			

Place steaks in plastic bag and set in bowl. Combine marinade ingredients and pour over steaks. Close bag with twist-tie. Marinate for 2 hours at room temperature or overnight in refrigerator. Remove steaks from marinade and barbecue over medium heat for 5-10 minutes on each side (depending on thickness). Baste with marinade throughout cooking. Meat will lose its pinkness when done. Serve pork on hamburger buns or kaisers. Serves 6.

Cornbread & Sausage Supper

1 lb	sausage	500g	2 tsp	baking powder	10 ml
1 cup	cornmeal	250 ml	½ tsp	salt	2 ml
2 cups	sour milk	500 ml	¼ cup	sugar	50 ml
1⅓ cups	flour	335 ml	1	egg	1
½ tsp	baking soda	2 ml	⅓ cup	shortening	75 ml

Oven fry sausage. When done, remove from oven and drain well. Grease a 9-inch (23 cm) square baking dish. Arrange sausage on bottom of pan. Set aside. Soak cornmeal in sour milk for 10-12 minutes. Sift together the flour, soda, baking powder, salt and sugar in mixing bowl. Cut in shortening. Beat egg and stir into cornmeal mixture. Add to dry ingredients. Pour batter over sausages in pan. Bake at 425F (218C) for 20 minutes. Serve hot with maple syrup. Serves 6.

Minute Meatballs & Spaghetti

When you don't have time to make meatballs.

1 lb	Italian sausage, mild	500g	¼ cup	parsley, chopped	50 ml
1 19-oz can	Italian stewed tomatoes	540 ml	12 oz	spaghetti, uncooked	375 g
¼ cup	tomato paste	50 ml	¼ cup	Parmesan cheese, grated	50 ml

Cut sausage into ½-inch (1 cm) slices. In skillet, brown sausages over medium heat for 5 minutes, turning once. Drain. In blender, purée tomatoes, if desired. Pour purée and tomato paste into skillet. On medium heat simmer until thickened. Stir in sausage and parsley. In a large pot of salted water, cook spaghetti for about 8 minutes or until tender but firm. Drain and return to pot. Add sauce and sausage and toss to coat. Sprinkle with Parmesan cheese. Serves 4-6.

Sweet and Sour Pork Chops

4	pork chops	4	½ cup	brown sugar	125 ml
1	onion, sliced	1	¼ cup	water	50 ml
¼ cup	white sugar	50 ml	1 tbsp	Worcestershire sauce	15 ml

Place chops in roaster. Bake at 350F (175C) for 20 minutes or until nearly done. In meantime, mix sauce ingredients together. Pour sauce over chops and cook ten minutes. Serves 4.

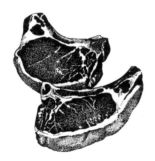

Graham Cracker Ham Loaf

4	eggs	4	2½ lb	ground ham	1.25 kg
2 cups	graham cracker crumbs	500 ml	1½ lb	ground pork	675 g

Sauce:

1 cup	brown sugar	250 ml	½ cup	water	125 ml
1 tsp	dry mustard	5 ml	1 10-oz can	tomato soup	284 ml
½ cup	vinegar	125 ml			

Mix eggs, crumbs and meat and shape into loaf. Place in a 3-quart (3 L) baking dish. Combine sauce ingredients; pour over ham loaf. Cover and bake in 350F (175C) for 1½ hours. Uncover and bake ½ hour longer, spooning sauce over loaf. Serves 8.

Sauerkraut-Zuurkoolschotel

1½ lb	sauerkraut	675 g	8 thin slices	lean bacon	8
4	juniper berries, crushed	4	4	frankfurters	4
½ lb	fat bacon, in one piece	225 g	2 lb	small potatoes, peeled and cooked	1 kg
4	thick slices ham, uncooked	4	1 small	piece bacon rind	
¾ cup	white wine	175 ml			

Place bacon rind in heavy pan and spread with sauerkraut and juniper berries. Place the fat bacon in centre of sauerkraut and arrange ham around it. Pour wine over sauerkraut and cover with lean slices of bacon. Cook covered for 1 hour over low heat. Add frankfurters and simmer for another 20 minutes. Arrange sauerkraut on a warm, flat dish. Slice the fat bacon and arrange on top. Garnish with the ham, frankfurters, whole potatoes and thinly sliced lean bacon. Discard rind. Serve with melted butter. Serves 6.

Orange Pork Tenderloin

2	lean pork tenderloins, ½ lb (250 g) each	2	½ tsp	black pepper	2 ml	
			2	cloves garlic, halved	2	
1 tsp	orange peel, grated	4 ml	1 tsp	cornstarch	5 ml	
½ cup	orange juice	125 ml	¼ tsp	salt	1 ml	
2 tbsp	fresh cilantro, chopped	30 ml	1 tsp	vegetable oil	5 ml	
			1 large	plantain, ripe, cut into ¼-inch slices	1	
2 tbsp	lime juice	30 ml				

Cut tenderloins across grain into ⅛-inch slices. Mix orange peel, orange juice, cilantro, lime juice, pepper and garlic in large bowl. Add pork slices. Cover and refrigerate 30 minutes. Remove pork from marinade. Stir cornstach and salt into remaining marinade; set aside. Heat oil in nonstick skillet over medium heat. Cook pork in oil about 4 minutes, stirring frequently, until no longer pink. Stir in plantain. Cook 2-3 minutes, stirring frequently. Stir in marinade mixture. Heat to boiling, stirring constantly. Boil and stir 1 minute.

Crunchy Pork Chops

¼ cup	butter	50 ml	1 cup	chicken stock	250 ml
3 cups	onions, thinly sliced	750 ml	1 cup	breadcrumbs	250 ml
⅓ cup	sweet red pepper	75 ml	½ cup	Mozzarella cheese, shredded	125 ml
½ tsp	salt	2 ml			
¼ tsp	pepper	1.5 ml	½ cup	Parmesan cheese, freshly grated	125 ml
¼ tsp	thyme, dried	1.5 ml			
6	pork loin chops	6	3 tbsp	butter, melted	45 ml

Cook onion over low heat in 2 tbsp (30 ml) of butter, stirring frequently until tender. Stir in red pepper, salt, pepper and thyme. Set aside. Melt remaining butter in fry pan. Brown chops in batches over moderate heat. Spread one half onion mixture in 8-cup (2 L) baking dish. Place chops on top, overlapping if necessary. Cover with remainder of onion mixture and chicken stock. Cover and bake at 400F (200C), basting 2-3 times, about 30 minutes. Combine breadcrumbs, cheeses and butter. Sprinkle over chops. Bake 10 minutes more. Garnish with red pepper and thyme.

Curried Pork Chops & Peaches

2 tbsp	shortening or oil	30 ml		¼ cup	butter	50 ml
6	pork loin or rib chops, 1 inch (2.5 cm) thick	6		¼ cup	flour	50 ml
				1 tsp	curry	5 ml
1 28-oz can	peach halves, drained	796 ml		2 cups	milk	500 ml
				1 6-oz can	sliced mushrooms, drained	180 ml
½ cup	onion, finely chopped	125 ml			salt	

Melt shortening in skillet; brown chops over medium heat. Place in an ungreased 13x9x2-inch (23x33x5 cm) dish. Arrange peach halves cut side down on meat. In medium skillet, cook and stir onion in butter until onion is tender. Stir in flour, salt, and curry powder. Cook over low heat, stirring until mixture is bubbly. Remove from heat. Stir in milk gradually. Heat to boiling, stirring constantly for one minute. Stir in mushrooms; pour over chops. Cover tightly and bake at 350F (175C) until meat is tender, about 20 minutes. Uncover and bake 15 minutes longer. Serves 6.

Grilled Pork Chops

Tender, mouth-watering chops—easy to make and very popular.

1	large onion, finely chopped	1		¼ cup	lemon juice	50 ml
				1 clove	garlic, crushed and minced	1
½ cup	water	125 ml				
⅓ cup	soy sauce	75 ml		6	pork loin chops, 1 inch (2.5 cm) thick	6
⅓ cup	brown sugar	75 ml				

In a shallow glass pan, combine onion, water, soy sauce, brown sugar, lemon juice and garlic. Set aside ⅓ cup for basting. Add pork chops to the remaining marinade, so that marinade covers chops. Refrigerate overnight. Drain and discard marinade. Grill chops, covered, over medium-hot heat for 4 minutes. Turn, baste with reserved marinade, and grill until juices run clear. Serves 6.

Ham Cups

1 8-oz carton	cottage cheese	250 g	2	eggs, slightly beaten		2
1 tbsp	canola oil	15 ml	½ cup	ham, diced		125 ml
1	small onion, minced	1	pinch	nutmeg		
				salt and pepper		
2 cups	mushrooms, chopped	500 ml	2 tbsp	butter, melted		30 ml
				parsley sprigs, for garnish		

Preheat oven to 400F (200C). Heat oil in a small saucepan. Add onion and cook gently until soft. Add the mushrooms and cook for 1-2 minutes, stirring constantly. Remove the saucepan from the heat and cool. Push the cottage cheese through a strainer into a bowl. Beat in the eggs, a little at a time. Add diced ham, onion, mushrooms and nutmeg to bowl. Season to taste. Brush 4 ramekins with the melted butter and divide the mixture equally among them. Place on cookie sheet and bake until well risen, brown and bubbly on top, about 20 minutes. Serve immediately. Garnish with parsley sprigs. Serve with hot French bread. Serves 4.

Ham Steak with Apples

1	thick slice ham, precooked	1	¼ cup	orange juice diluted with ½ cup (125 ml) water	50 ml
15	whole cloves	15	4	apples, cored and sliced	4
¾ cup	brown sugar	175 ml			

Stud the ham with cloves. Put the ham in open roasting pan. Cover bottom of pan with a little water. Bake for 25-35 minutes in 350F (175C) oven. Remove from the oven and spread ham with sugar—then cover with diluted juice. Return ham to oven, set at 400F (200C); allow 20 minutes for glazing. Watch carefully to avoid burning. Remove ham to hot platter and cook apple slices in pan drippings, for about 5 minutes, turning once. Serves 4.

Ham with Apricot Glaze

1	large ham (bone in)	1	1 tbsp	cornstarch	15 ml
½ cup	apricot jam	125 ml	1 tsp	cloves, whole	5 ml
⅓ cup	liquid honey	75 ml	pinch	cinnamon	
2 tbsp	real lemon juice	30 ml			

Remove excess fat from ham. Score surface of ham every 2 inches (5 cm) and place a whole clove in centre of each. To make the glaze combine all remaining ingredients and bring to a boil in a small saucepan. Bake ham in shallow pan at 350F (175C) for 2½ hours. During last ½ hour brush on glaze.

Hot Sausage Roll-Ups

| 12 | sausages | 12 | | mustard, as desired | |
| 12 slices | bread | 12 | | | |

Cook sausages on rack in pan in oven until browned. Remove from oven. Trim crusts from bread. Spread with mustard. Roll a sausage in each bread slice and secure with two well-spaced toothpicks. Slice in half or leave whole and place on a greased cookie sheet. Bake at 425F (220C) until bread is golden. Serve hot with a favourite dip.

Sausage & Sauerkraut Supper

| 1 19-oz can | sauerkraut | 540 ml | 1 lb | sausage | 500 g |

Arrange sausage in baking pan and bake until browned. Remove from oven and lift sausage from pan. Pour off grease. Spread sauerkraut over bottom of pan. Lay baked sausages on top of sauerkraut. Return to oven until all is heated, about 20 minutes. Serve with baked potatoes and other vegetables. Serves 4.

Chop Suey

4 tbsp	vegetable oil	60 ml	1	small green pepper	1
2 cups	leftover roast, ground in meat grinder	500 ml	2 cups	celery, sliced	500 ml
			1 cup	cold water	250 ml
			1 cup	mushrooms	250 ml
3 tbsp	soy sauce	45 ml	2 tbsp	cornstarch	30 ml
1 tbsp	brown sugar	15 ml	1 10-oz can	bean sprouts rinsed and drained	284 ml
3	medium onions	3			
2 cloves	garlic	2			

Place oil in pan. Heat and add onion, garlic, green pepper and celery. Stir and cook until tender. Add 1 cup (250 ml) cold water with cornstarch dissolved in it. Stir well together and add soy sauce and brown sugar, mushrooms, meat and bean sprouts. Stir well until flavours blend. Serve with hot rice or buttered noodles. Amounts can vary. Serves 4.

Favourite Beef Casserole

A very old recipe.

In the morning, cook ½ pound (250 g) medium noodles until barely tender. Drain and rinse. In a large skillet, sauté 3-4 chopped onions in 2 tbsp (30 ml) butter until tender, but not brown. Set aside. In same skillet, cook 2 lb (1 kg) ground chuck in 1 tbsp (15 ml) olive or salad oil, stirring to break meat into bits and adding 1 tsp (5 ml) salt, ½ tsp (2 ml) pepper, and ½ tsp (2 ml) thyme. In about 10 minutes, when the meat loses its colour, add to it the sautéed onion. In a 3-quart (3 L) casserole, arrange ⅓ of the noodles, then half of the meat mixture. Combine one can of condensed celery soup with ¼ cup (50 ml) milk. Pour half of this mixture over the meat. Repeat. Arrange rest of the noodles on top. Store in refrigerator. About 1¼ hours before serving, heat the oven to 350F (175C). Sprinkle 1½ cups (375 ml) grated Cheddar cheese over the noodles. Beat 3 eggs and pour them over the cheese. Bake uncovered one hour or until hot, bubbly and lightly browned with a delectable crisp top. Serves 8-10.

Chili

1 lb	ground beef	500 g			cayenne pepper	
1	onion, finely chopped	1	1 28-oz can	red kidney beans, with liquid	796 ml
1	sweet red pepper, finely chopped	1	1 19-oz can	tomatoes, with liquid	540 ml
1	green pepper, finely chopped	1	1 cup	romaine lettuce, shredded	250 ml
2 cloves	garlic, crushed	2	1 cup	Mozzarella cheese	250 ml
2 tbsp	chili powder	30 ml	1 cup	onion, chopped	250 ml
pinch	salt and pepper				

Sauté the beef, onions and bell peppers in a little oil in fry pan, until meat caramelizes and onion and peppers are tender. Add the garlic, chili, onion, pepper and cayenne.

Sauté over low heat 2 minutes. Add the kidney beans, tomatoes and salt. Bring all to a boil, then reduce heat and simmer uncovered for 30 minutes or longer. Serve chili in bowls. Shredded lettuce, cheese and chopped onions can be served in side bowls. Good with hot cornmeal muffins. Serves 6.

Quick Hamburg Supper

1½-2 lb	lean ground beef	750 g-1 kg		garlic, fresh or powdered, to taste
½ pkg	onion soup mix	½		pepper, to taste
1 10-oz can	golden mushroom soup	284 ml		oil

Place a little oil in fry pan. Heat and add meat. Mix and stir until meat is cooked and caramelized. Add onion soup mix, garlic and pepper. Blend all together. Add soup last. Stir well and transfer to baking dish. Let stand in warm oven until ready to serve. Serve with mashed potatoes, a vegetable and green salad. Serves 6.

Pot Roast

Rump roast is one of the most tasty cuts of beef.

5-6 lb	beef, rump roast	2.5-3 kg		pepper
3 tbsp	oil	45 ml		water
	garlic powder			flour

Heat heavy-bottomed pot on burner. Add oil to pot. Wash roast under cold water, removing excess fat. Place roast in hot pot, skin side down. Sear on all sides until well browned, watching carefully that it does not burn. When seared, season generously with garlic powder and pepper. Pour about 1½ cups (375 ml) of water in bottom of pot. Cover and cook until roast tests tender when pierced with fork. During cooking, check frequently and turn meat. Add water as required. During the last few minutes of cooking, let the water reduce to give a good rich brown gravy. Remove roast to a hot platter and cover with foil or an inverted bowl to keep it both hot and moist.

Make gravy in the pot by adding water and stirring down any browned pieces that will add flavour. Make a paste of flour and cold water and add to the drippings and water (use 1 tbsp (15 ml) flour and ¼ cup (50 ml) cold water for each cup of liquid in the pan). A little salt may be needed, but if the meat has browned sufficiently, salt is not necessary. Sliced onions add a nice touch. Slice roast in thin or thick slices (according to your preference) across the grain of the meat. Serves 10.

Oven-Baked Hash

An old supper dish—still used and enjoyed.

Using leftover roast beef, grind about 3 cups (750 ml) of meat in the coarse-grind unit of a meat grinder. Also grind cold, boiled potatoes that have been peeled. The quantity of potato should equal the amount of prepared meat. Grind onions, according to your taste. Add a little salt and pepper.

Toss all ingredients together; place in baking dish. Pour about 1 cup (250 ml) of beef or chicken stock over top. Dot generously with butter. Cook in 350F (175C) oven for 30-45 minutes. Top should be lightly browned. Good with brown gravy. Serves 6.

Judy's Lasagna

3 tbsp	olive oil	45 ml		½-1 cup	Parmesan cheese, grated	125-250 ml
1 clove	garlic	1		1 cup	onion, finely chopped	250 ml
2 tsp	salt	10 ml				
1 8-oz can	tomato sauce	250 g		1½ lb	ground beef	675 g
¾ cup	water	175 ml		1 28-oz can	tomatoes	796 ml
½ tsp	oregano	2 ml		1 6-oz can	tomato paste	168 ml
1 tbsp	parsley (optional)	15 ml				
1 lb	lasagna noodles	500 g		½ tsp	basil	2 ml
1	egg	1		1 tsp	sugar	5 ml
1 lb	Mozzarella cheese	500 g				
1 lb	Ricotta cheese	500 g				

Heat 2 tbsp (30 ml) oil in heavy saucepan. Sauté onion and garlic for 5 minutes, and stir in ground beef. Cook over medium heat until brown. Add salt, tomatoes, tomato paste, tomato sauce, water, sugar, parsley, basil and oregano. Bring sauce to boil and simmer for 45 minutes. Meanwhile, cook lasagna noodles, adding remaining oil to noodles while cooking to prevent sticking. Drain, rinse and cool. In bowl, blend Ricotta cheese and egg. Preheat oven to 375F (190C). Grease 13x9x2-inch (33x24x5 cm) baking pan. In pan, arrange alternate layers of sauce, lasagna noodles, Ricotta and Mozzarella, finishing with sauce. Sprinkle with Parmesan cheese to your own taste (between layers or just over top). Bake for 35 minutes. Let stand 10 minutes before serving. May be frozen. Serves 8-10.

Quick & Easy Shepherd's Pie

1 lb	lean ground beef	500 g	1 lb	vegetable combination (broccoli, cauliflower and carrots), thawed	500 g
1 10-oz can	Campbell's Cream of Mushroom and Garlic soup	284 ml	4	medium potatoes, or more	4
1 tbsp	Worcestershire sauce	15 ml			

In skillet over medium heat cook beef until browned. Pour off fat. In a shallow, 2-quart (2 L) dish, mix beef, ½ can soup, Worcestershire sauce and vegetables. Cook potatoes, mash and add the remaining soup, blending well. Spoon potato mixture over beef mixture. Bake at 400F (200C) for 20 minutes or until hot. Serves 6.

Meat Pie

This is a version of a supper dish that my mother, who was from the Margaree Valley, used to make.

Meat mixture:

3 lb	beef	1.4 kg	3 lb	chicken	1.4 kg
3 lb	pork	1.4 kg			

You can use any meat combination: deer, rabbit, partridge, but always include pork.

4	medium onions	4	¼ tsp	sage, more if desired	1.5 ml
1½ tsp	black pepper	7 ml	½ cup	water	125 ml
1-2 tsp	salt	5-10 ml			

Cut meat into chunks, removing skin and fat. Combine with other ingredients in a large pot. Stew slowly for 3-4 hours. Remove from heat. Cool. Remove all bones and gristle. Cut into small chunks. Grate raw onion into meat and mix with stock. Make a rich pastry. (See pages 325-326 for recipe.) Roll out as for any pie, making top and bottom crusts. Fill with meat mixture. Top crust can be made "fancy" with cut-outs. Bake pies at 350F (175C) until golden brown. Serve hot with cranberries. A few vegetables may be added to the filling. Makes 3 pies.

Beef Casserole

1½ cups	fusilli	375 ml	1 cup	cottage cheese	250 ml
1 lb	lean ground beef	500 g	8 oz	cream cheese	225 g
1 8-oz can	tomato sauce	250 ml	1 8-oz carton	sour cream	250 ml
1 tsp	salt	5 ml	½ cup	green onions, chopped	125 ml
1 tbsp	green pepper, chopped	15 ml			

Cook pasta as directed on package. Drain. Brown meat in a saucepan until caramelized, stirring often. Add tomato sauce and salt. Combine cottage cheese, cream cheese, sour cream, green onions and green pepper. Place half the pasta in a large casserole; top with cheese mixture, then the other half of the pasta, then the meat mixture. Bake at 350F (175C) for 30 minutes. Served with a tossed green salad and crusty rolls, this makes a satisfying meal. Serves 6.

Porcupine Meatballs

1 10-oz can	tomato soup	284 ml	½ cup	rice, uncooked, long-grain	125 ml
½ cup	water	125 ml	1 tsp	salt	5 ml
1½ lb	ground beef	675 g	½ tsp	pepper	2 ml
1 tbsp	onions	15 ml			

Blend soup and water in saucepan. One 19-oz (625 ml) can of tomatoes may be used instead of soup. Combine meat, onions, rice and seasonings. Shape into small meatballs. Heat the tomato mixture until it simmers. Add meatballs. Cook until rice is tender and meat cooked through. Serves 6.

Cheese-Topped Beef Pie

	pastry for single-crust, 9-inch (23 cm) pie		¼ cup	onion, chopped	50 ml
			¾ tsp	salt	3 ml
1 lb	lean ground beef	454 g	½ tsp	oregano, crushed	2 ml
½ cup	evaporated milk	125 ml	¼ tsp	pepper	1.5 ml
½ cup	ketchup	125 ml	1 cup	processed cheese, shredded	250 ml
⅓ cup	breadcrumbs, fine and dry	75 ml	1 tsp	Worcestershire sauce	5 ml

Preheat oven to 350F (175C). Line 9-inch (23 cm) pie plate with pastry. In a bowl, combine ground beef, milk, ketchup, breadcrumbs, onion, salt, oregano and pepper. Turn meat into pastry shell. Bake at 350F (175C) for 35-40 minutes. Toss cheese with Worcestershire sauce; sprinkle on pie. Bake 10 minutes more. Remove from oven; let stand 10 minutes before serving. Trim with pickle slices, if desired. Serves 6.

Hawaiian Meatballs

1 lb	ground beef	450 g	⅛ cup	vinegar	30 ml
⅔ cup	cracker crumbs	150 ml	½ cup	ketchup	125 ml
⅓ cup	minced onions	75 ml	½ cup	water	125 ml
1	egg	1	1 tbsp	soy sauce	15 ml
1 tsp	salt	5 ml	½ cup	maraschino cherries	125 ml
¼ cup	milk	50 ml	1 cup	pineapple chunks, drained	250 ml
2 tbsp	cornstarch	30 ml			
½ cup	brown sugar	125 ml			

Mix first 6 ingredients and shape into small balls. Brown in skillet. For sauce, combine next 6 ingredients and cook over medium heat. Add cherries and pineapple. Place meatballs in a small roasting pan or a slow cooker, and cover with sauce and fruit mixture. Bake at 300F (150C) for 30 minutes. Serve with rice. Serves 4-6.

Margaret's Sweet
& Sour Meatballs

2 lb	ground beef	1 kg	¼ tsp	pepper	1.5 ml
1 cup	cornflake crumbs	250 ml	½ tsp	garlic powder	2 ml
⅓ cup	parsley flakes	75 ml	⅓ cup	ketchup	75 ml
2	eggs	2	2 tbsp	onion	30 ml
2 tbsp	soy sauce	30 ml		oregano, to taste	

Beat eggs with spoon in bowl. Add all ingredients. Mix well and shape into small balls. Fry the meatballs or bake them in the oven on a cookie sheet for 20 minutes at 350-375F (175-190C) to brown evenly. Drain on paper towel.

Sauce:

1 cup	water	250 ml	¾ cup	ketchup	175 ml
1 cup	white sugar	250 ml	¼ cup	fruit juice	50 ml
½ cup	vinegar	125 ml	1 tbsp	cornstarch	15 ml

Mix first 5 ingredients and bring to a boil. Mix cornstarch with a little water and add. Cook until nicely thickened. Combine with meatballs and cook for 30 minutes at 350F (175C). The sauce will thicken as it cooks in the oven. Serves 8.

Applesauce Meatballs

¾ lb	ground beef	375 g	2 tbsp	onion, grated	30 ml
¼ lb	ground pork	125 g	¼ cup	water	50 ml
½ cup	breadcrumbs, soft	125 ml	⅓ cup	ketchup	75 ml
1	egg	1	1 tsp	salt	5 ml
1 cup	applesauce, unsweetened	250 ml	⅛ tsp	pepper	0.5 ml
			2 tsp	Worcestershire sauce	10 ml

Combine all ingredients except ketchup and water. Mix lightly. Form into 2-inch (5 cm) balls. Brown in hot vegetable oil. Place browned meatballs in casserole dish; cover with ketchup and water mixed together. Cover and bake in oven until meatballs are cooked through, about 20 minutes. Serves 4-6.

Beef Enchiladas

2 tbsp	vegetable oil	30 ml			pepper, to taste	
2	small onions	2		1 tsp	cumin	5 ml
1	sweet red pepper, sliced	1		6	flour tortillas, 6-inch (15 cm)	6
1	green pepper, sliced	1				
1 clove	garlic, crushed and minced	1		1 cup	Cheddar cheese, shredded	250 ml
2½-3 cups	roast beef, cut into cubes	625 ml-750 ml		½ cup	sour cream	125 ml
				2 tbsp	green onion, chopped	30 ml
2 cups	taco sauce	500 ml				

Place oil in fry pan. Over medium heat, cook onion, red and green pepper and garlic for about 3 minutes, until tender and crisp. Remove from heat; stir in roast beef and 1 cup (250 ml) taco sauce and season with pepper. Spoon about ¾ cup (175 ml) of the meat mixture down the centre of each tortilla. Sprinkle with 1 tbsp (15 ml) of the cheese. Fold the tortilla over filling, slightly overlapping edges. Arrange seam side up in 11x7-inch (2L) baking dish. Spoon remaining taco sauce over each tortilla. Spoon sour cream down centre. Add remaining cheese. Bake in oven for 350F (175C) for 30 minutes or until heated through. Garnish with chopped green onion. Serves 6.

Reuben Sandwiches

1	large corned beef brisket, pre-seasoned	1		Swiss or Muenster cheese, sliced	
1 cup	brown sugar	250 ml		onions, sliced	
1 cup	vinegar	250 ml		sauerkraut, drained	
2 cups	ketchup	500 ml		prepared mustard	
	salt, to taste			prepared horseradish	
1 loaf	rye bread	1			

In a large pot, simmer brisket slowly until tender. Let cool. Thinly slice across the grain. Arrange slices in a 9x13-inch (23x33 cm) baking dish. Combine brown sugar, vinegar and ketchup and any corn beef crumbs left from slicing. Pour sauce over corned beef slices and bake at 350F (175C) for 20 minutes. Serves 6-8. Serve with sliced rye bread and other ingredients.

The Great Nova Scotia Cookbook

Corned Beef Pickle

There is something really enjoyable about a hearty meal on a cold day. Many of us remember corned beef and cabbage with potatoes, carrots and parsnips—a wonderful winter treat. Our parents took great pride in pickling their own beef. The recipe below was a favourite.

3 gallons	boiling water	12 L	10 lb	brisket or top of round beef, cut in portions	5 kg
5 lb	coarse salt	2.5 kg			
2 oz	saltpetre	56 g			
¼ cup	brown sugar	50 ml			

Pour boiling water into a crock and mix in salt, saltpetre and brown sugar. Stir. Let stand overnight. In morning, strain through a cloth. Place meat in strained pickle, cover with a cloth and allow to remain in the pickle one day for each pound of meat. Turn the meat every day. This pickle may be used for corning beef tongue as well. The time allowed for pickling should be doubled. When ready to use, remove beef from pickle. Wash. Place in stewing pot and add cold water to cover. Add 4-5 peppercorns and 8-12 whole cloves. Cook slowly until meat is tender. Add vegetables—potato, cabbage, carrot, parsnip and turnip are good. Add cabbage during the last 15 minutes. Cook until all are tender.

Corned Beef Patties

Sir William Van Horne is remembered as the genius associated with the construction of the Canadian Pacific Railway. The following recipe is a version of the one he enjoyed in 1886 when his dining car service was launched.

1 can	bully beef	1		celery salt
1	large potato	1		parsley
1	large onion	1		flour
1	egg	1	dash	dry mustard
	pepper			bacon fat

Heat a small amount of bacon fat in an iron skillet. In a bowl, mash bully beef. Add cooked and coarsely mashed potato. Chop onion and add, along with egg, seasonings and flour. Stir all together. Make into generous-sized patties. Sprinkle a little dry mustard on both sides. Brown in hot fat on each side. Break an egg on top of each patty and allow to cook. Pan may be covered with a lid. Do not overcook. Serves 2-4.

Hachee-Dutch Hash

1½-2 lb	lean boneless beef, pork or veal, diced	750 g-1 kg	5 tbsp	flour	75 ml
			3 cups	beef broth	750 ml
			2	bay leaves	2
1 tsp	salt	5 ml	2	cloves	2
	fresh ground pepper		1 tsp	sugar	5 ml
4 tbsp	butter	60 ml	2 tbsp	vinegar	30 ml
2	large onions, cut into rings	2			

Toss the diced meat (leftover roast will do) with salt and pepper. Heat the butter and sauté the meat and onions over high heat until lightly browned. Add the flour and cook, stirring, for 2 minutes. Add the broth gradually, stirring up the brown bits in the bottom of the pan. Add the remaining ingredients. Cover and simmer slowly for 1½ hours. Serve with rice or baked potatoes. Serves 6.

Dinner in a Dish

2 lb	ground beef	1 kg		2 tbsp	flour	30 ml
1	medium onion	1		2 tsp	marjoram	10 ml
1 28-oz can	tomatoes, undrained	796 ml		1 tsp	salt	5 ml
				½ tsp	pepper	2 ml
3 cups	peas, frozen	750 ml		6 cups	potatoes, hot mashed, prepared with milk and butter	1.5 L
⅔ cup	ketchup	150 ml				
¼ cup	parsley, chopped	50 ml				
2 tsp	beef bouillon granules	10 ml		2	eggs	2

In a saucepan over medium heat, brown the beef and onion; drain. Add the next 9 ingredients. Mix well; cook and stir for 2 minutes. Pour into an ungreased, shallow, 3-quart (3 L) baking dish. Combine potatoes and eggs; mix well. Drop by the ½ cup (125 ml) onto beef mixture. Bake uncovered at 350F (175C) for 35-40 minutes or until mixture is bubbly and potatoes are lightly browned. Serves 8.

Shepherd's Pie

1 lb	lean ground beef or lamb	500 g		1 cup	beef or chicken broth	250 ml
1 tbsp	vegetable oil	15 ml		1 tbsp	tomato paste	15 ml
1 clove	garlic, chopped	1		2 tbsp	parsley, chopped	30 ml
2	shallots, sliced	2		1 cup	green peas, frozen	250 ml
1	medium onion, chopped	1		1 quart	potatoes, mashed	1 L
2 tbsp	flour	30 ml		8 tbsp	Cheddar cheese, grated	125 ml
1 tsp	salt	5 ml				
1 tsp	ground pepper, to taste	5 ml				

Place meat in fry pan and cook well, stirring frequently. Place oil in a heavy saucepan and sauté shallots, onion and garlic. Add flour. Stir in next 6 ingredients, mixing well. Add meat and mix. Place mixture in casserole. Spread mashed potatoes over meat. Sprinkle with cheese. Serves 6.

Texas Beef and Beans

3 lb	ground beef	1.4 kg	1½ cups	ketchup	375 ml
2	celery stalks	2	⅓ cup	prepared mustard	75 ml
3	medium onions	3	3	garlic cloves, crushed and minced	3
¾ cup	boiling water	175 ml			
2	beef bouillon cubes	2	1 tsp	salt	5 ml
1 lb	bacon, cooked and crumbled	450 g	½ tsp	pepper	2.5 ml
2 28-oz cans	baked beans with molasses	2 x 796 ml			

In a large fry pan or Dutch oven, cook beef, onions and celery until meat is no longer pink. Drain off fat. Dissolve beef bouillon cubes in the hot water and stir into meat mixture. Add beans, ketchup, mustard, garlic, salt and pepper. Stir in one half the bacon. Top with remainder of bacon. Cover and bake at 350F(175C) for about 2 hours or until thick. Serves 12.

Oven Swiss Steak

2 lb	round steak, boneless	1 kg	½ cup	celery, chopped	125 ml
⅓ cup	flour	75 ml	2 cups	carrots, sliced	500 ml
1 tsp	salt	5 ml	¼ cup	onion, chopped	50 ml
2 tbsp	shortening	30 ml	2 tsp	Worcestershire sauce	10 ml
1 28-oz can	tomatoes	796 ml	½ cup	Cheddar cheese, shredded	125 ml

Cut meat into serving size portions. Combine half of the flour and salt and pound mixture into meat. In a large skillet, melt shortening and lightly brown meat. Transfer meat to shallow baking dish. Combine reserved flour and meat drippings in skillet; add all remaining ingredients except cheese. Cook, stirring constantly until mixture boils; pour over meat. Sprinkle with cheese. Cover and bake at 350F (175C) until cheese has melted, about 20 minutes. Serves 6.

Stuffed Manicotti

1 lb	ground beef	500 g	1 cup	Mozzarella cheese, grated	250 ml
1	large onion, chopped	1	1 32-oz jar	spaghetti sauce	1 L
1 tsp	garlic powder	5 ml	14	manicotti shells, cooked and drained	14
½ cup	Cheddar cheese, grated	125 ml		oregano	
1 cup	cottage cheese	250 ml			
½ cup	mayonnaise	125 ml			

Brown ground beef, onion and garlic powder; drain and cool. Add Cheddar cheese, cottage cheese, mayonnaise and Mozzarella cheese. Carefully spoon into manicotti shells and place in a casserole dish; cover with spaghetti sauce. Sprinkle with oregano, extra Cheddar and Mozzarella cheeses. Cover and bake at 350 F (175C) for 15 minutes. Uncover and continue baking for an additional 15 minutes. Serves 6.

Meat and Noodle Casserole

1 lb	ground beef	500 g	1 cup	tomato soup	250 ml
3 tbsp	oil	45 ml	1½ cups	water	375 ml
2 cups	onion, chopped	500 ml	1 tsp	chili powder	5 ml
2 cups	celery, chopped	500 ml	1 6-oz pkg	chow mein noodles, coarsely chopped	180 g
1½ cups	mushrooms, chopped	375 ml		salt and pepper	

Brown meat in oil. Add onion and celery. When almost soft, add mushrooms. Mix in other ingredients, reserving ½ cup (125 ml) noodles. Pour into a greased shallow casserole and top with reserved noodles. Bake at 350F (175C) for about 45 minutes. Serves 6.

Tangy Beef Stroganoff

1 lb	sirloin steak	500 g	1 tbsp	red wine vinegar	15 ml
¼ cup	butter	50 ml	2 tsp	beef bouillon granules	10 ml
½ lb	mushrooms, sliced	250 g	½ tsp	salt	2 ml
½ cup	onion, sliced	125 ml	¼ tsp	pepper	1.5 ml
1 clove	garlic, minced	1	1 cup	sour cream	250 ml
2 tbsp	flour	30 ml		cooked noodles	
1 cup	water	250 ml		paprika	
1 tbsp	lemon juice	15 ml		fresh parsley, chopped	

Cut beef into ⅛-inch (0.3 cm) thick strips. In a large skillet over medium-high heat, cook beef in butter until no longer pink. Remove with slotted spoon and keep warm. In pan juices, cook mushrooms, onion and garlic until tender; stir in flour. Add water, lemon juice, vinegar, bouillon, salt and pepper; bring to a boil. Cook and stir for 2 minutes. Stir in sour cream and beef. Heat through; do not boil. Serve over hot noodles. Garnish with paprika and parsley. Serves 6.

Tourtière

Often served on Christmas Eve.

1 lb	ground beef	500 g	1 clove	garlic, crushed and chopped	1
1 lb	ground pork	500 g		salt and pepper	
2	small onions, chopped	2	½ cup	boiling water	125 ml
1 tsp	ground cloves	5 ml		pastry for 2 double-crust 9-inch (23 cm) pies	
1 tsp	ground cinnamon	5 ml			

Put meat, onion, garlic and spices in heavy frying pan. Add the boiling water and cook slowly until meat loses its pinkness, stirring constantly. Spread meat in pastry-lined pie plates and top with crusts. Seal edges and cut slits in top crusts. Bake at 450F (225C) for 30 minutes. Serve piping hot. Serves 8.

"Best" Meat Loaf

The name says it all.

1½-2 lb	lean ground beef	750g-1 kg	½ tsp	pepper	2 ml
¼ cup	brown sugar	50 ml	2 cups	fresh breadcrumbs	500 ml
¼ cup	ketchup	50 ml	1	large onion, chopped	1
1 tbsp	prepared mustard	15 ml			
2	eggs	2	1 tbsp	Worcestershire sauce	15 ml
⅔ cup	milk	150 ml	1 cup	cheese, shredded	250 ml
1 tsp	salt	5 ml	1 cup	carrots, shredded	250 ml

Place ground beef in large mixing bowl. In separate bowl, beat eggs, milk, salt, pepper and breadcrumbs. Add onions, carrot and cheese to egg mixture, mixing well. Add to ground beef. Pack into baking dish. Top with sauce made from sugar, prepared mustard and ketchup. Bake at 350F (175C) for 1 hour. Let stand 10 minutes before serving. Serves 8.

Stuffed Green Peppers

4	large green peppers	4	¼ tsp	dry mustard	1.5 ml
2 cups	ground beef or ground ham, cooked	500 ml	¼ tsp	garlic powder	1.5 ml
1 cup	rice, cooked	250 ml	4 oz	cheese slices, cut in half	125 g
½ cup	margarine, or less	125 ml	1½ cups	tomato juice	375 ml
2 tbsp	onions, minced	30 ml			

Rinse and cut peppers lengthwise into halves. Remove stems, fibre and seeds. Rinse. Cover with salted water and boil for 5 minutes. Remove peppers; invert to drain. Melt margarine; add beef or ham and blend in rice with onion and seasonings. Lightly fill peppers with meat-rice mixture, heaping slightly. Place in baking dish. Place half cheese slice on top of each pepper. Pour tomato juice around peppers. Bake at 350F (175C) for 20 minutes, and then increase heat to 400F (200C) for 10 minutes until cheese is slightly browned. Serves 4.

Meatloaf with Pineapple Sauce

1 19-oz can	pineapple, crushed	540 ml	6 tbsp	soy sauce	90 ml
1½ lb	lean ground beef	750 g	1 tbsp	Worcestershire sauce	15 ml
¾ cup	breadcrumbs, soft	175 ml	2	cloves garlic, minced	2
½ cup	onion, chopped	125 ml	1 tsp	salt	5 ml
			½ tsp	pepper	2 ml

Glaze:

1 tbsp	cornstarch	15 ml	3 tbsp	vinegar	45 ml
1 tsp	ginger	5 ml		reserved syrup and pineapple	
3 tbsp	soy sauce	45 ml			

Drain pineapple. Reserve syrup and ½ cup (125 ml) pineapple for glaze. Combine remaining pineapple, ground beef, breadcrumbs, onion, soy sauce, Worcestershire sauce, garlic, salt and pepper. Pack the mixture into a loaf pan and bake at 350F (175C) for 1 hour and 15 minutes. Near serving time, prepare the glaze. In a saucepan, combine cornstarch and ginger. Stir in reserved pineapple syrup, soy sauce and vinegar. Bring to boil for 1 minute. Stir in reserved pineapple. Spoon some of the glaze over meatloaf and serve the rest on the side.

Grilled Burgers

¼ cup	sour cream	50 ml	2½ lb	ground beef	1.25 kg
2 tsp	parsley flakes, dried	10 ml	10	hamburger buns	10
1 tsp	thyme, dried	5 ml		lettuce leaves	
1 tsp	salt	5 ml		tomatoes	
½ tsp	pepper	2 ml		onion	

In a large bowl, combine the first 5 ingredients; add beef and mix gently. Shape into 10 patties. Grill over medium coals for 4-5 minutes on each side or until meat is no longer pink inside. Serve on buns with lettuce, tomato and onion.

Stuffed Green Pepper Cups in the Microwave

An 850-watt microwave is required for this recipe.

1 lb	lean ground beef	500 g	3 tbsp	Parmesan cheese, grated and divided	45 ml
⅓ cup	onion, finely chopped	75 ml	1 tsp	salt	5 ml
1 15-oz can	tomato sauce, divided	470 ml	⅛ tsp	pepper	0.5 ml
¼ cup	water	50 ml	½ cup	instant rice, uncooked	125 ml
			4	medium green peppers	4

Crumble beef into a ½ quart (1.5 L), microwave-safe bowl. Add the onion. Cover and microwave on high for 3-4½ minutes or until meat is browned; drain. Stir in 1½ cups (375 ml) tomato sauce, water, 1 tbsp (15 ml) of the cheese, salt and pepper. Cover and microwave on high for 2-3 minutes. Stir in rice; cover and let stand for 5 minutes. Remove tops and seeds from the peppers; cut in half lengthwise. Stuff with meat mixture; place in an ungreased, microwave-safe, shallow 3-quart (3 L) or 9x13x2-inch (23x33x5 cm) dish. Spoon remaining tomato sauce over peppers; sprinkle with remaining cheese. Cover and microwave on high for 10-12 minutes or until peppers are tender. Let stand 5 minutes before serving. Serves 4.

Holubtsi (Cabbage Rolls)

1 lb	lean ground beef	500 g	3 tbsp	water	45 ml
2 lb	lean pork	1 kg		salt and pepper	
2 cups	rice, uncooked	500 ml	1	large cabbage	1
1	large onion, chopped finely	1	2 tbsp	vinegar	30 ml
			1 lb	bacon	500 g
1 10-oz can	tomato soup	284 ml			

Cook rice until tender, according to package instructions. Drain. Mix meat, rice, onion, salt, pepper and 1 cup (250 ml) boiling water. Scald cabbage in a pot of boiling water to which has been added the vinegar; cabbage leaves will separate easily and roll without breaking. Separate cabbage leaves. Remove hard core. Cut leaves in half. Place 1 tbsp (15 ml) filling on leaf and roll. Place in large baking dish. Mix can of tomato soup with 3 tbsp (45 ml) water and pour over cabbage rolls. Place bacon on top. Bake covered at 350F (175 degrees) for 2 hours. Remove cover during last 15 minutes. Serves 8-10.

Roast Veal

My mother's advice when preparing a roast of veal was, "Always add extra fat and, for goodness sake, don't let it burn!" Veal has a delicate flavour.

5 lb	veal roast	2.5 kg	½ tsp	pepper	2 ml
½ cup	vegetable oil	125 ml	1 tbsp	mustard	15 ml
⅓ cup	lemon juice	75 ml		spices as desired: sage and savoury, or basil and sweet marjoram.	
2 tsp	salt	10 ml			
1 tbsp	brown sugar	15 ml			

Sear the veal roast in oil on all sides until browned. Mix spices, sugar and lemon juice in a little water and spread over the surface of the meat. Keep a little water in pan throughout roasting. Cover roasting pan and bake at 325F (165C) until very tender, about 20 minutes per pound, basting occasionally. Remove cover during the last 30 minutes of cooking. Make gravy from the drippings. Serves 8-10.

Lamb Curry

2 lb	lamb (shoulder or leg), cubed	1 kg	½ cup	butter	125 ml
2 tbsp	flour	30 ml	1	lemon, diced	1
1½ tsp	salt	7 ml	2 tbsp	brown sugar	30 ml
1½ tbsp	curry powder	23 ml	2-3 tbsp	raisins	30-45 ml
2	large onions	2	1 tbsp	Worcestershire sauce	15 ml
2	apples, diced	2	2 cups	water	500 ml

Brown meat in butter. Remove from frying pan and place in heavy pot. Add flour to meat and stir with fork to coat. Brown onions in butter. Remove to pot with meat. Add remaining ingredients to pot. Cook on medium-low heat, simmering for 1½ hours. Serve over rice with chutney. Serves 4-6.

Leg of Lamb

Serve hot or cold.

1	leg of lamb	1	1	lemon	1
3 cloves	garlic	3	¼ cup	butter	50 ml
1 tsp	rosemary	5 ml		salt and pepper	
1 tsp	oregano (optional)	5 ml			

Preheat oven to 300F (150C). Wash meat, and dry thoroughly. Make slits in meat and press in small pieces of garlic until the whole surface is covered. Cut lemon into four pieces and rub surface of meat, pressing out all juice. Spread softened butter on meat and sprinkle with spices, salt and pepper. Place in a roasting pan with a little water and cover. Cook until meat has reached desired doneness—2-3 hours.

Braised Lamb and Onions

Onions build the flavour for this hearty stew.

2½ lb	lean lamb, trimmed	1.25 kg	2 cups	chicken stock	500 ml
2 tbsp	olive oil	30 ml	1 cup	dry white wine	250 ml
6	large onions, cut in wedges	6	1 tbsp	tomato paste	15 ml
			½ tsp	salt	2 ml
2	garlic cloves, slivered	2	¼ tsp	pepper	2 ml
			2 tbsp	butter, softened	30 ml
4	large carrots, cut in chunks	4	2 tbsp	all-purpose flour	30 ml
			¼ cup	fresh parsley, chopped	50 ml
1 tsp	paprika	5 ml			

Cut lamb into ¾-inch (2 cm) cubes. In Dutch oven heat half of the oil over high heat; brown lamb in batches, adding more oil if necessary. Remove lamb to plate and set aside. Add remaining oil to pan; cook onions, garlic, carrots and paprika over medium-low heat, stirring occasionally until slightly softened. Return lamb and any juices to pan; stir in stock, wine, tomato paste, salt and pepper. Bring to boil; reduce heat, cover and simmer for about 1½ hours or until lamb is tender, stirring occasionally. Blend butter with flour, and stir into pan juices; stir until thickened and smooth. Sprinkle with parsley. Serves 6.

Lamb Stew with Vegetables

2½ lb	boneless lamb shoulder	1.25 kg	¾ tsp	salt	3 ml
			½ tsp	pepper	2 ml
¼ cup	all-purpose flour	50 ml	1 lb	new potatoes (about 4)	500 g
3 tbsp	vegetable oil	45 ml			
3	onions, sliced	3	1 lb	green beans	500 g
2 cloves	garlic, minced	2	¾ cup	baby carrots	175 ml
2½ cups	beef stock	625 ml	1 cup	peas	250 ml
2 tbsp	tomato paste	30 ml			
1½ tsp	rosemary, crumbled and dried	7 ml			

Trim lamb; cut into bite-size cubes. In bowl, toss lamb with flour. In Dutch oven, heat half of the oil over medium-high heat; brown meat in batches, adding more oil if needed. Transfer to plate and set aside. Add onions and garlic to pan; cook, stirring occasionally, until softened. Add beef stock and tomato paste; bring to boil, stirring to scrape up brown bits. Return meat to pan along with rosemary, salt and pepper. Reduce heat to medium-low; cover and simmer for about 1 hour or until meat is tender. Scrub and cut potatoes into bite-size chunks. Trim green beans; cut into 1½-inch (4 cm) pieces. In saucepan of boiling salted water, cook potatoes for 6 minutes. Add carrots; cook for 2 minutes. Add green beans; cook until potatoes are tender. Drain vegetables and add to stew along with peas; heat through. Serves 6.

Braised Lamb Shanks

6 cups	white kidney beans, cooked	1.5 L		4 cups	dry white wine	1 L
6	lamb shanks	6		4 cups	chicken or lamb stock	1 L
1 tbsp	sea salt	15 ml		1 cup	tomatoes, diced	250 ml
1 tbsp	pepper	15 ml		4 cloves	garlic, finely chopped	4
½ cup	butter	125 ml		1 tbsp	fresh rosemary	15 ml
1 cup	smoked bacon, diced	250 ml		1 tbsp	fresh tarragon	15 ml
1 cup each	carrots, celery and onion, coarsely diced	250 ml		4 tbsp	olive oil	60 ml

Preheat oven to 350F (175C). Season the lamb shanks with sea salt and pepper. In heavy, ovenproof saucepan, melt the butter. Add the shanks and sauté until brown. Remove and set aside. Using the same pan, sauté bacon until brown; add and brown the celery, carrots and onion. Add the wine and stock. When this comes to a boil, sprinkle in the herbs, garlic and tomatoes. Stir and remove from heat. Place the lamb shanks in the cooking liquid. Cover and slowly braise in oven for 2-3 hours until the meat is tender. When ready to serve, heat the olive oil in a frying pan on low heat. Add the cooked beans and warm through. Divide the beans equally among the serving dishes. Season with a little salt and pepper, then place a lamb shank on each dish. Spoon the sauce over each shank. Sauce may be thickened with cornstarch. Serves 6.

Prune and Sausage Stuffing for Goose

There is more than one way to cook a goose. This is the best.

1 lb	pork sausage meat	500 g	½ tsp	nutmeg	2 ml
4 cups	wholewheat breadcrumbs, soft	1 L	1½ cups	prunes, chopped	375 ml
½ cup	onion, chopped	125 ml	½ cup	sour cream (optional)	125 ml
1 tsp	salt	5 ml		black pepper, to taste	
2 tsp	dried sage	10 ml	12 lb	goose	5.6 kg

Stir-fry sausage meat on low heat until pinkness disappears. Drain off fat. Combine next 8 ingredients with a fork and add sausage meat. Taste for seasoning. Mixture will be moist. For a drier dressing, eliminate the sour cream.

Rinse goose; dry inside and outside. Stuff cavity loosely with dressing, reserving ½ cup (125 ml) of the mixture to pack into the neck cavity. Truss the bird and then arrange on a rack in an open roast pan. Pierce breast in several places with a fork, and roast at 350F (175C) for 2 hours, pouring off fat at least twice during this period. Sprinkle with salt and reduce temperature to 325F (165C). Cover and roast slowly for 2½-4 hours. Test for doneness by pressing the thigh with fingers; flesh is soft when done. Remove goose to hot platter. Prepare gravy with well-skimmed juices. Serves 6-7.

Broiled Partridge

Split partridge down breast bone into halves. Have ready about ¼ cup (50 ml) or more of soft butter. Rub all surfaces with butter, then arrange partridge on broiler rack, skin side down, and broil for 10 minutes, adding a sprinkle of salt and pepper at halfway point. Turn halves, brush skin side with more butter and broil for 10-15 minutes more. Serves 2.

Roast Duck and
Wild Rice Stuffing

Wild rice complements the taste of duck.

4-5 lb	duckling, eviscerated	about 2.3 kg	2 tbsp	lemon juice	30 ml
			½ tsp	salt	2 ml
1	orange, quartered	1	3-4 tbsp	cooking sherry	45-60 ml

Wash and wipe duckling inside and outside, and stuff with orange quarters. Lace the openings and pin the neck skin to the back with a skewer. Arrange bird, breast side up, on a rack in a shallow pan. Sprinkle with lemon juice and salt. Roast at 325F (165C) for about 1½ hours. Pour off fat. Add sherry to the pan and continue roasting for 1-1¼ hours, basting occasionally. Skim fat from drippings and prepare gravy. Carve duck; discard orange quarters. Arrange meat on a bed of wild rice stuffing. Cover with foil and keep hot until serving time. Serves 6.

Stuffing:

1 cup	wild rice	250 ml	2 cups	water	500 ml
¼ cup	butter	50 ml	¼ tsp	salt	1.5 ml
¼ cup	onion, chopped	50 ml	¼ tsp	sweet basil	1.5 ml
½ lb	mushrooms, fresh and sliced	225 g	½ tsp	summer savoury	2 ml
1¼ cups	consommé	310 ml	½ cup	rye breadcrumbs	125 ml

Rice may be soaked in water overnight. Wash and drain rice. Slowly sauté rice, onion and mushrooms in melted butter. When rice begins to turn yellow, stir in other ingredients. Cover and simmer slowly for 1¼ hours or until all moisture is absorbed. Alternatively, bake in covered casserole in oven during last 1½ hours of duck's roasting time.

Fried Rabbit

1	rabbit, cut in pieces	1	1	egg	1
	salt and pepper		¼ cup	flour	50 ml
⅛ tsp	oregano, if desired	0.5 ml	½ cup	breadcrumbs, fine and dry	125 ml
2 tbsp	milk	30 ml			

Sprinkle each piece of rabbit with salt, pepper and oregano. Combine milk and egg. Beat slightly. Dip seasoned rabbit in flour, then in egg mixture and lastly in breadcrumbs. Brown on all sides in ½ inch (1.3 cm) of fat. Reduce heat and cover. Cook until tender. Uncover during the last 10 minutes to crisp the surface. Drain on paper towel. Serves 4.

Rabbit-Sausage Patties

6 lb	rabbit, dressed and cut up, bones removed	3 kg	¾ tsp	nutmeg	3 ml
			½ tsp	cinnamon	2 ml
2 tsp	salt	10 ml	1 cup	tart apple, grated and peeled	250 ml
1½ tsp	sage	7 ml	2 tbsp	oil	30 ml
1¼ tsp	pepper	6 ml			

In a bowl, combine meat, salt, sage, pepper, nutmeg and cinnamon. Mix well and refrigerate overnight. In a meat grinder or food processor, process the mixture in small batches until coarsely ground. Stir in apple. Shape into 16 patties. Heat oil in skillet. Cook patties over medium heat for 5 minutes on each side until no longer pink. Serves 8.

Venison Chops

8	venison chops	8		salt and pepper	
4 tsp	lemon juice	20 ml		vegetable oil	
¼ tsp	thyme	1.5 ml	¼ lb	mushrooms, fresh and sliced	125 g

Trim fat off chops and place in glass pan. Combine lemon juice and thyme, and marinate for an hour. Drain; reserve marinade. In a large skillet, heat vegetable oil. Place chops in hot oil and brown on both sides. Sprinkle with salt and pepper. Add sliced mushrooms and marinade. Cover and simmer over medium heat for 30 minutes. Uncover and cook for another five minutes.

A little butter drizzled over the chops, just before serving, adds to the flavour. Serve very hot. Serves 4.

Cheddar Spinach Quiche

Perfect for lunch or a light supper.

2 cups	sharp Cheddar, shredded	500 ml	3 slices	bacon, cooked and crumbled	3
2 tbsp	flour	30 ml	½ tsp	salt	2 ml
1 10-oz pkg	spinach, cooked, drained and chopped	280 g	dash	pepper	
			1 9-inch	pastry shell, unbaked	1
1 cup	milk	250 ml			
2	eggs, beaten	2			

In a medium-size bowl, toss cheese with flour. Add remaining ingredients, mixing well. Pour into pastry shell and garnish with additional bacon. Bake at 350F (175C) for about 1 hour.

Hash Brown Quiche

1 20-oz pkg	hash browns, refrigerated or frozen, shredded	625 g	6 cups	milk	1.5 L
			12	eggs	12
⅓ cup	melted butter	75 ml		cayenne pepper	
4 cups	mild Cheddar cheese, shredded	1 L		garlic salt	

Preheat oven to 425F (220C). Press hash browns into muffin cups to form crusts. Brush or drizzle with melted butter. Bake 25-30 minutes. Reduce oven temperature to 350 degrees (175C). Divide cheese among muffin cups. Whisk together milk, eggs, pepper and salt. Pour into muffin cups, and bake for 30-40 minutes or until toothpick inserted into centre comes out clean. Allow to cool before removing from pan. Serves 12.

Pizza Quiche

¾ lb	Italian-style hot pizza sausage	375 g	¼ cup	canned green chili peppers, finely chopped	50 ml
3	eggs	3	1 9-inch	pastry shell, unbaked	1
1¾ cups	hot milk	430 ml			
2 cups	Mozzarella cheese, shredded	500 ml			

Line 9-inch (23 cm) pie plate with pastry. Crumble sausage, removing from casing, if desired. In skillet, cook sausage until browned, breaking up with a fork; drain well. Beat eggs and stir in milk, sausage, cheese and chilies. Turn into pastry shell. Bake at 400F (200C) for 40-45 minutes or until knife inserted in centre comes out clean. Let stand 10 minutes before serving. Serves 6.

Quick Garden Frittata

1 tbsp	vegetable oil	15 ml		6	eggs, beaten	6
2 cups	potatoes, peeled and diced	500 ml		¼ cup	Parmesan cheese, grated	50 ml
1 cup	each, diced red pepper, zucchini and smoked ham	250 ml each				

Heat oil at medium-high in large, non-stick frying pan. Add potatoes and stir-fry until tender crisp. Add pepper, zucchini and ham; stir-fry for 3 minutes. In a bowl, whisk eggs lightly. Pour evenly over mixture in fry pan. Cover and cook at low to medium heat for 10 minutes or until mixture is almost set. Sprinkle with cheese, cover and cook 10 minutes or until surface is set. Place frittata under preheated broiler to lightly brown top. (Protect handle with foil). Cut in wedges. Serves 4.

Ham & Asparagus Quiche

1	refrigerated pie crust	1		3	eggs, beaten	3
2 tbsp	butter	30 ml		½ cup	milk	125 ml
1	large leek, sliced, heavy green tops discarded	1		¼ tsp	ground nutmeg	1.5 ml
				dash	hot sauce	
				8 oz	ham, chopped	250 g
8 oz	fresh asparagus spears, chopped	250 g		2	tomatoes, coarsely chopped	2

Sauté leek in butter until soft. Add asparagus and sauté 2 minutes. Add to pie crust. Mix remaining ingredients together, and pour into crust. Bake at 400F (200C) until a knife inserted in centre comes out clean.

Cheese-Egg Muffins

1 10-oz can	mushroom soup	284 ml	6	hard-boiled eggs, sliced	6
1 cup	cheese spread	250 ml	4-6 slices	bacon	4-6
			6	English muffins	6

Combine soup and cheese in the top of a double boiler; heat until cheese is melted. Stir well; fold in eggs. Top muffins with bacon, cover with cheese mixture and serve.

Creamy Pesto Sauce

2 cups	fresh basil leaves or fresh parsley	500 ml	½ tsp	pepper	2 ml
			2 tbsp	olive oil	30 ml
2 cloves	garlic, chopped	2	3 tbsp	butter	45 ml
¼ cup	pinenuts or walnuts	50 ml	¼ cup	all-purpose flour	50 ml
½ cup	Parmesan cheese, grated	125 ml	3 cups	milk	750 ml
			1 tsp	salt	5 ml
1 tsp	salt	5 ml	¼ tsp	nutmeg	1.5 ml

For pesto, combine fresh basil with garlic and nuts in blender or food processor. Blend until finely chopped. Blend in cheese, salt, pepper and olive oil. Reserve. Melt butter in a large saucepan. Add flour. Cook 3 minutes but do not brown. Add milk. Bring to a boil. Cook gently 5 minutes. Add salt, nutmeg and reserved pesto mixture. Remove from heat. Serve on pasta (spaghetti, fettuccine or linguine). Serves 6.

Triple-Cheese
Baked Spaghetti

6 oz	dry spaghetti	168 g	1 tsp	dried basil	5 ml
¾ cup	low-fat Ricotta cheese	175 ml	2 tsp	dried oregano	10 ml
			¼ tsp	black pepper	1.5 ml
½ cup	Romano cheese, finely grated	125 ml	4 oz	part-skim Mozzarella cheese, shredded	125 g
2 cups	prepared spaghetti sauce	500 ml			

Cook pasta according to package directions. Drain completely. Preheat oven to 350F (175C). In a large bowl, combine Ricotta and Romano cheeses, 1 cup spaghetti sauce, basil, oregano and pepper. Set aside remaining 1 cup (250 ml) spaghetti sauce. Mix cooked pasta with cheese mixture, stirring until pasta is distributed. Place in casserole dish coated with vegetable oil cooking spray. Top pasta and cheese mixture with shredded Mozzarella cheese. Cover with lid or foil and bake 20 minutes. Remove cover; continue baking until cheese bubbles. Remove from oven and let stand for 3 minutes. Cut into four large (or six small) servings. Top each portion with remaining spaghetti sauce before serving.

Macaroni and Cheese

A quick and nourishing meal, anytime.

2 cups	macaroni, uncooked	500 ml	4 tbsp	flour		60 ml
4 cups	milk	1 L	1½ lb	sharp Cheddar cheese, grated		750 g
1 tsp	salt	5 ml		breadcrumbs, buttered		

Cook macaroni according to directions on package. Drain. Mix salt and flour into Cheddar cheese. Grease a large casserole dish. Place in the dish alternating layers of macaroni and cheese. Make sure that the top layer is cheese. Pour milk in casserole—up to, but not covering, the top layer. Sprinkle buttered breadcrumbs over the casserole. Bake at 350F (175C) until bubbles appear and the top is golden brown. You may need to cover dish with foil. Serves 8.

Low-Fat Alfredo Sauce with Spaghetti or Fettuccine

3 cups	1% cottage cheese	750 ml	2 tsp	salt	10 ml
1½ cups	1% milk	375 ml	¼ tsp	white pepper, ground	1.5 ml
1 cup	Parmesan cheese, grated	250 ml	¹⁄₁₆ tsp	nutmeg	0.25 ml
1 lb	spaghetti or fettuccine	500 g	2 tbsp	parsley, chopped	30 ml
			1 tbsp	chives, chopped	15 ml

Purée the cottage cheese with the milk until very smooth. Cook the pasta of choice, drain, then add the cottage cheese mixture and Parmesan. Heat on a low setting, stirring often until hot throughout. Do not boil. Season with salt, pepper and nutmeg. Add the parsley and chives. Serve hot! Sautéed or steamed vegetables, chicken and shrimp may be added. Simply cook them in a separate pan and add to the drained pasta before adding the cheese mixture, or spoon them over the alfredo pasta as a garnish. Serves 6.

Bacon and Cheese Pizza

Basic Sweet Dough:

2 pkg	dry yeast	2	1 tsp	salt	5 ml
1 cup	water, lukewarm	250 ml	½ cup	sugar	125 ml
1 cup	milk	250 ml	2	eggs, beaten	2
2 tsp	sugar	10 ml	1 tsp	lemon rind, grated	5 ml
¼ cup	butter	50 ml	6 cups	flour	1.5 L

Soften the yeast in lukewarm water and 2 tsp (10ml) sugar. Scald milk; add butter, ½ cup sugar and salt. Cool to lukewarm and add yeast. Add half the flour to make thick batter. Add eggs and lemon rind. Beat well. Add enough flour to make a soft dough. Turn out onto a lightly floured board and knead until satin smooth. Place in a greased bowl and let rise until doubled in bulk. Punch down and roll out. Press dough into a pie pan up to the inner rim (not over the edge). Brush lightly with vegetable oil. Refrigerate if making crusts ahead of serving time; stack carefully and cover tightly with aluminum foil. Makes 6-8 pizzas.

Topping:
Cut 1 lb (500g) bacon into 1-inch (2.5cm) pieces, reserving 8 whole slices. Fry pieces and whole slices together until they begin to wrinkle and brown slightly at the edges. Drain. Separate pieces and slices.

Pizza Sauce:

1	medium onion, quartered and sliced	1	1 10-oz can	tomato soup	284 ml
1	small green pepper, chopped	1	¼ tsp	pepper	1.5 ml
			2 tsp	oregano	10 ml
3 tbsp	bacon drippings (or oil, if desired)	45 ml			

Sauté onion and green pepper in bacon drippings until onion is golden brown. Add soup and spices, and stir in bacon pieces.

To prepare pizza: spoon sauce onto prepared pizza dough, and arrange remaining bacon slices on top. Sprinkle with shredded Cheddar, Mozzarella or jack cheese.

Sweet & Sour Meatball Sauce

1 cup	brown sugar	250 ml		1 cup	water, divided	250 ml
½ cup	vinegar	125 ml		2 tbsp	soy sauce	30 ml
¼ cup	ketchup	50 ml		2 tbsp	cornstarch	30 ml

Place brown sugar, vinegar, ketchup and ½ cup (125 ml) water in pot and bring to a boil. Mix ½ cup (125 ml) water, soy sauce and cornstarch in a bowl and add to boiling stove-top mixture. Simmer to thicken. Pour over cooked meatballs and serve. Freezes well.

Sweet and Sour Sauce

An easy, versatile sauce.

1 cup	vinegar	250 ml		1 tbsp	cornstarch, dissolved in ¼ cup (50 ml) water	15 ml
1½ cups	brown sugar	375 ml				
1 cup	water	250 ml		1 14-oz can	pineapple tidbits, drained	398 ml
½ cup	pineapple juice	125 ml				

Heat vinegar and water, and add other ingredients. Stir until slightly thickened and mixture has boiled. Good with meatballs or ham.

Sweet Sauce for Sausages

½ cup	apricot jam	125 ml		½ tsp	Worcestershire sauce	2 ml
1 tbsp	Dijon mustard	15 ml		1 tbsp	cider vinegar	15 ml

Combine all ingredients in saucepan. Heat, stirring until jam melts. Brush sauce on barbecued sausages in last 5-10 minutes of cooking.

Red Barbecue Sauce

2 tbsp	brown sugar	30 ml		¾ cup	water	175 ml
1 tsp	salt	5 ml		2 tbsp	vinegar	30 ml
½ tsp	dry mustard	2 ml		1 clove	garlic, chopped	1
1 cup	ketchup	250 ml				

Combine all ingredients in a saucepan. Simmer 10 minutes. Makes 2 cups.

Basic Barbecue Sauce

½ cup	butter or vegetable oil	125 ml		1 tsp	salt	5 ml
				½ cup	water	125 ml
1 cup	vinegar	250 ml				

Mix the ingredients and heat. Stir well before basting. Brush or spray on meat several times during cooking.

Cucumber Dill Sauce
(for Cold Ham)

1 cup	cucumber, finely chopped, peeled and seeded	250 ml		¼ cup	sour cream	50 ml
				1	green onion, finely sliced	1
⅓ cup	mayonnaise or salad dressing	75 ml		⅛ tsp	salt	0.5 ml
				¼ tsp	dillweed, dried	1.5 ml

Combine all ingredients. Refrigerate until serving time. Serve with slices of cold ham.

Zesty Orange Sauce
(for Ham Steaks)

1 tbsp	brown sugar	15 ml		1 cup	orange juice	250 ml
1 tbsp	cornstarch	15 ml			orange rind, finely grated	
½ tsp	ground ginger	2 ml				

In a small saucepan, combine brown sugar, cornstarch and ginger. Stir in orange juice. Heat, stirring constantly, until sauce comes to a boil and becomes thick and smooth. Blend in orange rind. Serve with warm ham slices or steaks.

Apricot Glaze for Ham

½ cup	apricot jam	125 ml		1 tbsp	cornstarch	15 ml
⅓ cup	liquid honey	75 ml		1 tsp	cloves, whole	5 ml
2 tbsp	real lemon juice	30 ml		pinch	cinnamon	

Remove excess fat from ham. Score surface of ham every 2 inches (5 cm), place a clove in centre of each diamond and bake in shallow pan at 350F (175C) for 2 ½ hours. To make the glaze, combine all ingredients and bring to a boil in a small saucepan. During last ½ hour, brush on glaze.

Raisin Sauce for Baked Ham

¾ cup	brown sugar	175 ml		¼ cup	raisins, washed	50 ml
½ tbsp	dry mustard	8 ml		¼ cup	vinegar	50 ml
1 tbsp	flour	15 ml		1¾ cups	water	430 ml

Mix first 3 ingredients; add raisins, vinegar and water. Bring to boil. Serve with baked ham.

Raisin-Orange Sauce

My favourite.

½ cup	brown sugar	125 ml	1 tbsp	vinegar	15 ml
2 tsp	cornstarch	10 ml	1 tbsp	butter	15 ml
½ cup	hot water	125 ml	1	orange (juice and grated rind)	1
½ cup	raisins, seedless	125 ml			
½ tsp	salt	2 ml			

Mix sugar and cornstarch together in saucepan; stir in hot water and let cook gently, stirring constantly for 5 minutes. Add raisins, which have been washed and drained. Cook, stirring, for another 5 minutes. Add remaining ingredients. Serve with roast duck, goose, pork or ham. Makes about 1 cup.

Buttered Fruit Sauce

Rich and tangy.

1½ cups	pineapple (fresh or canned), drained, or orange wedges	375 ml	¼ cup	butter	50 ml
			pinch	ginger	
			¼ cup	brown sugar	50 ml

Sauté pineapple or orange wedges in butter until fruit is thoroughly heated. Add ginger and brown sugar. Cook until sugar melts. Serve hot. Serve with sweet potatoes, pork or baked ham.

Apple-Cider Raisin Sauce

1¼ cups	apple cider	310 ml		2 tsp	cornstarch	10 ml
¾ cup	raisins, seedless, washed	175 ml		1 tsp	dry mustard	5 ml
				⅓ cup	brown sugar	75 ml
½ tsp	lemon rind, grated	2 ml		2 tbsp	lemon juice	30 ml

Combine apple cider, raisins and rind in saucepan; cover and simmer 5 minutes. Blend together cornstarch, mustard, sugar and lemon juice. Stir into hot mixture and let cook gently until thick and clear. Serve warm. One tart apple, peeled and chopped, may be added with apple cider and raisins, if desired. Makes about 2 cups.

Tangy Tomato Sauce for Meats

3 cups	tomatoes, canned, with juice	750 ml		½ cup	sugar	125 ml
				1 tsp	cloves	5 ml
1 cup	celery, diced	250 ml		½ tsp	ground cinnamon	2 ml
1 cup	onion, diced	250 ml		1 tbsp	salt	15 ml
1 clove	garlic	1		¼ tsp	pepper	1.5 ml
⅓ cup	cider vinegar	75 ml		1 cup	cucumber relish	250 ml

Place all ingredients except relish in a saucepan and simmer, stirring frequently, about 45 minutes, until a good consistency is achieved. Add relish. Cool. Store in refrigerator. Use for spareribs, chops, hamburgers, etc. Makes 1 quart.

Glaze for Roast Pork

2 cups	pineapple marmalade	500 ml		⅓ cup	corn syrup	75 ml
				1 tsp	ground cloves	5 ml

Combine ingredients in saucepan over medium heat, stirring occasionally. Baste roast every 10-15 minutes for last hour of cooking time.

Hot Dog Onion Topper

Simply delicious.

3 tbsp	olive oil	45 ml		2 tsp	corn syrup	10 ml
1	large onion, sliced and chopped	1		2 tsp	cornstarch	10 ml
				1 tsp	salt	5 ml
8 cups	water	2 L		½ tsp	red pepper flakes	2 ml
¼ cup	tomato paste	50 ml		½ cup	vinegar	125 ml

Over medium heat, heat oil in a large saucepan. Add onion and sauté until soft. Add water, tomato paste, corn syrup, cornstarch, pepper flakes and salt. Stir well. Increase heat and bring to boil. Reduce heat and simmer for 45-50 minutes. Add vinegar and continue to simmer for 45-50 minutes. Sauce will thicken when liquid is reduced. Place generous amounts on barbecued hot dogs. Makes about 2 cups.

Maître d'Hôtel Butter
Sauce for Fish

¼ cup	butter	50 ml		1 tsp	salt	5 ml
2 tbsp	parsley, chopped	30 ml		¼ tsp	pepper	1.5 ml
2 tbsp	lemon juice	30 ml				

Melt butter and combine with other ingredients. Mix well and serve hot.

Quick Tartar Sauce

1 cup	Miracle Whip	250 ml	1 tsp	lemon juice	5 ml
¼ cup	sweet pickle relish	50 ml	½ tsp	onion flakes, dried	2 ml

Mix all together and serve.

Tartar Sauce

1	medium dill pickle	1	1 cup	mayonnaise	250 ml
1 tbsp	capers	15 ml	1½ tbsp	prepared mustard	23 ml
2 or 3	parsley sprigs, chopped	2 or 3	2 tbsp	onion, chopped	30 ml

Finely chop pickle and capers. Mix into mayonnaise. Add parsley, mustard and onion. Mix again.

Tartar Sauce for Fish

A standard accompaniment to many fish dishes.

1 cup	mayonnaise	250 ml	1 tbsp	green pepper, chopped	15 ml
2 tbsp	olives, chopped	30 ml	1 tsp	lemon juice	5 ml
2 tbsp	gerkins, chopped	30 ml	1 tsp	salt	5 ml
1 tbsp	parsley, chopped	15 ml	1 tsp	pepper	5 ml
1 tbsp	onion, chopped	15 ml			

Mix all together and serve cold.

MARINADES

We're all in such a hurry these days that any opportunity to save time is welcomed by today's cooks. Most meats can be combined with a marinade in a zippered plastic bag in the morning to be ready for the grill in the evening.

Teriyaki Marinade

⅓ cup	soy sauce	75 ml	1 tsp	ginger, fresh, minced	5 ml
2 tbsp	lemon juice	30 ml	1 tsp	garlic, minced and crushed	5 ml
2 tbsp	granulated sugar	30 ml			

Hot and Spicy Marinade

1/3 cup	hot salsa	75 ml	1/4 tsp	black pepper	1.5 ml
2 tbsp	red wine vinegar	30 ml	1/4 tsp	hot pepper sauce or flakes	1.5 ml
2 tsp	Dijon mustard	10 ml			
2 tsp	Worcestershire sauce	10 ml			

Thai Marinade

4 tbsp	fish sauce	60 ml	2 tsp	garlic, minced	10 ml
3 tbsp	lime juice	45 ml	2 tsp	ginger, minced	10 ml
2 tbsp	vegetable oil	30 ml	¼ tsp	hot chili pepper	1.5 ml
2 tbsp	sugar	30 ml			

Herbed Citrus Marinade

¼ cup	lemon or lime juice	50 ml		2 cloves	garlic, minced	2
2 tsp	lemon or lime rind, grated	10 ml		2 tbsp	rosemary, chopped	30 ml
				½ tsp	thyme, chopped	2 ml
2 tsp	Dijon mustard	10 ml		¼ cup	olive oil	50 ml

Denise's Meat Marinade

½ cup	soy sauce	125 ml		1 tsp	sugar	5 ml
¼ cup	water	50 ml		¼ tsp	ground ginger	1.5 ml
2 tbsp	vinegar	30 ml			garlic, to taste	
1 tbsp	vegetable oil	15 ml				

Beef Marinade

1 cup	vegetable oil	250 ml		¼ cup	Dijon mustard	50 ml
¾ cup	soy sauce	175 ml		1-2 tsp	black pepper, cracked	5-10 ml
½ cup	lemon juice	125 ml				
¼ cup	Worcestershire sauce	50 ml		2 cloves	garlic, minced	2

Blend all ingredients in blender. Will marinate 2-3 pounds of beef. Let sit in refrigerator 24-48 hours before cooking.

Lemon-Herb Chicken Marinade

¼ cup	lemon juice	50 ml	1 tbsp	Tabasco sauce	15 ml
⅓ cup	oil	75 ml	1 tbsp	sugar	15 ml
1 tbsp	onion, dried and minced	15 ml	2 tsp	chicken bouillon	10 ml
			1 tsp	thyme	5 ml
1 clove	garlic	1	¼ tsp	oregano	1.5 ml

Combine all ingredients. Marinate chicken for at least 4 hours before roasting, broiling, or grilling.

Pizza Sauce

1 cup	Italian tomatoes, seeded and drained	250 ml	2 tbsp	oregano, chopped	30 ml
			1 tsp	crushed red pepper	5 ml
1 tbsp	tomato paste	15 ml	1 tsp	sugar	5 ml
1 clove	garlic, minced	1	½ tsp	salt	2 ml
2 tbsp	basil, chopped	30 ml			

In a food processor, combine tomatoes, paste and garlic. Slowly add basil, oregano, red pepper, sugar and salt until blended. Refrigerate until ready to use. Makes 1 cup.

Fruit Chili Sauce

4 lb	ripe tomatoes	2 kg	1 cup	onion, chopped	250 ml
1 cup	peaches, peeled and finely chopped	250 ml	1 tbsp	hot red pepper	15 ml
			½ cup	seedless raisins	125 ml
1 cup	pears, unpeeled and finely chopped	250 ml	1½ cups	vinegar	375 ml
			1½ cups	sugar	375 ml
1 cup	apples, unpeeled and finely chopped	250 ml	1½ tbsp	coarse salt	22 ml
			¼ cup	whole mixed pickling spice	50 ml
1 cup	sweet red pepper, chopped	250 ml			

Blanch and peel tomatoes, then cut into pieces. Combine vegetables, fruits, vinegar, sugar, salt and spices (tied loosely in a cheesecloth bag). Bring to boil and cook until thick—40-50 minutes. Remove spice bag. Pour into hot, sterilized jars and seal immediately. Makes about 8 cups.

Chili Sauce

30	tomatoes, medium ripe	30	2 tbsp	coarse salt	30 ml
			4 cups	vinegar	1 L
2½ cups	onions, peeled and chopped	625 ml	1 tbsp	cloves	15 ml
			3 tbsp	whole allspice	45 ml
2½ cups	sweet red peppers, chopped	625 ml	1 tbsp	celery seed	15 ml
1½ cups	sugar	375 ml			

Blanch and peel tomatoes, then cut into pieces. Add remaining ingredients after tying spices loosely in a cheesecloth bag. Cook uncovered 2-2½ hours or until quite thick, stirring frequently. Remove spice bag. Pour into hot sterilized jars and seal immediately. Makes about 9 cups (2.25 L).

Cranberry Sauce

Plain, old fashion-style—no turkey dinner can be without.

4 cups	sugar	1 L	8 cups	cranberries	2 L
2 cups	water	500 ml			

Combine sugar and water in a large saucepan. Stir to dissolve. Bring to a boil for 5 minutes. Add cranberries. Cook in boiling syrup, without stirring until skins pop. Simmer to thicken. Pour into sterilized jars.

Light Peach Salsa

This is a wonderful accompaniment to almost any meat or fish dish.

4 cups	ripe peaches, peeled, pitted and finely chopped	1 L	2 cloves	garlic, finely chopped	2
½ cup	onions, finely chopped	125 ml	1½ tsp	cumin	8 ml
			¼ cup	white vinegar	50 ml
½ cup	red pepper, chopped	125 ml	1 tsp	lime rind, grated	5 ml
			3¾ cups	sugar	930 ml
4	jalapeño peppers, finely chopped	4	1 box	Certo light fruit pectin crystals	58 g
¼ cup	coriander, finely chopped	50 ml			

Measure prepared fruit into a large saucepan; add onions, peppers, coriander, garlic, cumin, vinegar and lime rind. Combine fruit pectin crystals with ¼ cup (50 ml) sugar. Stir pectin mixture into fruit mixture. Place saucepan over high heat and stir until mixture comes to a full boil. Stir in remaining sugar. Continue to cook and stir over high heat until mixture comes to a full, rolling boil. Boil hard 1 minute, stirring constantly. Remove from heat. Stir and skim foam for 5 minutes to prevent floating fruit. Pour quickly into warm, sterilized jars, filling ¼ inch from top. Seal while hot.

The Great Nova Scotia Cookbook

• VEGETABLES •

• Best •

• Traditional •

• Trendy •

Asparagus Parmesan

16	asparagus spears	16	1 cup	breadcrumbs, freshly made, crust removed	250 ml
1 tbsp	Parmesan cheese, grated	15 ml	½ tsp	garlic, peeled and minced	2 ml
1	large egg, beaten	1	½ tsp	salt	2 ml
1 tbsp	cold water	15 ml	pinch	ground white pepper	
½ cup	flour	125 ml			

Trim, peel and blanch the asparagus in boiling salted water for one minute. Remove and cool in cold water; drain well. Combine flour, salt and pepper. In a separate bowl, combine egg and water. In a separate bowl again, combine breadcrumbs, cheese and garlic. Dip the spears into the flour, then into the beaten egg mixture, then coat well with the breadcrumbs. In a frying pan heat the oil over medium-high heat, add half of the spears and sauté on all sides until golden in colour; drain on paper towels and keep warm while you cook the remaining spears. Serve with a marinara sauce and additional grated cheese over freshly-cooked, thin spaghetti. Asparagus vinaigrette, French dressing or hollandaise sauce are also suitable. Serves 4.

Asparagus

Simple and tasty!

20	large asparagus spears	20	salt	
6 tbsp	unsalted butter	90 ml	fresh ground pepper	
1	large lemon, for juice	1		

Trim asparagus to one length. Peel stems within three inches of tip with a vegetable peeler. In a saucepan, steam asparagus 3-4 minutes. Melt butter, cook slightly and stir in lemon juice. Pour over asparagus, and sprinkle with salt and pepper. Serves 4.

Asparagus with Lemon Butter & Pecans

Asparagus can be cooked earlier and baked just before serving.

6 lb	asparagus, trimmed and barely cooked	3 kg	1½ cups	pecan pieces, toasted	375 ml
6 tbsp	unsalted butter	90 ml		freshly ground pepper	
2 tbsp	lemon juice, to taste	30 ml			

Place the asparagus in a shallow baking dish that has been greased with some of the butter. Dot the asparagus with the remaining butter and sprinkle with the lemon juice. Sprinkle with pecans. Season with pepper and bake at 350F (175C) for about 10 minutes, just until heated through. Serves 12.

Fiddlehead Greens

Like dandelions, fiddleheads are free for the picking, but finding the right fern can be a problem. Fiddleheads grow in rich, moist soil near a river or stream. They can be distinguished from other ferns by their heads, which are wrapped in brownish, papery scales. The plants grow in clumps—just snap off the short ones (those less than 6 inches). Remove the papery scales from the heads, wash and boil until tender. Serve fiddleheads with a lot of butter, a little vinegar, and salt and pepper.

Cooked Dandelion Greens

No scarcity of these—they're everywhere.

Blanch dandelion greens in boiling water for five minutes. Cover with fresh boiling water and salt. Cover and cook until tender, about 10-15 minutes. Drain. Add pieces of crisp bacon or garlic croutons. Toss with a sprinkle of vinegar.

Green Beans with Ginger

1½ lb	green beans, fresh	675 g	3 tbsp	Chinese parsley	45 ml
1 piece	ginger, about 2-inches (5 cm) long and 1-inch (2.5 cm) wide, peeled and coarsely chopped	1		fresh coriander greens or cilantro, chopped	
			1 tsp	ground cumin	5 ml
			2 tsp	ground coriander	10 ml
6 tbsp	vegetable oil	90 ml	1¼ tsp	garam masala	6 ml
¼ tsp	ground turmeric	1 ml	2 tsp	lemon juice, to taste	10 ml
½ cup	fresh green chilis, washed and finely sliced (optional)	125 ml	1 tsp	salt, to taste	5 ml

Wash the green beans and trim the ends. Slice into thin rounds and set aside in a bowl. Put the ginger in a blender with 3 tbsp (45 ml) of water and blend at high speed until it is a smooth paste. Heat the oil in a 10-inch (25 cm) skillet over medium heat. While it is heating, pour in paste from blender and add turmeric. Fry, stirring constantly, for 2 minutes, then add the sliced green chilies and the parsley. After another minute, add the green beans and continue cooking and stirring for about a minute. Add the cumin, coriander, 1 tsp of the garam masala, lemon juice, salt and 3 tbsp (45 ml) of warm water. Cover skillet, turn flame very low, and let beans cook slowly for about 40 minutes, stirring every ten minutes or so. Serve in a warm dish, with ¼ tsp (1 ml) garam masala sprinkled on top. This dish goes well with nearly all meat and chicken dishes. Serve with plain, boiled rice. Serves 6.

Brussels Sprouts in Sauce

The sauce adds interest to this flavourful vegetable.

3 lb	Brussels sprouts	1.5 kg	1½ cups	white Cheddar cheese, old	375 ml
¼ cup	butter	50 ml	¾ tsp	ground nutmeg	3 ml
2	onions, chopped	2	½ tsp	salt	2 ml
¼ cup	flour	50 ml	½ tsp	pepper	2 ml
2 cups	warm milk	500 ml			

Trim Brussels sprouts; cut an X in base of each. In a large saucepan of boiling water, cook Brussels sprouts for 7-9 minutes or until tender crisp. Drain and chill under cold running water; press out excess water with towel. Cut in half, if large; place in shallow, greased 10-cup (2.5 L) casserole. In saucepan, melt butter over medium heat, cook onions, stirring occasionally, for 8-10 minutes or until softened. Stir in flour; cook, stirring for 1 minute. Add milk, and stir for 3-5 minutes or until thickened. Remove from heat. Stir in half the cheese, the nutmeg, salt and pepper; pour over sprouts. Cover and bake at 375F (175C) for about 40 minutes or until bubbly. Sprinkle with remaining cheese. Cook uncovered until golden. Serves 4.

Crumb-Topped Brussels Sprouts

1½ lb	Brussels sprouts, fresh	750 g	2 tbsp	Parmesan cheese, grated	30 ml
3 tbsp	butter, melted and divided	45 ml			
¼ cup	Italian-seasoned dry breadcrumbs	50 ml			

In a saucepan, cook Brussels sprouts in salted water until tender crisp, about 8-10 minutes, and drain. Place in an ungreased, shallow 1½-quart (2 L) baking dish. Drizzle with 2 tbsp (30 ml) butter. Combine breadcrumbs, Parmesan cheese and remaining butter; sprinkle over Brussels sprouts. Cover and bake at 325F (165C) for 10 minutes. Uncover and bake 10 minutes longer. Serves 8.

Marinated Sugar Snap Peas

2 lb	sugar snap peas, blanched	900 g		2 tbsp	tarragon leaves, fresh	30 ml
				½ cup	vegetable oil	125 ml
1	lemon, juice and zest	1				
2 tbsp	white wine vinegar	30 ml				

Mix ingredients together in a large bowl. Serve immediately or refrigerate. Serves 6-8.

Spicy Steamed Broccoli

2 heads	broccoli, chopped into bite-size pieces	2		2 tbsp	hot sesame oil	30 ml
				2 tbsp	lemon juice	30 ml
2 tbsp	soy sauce	30 ml		½ tsp	sesame seeds	2 ml

Steam the broccoli for 2-3 minutes. If you do not have a steamer, pour ½ cup (125 ml) water in a deep pot. Cover with aluminum foil, leaving enough slack that the foil forms a "bowl" around the rim. Carefully poke holes in the foil. Place the broccoli on the foil and cover. When steamed, place broccoli in a bowl, toss in the other ingredients and mix. Serves 6.

Coleslaw

1	medium cabbage, grated	1	¼ cup	whole milk	50 ml
1	medium carrot, grated	1	½ cup	Miracle Whip	125 ml
2 tbsp	onion, finely chopped	30 ml	¼ cup	buttermilk	50 ml
			1½ tsp	white vinegar	7 ml
⅓ cup	sugar	75 ml	2 tbsp	lemon juice	30 ml
¼ tsp	pepper	1 ml			

In a large bowl, combine cabbage, carrot and onion. In a separate bowl (or blender), combine sugar, pepper, milk, Miracle Whip, buttermilk, vinegar and lemon juice. Beat well in mixer. Add to grated ingredients. Mix well. Refrigerate for a few hours before serving. Serves 8.

Overnight Coleslaw

1⅓ cups	mayonnaise	335 ml	2 tbsp	milk	30 ml
3 tbsp	white vinegar	45 ml	dash	salt	
2 tbsp + 2 tsp	granulated sugar	40 ml	8 cups	cabbage, chopped	2 L
			½ cup	carrot, shredded	125 ml

Combine all ingredients, except the cabbage and carrots, in a large bowl and blend until smooth with an electric mixer. Add cabbage and carrots and toss well. Cover and chill overnight in the refrigerator. The flavours fully develop after 24-48 hours. Serves 8.

Peperanata

A delightful and nutritious dish.

1	large onion, cut in thick slices	1	3	celery stalks, cut up	3
½ cup	vegetable oil	125 ml	1 cup	peas, fresh or frozen	250 ml
1	small eggplant, peeled and cut into bite-size pieces	1	1½ cups	string beans, fresh or frozen, cut up	375 ml
4	green peppers, cut up	4		salt	
4	red peppers, cut up	4		pepper	
1	medium zucchini with peel, cut into bite-size pieces	1		bay leaf	
				oregano	
1 28-oz can	stewed tomatoes	796 ml	¼ cup	butter	50 ml
			2-3	bouillon cubes	2-3
			pinch	hot pepper, dried	

In a large saucepan, lightly brown onion in vegetable oil. Stir in the cut-up vegetables. Add tomatoes; stir again. Add salt, pepper, bay leaf and oregano to taste. Cook over low heat for approximately 1½-2 hours until vegetables are just tender. Stir the mixture frequently. Juice from tomatoes will have boiled away. When cooked, add butter, bouillon cubes, and dried hot pepper. Mix thoroughly. Serve as a side dish with any meal. May be kept for 1-2 weeks in refrigerator or may be frozen in small containers. Serves 8.

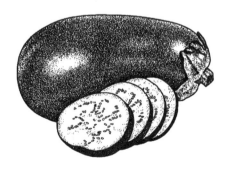

Hodge Podge

Any combination of garden-fresh vegetables can be combined to make this irresistible chowder. My favourites are string beans, peas, baby carrots and small new potatoes.

In a large saucepan, cook vegetables in a small amount of salted water until tender. Those requiring the longest cooking time should be started first. Reserve the cooking liquid. Add ¼ cup (50 ml) butter for every 6 cups (1.5 L) vegetables. Mix together. Add salt and pepper and reserved liquid. Add light cream or evaporated milk, sufficient for the number of servings. Heat to boiling. Serve piping hot. Allow for second and third helpings—it is just so delicious.

Couscous with Vegetables

The yellow Vidalia onion adds a touch of sweetness to this dish.

	vegetable cooking spray		¼ cup	fresh parsley, chopped	50 ml
1 tsp	olive oil	5 ml	1 tbsp	lime juice	15 ml
1¼ cups	zucchini, shredded	310 ml	¼ tsp	dried rosemary	1 ml
1¼ cups	carrots, shredded	310 ml	¼ tsp	salt	1 ml
½ cup	Vidalia onion, chopped	125 ml	1½ cups	couscous, cooked	375 ml
1	small sweet red pepper, seeded and sliced into thin strips	1			

Coat a large, nonstick skillet with cooking spray; add oil, and place over medium heat until hot. Add zucchini, carrot, onion and red pepper; sauté until crisp-tender. Transfer to a large bowl. Combine parsley, lime juice, rosemary and salt. Add to vegetables. Add couscous to vegetable mixture and stir well. Serve warm. Serves 8.

Three-Pepper Coulis

1	red pepper, seeded and chopped	1		1	orange pepper, seeded and chopped	1
1	yellow pepper, seeded and chopped	1		1 cup	cilantro leaves	250 ml
				¼ cup	olive oil	50 ml

Combine all ingredients in blender and serve.

Tomatoes Provençal

This elegant and colourful dish is especially good in the winter, when tomatoes are less flavourful.

Slice 2 large tomatoes in half and place sliced side up in shallow baking pan: Combine and sprinkle over the top of each tomato half:

1 tsp	olive oil	5 ml		½ tsp	dry oregano	2 ml
1 tsp	breadcrumbs	5 ml		½ tsp	basil, fresh	2 ml
1 tsp	Parmesan cheese, grated	5 ml		½ tsp	sesame seeds	2 ml
dash	garlic salt			pinch	ground red chili	

Place the tomato halves under a preheated broiler until very hot and the tops slightly browned. These can be baked ahead of time, covered with plastic wrap, then pulled out and broiled as the final step in dinner preparation. Serves 4.

Greek Stuffed Tomatoes

8	medium tomatoes (about 3½ lb)	8	¼ tsp	salt	1 ml
	vegetable cooking spray		2 tbsp	pinenuts	30 ml
½ cup	onion, chopped	125 ml	2 tbsp	fresh parsley, chopped	30 ml
1 clove	garlic, peeled and chopped	1	¼ tsp	dried basil	1 ml
			¼ tsp	pepper	1 ml
1½ cups	cooked rice	375 ml	2 oz	feta cheese, crumbled	56 g

Cut the top quarter off each tomato. Scoop out pulp, leaving ¼-inch (5 mm) thick shells. Discard seeds and chop pulp. Reserve 2 cups (500 ml) chopped pulp; discard remaining pulp or reserve for another use. Coat a large, nonstick skillet with cooking spray; place over medium heat until hot. Add onion and garlic and sauté until tender, being careful not to burn garlic. Remove from heat. Stir in cooked rice, reserved tomato pulp and remaining ingredients. Spoon rice mixture evenly into tomato shells. Arrange tomatoes in a large, shallow dish coated with cooking spray. Cover and bake at 350F (175C) for 20-25 minutes. Serves 8.

Baked Tomatoes

Slice the tops off tomatoes. Mix Italian seasoning with breadcrumbs, basil and a dash of salt. Spread breadcrumb mixture over cut section of tomatoes. Sprinkle with Parmesan cheese or dried mint. Add 1-2 pats of margarine. Bake for 15 minutes at 350-400F (175-200C).

Southern Corn Pudding

3 cups	corn, cut	750 ml		3 tbsp	melted butter	45 ml
3	eggs, slightly beaten	3		3 tbsp	sugar	45 ml
1 tsp	salt	5 ml		1⅛ cups	scalded milk	280 ml
⅛ tsp	pepper	0.5 ml				

Combine ingredients and pour into a greased 8x8-inch (20x20 cm) baking dish or into the cavity of a crown roast. Bake in a slow oven 325F (165C) for about 30-40 minutes or until firm.

Corn Pudding

1	onion	1		4	eggs	4
1	sweet red pepper, finely chopped	1		1 tbsp	sugar	15 ml
				2 tsp	Dijon mustard	10 ml
2 tbsp	butter	30 ml		1 tsp	salt	5 ml
4 cups	corn, fresh or frozen	1 L		½ tsp	baking powder	2 ml
¼ cup	flour	50 ml		¼ tsp	cayenne	1 ml
2 cups	milk	500 ml				

Butter a large baking dish. In a skillet, melt butter; sauté onion and red pepper for 5 minutes. Add corn, and cook for 3 minutes, stirring occasionally. Whisk flour and half cup of milk in bowl. Add remaining milk, eggs, sugar, mustard, salt, baking powder and cayenne. Stir into corn mixture. Transfer mixture into baking dish. Place baking dish in a shallow pan on rack in oven. Add enough water to shallow pan to come halfway up the sides of baking dish. Bake in 350F (175C) oven for about 1 hour or until set. If the top browns too quickly, cover with foil.

Mushrooms à la King

1 lb	fresh mushrooms	500 g	1 cup	whole milk	250 ml
2 tbsp	onion, chopped	30 ml	1 cup	chicken broth	250 ml
5 tbsp	butter	75 ml	3 tbsp	chopped pimento	45 ml
4 tbsp	flour	60 ml	2 tbsp	pimento juice	30 ml
	salt and pepper		2 tbsp	dry sherry	30 ml

Wash mushrooms and detach stems. Melt butter in skillet over medium heat. Add stems and onion. Stir-fry for 1 minute. Add caps and continue cooking for 2 minutes. Remove mushrooms from skillet. Stir in flour, salt and pepper. Add milk gradually and cook until thick, then stir in the chicken broth and remaining ingredients. Add mushrooms and taste for seasoning. Spoon into patty shells or serve over toast points. For a richer, thicker mixture, whisk 1 or 2 egg yolks with chicken broth, add to mixture and heat for 2-3 minutes. Serves 6.

Sautéed Mushrooms

If you like mushrooms, you'll love these.

½ lb	shiitake mushrooms	250 g	¼ lb	shallots, skins removed	125 g
½ lb	Italian portabello mushrooms	250 g	1 clove	garlic, skin removed	1
½ lb	matsutake mushrooms	250 g	1 bunch	thyme sprigs	1
8 tbsp	butter	125 ml		salt and fresh ground pepper, to taste	
¼ lb	pearl onions, skins removed	125 g			

Wipe mushrooms clean, discard the shiitake stems and cut ¼ inch (5 mm) off the portabello and matsutake stems. Slice shiitake and matsutake thinly, portabello thicker. Melt the butter in a sauté pan, add the onions, shallots and garlic cloves and cook over medium heat for about 5 minutes or until wilted, stirring occasionally. Add the mushrooms and sauté briefly. Add the thyme (leaves only), then season with salt and pepper. Garnish with whole sprigs of thyme. Serve immediately. Serves 6.

Creamed Hashed Potatoes

4	large potatoes, cooked, hot or cold, sliced	4		salt and pepper	
1¼ cups whole milk		310 ml	⅓ cup	butter	75 ml

Place butter in heated frying pan. Add potatoes. Spread over pan. Add milk and seasonings. Stir to mix well. Cook over low heat. Milk will gradually be absorbed by potatoes. Serve hot. Serves 6.

Hash Brown Party Patties

Another great way to serve hash browns.

8	hash brown patties	8	1 cup	whipping cream	250 ml
½ tsp	salt	2 ml	1 cup	Cheddar cheese, shredded	250 ml
½ tsp	garlic powder	2 ml			

Place patties in a greased 13x9x2-inch (33x23x4 cm) baking dish. Sprinkle with salt and garlic powder. Pour cream over patties. Bake uncovered at 350F (175C) for 50 minutes. Sprinkle with cheese. Bake 5-10 minutes longer or until potatoes are tender and cheese is melted. Serves 8.

Potatoes au Gratin

Cheese and potatoes make a great combination.

2 lb	potatoes	1 kg			salt and pepper	
4 oz	Roquefort cheese	125 g	¼ tsp	nutmeg		1 ml
½ cup	heavy cream	125 ml	¼ tsp	ground red pepper		1 ml
2 cups	milk	500 ml	½ clove	garlic, crushed		½
¼ cup	Monterey Jack cheese, shredded	50 ml	3 tbsp	butter		45 ml

Preheat oven to 325F (165C). In a wide mixing bowl, crush Roquefort cheese with 5 tbsp (75 ml) heavy cream until smooth and pliable. Stir in the milk and half the shredded cheese. Add a pinch of salt and pepper, nutmeg and red pepper. Rub a large gratin pan with garlic and butter. Peel and thinly slice potatoes. Fold into milk mixture, and spread out in an even layer in the prepared dish. Bake 1¼ hours on lower shelf without disturbing. Raise oven temperature to 400F (200C). Sprinkle with remaining cheese and heavy cream; bake 15 minutes longer or until golden brown on top. If not serving at once, reduce oven heat to 200F (100C). The cooked gratin can hold one hour or be reheated. Serves 6.

Fried Potatoes

Great for using up leftover potatoes!

4 cups	potatoes, sliced and cooked	1 L		salt and pepper	
	butter				

Melt enough butter to cover bottom of a hot, large, heavy frying pan. Add potatoes and reduce heat. Let potatoes brown and then turn as browning takes place. Season and serve hot. Finely chopped onion may be added to butter before potatoes. Serves 6.

Twice-Baked Potatoes

These are great to make ahead and have on hand. Children love them!

4	medium baking potatoes	4	2 tbsp	green onion, thinly sliced	30 ml
2 tbsp	butter	30 ml	½ tsp	salt	3 m
½ cup	sour cream	125 ml	⅛ tsp	pepper	0.5 ml
½ cup	Cheddar or Swiss cheese, shredded	125 ml			

Bake potatoes at 425F (220C) for 40-60 minutes or until done. Cut a lengthwise slice from the side of each potato; discard skin from slice. Scoop out the inside of each potato, leaving ½-inch shell. Set shells aside; mash potato. Add butter to potato. Beat in sour cream. Season with pepper. Stir in cheese and green onion. Spoon or pipe mashed potato mixture into potato shells. Place in a 10x6x2-inch (25x15x5 cm) baking dish. Cover and refrigerate for 24 hours, or wrap in moisture/vapour-proof wrap and freeze. When ready to use, bake uncovered in a 425F (220C) oven for 35 minutes or until lightly browned (bake frozen potatoes 1 hour). Sprinkle with paprika, if desired. Serves 4.

Potato Casserole

10	Yukon gold potatoes	10	**Topping:**		
2	onions, sliced	2	¼ cup	butter	50 ml
1 tsp	thyme	5 ml	2 cups	coarse breadcrumbs	500 ml
¾ tsp	salt and pepper	3 ml	¼ cup	parsley, chopped	50 ml

Peel and slice potatoes to make 8 cups (2 L). Spread half of the onion in greased 12-cup (3 L) casserole or 13x9 (3 L) baking dish. Top with half of the potatoes; sprinkle with half of the salt, pepper and thyme. Repeat layers. Make sauce by blending ¼ cup (50 ml) each of butter and flour in a saucepan over low heat; gradually stir in 2½ cups (625 ml) chicken or vegetable stock and 1 tbsp (15 ml) vinegar. Bake at 350F (175C) until browned on top and cooked throughout.

Potato Puffs and Bacon

3 cups	mashed potatoes, hot	750 ml		salt and pepper	
½ cup	milk	125 ml		bacon	
1	egg	1		paprika	
1 tbsp	butter	15 ml			

Mix first 6 ingredients together and beat well. Shape into balls. Wrap each in a slice of bacon. Place in a greased casserole dish. Bake in moderate oven for 30 minutes. Remove from oven. Sprinkle with paprika. Serve with green salad and hot biscuits. Serves 6.

Creamed Potatoes

8	medium potatoes	8	2 tbsp	butter	30 ml
1	large onion, diced	1		salt and pepper	
1½ cups	whole milk	375 ml	1 cup	breadcrumbs, buttered	250 ml
2 tbsp	flour	30 ml			

Peel and slice or dice potatoes. Cook in hot, salted water until barely tender. Drain and empty into casserole. Add diced onion, making sure to distribute well among potatoes. Over this, sprinkle flour. Add milk and butter. Sprinkle generously with salt and pepper. Cover with buttered breadcrumbs. Bake until potatoes and onion are tender, and sauce is creamy. Serves 8.

Cheesy Creamed Potatoes

Follow directions for creamed potatoes but add 2 cups (500 ml) grated Cheddar cheese to the potatoes, making sure to distribute the cheese well. (Cheese and flour can be mixed together.) Add milk and continue to follow same procedure. Evaporated milk makes an excellent substitute for the milk required in this recipe. Save the water drained off the potatoes to dilute the milk. Serves 6.

Yogurt Mashed Potatoes

Uses yogurt instead of cream—a great idea.

2 lb	potatoes, peeled	1 kg		1 cup	low-fat plain yogurt	250 ml
1 tsp	salt	5 ml		2 tbsp	butter, melted	30 ml

Add salt to potatoes in saucepan. Add water and boil until tender. Drain. Add yogurt to potatoes and mash with potato masher. Can be served plain or placed in pastry bag fitted with a decorative tip, and piped into a shallow baking dish. Drizzle melted butter over top. Broil 3 minutes or until browned. Serves 6.

Garlic Mashed Potatoes

1-3	garlic heads, whole	1-3		6 tbsp	butter	90 ml
1½ tbsp	olive oil	23 ml		2 tsp	white pepper	10 ml
	black pepper, to taste			⅔ cup	hot milk or cream	150 ml
4 lb	Idaho potatoes	2 kg				

Roast the garlic by cutting just the ends off the heads of the individual cloves, leaving the papery skin on and the root end intact. Drizzle olive oil over the cut end and sprinkle with black pepper. Add ½ inch (1 cm) water to a small oven-proof pan and place garlic in it, root end up. Bring the water to a boil on top of the stove and then place pan in a 350F (175C) oven for 45 minutes. When the garlic head is cool enough to handle just squeeze the plump cloves from their skins and push them through a sieve. Peel the potatoes and cook, covered in water, until a knife easily pierces the flesh. Mash the potatoes, adding the butter, white pepper, and hot milk or cream along with the mashed cloves of roasted garlic. Serves 8.

Harvard Beets

2 cups	beets, washed, boiled and diced (reserve ⅓ cup (75 ml) cooking liquid)	500 ml		1 tbsp	cornstarch	15 ml
				¼ cup	vinegar	50 ml
				2 tbsp	butter	30 ml
2 tbsp	white sugar	30 ml			salt, if desired	

In a saucepan, stir together sugar and cornstarch. Stir in reserved liquid, vinegar, butter and salt. Cook and stir until thickened. Add beets and heat. Serves 6.

Beet Sauce

4	medium beets, peeled and chopped	4		1	onion, chopped	1
					salt and ground black pepper	
8 cups	fish stock	2 L				
1	leek, white part only, chopped	1		½ cup	whipping cream	125 ml

In a saucepan, cook beets in fish stock with leek and onion until tender. Strain and place vegetable in food processor or blender. Add cream, and blend sauce until smooth. Reheat over medium heat until very hot.

Parsnip Scallop

Peel and slice four large parsnips. Boil for ten minutes. Remove from heat and drain. Set aside.

Cheese sauce:

2 tbsp	butter	30 ml
2 tbsp	flour	30 ml
2 cups	milk	500 ml
1 cup	sharp Cheddar cheese, grated	250 ml

Topping:

	cracker crumbs
	sharp Cheddar cheese, grated
	salt, as desired

Melt butter in a heavy saucepan. Add flour and blend, stirring continually for 3 minutes. Add milk gradually and heat thoroughly. Add grated cheese and stir until well combined. Remove from heat.

In a 1½-quart (2 L) baking dish, spread a layer of parsnips and a layer of cheese sauce alternately. Sprinkle with cracker crumbs and top with grated cheese. Bake at 350F (175C) for 30-40 minutes. Serves 4-6.

Glazed Parsnips

All dressed up and ready to enjoy.

6	medium parsnips	6	1 tbsp	brown sugar	15 ml
¼ cup	butter	50 ml	½ tsp	dry mustard	2 ml
	salt and pepper				

Peel parsnips and cut into slices. Melt butter in saucepan. Add parsnips, and season with salt and pepper. Cover and cook gently until parsnips are tender. Transfer to ovenproof dish. Mix brown sugar and mustard together, and sprinkle over parsnips. Bake at 350F (175C) until browned. These are excellent with ham or pork. Serves 6.

Skillet Sweet Potatoes

Change the spices to suit your own tastes.

1 lb	sweet potatoes, peeled and sliced	500 g	1 tbsp	honey	15 ml
			¼ tsp	salt	1 ml
½ tsp	orange peel, finely shredded	2 ml	¼ tsp	cinnamon	1 ml
			⅛ tsp	nutmeg	0.5 ml
½ cup	orange juice	125 ml			

In a large skillet, bring 1 inch (2.5 cm) of water to boil. Add sweet potatoes. Reduce heat. Cover and simmer for 20 minutes or until tender. Drain well. In a small bowl, combine orange peel, orange juice, honey, salt, cinnamon and nutmeg. Pour over drained potatoes in skillet. Cook and stir gently until bubbly. Simmer uncovered for 5 minutes or until potatoes are glazed, spooning sauce over potatoes occasionally. Serves 6.

Baked Sweet Potatoes

Scrub sweet potatoes and bake in oven until tender. Remove from oven and cut in halves lengthwise. Scoop out inside and place in bowl, leaving the skins intact. Mash the potatoes and add 1 tsp (5 ml) of butter and cream for each potato half. Season with salt and pepper. Refill skins and bake 5 minutes more.

Sweet Potato Oven Slices

Scrub sweet potatoes. Slice into ¼-inch (5 mm) slices. Place on oiled cookie sheet. Brush slices with butter or olive oil. Bake until tender. They will be puffy and lightly browned. Season as desired. Slicing a sweet potato into your next beef stew will add a subtle sweetness to the flavour.

Turnip and Apple Scallop

2 cups	turnip, peeled and thinly sliced	500 ml	6 tbsp	butter, melted	90 ml
2 cups	Red Delicious apples, thinly sliced	500 ml		salt and pepper	

Preheat oven to 400F (200C). Butter two 9-inch (23 cm) pie plates. Layer the turnip slices, alternating with apple slices, and brush with butter between each layer. Sprinkle with salt and pepper. Bake for 20 minutes, covered, then remove cover and bake 5 minutes more, or until slices are slightly browned. Serve hot on a bed of dandelion greens with crisp bacon.

Note: Preliminary blanching removes a turnip's strong taste.

Turnip and Potato Cakes

Mix together 1 cup (250ml) each of mashed turnip and potato; blend in 1 lightly beaten egg and a little chopped onion. Form into flat cakes on a floured surface. Pan fry in butter until nicely browned on both sides. Top each cake with a spoonful of heated chili sauce. Serves 4.

Baked Butternut Squash

2½ lb	butternut squash (about 2 medium)	1.25 kg		salt and pepper, to taste	
			¾ cup	pure maple syrup	175 ml
2 lb	Granny Smith apples (tart)	1 kg	¼ cup	butter, cut into pieces	50 ml
	freshly grated nutmeg		1½ tbsp	fresh lemon juice	23 ml

Preheat oven to 350F (175C). Peel the squash and quarter it lengthwise. Seed squash before cutting it crosswise into ¼-inch (5 mm) thick slices to yield about 6 cups (1. 5 L). Peel and quarter the apples, then remove the core. Cut crosswise into ¼-inch (5 mm) slices to yield about 6 cups (1.5 L). Cook squash in a large pot of boiling water until almost tender, about 3 minutes. Drain well. Combine squash and apples in 13x9x2-inch (33x23x5 cm) glass baking dish. Season generously with nutmeg, salt and pepper. Combine maple syrup, butter and lemon juice in small, heavy saucepan. Whisk over low heat until butter melts. Pour syrup over squash mixture and toss to coat evenly. Bake until squash and apples are very tender (about 1 hour), stirring occasionally. Cool 5 minutes. Can be made 1 day ahead; cover with foil and chill. Re-warm, covered, at 350F (175C) for about 30 minutes. Serves 8.

Stir-Fried Zucchini

3 tbsp	oil	45 ml	2 tbsp	soy sauce	30 ml
12	large mushrooms, sliced	12	¼ tsp	pepper	1.5 ml
			½ tsp	salt (optional)	2.5 ml
2	medium onions, sliced	2	½ tsp	sugar	2.5 ml
2	medium zucchini, thinly sliced	2			

Heat oil in a large skillet or wok. Add all ingredients. Stir-fry over high heat, about 8-10 minutes or until zucchini is tender crisp. Serves 4.

Glazed Ginger Carrots

The high level of beta-carotene in carrots lowers the risk of heart disease. Ginger is said to soothe the digestive tract.

3 cups	baby carrots, fresh	750 ml		1 tsp	ground ginger	5 ml
½ cup	water	125 ml		1 tbsp	lemon juice	15 ml
½ cup	apple juice	125 ml		2 tsp	brown sugar	10 ml
2 tsp	margarine	10 ml				

Cook the carrots in the water, juice, margarine and ginger over medium heat for 10-15 minutes. Reduce heat and add lemon juice and brown sugar, stirring for another 5 minutes. Serves 4.

Black Bean and Cheese Burritos

1 14-oz can	refried black beans	398 ml		2 cups	Monterey Jack cheese, shredded	500 ml
1 3½-oz can	green chilies	114 ml		1¾ cup	salsa	430 ml
8	flour tortillas	8				

Combine beans and chilies in a small saucepan. Heat until steaming. Spoon ¼ cup (60ml) of the bean mixture down the centre of a warm tortilla. Top with ¼ cup (60ml) cheese and 2 tablespoons of salsa. Fold and repeat. Serve with salsa. Makes 8 burritos.

Helene's Bean Casserole

½ lb	bacon, more or less	250 g	½ cup	ketchup		125 ml
1	large onion	1	1 tsp	dry mustard		5 ml
1½ lb	hamburger	675 g		salt and pepper, to taste		
2 19-oz cans	molasses beans	2x540 ml	pinch	garlic powder		
½ cup	molasses	125 ml		Worcestershire sauce, to taste		

Fry (or microwave) bacon and crumble. Fry onion and hamburger. Mix all ingredients together and bake at 350F (175C) for 30 minutes. Everyone will think they are eating homemade beans—the ones that take forever. Serves 8.

Baked Canned Pinto Beans

2 15-oz cans	pinto beans, with liquid	2x470 ml	1 tsp	prepared mustard	5 ml
2 tbsp	water	30 ml	½ tsp	chili powder	2 ml
2 tsp	cornstarch	10 ml	¼ tsp	salt	1 ml
½ cup	ketchup	125 ml	¼ tsp	coarse ground black pepper	1 ml
⅓ cup	white vinegar	75 ml	½ cup	bacon, cooked and crumbled	125 ml
⅓ cup	brown sugar	75 ml			
3 tbsp	onion, diced	45 ml			

Preheat oven to 350F (175C). Pour pinto beans into a casserole (with a lid). Dissolve the cornstarch in a small bowl with water. Add to the beans and stir. Add the remaining ingredients to the dish, stir well and cover. Bake for 90 minutes or until the sauce thickens. Stir every 30 minutes. After removing the beans from the oven, let them cool for 5-10 minutes before serving. Serves 8.

Baked Beans

Nova Scotians have long been known for their tradition of "beans on Saturday night." Most recipes include the same ingredients, but the secret of the goodness lies in the skill of the cook who, with one glance, knows when the beans are ready for the oven. The old tradition is showing signs of waning, but here and there on Saturday night you may still experience that great aroma and taste of baked beans.

1 lb	dry white beans (or any variety)	500 g	1 tsp	salt, more if desired	5 ml
½ cup	butter	125 ml	½ tsp	pepper	2.5 ml
1 tsp	dry mustard	5 ml		brown sugar, as desired	
1	onion, sliced	1			
½ cup	molasses (more or less if desired)	125 ml	1 piece	salt pork (optional)	1

On Friday night: Pick over dry beans; remove bad ones and debris. Rinse well; cover with water and soak overnight. (Some varieties do not require overnight soaking.) In the morning, drain, cover with fresh cold water and bring to a boil. Reduce heat and simmer until soft. Test for doneness by removing a few beans and blowing on them—if beans are done, the skins will lift. When cooked, drain and place in bean crock or baking dish. Some cooks like to place a piece of salt pork on the bottom of the pot; others place pork or bacon on top. Still others use only butter. Along with butter, add molasses, mustard, onion, salt and pepper and place on top of beans. Add enough water to barely cover. Cover bean crock and place in 300F (150C) oven. Bake 5-8 hours. Check now and then, and add cold water to keep liquid at level of beans. About 3 hours into the baking process taste for sweetness. If not sweet enough to your taste, add either molasses or brown sugar. (Too much molasses tends to harden the beans.) Make some coleslaw and serve with freshly baked brown bread, biscuits, cornbread or rolls. You will have a great supper and perhaps leftovers for Sunday. Serves 6.

· BREADS ·

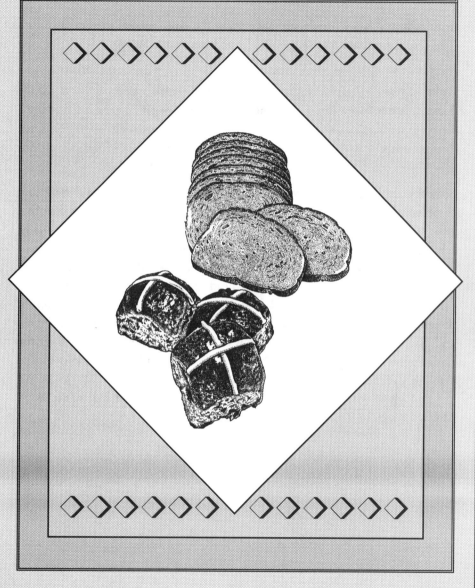

· Best ·

· Traditional ·

· Trendy ·

Standard Rolls

Yeast rolls and fancy breads are made using the same general method as bread. They usually contain more sugar and fat and sometimes an egg.

2 pkg	yeast	2	1 tsp	salt	5 ml
1 cup	water, lukewarm	250 ml	¼ cup	sugar	50 ml
2 tsp	sugar	10 ml	⅓ cup	shortening	75 ml
2 cups	milk	500 ml	8 cups	flour	2 L

Soften yeast in lukewarm water and sugar for 10 minutes. Scald milk and combine with salt, sugar and shortening. Cool to lukewarm, and add dissolved yeast. Add half the flour and beat until smooth. Add rest of flour gradually, mixing it thoroughly and adding just enough to prevent stickiness; the less flour used, the lighter the rolls. Turn out onto a floured board to knead. Let dough rest on board for about 10 minutes. Knead again until dough is smooth and elastic. Shape into a smooth ball, and place in a greased bowl. Grease top of dough, cover and let rise in warm place until double in bulk. Shape as desired and place on a greased pan. Brush tops of rolls with butter. Cover and let rise until double in bulk. Bake in a 350F (175C) oven until browned and cooked through, depending on size of rolls and pans.

For whole wheat rolls, use half whole wheat flour and half white flour. Makes 4 dozen rolls.

Methods of Shaping Rolls

Plain: Cut off small, uniform pieces, and fold under until top is smooth and dough is round. For crusty rolls, place 1 inch (2.5 cm) apart on baking sheet. For tall, soft rolls, place close together so that they touch.

Cloverleaf Rolls: Form dough into very small balls. Dip balls in melted butter and place 3 balls in each section of a muffin tin.

Crescent: Roll ball of dough into a circular shape about ¼ inch (5 mm) thick. Cut in pie-shaped pieces. Brush with melted butter and roll up, beginning at the wide end. Form into crescents on greased baking sheet.

Parker House: Roll dough to ¼-inch (5 mm) thickness; cut with floured 2-inch (5 cm) cutter. Make a line, just off centre of each round, with dull side of a knife. Brush with melted butter; fold each over so that top overlaps the bottom. Press edges together. Place rolls 1 inch (2.5 cm) apart.

Finger Rolls: Shape small pieces of dough into balls, then roll between palms of hands, keeping them smooth and uniform in size. Place 1 inch (2.5 cm) apart on baking sheet.

Basic Sweet Dough for Sweet Rolls and Fancy Breads

Versatile and always good.

2 pkg	yeast	2	1 tsp	salt	5 ml
1 cup	water, lukewarm	250 ml	½ cup	sugar	125 ml
2 tsp	sugar	10 ml	2	eggs, beaten	2
1 cup	milk	250 ml	1 tsp	lemon rind, grated	5 ml
¼ cup	butter	50 ml	6 cups	flour	1.5 L

Soften the yeast in lukewarm water and 2 tsp (10 ml) sugar. Scald milk; add butter, ½ cup sugar and salt. Cool to lukewarm and add yeast. Add half the flour to make thick batter. Add eggs and lemon rind. Beat well. Add enough flour to make a soft dough. Turn out on lightly floured board and knead until satin smooth. Grease top of dough. Place in greased bowl and let rise until doubled in bulk. When light, punch down. Let rise until dough doubles in bulk again. Make into 2 sweet breads or 3 dozen rolls. Bake at 350F (175C) for 25-30 minutes.

The basic sweet dough may be used to make fancy braids with fruit and nuts added.

Cinnamon Rings:
Roll out dough and spread with butter. Sprinkle with cinnamon and sugar and roll as jellyroll. Bake in loaf tins or slice and lay on greased cookie sheet.

Currant Buns:
Add 1 cup (250 ml) of raisins or currants to the dough when it rises the first time.

Hot Cross Buns:
Add 1 tbsp (15 ml) cinnamon and 1 cup (250 ml) of raisins to the dough when the eggs and lemon rind are added, or sift cinnamon with the first addition of flour.

Milk Rolls

More full-bodied than rolls made with water.

1 cup	milk, scalded	250 ml	1 pkg	yeast		1
2 tbsp	shortening	30 ml	2	eggs, beaten		2
¼ cup	sugar	50 ml	3 cups	flour		750 ml
½ tsp	salt	2 ml	½ cup	raisins, if desired		125 ml

Heat milk in a large saucepan. Remove from heat and add shortening, sugar and salt. Dissolve yeast in water and sugar according to package directions. Add to cooled milk mixture. Add eggs and about one third of flour. Beat well. Work in remainder of flour. Knead. Grease dough and place in a large bowl to rise until light. Punch down and add raisins, if using. Shape into rolls. Place in greased pan and grease each roll as you make it. Place close together. Let rise. When doubled in bulk, place in oven at 350F (175C). Bake 25-30 minutes or until nicely browned. Makes 2 dozen rolls.

Hot Cross Buns

An Easter favourite, year after year.

2 pkgs	yeast	2	2	eggs, beaten	2
1 cup	water, lukewarm	250 ml	1 tsp	lemon rind, grated	5 ml
2 tsp	sugar	10 ml	6 cups	flour	1.5 L
1 cup	milk	250 ml	1 tbsp	cinnamon	15 ml
¼ cup	butter	50 ml	½ tsp	ginger	2 ml
1 tsp	salt	5 ml	1 cup	raisins or currants	250 ml
½ cup	sugar	125 ml			

Add 2 tsp sugar to lukewarm water and stir. Sprinkle on yeast. Let rise. Scald milk, add butter and ½ cup sugar. Stir well and let cool to lukewarm. Add yeast mixture. Add about half the flour. Beat well. Add eggs and lemon rind. Add enough of the remaining flour to make a soft, sticky dough. Knead and form into a ball and place in a greased bowl. Cover and let rise in a warm place until double in bulk. Punch down and add raisins or currants. Shape into buns. Grease pan and arrange rolls, leaving a space for crusty rolls or placing close together for soft ones. Let rise until double in size. Bake at 350F (175C) until done, about 25-30 minutes. While still warm make crosses with vanilla-flavoured butter icing on top of each roll. Ice only enough for the day they will be eaten. Frost more, as they are needed. Makes 3 dozen rolls.

The Great Nova Scotia Cookbook

Rolled Cinnamon Buns

A perfect substitute for toast in the morning.

1 cup	milk	250 ml		2	eggs, beaten	2
1 cup	water, warmed	250 ml		7 cups	flour	1.75 L
2 pkg	yeast	2			cinnamon	
½ cup	shortening	125 ml			butter, softened	
½ cup	sugar	125 ml			brown sugar	
1½ tsp	salt	7 ml				

Scald milk and mix in sugar, shortening and salt. Dissolve yeast in water with a little sugar. When yeast mixture rises, add to milk mixture. Stir well. Add eggs and stir. Add flour gradually and beat until dough becomes stiff. Turn onto a board and knead. Grease dough and place in bowl to rise until double in volume. Turn out onto board. Roll out dough with rolling pin; make a rectangular shape. Spread surface with butter and sprinkle with brown sugar, making sure dough is entirely covered. Over top, sprinkle a good coating of cinnamon. Roll up dough as for jellyroll. Cut with sharp knife in 1½-inch (3.5 cm) slices. Pack slices into baking pan, laying them close together. Let rise until double. Bake at 350F (175C) for 25-30 minutes or until lightly browned. Makes 2 dozen rolls.

Whole Wheat
Parker House Rolls

A little more wholesome than standard rolls.

1 cup	milk	250 ml	1 tsp	sugar	5 ml
3 tbsp	brown sugar	45 ml	1 pkg	yeast	1
½ tsp	salt	2 ml	2¾ cups	whole wheat flour	675ml
3 tbsp	shortening	45 ml	1 cup	white flour	250 ml
½ cup	water, lukewarm	125 ml		butter	

Scald milk and stir in brown sugar, salt and shortening. Cool to lukewarm. Measure lukewarm water into a large bowl. Stir in sugar. Sprinkle in yeast. Let stand until dissolved then stir well. Stir in lukewarm milk mixture. Add 2 cups (500 ml) whole wheat flour and beat well. Mix in remaining whole wheat and white flour.

Turn out on floured board and knead until elastic. Place in greased bowl. Grease well and cover. Let rise in warm place, free from draft, until doubled in bulk, about 1¼ hour. Punch down dough. Turn onto floured board and knead until smooth. Roll out and spread with butter. Cut out rounds, as for biscuits. Crease each round with the dull side of knife. Fold at the crease of each roll and press edges together. Grease tops. Cover and let rise until double in bulk, about ¾ hour. Bake at 375F (190C) for 25-30 minutes.

Optional: Into a cup of water, mix about ¼ cup (60ml) sugar. Brush rolls with a pastry brush dipped in the sugar water and brush over hot rolls while still in pan. Return pan to oven to dry. Remove from oven immediately and remove rolls from pan.

If preferred, white flour may be substituted for the whole wheat flour called for in this recipe. Makes 2 dozen rolls.

Low-Fat Parker House Rolls

1 pkg	yeast	1
1 tsp	sugar	5 ml
½ cup	water	125 ml
½ cup	warm water	125 ml
1 cup	warm skim milk	250 ml
½ cup	sugar	125 ml

1 tsp	salt	5 ml
1	egg	1
5-6 cups	flour	1.25-1.5 L
7 tsp	vegetable oil	35 ml
3 tbsp	butter	45 ml

In a mixing bowl, dissolve yeast and 1 tsp (5 ml) sugar in water; let stand for 10 minutes. Add warm water, milk, salt and ½ cup sugar. Gradually add 2 cups (500 ml) flour; beat until smooth. Beat in egg and oil. Stir in remaining flour to make a soft dough. Turn onto a floured board. Knead until smooth and elastic. Place in a greased bowl; grease top and sides of dough well. Cover and let rise until double, about 1 hour. Punch down dough. Divide in half. Roll each half to ½ inch (1.3 cm). Cut with a floured cutter. Brush each roll with butter. Using the dull edge of a table knife, make an off-centre crease in each roll. Fold along crease, so that the large part is on the top. Press along folded edge. Place 2-3 inches (5-7 cm) apart on greased baking sheets. Cover and let rise until doubled. Bake at 350F (175C) for about 25-30 minutes or until golden brown. Brush with glaze.

Glaze:
Mix 2 tbsp (30 ml) sugar and ½ cup (125 ml) water. Brush over hot rolls before they are removed from pan. Return to oven to dry. Makes 3 dozen rolls.

Featherbed Rolls

This recipe appeared in an issue of the *Free Press Weekly* in 1958. They are described as light and delicious. Unlike most rolls they are mixed to a stiff batter and do not require kneading.

2 cups	milk, scalded	500 ml	4 cups	flour	1 L
¼ cup	butter	50 ml	1 pkg	yeast	1
¼ cup	sugar	50 ml	½ cup	warm water	125 ml
1½ tsp	salt	7 ml	1 tsp	sugar	5 ml
2	eggs, well beaten	2			

Melt butter in warm milk. Add salt and sugar. Dissolve yeast in water, add sugar, and add all to milk mixture. Add eggs and part of the flour. Beat well. Mix in remainder of flour with a mixing spoon. Let dough rise until light—about 2 hours. Beat down the risen dough. Place spoonfuls in buttered muffin tins, filling about ¾ full. Let rise again and bake 350F (175C) until done. Makes 2 dozen rolls.

Evaporated Milk Rolls

A heavy, dense roll with a distinctive taste.

¾ cup	evaporated milk	175 ml	4½-5 cups	flour	1 L-1.25 L
¾ cup	hot water	175 ml			
¼ cup	vegetable oil	50 ml	1 tbsp	yeast	15 ml
¼ cup	sugar	50 ml	½ cup	water	125 ml
1	egg, beaten	1	1 tsp	sugar	5 ml
1 tsp	salt	5 ml			

In a large pan or bowl, mix milk, water, oil, sugar, egg and salt. Stir well. Dissolve yeast in ½ cup water with 1 teaspoon sugar and combine with milk mixture. Beat in flour. Mix into ball and knead. Add extra flour if dough is too soft to handle. Shape into 1x3-inch (2.5x7.5 cm) rolls. Grease each roll and place 2 inches (5 cm) apart on baking sheet. Let rise until double in bulk. Bake in 350F (175C) oven until brown. Makes 2 dozen rolls.

Overnight Sticky Buns

3¾ cups	flour	930 ml	1	egg	1
⅓ cup	sugar	75 ml	½ cup	brown sugar	125 ml
¾ tsp	salt	3 ml	½ cup	corn syrup	125 ml
2 pkg	yeast	2	¾ cup	pecan halves	175 ml
1 cup	milk, lukewarm	250 ml	3 tbsp	butter or margarine	45 ml
			½ cup	pecans, chopped	125 ml
⅓ cup	butter or margarine, softened	75 ml	¼ cup	brown sugar	50 ml
			1 tbsp	cinnamon, as desired	15 ml

Dissolve yeast and ⅓ cup sugar in the milk. Mix 2 cups (500 ml) flour and salt. Add dissolved yeast mixture, butter and egg. Beat on low speed for 1 minute, scraping bowl frequently. Beat on medium speed for another minute, scraping bowl well. Stir in enough flour to make dough easy to handle. Turn dough out on a floured surface and knead for about 5 minutes until smooth and elastic. Place in greased bowl and grease dough well. Cover and let rise in warm place about 1½ hours or until double in bulk. In saucepan, heat ½ cup brown sugar, ½ cup margarine or butter to boiling. Remove from heat and add corn syrup. Spray or grease a 13x9x2-inch (33x23x5cm) Pyrex pan. Sprinkle with pecan halves; distribute evenly over the pan. When dough has completed rising, punch down and turn out onto a floured surface and roll into a 15x10-inch (37.5x25 cm) rectangle. Spread with 3 tbsp (45 ml) butter. Mix together chopped pecans, ¼ cup brown sugar and cinnamon, and sprinkle over the buttered dough. Tightly roll dough (starting at longer side). Pinch edges to seal. Slice roll into about 15 pieces, using a sharp knife. Place in pan, slightly apart and on top of pecan halves. Wrap pan in foil and refrigerate 12–48 hours. Bake in 350F (175C) oven until golden brown, about 30–35 minutes. Immediately invert pan onto serving plate, so that syrup runs down into buns. Remove pan. Care must be taken when baking so that syrup does not burn. Makes 15 rolls.

All Bran Rolls

A cross between a muffin and a roll.

1 cup	All Bran cereal	250 ml		1	egg	1
1 cup	boiling water	250 ml		1 pkg	yeast	1
¼ cup	shortening	50 ml		1 cup	lukewarm water	250 ml
1½ tsp	salt	7 ml		1 tsp	sugar	5 ml
½ cup	molasses	125 ml		2-3 cups	flour	500-750 ml

In a bowl, pour boiling water over All Bran, shortening, salt and molasses. Stir to blend. In another bowl, dissolve sugar in lukewarm water and add yeast. Beat egg and add to cooled bran mixture. Mix well and add dissolved yeast. Sift in flour in small quantities and beat with electric beater until a stiff dough is formed. Place dough in bowl, grease, cover and let rise until doubled in bulk. Form into rolls and place close together in pan. Bake in 350F (175C) oven for 25-30 minutes. This recipe may be doubled. Makes 2 dozen rolls.

Bran Refrigerator Rolls

2 pkg	yeast	2		1½ tsp	salt	7 ml
1 cup	lukewarm water	250 ml		1 cup	All Bran cereal	250 ml
1 cup	boiling water	250 ml		2	eggs, beaten	2
1 cup	shortening	250 ml		4 cups	flour, or more	1 L
¾ cup	sugar	175 ml				

Soak yeast in lukewarm water. In a large bowl, mix boiling water, shortening, sugar, salt and All Bran; stir until shortening melts; cool to lukewarm. Add eggs and yeast. Stir in enough flour to make stiff dough. Cover and place in refrigerator until needed. Form into balls, grease and place in muffin tins that have been well greased. Allow about 2 hours to rise. Bake in 350F (175C) oven for 20-25 minutes. Makes about 3 dozen rolls.

White Bread

Always a family favourite, hot from the oven.

1 pkg	yeast	1	2 tbsp	shortening	30 ml
½ cup	lukewarm water	125 ml	2 cups	water	500 ml
1 tsp	sugar	5 ml	1 tbsp	salt	15 ml
2 cups	milk	500 ml	12 cups	flour	3 L
¼ cup	sugar	50 ml			

Soften yeast in lukewarm water and 1 tsp (5 ml) sugar; let stand 10 minutes. Scald milk and add ¼ cup sugar, salt and shortening; add water and cool to lukewarm. Add yeast to cooled milk mixture. Add half the flour and beat with a spoon until almost smooth. Add rest of the flour gradually, mixing it in thoroughly and using just enough flour to prevent sticking. When dough is stiff, turn out on a floured board and knead until smooth and satiny. Shape into a smooth ball. Place in a greased bowl. Grease top of dough. Cover with clean dishtowel and let rise in a warm place until double in bulk. Punch down. Form into loaves. Cover and let rest about 15 minutes on board. Work into loaves again. Grease well with shortening and place in bread pans. Let rise until double in bulk. Bake in 350F (175C) oven until nicely browned, about 45-60 minutes; if turned out of pan, the loaf will sound hollow when tapped and will spring back when side is pressed lightly. Remove from oven and cool on racks. May be stored in plastic bags and frozen. Makes 4 loaves.

A note on bread making:
Yeast breads should not be baked in an oven registering higher than 350F. The uncooked loaves will continue to rise during the first 10 or 15 minutes in oven. If temperature is too high a crust will form too soon and prevent that rising period which will make bread heavy.

Crumpets

Hot toasted crumpets slathered with butter are delicious. Better still, drizzle them with maple syrup and eat them with a knife and fork.

½ cup	warm water	125 ml		½ tsp	salt	2 ml
1 pkg	yeast	1		2 cups	flour	500 ml
1 tsp	sugar	5 ml		½ tsp	baking soda (can be omitted; if so, omit the tepid water also)	2 ml
1 cup	milk	250 ml				
2 tbsp	butter	30 ml		1 tbsp	tepid water	15 ml

In large mixing bowl, combine warm water with yeast. Add sugar and stir to dissolve. Set aside. In small saucepan heat ½ cup (125 ml) of milk and the butter until butter melts. Remove from heat and stir in salt and remaining ½ cup (125 ml) of milk. Set aside to cool. Add milk mixture to yeast mixture and stir to blend. Mix in flour with a wooden spoon. The batter will be very lumpy. Cover the bowl with plastic wrap and secure with elastic band. Set aside to rise for 1½ hours or until the bubbling action slows and the mixture begins to collapse in on itself. Place four crumpet rings on a griddle, allowing the sides to touch. Spray all sides and set over medium heat. Dissolve the baking soda in tepid water and stir into batter. When griddle is hot, take up by scant quarter-cupfuls and pour into rings. (The batter will be thin and ropey.) Spread batter to the sides of rings with back of spoon. As the batter begins to set, carefully rotate rings to ensure even cooking. When the surface of the crumpets is covered with holes and no longer looks wet (about 3 minutes), remove the rings with tongs. Turn the crumpets over and continue cooking for about 1 minute, until the surface is lightly browned. Repeat with remaining batter, spraying the rings and griddle before each batch. Cool crumpets on a rack. Toast to serve. Do not split. Makes 10. If crumpet rings are not available, use tuna cans with both ends removed.

Porridge Brown Bread

A satisfying way to use up leftover porridge.

3 cups	rolled oats	750 ml
7½ cups	boiling water	1.9 L
1½ tbsp	salt	18 ml
3 tbsp	shortening	45 ml
1½ cups	molasses	375 ml

1 cup	cold water	250 ml
1½ tbsp	yeast	18 ml
1½ cups	warm water	375 ml
1 tsp	sugar	5 ml
6-8 cups	white flour	1.5-2 L

Add salt and 7½ cups boiling water to a large pot on the stove. Stir in rolled oats and boil until thick like porridge. Remove from stove and stir in shortening, molasses and cold water. This mixture can be made as much as a day in advance. It must be cooled. Dissolve yeast in warm water and sugar, and add to rolled oat mixture. Add about 4 cups (1 L) flour. Stir well and beat. Add two more cups (500 ml) and mix. Continue adding flour until dough is stiff enough to knead. It is not necessary to knead all of the dough at the same time. Smaller amounts are easier to work with. Gradually add flour until stiff dough forms. It will be sticky. Recombine dough into one ball. Grease with shortening and place in warm bowl in a warm spot, free from drafts. Cover with clean dish towel. Let rise until double in bulk. Punch down dough and divide into loaves as desired. Place in pans preferably with straight sides to support the dough and prevent "falling." The risen loaves can be tested for oven readiness by gently pressing dough with your fingers. If the depression remains, it's ready to bake. If the dough springs back, it should be left longer to rise. Place pans in a 350F (175C) oven and bake until loaves are brown. Baking time depends on size of loaf. If a loaf is turned out of pan it will sound hollow when tapped with finger. When done, remove from oven and place on racks to cool. Pack in plastic bags. Eat fresh or freeze. Makes 4 large or 7 small loaves.

Plum Loaf

Slow-rising—start early in the day. A Christmas special!

2 cups	warm water	500 ml
2 cups	milk	500 ml
2 tsp	salt	10 ml
¼ cup	sugar	50 ml
2 tbsp	shortening	30 ml

12 cups	flour	3 L
1 pkg	yeast	1
½ cup	water, lukewarm	125 ml
1 tsp	sugar	5 ml

Add lukewarm water and 1 tsp (5 ml) sugar to yeast and let stand 10 minutes. Scald milk and add ¼ cup sugar, shortening and salt; add water and cool to lukewarm. Add yeast to cooled milk mixture. Add half the flour and beat until almost smooth. Cover and let rise for about ½ hour or so. This batter is referred to as a sponge.

After sponge rises, beat and add the following combined ingredients:

1 cup	flour	250 ml
1 tbsp	cinnamon	15 ml
1 tsp	ginger	5 ml

1 cup	sugar	250 ml
3 cups	raisins, seedless	750 ml
2 cups	raisins, seeded	500 ml

Beat all together until dough is smooth. Gradually add more flour until stiff enough to handle. It will be somewhat sticky—keep a little flour on breadboard. Shape into a smooth ball. Place in a large pan or bowl, and let rise until double in bulk. This will take longer than white bread. Make sure dough is covered, free of drafts and in a warm place. A nice sunny window is ideal. When dough is ready, punch down. Mould into loaves. Grease with butter and place in greased pans. Let rise again until double in bulk. Bake at 350F (175C) for 50-60 minutes, depending on loaf size. Time of baking depends on size and number of loaves. Test for doneness by turning out a loaf and tapping for a hollow sound. Crust on sides should be firm enough to spring back when touched lightly. Two cups (500 ml) dried cranberries may be added with raisins , if desired. Makes 4 loaves.

Florence's Plum Loaf

Cinnamon and raisins make this a special treat.

1 pkg	yeast	1	1 tsp	ginger	5 ml
1 cup	warm water	250 ml	1 lb	raisins	500 g
1 tsp	sugar	5 ml	½ cup	molasses or 1 cup (250 ml) brown sugar	125 ml
10 cups	flour	1.4 kg			
1 tbsp	salt	15 ml			
1 tbsp	cinnamon	15 ml		water, to mix	

Combine yeast with warm water in which sugar has been dissolved. Place remaining ingredients in a large mixing bowl. Add enough warm water to form a soft dough. Knead until dough loses its stickiness. Let rise until double in bulk. Punch down and place in pans. Bake at 350F (175C) for 50-60 minutes. Makes 4 loaves.

Whole Wheat Bread

3 cups	skim milk	375 ml	½ cup	lukewarm water	125 ml
½ cup	shortening	125 ml	1 pkg	yeast	1
¼ cup	molasses	50 ml	4 cups	whole wheat flour	1 L
2 tsp	salt	10 ml	4 cups	white flour	1 L
1 tsp	sugar	5 ml			

In a small bowl, place ½ cup water and 1 tsp sugar. Stir well and add yeast. Scald milk; add shortening, molasses and salt. Cool. In a large bowl, combine yeast mixture with milk mixture. Beat together and add all unsifted whole-wheat flour. Beat thoroughly until smooth. Knead in white flour until stiff dough forms. Knead well. Place in greased bowl. Grease dough. Cover and let rise until doubled in bulk—about 2½ hours. Knead again. Divide into loaves. Cover and let rest about 15 minutes. Form into loaves and grease. Place in greased pans. Let rise until double in bulk. Bake at 350F (175C) for about 50-60 minutes. Makes 3 large loaves.

Rolled Oats Bread with Milk

1 cup	milk	250 ml		2 tbsp	molasses	30 ml
1 cup	hot water	250 ml		½ cup	lukewarm water	125 ml
2 cups	rolled oats	500 ml		1 tsp	sugar	5 ml
2 tbsp	sugar	30 ml		1 pkg	yeast	1
2 tsp	salt	10 ml		2 cups	pancake mix	500 ml
2 tbsp	oil	30 ml		2½-3 cups	flour	625-750 ml

To the lukewarm water add the 1 tsp (5 ml) of sugar and sprinkle yeast over top. Let stand. Mix together milk, hot water, rolled oats, sugar, salt, oil and molasses. Add 1 cup (250 ml) flour and beat until smooth and elastic. Add the yeast mixture. Work in the pancake mix. Add sufficient flour to make a soft dough. Knead on a floured board or in a bowl until smooth and elastic. Grease the top. Cover and let rise in a warm place until double in bulk, about an hour. Punch down dough. Turn out and knead until smooth. Divide into two equal portions. Cover and let rest 10 minutes. Shape each portion into a loaf and place in greased, 9x5x3-inch (23x13x8 cm) pans. Cover and let rise about 40 minutes or until double in bulk. Bake 35-40 minutes at 350F (175C). Makes 2 loaves.

French Bread

2 cups	warm water	500 ml		2 tsp	salt	10 ml
1 pkg	yeast	1		5¾ cups	flour	1.5 L
1 tbsp	sugar	15 ml		1	egg white	1

Measure warm water into warmed bowl. Sprinkle dry yeast over water. Stir until dissolved. Add sugar, salt and 3 cups (750 ml) flour. Stir to mix, then beat until smooth and shiny. Stir in 2½ cups (625 ml) more flour. Sprinkle remaining ½ cup (125 ml) flour on breadboard. More or less flour may be needed. Turn out dough onto a board and knead until satiny smooth, 5-7 minutes. Shape into smooth ball. Rub bowl lightly with shortening. Place dough into greased bowl. Grease top of dough. Cover and let rise until doubled—about an hour. Punch down. Divide in halves. Shape each half into a ball. Cover and let rise 5 minutes. Rub a little shortening on hands, then hand roll each ball of dough to form a long slender loaf—about 3 inches in diameter. Do this several times to make a well-shaped loaf. Place loaves 4 inches apart on a lightly greased baking sheet. With a sharp knife cut diagonal gashes about ¾ inch (2 cm) deep into the top of each loaf and let rise until a little more than doubled—about one hour. Bake at 350-375F (175-190C). After baking about 15 minutes brush with slightly beaten egg white. Repeat this after 10 minutes. After baking for about 30-35 minutes, remove from baking sheet. Cool. Makes 2 loaves.

Scottish Oat Bread

½ cup	water, lukewarm	125 ml		1 cup	whole bran cereal	250 ml
1 tsp	sugar	5 ml		2 tbsp	sugar	30 ml
1 pkg	yeast, or 1 tbsp (15 ml) yeast	1		2 tsp	salt	10 ml
				2 tbsp	oil	30 ml
1 cup	evaporated milk	250 ml		¼ cup	molasses	50 ml
1 cup	hot water	250 ml		¾ cup	raisins	175 ml
1 cup	rolled oats	250 ml		4-5 cups	flour	1-1.25 L

To the lukewarm water, add 1 tsp sugar and sprinkle the yeast over top. Let stand. Mix together evaporated milk, hot water, rolled oats, bran, sugar, salt, oil and molasses. Add 1 cup flour, beat until smooth. Add raisins. Add yeast mixture and beat. Gradually add enough flour to make soft dough. Knead on board until smooth and elastic. Place in greased bowl. Grease top. Cover and let rise in warm place until double in bulk. Punch down dough. Divide into 2 equal portions. Cover and let rest 10 minutes. Shape each portion into a round ball and put into 1 lb coffee cans. Cover and let rise until double in bulk, about one hour. Bake at 350F (175C) for about 45-50 minutes or until done. Makes 2 loaves.

Shredded Wheat Bread

1 pkg	yeast	1		2 tsp	salt	10 ml
½ cup	warm water	125 ml		3	shredded wheat biscuits, broken into pieces	3
1 tsp	sugar	5 ml				
3 cups	boiling water	750 ml				
¾ cup	molasses	175 ml		7 cups	flour	about 1.75 L
2 tbsp	shortening	30 ml				

Dissolve sugar, then yeast in the ½ cup (125 ml) warm water. Place shredded wheat in a large bowl. Add molasses, shortening, and salt. Pour boiling water over all. Combine well. Let cool. Add yeast. Mix in enough flour to make stiff dough. Let rise until doubled in bulk. Make loaves and place in baking pans. Bake at 350F (175C) for about 45-50 minutes or until done. Makes 3 loaves.

Plain Raisin Bread

No spice but lots of sugar.

1 pkg	yeast	1	¾ cup	sugar	175 ml
1 cup	water, lukewarm	250 ml	4 tbsp	shortening	60 ml
1 cup	milk	250 ml	¾ cup	raisins	175 ml
6 cups	flour	1.5 L ·	1 tsp	salt	5 ml

Dissolve 1 tsp sugar, then yeast in water. Scald milk and add sugar and shortening. Stir and cool. Add 2 cups (500 ml) flour. Beat until smooth. Cover and let rise for 1½ hours. Then add raisins, salt and remaining flour. Knead and let rise again for about ½ hour. Punch down. Form into loaves and place in pans. Let rise until doubled in bulk. Bake at 350F for 45-50 minutes or (175C). Makes 3 loaves.

Judy's Raisin Bread

Smells so wonderful when baking!

2 pkg	yeast	2	12 cups	flour	3 L
2 tsp	white sugar	10 ml	¼ cup	brown sugar	50 ml
1 cup	water, lukewarm	250 ml	2 tbsp	salt	30 ml
3 cups	water, lukewarm	750 ml	1 lb	raisins, or more	500 g
1 cup	molasses	250 ml	1 tbsp	cinnamon, if desired	15 ml
¼ cup	butter, melted	50 ml			

Dissolve white sugar and yeast in 1 cup lukewarm water. Combine 3 cups lukewarm water, molasses, butter, brown sugar, cinnamon and salt. Stir dissolved yeast into molasses mixture and add raisins. Stir flour into mixture and knead for 10-12 minutes. Place in a greased bowl and let rise to about double in bulk for about 2½ hours. Divide dough; form into loaves. Place into greased pans and let rise for 1 hour. Bake at 350F (175C) for about 1 hour. Brush with melted butter while hot. Makes 4 loaves.

Buttermilk Loaf

1⅓ cups	buttermilk	335 ml
2 tbsp	butter	30 ml
1 tbsp	liquid honey	15 ml
1	egg, beaten	1
2¼ cups	flour	550 ml

1½ cups	whole wheat flour	375 ml
1¼ tsp	rapid or quick-rising yeast	6 ml
¾ tsp	salt	3 ml
2 tsp	milk	10 ml

In a saucepan, heat buttermilk, butter and honey until butter starts to melt; let cool. Whisk in egg. In a large bowl, stir together 1¾ cups (430 ml) all-purpose flour, whole wheat flour, yeast and salt. With a wooden spoon, add buttermilk mixture and beat until smooth. Gradually stir in enough of the remaining flour to form slightly sticky dough. Turn out onto a lightly floured board. Knead for 8-10 minutes or until smooth and elastic, dusting with as much of the remaining flour as necessary to prevent sticking. Place in greased bowl. Grease top and cover; let rise in a warm place until doubled in bulk. Punch down dough; turn out on board. Press out into 10x9-inch (25x23 cm) rectangle. Starting at narrow end roll into a log; pinch along bottom to seal. Place seam side down in a greased 9x5-inch (2 L) loaf pan. Cover with towel; let rise until about ½ inch (1 cm) above pan. Brush top of loaf with milk. Bake in centre of oven at 350F (175C) for 40-45 minutes or until golden brown and loaf tests done. Remove from pan and cool on rack. Makes 1 loaf.

Quick Cheese Bread

No kneading and only one rising.

3 tbsp	sugar	45 ml		1 tsp	salt	5 ml
½ cup	water, warm	125 ml		½ tsp	dry mustard	2 ml
1 pkg	yeast	1		¼ tsp	dry sage, if desired	1 ml
	or			4 cups	flour	1 L
1 tbsp	yeast	15 ml		1½ cups	old Cheddar cheese, shredded	375 ml
1 14-oz can	evaporated milk, warm	385 ml				
2 tbsp	vegetable oil	30 ml				

In a large bowl, dissolve 1 tsp (5 ml) of sugar in warm water. Sprinkle yeast over top; let stand for 10 minutes. Stir in remaining sugar. In a separate bowl, stir together warm milk, oil, salt, mustard and sage. Stir into yeast mixture. Beat in 3 cups (750 ml) of the flour, 1 cup (250 ml) at a time, beating well after each addition. Using a wooden spoon, stir in cheese, then remaining flour until a sticky dough forms. Transfer to a 9x5-inch (2 L) loaf pan, patting top to make level. Cover dough with greased wax paper, then a towel, and put in a warm place for about 1¼ hours, until the dough rises just above top of pan. Bake in centre of oven at 350F (175C) for about an hour. Top will be brown and sides should sound hollow when tapped. Turn out on rack and cool. Makes 1 loaf.

Florence's Potato Spice Bread

Dense, spicy and sweet!

1½ cups	water, boiling	375 ml		½ cup	shortening	125 ml
1 cup	potatoes, well mashed	250 ml		1 tsp	baking soda	5 ml
				2 tbsp	salt	30 ml
2 cups	brown sugar, divided	500 ml		1 tsp	nutmeg	5 ml
				1 tsp	cinnamon	5 ml
2 pkg	yeast	2		1 lb	seedless raisins, sticky	500 g
½ cup	water, lukewrm	125 ml				
1 tsp	sugar	5 ml		3-4 cups	flour	750 g-1 kg
2 cups	milk	500 ml				

Combine boiling water, mashed potatoes and 1 cup brown sugar, and let cool. Dissolve ½ tsp sugar and yeast in lukewarm water. When yeast is light, add to potato mixture. Add about 1½ cups (375 ml) flour and beat. Let mixture rise for 20 minutes. Meanwhile scald milk; add shortening and 1 cup (250 ml) of brown sugar. When cool add to yeast mixture. Add spices, salt and soda sifted with 2 more cups (500 ml) of flour. Mix well. Add raisins. Work in sufficient flour to make stiff dough. Knead until smooth and satiny. Grease and let rise until doubled in bulk. Punch down and form into loaves. Grease well. Bake 350F (175C) for 45-50 minutes or until done. Makes 4 loaves.

Cracked Wheat Bread

1 pkg	yeast	1	4-5 tbsp	sugar	60-75 ml
3 cups	cracked wheat	750 ml	5½ cups	water, or water and scalded milk	1.4 L
10 cups	white flour	2.5 L			
1 tbsp	salt	15 ml	2 tbsp	molasses	30 ml
4 tbsp	shortening	60 ml			

Dissolve 1 tsp of the sugar in ½ cup (125 ml) of the water (or water and milk mixture); add yeast and let stand 10-15 minutes. Dissolve remainder of sugar, salt, shortening and molasses in the remaining 5 cups of water (or water and milk). Cool to lukewarm; add yeast mixture and stir, working in the flour and cracked wheat (well mixed with white flour) until the dough is dry enough to knead without sticking to the hands. Knead well for 10 minutes until dough is smooth. Set in greased bowl. Cover and set in warm place free from drafts; let rise for about 1¼ hours or until double in bulk. Punch down; form into ball. Let rise again for about 30 minutes. Turn out onto a board and divide into loaves. Let sit for 20 minutes or so. Reshape loaves again. Grease each loaf with shortening and place in loaf pans. Let rise until double in bulk and bake at 350F (175C) for 50-60 minutes, according to size of loaf. Test for doneness before removing from oven. Remove from oven and cool on racks. If desired, the cracked wheat may be softened for 15 minutes in lukewarm water and drained before it is added to the dough mixture; this makes a softer bread. Makes 3-4 loaves.

Light Rye Bread

1 cup	water, lukewarm	250 ml		¼ cup	brown sugar	50 ml
1 tsp	sugar	5 ml		2 tsp	salt	10 ml
1 tbsp	yeast	15 ml		2 cups	rye flour	500 ml
1½ cups	buttermilk	375 ml			white flour, unbleached, as required	
¼ cup	butter or margarine, melted	50 ml				

Combine water, sugar and yeast and let stand for 10 minutes. In a mixing bowl, combine buttermilk, margarine, brown sugar, salt and yeast mixture. Add rye flour and mix well. Add white flour until dough is stiff enough to be turned onto floured board. Knead for 10 minutes, place in a greased bowl, cover and let rise until doubled. Form into 2 round or oblong loaves on a cookie sheet and let rise until doubled. Bake at 400F (200C) for 25 minutes. Makes 2 loaves.

Light Rye Bread II

1 cup	water, warm	250 ml		7 cups	water, warm	1.75 L
1 tsp	sugar	5 ml		5-6 cups	white flour, as required	1.25-1.5 L
2 tbsp	yeast	30 ml				
8 tsp	salt	40 ml		6 cups	rye flour	1.5 L
3 tbsp	margarine	45 ml				

Combine water, yeast and sugar and let stand for 10 minutes. Measure 6 cups (1.5 L) rye flour and salt in bowl. Cut in margarine as for piecrust. Add yeast mixture. Stir until well blended. Gradually add white flour to make a stiff dough. Knead for 10 minutes. Form into round ball. Coat with margarine. Cover with damp towel. Let rise 1½-2 hours. Shape into long loaves and place on greased and floured cookie sheets. Let rise 20 minutes. Bake at 375F (190C) for 45 minutes. Makes 4 loaves.

Cholla Bread

My mother often spoke of the delicious Challah or Cholla (egg bread) made by her Jewish neighbours in Glace Bay. Unfortunately, however, the recipe she used has been lost.

2 cups	milk	500 ml		1 tbsp	salt	15 ml
⅓ cup	butter	75 ml		4	eggs	4
¼ cup	water	50 ml		1 tbsp	cold water	15 ml
3½ cups	flour, unsifted	875 ml		½ tsp	poppy or sesame seeds	2 ml
2 pkgs	active dry yeast	2				
¼ cup	sugar	50 ml				

In a saucepan, heat milk, butter, and water until blended. In a large bowl, combine about 3 cups flour, yeast, sugar and salt. Blend in milk mixture and beat for 2 minutes with mixer at medium speed. Separate 1 egg, reserving yolk, and blend egg white and 3 eggs into batter. Add enough flour to make soft dough. Turn out onto floured board and knead until smooth. Place dough in greased bowl, turning once to grease top. Cover and let rise in warm place until doubled in bulk. Punch down. Turn onto floured board and divide into 2 pieces, one twice the size of the other. Divide larger piece into thirds, rolling each into a 15-inch (38 cm) rope. Braid tightly. Seal ends by pinching. Divide smaller rope into thirds and roll into 13-inch (33 cm) ropes. Braid. Place smaller braid on larger and seal ends. Place diagonally on greased baking sheet. Beat reserved yolk with water and brush loaf. Let rise until doubled. Sprinkle with seeds. Bake at 375F (190C) for 25-30 minutes. Makes 1 large loaf.

Portuguese Sweet Bread

1 tsp	sugar	5 ml	½ cup	potatoes, cooked and mashed	125 ml
¼ cup	water, warm	50 ml	¼ lb	butter	125 g
2 tbsp	sugar	30 ml	1½ tsp	salt	7 ml
2 cups	whole milk	500 ml	5	eggs	5
6 cups	flour	1.5 L	2 pkgs	yeast	2
1¼ cups	sugar	300 ml			

Potatoes should be cut in cubes, boiled using no salt and mashed using no milk or butter; allow to come to room temperature. Dissolve 1 pkg yeast and 1 tsp (5 ml) sugar in warm water. Add to potatoes along with 2 tbsp (30 ml) of sugar. Let stand about ½ hour until this mixture rises. In a mixing bowl, combine 2 cups (500 ml) of flour, 1 pkg yeast, 1¼ cups (300 ml) sugar and salt. Heat butter, add to flour, and mix until smooth. Beat eggs and add to mixture, along with potato mixture. Add remaining flour in sufficient quantities until dough is no longer sticky. Turn out onto a lightly floured board and knead for 6-10 minutes. Place in greased bowl, turning to grease top, cover bowl with plastic wrap and let rise until doubled. Mold into buns or round loaves. Let rise again. Brush flour, melted butter and milk, or egg white and sugar, over tops of buns or loaves. Bake at 350F (175C) until golden brown, about 40-45 minutes. Remove to rack and cool. Makes 3 loaves.

German Rye Bread

2 pkgs	yeast	2	½ cup	molasses	125 ml
½ cup	water, warm	125 ml	2 tbsp	butter	30 ml
1½ cups	milk, lukewarm	375 ml	3¼ cups	rye flour	800 ml
2 tbsp	white sugar	30 ml	2½ cups	bread flour	625 ml
1 tsp	salt	5 ml			

Dissolve yeast in warm water. In a large bowl, combine milk, sugar and salt. Use a mixer to beat in molasses, butter, yeast mixture and 1 cup (250 ml) rye flour. Use wooden spoon to mix in the remaining rye flour. Add white flour by stirring until the dough is stiff enough to knead. Knead 5-10 minutes, adding flour as needed. If the dough sticks to your hands or board, add more flour. Cover dough and let rise 1–1½ hours or until doubled. Punch down dough and divide to form two round loaves. Let loaves rise on a greased baking sheet until doubled, about 1½ hours. Preheat oven to 375F (190C). Bake for 30-35 minutes. Makes 2 loaves.

Third Bread

2 cups	water, warm	500 ml	1 cup	rye flour	250 ml
1 pkg	yeast	1	3 cups	white flour	750 ml
½ cup	molasses	125 ml	1 cup	yellow cornmeal	250 ml
1 tsp	salt	5 ml			

In a large bowl, stir the yeast into warm water and let stand for 5 minutes to dissolve. Add the molasses and salt and stir well. Beat in the rye flour, white flour and cornmeal. Cover and put in a warm place until the dough doubles in bulk. Beat again briefly and divide into two loaves. Place in greased loaf pans, cover and let double in bulk once again. Preheat oven to 375F (190C). Bake bread for about 45 minutes. Remove from pans and cool on racks. No kneading required. Makes 2 loaves.

Cornmeal Bread

1½ cups	cornmeal	375 ml	1 pkg	yeast	1
4 tbsp	butter	60 ml	¼ cup	water, warm	50 ml
1¾ tsp	salt	9 ml	½ cup	milk	125 ml
1½ cups	water, boiling	375 ml	3-4 cups	flour	875 ml-1 L

Place cornmeal, butter and salt in a large bowl. Add boiling water and stir until butter is melted. Set aside to cool until just warm. Dissolve yeast in warm water. Stir into cornmeal mixture and blend well. Stir in milk and add flour one cup (250 ml) at a time, blending well to form a dough. Turn dough onto a lightly floured board and knead for 5-10 minutes, adding flour as necessary to keep dough from sticking. Place dough in oiled bowl, cover with damp cloth and let rise until doubled in size. Punch down and knead 5 minutes. Return to bowl and allow to rise until doubled again. Knead for 1-2 minutes. Place in a 9-inch round baking pan and cover. Let rise about 40 minutes or until doubled in size. Bake 45-50 minutes at 350F (175C), or until bread pulls away from the edges of the pan. Makes 1 loaf.

Portuguese Corn Bread

1½ cups	cornmeal	375 ml		1 tsp	sugar	5 ml
1½ tsp	ground pepper	7 ml		¼ cup	hot water	50 ml
1½ tsp	salt	7 ml		1 tbsp	olive oil	15 ml
1 cup	boiling water	250 ml		2 cups	bread flour	500 ml
1 pkg	rapid-rise yeast	1				

Mix 1 cup (250 ml) cornmeal, pepper and salt in the large bowl of an electric mixer fitted with dough hook. Add boiling water and mix until smooth. Let cool to lukewarm. Mix in yeast and sugar, then hot water and oil (that has cooled to lukewarm). Mix in remaining ½ cup (125 ml) cornmeal. Add 1 cup (250 ml) flour and mix until smooth and elastic, about 5 minutes. Cover bowl with damp towel and let dough rise in warm, draft-free area until puffy, about 45 minutes. Grease 9-inch (23 cm) metal pan with oil. Knead enough bread flour into dough to make it non-sticky. Knead on a floured surface until smooth and elastic, about 5 minutes. Knead into a ball. Place in pan. Flatten to fill bottom of pan. Cover with towel; let rise in warm, draft-free area until doubled in size, about 1 hour. Preheat oven to 350F (175C). Score top of bread in a tick-tack-toe pattern. Bake until bread is light brown on top and sounds hollow when tapped on bottom, about 45 minutes. Remove from pan; cool on rack. Serve warm or at room temperature. Can be made 1 day ahead. If so, cool bread and wrap. Before serving, wrap in foil and warm in 350F (175C) oven for 15 minutes. Makes 1 loaf.

Twelve-Grain Bread
for Breadmaker

1⅓ cups	water	325 ml		2 cups	white flour	500 ml
3 tbsp	honey	45 ml		¾ cup	whole wheat flour	175 ml
2 tbsp	butter or margarine	30 ml		¾ cup	12 grain cereal	175 ml
1½ tsp	salt	7 ml		2 tsp	breadmaker yeast	10 ml

The 12-grain cereal may be purchased at a health food store. Follow the directions for your breadmaker.

Brioche

2 pkgs	yeast	2	½ cup	sugar	125 ml
1 cup	warm milk	250 ml	1½ tsp	salt	7 ml
⅔ cup	butter	150 ml	1	lemon rind, grated	1
1	egg	1			
4	egg yolks	4	5½ cups	white flour	1.4 L

In a large mixing bowl, stir sugar and yeast into milk and let stand for 5 minutes to dissolve. Add butter, egg, egg yolks, lemon rind and about 2½ cups (625 ml) flour. Beat thoroughly, then add as much of the remaining flour as necessary for dough to handle easily. Turn out onto a lightly floured board. Knead for a minute or two and let rest for 10 minutes. Continue to knead until smooth and elastic. Put the dough in a large, buttered bowl, cover, and let rise in a warm place until doubled in bulk. Punch down and let it rise again until slightly less than doubled in bulk (at least 4 hours) or place in a covered bowl in the refrigerator overnight. Butter a loaf pan and a 6-cup muffin pan and form loaf and rolls to fill pans one-third full. Cover and let double once again. Preheat oven to 375F (190C). Bake bread, allowing 20 minutes for the muffins and 45 minutes for the bread. Remove from pans and cool on racks. Makes 1 loaf and 6 muffins.

Stollen

A rich, sweet dough—well suited to festive trimmings.

1 pkg	yeast	1
¼ cup	water, warm	50 ml
¾ cup	warm milk	175 ml
¼ cup	granulated sugar	50 ml
½ tsp	salt	2 ml

4 tbsp	butter, softened	60 ml
2	eggs	2
3 cups	flour	750 ml
1 tbsp	lemon rind, grated	15 ml
½ cup	almonds, chopped	125 ml
¾ cup	candied fruit	175 ml

Glaze:

1 cup	icing sugar	250 ml
2 tbsp	lemon juice	30 ml
1-2 tbsp	water	15-30 ml

Stir yeast into warm water and let stand to dissolve. Mix the milk, sugar, salt, butter and eggs in a large mixing bowl. Add dissolved yeast; beat thoroughly and add 1½ cups (375 ml) of flour, beating until well blended. Cover the bowl and let rise in warm place for about 1 hour. Add enough of the remaining flour so the dough is easy to handle. Cover and chill in the refrigerator for about 30 minutes. Turn out onto a floured board and knead for a few minutes with lemon rind, almonds and candied fruit. Pat one half the dough into an oval ¼ inch thick. Fold the dough in half lengthwise, bringing the upper half not quite to the edge of the lower half. Press down along the edge to secure. Repeat for another loaf. Place on buttered cookie sheets; cover and let double in bulk. Preheat oven to 375F (190C). Bake stollen for 35 minutes. Mix the sugar, lemon juice and 1-2 tbsp (15-30 ml) water, and glaze the loaf while it is still warm. Decorate with garnish of candied fruit and nuts. Makes 2 loaves.

Stollen Dough
Coffee Cake

Prepare the dough for stollen, omitting the lemon rind, almonds, and candied fruit. Roll it in a log about 1 inch (2.5 cm) in diameter. Cut off 1-inch (2.5 cm) pieces and form them into balls. Dip each ball into melted butter, then in a sugar-cinnamon mixture—using 1 tbsp (15 ml) of cinnamon to ½ cup (125 ml) sugar. Arrange the dough in 2 layers in a buttered 10-inch (25 cm) tube pan, sprinkling each layer with raisins. Bake at 350F (175C) for 50-60 minutes.

Breakfast Wreaths

Great anytime.

2 pkgs	yeast	2	½ tsp	cinnamon	2 ml
1 cup	milk, lukewarm	250 ml	¼ cup	chopped nuts, if desired	50 ml
4 cups	flour	1 L			
1 cup	butter	250 ml	2 tbsp	orange peel, grated	30 ml
½ cup	sugar	125 ml	½ cup	raisins	125 ml
2	eggs	2	½ cup	candied cherries	125 ml
1 tsp	salt	5 ml			

Dissolve yeast in lukewarm milk. Add 1 cup of flour to the dissolved yeast mixture and mix well. Cover and allow to rise in a warm place until light—about 30 minutes. Cream the butter, add the sugar and continue to cream until light and fluffy. Add eggs, one at a time, beating after each addition. Beat in yeast mixture. Add remaining 3 cups (750 ml) of flour, which has been sifted with salt and cinnamon. Add nuts, peel, raisins and cherries. Mix well. Place the dough in a greased bowl, cover and allow to rise in warm place until double in bulk. Place on floured board and knead until smooth and elastic. Roll dough to ½ inch (1 cm) thickness and cut into narrow strips. Flour hands and roll strips between palms until 8 inches (20 cm) long. Braid the strips 3 at a time. Shape into wreath. Let rise 30 minutes. Bake at 350F (175C) oven 20-30 minutes. Frost with white icing. Decorate with cherries and nuts. Makes 2 wreaths.

Homemade Bagels

2 cups	warm water	500 ml		3 quarts	water with 1 tbsp (15 ml) sugar	3 L
2 pkgs	yeast	2			cornmeal	
3 tbsp	sugar	45 ml		1	egg yolk, beaten with 1 tbsp (15 ml) water	1
3 tsp	salt	15 ml				
5¾ cups	all-purpose flour, unsifted	1.4 L				

Combine water and yeast in the large bowl of an electric mixer; let stand 5 minutes. Stir in sugar and salt; gradually mix in 4 cups of the flour. Beat at medium speed for 5 minutes. With a spoon, mix in about 1¼ cup (300 ml) more flour to make stiff dough. Turn out onto a floured board and knead until smooth, elastic and no longer sticky, about 15 minutes; add more flour as needed (dough should be firmer than for most other yeast breads). Place in a greased bowl, cover and let rise in a warm place until almost double, about 40 minutes. Knead dough lightly, then divide into 12 equal pieces. To shape, knead each piece, forming it into a smooth ball. Holding ball with both hands, poke your thumbs through the centre. With one thumb in the hole, work around perimeter, shaping bagel like a doughnut, 3-3½ inches (8-9.5 cm) across. Place shaped bagels on a lightly floured board, cover lightly, and let stand in a warm place for 20 minutes. Bring the water and sugar mixture to boiling in a 4 or 5-qt (4 or 5 L) pan; adjust heat to keep it boiling gently.

Lightly grease a baking sheet and sprinkle with cornmeal. Gently lift one bagel at a time and drop into water; boil about 4 at a time, turning often, for 5 minutes. Lift out with a slotted spatula, drain briefly on a towel, and place on the baking sheet. Brush bagels with the egg yolk glaze and bake in a 400F (200C) oven for about 35-40 minutes or until well browned and crusty. Cool on a rack.

Whole Wheat Bagels:

Follow basic recipe, omitting sugar; use 3 tbsp (45 ml) honey instead. In place of the flour, use 2 cups (500 ml) whole wheat flour, ½ cup wheat germ (125 ml), and about 2¾ cups (680 ml) all-purpose flour. Mix in all the whole wheat flour and wheat germ, and 1¼ cups (300 ml) all-purpose flour before beating dough. Then mix in about 1½ cups (375 ml) more all-purpose flour, knead and continue as directed.

Pumpernickel Bagels:
Follow basic recipe, omitting sugar; instead use 3 tbsp (45 ml) dark molasses. In place of flour use 2 cups (500 ml) each rye and whole wheat flours and about 1¾ cups (4300 ml) all-purpose flour. Add all of the rye and 1 cup (250 ml) each of the whole wheat and all-purpose flours before beating dough. Then add remaining 1 cup of whole wheat and about ¾ cups more all-purpose flour; knead and continue as directed.

More Bagel Variety:
Try adding ½ cup (125 ml) instant toasted onion to the whole wheat or basic bagels; add it to the yeast mixture along with the sugar and salt. Or sprinkle ½ tsp (2 ml) poppy or sesame seeds or ¼ tsp (1 ml) coarse salt on each glazed bagel before baking. Or add 1 tbsp (15 ml) caraway seed to pumpernickel bagels, then sprinkle with ½ tsp (2 ml) more caraway seed before baking.

Some like to use a beaten egg to replace some of the required water or milk.

Butter Bagels

Combine:

1 cup	milk, scalded	250 ml
¼ cup	butter	50 ml

1 tbsp	sugar	15 ml
1 tsp	salt	5 ml

When the mixture is lukewarm, add and dissolve for 3 minutes:

Blend in:

2	eggs	2
3¾ cups	flour	930 ml

1 pkg	yeast	1

Knead this soft dough for 10 minutes, adding more flour if necessary to make it firm enough to handle. Let rise, covered in a greased bowl, until doubled in bulk. Punch down and roll into a rectangular shape. Divide into 18 pieces. Roll each piece into a rope 7 inches long, and taper and overlap the ends, to form a doughnut-shaped ring. Let rise, covered, on a floured board about 15 minutes. Drop rings, one at a time, into a solution of:

2 quarts	water, almost boiling	2 L
1 tbsp	sugar	15 ml

As the bagels surface, turn them over and cook about 3 minutes longer. Skim out and place on an ungreased baking sheet. Coat with beaten egg whites. Bake in a preheated 400F (200C) oven 20-25 minutes until golden and crisp. To the basic dough, try adding spices, dried onion flakes or currants. Poppy seeds or sesame seeds may be shaken on before baking.

English Muffins

1 cup	water	250 ml		1 tsp	salt	5 ml
¾ cup	milk	175 ml		3½-4 cups	flour	875 ml-1 L
3 tbsp	butter	45 ml		2 tbsp	cornmeal butter	30 ml
1¾ cups	flour	430 ml				
1 pkg	yeast	1				
2 tbsp	sugar	30 ml				

Heat water, milk and butter to 120F (48C). In the large bowl of an electric mixer, combine 1¾ cups (430 ml) flour, yeast, sugar, salt and warmed water mixture. Mix well until smooth. Add 3½ cups (875 ml) flour. Continue mixing until smooth. If still sticky, knead in more flour to make a stiff dough. Place dough in greased bowl. Cover and let rise in a warm place for 30 minutes. Punch down and turn onto a board sprinkled with cornmeal. Roll dough ½ inch (1.3 cm) thick. Cut with a floured 3-inch (7 cm) round cookie cutter. Cover. Let rise 30 minutes. Preheat skillet on medium-low heat and lightly butter. Brown muffins, cornmeal side down, 15-20 minutes. Turn and cook for 15-20 minutes longer. Cool on wire rack. Makes 18-20 muffins.

Scuffles

1 pkg	yeast	1		1 cup	butter or margarine	250 ml
¼ cup	water, lukewarm	50 ml		½ cup	milk	125 ml
3 cups	flour	750 ml		2	eggs, slightly beaten	2
3 tbsp	white sugar	45 ml		1 cup	white sugar	250 ml
½ tsp	salt	2 ml		2 tbsp	butter or margarine	30 ml

Soak yeast in lukewarm water for 10-15 minutes. As you would for piecrust, mix flour, sugar, salt and margarine. Then add milk, eggs and softened yeast. Knead dough until smooth. Place in a bowl and let stand in refrigerator overnight. Divide the dough into 4-6 parts. Roll out dough as you would a pie crust and sprinkle both sides of the dough with a mixture of 1 cup (250 ml) white sugar and 2 tbsp (30 ml) melted butter. Cut in 8 or 12 wedges as you would a pie. Roll up each wedge from wide end to the narrow end. Bake 15 minutes at 350F (175C). This dough does not need to rise before baking.

Bread Pretzels or Sticks

Combine in a mixing bowl:

1 cup	water, lukewarm	250 ml
1 pkg	yeast	1

When dissolved, add and beat at least 3 minutes:

1½ cups	flour	375 ml		½ tsp	salt	2 ml
2 tbsp	butter, softened	30 ml		1 tbsp	sugar	15 ml

Sift in:

1¼ cups flour		300 ml

Knead dough until it loses its stickiness. Let rise in greased, covered bowl until doubled in bulk. Punch down and divide into 12 equal pieces for pretzels or 36 pieces for sticks. With your palm, roll the 12 pretzel pieces into 18-inch (45 cm) lengths, about pencil thickness, tapering the ends slightly. Loop into a twisted pretzel shape. Place on an ungreased baking sheet and let rise until almost double in bulk. Preheat oven to 475F (245C). In a non-aluminum pot, have ready an almost-boiling solution of:

4 cups	water	1 L
5 tbsp	baking soda	75 ml

With a slotted spoon, carefully lower the pretzels into the hot solution for a minute or until they float to the surface. Return them to the baking sheet. Sprinkle with coarse salt. Bake until crispy and brown, about 12 minutes (sticks take less time). They are best served at once, but will keep for a few days in an airtight container.

Rivel Kuchen— German Coffee Cake

1 pkg	yeast	1	1½ cups	white sugar	375 ml
¼ cup	water, warm	50 ml	3 cups	water	750 ml
1 tsp	white sugar	5 ml	3 tbsp	all-purpose flour	45 ml
2 cups	milk	500 ml	¾ cup	milk	175 ml
½ cup	sugar	125 ml	1½ tsp	allspice	7 ml
½ cup	shortening	125 ml	1 cup	all-purpose flour	250 ml
2 tsp	salt	10 ml	¼ cup	butter or margarine	50 ml
2	eggs, well beaten	2	1 tbsp	white sugar	15 ml
7 cups	all-purpose flour	1.75 L	¼ tsp	ground cinnamon	1 ml

Dissolve yeast in ¼ cup (50 ml) warm water to which 1 tsp (5 ml) of sugar has been added. Scald milk; add ½ cup sugar, shortening and salt. Cool to lukewarm. Beat in eggs. Add flour (enough to make medium thick batter) and beat well. Add yeast mixtures. Beat well. Stir in the remaining flour. When too thick to mix by spoon, pour onto a floured board. Knead dough until smooth and elastic. Put dough into greased bowl, and let rise until double in size. Divide into 2 parts. Knead each down, and roll out to fit 13x9-inch (33x23 cm) pan. While dough is rising, prepare the following: Put 1½ cups (375 ml) sugar into heavy skillet and brown, stirring all the time. Add 3 cups water. Cook until sugar is dissolved. Stir together 3 tbsp (45 ml) flour and ¾ cup (175 ml) milk; add to the sugar water. Cook until mixture is thick like gravy. Cool. Add allspice. Spread on unbaked coffee cakes. Mix 1 cup flour, butter or margarine, sugar, and cinnamon until crumbly. Sprinkle rivels mixture over coffee cake. Bake at 350F (175C) for 25 minutes, or until golden brown.

Shortcake Biscuits

This recipe was given to me by my sister-in-law, Elda Foster, who lives in the Annapolis Valley near a huge field of luscious strawberries.

2 cups	flour	500 ml		1 tsp	salt	5 ml
⅓ cup	sugar	75 ml		½ cup	shortening	125 ml
3½ tsp	baking powder	17 ml		1 cup	milk	250 ml

Sift flour, sugar, baking powder and salt into mixing bowl. Cut in shortening. Add milk. Stir together and turn out onto a floured board and knead. Roll ¾ inch thick. Bake at 425F (220C) for 14-16 minutes.

Marion's Mile-High Biscuits

3 cups	flour	750 ml		4½ tsp	baking powder	22 ml
¾ tsp	cream of tartar	3 ml		2 tbsp	sugar	30 ml
¾ tsp	salt	3 ml		¾ cup	shortening	175 ml
1	egg	1		1 cup	milk	250 ml

In a mixing bowl, sift together flour, cream of tartar, salt, baking powder and sugar. Cut in shortening. Add egg to milk and beat together with fork. Stir into dry ingredients. Turn out on board and knead 3 minutes. Cut with round cutter. Bake at 450F (230C) for about 12 minutes.

Cheese Scones

No rolling! No cutting!

3 cups	flour	750 ml		2 cups	old cheese, grated or cut in small pieces	500 ml
2 tbsp	sugar	30 ml				
4 tsp	baking powder	20 ml		1 cup	milk	250 ml
½ tsp	salt	2 ml		1 tbsp	vinegar	15 ml
½ tsp	baking soda	2 ml		1	egg	1
½ cup	butter, cut in small pieces	125 ml				

In a bowl combine flour, sugar, baking powder, soda and salt. With pastry blender cut in butter until crumbly. Cut in cheese. In small bowl, whisk together milk, vinegar and egg. Add egg mixture to dry mixture, gently stirring with fork until moistened. Spoon into 12 mounds on lightly greased baking sheet. Bake at 300F (200C) for 20-25 minutes or until lightly browned.

Allison's Biscuits Supreme

The secret to good biscuits is a hot oven.

2 cups	flour, sifted	500 ml		2 tsp	sugar	10 ml
½ tsp	salt	2 ml		½ cup	shortening	125 ml
4 tsp	baking powder	20 ml		⅔ cup	milk, less 1 tbsp (15 ml)	150 ml
½ tsp	cream of tartar	2 ml				

Measure flour, salt, baking powder, cream of tartar and sugar in mixing bowl. Add shortening and cut into dry ingredients with a pastry blender. Scoop a well in flour mixture and add milk all at once. Stir until dough follows fork around bowl. Turn out onto a board and knead gently about 15 times. Roll to desired thickness. Cut into rounds. Bake at 450-475F (230-243C) for 15 minutes.

Cheddar Cheese Biscuits:
Add ½ cup (125 ml) grated old Cheddar cheese after the shortening has been cut into the dry ingredients.

Maple Cakes

A plain biscuit, but all dressed up.

7 tbsp	butter, divided	105 ml		2 tsp	baking powder	10 ml
½ cup	maple syrup	125 ml		½ tsp	salt	2 ml
1 cup	white flour	250 ml		⅓ cup	milk	75 ml

Melt 4 tbsp (60 ml) butter and pour into a 8x8-inch (20x20 cm) cake pan. Stir in maple syrup. Sift flour, baking powder and salt into a small bowl. Cut in 3 tbsp (45 ml) butter until it resembles cornmeal. Stir in milk. Gently knead the dough in bowl, enough to form a ball. Pat on board to about ½-inch thickness (1 cm). Cut with biscuit cutter. Place on mixture in pan. Bake at 375F (190C) for 15 minutes. Can be enjoyed as a dessert or a breakfast surprise.

Whole Wheat Biscuits

1 cup	whole wheat flour	250 ml		¼ cup	shortening	50 ml
1 cup	white flour	250 ml		⅞-1 cup	milk	220-250 ml
4½ tsp	baking powder	22 ml		2 tsp	sugar, if desired	10 ml
½ tsp	salt	2 ml				

Mix and sift dry ingredients. Cut in shortening. Make a hollow in the centre of dry ingredients. Add milk slowly to make a soft dough. When liquid is all added, stir vigorously until dough comes away from sides of bowl—about 5-6 strokes of the spoon. Dough should be soft, not sticky. Knead dough on a lightly floured board for a few seconds. Cut dough with floured cutter and place in pan. Bake at 450F (225C) for 12-15 minutes until biscuits are nicely browned.

Tea Biscuits

Jean Taggart has served countless numbers of these delicious biscuits to family and friends.

2 cups	flour	500 ml		2 tsp	sugar	10 ml
½ tsp	salt	2 ml		½ cup	butter	125 ml
4 tsp	baking powder	20 ml		⅔ cup	milk	150 ml
¼ tsp	cream of tartar	1 ml				

Sift dry ingredients together in a bowl. Cut butter into dry ingredients, until mixture resembles coarse crumbs. Add milk all at once. Stir with fork until mixture leaves sides of bowl. Knead 10 times on lightly floured board. Roll or pat dough to ½-inch (1 cm) thickness. Cut with floured biscuit cutter. Bake at 450F (230C) for 10-12 minutes.

Buttermilk Biscuits

2 cups	all-purpose flour	500 ml		5 tbsp	vegetable shortening, chilled	75 ml
4 tsp	baking powder	20 ml		2 tbsp	butter or margarine, chilled	30 ml
¾ tsp	salt	3 ml				
½ tsp	baking soda	2 ml		1 cup	buttermilk	250 ml

Preheat oven to 425F (220C). In a large bowl, sift the flour, baking powder, salt and baking soda. Blend the shortening and butter into the flour mixture until coarse crumbs form. Add the buttermilk, mixing with a fork until a dough forms. Place the dough on a floured surface, form into a ball and knead a few times just until smooth. (You can make the dough a few hours ahead and refrigerate until ready to use.) Pat the dough to a ¾-inch thickness. Using a 2-inch biscuit cutter, cut out the biscuits. Place on an ungreased baking sheet. Reform trimmings to ¾ inch (2 cm) thick, and cut more biscuits. Repeat until all dough is used. Bake the biscuits until golden, 12-15 minutes. For added flavour and richness, brush the tops with melted butter. Serve hot!

Cloud Biscuits

For light and fluffy biscuits, just add an egg.

2 cups	flour	500 ml	⅔ cup	milk	150 ml
4 tsp	baking powder	20 ml	1	egg	1
1 tbsp	sugar	15 ml	½ cup	shortening	125 ml
½ tsp	salt	2 ml			

Sift dry ingredients. Cut in shortening until it resembles coarse crumbs. Combine milk and egg. Add to flour mixture all at once. Stir until dough follows flour around bowl. Turn out onto floured board. Knead gently with heel of hand 20 times. Roll out to ¾-inch (2 cm) thickness. Dip cutter in flour and cut straight down. Bake at 450F (230C) for 10-14 minutes.

Creamy Biscuits

2 cups	flour	500 ml	½ cup	sour cream	125 ml
2½ tsp	baking powder	12 ml	½ cup	milk	125 ml
½ tsp	salt	2 ml	2-3 tbsp	butter, melted	30-45 ml
2 tsp	sugar	10 ml			

Preheat oven to 425F (220C). Sift together flour, baking powder, salt and sugar. Make a well in the centre and add blended sour cream and milk. Mix only until soft dough is formed. Turn onto a lightly floured board and knead gently for 5-6 seconds. Gently pat or roll to 1-inch (2.5 cm) thickness and cut out with floured cutter. Dip each side in the melted butter, and place 2 inches (5 cm) apart on an ungreased sheet and bake 15-20 minutes.

Scottish Oat Scones

We owe our Scottish ancestors for these old favourites.

1½ cups	all-purpose flour	375 ml		½ cup	currants	125 ml
2 cups	rolled oats	500 ml		1	egg, beaten	1
¼ cup	white sugar	50 ml		½ cup	butter or margarine, melted	125 ml
4 tsp	baking powder	20 ml				
½ tsp	salt	2 ml		⅓ cup	milk	75 ml

Combine flour, oats, sugar, baking powder, salt and currants in a large bowl. Mix well. Make a well in centre. Beat egg until frothy, and mix in melted butter or margarine and milk. Pour into well. Stir to make a soft dough. Pat dough into two 6-inch (15x17.5 cm) circles. Transfer to greased baking sheet. Score each top into 8 pie-shaped wedges. Bake at 425F (220C) for 15 minutes, until risen and browned.

Raisin Scones

A little lighter than the Scottish scones.

2⅓ cup	flour	585 ml		2	eggs	2
6 tbsp	butter	90 ml		2 tsp	sugar	10 ml
2½ tsp	baking powder	12 ml		½ cup	raisins	125 ml
5 tbsp	milk	75 ml			sugar for topping	
½ tsp	salt	2 ml				

Preheat oven to 450F (225C). In a large bowl, sift flour, baking powder, salt and 2 tsp (10 ml) sugar. Cut butter into flour until mixture resembles cornmeal. Blend in raisins. Separate 1 egg, reserving 1 tbsp (15 ml) egg white. Beat eggs and milk and stir into flour mixture. Roll out dough on floured surface. Cut into 3-inch (7.5 cm) squares, then cut each square into 2 triangles. Arrange on cookie sheet. Brush with reserved egg white that has been slightly beaten. Sprinkle with sugar. Bake 10-15 minutes until golden brown.

Bran and Oat Scones

1 cup	Nabisco bran cereal	250 ml
1 cup	rolled oats, quick cooking	250 ml
½ cup	raisins	125 ml
1 cup	plain yogurt	250 ml
1 cup	flour	250 ml
¼ cup	sugar	50 ml

1 tbsp	baking powder	15 ml
1 tsp	baking soda	5 ml
½ tsp	salt	2 ml
½ tsp	cinnamon	2 ml
¼ tsp	nutmeg	1 ml
⅓ cup	butter	75 ml

Topping:

¼ cup	bran cereal	50 ml
2 tbsp	milk	30 ml

Combine cereal, oats, raisins and yogurt; let stand to soften. Combine flour, sugar, baking powder, soda, salt, cinnamon and nutmeg in a large bowl. Cut in butter until crumbly. Add cereal mixture and stir just until moistened. Turn out onto a floured board and knead 10 times. Place on a greased cookie sheet and flatten to a 9-inch (23 cm) circle. Score surface into 12 wedges. Spoon topping over surface. Bake at 425F (220C) for about 20-25 minutes or until done.

Pineapple Coconut Scones

Sometimes you can improve on perfection.

2 cups	white flour	500 ml
1 cup	whole wheat flour	250 ml
2 tsp	baking powder	10 ml
½ cup	butter	125 ml
½ cup	coconut, dried and unsweetened	125 ml

1	egg	1
1 cup	honey	250 ml
½ cup	pineapple, canned, drained and crushed	125 ml
⅓ cup	milk	75 ml

Blend together white flour, baking powder and whole wheat flour in a large bowl. Rub in butter until it resembles cornmeal. Stir in coconut. Blend together egg, honey, pineapple and milk in a small bowl. Lightly stir liquids into flour mixture until blended. Do not overmix. Turn out onto a floured board, and knead gently to form a 2½x12-inch (7.5x30 cm) log. With a sharp knife, cut off rounds 1 inch (2.5 cm) wide. Place on greased cookie sheet. Bake at 425F (220C) for 15 minutes until lightly browned.

Spicy-Oat Scones

When the family gets a whiff of these oat scones cooling on the kitchen table, they'll all come running.

1½ cups	sifted flour	375 ml
3 tbsp	baking powder	45 ml
½ tsp	salt	2 ml
2 tbsp	sugar	30 ml
¼ tsp	nutmeg	1 ml
¼ tsp	allspice	1 ml

½ tsp	lemon rind, grated	2 ml
⅓ cup	butter	75 ml
½ cup	rolled oats	125 ml
½ cup	currants	125 ml
⅔ cup	milk	150 ml

Sift flour, baking powder, salt, sugar and allspice. Stir in nutmeg and lemon rind. Cut in butter until the mixture resembles cornmeal. Stir in rolled oats and currants. Add milk and mix lightly until dough leaves the sides of bowl. Turn dough out onto board and knead for a few seconds. Roll out dough to ½-inch (1 cm) thickness. Brush with melted butter and sprinkle with sugar. Cut into triangles and place on baking sheet. Bake at 450F (230C) for 20-30 minutes. Cool on rack. Serve warm with butter.

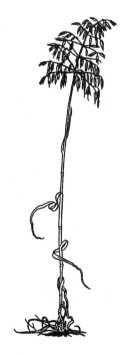

Bannock

An old Scottish favourite that never disappoints.

3 cups	all-purpose flour	750 ml		1½ cups	water	375 ml
1 tsp	salt	5 ml			blueberries or	
2 tbsp	baking powder	30 ml			raisins, if desired	
¼ cup	butter or margarine, melted	50 ml				

Measure flour, salt and baking powder into a large bowl. Add blueberries or raisins. Stir to mix. Pour melted butter and water over flour mixture. Stir with a fork to make a ball. Turn dough out onto a lightly floured surface, and knead gently about 10 times. Pat into a flat circle ¾-1 inch (2-2.5 cm) thick. Cook in a greased frying pan over medium heat, allowing about 15 minutes for each side. Use two lifters for easy turning. May also be baked on a greased baking sheet at 350F (175C) for 25-30 minutes. Makes 1 loaf.

Traditional Irish Soda Bread

Contains no shortening.

1 lb	whole wheat flour	450 g		10 oz	buttermilk or sour milk	300 ml
1 tsp	baking soda	5 ml				
1 tsp	salt	5 ml				

Sift the flour, baking soda and salt in a bowl. Add milk and mix to a smooth dough with your hands. If you do not have buttermilk or sour milk, add a little vinegar or lemon juice to fresh milk. Place on a floured board, knead lightly and roll into a round shape. Place on a greased baking sheet and cut a deep cross in the centre. Bake at 400F (200C) for about 40 minutes. The bread should sound hollow when tapped. If the bottom seems under-done, turn it upside down and bake for a few minutes more. Wrap the freshly cooked bread in a clean tea towel as it cools. This helps to keep the crust soft.

Irish Soda Bread

A quick bread that rises in the oven.

4 cups	flour	1 L	1 tbsp	sugar	15 ml
2 tsp	baking powder	10 ml	¼ cup	shortening	50 ml
1 tsp	baking soda	5 ml	1¾-2 cups	buttermilk	430-500 ml
½ tsp	salt	2 ml			

Measure dry ingredients and sift together. Cut in shortening. Stir in buttermilk to make stiff dough. Knead slightly and form into round loaf. Set on a greased cookie sheet. Cut a deep cross in the top with a wet knife. Shake a dusting of flour on top. Bake at 400F (200C) for 15 minutes. Reduce heat to 350F (175C) and continue baking 40 minutes. The deep cross-cut in the top helps to reduce baking time. Serve warm with assorted cheeses.

Dough Boys or "Grunt"

No need for bread when these dumplings are added to a stew.

2 cups	flour	500 ml	2 tbsp	shortening	30 ml
4 tsp	baking powder	20 ml	1 cup	milk	250 ml
½ tsp	salt	2 ml			

In a mixing bowl, sift together flour, baking powder and salt. Cut in shortening. Add milk and stir only until combined. Add dough by dessert spoon. Dip the spoon into liquid of stew to clean off dough before dipping into dough again. Care must be taken to have only enough liquid to almost cover vegetables, so that dumplings sit on the vegetables rather than float on the liquid. When all the dumplings are added, wait a minute, then cover with a tight-fitting lid. Do not lift the lid for about 10 minutes. Seasoning such as savoury, parsley or onion powder may be added to the dough if it is to be used with meat stews. These dumplings may be used with boiled fruits—if so, flavour with lemon zest or cinnamon. Add 2 tbsp sugar to the dumpling dough. This dessert is often referred to as "grunt."

All Bran Molasses Hot Bread

Fragrant, hearty and tempting.

1 cup	All Bran cereal	250 ml	1	egg	1
½ cup	raisins, seedless	125 ml	1 cup	flour	250 ml
2 tbsp	shortening	30 ml	1 tsp	baking soda	5 ml
½ cup	molasses	125 ml	½ tsp	salt	2 ml
¾ cup	hot water	175 ml	½ tsp	cinnamon, if desired	2 ml

Measure All Bran, raisins, shortening and molasses into mixing bowl. Add hot water. Stir until shortening is melted. Add egg and beat well. Sift together flour, soda, salt and cinnamon. Add to All Bran mixture, stirring only until combined. Fill empty, well-greased cans—any size that will make attractive round slices—or an 8x8-inch pan. Grease and line with brown paper or parchment. Fill only about ⅔ full. Bake in moderate oven: 350F (175C). Serve hot. Great with baked beans. Good in the lunch box, spread with cream cheese.

Hilda's Pumpernickel

In a large bowl, combine:

2½ cups	Red River cereal	625 ml	⅓ cup	molasses	75 ml
2 cups	whole wheat flour	500 ml	1 tsp	salt	5 ml
3 tbsp	baking soda	45ml	3 cups	hot water	750 ml

Pour mixture into greased loaf pan and let it sit at room temperature for 2 hours. Then bake at 225F (110C) for 2 hours.

Sylvia's Hobo Bread

Inexpensive with a great flavour.

In a large mixing bowl, pour 1½ cups (375 ml) hot water over 3¾ cups (930 ml) washed sultana raisins. Stir in 4 tsp (20 ml) soda. Add ¼ cup (50 ml) butter and stir. Add 1¼ cup (310 ml) brown sugar, 1½ cup (375 ml) white sugar, and 2 tsp (10 ml) vanilla. When cool add 4 cups (1 L) flour and 2 beaten eggs. Mix well. Grease 6 cans (19 oz/540 ml). Line with greased brown paper or parchment. Bake at 350F (175C) for 45-60 minutes. Let stand for a few minutes, then take loaves out of cans. Serve sliced and buttered. Keeps and freezes well.

Andrea's Dutch Rye Bread

A definite tang of molasses and a chewy texture.

4 cups	flour	1 L	3 tsp	baking soda	15 ml
1 9½-oz box	Quaker natural bran	300 g	2 tsp	salt	10 ml
			3 cups	molasses	750 ml
4 cups	Red River cereal	1 L	7 cups	boiling water	1.75 L

Mix all ingredients in a large mixing bowl and pour into greased floured pans, filling ¾ full. Place foil over pans. Bake 1 hour at 350F (175C) and for another hour at 325F (165C).

Carrot Muffins

These are very special muffins.

Mix and set aside:

2 cups	carrots, grated	500 ml		½ cup	coconut, finely ground	125 ml
⅔ cup	raisins, washed and drained	150 ml		1	large apple, grated	1
⅔ cup	pecans, freshly roasted and ground fairly fine	150 ml				

In a small bowl, combine and set aside:

4	eggs, well beaten	4
1 cup	vegetable oil	250 ml
2 tsp	vanilla	10 ml

In a large mixing bowl, combine:

2 cups	flour	500 ml		¼ tsp	cloves, ground	15 ml
1¼ cups	white sugar	310 ml		2 tsp	cinnamon	10 ml
2 tsp	baking soda	10 ml		½ tsp	salt	2 ml

Mix prepared fruit into flour mixture; stir so that fruit is well dusted. Stir egg mixture into flour-fruit mixture. Blend. Spoon into muffin pans well coated with cooking spray. Bake at 350F (175C) for about 20 minutes or until done. Makes about 16 large muffins.

Corn Muffins or Johnny Cake

Try as you will, you really can't improve on this basic recipe.

¾ cup	sugar	175 ml	¾ cup	milk	175 ml
1	egg	1	1½ cups	white flour	375 ml
½ cup	butter or margarine	125 ml	1 tsp	baking powder	5 ml
¾ cup	cornmeal	175 ml	½ tsp	salt	2 ml

Cream butter with sugar. Add egg, milk and cornmeal. Add other sifted, dry ingredients. Bake at 400F (200C) for 20-30 minutes. This recipe may be used for muffins or may be placed in an 8x8-inch (20x20 cm) pan and cut into large squares. Serve hot with butter and molasses. Makes 1 dozen muffins or 1 cake.

Chunky Apple Muffins

3 cups	white sugar	750 ml	1½ tsp	salt	7 ml
1½ cups	vegetable oil	375 ml	½ cup	nuts (optional)	125 ml
4½ cups	apple, chopped	1.25 L	3	eggs	3
4½ cups	flour	1.25 L	1 tbsp	vanilla	15 ml
1 tbsp	baking soda	15 ml	1½ cups	raisins	375 ml
1 tbsp	cinnamon	15 ml			
1½ tsp	nutmeg	7 ml			

Sift dry ingredients together. Add chopped apple and stir. Make a well in dry ingredients. Mix liquid ingredients together. Add all at once to dry ingredients. Bake at 350F (175C) for approximately 25 minutes. Makes 2 dozen.

Applesauce Oatmeal Muffins

½ cup	white flour	125 ml	¼ cup	brown sugar	50 ml
½ cup	whole wheat flour	125 ml	1	egg	1
3 tsp	baking powder	15 ml	¼ cup	vegetable oil	50 ml
½ tsp	cinnamon	2 ml	⅓ cup	milk	75 ml
½ tsp	salt	2 ml	⅔ cup	applesauce, sweetened	150 ml
¼ tsp	nutmeg	1 ml			
¾ cup	rolled oats	175 ml			

In mixing bowl, sift white flour, baking powder, cinnamon and salt. Stir in whole wheat flour and nutmeg. In a separate bowl whisk together egg, oil and milk. Stir in applesauce. Pour into dry ingredients. Stir until moistened. Do not overmix. Fill greased muffin cups ⅔ full. Bake at 375F (190C) for 20 minutes. Makes 1 dozen.

Banana Bran Muffins

Bananas add flavour and moisture.

2	eggs	2	½ tsp	salt	2 ml
⅔ cup	bananas, mashed	150 ml	¾ cup	bran	175 ml
¾ cup	vegetable oil	175 ml	1 tsp	baking powder	5 ml
⅓ cup	buttermilk or sour milk	75 ml	½ tsp	baking soda	2 ml
1¼ cups	whole wheat flour	300 ml	¾ cup	brown sugar	175 ml

Mash bananas with fork. Beat eggs with fork. Place bananas, eggs, buttermilk, oil and sugar in a bowl and beat together. In a large bowl, sift dry ingredients. Add liquids to dry ingredients and stir until just moistened. Turn into muffin pans, and bake at 375F (190C) for 20 minutes. Makes 1 dozen.

Banana Nut Muffins

2 cups	flour	500 ml		1	egg, beaten	1
¼ cup	sugar	50 ml		⅓ cup	vegetable oil	75 ml
1 tbsp	baking powder	15 ml		¾ cup	bananas, crushed	175 ml
½ tsp	salt	2 ml		¾ cup	walnuts, crushed	175 ml
1 cup	milk	250 ml		1 tsp	vanilla	5 ml

Spray a 12-cup muffin pan with non-stick cooking spray. Sift flour, sugar, baking powder and salt into a medium-sized bowl, making a well in the centre. Mix milk, egg, oil, banana, walnuts and vanilla in small bowl. Pour liquid mixture into dry ingredients. Mix batter until just moistened. Do not overmix. Spoon batter into muffin pan. Bake in a 400F (200C) oven until a toothpick inserted into the muffins in centre of pan comes out clean and muffins are golden brown. Makes 1 dozen.

Banana Chocolate Chip Muffins

Especially for the chocolate chip lovers.

1¾ cups	flour (all-purpose or whole wheat)	430 ml		⅓ cup	oil or melted margarine	75 ml
½ cup	sugar	125 ml		1 cup	bananas (3 medium), overripe and mashed	250 ml
4 tsp	baking powder	20 ml				
½ tsp	salt	2 ml				
½ cup	chocolate chips	125 ml		¼ cup	nuts (optional)	50 ml
2	eggs	2				

Sift flour, sugar, baking powder and salt in a large bowl. Make a well in centre. In a separate bowl, mix liquid ingredients, banana, chocolate chips and nuts if using. Add liquid ingredients to dry ingredients. Combine only until moistened. Fill muffin tins ⅔ full. Bake in preheated oven at 400F (200C) for 15-20 minutes. Makes 1 dozen.

Old-Fashioned
Blueberry Muffins

2 cups	white flour	500 ml	2	eggs, at room temperature		2
2½ tsp	baking powder	12 ml				
½ tsp	salt	2 ml	¾ cup	buttermilk, at room temperature		175 ml
½ cup	white sugar	125 ml				
½ cup	brown sugar	125 ml	2 cups	wild blueberries		500 ml
6 tbsp	butter, softened	90 ml	2 tbsp	lemon juice		30 ml

Topping (optional). Combine the following:

½ tsp	cinnamon	2 ml
4 tsp	sugar	20 ml
¼ cup	walnuts, ground	50 ml

Preheat oven to 400F (200C). Spray muffin tins with nonstick cooking spray. In small bowl make topping; set aside. Sift flour, salt and baking soda in a large bowl. In a medium bowl, cream butter and sugars. Beat in eggs. Add buttermilk and lemon juice. Pour wet mixture over dry mixture. Stir just until moistened. Fold in blueberries. Pour into muffin tins. Add topping. Bake for 20-25 minutes. Makes 1 dozen 3-inch muffins.

Blueberry Corn Muffins

1¼ cups	cornmeal	310 ml	1	egg		1
1 cup	flour	250 ml	1 cup	buttermilk or sour milk		250 ml
¼ cup	white sugar	50 ml				
¼ cup	brown sugar, packed	50 ml	3 tbsp	orange rind		45 ml
1 tsp	baking soda	5 ml	1½ cups	blueberries, fresh or frozen		375 ml
½ tsp	salt	2 ml				
¾ cup	oil	175 ml	2 tbsp	lemon juice		30 ml

In a large mixing bowl, sift flour, soda, salt and white sugar. Stir in cornmeal and brown sugar. In another bowl whisk egg, milk, oil and lemon juice. Add liquids to dry ingredients, stirring until blended. Fold in blueberries and orange rind. Spoon into greased muffin tins and bake at 425F (220C) for about 20 minutes. Makes 1 dozen muffins. Note: Additional orange rind may be sprinkled on top.

Blueberry Muffins

This recipe comes from a time when we picked our berries by the bucket.

¾ cup	brown sugar	175 ml	1 tbsp	baking powder	15 ml
1 tbsp	butter, melted	15 ml	¼ tsp	salt	1 ml
1	egg, beaten	1	1½ cups	blueberries	375 ml
½ cup	milk	125 ml	2 tbsp	flour	30 ml
1½ cups	flour	375 ml	2 tsp	vanilla	10 ml

Cream sugar and butter. Add beaten egg and vanilla. Sift together flour, baking powder and salt, and add to egg mixture. Toss blueberries with 2 tbsp flour and stir gently into batter. Bake in muffin pans that have been greased and floured. Fill about ⅔ full. Bake at 425F (220C) for about 12 minutes. Serve hot with fresh butter. Makes 1 dozen.

Blueberry Lemon Muffins

1 cup	margarine	250 ml	½ cup	cornmeal	125 ml
1½ cups	sugar	375 ml	1 tsp	baking soda	5 ml
4	eggs	4	2 tsp	baking powder	10 ml
1 tsp	vanilla	5 ml	1½ cups	blueberries	375 ml
3 tbsp	lemon juice	45 ml	1	lemon rind, grated	1
1 cup	milk	250 ml			
2½ cups	flour	625 ml	½ tsp	salt	2 ml

Sift flour, soda, baking powder and salt into a large mixing bowl. Cream margarine and sugar. Add eggs one at a time, beating well after each addition. Add milk, vanilla and lemon juice. Stir in cornmeal, blueberries and lemon rind. Add liquid mixture to flour mixture, mixing only until combined. Pour into sprayed muffin pans. Bake at 350F (175C) for 20 minutes. Makes 1 dozen.

Bran Muffins

1	egg, beaten	1	1 cup	flour	250 ml
1 cup	milk	250 ml	3 tsp	baking powder	15 ml
3 tbsp	oil	30 ml	½ tsp	salt	2 ml
2 tbsp	molasses	30 ml	⅓ cup	brown sugar	75 ml
1½ cups	bran	375 ml	1 cup	raisins (optional)	250 ml

Combine egg, milk, oil and molasses. Stir in bran and let stand 5 minutes. Sift together flour, baking powder and salt. Mix in brown sugar and raisins, if using. Add bran mixture to dry ingredients, stirring until combined. Do not beat or overmix. Spoon into greased muffin tins. Bake at 400F (200C) for 20 minutes. Makes 1 dozen.

Raisin Bran Muffins

These bran muffins can't get any better!

1 cup	cooking oil	250 ml	5 tsp	baking soda	25 ml
3 cups	sugar	750 ml	4 tsp	salt	20 ml
4	eggs	4	2 tsp	cinnamon	10 ml
1 quart	buttermilk or sour milk	1 L	1 tsp	nutmeg	5 ml
5 cups	flour	1.25 L	1 15-oz box	Raisin Bran cereal	450 g

Mix in order given. Bake at 375F (190C) until done. This dough keeps well in refrigerator for 6-8 weeks. Makes 4-5 dozen.

Spicy Bran Muffins

3 cups	bran flakes	750 ml	½ tsp	salt	2 ml
1 cup	boiling water	250 ml	2½ tsp	baking soda	12 ml
2	eggs, beaten	2	1 tsp	cinnamon	5 ml
1¾ cups	buttermilk	430 ml	1 tsp	allspice	5 ml
½ cup	vegetable oil	125 ml	½ cup	apple, grated	125 ml
½ cup	molasses	125 ml	1 cup	raisins	250 ml
2½ cups	flour	625 ml	1	orange rind, grated	1
¼ cup	brown sugar	50 ml			

In a large bowl, combine bran flakes and boiling water. Stir and set aside to cool. Combine the eggs, buttermilk, oil and molasses. Combine with bran mixture. Fold dry ingredients into the bran mixture. When partially mixed, fold in apple, raisins and grated orange rind. Fill muffin tins to top. Bake at 400F (200C) for about 20 minutes. Makes 1 dozen large muffins.

Sylvia's Refrigerator Bran Muffins

Keep muffins on hand for busy lifestyles.

Pour 2 cups (500 ml) boiling water on:

2 cups	All Bran cereal	500 ml
2 cups	Bran Flakes cereal	500 ml

Let stand 10 minutes.

Add and mix well together:

1 cup	margarine	250 ml
3 cups	white sugar	750 ml
4	eggs, beaten	4
4 cups	buttermilk	1 L
3 cups	dates, cooked and cooled	750 ml

Add last:

5 cups	flour	1.25 L
5 tsp	baking soda	25 ml
2 tsp	salt	10 ml

Mix all until combined. Store batter in refrigerator. Can be used when needed. Bake at 350F (175C). Makes 3 dozen.

Wheat Germ Muffins

A crunch in every bite.

1¾ cups	flour	430 ml
4 tsp	baking powder	20 ml
1 tsp	salt	5 ml
¼ cup	sugar	50 ml
⅔ cup	wheat germ	150 ml

2	eggs	2
1 cup	milk	250 ml
⅓ cup	shortening, melted, or vegetable oil	75ml

Sift flour, baking powder, salt and sugar in mixing bowl. Add wheat germ. Stir together to mix. Beat together eggs, milk and oil. Add to dry ingredients. Stir only until well combined. Pour batter into well-greased muffin tins. Bake at 400F (200C) for 20 minutes. Serve warm. Makes 1 dozen muffins.

Natural Bran Muffins

¼ cup	shortening	50 ml	1 cup	flour	250 ml
½ cup	brown sugar, firmly packed	125 ml	1½ tsp	baking powder	7 ml
			½ tsp	baking soda	2 ml
¼ cup	molasses	50 ml	½ tsp	salt	2 ml
2	eggs, unbeaten	2	1½ cups	wheat bran	375 ml
1 cup	milk	250 ml	½ cup	raisins	125 ml

Cream shortening and sugar. Add molasses and eggs and beat together well. Add milk, then bran. Combine flour, baking powder, soda and salt. Add to liquid ingredients. Add raisins, if desired. Place in greased muffin pans. Bake at 375F (190C) for 18-20 minutes. Makes 1 dozen large muffins.

Fruit Cheesecake Muffins

Sometimes gilding the lily works.

⅓ cup	cream cheese	75 ml	2 cups	flour	500 ml
2 tbsp	icing sugar	30 ml	2 tsp	baking powder	10 ml
⅓ cup	butter, softened	75 ml	¼ tsp	salt	1 ml
⅔ cup	brown sugar, packed	150 ml	⅔ cup	milk	150 ml
			⅓ cup	whole fruit jam	75 ml
1	egg	1	2 tbsp	pecans, finely chopped	30 ml
1 tsp	orange rind, grated	5 ml			

Blend cream cheese with icing sugar; set aside. In bowl, cream butter and brown sugar; beat in egg and orange rind. Combine flour, baking powder and salt; add to creamed mixture alternately with milk, stirring just until blended. Do not overmix. Spoon into large greased muffin tins, filling halfway to top. Add 1 tsp (5 ml) of jam to each; top with cream cheese mixture. Sprinkle with nuts. Bake at 375F (190C) for 25-30 minutes, or until firm to touch. Immediately remove from tins. Makes 1 dozen muffins.

Date-Orange Muffins

¾ cup	dates, loosely packed	175 ml
1	orange, unpeeled	1
½ cup	orange juice	125 ml
2	eggs	2
½ cup	cold butter, cut in small pieces	125 ml

1 cup	whole wheat flour	250 ml
1¼ cups	white flour	310 ml
2 tsp	baking powder	10 ml
1 tsp	baking soda	5 ml
½ tsp	salt	2 ml

Mix dates with ½ cup (125 ml) of the white flour. Place in blender and process until dates are evenly chopped in pieces. Cut unpeeled orange into 8 1-inch pieces and remove seeds. Add to blender and process until finely cut. Add orange juice, eggs and butter. Blend until smooth. Stir together remainder of white flour, whole wheat flour, baking powder, soda and salt. Add to ingredients in blender. Process until just moistened. Fill muffin tins ¾ full. Bake in at 400F (200C) until tops are firm to touch, approximately 20 minutes. Makes 1 dozen muffins.

Lemon Muffins

1¾ cups	flour	430 ml
½ cup + 3 tbsp	sugar	170 ml
1 tbsp	baking powder	15 ml
½ tsp	salt	2 ml

1	egg	1
⅔ cup	milk	150 ml
1 tbsp	lemon zest	15 ml
1 tbsp	lemon juice	15 ml
⅓ cup	oil	75 ml

Combine flour, ½ cup (125 ml) sugar, baking powder and salt in a medium-sized bowl. Beat egg lightly in small bowl. Stir in milk, 2 tsp (10 ml) lemon zest, lemon juice and oil. Add liquid to flour mixture, stir just until moistened. Fill greased muffin cups ⅔ full. Combine remaining 3 tbsp sugar and 1 tsp lemon zest. Sprinkle over tops of muffins. Bake at 400F (200C) for 20 minutes. Makes 1 dozen muffins.

Lemon Poppy Seed Muffins

Poppy seeds add crunch and interest.

1 cup	white sugar	250 g	½ cup	poppy seeds	125 ml
¼ cup	butter or margarine, softened	50 ml	2 tbsp	lemon rind	30 ml
			2½ cups	flour	625 ml
2	eggs	2	1 tbsp	baking powder	15 ml
1½ cups	plain yogurt	375 ml	½ tsp	salt	2 ml

Cream sugar, butter and eggs in a large bowl until smooth. Stir in yogurt, poppy seeds and lemon rind. Mix flour, baking powder and salt in a separate bowl. Stir into creamed mixture, until just moistened. Fill greased muffin tins. Bake at 400F (200C) for 20 minutes or until firm to touch. Cool in tins for 5 minutes before removing to wire rack. Makes 1 dozen muffins.

Lemony Cheese Muffins

A very tart flavour.

1 cup	creamed cottage cheese	250 ml	¼ cup	liquid honey	50 ml
			1½ cups	flour	375 ml
1 cup	100% Bran cereal	250 ml	⅓ cup	sugar	75 ml
2 tbsp	milk	30 ml	1½ tsp	baking powder	7 ml
1	small lemon, seeded	1	½ tsp	baking soda	2 ml
2	eggs, lightly beaten	2	½ tsp	salt	2 ml
¼ cup	butter	50 ml			

Grind whole lemon in blender. Add cottage cheese and process until smooth. Stir in cereal and milk. Let stand 5 minutes. Stir in eggs, butter and honey. Sift and combine all other ingredients in a large bowl. Stir cereal mixture into dry ingredients only until moistened. Spoon into muffin cups, filling to the top. Bake at 400F (200C) until brown. Cool on rack. Store in an airtight container. These freeze well. Makes 1 dozen muffins.

Maple Syrup Muffins

The maple syrup flavour works its magic.

2 cups	flour	500 ml	½ cup	milk	125 ml
4 tsp	baking powder	20 ml	½ cup	maple syrup	125 ml
½ tsp	salt	2 ml	¼ cup	melted shortening or oil	50 ml
1	egg, beaten	1			

Sift dry ingredients into bowl. To beaten egg, add milk, maple syrup and oil. Stir liquid ingredients into dry ingredients. Mix only enough to combine. Fill well-greased muffin tins two-thirds full. Bake at 400F (200C) for 20 minutes. Serve warm with more maple syrup. Makes 1 dozen muffins.

Orange Yogurt Muffins

2 cups	flour	500 ml	2 tbsp	honey	30 ml
1 tsp	baking powder	5 ml	2	eggs	2
½ tsp	baking soda	2 ml	1¼ cups	plain yogurt, room temperature	310 ml
¼ tsp	salt	1 ml			
¼ cup	sugar	50 ml	¼ cup	butter, melted	50 ml
			1 tbsp	orange rind, grated	15 ml

Orange Syrup:

5 tbsp	orange juice	75 ml
⅓ cup	sugar	75 ml
3 tbsp	water	45 ml

Combine flour, baking powder and salt; set aside. In another bowl, combine sugar, honey, eggs, yogurt, butter and rind. Add dry ingredients and mix. Spoon into greased muffin tins. Bake at 375F (190C) for 15 minutes or until wooden pick in centre tests done. To make syrup, combine ingredients in a saucepan; boil 1 minute. Drizzle syrup over warm muffins. Makes 1 dozen muffins.

Pumpkin Muffins

A reminder of harvest time.

1½ cups	whole wheat flour	375 ml		½ tsp	nutmeg	2 ml
½ cup	sugar	125 ml		1	egg	1
2 tsp	baking powder	10 ml		½ cup	milk	125 ml
½ tsp	salt	2 ml		½ cup	pumpkin, canned	125 ml
½ tsp	cinnamon	2 ml		¼ cup	butter, melted	50 ml
1 tsp	ginger	5 ml		½ cup	raisins, seedless	125 ml

In a large bowl, sift together flour, sugar, baking powder, salt, cinnamon and ginger. Stir in whole wheat flour. Beat egg in a small bowl; add milk, pumpkin, nutmeg and melted butter. Add all at once to dry ingredients, stirring until just moistened. Stir in raisins. Place in muffin tins. Bake at 400F (200C) for 20 minutes. Note: Vegetable oil may be used instead of butter. Makes 1 dozen muffins.

Spicy Pumpkin Muffins or Loaf

Recipe can be doubled to make muffins and a loaf.

2	eggs	2		1 tsp	baking soda	5 ml
⅔ cup	brown sugar, packed	150 ml		½ tsp	salt	2 ml
				1 tsp	cinnamon	5 ml
½ cup	vegetable oil	125 ml		½ tsp	nutmeg	2 ml
1 cup	pumpkin, canned	250 ml		½ cup	golden raisins	125 ml
1½ cups	flour	375 ml		½ cup	nuts (optional)	125 ml
1 tsp	baking powder	5 ml				

In the large bowl of an electric mixer, beat together eggs, sugar and oil. Beat in pumpkin. In separate bowl, sift together flour, baking powder, soda, salt and spices. Stir into creamed mixture. Stir in raisins and nuts. Spoon into muffin tins or loaf pan. Bake at 350-375F (175-190C) for 20-25 minutes. Turn out on rack to cool. Store in plastic wrap. Can be frozen. Makes 1 dozen muffins.

Big Batch Pumpkin
Pecan Muffins

There's something special about pecan and pumpkin combined.

4 cups	flour	1 L		2 tbsp	orange rind, grated	30 ml
1½ cups	brown sugar	375 ml		4	eggs	4
4 tsp	baking powder	20 ml		1 14-oz can	pumpkin	398 ml
2 tsp	cinnamon	10 ml				
1 tsp	baking soda	5 ml		1 cup	orange juice	250 ml
1 tsp	ginger	5 ml		¾ cup	butter or margarine, melted	175 ml
1 tsp	nutmeg	5 ml				
1 tsp	salt	5 ml		1½ cups	chopped pecans, divided	375 ml
½ tsp	cloves	2 ml				
½ tsp	allspice	2 ml				

Spray muffin tins with cooking spray. Sift together flour, baking powder, cinnamon, soda, ginger, cloves, allspice and salt. Stir brown sugar and nutmeg into sifted dry ingredients. Add ¾ cup nuts and orange rind to dry mixture and stir to coat. Whisk together eggs, pumpkin, orange juice and butter. Stir liquid mixture into dry ingredients, just until moistened. Spoon into muffin pans, filling each one to top. Sprinkle remaining pecans on top, pressing slightly into batter. Bake at 375F (190C) for 20-25 minutes or until firm to touch. Cool in pan for 5 minutes. Remove from pans and finish cooling on racks. Store in tightly covered containers or freeze. Makes 2 dozen muffins.

Rhubarb Muffins

1¼ cups	brown sugar	300 ml	½ cup	walnuts, chopped (optional)	125 ml
½ cup	salad oil	125 ml	2½ cups	flour	625 ml
1	egg	1	1 tsp	baking soda	5 ml
2 tsp	vanilla	10 ml	1 tsp	baking powder	5 ml
1 cup	buttermilk	250 ml	½ tsp	salt	2 ml
1½ cups	rhubarb, diced	375 ml			

In a large bowl, combine sugar, oil, egg, vanilla and buttermilk; beat well. Stir in rhubarb and walnuts. In a separate bowl, stir together flour, soda, baking powder and salt until thoroughly blended. Stir dry ingredients into rhubarb mixture just until blended. Spoon batter into greased muffin cups, filling them about ⅔ full. Scatter cinnamon topping over filled cups and press lightly into batter. Bake at 400F (200C). Makes 1 dozen muffins.

For Cinnamon Topping: Combine 1 tbsp (15 ml) melted butter or margarine with ⅓ cup (75 ml) sugar and 1 tsp (5 ml) ground cinnamon.

Rhubarb Sticky Muffins

1 cup	rhubarb, finely cut	250 ml	1½ cups	flour, sifted	375 ml
¼ cup	butter, softened	50 ml	2 tsp	baking powder	10 ml
1 cup	brown sugar	250 ml	½ tsp	salt	2 ml
⅓ cup	white sugar	75 ml	½ tsp	nutmeg	2 ml
⅓ cup	butter, softened	75 ml	½ cup	milk	125 ml
1	egg	1			

Combine rhubarb, ¼ cup (50 ml) butter and brown sugar in a small bowl, and mix with a fork until blended. Spoon mixture evenly into prepared and oiled muffin tins. Beat ⅓ cup (75 ml) butter, sugar, nutmeg and egg together until fluffy. Sift together flour, baking powder and salt, and add to butter/sugar alternating with milk. Stir just to blend. Spoon the mixture on top of rhubarb mixture in tins. Bake at 350F (175C) for 20-25 minutes. Invert muffin pan on rack and let stand on top of muffins for a few minutes so that all of the rhubarb mixture runs out. Makes 1 dozen muffins.

Helene's Carrot Muffins

1¼ cups	oil	310 ml	2 tsp	vanilla	10 ml
4	eggs	4	3 cups	flour, sifted	750 ml
2 cups	white sugar	500 ml	2 tsp	baking powder	10 ml
3 cups	carrots, shredded	750 ml	2 tsp	baking soda	10 ml
1 cup	raisins	250 ml	1 tsp	salt	5 ml
1 cup	walnuts	250 ml	1 tsp	cinnamon	5 ml

Mix first four ingredients. Add next three; add flour, baking powder, baking soda, salt and cinnamon. Bake for 20 minutes at 350 F (175C). Makes 1 dozen large muffins.

Sweet Potato-Pecan Muffins

6 tbsp	butter, softened	90 ml	½ tsp	salt	2 ml
⅔ cup	sugar	150 ml	⅔ cup	milk	150 ml
1	large egg	1	1	sweet potato, about ½ lb (250 g), peeled and finely grated	1
1 tsp	vanilla extract	5 ml			
1¾ cups	all-purpose flour, unsifted	430 ml	⅔ cup	pecans, chopped	150 ml
1½ tsp	baking powder	7 ml			

Heat oven to 375F (190C). Grease muffin cups. In a large bowl, with electric mixer on medium speed, beat butter and sugar until light and fluffy. Beat in egg, milk and vanilla until blended. In medium-size bowl, combine flour, baking powder and salt, and add to the butter mixture, beating just until combined. Fold in sweet potatoes and pecans. Using ice-cream scoop or large spoon, divide batter among greased muffin cups. Bake muffins 25-30 minutes or until centres spring back when lightly pressed with fingertip. Cool muffins in pan on wire rack 5 minutes. Remove muffins from pan and serve warm. Makes 1 dozen muffins.

Whole Wheat
Raspberry Muffins

1 cup	whole wheat flour	250 ml	¼ cup	oil	50 ml
1 cup	white flour	250 ml	¾ cup	milk	175 ml
1 tbsp	baking powder	15 ml	1½ cups	raspberries, fresh or frozen	375 ml
½ tsp	salt	2 ml			
1	egg	1	2 tsp	lemon rind	10 ml
½ cup	honey	125 ml			

Preheat oven to 400F (200C). In a large bowl, combine two flours, baking powder and salt. Do not attempt to sift whole wheat flour. Make a well in the centre of dry ingredients, and pour in the combined egg, honey, oil, milk and lemon rind. Stir until all moistened. Add raspberries carefully to avoid breaking them. Spoon into oiled muffin tins. Bake for 15-20 minutes. Blueberries can be substituted. Makes 1 dozen muffins.

Pineapple Banana Muffins

3 cups	flour	750 ml	3	eggs	3
2 cups	sugar	500 ml	2 cups	bananas (about 5), mashed	500 ml
1 cup	nuts or raisins, chopped	250 ml	1¼ cups	crushed pineapple, undrained	310 ml
1 tsp	baking soda	5 ml			
1 tsp	salt	5 ml	1 cup	vegetable oil	250 ml
1 tsp	cinnamon	5 ml			

In a large bowl, sift flour, sugar, baking soda, salt and cinnamon. Add nuts. In a separate bowl, beat eggs; stir in bananas, pineapple and oil until well blended. Add to dry ingredients. Stir just until moistened. Spoon into large, greased muffin cups, filling them about ⅔ full. Bake in 350F (175C) oven for 20-30 minutes, or until firm to touch. Makes 30 muffins.

Maple Cinnamon Bran Buns

1 cup	milk	250 ml
1 cup	whole bran cereal	250 ml
2 cups	flour	500 ml
3 tbsp	sugar	45 ml
4 tsp	baking powder	20 ml
½ tsp	salt	2 ml
½ cup	shortening	125 ml
2 tbsp	butter	30 ml

Filling:

½ cup	brown sugar	125 ml
2 tsp	cinnamon	10 ml
½ cup	raisins	125 ml

Topping:

2 tbsp	butter	30 ml
¼ cup	brown sugar	50 ml
¼ cup	maple syrup	50 ml

Combine cereal and milk; let stand 5 minutes. Combine flour, sugar, baking powder and salt. Cut in shortening until crumbly. Mix with cereal mixture and stir until just moistened. Turn out onto a floured board and knead about 10 times or until smooth. Roll out to make a rectangle about 12 inches long. Brush with butter. Sprinkle with mixture of brown sugar, cinnamon and raisins. Roll up from long side, jellyroll style. Seal edges. Cut in 12 slices. Combine topping ingredients and divide evenly among 12 muffin cups. Place each piece, cut-side down, in a cup. Bake at 400F (200C) until browned, about 20 minutes. Watch carefully— they burn quickly. Cool on rack. Serve upside down. Makes 1 dozen muffins.

Strawberry Maple Muffins

1½ cups	flour	375 ml
¼ cup	sugar	50 ml
1 tbsp	baking powder	15 ml
½ tsp	salt	2 ml
¼ cup	butter, melted, or oil	50 ml
1	egg, beaten	1

½ cup	milk	125 ml
½ cup	maple syrup	125 ml
¾ cup	quick oats or oat bran	175 ml
1 cup	strawberries, fresh or frozen, diced	250 ml

Sift and mix flour, sugar, baking powder and salt together. Blend butter, egg, milk, syrup and oats. Stir into dry ingredients until all ingredients are moistened. Fold in strawberries. Fill muffin pans ⅔ full. Bake at 400F (200C) for 35-40 minutes. Makes 1 dozen muffins.

Gingerbread Cupcakes

Light and delicious!

⅔ cup	shortening	150 ml		1 tsp	ginger	5 ml
⅔ cup	white sugar	150 ml		½ tsp	cinnamon	2 ml
½ cup	molasses	125 ml		1 tsp	cloves	5 ml
2	eggs	2		1 tsp	baking soda	5 ml
2 cups	flour	500 ml		⅔ cup	boiling water	150 ml
1 tsp	salt	5 ml				

Cream shortening and sugar. Add molasses and eggs. Beat. Add dry ingredients, sifted together. Add boiling water last. Mix well. Drop into cupcake tins (a little smaller than muffin tins). Bake at 350F (175C) for 20-25 minutes.

Chocolate Cupcakes

1½ cups	flour	375 ml		½ cup	cocoa	125 ml
1 tsp	baking soda	5 ml		½ tsp	salt	2 ml
½ cup	margarine	125 ml		1½ cups	white sugar	375 ml
2	eggs	2		2 tsp	vanilla	10 ml
½ cup	buttermilk	125 ml		½ cup	hot water	125 ml

Cream margarine and sugar until light and fluffy. Add eggs, one at a time, beating after each. Add vanilla. Sift together flour, cocoa, soda and salt. Blend with egg mixture. Add liquid alternating between buttermilk and hot water. Put in greased cupcake pans. Bake at 350F (175C) for 20-25 minutes.

Party Cupcakes

2½ cups	flour	625 ml		4	eggs	4
2¼ tsp	baking powder	11 ml		1 cup	milk	250 ml
½ tsp	salt	2 ml		1 cup	semi-sweet chocolate chips, miniature	250 ml
1 cup	butter, softened	250 ml				
1½ cups	sugar	375 ml				
2 tsp	vanilla	10 ml				

Combine flour, baking powder and salt. Sift together in a bowl. In a mixing bowl, beat butter, sugar and vanilla until creamy. Add eggs, beating well after each. Blend in flour mixture alternately with milk. Stir in ¾ cup (175 ml) chocolate chips. Spoon batter into 24 paper-lined muffin cups. Bake at 375F (190C) until tops spring back when lightly touched, approximately 25 minutes. If to be used for a party, frost with butter cream frosting. Tint in different colours and decorate as desired. Place a birthday candle on each.

Daffy Cupcakes

¾ cup	sugar	175 ml		2 tsp	baking powder	10 ml
½ cup	butter	125 ml		¼ tsp	salt	1 ml
2	eggs, unbeaten	2		1 tsp	vanilla	5 ml
2 cups	flour	500 ml				

Cream sugar and butter. Add eggs and vanilla. Beat. Add sifted dry ingredients. Turn out onto a floured board and roll out as for cookies. Cut with a large cookie cutter. Fit cookies into cupcake pans. Place a teaspoon of jam onto each cookie in the pans. Bake at 350F (175C) for 20-25 minutes.

Quick Chocolate Chip
Cream Cheese Cupcakes

Mix according to package directions.

1	chocolate cake mix	1

Filling:

8 oz	cream cheese, softened	250 g
1	egg	1
½ cup	sugar	125 ml

Cream above ingredients together and add:

1 8-oz pkg	chocolate chips	225 g

Fill lined muffin tins ¾ full with cake mixture. Add 1 tbsp (15 ml) cream cheese mixture. Bake at 350F (175C) for 15-20 minutes. Makes 30-36 cupcakes.

Cream Puffs

½ cup	butter	125 ml	4	eggs	4
1 cup	boiling water	250 ml	1 cup	flour	250 ml

Put butter and water in a saucepan and heat to boiling. Sift in flour all at once and beat vigorously. Cook until mixture leaves the side of the pan as you stir. When slightly cooled, add unbeaten eggs, one at a time, beating thoroughly after each addition. The mixture should be stiff enough to hold its shape. Drop by spoonfuls onto greased baking sheet, keeping mounds circular in shape and piled in centre. Bake at 375F (190C) for about 45 minutes, until no drops of moisture remain. One may be removed from oven to test. When cool make a slit in side and fill with sweetened whipped cream or any cream filling. Dust top with powdered sugar. Simply delicious!

Helene's Philly Cream Puffs

1 cup	water	250 ml		1 tsp	vanilla	5 ml
½ cup	margarine	125 ml		1 cup	whipping cream, whipped	250 ml
1 cup	flour	250 ml				
¼ tsp	salt	1 ml		2	bananas, sliced	2
4	eggs	4		1 oz	unsweetened chocolate	30 g
2 8-oz pkgs	cream cheese, softened	2x250 g				
				1 tbsp	milk	15 ml
1½ cups	powdered sugar	375 ml				

Bring water and margarine to a boil. Add flour and salt; stir vigorously over low heat until mixture forms a ball. Remove from heat. Add eggs, one at a time, beating well after each addition. Drop ten ½ cups of dough on lightly greased cookie sheet. Bake at 400F (200C) for 50-55 minutes or until golden brown. Remove immediately from cookie sheet and cool. Combine cream cheese, 1 cup powdered sugar and vanilla, mixing until well blended. Reserve ½ cup (125 ml) cream cheese mixture; fold whipped cream and bananas into remaining mixture. Chill. Carefully cut the tops of each puff and fill with whipped cream mixture. Replace top. Melt chocolate. Add remaining sugar, chocolate and milk to reserved cream cheese mixture. Mix well. Spread over each puff.

Molasses Puffs

1	egg	1		½ tsp	baking soda	2 ml
½ cup	sugar	125 ml		½ tsp	ground ginger	2 ml
½ cup	molasses	125 ml		¼ tsp	nutmeg	1 ml
¼ cup	shortening, softened	50 ml		¼ tsp	salt	1 ml
1 cup	flour	250 ml		¼ tsp	cinnamon	1 ml
¼ tsp	salt	1 ml		½ cup	boiling water	125 ml

Beat together in a mixing bowl the egg, sugar, molasses and shortening. Mix in sifted dry ingredients. Finally, add hot water. Combine well but do not overmix. Fill muffin tins ⅔ full. Bake at 350F (175C) for 20-30 minutes.

Delicious Butter Tarts

Pastry:		
1½ cups	flour	375 ml
¼ tsp	salt	1 ml
½ cup	butter and shortening, mixed	125 ml
1 tsp	vinegar	5 ml
1	egg yolk	1
	water, chilled	

Filling:		
2 tbsp	butter	30 ml
1	egg	1
1 tsp	vinegar	5 ml
1 tsp	vanilla	5 ml
	salt	
⅓ cup	currants, raisins, coconut or pecans	75 ml

In a large bowl, sift flour and salt. Blend in butter and shortening with pastry blender until mixture becomes fine crumbs. Mix egg yolk, vinegar and water in measuring cup, adding enough water to equal ⅓ cup (75 ml) of liquid altogether. Add egg mixture gradually to the crumb mixture and mix together enough so that it holds together. Refrigerate for at least one hour. To make filling, whisk all ingredients together except fruit. Set aside. Roll out pastry and cut out circles to fit muffin tins—a 4-inch (10 cm) cutter will do. Fit circles of dough into muffin tins. Divide the fruit or nuts among the tart shells. Spoon filling into each tart shell, filling about ¾ full. Bake at 450F (230C) until filling rises and is bubbly. Let stand for 1 or 2 minutes, and remove from pan.

Raised Doughnuts

½ cup	oil	125 ml
2	eggs, well beaten	2
1 tsp	vanilla	5 ml
1 tsp	salt	5 ml

½ cup	sugar	125 ml
2 cups	water, warm	500 ml
1 pkg	yeast (instant)	1
4-5 cups	flour	1-1.25 L

Dissolve sugar in warm water. Add the oil, eggs, vanilla and salt. Combine flour with instant yeast. Add to liquids, mixing in a little flour at a time to make a soft dough. Let rise and punch down and let rise again, then roll out dough and cut with doughnut cutter. Let rise until doubled. Deep-fry in hot lard or oil.

Doughnuts

Makes 6 dozen wonderful doughnuts.

2 cups	sugar	500 ml	2 tsp	salt	10 ml
⅞ cup	butter	220 ml	1 tsp	nutmeg	5 ml
6	eggs	6	¼ tsp	cinnamon	1 ml
2 cups	milk	500 ml	2 tsp	vanilla	10 ml
8 cups	flour	2 L	4 lbs	lard, for frying	2 kg
4 tbsp	baking powder	60 ml		ginger	

Cream butter and sugar. Beat in eggs, one at a time. Stir in milk and vanilla. Add sifted dry ingredients. Chill. Can be left in fridge overnight. When ready to fry, heat at least 4 lb (2 kg) lard in a heavy cooking pot. (Lard makes a lighter doughnut than shortening.) Add a pinch of ginger to the fat. Fat must be very hot, about 365F (178C). Roll out dough, preferably on a floured pastry cloth, which requires less flour and so makes a lighter doughnut). Cut with doughnut cutter. Save centres and re-roll with scraps of dough. Fry in hot lard (very carefully). Turn once, only after one side is brown. After both sides have browned, remove from fat with slotted metal spatula. Let drain on paper towel or brown paper bag.

When cooled (but not cold) shake in a paper bag with sugar (and cinnamon), if desired. When no thermometer is available to test for proper frying temperature, drop a small cube of bread about 1-inch (2.5 cm) square into the fat. If the cube browns in 60 seconds the temperature of the fat will be about 365F (178C).

Hilda's Oliebollen: Dutch Doughnuts

1 pkg	yeast	1	½ tsp	vanilla	2 ml
3 tbsp	sugar	45 ml	1 tsp	salt	5 ml
½ cup	milk, lukewarm	125 ml	4 cups	flour	1 L
2	eggs, well beaten	2	2 cups	seedless raisins	500 g
1½ cups	milk, lukewarm	375 ml		cooking oil, for frying	

Soak yeast, sugar and ½ cup milk for 10 minutes. Mix with eggs, remaining milk, vanilla and salt. Slowly beat in flour. Add raisins. Cover bowl and let rise 1½ hours. Punch down. Let rise again for 1½ hours. Drop by heaping teaspoonfuls into hot cooking oil. Turn if necessary. Some balls will turn by themselves when cooking. Remove from oil with a straining spoon. Sprinkle with fine sugar while still hot. Can be eaten hot or cold. Makes about 5 dozen. (Note: Use only cooking oil for frying.)

Jessie's Brown Sugar Doughnuts

You could always count on Jessie Wright for a good doughnut.

2	eggs	2	½ cup	milk	125 ml
1 cup	brown sugar	250 ml	3 cups	flour	750 ml
3 tbsp	butter, melted	45 ml	2 tsp	cream of tartar	10 ml
1 tsp	nutmeg	5 ml	1 tsp	baking soda	5 ml
1 tsp	vanilla extract	5 ml	½ tsp	salt	2 ml
1 tsp	lemon extract	5ml	4 lbs	lard, for frying	2 kg

Beat eggs until light. Gradually beat in brown sugar and melted butter. Add nutmeg and flavourings. Stir in milk. Add sifted dry ingredients and mix until combined. Roll out onto a floured board and cut with a doughnut cutter. Heat lard in a heavy pot to about 365F (178C). (See "Doughnuts" recipe for how to test temperature without a thermometer.) Fry doughnuts on one side until brown; turn and brown on other side. Drain on paper towel. Makes 2 dozen.

Gumdrop Loaf

Jean Curtis uses dates to make this loaf just a little different.

½ cup	butter	125 ml	1 tsp	vanilla	5 ml
1 cup	white sugar	250 ml	1 tsp	almond extract	5 ml
2	eggs, beaten	2	1½ cups	dates, chopped	375 ml
¾ cup	milk	175 ml	1½ cups	gumdrops, chopped (black ones removed)	375 ml
2 cups	flour	500 ml			
2 tsp	baking powder	10 ml			
¼ tsp	salt	1 ml			

Cream butter and sugar. Add eggs, milk and flavourings, beating well. Sift dry ingredients, saving about ½ cup (125 ml) flour to dust dates and gumdrops. Add dry ingredients to liquid batter. Fold in floured fruit. Pour into a 13x4-inch (33x10.5 cm) pan. Bake for 1¼ hours at 350F (175C).

Coconut-Cherry Banana Loaf

2	eggs	2	1½ tsp	baking powder	7 ml
1 cup	white sugar	250 ml	½ tsp	baking soda	2 ml
½ cup	margarine, melted	125 ml	½ tsp	salt	2 ml
1 cup	bananas, mashed	250 ml	½ tsp	almond flavouring	2 ml
1½ cups	flour	375 ml	½ cup	walnuts	125 ml
½ cup	coconut (fine)	125 ml	½ cup	maraschino cherries	125 ml

Beat eggs until light and frothy. Add sugar and melted butter; beat well. Stir in mashed bananas and almond flavouring. Mix dry ingredients, and coconut, walnuts and cut-up cherries. Stir until well mixed; pour over first mixture. Stir just to combine. Pour into a 9x5x3-inch (23x12x7 cm) greased pan. Bake at 350F (175C) for 1 hour. Let stand in pan for 10 minutes.

Blueberry Orange Nut Loaf

⅔ cup	butter	150 ml		1 cup	milk	250 ml
1 cup	sugar	250 ml		1¼ cups	blueberries	310 ml
3	eggs, separated	3		2 tsp	orange rind, grated	10 ml
3 cups	flour, save some to flour berries	750 ml		½ cup	walnuts, chopped	125 ml
3 tsp	baking powder	15 ml			brown sugar, for topping	
¼ tsp	salt	1 ml				

Cream sugar and butter and beat in egg yolks. Add milk, beat well. Sift flour, baking powder and salt. Add dry ingredients to milk mixture. Stir in blueberries and orange rind, which have been lightly floured. Last, fold in beaten egg whites and pour mixture into floured loaf pan. Sprinkle top with a little brown sugar and chopped walnuts. Press into batter. Bake at 350F (175C) for 30-40 minutes.

Apple Gingerbread Loaf

1 cup	boiling water	250 ml		1½ cups	flour	375 ml
1½ cups	bran cereal	375 ml		1 tsp	baking powder	5 ml
¼ cup	butter	50 ml		1 tsp	baking soda	5 ml
2 tbsp	molasses	30 ml		½ tsp	ginger	2 ml
2	eggs, lightly beaten	2		½ tsp	cinnamon	2 ml
½ cup	brown sugar, firmly packed	125 ml		½ tsp	nutmeg	2 ml
2	medium apples, peeled and chopped	2		¼ tsp	salt	1 ml

Pour boiling water over cereal and butter in bowl, stirring until butter melts. Stir in molasses and cool. Stir in eggs, brown sugar and chopped apples. Combine remaining dry ingredients in a large bowl. Stir bran mixture into dry ingredients until moistened. Pour into greased and lined, 9x5-inch (23x13 cm) loaf pan. Bake at 350F (175C) until it tests done. Cool on rack for 10 minutes, then turn out to cool.

Banana Bran Bread

1 cup	bananas (2-3 medium), mashed	250 ml		⅓ cup	vegetable oil	75 ml
				2 cups	flour	500 ml
1 cup	bran	250 ml		½ cup	apricots, dried and chopped	125 ml
1 cup	milk	250 ml				
2	eggs, slightly beaten	2		½ cup	walnuts, chopped	125 ml
				1 tbsp	baking powder	15 ml
½ cup	brown sugar, packed	125 ml		½ tsp	salt	2 ml

Combine bran and milk. Let stand 5 minutes. Stir in bananas, eggs, sugar and oil. Sift dry ingredients into a large bowl. Add apricots and walnuts. Stir cereal mixture into flour mixture until combined. Pour into 9x5-inch (23x13 cm) pan. Bake at 350F (175C) for about 1 hour. Cool in pan for 10 minutes. Remove from pan and cool on rack.

Grape Nuts Bread

An old recipe, very plain—serve with cream cheese.

1 cup	brown sugar	250 ml		4 tsp	baking powder	20 ml
2	eggs	2		2 cups	flour	500 ml
1 cup	Grape Nuts cereal	250 ml		½ tsp	salt	2 ml
2 cups	milk	500 ml				

Heat grape nuts and milk, stirring often to prevent burning. Cool. Cream sugar and eggs; add cooled grape nuts mixture. Add sifted dry ingredients: flour, baking powder and salt. Mix together lightly. Pour into a loaf pan. Bake at 350F (175C) for 40 minutes.

Zucchini Nut Loaf

A delicious way to use this versatile vegetable.

2 cups	zucchini, grated	500 ml	1 tsp	baking soda	5 ml
2 cups	sugar	500 ml	1 tsp	baking powder	5 ml
3	eggs	3	1 tsp	nutmeg	5 ml
1 cup	vegetable oil	250 ml	¾-1 tsp	lemon rind, grated	4-5 ml
3 cups	flour	750 ml	1 cup	walnuts, crushed	250 ml
2 tsp	cinnamon	10 ml	¾ tsp	salt	3 ml

In a mixing bowl, beat together zucchini, sugar and eggs. Add oil, lemon rind and nutmeg. Sift together flour, cinnamon, soda, baking powder and salt. Add dry ingredients to zucchini mixture. Stir together only to combine. Fold in walnuts. Pour into two loaf pans. Bake at 325F (165C), approximately 1 hour. Let stand in pan for 10 minutes before turning out to cool.

Steamed Blackbread

2 cups	sour milk or buttermilk	500 ml	pinch	salt	
½ cup	molasses	125 ml	2 tsp	baking soda	10 ml
1 tbsp	vegetable oil	15 ml	1½ cups	all-purpose flour	375 ml
3 tbsp	white sugar	45 ml	2 cups	graham flour	500 ml

Use a canning kettle, and invert the wire rack. Fill with water to just below the wire rack. Bring water to a boil. In a large bowl, mix together molasses, oil, milk, sugar, salt and baking soda. Stir in flours. Divide batter into two 1-lb coffee cans. Place a double thickness of aluminum foil over top, and secure with rubber bands. Keep water at a slow boil, and steam for one hour.

Irish Barm Brack

Ask the Irish neighbours in for tea!

1¾ cups	black tea, cold	430 ml		¼ cup	citron	50 ml
1 cup	light brown sugar	250 ml		1¼ cups	self-rising flour	310 ml
1¼ cups	golden raisins	310 ml		1	egg, beaten	1

Put the tea, sugar, raisins and peel into a bowl; cover and leave to soak overnight. Preheat oven to 350F (175C). Grease and flour an 8-inch round pan. Sift the flour into the fruit mixture, add the egg and beat well. Pour into the pan and bake at 350F (175C) for 1 hour or until a toothpick inserted in centre comes out clean. Watch for burning. Turn out onto a wire rack.

Sticky Lemon Bread

⅓ cup	margarine, softened	75 ml		¼ tsp	salt	1 ml
⅔ cup	sugar	150 ml		1 8-oz carton	lemon low-fat yogurt	1
¼ cup	egg substitute	50 ml				
1 tsp	lemon rind, grated	5 ml				
2 tsp	vanilla extract	10 ml		Glaze:		
2¼ cups	flour	550 ml		½ cup	sugar	125 ml
¾ tsp	baking powder	3 ml		½ cup	lemon juice, fresh	125 ml
½ tsp	baking soda	2 ml				

Cream margarine with mixer; gradually add sugar, beating at medium speed until light and fluffy (about 5 minutes). Add egg substitute, lemon rind and vanilla; beat until well blended. Combine flour, baking powder, baking soda and salt. With mixer running at low speed, add to creamed mixture, alternating with yogurt beginning and ending with the flour mixture. Pour batter into a loaf pan coated with baking spray. Bake at 350F (175C) for 55 minutes or until wooden pick inserted in centre comes out clean. Remove from oven and place on a wire rack to cool.

For Glaze: Combine sugar and lemon juice in a saucepan; bring to a boil, and cook 1 minute. Remove from heat. Pierce top of bread several times with a fork. Pour sugar mixture over bread; cool in pans 10 minutes. Remove from pan; cool completely on a wire rack.

Date Pecan Tea Bread

2½ cups	dates, chopped	625 ml	2 tbsp	butter	30 ml
1½ cups	boiling water	375 ml	1¼ cups	sugar	310 ml
1½ tsp	baking soda	7 ml	2	eggs	2
1¾ cups	flour	430 ml	2 tsp	vanilla	10 ml
¼ tsp	cloves	1 ml	1½ cups	pecans, coarsely chopped	375 ml
¼ tsp	cinnamon	1 ml			
¼ tsp	nutmeg	1 ml	½ tsp	salt	2 ml

Place dates in a bowl and cover with boiling water. Add nutmeg, cinnamon and cloves and stir together well. In a mixing bowl, cream butter and sugar. Beat in eggs and vanilla. Sift flour, soda, and salt and add to butter mixture, alternating with date mixture. Stir in pecans. Pour into a greased and floured 9x5x3-inch (23x13x5 cm) loaf pan. Bake at 350F (175C) for 65-75 minutes or until a toothpick inserted in the centre comes out clean. Let stand for 5-10 minutes before removing from pan. Then turn out onto rack and cool. Serve with cream cheese spread.

Cinnamon Coffee Cake

Filling mixture:					
¼ cup	brown sugar, packed	50 ml	½ cup	butter	125 ml
¼ cup	chopped nuts	50 ml	1 cup	white sugar	250 ml
1 tsp	cinnamon	5 ml	2	eggs	2
			1 tsp	vanilla	5 ml
			2 cups	brown sugar	500 ml
			1 tsp	baking powder	5 ml
			1 tsp	baking soda	5 ml
			1 cup	sour cream	250 ml

Preheat oven to 350F (175C). Butter a 10-inch tube pan. For filling, combine brown sugar, nuts, and cinnamon; set aside. In a bowl, cream butter and white sugar until light and fluffy. Beat in eggs, one at a time, and add vanilla. Sift together flour, baking powder and soda. Add to creamed mixture alternating with sour cream. Spread half the batter in the pan. Sprinkle filling on top. Press slightly into dough. Add remaining batter and bake 40-50 minutes.

Steamed Brown Bread

This has been a favourite throughout several generations.

1 cup	white flour	250 ml		1 tsp	baking powder	5 ml
1 cup	whole wheat flour	250 ml		1 tsp	salt	5 ml
1 cup	cornmeal	250 ml		¾ cup	molasses	175 ml
1 tsp	baking soda	5 ml		2 cups	milk	500 ml

Mix dry ingredients together; add molasses, then milk. Pour into an oiled mold lined with parchment or brown paper. Cover tightly, and steam in a large, covered pot for three hours. Coffee cans are great if molds are not available. This is delicious with homemade baked beans on Saturday night.

Lemon Bread

3 cups	flour	750 ml		1 tbsp	lemon peel, grated	15 ml
2 cups	sugar	500 ml		4	eggs	4
1½ tsp	baking powder	7 ml		1 cup	milk	250 ml
1 tsp	salt	5 ml		1 cup	vegetable oil	250 ml

Preheat oven to 350F (175C). Mix together dry ingredients. Add wet ingredients and mix until just blended. Grease and flour two 4x9-inch (10x23 cm) pans. Fill ¾ full with mixture. Bake for 35-40 minutes or until golden brown.

For Glaze: Heat ⅔ cup (150 ml) sugar and ½ cup (125 ml) lemon juice in small saucepan until sugar dissolves.

When loaves are done, puncture tops several times with a fork, and cover with glaze. Remove from pans when cool. Slice and serve.

Cranberry Bread

A Christmas specialty.

2	eggs, beaten	2	1 tsp	salt	5 ml
1 cup	orange juice	250 ml	1 tbsp	baking powder	15 ml
¼ cup	water	50 ml	2 cups	sugar	500 ml
2	orange rinds, grated	2	1 cup	nuts, chopped	250 ml
¼ cup	butter, melted	50 ml	2 cups	cranberries, chopped	500 ml
4 cups	flour	1 L			

Combine first five ingredients. Sift dry ingredients and add nuts and cranberries. Blend well with creamed mixture. Turn into 2 greased and parchment-lined loaf pans. Bake at 325F (165C) for 40 minutes. Lower heat to 300F (150C) and bake 40 minutes more. Remove bread from pans and peel off paper before cooling. Can be frozen.

Ruby's Lemon Loaf

Fresh lemon juice provides the zing.

1 cup	sugar	250 ml	½ cup	milk	125 ml
½ cup	shortening	125 ml	1½ cups	flour	375 ml
2	eggs	2	1 tsp	baking powder	5 ml
1	lemon rind, grated	1	juice	of 1 lemon	
½ tsp	salt	2 ml	¼ cup	sugar	50 ml

Cream 1 cup sugar and shortening. Beat in eggs, one at a time. Mix in rind and milk. Last, add sifted flour, baking powder and salt. Pour into loaf pan and bake at 350C (175C) for about an hour. Remove from oven. Dissolve remaining sugar in lemon juice and drizzle over loaf. Place in oven for an additional 5-8 minutes.

Cranberry Orange Bread

½ cup	butter	125 ml
1 cup	sugar	250 ml
2	eggs	2
½ cup	milk	125 ml
2 cups	flour	500 ml
2 tsp	baking powder	10 ml

½ tsp	salt	2 ml
1 cup	cranberries, fresh or frozen, coarsely chopped	250 ml
1½ tsp	orange peel, grated	7 ml
½ cup	pecans, chopped	125 ml

Cream butter and sugar until light. Beat in eggs, one at a time. Add milk. In a separate bowl, combine flour, baking powder and salt. Fold in cranberries, orange peel and pecans. Add to butter mixture, stirring until just moistened. May be baked in mini loaf pans. Grease and flour pans. Bake at 375F (190C) until a pick inserted in each pan comes out clean, approximately 30 minutes. Time will vary depending on size of pan. Cool on racks. Glaze. Makes 6-8 mini loaves.

For orange glaze: Combine 1 cup (250 ml) icing sugar and 4 teaspoons (20 ml) orange juice in small bowl. Stir. Drizzle over each loaf.

Bea's Blueberry Orange Loaf

2 cups	flour	500 ml
2 tsp	baking powder	10 ml
½ tsp	salt	2 ml
½ tsp	baking soda	2 ml
¾ cup	sugar	175 ml
1 tbsp	orange rind, grated	15 ml
¼ cup	orange juice	50 ml

¼ cup	butter, melted	50 ml
¾ cup	milk	175 ml
1	egg, beaten	1
1 cup	blueberries, washed and dried well	250 ml
½ cups	nuts	125 ml

Sift first five ingredients into a bowl. Combine next five ingredients together and fold into dry ingredients. Mix well. Grease or spray a 9x4x3-inch (23x10x8 cm) loaf pan and spread ⅓ cup of batter into pan. Sprinkle with ½ of the berries and nuts. Add another third of the batter, then the remaining berries and nuts. Top with remaining third of batter. Bake at 350F (175C) for about 50 minutes or until it tests done. Frost when cool, if desired.

· DESSERTS ·

· Best ·

· Traditional ·

· Trendy ·

Summer Fruit Tart

1 sheet	frozen puff pastry 12x12 inch (30x30 cm)	1	2 tbsp	butter, melted	30 ml
			¼ cup	heavy cream	50 ml
1	egg	1	½ cup	almonds, ground	125 ml
1	egg yolk	1	1	peach, thinly sliced	1
⅓ cup	sugar	75 ml	1	plum, thinly sliced	1
1 tbsp	flour	15 ml	½ cup	raspberries	125 ml

Preheat oven to 400F (200C). Cut a 12-inch (30 cm) circle from the sheet of puff pastry; cut trimmings into ¼-inch (0.75 cm) strips. Brush edges of the circle with egg yolk and place the ¼-inch pastry strips all along the outer edge. Prick tart bottom with a fork; refrigerate one hour. Mix egg, sugar, flour, butter, cream and ground almonds; set aside. Bake tart for about 10 minutes or until it rises and turns slightly golden. Fill tart with almond mixture, and bake 10 minutes until filling is set. Arrange fruit in a circle around the edge of tart.

Fresh Strawberry Pie

Strawberries are in season in Nova Scotia for only a short time, so hurry to enjoy them.

4 cups	strawberries, hulled and washed	1 L	1 tsp	lemon juice	5 ml
			1	baked pie shell	1
½ cup	sugar	125 ml		whipping cream	
2 tbsp	cornstarch	30 ml		sugar	
1 cup	water	250 ml		vanilla	

Crush 1 cup of strawberries and place in saucepan. Mix sugar and cornstarch and add to water. Add this mixture to the strawberries. Cook over medium heat until thick and clear. Remove from heat. Add lemon juice. Allow to cool. Arrange remaining berries in cooked pie shell so that pointed ends are up. Pour cooked mixture over the raw berries. Refrigerate for 2-3 hours. Serve with whipped cream flavoured with sugar and vanilla.

Apple Pie

Everyone should bake an apple pie at least once in their life.

Prepare pie crust and chill in refrigerator until ready to use. Wash, peel and slice about 4 cups (375 ml) of apples (enough to fill a pie plate). My favourite apples are the yellow or golden Gravensteins in early fall and Cortlands in the winter.

Grease pie plates with butter. Roll out dough to fit the plate, taking care not to stretch it but removing air bubbles that may form under it. Place apples in a bowl. Sprinkle with ¾-1 cup (180-250 ml) sugar, depending on tartness of apples. Mix well to coat apples. Transfer sugared apple slices to pastry-lined pie plate. Press lightly to pack. Form a slight depression in centre to allow the centre of pie to cook faster and the juice to gather as the apples cook. This will prevent the juice from spilling over in the oven.

Sprinkle apples generously with nutmeg, 1 tbsp (15 ml) of lemon juice and a shake of salt. Dot apples with small pieces of butter. Dampen the outer edges of the crust with water to seal the top crust.

Roll out the pastry for the top crust. Handle the dough gently, so as not to stretch it. Fold crust over in half and mark "vents" in the dough with a sharp knife. Gently lift the folded crust onto the pie so that it covers one half, then lift the folded portion over to cover edges and seal; edges may be fluted or crimped. Sprinkle cold water over surface of pie. Gently press crust over apples.

Place pie on lowest rack in a 425F (218C) oven. Bake for 10-12 minutes. Lower heat to 325-350F (165-175C) and bake approximately 35-45 minutes more. Test with a toothpick inserted into one of the vents. Apples should be soft and mushy and juice bubbling. Remove pies from oven and cool on racks.

Apple pie may be served plain or with slices of Cheddar cheese, whipped cream or ice cream.

Berry Pies

Make crust for 2-crust pie. Top crust can be done in lattice style if desired. Roll out pastry for bottom crust. Fit into well-greased pie pan. To prepare filling, mix the first three ingredients in a bowl:

3 cups	berries (blueberries, raspberries, strawberries, etc.)	750 ml	2½ tbsp	quick-cooking tapioca or ¼ cup (50 ml) flour	38 ml
¾-1 cup	sugar, depending on tartness of fruit	180-250 ml	1 tbsp	lemon juice	15 ml
			pinch	salt	
			3 tbsp	butter	45 ml

Pour fruit into 8-inch pie plate lined with pastry. Heap berries toward the outer edges of pie, leaving the centre more shallow. Place small pieces of butter over berries and drizzle with lemon juice. Shake a sprinkle of salt over all. Dampen edges of bottom crust with cold water. Cut vents into top crust and lay crust on top of fruit. Seal crusts carefully. Edges may be fluted. Bake on lower rack at 425F (220C) for 10 minutes. Reduce heat to 350F (175C) and bake until juice bubbles through vents, about 35-45 minutes. If berries are very tart, use tapioca rather than flour for thickening.

Raisin Pie

Raisin pie has been an old standby for many years, since earlier generations usually had a supply of raisins on hand and raisin pies are simple to make.

Make pastry for a 2-crust pie. Prepare raisin filling:

2 cups	raisins	500 ml	pinch	salt	
2 cups	boiling water	500 ml	1 tsp	vanilla, if desired	5 ml
½ cup	sugar	125 ml	1	lemon or orange	1
2 tbsp	flour	30 ml		butter	

Place raisins and water in saucepan. Mix together sugar and flour and add to raisins and water. Boil for 1 minute, stirring constantly. Remove from heat. Add juice and grated orange or lemon rind. Pour mixture into a pie plate that has been previously buttered and lined with pastry. Dot filling with butter and bake at 425F (220C) for 10 minutes; reduce heat to 350F (175C) and bake 20-30 minutes longer.

Rhubarb Pie

Prepare pie crust for a 2-crust pie.

4 cups	rhubarb, cut in pieces	1 L	4 tbsp	minute tapioca	60 ml
				pie crust for 2-crust pie	
1½ cups	sugar	375 ml			
⅛ tsp	salt	0.5 ml		butter	
				sugar	

Roll out pastry for the bottom of a 9-inch (23 cm) pie plate. Butter pie plate and line with pastry. In a bowl, combine rhubarb, sugar, tapioca and salt. Turn into pie shell. Roll out top crust. Fold in half and cut out vents. Dampen edges of lower crust. Place top crust over fruit and press edges of top and bottom crusts together, sealing well. Crimp or flute edges. Sprinkle cold water over top crust and sprinkle on some granulated sugar. Bake on lowest rack of 425F (220C) oven for 10 minutes. Reduce heat to 350F (175C) and cook until browned and juice bubbles around vents, about 50-60 minutes.

Rhubarb Custard Pie

Prepare and bake 1 pie shell. Make filling:

2 cups	rhubarb, chopped	500 ml		1 tbsp	cornstarch	15 ml
3	eggs, separated	3		½ tsp	vinegar	2 ml
1 cup	sugar	250 ml		6 tbsp	sugar	90 ml
1 tbsp	butter	15 ml				

Cook rhubarb in top part of double boiler. When rhubarb is soft, add sugar mixed with cornstarch. Cook until creamy. Add butter. Remove from heat and pour rhubarb mixture over beaten egg yolks, mixing quickly and constantly. Return to hot water and cook to thicken egg yolks. Cool. Pour into baked pie shell. Make meringue by beating egg whites and vinegar in a bowl until stiff and frothy. Add sugar gradually until sugar is dissolved and meringue is stiff. Spread meringue on top and bake at 350F (175C) until light brown, approximately 10-12 minutes.

Cranberry Pie

3½ cups	cranberries	875 ml		2 tbsp	butter	30 ml
1½ cups	sugar	375 ml		3 tbsp	orange or apple juice	45 ml
1½ tbsp	flour	22 ml				
¼ tsp	salt	1 ml				

Chop cranberries and mix in a bowl with other ingredients. Turn into an unbaked piecrust. Arrange strips of piecrust across the top. Brush piecrust with cold water. Bake at 425F (220C) for 10 minutes, then reduce heat to 350F (175C) and bake until filling bubbles, approximately 35-45 minutes more.

Apple and Cranberry Crumb Pie

			Topping:		
1½ cups	cranberries	375 ml			
1 cup	sugar	250 ml	½ cup	flour	125 ml
1½ tbsp	quick-cooking tapioca	22 ml	¼ cup	brown sugar	50 ml
			¼ tsp	cinnamon	1 ml
dash	salt		¼ cup	butter	50 ml
4 cups	apples, thinly sliced	1 L			
1	pie crust, unbaked	1			

Put cranberries through food chopper or blender; combine with apples. Mix sugar, tapioca and salt, and combine with cranberry-apple mixture. Turn into an unbaked pie shell. Make topping by mixing flour, brown sugar and cinnamon. Cut in butter until mixture resembles coarse crumbs. Sprinkle on top of pie. Bake for 10 minutes at 450F (225C). Reduce heat to 350F (175C) and bake until apples are tender, approximately 35-45 minutes more. If crumbs brown too quickly, reduce heat or place foil over pie.

Sour Cherry Pie

There were a few cherry trees on the farm where I grew up. I was assigned the task of removing the pits of this fruit—each and every one. The delicious pies my mother made were enough reward for this tedious chore.

4 cups	fresh cherries	1 L	2 tbsp	butter	30 ml
3 tbsp	tapioca	45 ml		pastry for one crust and a lattice top	
1⅓ cups	sugar	335 ml			

Wash, drain and pit cherries. Place in bowl and mix in sugar and tapioca. Let this mixture stand for 15 minutes. Pour fruit into pastry-lined pie plate. Dot with butter. Cover with pastry strips. Place in a 450F (230C) oven and bake for 10 minutes. Reduce heat to 350F (175C) and continue to cook until cherries are tender and crust is golden, approximately 35-45 minutes. Use tapioca rather than flour because the high acidity of the cherries can neutralize the thickening effect of the flour.

Vinegar Pie

Very popular years ago when lemons were scarce and expensive.

⅓ cup	vinegar	75 ml	1	baked pie shell	1
1 cup	sugar, divided	250 ml			
1¾ cups	water	430 ml		Meringue:	
6 tbsp	flour	90 ml	3	egg whites	3
3	egg yolks, beaten	3	½ tsp	vinegar	2 ml
¼ cup	water	50 ml	6 tbsp	sugar	90 ml
1 tsp	lemon extract	5 ml			

Stir vinegar, ½ cup (125 ml) sugar and 1¾ cups water into a saucepan. Bring to a boil over medium heat. In a small bowl mix the other ½ cup sugar with flour. Beat egg yolks in ¼ cup water, add lemon and whisk together with flour and sugar thoroughly. Stir egg mixture slowly into vinegar mixture. Let it come to boil and thicken. Pour into baked pie shell. Make meringue by beating egg whites and vinegar in a bowl until stiff and frothy. Add sugar gradually, beating until stiff and sugar is dissolved. Spread over pie. Bake at 350F (175C) until browned, approximately 10-12 minutes.

Shoofly Pie

1½ cups	flour	375 ml	½ tsp	baking soda	2 ml
1 cup	brown sugar, firmly packed	250 ml	⅔ cup	hot water	150 ml
			⅔ cup	molasses	150 ml
½ cup	butter	125 ml	1	pastry shell, 9 inch (23 cm), unbaked	1
¼ tsp	salt	1 ml			

Preheat oven to 350F (175C). Combine the flour, brown sugar, butter and salt. Rub the mixture between the hands to form crumbs. Set aside. Dissolve the baking soda in the water and combine with molasses. Pour this mixture into pastry shell. Sprinkle evenly with crumb mixture. Place pie in oven and bake for 30-40 minutes or until filling is set. Remove from oven and cool on rack.

Buttermilk Pie

Buttermilk was popular as a drink years ago, but it also found its way into pie.

1 cup	buttermilk	250 ml		½ cup	butter	125 ml
2 tsp	vanilla	10 ml		1⅔ cups	sugar	420 ml
1 tbsp	lemon juice	15 ml		3 tbsp	flour	45 ml
⅛ tsp	nutmeg	0.5 ml		4	eggs	4

Mix buttermilk, vanilla, lemon juice and nutmeg. Set aside. Beat eggs lightly and add butter, sugar and flour. Beat again, adding buttermilk mixture. Pour into an unbaked pie shell. Bake at 350F (175C) until centre is firm and top is golden brown, approximately 50 minutes.

Pecan Pie

4	eggs	4		1½ cups	corn syrup	375 ml
1 cup	sugar	250 ml		1 tsp	vanilla	5 ml
¼ cup	flour	50 ml		1 cup	pecans, halved	250 ml
½ tsp	salt	2 ml		1	9-inch single crust	1

Prepare crust, fluting edges to make a stand-up edge. Preheat oven to 350F (175C). Beat eggs slightly in a medium-size bowl. Stir in sugar, flour, salt, corn syrup and vanilla. Pour into an unbaked pie shell. Arrange pecans on top to form pattern, or chop pecans coarsely and sprinkle into shell before adding filling. Bake at 350F (175C) for 45 minutes or until set but still soft. Do not overbake—filling will set as it cools. Serve with whipped cream if desired.

Pumpkin Pie

Everyone wants pumpkin pie to finish off a Thanksgiving dinner, but it is a nice addition to any harvest-time meal.

2 cups	brown sugar	500 ml
5	eggs	5
⅓ cup	flour	75 ml
1 28-oz can	pumpkin	796 ml
1 14-oz can	evaporated milk plus enough whole milk to make 3⅓ cups (835 ml)	385 ml

2 tsp	ginger	10 ml
1 tsp	cinnamon, more if desired	5 ml
¼ tsp	cloves	1 ml
1 tsp	salt	5 ml
2-3	9-inch (23 cm) pie crusts	2-3

Prepare crusts for 2 to 3 single-crust pies. Flute edges. Preheat oven to 425F (220C). Measure brown sugar into a large bowl. Add flour, ginger, cinnamon, cloves and salt. Mix together well. Stir in eggs, pumpkin and milk and beat well. Pour into unbaked pie shells. Place in a 425F (220C) oven on bottom rack for 10 minutes. Reduce heat to 350F (175C), or to 325F (165C) if pies are browning quickly. Bake 30-45 minutes or until a silver knife inserted in centre comes out clean. Remove from oven and cool on racks. When ready to serve, spread with vanilla-flavoured whipped cream and sprinkle with cinnamon. Filling will keep in refrigerator for a day or two. Note: When buying canned pumpkin, be sure not to buy "pumpkin pie filling," which is unsuitable for this recipe.

Butterscotch Pie

¼ cup	butter	50 ml
¾ cup	brown sugar	175 ml
2 cups	milk	500 ml

Mix above ingredients in saucepan. Cook and stir on low heat until sugar is melted. Remove from heat.

6 tbsp	brown sugar	90 ml
6 tbsp	flour	90 ml
¼ tsp	salt	1 ml
3	egg yolks	3
1 tsp	vanilla	5 ml
1	pie shell, baked	1

Meringue:

3	egg whites	3
½ tsp	vinegar or pinch of cream of tartar	2 ml
6 tbsp	sugar	90 ml

In a small bowl, mix together sugar, flour and salt. Reheat milk mixture in double boiler. Add a small amount of warm milk mixture to the dry ingredients, making a paste. Add paste to remainder of milk in double boiler. Beat egg yolks slightly and whisk into hot mixture, beating well, then add to double boiler. Mix well and cook until thickened, stirring constantly. Add vanilla. When thick, cover saucepan and cook for 20 minutes longer. Remove from heat. Add vanilla. Pour into a pie shell. Make meringue by adding vinegar or cream of tartar to beaten egg whites. Beat into a firm froth and gradually add sugar, a little at a time, beating until meringue is firm and satiny. Spread on top of filling, making sure it touches the crust. Bake at 350F (175C) until golden, about 10 minutes. Chill completely. For a butterscotch banana pie or a butterscotch peach pie, slice bananas or peaches into bottom of pie shell before pouring in filling. Use whipped cream for topping.

Butterscotch Pie II

1	pie shell, baked	1	4	eggs, separated	4
½ cup	flour	125 ml	3 tbsp	butter	45 ml
1 cup	brown sugar	250 ml	1 tsp	vanilla	5 ml
2½ cups	milk, hot	625 ml	⅓ cup	granulated sugar	75 ml

Stir together brown sugar and flour in heavy saucepan. Slowly whisk in milk until smooth. Cook, stirring almost constantly over medium heat for about 5 minutes or until thick and smooth; reduce heat to low and cook 5 minutes longer, stirring often. Beat egg yolks and stir into them a little of the hot mixture. Pour egg mixture into pan, stirring constantly, and cook 3 minutes longer. Stir in butter and vanilla. Pour into baked pie shell. Beat egg whites until foamy; gradually beat in granulated sugar until soft peaks form. Mound meringue on top of filling, spreading out to edge of crust to keep it from shrinking. Bake at 350F (175C) for 7-10 minutes or until golden. Cool.

Old-Time Sugar Pie

1½ cups	brown sugar	375 ml	½ tsp	salt	2 ml
¼ cup	flour	50 ml		whipped cream	
1½ cups	whole milk or evaporated milk	375 ml			

Mix sugar and flour. Add milk, and stir well. Pour into an unbaked pie shell. Bake on bottom shelf of a 350F (175C) oven. When cooked, a knife inserted in centre will come out almost clean. Serve with whipped cream. Maple sugar makes a wonderful substitute for the brown sugar.

Chocolate Cream Pie

2 cups	milk	500 ml			hot coffee, enough to make a paste	
1 cup	brown sugar	250 ml				
3 tbsp	cornstarch, heaping	45 ml		2	egg yolks	2
				3 tsp	vanilla	15 ml
3 tbsp	flour	45 ml		1 tbsp	butter, heaping	15 ml
½ tsp	salt	2 ml		1	pie shell, baked	1
½ cup	cocoa	125 ml			whipped cream	
2 tbsp	butter, very soft	30 ml			chocolate shavings	

Scald 1¾ cups (430 ml) milk. In a double boiler combine brown sugar, cornstarch, flour and salt and slowly add reserved ¼ cup (50 ml) milk. Mix to a paste, adding a little more cold milk if necessary. Add the hot milk slowly, stirring well. Mix cocoa, butter and hot coffee to a paste. Add to hot milk mixture in double boiler, stirring constantly until bubbles appear on surface. Beat egg yolks and mix into them a little of the hot mixture from double boiler. Add to double boiler and cook for about 10 minutes, stirring constantly. This mixture will become very thick. Remove from heat and stir in butter and vanilla. Beat for a few seconds. Let cool. Pour into baked pie shell. Allow to remain in refrigerator for a few hours. When ready to serve, spread whipped cream over top. Add a few chocolate shavings over cream.

Vanilla Cream Pie

There is nothing quite as delicious as the delicate flavour of cream pie. This recipe was popular years ago if great grandmother's hens were laying.

⅔ cup	sugar	150 ml		3	eggs, separated and slightly beaten	3
½ tsp	salt	2 ml		1 tbsp	vanilla	15 ml
1 tbsp	flour	15 ml		1 tbsp	butter	15 ml
2½ tbsp	cornstarch	38 ml		1	9-inch (23 cm) pie shell, baked	1
3 cups	milk	750 ml				

Meringue:

3	egg whites	3
¼ tsp	cream of tartar	1 ml
6 tbsp	sugar	90 ml

Place milk in a saucepan over moderate heat. Heat until lukewarm and add the sugar, salt, flour and cornstarch. Stir constantly until mixture thickens and boils for 1 minute. Remove from heat and stir about 1 cup (250 ml) of mixture into the egg yolks. Blend back into mixture in saucepan. Boil for 1 minute only, stirring constantly. Remove from heat and add vanilla and butter. Cool, stirring occasionally. Pour into pie shell and chill thoroughly. Meanwhile make meringue by beating egg whites with cream of tartar; gradually beat in sugar. Continue to beat until mixture is stiff and glossy. Spread meringue lightly on top of filling, bringing it to the edge of crust to prevent meringue from shrinking. Swirl and pull up points in the meringue for added decoration. Bake at 375F (190C) for 8-10 minutes until lightly browned. Let cool at room temperature.

Variations to Cream Pie

Banana Cream Pie: Arrange a layer of sliced bananas in pie shell before pouring in cream filling.

Coconut Cream Pie: Fold ¾ cup (175 ml) flaked coconut into filling just before pouring into pie shell.

Coconut Cream Pie

Deliciously sweet!

3 cups	milk	750 ml		⅔ cup	coconut	150 ml
3	egg yolks, beaten	3		1 tbsp	butter	15 ml
1 cup	sugar	250 ml		1 tsp	vanilla, or more	5 ml
⅓ cup	cornstarch	75 ml		1	10-inch (25 cm) pie shell, baked	1
pinch	salt					

Topping

3	egg whites	3		⅓ cup	sugar	85 ml
⅛ tsp	cream of tartar	0.5 ml		½ tsp	vanilla	2 ml
pinch	salt			2 tbsp	coconut	30 ml

Combine and heat milk and yolks in saucepan, stirring constantly. Mix sugar, cornstarch and salt; add to heated milk mixture. Cook until thickened, then one minute more. Remove from heat and add coconut, butter and vanilla. Pour into cooled pie shell. Beat egg whites, cream of tartar and salt until frothy; add sugar very gradually and beat until peaks form. Add vanilla. Spread meringue over filling, taking care to spread meringue to crust. Sprinkle with coconut and bake at 325F (165C) for about 12-15 minutes or until a delicate brown.

Peaches and Cream Pie

¾ cup	sugar	175 ml
1½ cups	fresh peaches, chopped	375 ml
1 pouch	unflavoured gelatin	1
¼ cup	cold water	50 ml

½ cup	hot water	125 ml
1 tbsp	lemon juice	15 ml
dash	salt	
½ cup	heavy whipping cream, whipped	125 ml
1	9-inch (23 cm) pie shell, baked and cooled	1

Mix sugar and peaches and let sit. Soften gelatin in cold water, then dissolve in hot water. Cool. Add peach mixture, lemon juice and salt. Chill until partially set. Fold in whipped cream. Pour into pie shell and refrigerate. Note: Fresh strawberries or a mixture of the two fruits can be substituted for peaches.

Lemon Pie

3	eggs, separated	3
1 cup	sugar	250 ml
⅓ cup	flour	75 ml
½ tsp	salt	2 ml
¼ cup	lemon juice	50 ml
1 tsp	lemon rind, grated	5 ml

1½ cups	water	375 ml
1 tsp	butter	5 ml
1	9-inch (23 cm) pie shell, baked	1
	sugar, to taste	

Beat egg yolks. Gradually stir in the 1 cup sugar. Add flour, salt, lemon juice and rind. Cook in the top of a double boiler over boiling water. When mixture begins to cook, gradually add water. Continue to cook over boiling water until smooth and thickened, stirring constantly. Remove from heat. Add butter. Cool. Pour into pastry shell. Beat egg whites and sugar (to taste) until stiff. Cover pie evenly with meringue. Bake at 375F (190C) for 8-10 minutes until lightly browned. Let cool before serving.

Key Lime Pie with Meringue

3-4	eggs, separated	3-4
1 10½-oz can	condensed milk	300 ml
½ cup	lime juice and zest from 1 lime	125 ml
1	pie shell, baked	1

Meringue:		
3	egg whites	3
¼ tsp	cream of tartar	1 ml
6 tbsp	sugar	90 ml

Beat egg yolks until smooth. Add condensed milk, lime juice and lime zest. Beat together well. Pour into pie shell. Make meringue by beating together egg whites and cream of tartar until frothy. Gradually add sugar a little at a time, beating after each addition. Continue until meringue is stiff and stands in peaks. Place on rack in top third of oven at 350F (175C). Bake until golden brown, approximately 15 minutes. A drop or two of green food colouring may be added to the milk and lime juice filling, if desired.

Key Lime Pie

| 1 10½-oz can | sweetened condensed milk | 300 ml |
| 4 | egg yolks | 4 |

| 4 oz | key lime juice | 125 ml |
| 1 | 9-inch (23 cm) graham cracker pie shell (recipe follows) | 1 |

In mixing bowl on low speed, blend condensed milk and egg yolks. Slowly add key lime juice and mix well. Pour ingredients into the pie shell and bake at 350F (175C) for about 15 minutes. Chill and serve. Optional garnish: Whipped cream and raspberry or mango purée is a wonderful addition!

Hot Water Pastry

A good recipe for beginners.

1 cup	shortening	250 ml		1 tsp	salt	5 ml
½ cup	boiling water	125 ml		½ tsp	baking powder	2 ml
3 cups	flour	750 ml				

Pour boiling water over shortening. Stir well. Cool. Sift dry ingredients together and stir into the cooled shortening mixture. Work into a ball. Refrigerate.

Pastry

3 cups	flour, sifted	750 ml		1 cup	shortening	250 ml
1 tbsp	sugar	15 ml		¼ cup	cold water	50 ml
2 tsp	salt	10 ml			butter	

Combine flour, sugar and salt. Cut in shortening until mixture is the consistency of coarse crumbs. Add enough cold water to make mixture hold together in the palm of hand. Let stand in refrigerator overnight for best results. Roll out pastry, butter it, fold over and roll again; repeat. Handle very gently. Keep refrigerated until ready to use. Use as little flour as possible.

Wild Berry Tart

Pastry:		
1⅓ cups	flour	335 ml
3 tbsp	sugar	45 ml
½ tsp	salt	2 ml
⅔ cup	butter	150 ml
⅓ cup	whipping cream, chilled	75 ml

Filling:		
½ cup	butter, softened	125 ml
½ cup	sugar	125 ml
4	eggs	4
2 tsp	vanilla	10 ml
1 cup	flour	250 ml
3 cups	fresh blueberries or fresh or frozen raspberries	750 ml

Make pastry by mixing all ingredients and refrigerate until thoroughly chilled. Choose a 10- or 11-inch (25x28cm) tart pan with a removable bottom. Roll out dough to fit tart pan. Prick bottom of pastry and cover with foil. Fill with pie weights or dried beans. Bake in bottom third of oven at 375F (190C) for 15-20 minutes. Lift out weights and foil and continue to bake until golden brown. Let cool. In a large bowl, beat butter with sugar. Beat in eggs, one at a time. Beat in vanilla. Stir in flour. Fold in berries. Spread filling evenly over tart shell. Bake at 350F (175C) for about 45 minutes or until set. Let cool on rack. Yields about 12 servings. May be garnished with dollops of whipped cream and fruit.

Simple Strawberry Tart

1 pkg	instant vanilla pudding (4 servings size)	1		4 cups	whole fresh strawberries	1 L
½ cup	milk	125 ml		½ cup	apple jelly	125 ml
2 tsp	orange rind, grated	10 ml		1	9-inch (23 cm) pie crust, baked	1
½ cup	prepared whipped cream	125 ml				

Prepare the instant pudding as directed, using only ½ cup (125 ml) milk. Mixture will be thick. Fold in the orange rind and whipped cream. Spread crust with pudding filling. Wash and thoroughly dry strawberries. Set most perfect berry aside for centre. Hull remaining berries and cut in half lengthwise. Working from outside edge of tart to centre, place berries on filling, cut side up pointing toward edges of tart; put perfect berry in centre. Melt apple jelly over low heat. Spoon over strawberries as a glaze. Chill.

Elda's Butterscotch Pie Filling

2 cups	milk	500 ml		1 tbsp	vanilla	15 ml
1 cup	brown sugar	250 ml		¼ cup	butter	50 ml
¼ cup	flour	50 ml		¼ tsp	cream of tartar	1 ml
2	eggs, separated	2		5 tbsp	sugar	75 ml

Combine 1½ cups milk with brown sugar and heat in double boiler. Stir while heating until sugar is dissolved. In a separate bowl, beat egg yolks, mixing with the remaining ½ cup milk and flour. Add to the milk-sugar mixture. Cook and stir until thickened. Add vanilla and butter and blend until smooth. Pour into a baked pie shell. Make meringue by beating together egg whites and cream of tartar until frothy. Gradually add sugar a little at a time, beating after each addition until meringue is stiff. Bake at 350F (175C) for 10-15 minutes.

Fresh Fruit Flan

Always an attractive dessert.

To prepare a rich egg-tart dough, combine:

1 cup	flour	250 ml
2 tbsp	sugar	30 ml
½ tsp	salt	2 ml

Work in:

6 tbsp	butter, softened	90 ml

Make a well in dry mixture and add:

1	egg yolk	1
½ tsp	vanilla	2 ml
1 tbsp	lemon juice or water	15 ml

Stir until mixture forms one blended ball. Cover and refrigerate for at least 30 minutes. Roll dough to ⅛-inch thickness (0.3 cm) as for pie dough. Line 10-inch (25 cm) pan. Prick well with fork. Chill for 15 minutes. Bake at 425F (220C) for 7-10 minutes. Cool.

Fruit filling for flan:

1 8-oz pkg	cream cheese	250 ml
½ cup	icing sugar, sifted	125 ml
1 tsp	vanilla	5 ml
½ cup	whipping cream	125 ml

2 cups	strawberries, halved	500 ml
1	kiwi fruit, sliced	1
½ cup	red currant jelly	125 ml
1 tbsp	lemon juice	15 ml

Beat cream cheese, icing sugar and vanilla together until smooth. Whip cream until stiff and fold into cheese mixture. Spread evenly in baked crust. Chill. Arrange strawberry halves and sliced kiwi attractively over cheese mixture. Melt jelly and lemon juice together. Brush or spoon over fruit to glaze. Chill. Serve flan at room temperature.

Almond-Filled Chocolate Torte

⅓ cup	cake flour, sifted	75 ml
3 tbsp	cocoa	45 ml
¼ cup	white sugar	50 ml
6	egg whites	6
½ tsp	cream of tartar	2 ml
¼ tsp	salt	1 ml
1 tsp	vanilla extract	5 ml
½ cup	white sugar	125 ml
	icing sugar, sifted	

Almond Filling:

5 tsp	cornstarch	25 ml
¼ tsp	salt	1 ml
¼ cup	white sugar	50 ml
1 cup	milk	250 ml
2	eggs, beaten	2
2 tbsp	Amaretto (almond liqueur)	30 ml

Preheat oven to 375F (190C). Sift flour, cocoa and ¼ cup (50 ml) white sugar together. Beat egg whites with cream of tartar and salt until soft peaks form, and gradually add ½ cup (125 ml) sugar, beating until stiff and shiny; add vanilla. Gradually sift dry mixture over beaten egg whites and gently fold in. Spoon batter into an ungreased 9x5-inch (23x13cm) loaf pan. Bake for 25 minutes. Invert pan and cool completely. Remove cake and cut it into 3 layers.

To make almond filling: Combine sugar, cornstarch and salt in a saucepan. Mix eggs and milk together and stir them into the sugar mixture. Cook over medium heat, stirring constantly until thick and bubbling. Cook for an additional 2 minutes. Remove from heat, add the almond liqueur and stir well. Cover the surface of the filling with plastic wrap and chill completely before using.

Spread almond filling between the layers and dust top with sifted icing sugar. Makes about 10 servings.

Southern Pecan Pie

If both light and dark corn syrup are not available, either one will do.

3	eggs, slightly beaten	3	1 tbsp	flour	15 ml
¾ cup	dark corn syrup	175 ml	1 cup	pecans	250 ml
¾ cup	light corn syrup	175 ml	1 tsp	sugar	5 ml
2 tbsp	butter, melted	30 ml	1	9-inch (23 cm) pie shell, unbaked	1
¼ tsp	salt	1 ml			
1 tsp	vanilla	5 ml			

Mix the flour, sugar, salt and butter. Blend in the syrups, eggs and vanilla. Spread the pecans over the bottom of the pie shell and pour in the mix. Bake in a 325F (180C) oven for one hour or until firm.

Graham Cracker Crust

1¼ cups	graham cracker crumbs	310 ml	2 tbsp	sugar	30 ml
			⅓ cup	butter, melted	75 ml

Heat oven to 375F (190C). In mixing bowl combine graham cracker crumbs and sugar; stir in butter until blended. Press mixture firmly and evenly over bottom and sides of a 9-inch pie plate. Bake 10 minutes until browned. Cool completely on wire rack.

Basic Pie Pastry

2 cups	flour, sifted	500 ml		1 cup	shortening	250 ml
¾ tsp	salt	3 ml		4 tbsp	water, cold	60 ml

Combine flour and salt. Cut in shortening until mixture consists of lumps the size of peas. Do not overmix. Sprinkle with cold water, 1 tbsp (15 ml) at a time, mixing lightly. Turn out onto a floured board, form into firm ball, halve dough and flatten. Chill in refrigerator until ready to use.

Pie Pastry with Butter and Lard

2 cups	flour	500 ml		⅓ cup	lard	75 ml
1 tsp	salt	5 ml		⅓ cup	butter	75 ml
½ tsp	baking powder	2 ml			ice water	

Mix flour, salt and baking powder. Work in lard and butter until mixture resembles very small peas. Sprinkle in up to ⅓ cup (75 ml) of ice water, stirring lightly until dough will hold together. Chill for at least 30 minutes.

Quiche Pastry (Cream Cheese)

Easy to handle, never tough.

½ cup	butter or hard margarine	125 ml		4 oz	cream cheese, softened	125 g
				1 cup	flour, more or less	250 ml

Beat butter and cream cheese until smooth and light. Knead in flour. Suitable for one 9-inch (23 cm) pie or 24 tarts.

Pie Crust Pastry

5 cups	flour	1.25 L	1 lb	shortening or lard	454 g
2 tsp	salt	10 ml	1	egg	1
1 tsp	baking powder	5 ml	2 tbsp	vinegar	30 ml
3 tbsp	brown sugar	45 ml		cold water	

Measure dry ingredients into a large bowl. Stir. Cut in shortening using a pastry blender until mixture is moist and crumbly. Break egg into measuring cup and beat. Add vinegar and enough cold water to make one cup (250 ml) in total. Pour slowly over flour mixture. Stir with fork. Pack together with hands until it forms a ball. Makes enough crust for 4 (2-crust) pies. Can be refrigerated for up to 2 weeks wrapped in plastic, or frozen.

No Fail Pastry
with Egg and Vinegar

2 cups	flour	500 ml	1	egg	1
¾ tsp	salt	3 ml	2 tbsp	cold water	30 ml
1 cup	shortening, room temperature	250 ml	1 tbsp	white vinegar	15 ml

Combine flour and salt. Cut in shortening until mixture resembles large peas. Beat egg, water and vinegar together. Pour all of the liquid over flour mixture. Stir together until mixture is moistened. Form into ball with hands. Divide dough in half; shape into balls. Flatten each ball; wrap and chill.

Cheese Pastry

1½ cups	flour	375 ml		¾ cup	sharp cheese, grated	175 ml
¼ tsp	salt	1 ml		2 tbsp +2 tsp	water	40 ml
½ cup	shortening	125 ml				

Sift flour and salt together into bowl. Work shortening into flour with a fork or pastry blender until mixture resembles small peas. Stir in cheese. Add water, 1 tbsp (15 ml) at a time. Stir lightly. Form into ball with hands. Chill.

Three Double-Crust Pastry with Lard, Egg and Vinegar

5½ cups	flour	1.4 L		1 tbsp	vinegar	15 ml
1 tsp	salt	5 ml		1	egg	1
1 lb	lard	454 g			water, cold	

Combine flour and salt. Do not sift. Cut in lard with pastry blender, leaving a few larger pieces among smaller ones. Mixture should resemble coarse oatmeal. Mix together egg and vinegar. Add enough cold water to make 1 cup (250 ml). Add to flour mixture, a little at a time. Add only enough liquid to hold dough together. Work in all crumbs and form dough into ball. Chill. Roll out to fit pie plate. Let it fit loosely into pie plate; do not stretch. Makes enough for 3 (2-crust) pies.

Mom's Strawberry Shortcake

There's nothing like it!

Shortcake:

2 cups	flour	500 ml		1	egg	1
4 tsp	baking powder	20 ml			milk	
½ tsp	salt	2 ml		2 quarts	strawberries	2 L
2 tbsp	sugar	30 ml			sugar, to taste	
½ cup	shortening	125 ml		1 pint	whipping cream	500 ml
					vanilla, to taste	

Sift flour, baking powder, salt and sugar into a mixing bowl. Cut in shortening. Break egg into a measuring cup and beat with a fork, adding enough milk to make 1 cup (250 ml) of liquid. Stir into flour mixture. Mix together quickly and, turn out onto a board and knead for a few strokes. Pat out dough to about 1-inch (2.5 cm) thickness and, with a sharp knife, cut into squares. Arrange on baking pan and bake at 425F (220C) until golden brown and done in centre. Remove from oven. Cool on rack.

Wash and hull strawberries. Reserve a few whole berries and a few sliced berries for garnish. Mash berries in bowl and add sugar to taste. Set aside. Whip cream in mixing bowl, add sugar and a little vanilla to taste. Keep cold until ready to serve.

Split shortcake in two and place bottom halves in serving dishes. Place on each a dollop of whipped cream and a large spoonful of mashed berries. Replace tops. Repeat for top halves. Top each shortcake with a whole berry and a few sliced berries.

Double Treat Shortcake: Raspberry and Rhubarb

3 cups	rhubarb	750 ml
¾ cup	sugar	175 ml
2 tbsp	water	30 ml

Combine ingredients in a saucepan; cover. Place over low heat until mixture begins to boil. Simmer until tender. Chill.

2 cups	raspberries, fresh or frozen	500 ml	1 tsp	salt	5 ml
			2 tbsp	sugar	30 ml
½ cup	sugar	125 ml	¼ cup	shortening	50 ml
2 cups	flour	500 ml	1 cup	milk	250 ml
4 tsp	baking powder	20 ml	2 tbsp	butter, softened	30 ml

Place raspberries in a bowl. Sprinkle with sugar and let stand while preparing and baking shortcake. Sift dry ingredients in a bowl. Cut in shortening. Add milk and mix with fork to make a soft, puffy dough. Turn onto lightly floured board and knead gently about 10 times. Divide dough in two. Pat half into an 8-inch (20 cm) round pan. Spread with butter. Pat remaining dough into an 8-inch (20 cm) round and place on top of other round. Bake at 450F (230C) for 15-20 minutes or until done. Remove from oven and place on rack. Cut shortcake into 5 wedges.

1 cup	whipping cream, whipped	250 ml		icing sugar and vanilla, to taste

To serve: In serving dishes, spread whipped cream and then rhubarb sauce on bottom half of each wedge. Cover with top of each wedge, and spread with a layer of whipped cream and raspberries.

Saucy Rhubarb Dumplings

Another way to enjoy versatile rhubarb.

5 cups	rhubarb or	1.25 L
3 cups	rhubarb plus 2 cups (500 ml) sliced strawberries	750 ml
¾ cup	sugar	175 ml

2 tbsp	cornstarch	30 ml
½ cup	water	125 ml
2 tbsp	butter	30 ml

Place rhubarb in deep skillet or heavy pot. (If using frozen rhubarb let it thaw.) Mix sugar and cornstarch together. Add to rhubarb. Add water and butter. Bring to boil, stirring gently. Boil 1 minute. Reduce heat to low.

To make dough:

1 cup	flour	250 ml
2 tsp	baking powder	10 ml
½ tsp	salt	2 ml
½ cup	milk	125 ml

1 tsp	sugar	5 ml
2 tbsp	butter	30 ml
	cream	

Combine dry ingredients in a bowl. Cut in butter. Add milk, stirring until just blended. Drop by small spoonfuls onto simmering rhubarb. Cover and cook for 20 minutes, or until dough is cooked through. Serve warm with pouring cream.

Fruit Fool

"Fools" may be made from fresh or cooked fruits. Fruit combinations are equally delicious. Some favourites are applesauce, rhubarb, gooseberry, apricot and currant. Make a purée of whatever fruit you have. You will need 1 cup (250 ml) of fruit for each cup of whipped cream. Fold cream into fruit and add 1½ tsp (7 ml) grated lemon rind or ½ tsp (2 ml) almond flavouring. Place mixture in serving bowl. Sprinkle top with crumbled coconut macaroons. Chill thoroughly. Serve with ladyfingers.

Rhubarb Fool

7 cups	fresh rhubarb, trimmed and cut into 1-inch pieces	1.75 L		¼ tsp	mace	1 ml
				3 tbsp	unsalted butter, melted	45 ml
1 cup	gingersnaps, crushed	250 ml		1 cup	whipped cream or	250 ml
				2 cups	vanilla ice cream	500 ml
⅔ cup	sugar	150 ml			water	
½ tsp	cinnamon	2 ml				

Place rhubarb in a large saucepan; add about 1 cup (250 ml) water—just enough to prevent rhubarb from sticking. Cover and cook about 10 minutes over medium heat, stirring occasionally, until tender (not mushy). Combine crushed gingersnaps with sugar and spices; add melted butter, and mix well. Lightly grease a 1-quart baking dish, add a layer of the rhubarb, and sprinkle with some of the crumb mixture. Repeat layering, ending with the crumbs. Bake at 350F (175C) for 15 minutes. Let cool slightly but serve warm, with whipped cream or vanilla ice cream. Serves 8.

Ruby Rhubarb Dessert

2 cups	rhubarb juice	500 ml
1 3-oz pkg	strawberry Jell-O	90 g

Bring rhubarb juice to a boil. Remove from heat and add Jell-O powder. Stir until dissolved. Chill until set. If desired, fold in fruit when Jell-O is partially set.

Blueberry Buckle

A great old-time dessert.

½ cup	shortening	125 ml	2 cups	blueberries, fresh	500 ml
½ cup	sugar	125 ml	¼ tsp	salt	1 ml
1	egg, beaten	1	2½ tsp	baking powder	12 ml
2 cups	flour	500 ml	1 tsp	vanilla	5 ml
½ cup	milk	125 ml			

Cream shortening and sugar. Add egg and vanilla. Mix well. Sift flour, baking powder and salt, and add to creamed mixture alternating with milk. Pour into an 8-inch (20 cm) square pan. Sprinkle blueberries over batter.

Make a topping of:

½ cup	white sugar	125 ml	½ tsp	cinnamon	2 ml
½ cup	flour	125 ml	¼ cup	butter	50 ml

Mix ingredients into a crumbly mixture and sprinkle over blueberries. Bake at 350F (175C) for 1 hour.

Upside Down Apple Cake

3 tbsp	butter	45 ml	1⅛ cups	flour	280 ml
⅓ cup	sugar	75 ml	2 tsp	baking powder	10 ml
1	small egg	1	2-3	apples	2-3
¼ tsp	salt	1 ml		cinnamon or nutmeg, as desired	
½ cup	milk	125 ml			
1 tsp	vanilla	5 ml			

Cream butter and sugar. Add egg and vanilla. Beat well. Sift flour, baking powder and salt together; add, alternating with milk, to first mixture. Pare and very thinly slice apples. Cover a well-greased 8x8-inch (20 cm) pan with apples and sprinkle with sugar and cinnamon or nutmeg. Spread cake mixture on top. Bake at 350F (175C) for 30-40 minutes. Invert on plate and serve with whipped cream or ice cream. This recipe is good with blueberries or other fruits.

Apple Crisp

On a cold winter day, what could be better than apple crisp for dessert?

1 cup	flour	250 ml		½ cup	butter	125 ml
1 cup	rolled oats	250 ml		6 cups	apples, peeled and sliced	1.5 L
1 cup	brown sugar, lightly packed	250 ml		¼ cup	water	50 ml
1 tsp	cinnamon	5 ml			salt	

Mix together flour, rolled oats, brown sugar, and cinnamon. Cut in butter. Set aside. Spread apples into a greased 9x9-inch (23 cm) pan. Pour water over apples and sprinkle with a little salt. Cover with crumbs, patting firmly. Bake at 350F (175C) for 35-40 minutes or until apples are tender. Serve warm. Good with ice cream.

Blueberry Grunt

Fluffy dumplings, floating in a rich blue sauce. Don't let the name put you off.

Sauce:

4 cups	blueberries, fresh or frozen	1 L		¾ cup	sugar	175 ml
				2 tbsp	lemon juice	30 ml
1½ cup	water	375 ml				

Combine ingredients in a large, covered saucepan. Heat to boiling. Immediately add dumplings.

Dumplings:

2 cups	flour	500 ml		1 tbsp	sugar	15 ml
4 tsp	baking powder	20 ml		2 tbsp	butter	30 ml
½ tsp	salt	2 ml		1 cup	milk	250 ml

Sift dry ingredients into a mixing bowl. Work in butter. Add milk gradually, while mixing with a fork. Do not overmix. Drop small spoonfuls into hot sauce in pot. Cover tightly. Cook for 15 minutes without lifting cover.

Poached Granny Smith Apples

A lovely substitute for applesauce.

6	Granny Smith apples	6	4 cups	water	1 L
juice	of 1 lemon	1	1 8-oz jar	ginger jelly	250 g
2 cups	sugar	500 ml	1	lemon, thickly sliced	1

Peel apples, taking care to leave stems intact, and brush them with lemon juice to keep them from turning brown. Combine sugar and water in a large pot, bring to a boil; cook until sugar is completely dissolved. Stir in ginger jelly and add apples and lemon slices. Poach for about 20 minutes or until the fruit is easily pierced with a sharp knife. Remove the fruit from the pot and boil remaining liquid to reduce by half. Cool and pour over the fruit. Serve warm or at room temperature.

Apple Crunch

1½ lb	Macintosh apples, tart	750 g	Topping:		
1 tbsp	brown sugar	15 ml	1 cup	rolled oats	250 ml
1 tsp	cinnamon	5 ml	¼ cup	brown sugar	50 ml
2 tbsp	cold water	30 ml	¼ cup	whole wheat flour	50 ml
	butter		2 tbsp	wheat germ	30 ml
	ice cream, yogurt or Cheddar cheese (optional)			salt	
			3 tbsp	butter, melted	45 ml

Grease a shallow baking pan with butter. Pare, quarter and core apples and slice thinly. Mix the cinnamon with sugar. Layer apples in dish and sprinkle each layer with spice-sugar mixture. Sprinkle the water over all. To make topping, mix oats, sugar, flour and salt in a bowl. Stir in melted butter with a fork until thoroughly mixed. Sprinkle the topping evenly over the apples. Bake at 375F (190C) for about 1 hour or until apples are tender and topping is crisp and browned. Serve plain or with ice cream, yogurt or Cheddar cheese.

Apple Slices

An Annapolis Valley recipe. Everyone asks for seconds and wishes for thirds.

Crust:

3 cups	flour	750 ml	1 cup	shortening	250 ml
1 tbsp	sugar	15 ml	1	egg, separated	1
1 tsp	salt	5 ml		milk	

Filling:

⅔ cup	Cornflakes, crushed	150 ml	1½ cups	sugar	375 ml
5 cups	apples, peeled and sliced	1.25 L	1 tsp	cinnamon	5 ml

Glaze:

1 cup	icing sugar	250 ml	2 tbsp	lemon juice	30 ml

Sift together flour, sugar and salt. Cut in shortening. Put egg yolk in measuring cup and add enough milk to make ⅔ cup (150 ml) of liquid. Add to flour mixture and mix until dough shapes into a ball. Roll out half of dough to a 15x11-inch (38x28 cm) rectangle; transfer to baking pan. Cover with Cornflakes, then with apple slices. Mix sugar and cinnamon; sprinkle over apples. Roll out other half of dough for top crust. Place over apples and pinch edges of top and bottom crusts together. Mark several vents in crust. Bake at 375F (190C) for 40 minutes. Combine glaze ingredients. While hot, drizzle glaze over top. Cut into squares. Serve.

Cool Fruit Delight

1 cup	graham wafer crumbs	250 ml	1 cup	mini marshmallows	250 ml
¼ cup	margarine, melted	50 ml	1 28-oz can	fruit cocktail, drained	796 ml
¼ cup	sugar	50 ml	2 cups	sour cream	500 ml

Combine graham wafers and sugar. Add melted margarine. Press mixture onto bottom of springform pan. Combine marshmallows, fruit cocktail and sour cream. Blend well and pour over crust. Chill several hours or overnight. Makes about 12 servings.

Apple Pandowdy

5 cups	sliced apples	1.25 L	
1 cup	brown sugar	250 ml	
¼ tsp	salt	1 ml	
1½ cups	water	375 ml	
½ tsp	nutmeg	2 ml	
½ tsp	cinnamon	2 ml	
¼ cup	flour	50 ml	
2 tbsp	butter	30 ml	
1 tbsp	vinegar	15 ml	
1 tsp	vanilla	5 ml	

Dough:

1 cup	flour	250 ml
2 tsp	baking powder	10 ml
¾ tsp	salt	3 ml
¾ cup	milk	175 ml
3 tbsp	shortening	45 ml

Place apples in the bottom of a greased 8x12-inch (20x30 cm) pan. Make sauce by placing brown sugar, salt, flour, water, vinegar and butter in a saucepan. Cook until thick. Remove from heat and add spices and vanilla. Pour over apples in pan. Prepare dough by combining flour, baking powder and salt. Mix in shortening, then milk. Combine as for biscuits. Drop in rough mounds on top of apples and sauce in pan. Bake at 375F (190C) for about 40 minutes. Serve warm with whipped cream or ice cream.

Fruit Soufflé

¾ cup	fruit purée, fresh or canned	175 ml	pinch	salt	
				sugar, to taste	
1 tbsp	lemon juice, fresh	15 ml	3	egg whites	3

Butter a 1-quart (1 L) soufflé dish and sprinkle with sugar. Heat the fruit purée in a small pan. Add the lemon juice, salt and sugar, and stir to blend; remove from heat. Beat the egg whites until stiff but not dry, and stir them into the hot purée until evenly blended. Spoon into soufflé dish and bake at 350F (175C) for 20-25 minutes. Serve immediately.

Canned applesauce, apricots, sour cherries, pineapple, fresh berries, apricots, pears or peaches can be used. Whatever is used, the fruit should be well drained.

Fruit Crumble

A candy-like topping the youngsters will love.

3 cups	rhubarb or apples diced, blueberries	750 ml	¾ cup	sugar	175 ml
			¼ cup	water	50 ml

Mix above ingredients in baking pan. Set aside.

1 cup	brown sugar	250 ml	½ cup	butter	125 ml
1 cup	flour	250 ml	1 tsp	vanilla	5 ml

Mix flour, brown sugar and butter together until crumbly. Stir in vanilla. Spread crumbs on fruit, and bake at 350F (175C) until fruit is bubbling and crumbs are browned. Serve hot or cold with cream, ice cream or custard sauce. If using apples, add 1 tsp cinnamon to the first layer in baking dish.

Banana Hawaiian Dessert

1 cup	heavy cream	250 ml	8	firm bananas, cut into 1-inch pieces	8
1 cup	sour cream	250 ml			
2 tbsp	icing sugar	30 ml	1 cup	flaked coconut	250 ml

Whip heavy cream until stiff. Add sour cream and sugar. Beat at low speed until blended. Dip bananas in creamed mixture, coating well. Roll in coconut. Pile in dessert dishes and tuck 2 slices of ripe strawberries on the top.

Death by Chocolate

Take a chance on this one.

1	chocolate cake mix, 2-layer size	1	4 cups	milk	1 L
⅔ cup	Kahlua liqueur	150 ml	2 8-oz tubs	frozen whipped topping, thawed	2x250 g
2 pkgs	instant chocolate pudding, 4-serving size	2	6 1½-oz bars	Skor chocolate bars, finely ground	6x38 g bars

Prepare cake according to package directions. Bake in 2 greased 8-inch (20 cm) round cake pans. Cool. Drizzle one of the cooked cakes with Kahlua. Cut in 1-inch (2.5 cm) squares. Transfer to 6-quart (6 L) glass trifle bowl. Drizzle second cake with Kahlua. Cut in 1-inch (2.5 cm) squares. Set aside. Beat pudding mix and add milk until smooth but not thick. Pour ½ the pudding over cake in bowl. Spread with ½ whipped topping. Sprinkle ½ crushed Skor bars over topping. Repeat layers beginning with reserved cake pieces. Chill until ready to serve. Serves 20 people.

Fairy Dream Dessert

1 cup	water	250 ml	1	egg yolk, slightly beaten	1
½ cup	sugar	125 ml	6	marshmallows	6
1	lemon, juice and rind	1	1	egg white, stiffly beaten	1
2 tbsp	cornstarch	30 ml			

Combine water, sugar, cornstarch and lemon in double boiler. Bring to boil. Boil for 6 minutes. Mix a portion of hot mixture to beaten egg yolk; add to mixture and boil 1 more minute. Remove from heat and stir in marshmallows. Stir until melted and then fold in beaten egg white. Chill and serve.

Luscious Dessert

2 cups	flour	500 ml		1 lg pkg	instant lemon pudding	1
1 cup	margarine	250 ml		1 cup	milk	250 ml
½ cup	nuts, chopped	125 ml			coconut	
1 8-oz pkg	cream cheese	250 g			nuts	
1 cup	icing sugar	250 ml				
2 cups	Cool Whip or Dream Whip, divided	500 ml				

Mix together flour and margarine. Stir in nuts. Press into a 9x12-inch (22x33 cm) pan. Bake at 325F (160C) for 25 minutes or until lightly browned. Cool. Cream together cream cheese and icing sugar; add 1 cup Cool Whip or Dream Whip. Mix well and spread over crust. Add milk to lemon instant pudding and whip. Pour over cheese mixture. Spread remaining Cool Whip over lemon mixture. Top with coconut and nuts. Chill.

Caramel Banana Sundaes

3 tbsp	brown sugar	45 ml		¼ tsp	cinnamon, if desired	1 ml
2 tbsp	butter	30 ml		2	firm bananas, cut in ½-inch slices	2
2 tbsp	whipping cream	30 ml				
1 tsp	vanilla	5 ml				

In skillet, combine brown sugar, cream, butter, vanilla and cinnamon. Bring to a boil, stirring constantly. Cook for 2 minutes. Remove from heat, add bananas and stir until coated. Keep warm. Serve warm over ice cream.

Jean's Super Dessert

This Cape Breton recipe from Jean Curtis' kitchen is light and delicious!

1 pkg	orange Jell-O	85 g	1 19-oz can	pineapple, crushed and drained	540 ml
16 oz	dry cottage cheese	500 ml			
1 cup	sour cream	250 ml	4 cups	Cool Whip	1 L

Sprinkle Jell-O powder in a large bowl. Add cottage cheese and sour cream, stirring well. Mix in crushed pineapple. Fold in Cool Whip. Chill for a few hours before serving.

Crêpes

3	eggs	3	½ tsp	salt	2 ml
1 cup	milk	250 ml	3 tbsp	butter, melted	45 ml
1 cup	white flour	250 ml		vegetable oil	

Process first 5 ingredients in a food processor or blender until smooth. If desired whisk ingredients together by hand. Heat an 8-inch (20 cm) fry pan or crêpe pan over medium-high heat. Brush pan lightly with oil. Oil pan as needed, every 3-4 crepes. Pour about ¼ cup (50 ml) batter into hot pan, tipping it to distribute batter evenly. Cook about 30 seconds, until crêpe has separated from sides of pan and bottom is very slightly browned. Flip crêpe and cook on other side for about 10 seconds. Remove to plate and cover with damp tea towel to prevent drying. Reheat fry pan, pour in more batter and continue process. Fill as desired.

Coconut Custard

4	eggs	4	3 cups	milk	750 ml
½ cup	sugar	125 ml	2 tsp	vanilla	10 ml
¼ tsp	salt	1 ml	1 tsp	nutmeg	5 ml
½ cup	coconut	125 ml		shortbread	

Beat eggs slightly, and add sugar and salt. Stir, then add milk and vanilla. Strain. Add coconut and nutmeg and pour into a buttered Pyrex baking dish. Sprinkle a little nutmeg on top. Put the dish into a pan of water and bake in a 350F (175C) oven until knife comes out clean when inserted in centre. Top it off with thick, buttery shortbread.

Peach Custard Kuchen

1 cup	flour	250 ml	¼ cup + 2 tbsp	sugar	80 ml
2 tbsp	sugar	30 ml			
	salt		1 tsp	cinnamon	5 ml
⅛ tsp	baking powder	0.5 ml	2	egg yolks	2
¼ cup	margarine	50 ml	1 cup	whipping cream	250 ml
1½ cups	sliced peaches, fresh, canned or frozen, drained	375 ml			

Preheat oven to 400F (200C). Sift first four ingredients. Work in margarine until mix is crumbly. Put in bottom of pan and halfway up sides of an ungreased pan. Arrange peaches on top. Mix ¼ cup and 2 tbsp (90 ml) sugar and cinnamon. Sprinkle over peaches. Bake 15 minutes. Blend egg yolks and whipping cream. Pour over peaches. Bake until crust is set and edges brown—25-30 minutes. Serve warm.

Pineapple Tapioca

2½ cups	pineapple juice	625 ml		¼ tsp	salt	1 ml
½ cup	sugar	125 ml		1 cup	pineapple, crushed and drained	250 ml
¼ cup	quick-cooking tapioca	50 ml				

Cook first four ingredients over low heat, stirring constantly until mixture boils. Remove from heat. Cool. Fold in 1 cup drained, crushed pineapple. Spoon into dessert dishes.

Trifle

There are many versions of this dessert. Try this one.

1 pkg	vanilla pudding and pie filling (6 serving-size)	1		2	sponge layer cakes	2
3 cups	milk	750 ml		⅔ cup	raspberry jam, seedless	150 ml
	sherry, to taste			⅔ cup	heavy whipped cream	150 ml
2 14-oz cans	pears, drained and crushed (reserve ⅓ cup (75 ml) syrup)	2x398 ml				
	cherries					

Prepare pudding, using 3 cups of milk. Cool. Add sherry. In an attractive bowl, place 1 sponge cake; cover with ½ the jam and ½ the pears. Spread half the pudding over cake. Top with second sponge cake. Repeat layers. Sprinkle with reserved syrup, top with whipped cream and garnish with cherries.

English Trifle

1½ loaves	pound cake	1½	4 cups	fresh and/or canned fruit, sliced: kiwi, fresh berries, pineapple, mandarin oranges, bananas	1 L
1¾ cups	raspberry, orange or apricot jam	430 ml			
1 cup	cream sherry	250 ml	1 cup	heavy cream, whipped, sweetened	250 ml
⅓ cup	sugar	75 ml			
¼ cup	cornstarch	50 ml		maraschino cherries, for garnish	
½ tsp	salt	2 ml			
2¾ cups	milk	680 ml		slivered almonds, toasted, for garnish	
2 tbsp	margarine	30 ml			
1 tsp	vanilla	5 ml		icing sugar	

Cut pound cake into cubes. Place half of cake cubes in bottom of serving bowl and spread with jam. Layer remaining cake and spread with remaining jam. Sprinkle the cake with sherry; cover and refrigerate overnight. To create the custard, use a large saucepan and stir together sugar, cornstarch and salt over low heat. Gradually stir in milk. Continue stirring and bring to a boil over medium heat. Boil one minute, then stir in margarine and vanilla. Cover cake/jam mixture first with three-quarters of fruit mixture, then with custard. Chill until firm. Just before serving, layer remaining fruit and top with whipped cream, slightly sweetened with icing sugar. Garnish with cherries and slivered almonds. Serves 6-8.

Steamed Plum Pudding

This pudding, with its rich, distinctive flavour, dates back to my grandmother, Ellen Foster. Passed on to me by my mother, it has remained inseparable from the Carter's Christmas dinner for fifty years.

1 cup	sour milk or (1 tbsp (15 ml) vinegar added to 1 cup (250 ml) milk)	250 ml		¼ cup	figs (sliced and packed)	50 ml
1 cup	molasses	250 ml		1½ cup	sultana raisins	375 ml
				1 cup	currants	250 ml
2 ½ cups	flour	625 ml		1-2 cups	seeded raisins (packed)	250 ml-500 ml
2 tsp	baking soda	10 ml		1 cup	dates (sliced and packed)	250 ml
¼ tsp	cloves	1 ml				
¼ tsp	cinnamon	1 ml		1 cup	cherries (red and green, halved)	250 ml
¼ tsp	nutmeg	1 ml				
½ tsp	salt	2 ml		1-2 tbsp	candied ginger, sliced thinly	15 ml-30 ml
1 cup	suet	250 ml				

Line coffee tins or pudding pans with parchment. It is not necessary to grease parchment, but a little shortening on sides of cans helps to hold parchment in place. Cut out circles of parchment to cover cans while steaming. Allow two circles for each can. Grease these very well on each side so that steam will not enter the cans. Secure covers over cans with rubber bands.

Place large steamer or preserving canner on heat. Cover bottom of pot with a rack and fill with enough water to extend up the pudding cans to about ½ their height. Heat water and have it boiling, when the pudding is ready. The steamer must have a tight cover.

To make pudding, prepare fruit first. Wash sultana raisins and currants and drain well. Seeded raisins must be separated. Slice fruits as required. You may add nuts if desired. Use a small amount of the required flour to dust fruit. Mix well.

Place soured milk in a large basin. Add molasses and stir until combined well. Sift in flour with soda, salt and spices. (Do not use more than the suggested amount of spices.) Stir until both mixtures are well combined.

continued...

Add floured fruit and mix well. Stir in suet last and mix well to distribute. Fill lined pudding cans ⅔ full (the pudding will rise to fill the cans). Shake down batter to avoid any air pockets. Follow directions for covering pudding cans and place them in canner.

This is a fairly versatile recipe. You may even make 4 times the quantity and use the extra for gifts and sales. Adjust the fruit according to taste. The can sizes may vary depending on use.

Steam for 3 hours, checking water in canner hourly and adding more water if necessary. After 3 hours, remove puddings from canner, remove paper from tops, and turn out on racks to cool. Sprinkle with rum, if desired, and wrap in rum-soaked cloths to store. They also freeze well.

Reheat in double boiler at serving time. Traditionally, hard sauce makes the perfect accompaniment to this perfect pudding.

Hard Sauce

Proportions may vary according to one's taste. The basic ingredients are always icing sugar (sifted), butter, vanilla, and a little salt. Blend 2 cups (500 ml) icing sugar and ¾ cup (175 ml) butter (soft but not melted) until a ball forms—this will take quite a while. Add salt and vanilla, to taste. The more blending and mixing, the nicer it becomes. Keep warm until ready to serve or it will harden. For Christmas Pudding, mold sauce with small fancy cutters and place on portions of pudding. Add a whole maraschino cherry on top.

Rhubarb Pudding

3 cups	rhubarb, chopped	750 ml		¼ tsp	nutmeg	1 ml
¾ cup	sugar	175 ml		½ cup	milk	125 ml
½ cup	Cornflakes, coarsely crushed	125 ml		¾ cup	sugar	175 ml
				1 tbsp	cornstarch	15 ml
¼ cup	flaked coconut	50 ml		¼ tsp	salt	1 ml
¾ cup	flour	175 ml		½ cup	hot orange juice	125 ml
1 tsp	baking powder	5 ml		3 tbsp	butter, softened	45 ml
¼ tsp	salt	1 ml				

Grease an 8x8-inch (20x20 cm) square pan and put in rhubarb. In a medium-size bowl, combine butter and ¾ cup (175 ml) sugar. Add cereal and coconut. In a small bowl, mix together flour, baking powder, ¼ tsp (1 ml) salt and nutmeg. Add to sugar-butter mixture, alternating with milk. Drop dough on top of rhubarb and spread as evenly as possible. Combine ¾ cup (175 ml) sugar, cornstarch, and ¼ tsp (1 ml) salt. Sprinkle over batter. Pour hot orange juice over all. Bake at 350F (175C) for 45 minutes or until cake is baked and rhubarb is tender. Serve warm with cream.

Blueberry Pudding

2 cups	blueberries	500 ml		½ cup	milk	125 ml
1 cup	flour	250 ml		2 tsp	vanilla	10 ml
1 tsp	baking powder	5 ml		1 cup	sugar	250 ml
½ tsp	salt	2 ml		1 tbsp	cornstarch	15 ml
3 tbsp	shortening, melted	45 ml		1 cup	boiling water	250 ml
¾ cup	sugar	175 ml				

Place berries in an 8-inch (20 cm) square pan. Sift together flour, baking powder, salt and ¾ cup (175 ml) sugar. Cut in shortening. Add milk and vanilla. Spread over berries. Mix cornstarch and 1 cup sugar and sprinkle over batter. Pour 1 cup (250 ml) hot water over all. Bake at 350F (175C) for about 45 minutes. Serve hot or cold with whipped cream or ice cream. Raspberries, strawberries or rhubarb can be substituted for blueberries.

Chocolate Pudding Dessert

1 cup	flour	250 ml		2 tbsp	butter, melted	30 ml
½ cup	sugar	125 ml		1 tsp	vanilla	5 ml
2 tsp	baking powder	10 ml		½ cup	sugar	125 ml
1½ tbsp	cocoa	23 ml		½ cup	brown sugar	125 ml
¼ tsp	salt	1 ml		3 tbsp	cocoa	45 ml
½ cup	milk	125 ml		1 cup	cold water	250 ml

Sift together flour, sugar, baking powder, cocoa and salt in a mixing bowl. Make a well in centre and add milk, melted butter and vanilla. Beat until smooth. Turn batter into a greased baking dish. Mix together the sugars and cocoa and sift over the mixture in pan. Over this, pour 1 cup (250 ml) cold water. Bake for 45 minutes at 350F (175C). Turn upside down to serve. Serve with whipped cream. Serves 6.

Fudge Pudding

The pudding that makes its own sauce!

1 cup	flour	250 ml		2 tbsp	butter, melted	30 ml
¾ cup	sugar	175 ml		½ cup	nuts	125 ml
2 tbsp	cocoa	30 ml		¾ cup	packed brown sugar	175 ml
2 tsp	baking powder	10 ml				
¼ tsp	salt	1 ml		2 tbsp	cocoa	30 ml
½ cup	milk	125 ml		1¾ cups	hot water	430 ml

Stir together flour, sugar, cocoa, baking powder and salt in a bowl. Add milk, butter and nuts. In separate bowl, mix together and pour into an 8-inch (20 cm) square pan. Mix sugar and cocoa together. Add water and stir to dissolve sugar. Pour over batter but do not stir. Bake uncovered at 350F (175C) for 40 minutes until batter has risen above sauce. Serves 6.

Cottage Pudding

1½ cups	flour	375 ml	¾ cup	sugar	175 ml
1½ tsp	baking powder	7 ml	1	egg	1
½ tsp	salt	2 ml	1 tsp	vanilla	5 ml
¼ cup	shortening	50 ml	½ cup	milk	125 ml

Sift flour, baking powder and salt together. Cream shortening and sugar. Add egg and vanilla. Add dry ingredients, alternating with milk. Turn into a 9-inch (23 cm) square pan. Bake at 350F (175C) for about 40 minutes. Cut into squares and serve with your favourite brown sugar sauce. Vinegar sauce is also good.

Lemon Pudding

A fluffy soufflé resting on a layer of creamy custard sauce.

3 tbsp	flour	45 ml	1 cup	milk	250 ml
⅔ cup	sugar	150 ml	1	lemon, grated rind and juice	1
1 tbsp	butter	15 ml			
2	egg yolks, beaten	2	2	egg whites, stiffly beaten	2

Cream together flour, sugar and butter. Add beaten egg yolks, milk and lemon. Fold in egg whites. Turn into a buttered baking dish and set in a pan of hot water. Bake at 350F (175C) for about 45 minutes.

Rice Custard Pudding

Now this pudding goes back a long, long time.

Beat 3 eggs well and add:

3 cups	rice, cooked	750 ml	¼ tsp	salt	1 ml
1 cup	brown or white sugar	250 ml	2 cups	milk	500 ml
			1 cup	raisins	250 ml

Pour into a 1-quart (1 L) casserole and set in a pan of water 1 inch (2.5 cm) deep. Bake at 350F (175C) until set—about 1¼ hour. Serves 8.

Creamy Rice Pudding

The texture is smooth and rich.

½ cup	long grain rice	125 ml	1½ tsp	vanilla	7 ml
1 14-oz can	evaporated milk	385 ml		raisins, if desired	
1⅓ cups	water	335 ml		nutmeg	
2	eggs	2		cream	
⅓ cup	sugar	75 ml			

In a heavy saucepan, combine rice with milk and water. Cook and stir until mixture boils. Reduce heat to low and cook covered for 40 minutes, stirring frequently. Beat eggs and add sugar. Beat again. Stir into hot rice and cook until thickened. Remove from heat. Add vanilla. Add raisins, if desired. Serve with nutmeg and cream.

Baked Rice Pudding

Without eggs!

4 cups	milk	1 L		3 tbsp	rice	45 ml
½ tsp	salt	2 ml		½ cup	raisins, if desired	125 ml
⅔ cup	sugar	150 ml				

Preheat oven to 300F (150C). Put all ingredients in a buttered dish and stir to mix. Bake for 3½ hours, stirring 3 times during the first hour to prevent rice from settling to the bottom. Add raisins, if desired. Serve warm or cold with a shake of nutmeg added at the table.

Raisin Caramel Pudding

1 cup	flour	250 ml		1 cup	raisins	250 ml
2 tsp	baking powder	10 ml		1 cup	brown sugar	250 ml
pinch	salt			1 tbsp	butter	15 ml
⅓ cup	brown sugar	75 ml		2 cups	boiling water	500 ml
½ cup	milk	125 ml				

Mix together flour, baking powder, salt and ⅓ cup (75 ml) brown sugar. Add milk and raisins and mix just to moisten. Turn into baking dish. Mix together 1 cup (250 ml) brown sugar, butter and boiling water. Pour this mixture over batter in baking dish. Bake at 350F (175C) for 30 minutes. Makes about 6 servings.

Pumpkin Gingerbread Pudding

This pudding takes the cake!

⅔ cup	margarine	150 ml
½ cup	brown sugar	125 ml
1	egg	1
½ cup	pumpkin, cooked	125 ml
⅓ cup	molasses	75 ml
2 cups	flour	500 ml
1 tsp	baking soda	5 ml

1 tsp	cinnamon	5 ml
1 tsp	ginger	5 ml
¼ tsp	cloves	1 ml
¼ tsp	salt	1 ml
⅔ cup	sour milk	150 ml
½ cup	raisins (optional)	125 ml

In the large bowl of an electric mixer, cream margarine and brown sugar. Beat in egg, molasses and pumpkin. Sift flour, soda, and spices together and add, alternating with sour milk. Stir in raisins, if desired. Pour into 9-inch (23 cm) square pan. Bake at 350F (175C) for about 40 minutes. Can be served with caramel sauce.

Caramel Sauce:

½ cup	margarine	125 ml
1¼ cups	brown sugar, packed	310 ml

2 tbsp	corn syrup	30 ml
½ cup	whipping cream	125 ml

In a medium-size saucepan over medium heat, melt margarine. Stir in brown sugar and corn syrup. Bring to boil, stirring constantly, until sugar dissolves. Stir in whipping cream. Return to boil and remove from heat.

Orange Bread Pudding

8 cups	bread, cubed	2 L		⅓ cup	orange juice concentrate	75 ml
5	eggs	5				
1 10½-oz can	sweetened condensed milk	300 ml		2 tbsp	orange rind, grated	30 ml
3 cups	milk	750 ml			cream, custard sauce or maple syrup	

Place bread cubes in a greased 13x9-inch (33x23 cm) pan. In a large bowl, beat together eggs, condensed milk, milk, orange juice and rind. Pour egg mixture over bread cubes. Let stand 10 minutes. Bake at 325F (165C) until pudding begins to puff, about 40 minutes. Serve with cream, custard sauce or a little maple syrup.

Butterscotch Bread Pudding

1 cup	brown sugar	250 ml		4	eggs, beaten	4
5-6 slices	stale bread, buttered and cut into cubes	5-6		1⅓ cups	milk	335 ml
					salt	
				1 tsp	vanilla	5 ml

Butter the inside top of a double boiler. In it place brown sugar and bread cubes. Beat eggs with milk, salt and vanilla. Pour egg mixture over bread and sugar. Do not stir. Cook over boiling water, covered, for 1 hour. Delicious served with ice cream.

Gingersnap-Vanilla Cheesecake

32	crisp gingersnap cookies, crushed	32		2 tbsp	cornstarch	30 ml
				1 cup	honey	250 ml
2 tbsp	white sugar	30 ml		1 tbsp	vanilla extract	15 ml
1	egg white	1		1 cup	egg substitute, fat-free	250 ml
4 oz	cream cheese, reduced fat	125 ml				
				16 oz	cottage cheese, low-fat	500 ml
1 cup	ricotta cheese	250 ml				

Preheat oven to 350F (175C). In a food processor or blender, crush the gingersnaps with sugar. Add the egg white and process long enough to moisten the mixture. Press the crumbs onto the bottom and up the sides of an 8-9-inch (20-23 cm) springform pan, forming a thin layer. If crumbs are too sticky, use a sheet of waxed paper between the crust and your fingers to press the crumbs into place. Bake 10-12 minutes until the crust is brown and firm to the touch. Remove from the oven. If the crust slides down the side of the pan, use a rubber spatula or the back of a spoon to press it in place. Reduce oven to 300F (150C). Fill an ovenproof dish with about 1 inch (2.5 cm) of warm water and place it at the back of the oven to provide steam for the cheesecake while it bakes. Clean the food processor or blender. Add cream, cottage and ricotta cheeses and cornstarch. Blend until the mixture is smooth. Add honey and vanilla and blend again. Add egg substitute, blending until the mixture is smooth and evenly coloured. Pour into the prepared crust. Bake 20 minutes on the lowest rack of the oven. Reduce oven temperature to 250F (120C) and bake 60 minutes longer or until the sides are set and the centre is fluid but not sloshing. Turn the oven off and allow the cake to cool 1 hour in the oven. Remove and cool to room temperature. Chill, covered, overnight before slicing. The cake will continue to set in the refrigerator so don't worry if the centre doesn't appear to be firm when you remove it from the oven. If desired, serve the cheesecake with a sauce made from thawed frozen strawberries or raspberries. Place the berries in a food processor or blender and purée until smooth. Add sugar, to taste.

Black Forest Cheesecake

1¼ cups	graham wafer crumbs	310 ml		8 1-oz squares	Baker's semi-sweet chocolate, melted	8x30 g
⅓ cup	butter	75 ml		4	eggs	4
¼ cup	sugar	50 ml		2 tsp	vanilla	10 ml
3 8-oz pkgs	cream cheese, softened	3x250 g		1 19-oz can	cherry pie filling	540 ml
1 10½-oz can	sweetened, condensed milk	300 ml			whipped cream	
					chocolate curls	

Combine crumbs, butter, and sugar; press into a 9-inch (23 cm) springform pan. In a large mixing bowl, beat cheese until fluffy. Gradually beat in sweetened condensed milk, chocolate, eggs and vanilla until smooth. Pour into prepared pan. Bake at 300F (150C) for 65 minutes or until cake springs back when lightly touched. Cool and chill. Top with cherry pie filling; garnish with whipped cream and chocolate curls.

Banana-Split Dessert

Great pot-luck pleaser!

¼ cup	brown sugar	50 ml		2	eggs	2
½ cup	butter	125 ml		¾ cup	butter	175 ml
2 cups	graham wafer crumbs	500 ml		1 10-oz can	mandarin oranges	284 ml
1 19-oz can	pineapple, crushed	540 ml		3	large bananas	3
4 cups	icing sugar	1 L		2 cups	whipping cream, or topping	500 ml

In a saucepan over medium heat, melt ½ cup butter. Stir in crumbs and sugar. Transfer into an ungreased 13x9-inch (22x33 cm) pan. Bake at 350F (175C) for 10 minutes. Cool. Spread pineapple evenly over crust. Put sugar, eggs, butter and vanilla into mixing bowl; beat for 10 minutes. Spread over pineapple. (This mixture may be heated in double boiler; when thickened, remove from heat.) Cool. Place well-drained oranges evenly over filling. Layer thin slices of banana over top. Whip cream. Spread over banana layer. Sprinkle with a mixture of graham wafer crumbs, chopped nuts, cherries, chocolate chips, and butterscotch, chocolate or strawberry sundae sauce of choice. Serves a crowd.

No-Bake Raspberry Cheesecake

Crust:

½ cup	butter	125 ml	¼ cup	brown sugar	50 ml
2 cups	graham wafer crumbs	500 ml			

Filling:

3 oz	raspberry Jell-O	90 g	¾ cup	icing sugar	175 ml
1 cup	boiling water	250 ml	2 pouches	Dream Whip (or 4 cups (1 L) prepared topping)	2
15 oz	frozen raspberries, partially thawed	470 g			
2 8-oz pkgs	cream cheese	2x250 g	1 cup	milk	250 ml

Melt butter in a saucepan. Stir in crumbs and sugar. Pack into a greased 9x13-inch (23x33 cm) pan. Bake at 350F (175C) for 10-12 minutes. Dissolve Jell-O in water. Stir in berries. Chill Jell-O until syrupy. Beat cream cheese and icing sugar. Prepare Dream Whip according to directions, using milk, and fold into cream cheese mixture. Fold into Jell-O mixture. Pour on crust and chill. Makes 15 servings.

Black Forest Brownie Dessert

1 pkg	brownie mix	440 g	½ cup	whipping cream	125 ml
1 cup	cream cheese, softened	250 ml	1 19-oz can	cherry pie filling	540 ml
⅓ cup	white sugar	75 ml	2 squares	unsweetened chocolate, melted	2 oz
1 tsp	vanilla	5 ml			

Prepare brownie mix according to directions. Spread batter in a well greased 9x13-inch (23x33 cm) pan. Bake in a 350F (175C) oven for 15 minutes. Remove from oven and place on a rack to cool. In a small bowl, combine cheese, sugar and vanilla. Beat until smooth. Whip whipping cream separately and fold into mixture. Spread over baked and cooled brownie. Top with cherry pie filling. Cut into squares and chill. Before serving, drizzle each serving with chocolate.

The Great Nova Scotia Cookbook

Judy's Almond Cheesecake

A subtle, light dessert.

2 8-oz pkgs	cream cheese	2 250 g pkgs
⅔ cup	sugar	150 ml
3	eggs	3
½ cup	almonds, ground and blanched	125 ml

Crust:

¾ cup	graham-cracker crumbs	175 ml
¼ cup	butter	50 ml

½ tsp	almond extract	2 ml
⅛ tsp	salt	0.5 ml
1 cup	sour cream (light, if preferred)	250 ml
1 tsp	vanilla	5 ml
3 tbsp	sugar	45 ml
	almonds, slivered	

½ cup	almonds, ground	125 ml
3 tbsp	sugar	45 ml

Combine crumbs, butter, almonds and sugar. Press into an 8-9-inch (20-23 cm) springform pan, making sure to press 1 inch (2.5 cm) up the sides. Chill. Beat cheese until fluffy. Beat in ⅔ cup (150 ml) sugar. Add eggs, one at a time, beating well after each addition, then beat until smooth. Stir in almonds, almond extract and salt. Pour into crust and bake at 350F (175C) for 45 minutes. Remove from oven and let stand on a rack for 20 minutes. Combine sour cream, 3 tbsp (45 ml) sugar and vanilla. Spread on cake. Put back in oven and bake 10 minutes longer. Cool on a rack, then refrigerate. Run spatula around edge of cake to loosen. Remove sides of pan. Sprinkle with slivered almonds.

Apple Danish Cheesecake

1 cup	all-purpose flour	250 ml		¼ tsp	cream of tartar	1 ml
¾ cup	almonds, ground	175 ml		1	egg	1
¼ cup	white sugar	50 ml		⅓ cup	brown sugar, packed	75 ml
½ cup	margarine or butter, cold	125 ml		1 tbsp	all-purpose flour	15 ml
¼ tsp	almond extract	1 ml		1 tsp	ground cinnamon	5 ml
8 oz	cream cheese	250 g		4 cups	tart apples, peeled and thinly sliced	1 L
¼ cup	white sugar	50 ml		⅓ cup	almonds, slivered	75 ml

Using the first 5 ingredients make dough. Shape dough into a ball, and gently press against the bottom and up the sides of a 9-inch (23 cm) springform or cake pan. Refrigerate for 30 minutes.

To make filling: In a medium-size mixing bowl, beat cream cheese, sugar, and cream of tartar until smooth. Add egg; beat on low just until combined. Pour over crust.

To make topping: In another medium-size bowl, combine brown sugar, flour and cinnamon. Add apples and stir until coated. Spoon over the filling. Sprinkle with slivered almonds.

Bake at 350F (175C) for 40-45 minutes or until golden brown. Cool on a wire rack for 10 minutes. Carefully run a knife around edge of pan to loosen; cool 1 hour longer. Refrigerate overnight. Remove from pan.

Berry Crisp Cheesecake

Crust:

1 cup	flour	250 ml
1¼ cups	brown sugar	310 ml
¾ cup	quick rolled oats	175 ml
2 tbsp	lemon rind, grated	30 ml
½ cup	butter, softened	125 ml

Filling:

3 8-oz pkgs	cream cheese light or regular	3x250 g
¾ cup	sugar	175 ml
3	eggs	3
2 cups	strawberries and blueberries, mixed fresh or thawed	500 ml

To make crust, mix flour, brown sugar, oats and lemon rind; cut in butter until mixture is crumbly. Press on bottom of a 9-inch (23 cm) springform pan. Bake at 350F (175C) for 30 minutes. Cool for 10 minutes. Crust will harden as it cools. While crumb mixture is in pan, crush into small chunks, using a fork; reserve 1 cup (250 ml). Press mixture onto bottom and 1 inch (2.5 cm) up sides of pan.

For filling: Beat cream cheese and sugar until very smooth. Beat in eggs, one at a time, just until blended. Pour over crumb crust. Place fruit on top of cheese filling and sprinkle reserved crumb mixture on top. Bake 60-70 minutes, or until centre is just set. Remove from oven and run a knife around sides of pan to loosen. Cool on a wire rack at room temperature. Chill overnight. Icing sugar may be shaken through a sieve over the surface of cheesecake for an attractive finish.

Chocolate Chip Cheesecake

1½ cups	cream-filled chocolate cookies, finely crushed	375 ml	3	eggs	3
			2 tsp	vanilla	10 ml
3 tbsp	butter, melted	45 ml	1 cup	semi-sweet mini chocolate chips, divided	250 ml
3 8-oz pkgs	cream cheese, softened	3x250 g			
			1 tsp	flour	5 ml
1 10½-oz can	sweetened condensed milk	300 ml			

Preheat oven to 300F (150C). Combine cookie crumbs and butter; press firmly on bottom of 9-inch (23 cm) springform pan. In a large mixing bowl, beat cream cheese until fluffy. For best distribution of chocolate chips throughout cheesecake, do not oversoften or overbeat cream cheese. Beat in condensed milk, eggs and vanilla. In a small bowl, toss ½ cup (125 ml) chips with flour to coat, and stir into cheese mixture. Pour into prepared pan. Sprinkle remaining chips over top. Bake 1 hour or until cake springs back when lightly touched. Cool, then chill. Garnish if desired. Refrigerate leftovers. Makes one cheesecake.

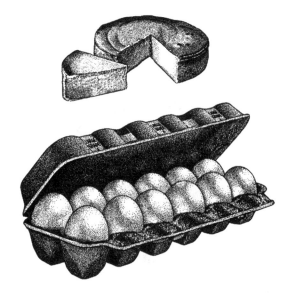

Cranberry Cheesecake

¾ cup	sugar	175 ml
2 tbsp	cornstarch	30 ml
1 cup	cranberry juice	250 ml
1½ cups	cranberries, fresh or frozen	375 ml

Filling:

4 8-oz pkgs	cream cheese, softened	4x250 g
1 cup	sugar	250 ml
3 tbsp	flour	45 ml

Crust:

¾ cup	graham wafer crumbs	175 ml
3½ tbsp	sugar	52.5 ml
3 tbsp	butter	45 ml

4	eggs	4
1 cup	eggnog	250 ml
3 tsp	vanilla	45 ml

Prepare sauce by placing sugar, cornstarch, cranberry juice and cranberries in a saucepan. Bring to a boil. Reduce heat; cook and stir over medium heat for 2 minutes. Remove from heat; set aside. In a small bowl, combine cracker crumbs and sugar; stir in butter. Press into a greased 9-inch (23 cm) springform pan. Bake at 325F (175C) for 10 minutes. Cool on a rack. In a mixing bowl, beat cream cheese and sugar until smooth. Add eggs and beat on low just until combined. Add eggnog and vanilla, and beat just until blended. Pour two-thirds of the filling over the crust. Top with half of the cranberry mixture. Cover and chill remaining cranberry mixture. Carefully spoon remaining filling on top. Bake at 325F (165C) for 60-70 minutes or until centre is almost set. Cool on a wire rack for 10 minutes. Carefully run a knife around edge of pan to loosen; cool 1 hour longer. Refrigerate overnight. Remove sides of pan. Spoon remaining cranberry mixture over cheesecake. Serves 12.

Apple Streusel Cheesecake

Crust:

½ cup	butter, softened	125 ml
⅓ cup	sugar	75 ml
1 cup	flour	250 ml

Filling:

3	apples	3	½ cup	brown sugar, packed	125 ml
¼ cup	sugar	50 ml	2	eggs	2
2 tbsp	butter	30 ml	1 cup	sour cream	250 ml
2 tbsp	whipping cream	30 ml	1	lemon, juice and rind	1
1 8-oz pkg	cream cheese, softened	250 g			

Topping:

½ cup	flour	125 ml	¼ tsp	cinnamon	1 ml
¼ cup	brown sugar, packed	50 ml	½ cup	butter, softened	125 ml

Crust: Heat oven to 350F (175C). Cream butter and sugar together. Blend in flour. Press on bottom and ½-inch (1 cm) up sides of greased 9-inch (23 cm) springform pan. Bake 12 to 15 minutes or until slightly golden.

Filling: Meanwhile peel, core and halve apples; cut into ⅓-inch thick slices. In frypan, melt granulated sugar with butter over medium heat; cook apples for 3 to 5 minutes or just until tender and lightly browned. Add cream and cook, stirring occasionally, for 5 minutes. Set aside. In a large bowl, with an electric mixer, beat cream cheese with brown sugar until smooth. Beat in eggs, one at a time, until just blended. Beat in sour cream, lemon rind and juice. Using a slotted spoon, arrange apples over crust; cover with cheese mixture.

Topping: Mix ingredients until crumbly. Sprinkle over filling. Bake 45 minutes or until centre is just set. Cool thoroughly at room temperature. Chill at least 4 hours or overnight. Makes 12 servings.

As an alternative to the topping recipe above, sprinkle 1½ cups (375 ml) ground walnuts over filling and add ¼ tsp (1 ml) of cinnamon to the apple mixture.

Coconut-Fruit Cheesecake

1 cup	coconut, flaked	250 ml
¼ cup	almonds, chopped	50 ml

2 tbsp	butter, melted	30 ml

In a small bowl, combine coconut and almonds. Stir in butter. Press into a greased 9-inch springform pan. Bake at 350F (175C). Cool on a wire rack.

Filling:

2 8-oz pkgs	cream cheese, softened	2x250 g
1 cup	sugar	250 ml
3 tbsp	cornstarch	45 ml
3	eggs	3

1 cup	sour cream	250 ml
3 tbsp	lemon juice	45 ml
2 tsp	vanilla	10 ml
¼ tsp	almond extract	1 ml
	kiwi	
	cherries	

In a mixing bowl, beat cream cheese and sugar until smooth. Add cornstarch and beat well. Add eggs and beat on low speed until combined. Add sour cream, lemon juice and extracts. Beat until just blended. Pour over crust. Bake at 350F (175C) for 45-50 minutes or until centre is almost set. Just before serving, garnish with kiwi slices and cherries.

Chocolate Sauce

As rich as it should be.

⅓ cup	water	75 ml
⅓ cup	sugar	75 ml
⅓ cup	corn syrup	75 ml

½ cup	whipping cream	125 ml
8 oz	bitter chocolate	250 g

Bring sugar, water and corn syrup to a boil in a small saucepan. Cook and stir for 1 minute. In a separate saucepan, bring cream to a boil; watch very carefully. Remove cream from heat and stir in chocolate until melted. Blend in sugar syrup. Makes 2 cups. Use immediately.

Blueberry Sauce

16 oz	blueberries, fresh or frozen	500 g	½ cup	sugar, or more to taste	125 ml
2 tbsp	fresh lemon juice, or more to taste	30 ml			

Combine ingredients in a medium-sized saucepan. Cover and cook over medium heat until berry juices are released, about 1-2 minutes. Stir to moisten all the berries; cover again, and cook 3 more minutes. Uncover and cook just until the mixture has come to a full rolling boil. Boil for 1 minute. Cool. Adjust flavour with additional teaspoons of sugar and/or drops of lemon juice. Serve as a compote-like sauce, or purée in a food processor and strain, if desired, for a more uniform consistency. Sauce may be refrigerated in a covered container for a week or frozen for 6 months.

Praline Sauce

1½ cups	brown sugar	375 ml	¼ cup	butter	50 ml
⅔ cup	corn syrup	150 ml	1 5-oz can	evaporated milk	160 g

Combine sugar, syrup and butter; heat to boiling. Remove from heat and cool. When lukewarm, add milk. Blend well. Store in jars in refrigerator. Serve over ice cream with pecans, walnuts or peanuts. Also good for dessert crêpes.

The Great Nova Scotia Cookbook

Brown Sugar Cream

½ cup	cream	125 ml	¼ cup	butter	50 ml
½ cup	brown sugar	125 ml	1 tsp	vanilla	5 ml

Stir first 3 ingredients over boiling water for about 15 minutes. Add vanilla, to taste, when cool.

Blueberry-Rhubarb Sauce

A blend of flavours that tastes like a new fruit.

4 cups	rhubarb	1 L	¾ cup	water	175 ml
4 cups	blueberries	1 L	2 tbsp	lemon juice	30 ml
1½ cups	sugar	375 ml			

Cut rhubarb into ¾-inch slices. Put all ingredients into a large saucepan. Stir until most of the sugar is dissolved. Cook over medium heat until mixture comes to a boil. Boil for 3-5 minutes. Pour hot sauce into sterilized jars and refrigerate. Delicious on ice cream. Makes 6 cups.

Ginger Sauce for Puddings

1 cup	sugar	250 ml	1 tsp	vanilla	5 ml
1 cup	water	250 ml	1 tbsp	ginger, grated	15 ml
1	egg yolk	1	1 tbsp	butter	15 ml

Boil sugar and water for 5 minutes. Pour syrup slowly over beaten egg yolk, stirring constantly. Cook until mixture is slightly thickened. Add vanilla, ginger and butter. Serve hot. This sauce goes well with steamed puddings.

Fudge Sauce

1 cup	sugar	250 ml	pinch	salt		
¼ cup	cocoa	50 ml	½ cup	pecans, chopped	125 ml
1 tbsp	flour	15 ml	1 tsp	vanilla	5 ml
½ cup	milk	125 ml				

Combine all ingredients except pecans and vanilla. Boil for 2 minutes, stirring constantly. Add pecans and vanilla. Serve warm. Store in refrigerator; reheat over hot water.

Vinegar Sauce for Desserts

This old recipe has virtually disappeared from today's cookbooks. For those of us who remember its distinctive tart taste, it brings back pleasant memories of sauces our mothers served over hot gingerbread, spice cakes, cottage puddings and even Christmas pudding. Just in case it drops out of memory, it is included here.

1¼ cups	warm water	310 ml	3 tbsp	vinegar	45 ml
½ cup	brown sugar	125 ml		salt	
4 tsp	cornstarch	20 ml	2 tbsp	butter	30 ml

Place warm water in a saucepan. Mix together cornstarch, sugar and salt. Add to water gradually, stirring constantly. Bring to boil and cook until thickened and clear. Remove from heat and add vinegar and butter. Serve hot.

Lemon juice or orange juice can be used instead of vinegar. Reduce sugar if using orange juice.

Raspberry Sauce

2 cups	fresh raspberries or (1 pkg (425 g) frozen raspberries, defrosted)	500 ml		¼ cup	lemon juice	50 ml
				¼ cup	cornstarch	50 ml
½ cup	white wine	125 ml		¼ cup	water	50 ml
½ cup	white sugar	125 ml				

Place raspberries in a medium-sized nonreactive saucepan. Crush berries and add wine, sugar and lemon juice. Bring to a boil over medium-high heat; reduce heat and simmer uncovered. Meanwhile, whisk together cornstarch and water in a cup. Whisk in a few tablespoons (25 ml) of the raspberry mixture. Whisk in the same amount again. Pour cornstarch mixture into saucepan and simmer, stirring constantly until thickened. If a thinner sauce is desired, stir in a little apple juice.

Lemon Sauce

Delicious over gingerbread.

1 cup	sugar	250 ml		2	lemons, juice and grated peel	2
1 tbsp	cornstarch	15 ml				
½ tsp	salt	2 ml		1 cup	water	250 ml
3	eggs, slightly beaten	3		2 tbsp	butter	30 ml

Combine sugar, cornstarch and salt. Add eggs, lemon juice, peel and water. Cook in double boiler until thick, stirring constantly.

Fruit Salad Dressing

½-¾ cup	pineapple juice	125-175 ml	1 tbsp	butter	15 ml
3 tbsp	flour	45 ml	1	egg	1
3 tbsp	sugar	45 ml	1 cup	whipping cream	250 ml

Mix flour and sugar and enough of the juice to make a smooth paste. Heat remaining juice; add flour mixture. Cook until thickened, stirring constantly in double boiler. Add beaten egg, then butter, and continue to stir until well blended. Remove from heat. Cool. Whip cream and add when ready to serve. Serve on fruit salads.

Vanilla Custard Sauce

1½ cups	milk	375 ml	½ tsp	vanilla, or more	2 ml
2 tbsp	sugar	30 ml	3	egg yolks	3

Put milk and sugar in a double boiler, heat and stir until dissolved. In a bowl, beat egg yolks until light in colour, and gradually stir in heated milk. Return to hot water and stir with wooden spoon over gentle heat, until creamy. Strain into bowl. Add vanilla. Sprinkle with a little sugar and cool. (The sugar melts and helps to prevent a skin from forming.) Should custard curdle, beat briskly for a few seconds.

Brown Sugar Butter Sauce

Cream in small saucepan: ¼ cup (50 ml) butter and 1 cup (250 ml) brown sugar. Gradually add 1 cup (250 ml) milk. Place on heat and stir until it boils. Remove from heat and add 1 tsp (5 ml) vanilla. Serve warm.

Foaming Butterscotch Sauce

¼ cup	butter	50 ml	½ cup	milk	125 ml
1 cup	brown sugar	250 ml	pinch	salt	
2	eggs, separated	2	1 tsp	vanilla	5 ml

Blend together butter and brown sugar; add well-beaten egg yolks. Mix well and add milk; stir and cook in double boiler until mixture thickens slightly. Beat egg whites until stiff but not dry; add pinch of salt and slowly beat into hot mixture. While still beating, add vanilla. Serve warm.

Foamy Sauce

Cream ½ cup (125 ml) butter until soft. Beat in 1 cup (250 ml) sifted icing sugar, 1 egg and 1 tsp (5 ml) vanilla. Place mixture in a double boiler and beat over hot water until mixture thickens. Beat again and serve at once. Do not reheat. Can be served cold.

Hard Sauce

Hard to beat!

Proportions may vary according to one's taste. The basic ingredients are always icing sugar (sifted), butter, vanilla, and a little salt. Blend 2 cups (500 ml) icing sugar and ¾ cup (175 ml) butter (soft but not melted) until a ball forms—this will take quite a while. Add salt and vanilla, to taste. The more blending and mixing, the nicer it becomes. Keep warm until ready to serve or it will harden. For Christmas Pudding, mold sauce with small fancy cutters and place on portions of pudding. Add a whole maraschino cherry on top.

Ginger Ice Cream

Ginger Syrup:

⅓ cup	water	75 ml
¼ cup	sugar	50 ml
3 tbsp	ginger, minced or grated	45 ml

Milk Mixture:

1 cup	whole milk	250 ml
2 tbsp	sugar	30 ml
2 tsp	preserved ginger, drained and finely minced	10 ml

Custard Mixture:

3	large egg yolks	3
¼ cup	sugar	50 ml

1 cup	whipping cream	250 ml
½ tsp	lemon juice, freshly squeezed and strained	2 ml

To make the syrup, heat the water and sugar in a small saucepan over medium heat, stirring to dissolve the sugar. When the sugar is dissolved, add the fresh ginger. Stir and bring the mixture to boil over medium heat. Reduce heat and simmer the syrup uncovered for 5 minutes. Remove pan from heat.

In another pan, combine the milk, sugar and ginger. Stir over medium heat until the milk comes to a scalding temperature, just short of a boil, then remove the pan from heat. Add the fresh ginger syrup into the milk mixture and stir well to blend. Cover and steep for 20 minutes.

In a small bowl beat the egg yolks and sugar until the mixture is pale yellow, thick, and falls in ribbons from the beater. Put the cream in a medium-size bowl and cover with a strainer.

Bring the milk mixture to scalding again, stirring. Slowly add ¼ cup (50 ml) of the scalded milk to the egg mixture and then pour the egg mixture back into the remaining milk. Cook over moderate heat, whisking slowly, until the mixture reaches a custard consistency. Do not let the mixture boil. Pour the custard through the strainer into the bowl of cream. Discard the ginger solids. Allow the mixture to cool completely, stirring occasionally. Once cool, the mixture may be sealed airtight and refrigerated for 1-2 days before freezing. Just before freezing, add the lemon juice and stir well. Freeze in an ice-cream maker or shallow tray for 2 hours. Beat with a food processor and freeze again. Repeat this procedure. When freezing process is completed, pack the ice cream into a plastic container, pressing it down to eliminate air bubbles. Press a piece of plastic wrap directly on the surface of the ice cream to prevent formation of ice crystals. Freeze for two more hours, but allow to thaw slightly in the fridge before serving.

Chocolate Velvet Ice Cream

12	egg yolks	12
5 tbsp	sugar	75 ml
1 tbsp	vanilla	15 ml
pinch	salt	
3½ cups	light cream	875 ml

5 tbsp	honey	75 ml
12 oz	extra-bittersweet chocolate	340 g
½ cup	cocoa, sifted	125 ml

Combine yolks, sugar, and salt in a heavy saucepan. Whisk and blend in cream and honey. Stir constantly over medium-low heat until thick enough to coat the back of a spoon. Do not boil. Remove from heat and add chocolate, stirring until dissolved. Whisk in cocoa and vanilla. Strain. Process mixture in an electric ice cream maker according to manufacturer's instructions. Freeze in container until firm, at least 2 hours. Makes 1½ quarts (1.5 L). If ice cream maker is not available, mixture may be placed in bowl and set in freezer. Stir every 15 minutes until frozen.

Homemade Freezer Ice Cream

Place 1 can of evaporated milk (385 ml) in the large bowl of an electric mixer. Place in freezer. Let freeze until a thick slush forms. Meanwhile, in the top of a double boiler, over boiling water, place the following ingredients beaten together:

3	eggs, well beaten	3
1 cup	cream or evaporated milk or whole milk	250 ml

¾ cup	white sugar	175 ml
¼-½ tsp	salt	1-2 ml
3 tsp	vanilla	15 ml

Cook and stir custard until mixture lightly coats spoon. Remove from heat and cool. In the large bowl of electric mixer, beat the partially frozen evaporated milk (if using cream, freezing is not necessary) with 2 tbsp (30 ml) lemon juice, until it is the consistency of whipped cream. Beat in cold custard mixture, to which has been added the vanilla. Two or three cups of fresh fruit such as strawberries, blueberries or raspberries may be added. Frozen fruits will cause ice crystals to form in ice cream. Grape nuts cereal added is also delicious. Place ice cream in freezer. Stir well every fifteen minutes until hard. Transfer to an ice cream container and store in freezer.

Fruit Sherbet

1	envelope gelatin	1	pinch	salt	
¼ cup	sugar	50 ml	2 tbsp	sugar	30 ml
2 cups	fruit, puréed fresh, cooked or canned	500 ml	2 tbsp	fresh lemon juice	30 ml

Sprinkle the gelatin over ¼ cup (50 ml) water and let it soften for 5 minutes. Put the sugar and ¾ cup (175 ml) water in a pan, stir in the gelatin, and cook over low heat until it dissolves. Add the fruit purée, salt and sugar, to taste. Cook, stirring, until the sugar has dissolved. Remove from heat and add lemon juice. Freeze in two ice cube trays or a metal bowl in the refrigerator freezer.

Cantaloupe Sorbet

2 cups	cantaloupe, chopped	500 ml	3 tbsp	sugar	45 ml
½ cup	cream	125 ml	1¼ cups	orange juice	310 ml
3 tbsp	lemon juice	45 ml	¼ cup	sugar	50 ml
2	egg whites (preferably egg substitute)	2		cantaloupe halves	

Combine cantaloupe and cream in a blender. Process until smooth. Stir in lemon juice. Transfer to a 9x9-inch (23 cm) baking pan and freeze. Place orange juice and ¼ cup (50 ml) sugar in saucepan. Bring mixture to a boil. Simmer for about 1 minute. Remove from heat and cool.

Beat egg whites until frothy. Add the 3 tablespoons (45 ml) sugar and beat until stiff. Meanwhile, break up frozen mixture and place in an electric mixing bowl. Beat until smooth. Quickly fold in egg whites. Turn into baking pan again. Cover and freeze 3 or 4 hours. Serve on chilled cantaloupe halves. Serves 4-6.

• CAKES •

• Best •

• Traditional •

• Trendy •

Elda's Carrot Pineapple Cake

2 cups	white sugar	500 ml		2 tsp	baking soda	10 ml
½ cup	brown sugar	125 ml		¾ tsp	salt	3 ml
1½ cups	oil	375 ml		2 cups	raw carrots, grated	500 ml
3	eggs	3		1 cup	raisins	250 ml
1 cup	pineapple, crushed	250 ml		1 cup	walnuts pieces	250 ml
				1 cup	coconut	250 ml
3 cups	flour, sifted	750 ml		2 tsp	vanilla	10 ml

Cream sugars, oil and eggs, adding eggs one at a time. Add pineapple. Sift flour, baking soda, and salt together. Add gradually to creamed mixture. Add raisins, carrots, walnuts and coconut. Add vanilla. (Use a small amount of the flour to dust raisins, nuts and coconut.) Bake at 350F (175C) for about 70 minutes in a well-greased tube pan. Frost with cream cheese icing (see recipe on page 423).

Queen of Pound Cakes

Very moist.

1 cup	butter, softened	250 ml	1 cup	sour cream	250 ml
2¾ cups	sugar	680 ml	2 tsp	vanilla	10 ml
6	eggs	6	1 tsp	lemon extract	5 ml
3 cups	flour	750 ml	1 tsp	lemon rind, grated	5 ml
½ tsp	salt	2 ml		icing sugar	

Cream butter and sugar together and beat until light. Add the eggs, one at a time, and beat. Add the dry ingredients, alternating with sour cream. Add flavourings and rind. Bake in a 10-inch (25 cm) tube pan or large loaf pan at 350F (175C). Test after 1 hour. Dust with icing sugar.

Lemon Pound Cake

1 cup	shortening	250 ml	3 cups	flour	750 ml
2 cups	sugar	500 ml	1 tsp	salt	5 ml
1 cup	water	250 ml	1 tsp	baking powder	5 ml
2	eggs	2	2 tbsp	lemon extract	30 ml

Cream shortening and sugar. Add eggs, one at a time, beating after each addition. Add water, alternating with dry ingredients. Add lemon extract. Bake in a tube pan at 350F (175C) for 1 hour.

Orange Pound Cake

1 cup	shortening	250 ml		2 cups	cake flour, sifted	500 ml
1¼ cups	sugar	310 ml		1 tsp	baking powder	5 ml
1 tsp	vanilla	5 ml		½ tsp	salt	2 ml
1 tsp	orange peel, grated	5 ml		¼ tsp	ground mace	1 ml
4	eggs	4		¼ cup	milk	50 ml

In mixing bowl, blend shortening, sugar, vanilla, and orange peel. Blend in eggs. Combine the flour, baking powder, salt and mace in separate bowl; add these—alternating with the milk—to the shortening-sugar mixture. Beat well. Spread batter in a well-greased 9x5x3-inch (23x13x8 cm) loaf pan. Bake at 325F (160C) for about 1¼ hours or until cake tests done. Cool 15 minutes; remove cake from pan and cool completely on rack.

Golden Pound Cake

1¼ cups	shortening	310 ml		⅔ cup	milk	150 ml
2 cups	sugar	500 ml		1 tsp	vanilla	5 ml
5	eggs	5		1 tsp	lemon extract	5 ml
2½ cups	flour, sifted	625 ml			icing sugar	
1¼ tsp	baking powder	6 ml				
½ tsp	salt	2 ml				

In a mixing bowl, blend shortening and sugar thoroughly. Add eggs, one at a time, beating well after each addition. Combine flour, baking powder and salt, and add to the shortening-sugar mixture alternating with the milk and flavourings. Beat until mixture is smooth. Turn batter into a well-greased and floured 10-inch (25 cm) fluted tube pan. Bake at 325F (160C) for 1 hour or until cake tests done. Cool 1 hour; remove cake from pan and cool completely on rack. To serve, sprinkle cake with icing sugar.

Sponge Cake

6	eggs	6	1 tsp	lemon rind, grated	5 ml
1 cup	white sugar	250 ml	1 cup	cake flour	250 ml
¼ cup	water	50 ml	½ tsp	cream of tartar	2 ml
1 tsp	lemon extract	5 ml	¼ tsp	salt	1 ml

Separate the eggs. In a large mixing bowl, beat egg yolks until very thick and lemon-coloured. Beat in sugar gradually. Add water, lemon extract and lemon rind. Beat in flour. In another bowl, beat egg whites until frothy, then add cream of tartar and salt. Beat mixture until whites are stiff but not dry. Fold this whipped mixture into yolk mixture. Pour batter into an ungreased 9-inch (23 cm) tube pan. (It's important that the pan not be greased; a sponge cake needs a dry surface to "cling to" as it rises.) Bake at 325F (165C) for approximately 1 hour.

Butter Cake

1½ cups	white sugar	375 ml	4	eggs	4
2 cups	butter	500 ml	1 tbsp	vanilla extract	15 ml
4½ tsp	baking powder	22 ml	1 tbsp	almond extract	15 ml
1 tsp	salt	5 ml	2 cups	milk	500 ml
3 cups	all-purpose flour	750 ml			

Preheat oven to 350F (175C). Lightly grease and flour one 9-inch or 10-inch bundt pan. With a spatula, cream butter and sugar together until light and fluffy. Add eggs all at once and beat well. Sift the flour, baking powder and salt together. Add to butter mixture along with 1 cup of the milk. Continue to beat well (the batter will be thick). Add the remaining 1 cup of milk along with the vanilla and almond extracts. Pour batter into the prepared pan. Bake for 1 hour, or until the cake tests done.

Best Butter Cake

Moist and buttery cake made from readily available ingredients.

3 cups	all-purpose flour	750 ml		1 cup	buttermilk	250 ml
2¾ cups	white sugar, divided	680 ml		1⅓ cups	butter	335 ml
				4 tsp	vanilla extract	20 ml
½ tsp	baking soda	2 ml		4	eggs	4
1 tsp	salt	5 ml		3 tbsp	water	45 ml
1 tsp	baking powder	5 ml				

Preheat oven to 325F (165C). Grease and flour one 9-inch or 10-inch (25 cm) bundt pan. Blend together on the low speed of an electric mixer flour, 2 cups (500 ml) of the sugar, salt, baking powder, baking soda, buttermilk, 1 cup (250 ml) of the butter, 2 tsp (10 ml) of the vanilla, and the eggs. Beat for 3 minutes at medium speed. Pour batter into prepared pan. Bake for 60 minutes. Turn out on rack. Place on serving plate.

Butter Sauce:

In a saucepan, combine the remaining ¾ cups sugar (175 ml), ⅓ cups butter (75 ml), 2 tsp (10 ml) vanilla, and the water. Cook over medium heat until fully melted and combined; do not boil. Prick 10-12 holes in the still-warm baked cake. Slowly pour sauce over cake. Cool and serve.

Washington Pie

This is not a pie as the name implies, but rather a 2-layer cake. There are as many versions as there are ways to serve it, but this is the one we were familiar with at home.

2 cups	flour	500 ml	1 cup	sugar	250 ml
2 tsp	baking powder	10 ml	2	eggs	2
½ tsp	salt	2 ml	¾ cup	milk	175 ml
½ cup	butter	125 ml	2 tsp	vanilla	10 ml

Sift together flour, baking powder and salt. Set aside. In a mixing bowl, cream butter. Add sugar gradually and cream mixture until light. Beat in eggs and vanilla. Add the flour mixture in three parts, alternating with milk. Stir after each addition, until batter is smooth. Spread batter in two 8-inch (20 cm) layer cake pans (lined with parchment or sprayed with cooking spray). Bake at 375F (190C) for about 25 minutes, or until the cakes test done. When cool fill with a layer of good raspberry jam. The top may be frosted with a white butter icing or dusted with icing sugar. Most delicious of all is a thick layer of sweetened, vanilla-flavoured whipped cream spread over the top—leave the sides exposed.

Angel Food Cake

Lovely served with any fresh fruit.

1¼ cups	cake flour	310 ml	1 tsp	cream of tartar	5 ml
1¾ cups	white sugar	430 ml	½ tsp	vanilla extract	2 ml
¼ tsp	salt	1 ml	½ tsp	almond extract	2 ml
1½ cups	egg whites	375 ml			

Beat egg whites until they form stiff peaks, then add cream of tartar, vanilla extract, and almond extract. Sift together flour, sugar and salt. Repeat five times. Gently combine the egg whites with the dry ingredients, then pour into an ungreased 10-inch tube pan. Place cake pan in a cold oven. Set the oven to 325F (165C). Bake for about one hour, or until cake is golden brown. Invert cake, and allow it to cool in the pan. When thoroughly cooled, remove from pan.

Glazed Lemon Bundt Cake

A simply lovely dessert.

1 cup	butter or margarine, softened	250 ml		2 tsp	baking powder	10 ml
				½ tsp	salt	2 ml
2 cups	sugar	500 ml		1 cup	milk	250 ml
4	eggs	4				
1 tbsp	lemon rind, finely grated	15 ml		**Glaze:**		
				⅓ cup	lemon juice	75 ml
2 tsp	vanilla	10 ml		1 tbsp	water	15 ml
3 cups	flour	750 ml		¾ cup	sugar	175 ml

In a mixing bowl, cream butter and sugar. Add the eggs one at a time, beating well after each addition. Beat in lemon rind and vanilla. Combine flour, baking powder and salt; add to the creamed mixture, alternating with milk. Pour into a greased, floured 10-inch fluted tube pan. Bake at 350F (175C) for 50 to 60 minutes or until a toothpick inserted near the centre comes out clean. Cool for 10 minutes; invert on a wire rack. Cook 10 minutes longer. Place rack on waxed paper. Combine glaze ingredients; drizzle over the warm cake. Cool completely before serving.

Cream Cake

This old recipe goes back to the time when farmers themselves separated the cream from the skim milk. The cream was used in place of shortening. For special occasions, my mother often doubled or even tripled the quantities and baked it in a large, oven-size biscuit pan. Her nephew called it Aunt Gertie's "yard cake."

2	eggs	2		1⅓ cups	flour	325 ml
1 cup	sugar	250 ml		2 tsp	baking powder	10 ml
1 cup	cream	250 ml		½ tsp	salt	2 ml
1 tsp	vanilla	5 ml				

Beat eggs and add sugar gradually, beating well after each addition. Add cream and vanilla. Beat again. Fold in sifted flour, baking powder and salt. Turn into an 8x8-inch (20x20 cm) square pan. Bake at 350F (175C) about 45 minutes or until top springs back when pressed with finger. Note: No butter or shortening required.

Hot Milk Cake

A nice big cake. I always make it in the electric mixer. Baked in a 13x9-inch (33x23 cm) pan, it can become a big bunny cake for Easter or a heart cake for Valentine's Day. Baked in a 9" tube pan, it makes a deep birthday cake.

5	eggs	5		2 cups	flour	500 ml
2 cups	sugar	500 ml		2 tsp	baking powder	10 ml
1 cup	milk, boiled	250 ml		½ tsp	salt	2 ml
⅓ cup + 1 tbsp	butter, melted	100 ml		2 tsp	vanilla	10 ml

Heat 1 cup milk and butter together. Sift dry ingredients: flour, baking powder and salt. Set aside. Separate eggs. In a small bowl, beat egg whites until stiff and gradually beat in 1 cup (250 ml) of sugar by teaspoons. Beat until fluffy and until sugar is dissolved. In large bowl, beat egg yolks until light in colour. Gradually add 1 cup (250 ml) sugar by teaspoons and beat until sugar is dissolved. Combine mixture by adding beaten egg whites and sugar to egg yolk mixture in the larger bowl. Beat well again. Add hot milk and butter. Beat vigorously. Add vanilla. Add flour mixture and beat again until well mixed. Turn into pan that has been lined with wax paper or parchment. Bake at 350F (175C) in centre of oven for 50 minutes, or until cake tests done. Remove from oven. Allow to set for 10-15 minutes and turn onto a rack. Frost and/or decorate.

Delicious Cake

1 cup	butter	250 ml		1	egg	1
2 cups	sugar	500 ml		1 cup	flour with 2 tsp (10 ml) baking powder and 1 tsp (5 ml) salt	250 ml
½ cup	boiling water	125 ml				
½ cup	milk	125 ml				
1 cup	flour	250 ml		1	egg	1
1	egg	1		2 tsp	vanilla	10 ml
1 cup	flour	250 ml				

Cream butter and sugar. Mix water and milk, and add this mixture to sugar and butter. Add remainder of ingredients in the order given above. (Yes, there really are 3 cups of flour and 3 eggs in this recipe.) Pour into an 8x8-inch (20x20 cm) pan or tube pan lined with wax paper. Bake in a 350F (175C) oven for 1 hour.

Pineapple-Mandarin Cake

This well-dressed cake is perfect for a special occasion.

2½ cups	all-purpose flour or 2¾ cups (680 ml) cake flour	625 ml
1 tbsp	baking powder	15 ml
1 tsp	salt	5 ml
⅔ cups	shortening	150 ml
1½ cups	white sugar	375 ml
3	eggs	3
2 tsp	vanilla extract	10 ml
1⅓ cups	milk	325 ml

Frosting:

½ cup	butter or margarine, softened	125 ml
4 cups	icing sugar, sifted	1 L
¼ cup	light cream	50 ml
2 tsp	lemon juice	10 ml
1 10-oz can	mandarin oranges, drained	284 ml
1 14-oz can	crushed pineapple, drained	398 ml

Combine flour, baking powder, and salt. Stir well to blend. In a large bowl, cream shortening, white sugar, eggs, and vanilla; beat until light and fluffy. Add flour mixture to creamed mixture, alternating with milk, making three dry and two liquid additions; combine lightly after each. Spread batter evenly into 2 greased and floured 8-inch (20 cm), round layer cake pans. Bake at 350F (175C) for 35-40 minutes, or until toothpick inserted in centre comes out clean. Cool cake in pan for 10 minutes, then turn out on a wire rack to cool completely. **Frosting:** Cream butter or margarine. Gradually blend in icing sugar, cream, and lemon juice. Beat until light and creamy. Fill and frost the cake. Decorate top with a ring of well-drained mandarin orange segments. Fill centre with well-drained crushed pineapple. Decorate centre with a few additional orange sections.

Dream Cakes

As light as a sweet dream.

1	egg	1	¼ tsp	salt	1 ml
1 cup	white sugar	250 ml	½ cup	milk	125 ml
1 cup	flour	250 ml	1 tbsp	butter	15 ml
1 tsp	baking powder	5 ml	1 tsp	vanilla	5 ml

Heat milk and butter together. In the meantime beat together egg, sugar and vanilla. Add sifted dry ingredients. Last, fold in hot milk and butter. Pour into an 8x8-inch (20 cm square) pan lined with greased parchment. Bake at 350F (175C). Test after 40 minutes. Remove from oven and spread with topping.

Topping:

3 tbsp	butter	45 ml	2 tbsp	milk	30 ml
2 tbsp	brown sugar	30 ml	½ cup	coconut	125 ml

Mix all together and spread on cake. Return cake to oven until topping bubbles. Remove from oven and lift—do not turn—out of pan. Cut in squares with a sharp knife while cake is still warm.

Jelly Roll

3	eggs, well beaten	3	½ tsp	baking soda	2 ml
¾ cup	sugar	175 ml	1 tsp	vanilla	5 ml
1 cup	flour	250 ml	1 tbsp	hot water	15 ml
½ tsp	salt	2 ml		dark red jelly	
1 tsp	cream of tartar	5 ml			

Beat eggs in a large mixing bowl. Add sugar gradually, beating well after each addition. Add sifted dry ingredients. Stir together gently and fold in hot water and vanilla. Spread in a jellyroll pan lined with parchment. Bake at 375-400F (190-200C) for 12-15 minutes. Turn out onto a clean tea towel sprinkled with sugar. Spread cake generously with dark red jelly. Work quickly to roll up. Set the roll, still wrapped, on a rack, placing it so that the edge where the seal ends is on the bottom. Cool and slice as needed. The edges of the cake may be removed before rolling, if desired.

Tomato Soup Cake

½ cup	shortening	125 ml	2 tsp	cinnamon	10 ml
1 cup	sugar	250 ml	½ tsp	cloves	2 ml
1 10-oz can	tomato soup	284 ml	2 tsp	baking powder	10 ml
1½ cups	flour	375 ml	½ tsp	salt	2 ml
½ tsp	baking soda	2 ml	1 cup	raisins	250 ml

Cream shortening and sugar. Beat in soup. Add sifted dry ingredients. Fold in raisins. Pour into a greased and floured 8-or 9-inch (20 cm or 23 cm) square pan. Bake at 350F (175C) for 35-40 minutes. May be iced when cool.

Fresh Apple Cake

Double the recipe—your family will love it.

Prepare and let stand 10 minutes:

1¾ cups	sliced apples	425 ml		1 cup	white sugar	250 ml

Mix the following ingredients thoroughly, then add them to the apple mixture:

½ cup	vegetable oil	125 ml
1	egg	1

Sift together, then add to above ingredients:

1½ cups	flour	375 ml		1 tsp	cinnamon	5 ml
½ tsp	salt	2 ml		½ tsp	nutmeg	2 ml
1 tsp	baking soda	5 ml		½ tsp	allspice	2 ml

Last, fold in ½ cup (125 ml) raisins. Pour into a 9x9-inch (23 cm) pan. Bake at 350F (175C) for 35-40 minutes. This cake may be eaten warm or cold. It is delicious served warm with a brown sugar butter sauce.

Cranberry Swirl Cake

Make your favourite white layer cake. After turning batter into layer pans, with a fork break up one cup of cranberry sauce. Sprinkle sauce over top of batter. With a spatula make zigzag lines through batter. Bake as desired. Frost with your favourite icing.

Apple Bundt Cake

This is a moist cake with substance.

1 cup	vegetable oil	250 ml		½ tsp	salt	2 ml
½ cup	butter or margarine, softened	125 ml		1 tsp	vanilla extract	5 ml
				2 cups	apples, peeled and diced	500 ml
1½ cups	white sugar	375 ml		1 cup	coconut	250 ml
3	eggs	3		1 cup	raisins	250 ml
3 cups	all-purpose flour	750 ml		1 cup	walnuts, chopped	250 ml
1 tsp	baking soda	5 ml				

Glaze:

1 cup	brown sugar	250 ml
½ cup	butter or margarine	125 ml
¼ cup	milk	50 ml

Preheat oven to 325F (165C). Grease and flour one 10-inch (25 ml) tube pan. Combine oil, butter or margarine, sugar and eggs. Beat well with a mixer. Add flour, baking soda, salt and vanilla; mix well. Stir in apples, coconut, raisins, and walnuts. Pour batter into a prepared pan. Bake for 90 minutes. Remove cake from oven. Let it cool in the pan for a few minutes, then remove. **Glaze:** In a small saucepan, heat brown sugar, butter or margarine, and milk. Bring mixture to boil, and stir for 1 minute. Pour over warm cake.

Spicy Apple Cake

1½ cups	butter, softened	375 ml		2 tsp	ground cinnamon	10 ml
4½ cups	icing sugar, sifted	1.125 L		1 tsp	ground allspice	5 ml
				16	caramels	16
1 tbsp	vanilla extract	15 ml		1½ cups	apples, peeled and coarsely chopped	375 ml
6	eggs	6				
3¼ cups	all-purpose flour	810 ml				

Preheat oven to 325F (165C). Grease a 10-inch tube or bundt pan. Unwrap and cut each caramel into 8 pieces. In a large mixing bowl, cream the butter, icing sugar and vanilla until light and fluffy. Add the eggs, one at a time, beating well after each one. Gradually add the flour, ground cinnamon and ground allspice to the egg mixture. Blend at low speed until thoroughly combined. By hand, stir in the caramel pieces and the chopped apples. Pour into greased pan. Bake at 325F (165C) for 85-90 minutes or until cake tester comes out clean. Cool upright in pan for 15 minutes before inverting onto a serving platter. Serve cake warm or cool. If desired, top slices with ice cream and caramel sauce.

Simple Blueberry Cake

5 tbsp	shortening	75 ml		1¾ cups	flour	425 ml
1 cup	sugar	250 ml		2 tsp	baking powder	10 ml
2	eggs	2			salt, to taste	
⅔ cup	milk	150 ml		2 cups	blueberries	500 ml

Cream shortening, sugar, and eggs. Combine flour, baking powder and salt. Add milk and flour mixture alternately to creamed mixture. Add blueberries, slightly floured. Line pan with wax paper and flour it. Bake at 350F (175C) for 35-45 minutes. This is yummy served warm with butter sauce or brown sugar sauce.

Blueberry Cake

A winner with blueberry lovers!

¼ cup	shortening	50 ml
¾ cup	sugar	175 ml
1	egg	1
¾ cup	milk	175 ml
1 tsp	vanilla	5 ml
2 cups	flour	500 ml
3 tsp	baking powder	15 ml

1 tsp	salt	5 ml
2 cups	blueberries	500 ml
Topping:		
½ cup	brown sugar	125 ml
⅓ cup	flour	75 ml
¼ cup	butter, melted	50 ml
1 tsp	cinnamon	5 ml

Prepare tube pan. Cream shortening and sugar. Add egg, milk and vanilla. Sift dry ingredients together and add to milk mixture. Fold in blueberries using a little of the flour to dust berries. Pour into pan. Blend sugar, cinnamon, butter and flour and sprinkle on top of batter. Bake at 350F (175C) until the cake tests done, approximately 40 minutes. Do not turn out of pan.

Margaret's Gumdrop Cake

1½ cups	sugar	375 ml
1 cup	butter	250 ml
4	eggs	4
3 cups	flour	750 ml
2 tsp	baking powder	10 ml
1 tsp	salt	5 ml

1 cup	milk	250 ml
1 tsp	vanilla	5 ml
1 tsp	lemon rind, grated	5 ml
3 cups	gumdrops	750 ml
1 cup	light raisins	250 ml

Cream butter, sugar, eggs, vanilla, and lemon rind. Sift together flour, baking powder and salt, and add to creamed ingredients alternating with milk. Add gumdrops and raisins. Place a pan of water in the oven with the cakes. Cook at 325F (165C) for 1 hour and 15 minutes. Check every 10 minutes after the hour. Note: Gumdrops must be cut up finely into flour with a knife, not scissors. Do not use the black candies. This recipe makes three cakes using greased and floured poppycock pans. One large loaf pan may be used—just cook the cake longer.

Gumdrop Cake

½ cup	butter	125 ml	2 tsp	baking powder	10 ml
1 cup	sugar	250 ml	½ tsp	salt	2 ml
2	eggs	2	1 lb	gumdrops	500 g
¾ cup	milk	175 ml	¾ cup	raisins	175 ml
2 cups	flour	500 ml			

Cut gumdrops into slices, making sure to remove the black ones. Wash and drain raisins. Use a little of the required flour to dust gumdrops and raisins. Cream butter and sugar. Add eggs one at a time, beating well after each. Add milk and beat. Sift together remaining flour, baking powder and salt. Last, fold in floured ingredients. Spoon into pan. Bake at 325F (165C) for 45-60 minutes. Frost with vanilla butter icing.

Pineapple Gumdrop Cake

1 lb	gumdrops (black ones removed)	500 g	2 tsp	vanilla	10 ml
			1 tsp	lemon rind, grated	5 ml
½ lb	raisins	250 g	3 cups	flour	750 ml
1 cup	butter	250 ml	2 tsp	baking powder	10 ml
2 cups	white sugar	500 ml	½ tsp	salt	2 ml
3	eggs	3	½ cup	warm milk	125 ml
1 cup	crushed pineapple, drained	250 ml			

Cut gumdrops into small pieces. Mix with raisins. Flour mixture with ½ cup (125 ml) of the flour. Cream butter and sugar; add beaten eggs, drained pineapple, vanilla and lemon rind. Beat. Sift dry ingredients together and mix, alternating with milk, into the creamed mixture. Add gumdrops and raisins last. Bake in tube pan, lined with wax paper, for about 1½ hours at 325F (165C).

Pecan-Buttermilk Layer Cake

½ cup	butter or margarine	125 ml	5	eggs, separated	5
			2 tsp	baking soda	10 ml
½ cup	vegetable oil	125 ml	2 cups	all-purpose flour	500 ml
½ cup	shortening	125 ml	½ cup	flaked coconut	125 ml
2 cups	white sugar	500 ml	1 cup	buttermilk	250 ml
1 tsp	vanilla extract	5 ml	1 cup	pecans, chopped	250 ml

Preheat oven to 325F (165C). Grease three 9-inch round cake pans. Beat egg whites until stiff but not dry. Combine baking soda and buttermilk, and let stand a few minutes. In a large bowl, cream sugar, butter or margarine, oil and shortening. Add egg yolks one at a time, beating well after each addition. Mix buttermilk mixture, alternating with flour, into creamed mixture. Stir in vanilla. Fold egg whites into batter. Gently stir in pecans and coconut. Divide into prepared pans. Bake for 25-30 minutes or until cake tests done.

Lemon Poppyseed Cake

1¼ cups	all-purpose flour	310 ml	2 tbsp	butter, unsalted	30 ml
⅔ cup	sugar	150 ml	1 cup	skim milk	250 ml
½ cup	cornstarch	125 ml	2 tsp	lemon zest	10 ml
1 tbsp	poppy seeds	15 ml	2 tsp	vanilla extract	10 ml
2¼ tsp	baking powder	11 ml	1	large egg	1
1 tsp	salt	5 ml			

Preheat oven to 350F (175C). Grease and flour an 8-inch (20 cm) baking pan. Combine first 6 ingredients in a bowl. Using a fork, blend in butter. Combine remaining ingredients in another bowl. Stir milk mixture into flour mixture, just until blended. Pour batter into prepared pan. Bake 35 minutes, or until a tester comes out clean when inserted in centre. Remove from pan and cool on a rack.

Cherry Pound Cake

1 cup	butter	250 ml		1 tsp	baking powder	5 ml
2 cups	sugar	500 ml		¾ cup	warm milk	175 ml
3	eggs	3		2 tsp	vanilla	10 ml
3 cups	flour	750 ml		1 tsp	lemon zest	5 ml
1 tsp	salt	5 ml		2 cups	maraschino cherries, cut up	500 ml

Cream butter and sugar well. Add lemon zest and vanilla. Add well-beaten eggs. Sift together flour, salt and baking powder, then, alternating with the milk, add to the butter mixture. Last, add cherries, cut up and floured. Pour into greased loaf pan. Bake at 325F (160C) until cake tests done, about two hours.

Cream Cheese Pound Cake

12 oz	cream cheese, softened	375 g		¼ tsp	salt	1 ml
				1 tsp	vanilla	5 ml
1 cup	unsalted butter, softened	250 ml		1 cup	candied fruit: cherries and pineapple, coarsely chopped	250 ml
3 cups	granulated sugar, divided	750 ml				
6	eggs, separated	6		⅔ cup	pecans, toasted and chopped	150 ml
3 cups	cake flour	750 ml				

Beat cream cheese, butter and vanilla in a large bowl until smooth; gradually beat in 2½ cups (625 ml) of sugar. Add egg yolks, one at a time, beating after each addition, until light and fluffy. Mix in flour and salt, reserving ½ cup (125 ml) flour to dust fruit. In a large bowl and using clean beaters, beat egg whites to soft peaks. Gradually add remaining ½ cup (125 ml) sugar, and beat into remaining egg whites. Fold in chopped fruit and pecans dusted with flour. Pour batter into greased and floured 12-cup (3 L) fluted cake pan. Bake at 325F (165C) until toothpick inserted in centre of cake comes out clean, about 1½ hours. Cool on wire rack for 20 minutes.

Blueberry Peach Pound Cake

½ cup	butter, softened	125 ml		2¼ cups	fresh peaches, peeled and cut into ½-inch (1 cm) pieces	550 ml
1¼ cups	sugar	300 ml				
3	eggs	3		2 cups	blueberries, fresh	500 ml
¼ cup	milk	50 ml		2 tsp	baking powder	10 ml
2½ cups	cake flour	625 ml			icing sugar	
¼ tsp	salt	1 ml				

In a mixing bowl, cream butter and sugar. Beat in eggs, one at a time. Beat in milk. Combine the flour, baking powder, and salt. Add to creamed mixture. Stir in peaches and blueberries. Pour into a greased and floured 10-inch (25 cm) fluted tube pan. Bake at 350F (175C) for 60-70 minutes or until a toothpick inserted near the centre comes out clean. Cool in pan for 15 minutes; remove to a wire rack. Dust with icing sugar, if desired.

Sultana Loaf Cake

1 cup	butter	250 ml		2¾ cups	flour	675 ml
1 cup	sugar	250 ml		1 tsp	baking powder	5 ml
2	eggs	2		½ tsp	salt	2 ml
½ cup	orange juice	125 ml		2 cups	raisins	500 ml
1 tsp	vanilla	5 ml				

Cream butter and blend in sugar. Add eggs, one at a time, beating after each addition. Stir in orange juice and vanilla. Reserve ½ cup (125 ml) of flour to dust raisins. Combine remaining flour, baking powder and salt, and add to mixture. Stir in flour-dusted raisins. Bake in a loaf pan at 325F (160C) for about 1 hour. Heat may need to be increased to 350C (175C).

Pear-Nut Cake

4 cups	pears, peeled, cored and chopped	1 L	1 tsp	ground nutmeg	5 ml
			1 tsp	cinnamon	5 ml
2 cups	white sugar	500 ml	½ tsp	ground cloves	2 ml
3 cups	all-purpose flour, sifted	750 ml	4	egg whites	4
			⅔ cup	canola oil	150 ml
1 tsp	salt	5 ml	1 cup	pecans, chopped	250 ml
1½ tsp	baking soda	7 ml			

Combine pears and sugar and let stand for one hour. Preheat oven to 325F (165C). Spray a 10-inch bundt pan with non-stick cooking spray. Beat the egg whites lightly and combine them with the oil, chopped pecans and pear mixture. Stir together the flour, salt, baking soda, nutmeg, cinnamon and cloves. Stir into the pear mixture. Pour batter into the prepared bundt pan. Bake at 325F (165C) for 1 hour and 10 minutes. Remove from oven and let cool on a wire rack for 10 minutes before removing from pan.

Date Cake

1	orange	1	1 cup	raisins	250 ml
1 tsp	nutmeg	5 ml	½ lb	dates	250 g
1 tsp	cinnamon	5 ml	2 cups	water	500 ml

Place above ingredients together in saucepan. Bring to boil for 15 minutes, stirring often. Cool.

Add:

½ cup	oil	125 ml	2 tsp	baking soda	10 ml
2 tsp	vanilla	10 ml	½ tsp	salt	2 ml
2 cups	whole wheat flour	500 ml			

Mix all together. Pour into a 9x9-inch (23x23 cm) pan. Bake at 350F (175C) for 1 hour.

Harvest Cake

1 cup	vegetable oil	250 ml	1 tsp	baking soda	5 ml
3	eggs	3	1 tsp	ground nutmeg	5 ml
2 cups	cooked, puréed pumpkin	500 ml	1 tsp	ground allspice	5 ml
			1 tsp	ground cinnamon	5 ml
1 tsp	vanilla extract	5 ml	½ tsp	ground cloves	2 ml
2½ cups	white sugar	625 ml	¼ tsp	salt	1 ml
2½ cups	all-purpose flour	625 ml	1 cup	nuts, chopped	250 ml
				icing sugar	

Preheat oven to 350F (175C). Grease a 10-inch bundt or tube pan. Cream oil, beaten eggs, pumpkin and vanilla together. Sift the flour, sugar, baking soda, ground nutmeg, ground allspice, ground cinnamon, ground cloves and salt together. Add the flour mixture to the pumpkin mixture and mix until just combined. Stir in chopped nuts. Pour batter into the prepared pan. Bake at 350F (175C) for 1 hour or until a toothpick inserted in the middle comes out clean. Let cake cool in pan for 5 minutes then turn out onto a plate and sprinkle with icing sugar.

Crumb Cake

2 cups	flour	500 ml	1 tsp	cloves	5 ml
1 cup	white sugar	250 ml	1 tsp	cinnamon	5 ml
¾ cup	butter	175 ml	1	egg	1
1 cup	sour milk	250 ml	1 cup	raisins	250 ml
1 tsp	baking soda	5 ml	1 cup	currants	250 ml
½ tsp	salt	2 ml			

Mix flour, sugar, and butter to the consistency of crumbs. Reserve 1 cup (250 ml) of crumb mixture. Mix remainder of crumbs with all remaining ingredients. Pour into a 9x13-inch (22x33 cm) pan. Sprinkle top of cake with remaining crumbs. Bake in a 350F (175C) oven for 1 hour.

Note: To make sour milk, add 1 tbsp (15 ml) vinegar or lemon juice to milk.

Rum and Raisin Cake

½ cup	golden raisins	125 ml	1 tbsp	cornstarch	15 ml
½ cup	sultana raisins	125 ml	2 tsp	baking soda	10 ml
1 tbsp	rum extract	15 ml	1 tsp	ground cinnamon	5 ml
½ cup	butter or	125 ml	½ tsp	ground nutmeg	2 ml
	margarine, softened		¼ tsp	salt	1 ml
1 cup	white sugar	250 ml	1 tbsp	cocoa	15 ml
2	eggs	2	1½ cups	applesauce	375 ml
1 cup	all-purpose flour	250 ml	¼ cup	walnuts, if desired	50 ml
1 cup	whole wheat flour	250 ml			

Place the raisins in a small bowl with the rum and let sit overnight. Preheat oven to 350F (175C). Grease and flour a 9x13-inch (22x33 cm) baking pan. In a large bowl, cream the butter or margarine with the sugar. Beat in the eggs, then the applesauce. In another bowl, stir together the flours, cornstarch, baking soda, spices, salt, and cocoa. Beat into the creamed ingredients. Stir in the raisins, along with any rum that was not absorbed, and the walnuts, if desired. Turn batter into the prepared pan. Bake for 25 minutes or until cake tests done. Let cool on rack.

Hilda's Dutch Botercake

Memories of Holland in every bite!

1⅛ cups	butter or	280 ml	1 tbsp	white sugar	15 ml
	margarine, softened		1 tsp	salt	5 ml
1⅛ cups	white sugar	280 ml	5	eggs	5
1¼ tsp	vanilla sugar	6 ml	1⅛ cups	all-purpose flour	280 ml
1	lemon rind, grated	1	1 tsp	baking powder	5 ml

Preheat oven to 350F (175C). Grease and flour one 10-inch (25 cm) loaf pan. Mix grated lemon rind with 1 tbsp (15 ml) sugar. Beat butter and sugar with vanilla sugar, and lemon rind until the mixture becomes white and fluffy. Add eggs one at a time mixing after each one. Mix flour, salt and baking powder together and then carefully fold into the butter and egg mixture. Pour batter into a prepared loaf pan. Bake cake for 60-75 minutes or until a knife inserted in the middle comes out clean.

Banana Layer Cake
with Cream Cheese Frosting

2 cups	flour	500 ml
1½ tsp	baking powder	7 ml
1 tsp	baking soda	5 ml
½ tsp	salt	2 ml
1½ cups	sugar	375 ml
½ cup	margarine	125 ml

½ cup	buttermilk or sour milk	125 ml
1 cup	ripe bananas, mashed	250 ml
2	eggs	2
2 tsp	vanilla	10 ml

Combine flour, baking powder, soda and salt in a large mixing bowl. Add sugar, margarine, ¼ cup (50 ml) buttermilk and bananas. Beat at medium speed for 2 minutes. Add eggs, vanilla, and remaining buttermilk. Beat at medium speed for 1 minute. Spread batter evenly between 2 greased 9-inch (23 cm) round layer cake pans. Bake at 350F (175C) for 30-40 minutes or until the cakes test done. Cool 10 minutes on racks, then remove from pans and cool on racks. Put layers together with cream cheese icing. (See recipe at the beginning of "Cakes" section.)

Cranberry Bundt Cake

¾ cup	butter or margarine	175 ml
1½ cups	sugar	375 ml
3	eggs	3
1½ tsp	almond extract	7 ml
3 cups	flour	750 ml
¾ tsp	salt	3 ml

1½ tsp	baking powder	7 ml
1½ tsp	baking soda	7 ml
1½ cups	sour cream	375 ml
½ cup	walnuts, chopped	125 ml
1 16-oz can	whole cranberries	450 g

Cream butter and sugar. Add eggs, one at a time. Beat in almond extract. Sift together dry ingredients. Add to creamed mixture, alternating with sour cream. Beat well after each addition. Spoon ⅓ batter into greased and floured bundt pan. Spread half the cranberries and half the nuts over the batter. Repeat, ending with batter. Bake at 350F (175C) for approximately 1 hour. Serves 12.

Drizzle on top of cooled cake a mixture of:

¾ cup	powdered sugar	175 ml
1 tbsp	orange juice	15 ml

½ tsp	almond extract	2 ml

Spice Cake

½ cup	shortening or butter	125 ml	2½ tsp	baking powder	12 ml
1 cup	white sugar	250 ml	½ tsp	salt	2 ml
2	eggs, unbeaten	2	1 tsp	cinnamon	5 ml
⅓ cup	molasses	75 ml	½ tsp	cloves	2 ml
1 cup	milk	250 ml	1 tsp	vanilla	5 ml
2-2½ cups	flour	500-550 ml			

Cream shortening (or butter) and sugar. Add eggs and molasses. Beat. Add milk and vanilla slowly and beat. Sift dry ingredients together and add to creamed mixture. Bake at 350F (175C) in a 9x9-inch (23x23 cm) pan for approximately 30 minutes.

Oatmeal Cake

1½ cups	boiling water	375 ml	½ tsp	salt	2 ml
1 cup	quick-cooking oatmeal	250 ml	1 cup	brown sugar	250 ml
			1 cup	white sugar	250 ml
1½ cups	flour	375 ml	2	eggs	2
1 tsp	cinnamon	5 ml	½ cup	salad oil	125 ml
1 tsp	baking soda	5 ml	1 tsp	vanilla	5 ml

Pour boiling water over oatmeal and let stand. Sift together flour, cinnamon, baking soda and salt; add these dry ingredients to sugars, eggs, vanilla, and oil, then add oatmeal. Mix well; pour into a greased and floured bundt pan. Bake at 350F (175C) for 30-40 minutes.

Topping:

1 cup	brown sugar	250 ml	1 tsp	vanilla	5 ml
½ cup	evaporated milk	125 ml	½ cup	nuts, chopped	125 ml
½ cup	butter	125 ml	1 cup	coconut	250 ml

Dissolve the sugar in the milk. Add the butter and cook, stirring constantly until mixture boils and becomes thick. Take from heat and add vanilla, nuts, and coconut. Pour over cake while hot.

Blueberry Gingerbread

½ cup	margarine	125 ml	2 tsp	ginger	10 ml
½ cup	brown sugar	125 ml	1 tsp	cinnamon	5 ml
2	eggs, beaten	2	½ cup	sour cream	125 ml
2 cups	flour	500 ml	½ cup	molasses	125 ml
1 tbsp	baking powder	15 ml	1½ cups	blueberries, fresh or frozen	375 ml
¼ tsp	salt	1 ml			

Preheat oven to 350F (175C). Grease and flour an 8-inch (20 cm) square pan. Cream margarine, and add sugar. Add eggs and beat. Sift together dry ingredients and add, alternating with the sour cream and molasses combined. Fold in blueberries. Pour into prepared pan. Bake for approximately 40 minutes.

Old Country Gingerbread

You can't beat it!

½ cup	sugar	125 ml	1 tsp	cinnamon	5 ml
½ cup	shortening	125 ml	2 tsp	ginger	10 ml
2	eggs	2	½ tsp	cloves	2 ml
1 cup	molasses	250 ml	½ tsp	salt	2 ml
2½ cups	flour	625 ml	1 cup	hot water	250 ml
1½ tsp	baking soda	7 ml			

Cream sugar and shortening. Add eggs and molasses and beat. Add dry ingredients, sifted together. Lastly add hot water. Beat well. Batter will be thin. Use a 9x9-inch pan for thick cake—a 13x9-inch will do. Bake at 325F-350F (165-175C) for 40 minutes. Can be served plain or with whipped cream, butterscotch sauce or butter. Absolutely delicious.

Sour Cream
Raspberry Cake

1½ cups white flour	375 ml
1 cup	white sugar	250 ml
1½ tsp	baking powder	7 ml
½ cup	butter	125 ml
1	egg	1

2 tsp	vanilla	10 ml
2	egg yolks	2
2 cups	sour cream	500 ml
3 cups	raspberries, fresh	750 ml

Sift flour, ½ cup (125 ml) sugar, and baking powder into a large bowl. Melt butter and stir into flour mixture. Beat egg and 1 tsp (5 ml) vanilla together and stir into flour mixture. Form into a ball and spread over bottom of a buttered 10" (25 cm) springform pan. Wisk together egg yolks, sour cream, ½ cup (125 ml) sugar and 1 tsp vanilla. Spread raspberries over cake base. Top cake with sour cream mixture. Bake for 1 hour and 10 minutes at 375F (190C). Cool and refrigerate at least 2 hours until firm. Serves 8-10.

Queen Elizabeth Cake

Fit for a queen.

1½ cups	dates, chopped	375 ml		3	eggs	3
1½ tsp	baking soda	7 ml		1 tsp	vanilla	5 ml
1½ cups	water, boiling	375 ml		2½ cups	flour	625 ml
¾ cup	butter	175 ml		1½ tsp	baking powder	7 ml
½ cup	white sugar	125 ml		½ tsp	salt	2 ml
1 cup	brown sugar	250 ml				

Put dates in a saucepan and cover with boiling water. Place saucepan contents on moderate heat and boil for about 1 minute. Stir in soda. Turn off heat and set aside to cool. Cream butter and sugars. Add eggs and vanilla and beat well until light. Add sifted dry ingredients. Mix well. Last, turn in cooled date mixture and combine well. Turn into a greased 9x13-inch (22x23 cm) pan. Bake at 325F (160C) for 45 minutes.

Topping:

⅓ cup	butter	75 ml	3 tbsp	milk	45 ml
1 cup	brown sugar	250 ml	1 cup	coconut	250 ml

Heat butter, brown sugar and milk in saucepan. Stir well. Heat to boiling and continue to stir. Remove from heat. Stir in coconut. Spread over cake. Return to oven until topping begins to bubble. May be left in pan. Good warm or cold.

Pineapple Coconut Cake

½ cup	shortening	125 ml		2½ tsp	baking powder	12 ml
1 cup	sugar	250 ml		½ tsp	salt	2 ml
2	eggs	2		¾ cup	milk	175 ml
2 cups	cake flour	500 ml		1 tsp	vanilla	5 ml

Blend shortening, sugar, salt, vanilla and eggs. Sift flour and baking powder and add to creamed mixture, alternating with milk. Pour into two greased layer pans. Bake at 350F (175C) for 25 minutes.

Pineapple Filling:
Mix 2 tbsp (30 ml) cornstarch with ½ cup (125 ml) sugar. Add 2 cups (500 ml) crushed pineapple (juice and fruit). Add 1 tbsp (15 ml) lemon juice. Cook slowly until thick and clear. Save ½ cup (125 ml) filling to decorate top of cake. Spread remainder between cake layers.

Cover top and sides of cake with 7-minute frosting. (See "Frostings" section for recipe.) Sprinkle top and sides of cake with coconut. Decorate top of cake with the ½ cup (125 ml) pineapple filling.

Helene's Chocolate Cake

This cake is really delicious and very moist. This recipe tends to dry out if you double it, so stick with the single and you won't be disappointed.

½ cup	rolled oats	125 ml		1 cup	flour	250 ml
1 cup	boiling water	250 ml		4 tbsp	cocoa	60 ml
½ cup	margarine	125 ml		1 tsp	baking powder	5 ml
1½ cups	brown sugar	375 ml		1 tsp	baking soda	5 ml
2	eggs	2		pinch	salt	
1 tsp	vanilla	5 ml				

Combine rolled oats and boiling water. Let stand. Combine margarine, brown sugar, eggs, and vanilla. Add flour, cocoa, baking powder, soda, and salt. Add oat mixture and blend. Bake in an 8x8-inch (20x20 cm) pan at 350F (175C) for 30 minutes. Frost with your favourite icing.

Diane's Chocolate Mayonnaise Cake

This is unforgettable!

1 cup	mayonnaise	250 ml	2 cups	flour	500 ml
1 cup	cold water	250 ml	4 tbsp	cocoa	60 ml
1 cup	white sugar	250 ml	1 tsp	baking soda	5 ml
1 tsp	vanilla	5 ml	¼ tsp	salt	1 ml

Preheat oven to 350F (175C). Mix mayonnaise and water. In a separate bowl, sift dry ingredients and add to wet mixture. Blend well. Pour into a greased and floured pan. Bake for 30 minutes. Remove from oven and cool. Top with Irish Coffee Icing. (See "Frostings" section for recipe).

Ruby's Red Devil's Food Cake

Preheat oven to 350F (175C). Prepare a 9x13-inch (22x33 cm) pan.
Sift the following ingredients into a large mixing bowl:

1¾ cups	cake flour	425 ml	1 tsp	salt	5 ml
1½ cups	sugar	375 ml	⅓ cup	cocoa	75 ml
1¼ tsp	baking soda	6 ml			

Add:

½ cup	shortening, softened	125 ml		Beat 2 minutes, and add:	
			2	eggs	2
			2 tsp	vanilla	10 ml
⅔ cup	milk	150 ml	⅓ cup	milk	75 ml

Beat 2 minutes. Pour into pan. Bake for 35-40 minutes until cake tests done. Top with chocolate icing and a sprinkle of ground nuts.

Devil's Food Cake

Everyone will agree that this cake is "wicked."

3 1-oz squares	unsweetened chocolate	3x30 g	1¾ cups	brown sugar, firmly packed	425 ml
2¼ cups	cake flour, sifted	550 ml	3	large eggs	3
			2 tsp	vanilla	10 ml
2 tsp	baking soda	10 ml	1 cup	sour milk	250 ml
½ tsp	salt	2 ml	1 cup	boiling water	250 ml
½ cup	butter	125 ml			

Melt chocolate in a small bowl over hot (not boiling) water. Cool. Grease and flour two 9-inch (23 cm) cake pans or one 13x9x2-inch (33x23x4 cm) baking pan. Heat oven to 350F (175C). In a large bowl, beat butter until smooth. Add brown sugar and eggs, and beat at high speed for 5 minutes. Beat in vanilla and cooled chocolate. Stir in dry ingredients, alternating with sour milk, until batter is smooth. Stir in boiling water. Batter will be thin. Pour into pans. Bake the layer cakes at 350F (175C) for 35 minutes or until centres spring back when pressed lightly. Cool cake in pans on rack for 10 minutes. Turn out onto rack and finish cooling.

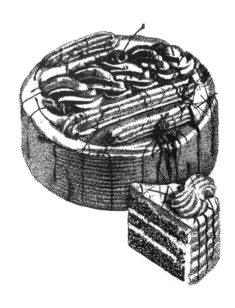

Chocolate Carrot Cake

This is a dense cake, moist and rich in flavour.

2½ cups	flour	625 ml		2	eggs	2
¾ cup	cocoa	175 ml		¼ cup	corn syrup	50 ml
1½ tsp	baking powder	7 ml		1 tsp	vanilla	5 ml
1 tsp	salt	5 ml		3 cups	carrots, shredded	750 ml
1 tsp	baking soda	5 ml		1 14-oz can	pineapple, crushed and undrained	398 ml
1 tsp	cinnamon	5 ml				
½ tsp	nutmeg, ground	2 ml			chocolate glaze	
½ cup	vegetable oil	125 ml			walnuts, chopped	
1 cup	brown sugar, packed	250 ml				

In a large bowl, mix flour, cocoa, baking powder, soda, salt, cinnamon and nutmeg; set aside. In a medium-sized bowl whisk together oil, brown sugar, eggs, corn syrup and vanilla until smooth. Stir in carrots and undrained pineapple. Add to flour mixture, stirring just until moistened. Pour into a 12-cup (3 L) bundt or tube pan. Bake in a preheated 350F (175C) oven for 60-65 minutes or until a cake tester inserted in centre comes out clean. Cool in pan for 10 minutes. Remove from pan and cool completely. Spoon chocolate glaze over cake so that glaze runs down sides of cake. Sprinkle with chopped walnuts.

Chocolate Glaze:
Sift together 1 cup (250 ml) icing sugar and 2 tbsp (30 ml) cocoa. Gradually stir in 2-3 tbsp (30-45 ml) boiling water. Add 1 tsp (5 ml) vanilla.

Sachertorte—Chocolate Cake

5 1-oz	semisweet chocolate	5x30 g	¾ cup	butter or margarine, softened	175 ml
squares					
¾ cup	white sugar	175 ml	5	eggs, separated	5
			¾ cup	all-purpose flour	175 ml

Preheat oven to 325F (165C). Have all ingredients at room temperature. Melt the chocolate in a double boiler over hot water. Remove from heat and let cool. Separate the eggs. Cream the butter and sugar together until light and fluffy. Gradually beat in the egg yolks until light in colour. Add the melted, cooled chocolate, and beat. Gradually add the sifted flour to the batter. Beat the egg whites until stiff but not dry, and fold them into the mixture. Pour batter into an ungreased 9-inch (23 cm) springform pan. Bake at 325F (165C) for 50-60 minutes. Allow cake to cool completely before removing from the pan. Slice cake horizontally. Insert a filling of puréed jam between the layers. Cover top and sides with warm Sachertorte icing. (See "Frostings" section for recipe.)

Chocolate Log

⅔ cup	flour	150 ml		2 tbsp	water	30 ml
¼ tsp	baking soda	1 ml		¼ cup	liquid baking chocolate, unsweetened	50 ml
¼ tsp	salt	1 ml				
4	eggs	4		2 cups	whipping cream, whipped and sweetened	500 ml
1 cup	sugar	250 ml				

Grease a 15x10-inch (38x25 cm) jellyroll pan and line with parchment paper or waxed paper. Grease again. Combine flour, soda, and salt. Beat eggs in the small bowl of an electric mixer, at high speed, until light coloured (about 5 minutes). Gradually add sugar, beating until thick. Blend in water and chocolate. Fold dry ingredients into egg mixture, gently but thoroughly. Spread in prepared pan. Bake at 350F (175C) for 15-17 minutes or until cake springs back when touched lightly. Loosen edges and immediately turn out of pan onto a tea towel generously sprinkled with sifted icing sugar. Remove paper. Spread evenly with whipped cream. Roll. Frost log completely with Chocolate Butter Icing (see recipe in "Frostings" section). Score with fork to resemble bark. Any filling suitable for cakes may be substituted for whipped cream.

Sour Cream Chocolate Cake

2 cups	cake flour	500 ml		½ cup	butter or margarine	125 ml
1 tsp	baking soda	5 ml				
½ tsp	salt	2 ml		1½ cups	white sugar	375 ml
½ cup	boiling water	125 ml		2	eggs	2
3 1-oz squares	unsweetened chocolate	3x30 g		1 tsp	vanilla extract	5 ml
				⅔ cup	sour cream	150 ml

Preheat oven to 350F (175C). Grease two 9-inch (23 cm) round cake pans. Sift flour, baking soda and salt. Mix boiling water into broken chocolate. Stir well. Cream together butter and sugar; add eggs, and beat well. Blend in the chocolate mixture. Then add the flour mixture, alternating with the cream; beat after each addition. Add vanilla, and pour into pans. Bake at 350F (175C) for 30 minutes or until cake tests done. Mint-flavoured icing goes well with this cake.

Chocolate Applesauce Cake

This cake has no eggs, so it's very dense.

½ cup	butter or margarine	125 ml	¼ cup	cocoa powder, unsweetened	50 ml
1¼ cups	white sugar	300 ml	2 tsp	baking soda	10 ml
½ cup	milk	125 ml	1 tsp	cinnamon, ground	5 ml
1½ cups	applesauce, sweetened or unsweetened	375 ml	1 tsp	nutmeg, ground	5 ml
			⅛ tsp	salt	0.5 ml
			1 cup	raisins	250 ml
¼ cup + 2 tbsp	dark rum, divided	80 ml	1 cup	pecans, coarsely chopped	250 ml
2 cups	all-purpose flour	500 ml			

In a bowl, cream the butter or margarine with the sugar. Beat in the milk, applesauce and 2 tbsp (30 ml) of rum. In another bowl, stir together the flour, cocoa, baking soda, spices, and salt. Beat into the creamed mixture and then stir in the raisins and pecans. Turn the batter into a greased and floured 9x13-inch (23x33 cm) baking pan. Bake the cake in a preheated 350F (175C) oven for 45 minutes or until it tests done with a toothpick. Immediately after removing the cake from the oven, sprinkle it with the remaining ¼ cup (50 ml) rum. Let cool on a rack. This cake improves if allowed to sit for a day of so before being eaten.

Easy Chocolate Bundt Cake

1	2-layer chocolate cake mix (Devil's Food is best)	1	½ cup	vegetable oil	125 ml
			½ cup	warm water	125 ml
			1 cup	sour cream	250 ml
1 pkg	chocolate pudding (4-serving size)	1	4	eggs	4
			1 cup	chocolate chips	250 ml

Mix all ingredients together. Pour into a greased and floured bundt or angel food cake pan. Bake at 350F (175C) for 1 hour. Frost or dust with icing sugar.

Chocolate-Mint Cake

2 cups	cake flour, sifted	500 ml		3 1-oz squares	unsweetened chocolate, melted and cooled	3x30 g
1⅔ cups	sugar	400 ml		½ cup	shortening	125 ml
1½ tsp	baking soda	7 ml		3	eggs	3
1 tsp	salt	5 ml		⅔ cup	milk	150 ml
½ tsp	baking powder	2 ml		1 tsp	peppermint or vanilla flavouring	5 ml
⅔ cup	milk	150 ml				

In mixing bowl, combine cake flour, sugar, baking soda, salt, and baking powder. Add ⅔ cup (150 ml) milk, shortening and melted chocolate. Beat with electric mixer at medium speed for 2 minutes. Add eggs, the remaining ⅔ cup (150 ml) milk, and the peppermint. Beat for 2 minutes more. Pour batter into 2 greased and floured 9x1½-inch (23x4 cm) round layer pans or a 13x9-inch (33x23x5 cm) baking pan. Bake at 350F (175F) for 35 to 40 minutes or until cake tests done. Cool for 15 minutes; remove from pans.

Chocolate Cake in a Frying Pan

5 tbsp	cocoa	75 ml		½ cup	sour milk: add 1 tsp (5 ml) vinegar to milk	125 ml
2 cups	sugar	500 ml		2 tsp	vanilla	10 ml
½ cup	butter	125 ml		½ tsp	salt	2 ml
1 cup	boiling water	250 ml		2 cups	flour	500 ml
2	eggs	2		2 tbsp	baking soda	30 ml

Combine cocoa, sugar, butter and boiling water. Add the eggs, sour milk, baking soda, vanilla, salt and flour. Batter will be very thin. Pour into a 12-inch (30 cm) cast-iron frying pan lined with parchment paper, and bake at 350F (175C) for 1 hour.

The Great Nova Scotia Cookbook

Chocolate Cookie Cake

1	2-layer white cake mix	1
½ cup	vegetable oil	125 ml
4	large eggs	4
1 cup	water	250 ml
1 cup	cream-filled chocolate cookies, coarsely crushed	250 ml

Icing:

1 cup	icing sugar	250 ml
2 tbsp	butter or hard margarine, softened	30 ml
1½ tbsp	water	25 ml
½ tsp	vanilla	2 ml
1 oz	unsweetened chocolate, cut up and melted	30 g

Combine cake mix, oil, eggs and water in a large bowl. Beat on low to moisten, then beat on medium for 2 minutes until smooth. Stir in crushed cookies. Grease and flour a 12-cup (2.7 L) bundt pan. Bake at 350F (175C) for about 45-55 minutes until an inserted wooden pick comes out clean. Cool. Place on rack.

Icing:
Stir first four ingredients vigorously until smooth. Spoon over cake, allowing some to run down sides. Drizzle chocolate over icing.

Deep Chocolate Raspberry Cake

6 1-oz squares	semisweet chocolate	6x28 g
6 1-oz squares	unsweetened chocolate	6x28 g
7	eggs, separated	7
1 cup	all-purpose flour	250 ml
1 cup	butter or margarine	250 ml
2 cups	white sugar	500 ml

2 tsp	vanilla extract	10 ml
6 1-oz squares	semisweet chocolate	6x28 g
¾ cup	heavy cream	175 ml
1 4-oz pkg	frozen raspberries, thawed	125 g
3 tbsp	raspberry jam, seedless	45 ml
	fresh raspberries	

Preheat oven to 300F (150C). Line two 9-inch (23 cm) cake pans with wax paper. Melt 6 oz of semisweet and 6 oz of unsweetened chocolate in the top of a double boiler or in a microwave. Cool, and beat in egg yolks. In a large bowl, beat butter or margarine, 1½ cups (375 ml) sugar, and vanilla until light and fluffy. Add chocolate mixture, and continue beating until smooth. Stir in flour until combined. In another bowl, beat egg whites until foamy. Gradually beat in ½ cup sugar (125 ml) until soft peaks hold. Fold whites into chocolate batter in three additions. Pour batter into prepared pans, and smooth tops. Bake until a toothpick inserted into the centre of each cake comes out with moist crumbs, about 45 minutes. Cool in pans.

Frosting:
In a saucepan, bring cream just to a boil. Chop 6 oz semisweet chocolate, and stir into the cream. Remove saucepan from heat and continue stirring until smooth. Pour out frosting into bowl, and press sheet of plastic wrap directly against surface of chocolate to prevent formation of a skin. Refrigerate until thick enough to spread.

Filling:
Drain the thawed raspberries, if necessary, and combine with the jam. Sandwich raspberry filling between the cake layers. Spread top and sides with chocolate frosting. Decorate with fresh raspberries.

Prize Dark Fruit Cake

This is a wonderful recipe. It won second prize in a province-wide contest in 1989. It was given to me in 1948 by Allison McMullen of Truro. It belonged to her sister, who was a home economics instructor at the Provincial Normal College in Truro. It is my favourite and I make it every year.

Prepare and mix together:

½ lb	mixed fruit	250 g	2¼ cups	brown sugar	550 ml
½ lb	figs, thinly sliced	250 g	1 lb	butter	454 g
3 lb	currants, picked over, rinsed and well drained	1.5 kg	12	eggs, extra large	12
			1 cup	thick strawberry jam, no pectin	250 ml
2 lb	raisins, picked over, rinsed and well drained	1kg	1 tsp	almond extract	5 ml
			1 tsp	rose flavouring	5 ml
¼ lb	red cherries, halved	125 g	2 tbsp	milk	30 ml
¼ lb	green cherries, halved	125 g	4½ cups	flour, more if needed	1.125 L
1 lb	dates, sliced	500 g	1 tsp	baking soda	5 ml
½ lb	almonds, thinly sliced and toasted	250 g	1 tsp	cinnamon	5 ml
			1 tsp	mace	5 ml
¼ lb	candied ginger, thinly sliced	125 g	1 tsp	cloves	5 ml
			1 tsp	salt	5 ml

Place all fruit in a large basin. Use part of the flour in recipe to dust fruit, making sure that each piece of fruit is covered. Set aside. Cream butter and blend in brown sugar. Drop in eggs one at a time, beating well after each addition. If extra large eggs are not readily available, add an extra one or even two. Add jam and stir well. Mix in milk and flavourings. Place remaining flour in sifter along with soda, salt, cinnamon, mace and cloves. Mix very carefully into batter. Last, add fruit and mix very carefully to distribute well. If the batter has a slightly curdled appearance it needs more flour. Add very little and then stir. Repeat until the batter has a smooth opaque appearance; it should be thick enough to just move off a spoon.

Preparations of pans and cooking:
Steam fruitcake for best results. Round tins are much preferred for steaming.

continued...

Cut 3 layers of heavy brown paper to fit bottoms of pans and make strips of paper to fit around sides. Grease well. Cut circles two or three inches larger than tops. Grease tops extremely well on both sides to prevent steam from entering cakes. Pack fruit cake batter into pans, filling about ⅔ full. Tap the pan several times to remove air. Place greased paper over top, secure with a rubber band, and tie with strong string, wrapping 2-3 times around. Allow a little fullness over the tin to help steam from condensing into "puddles" on top of cakes.

Place the pans in a steamer or canning pot deep enough for the height of the tins. You may need more than one steamer, depending on the size of your baking pans. Place the pans on racks in the bottom of the pot to keep cakes off the bottom of steamer. Pour and heat enough water to cover about half the height of the cake tins. Never cover the tins with water. The level of water must be maintained throughout cooking—about 3 hours. Have water in steaming pot boiling rapidly before placing the tins in water. Cover the steamer pots with tightly fitting covers, so that as little steam escapes as possible. After 3 hours of steaming, carefully remove cans from water. Set on racks, and remove paper from tops. Turn out cakes and remove liners while hot. If the cakes appear quite damp, they can be dried off in a warm oven for a few minutes. If the cakes appear dry, do not place them in oven.

When cold, sprinkle a little rum over cake surfaces to prevent mould from developing. Wrap the cakes in rum-soaked cloths and store in crocks to ripen. Check cakes for moistness by opening the wrappings periodically. They will keep well stored in a cool, dry place for a week or two—any longer and they should be frozen. (Fruitcakes do not store well in a refrigerator.) Wrap in foil and place in plastic bags to freeze. Fruit cake cuts easily if slightly frozen.

The Great Nova Scotia Cookbook

Gertrude Foster's Dark Fruit Cake

"Gertie," as she was affectionately known, is remembered as one of the best cooks in Princeport, a small community on the eastern side of the Shubenacadie River. And she was my mother! When a wedding was to take place, Gertie was sure to be asked to make the groom's cake. She would don a clean, starched apron, and, with love and care, present the cake on the special day.

2 lb	seeded raisins	1 kg		1 cup	molasses	250 ml
1 lb	seedless raisins	500 g		6	eggs	6
1 lb	currants	500 g		¾ lb	butter	375 g
¼ lb	mixed peel	125 g		¼ cup	milk	50 ml
¼ lb	mixed fruit	125 g		3¾ cups	flour, or more	925 ml
3 oz	ginger	90 g		1 tsp	baking soda	5 ml
1 cup	strawberry jam, no pectin	250 ml		½ tsp	salt	2 ml
				1 tsp	cinnamon	5 ml
1 cup	red cherries	250 ml		1 tsp	cloves	5 ml
½ cup	green cherries	125 ml		1 tsp	nutmeg	5 ml
2 cups	brown sugar	500 ml		1 tsp	allspice	5 ml

Wash and drain the seedless raisins and currants. Separate seeded raisins. Place all fruit in a large bowl. Use 1½ cups (375 ml) of the flour to dust fruit. Cover and set aside. In another large bowl, cream butter and add sugar gradually. Add eggs one at a time and beat after each addition. Add molasses, jam and milk and beat again. Sift together flour, soda, salt and spices, and add to the creamed mixture. More flour may be added to make a thick batter. The batter should have an opaque, not a curdled appearance. It should be thick enough to barely slide off a spoon. Combine all fruit and batter. Pack in round tins (the best shape for steaming) lined with heavy, greased, brown paper. Tie greased brown paper securely over tops with string. Place in steamer and steam for three hours. Remove from steamer. Let tins sit on racks for 15 minutes. Remove cakes from tins. Remove paper. If very moist, dry off in a very slow oven for 15 minutes. Cakes can be wrapped in rum soaked cloths and stored for two weeks, preferably in a crock. More rum can be added to cloths to prevent mould from forming. Cakes may be frozen. Cakes cut easily if slightly frozen.

Light Christmas Fruit Cake

This recipe was published in an issue of the *Winnipeg Free Press* in November 1957. I made it for Christmas that very year and it is still one of my most treasured recipes. The clipping is now old and tattered, worn from its annual usage. This fruitcake is pleasing to the taste, beautiful to the eye, and rich in flavour and colour.

1 cup	butter	250 ml		1 cup	candied red cherries	250 ml
1¼ cups	sugar	300 ml		½ cup	candied green cherries	125 ml
5	eggs	5				
3 cups	sifted flour	750 ml		1 cup	candied pineapple mix (red, green and yellow)	250 ml
1 tsp	salt	5 ml				
2 tsp	vanilla	10 ml				
2 tsp	lemon rind, grated	10 ml		1½ cups	slivered almonds, toasted	375 ml
3 cups	bleached (golden) sultana raisins	750 ml		1 cup	crushed pineapple, undrained	250 ml
2 cups	slivered citron	500 ml				

Prepare fruit and pan:

Wash raisins, drain well and dry on towel. Cut citron into thin slivers. Halve cherries, leaving about one third of them whole. Dice the candied pineapple. Spread almonds in pan and place in oven for a few minutes to crisp slightly; watch them very carefully. Place all fruit in a large bowl and cover with a towel until ready to use. Just before using, sift about 1 cup of the measured flour over fruit and nuts. Mix well to coat each piece.

Line a square pan 8x8x4 inches (20x20x10 cm) with heavy duty foil or thin layers of heavy brown paper with the top layer well greased with vegetable oil. Preheat oven to 275F (135C). Place two tins of water in back of oven to provide steam during the baking. During the last hour of baking, another two tins of water may be placed at the front of oven, but be careful not to disturb cake.

Method:

Cream butter very well. Gradually add sugar, a spoonful at a time, and beat after each addition until sugar is dissolved and blended with the butter. Add eggs, one at a time, beating well and scraping sides of bowl, until all eggs are beaten in. Add vanilla and grated lemon rind. Add crushed pineapple and stir well. Add flour and salt sifted together. Finally add floured fruit and nuts. Stir all together well, using a folding method until each piece of fruit is blended into the batter. Turn batter into prepared pan—making sure to push batter into each corner and spread evenly over pan. Thump the pan on counter to remove air pockets. Bake 3 to 3½ hours.

Cake must be checked during baking. Edges may become dark before centre is cooked. If this happens, place a piece of foil over the darkened area. When done, the centre will spring back when touched lightly. Remove from oven. Let cake stand on a rack in the pan until cooled. Wrap and store. Makes one 4-pound to 5-pound cake.

Note: No baking powder is required.

Canada War Cake

This was a popular recipe during World War Two when butter and sugar were rationed.

2 cups	sugar	500 ml	1 tsp	salt	5 ml
2 cups	water	500 ml	1 tsp	cinnamon	5 ml
2 tbsp	shortening	30 ml	1 lb	raisins	500 g

Boil the above ingredients together for five minutes, stirring frequently. When cool, add:

3 cups	flour	750 ml
1 tsp (heaping)	baking soda	5 ml

Bake at 275 F (135C). Let stand a few days. This cake does not require frosting.

Wartime Cake

An old recipe from the days of World War One.

1 lb	raisins	500 g	1 tbsp	baking soda	15 ml
3 cups	cold water	750 ml	¾ tsp	salt	3.5 ml
1¾ cups	sugar	425 ml	1 tsp	cinnamon	5 ml
½ cup	lard	125 ml	1 tsp	cloves	5 ml
4 cups	flour	1 L	1 tsp	nutmeg	5 ml

In a saucepan, combine raisins and water. Bring to boil and boil for 15 minutes. Add lard and sugar. Stir to melt lard and dissolve sugar. Cool. Sift dry ingredients together and fold into the raisin mixture. Pour into 2 greased loaf pans and bake at 325F (165C) until done. More fruit may be added.

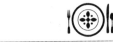

Yum Yum Cake

No eggs, no milk.

Boil 1 lb (500 g) raisins in 2 cups (500 ml) water for 15 minutes. Add ½ cup (125 ml) lard or butter. When melted, add 1 cup (250 ml) cold water and 2 cups (500 ml) sugar, 1 tsp (5 ml) nutmeg, 1 tsp (5 ml) allspice, ½ tsp (2 ml) cloves, 1 tsp (5 ml) lemon, 1 tsp (5 ml) vanilla, 1 tsp (5 ml) salt, and 1 tbsp (15 ml) baking soda dissolved in a little hot water. When cold add 4½ cups (1125 ml) flour. An 8x8-inch (20x20 cm) or 9x9-inch (23x23 cm) pan will make a nice deep cake. Bake at 325F (165C) for 1-1½ hours.

Florence's White Fruit Cake

Florence was the wife of one of the Yuill Brothers—famous potato growers in Old Barns, Colchester County.

1 lb	butter	454 g	1 tsp	salt	5 ml
2 cups	sugar	500 ml	½ lb	mixed peel	250 g
8	eggs, separated	8	½ lb	almonds, toasted	250 g
1	lemon, rind and juice	1	¼ lb	red and green cherries, halved	125 g
4 cups	flour, or more	1 L	1 lb	golden sultana raisins	500 g
1 tsp	baking powder	5 ml			

Cream butter and sugar. Add well-beaten egg yolks. Add lemon juice and rind. Add sifted flour (saving a little to dust the fruit), salt, and baking powder, alternating with stiffly-beaten egg whites. Fold in the floured fruit and almonds. Bake at 275F (135C) for 1½ hours. Makes 2 loaf-size cakes.

Cheap Christmas Fruit Cake

2 cups	brown sugar	500 ml	2 tsp	cloves	10 ml
4 tbsp	shortening	60 ml	2 tsp	nutmeg	10 ml
½ lb	seeded raisins	250 g	2 cups	hot water	500 ml
½ lb	seedless raisins or currants	250 g	¼ lb	any other kind of fruit you wish	125 g

Combine the above ingredients and boil five minutes. Cool. Add:

2 tsp	baking soda dissolved in a little hot water	10 ml	1 cup	nut meats, broken	250 ml
			3 cups	flour	750 ml
2 tbsp	molasses	30 ml	1 tsp	salt	5 ml
2 tbsp	marmalade	30 ml			

Bake at 275F (135C) for 1-1½ hours. Makes one large cake or two smaller ones. This cake improves with age.

Christmas Nut Cake

1 cup	sugar	250 ml		¼ lb	filbert nuts, chopped	125 g
1 cup	butter	250 ml		3	pineapple slices, cut in small pieces	3
2	eggs, well beaten	2				
¼ cup	milk	50 ml		½ cup	red cherries, halved	125 ml
1½ cups	flour, or more	375 ml		½ cup	green cherries, halved	125 ml
2 tsp	baking powder	10 ml				
1 tsp	salt	5 ml		2 tsp	rose extract	10 ml
½ lb	pecans, coarsely chopped	250 g		1 tsp	vanilla extract	5 ml
				2 tsp	orange rind, grated	10 ml
¼ lb	Brazil nuts, cut in large slices	125 g				

In a large bowl, cream butter and sugar. Beat in eggs, milk, and extracts. Reserve about ⅔ cup (150 ml) flour to flour fruit and nuts. Sift in flour, salt and baking powder. Blend well by beating at low speed. Fold in floured fruit and nuts and orange rind. If batter looks somewhat curdled, add more flour until a smooth texture appears. Add small amounts each time. Bake at 275F (135C) for 1-1½ hours or until it tests done. Baking time will depend on the size of pan or pans. Cool on a rack.

Cream Cheese Icing for a Layer Cake

2 8-oz pkgs	cream cheese, softened	2x250 g		1½-2 cups	icing sugar, sifted	375-500 ml
¼ cup	butter or margarine	50 ml		1 tsp	vanilla	5 ml

Beat cream cheese, butter and vanilla together on medium speed of electric mixer. Add icing sugar, beating until smooth.

Cream Cheese Pecan Frosting

1 8-oz pkg	cream cheese	250 ml		4 cups	icing sugar	1 L
				1 tsp	vanilla	5 ml
½ cup	butter or margarine	125 ml		1 cup	pecans, chopped	250 ml

Beat together cream cheese, butter, vanilla and sugar. Stir in chopped pecans. Spread on cake. Can be also used as a filling.

Coconut-Pecan Frosting

1 cup	evaporated milk	250 ml		½ cup	butter	125 ml
1 cup	sugar	250 ml		1 tsp	vanilla	5 ml
3	egg yolks, lightly beaten	3		1⅓ cups	coconut, flaked	325 ml
				1 cup	pecans, chopped	250 ml

Combine milk, sugar, egg yolks, butter and vanilla in a saucepan; cook and stir over medium heat until thickened. Remove from heat; stir in coconut and pecans. Beat until frosting is cool and reaches the desired consistency for spreading.

Fluffy White Frosting

1½ cups	white sugar	375 ml		2 tbsp	corn syrup	30 ml
¼ cup	water	50 ml		¼ tsp	salt	1 ml
2	eggs	2		1 tsp	vanilla	5 ml

Combine first five ingredients in the top of a double boiler and beat until well blended. Place over hot water and cook, beating constantly at high speed with an electric mixer, about 7 minutes, or until mixture triples and forms high peaks. Remove from heat. Beat in vanilla. Spread on cake. This frosting may be tinted to the colour of your preference.

Caramel Fudge Icing

1½ cups	brown sugar	375 ml		¼ tsp	salt	1 ml
½ cup	milk	125 ml				

Boil slowly to a soft ball stage at 236F (115C). Add 3 tbsp butter (45 ml). Cool and add 1 tsp vanilla (5 ml). Beat until mixture is spreadable. Thin icing with a little cream if it becomes too thick.

Seven-Minute Frosting

2	egg whites	2		¼ cup	water	50 ml
1 cup	sugar	250 ml		1 tsp	vanilla	5 ml
⅛ tsp	cream of tartar	0.5 ml				

Combine first four ingredients in the top of a double boiler. Place over boiling water and beat with electric beater until mixture hold its shape. Fold in vanilla. Tint with colouring, if desired. If frosting becomes sugary, beat in a little lemon juice.

Seven-Minute White Icing

A very fluffy, delightful icing that never fails. Make it in a double boiler.

2	egg whites, unbeaten	2		¼ tsp	cream of tartar	1 ml
				1½ tsp	light corn syrup	7 ml
1½ cups	sugar	375 ml		1 tsp	vanilla	5 ml
5 tbsp	cold water	75 ml				

Heat first five ingredients over rapidly boiling water, beating constantly for 7 minutes. Remove icing from heat. Add vanilla. Continue to beat until icing is the right consistency to spread. Add ½ cup (125 ml) chopped nuts or grated coconut, if desired.

Fluffy Buttercream Frosting

2 cups	icing sugar, unsifted	500 ml		½ tbsp	water	8 ml
½ tsp	vanilla	2 ml		3 tbsp	butter or margarine, softened	45 ml
1	egg white	1				

Combine all ingredients in a bowl. Beat at low speed to mix. Beat at high speed until smooth and fluffy, approximately 5-10 minutes. If too stiff, beat in a few drops of water.

Almond Filling

¼ cup	white sugar	50 ml		2	eggs	2
5 tsp	cornstarch	25 ml		2 tbsp	Amaretto (almond liqueur)	30 ml
¼ tsp	salt	1 ml				
1 cup	milk	250 ml				

Combine sugar, cornstarch, and salt in a saucepan. In a separate bowl, beat eggs and mix together with milk. Stir into dry mixture. Cook over medium heat, stirring constantly, until thick and bubbling. Cook for 2 minutes more. Remove from heat; add almond liqueur and stir will. Cover surface of filling with plastic wrap to prevent film from forming and chill completely before using.

Decorator Frosting

1 cup	shortening	250 ml		3-5 tbsp	milk	45-75 ml
4 cups	icing sugar	1 L		1½ tsp	almond extract	8 ml

Combine all ingredients in a mixing bowl. Beat on low speed of an electric mixer until well blended and very smooth.

Diane's Irish Coffee Icing

1 tbsp	instant coffee	15 ml		⅔ cup	butter	150 ml
2 tbsp	Irish whiskey or Kahlua	30 ml		1 tsp	vanilla	5 ml
2¾ cups	icing sugar	675 ml				

Stir dry coffee into whisky or Kahlua until coffee is dissolved. Beat coffee mixture, icing sugar, butter and vanilla with an electric mixer on medium speed until blended.

Fondant Frosting

3 cups	white sugar	750 ml		1 tsp	vanilla extract	5 ml
½ cup	light corn syrup	125 ml		⅛ tsp	almond extract	0.5 ml
¾ cup	water	175 ml		½ tsp	salt	2 ml
2	egg whites	2				

Cook sugar, corn syrup, and water in a saucepan over low heat, stirring constantly until sugar dissolves. Cover, then cook for 2-3 minutes longer. Uncover and continue cooking to the firm ball stage at 244-248F (118-120C). Remove from heat. Beat egg whites in a large mixing bowl with the vanilla extract, almond extract and salt until stiff but not dry; pour hot syrup in a slow, steady stream over beaten egg whites, beating constantly. Continue beating until frosting stands in peaks and begins to lose its gloss, about 10 minutes. If necessary, thin with a few drops of cream. Makes enough to frost one 9x13-inch (23x33 cm) cake.

Cream Cheese Icing

1 lb	icing sugar	450 g		¼ cup	margarine or butter	50 ml
1 8-oz pkg	cream cheese	250 g		1 tsp	lemon extract	5 ml

Mix all ingredients together until smooth. Spread over cooled cake.

Cream Cheese Glaze

2 oz	cream cheese, softened	60 g		2 tsp	lemon juice	10 ml
1 cup	icing sugar	250 ml				

Mix ingredients together, and frost the cake. Garnish as desired with glazed fruit (such as cherries and pineapple) or pecan halves.

Cocoa Cream Cheese Frosting

¾ cup	cream cheese, softened	175 ml		2 tsp	vanilla	10 ml
				2¾ cups	icing sugar	675 ml
¼ cup	butter, softened	50 ml		3 tbsp	cocoa	45 ml

In a large mixing bowl, beat cream cheese, butter and vanilla until smooth. Sift together icing sugar and cocoa and beat into creamed cheese mixture until smooth.

Chocolate Butter Icing

¼ cup	butter	50 ml	2 cups	icing sugar	500 ml
2 tbsp	milk	30 ml	2 tbsp	liquid baking chocolate	30 ml
1 tsp	vanilla	5 ml			

Combine all ingredients and beat well.

Chocolate Frosting

Quick, simple, and delicious!

½ cup	butter or margarine	125 ml		icing sugar	
¼ cup	cocoa	50 ml	1 tsp	vanilla	5 ml
¼ cup	milk	50 ml			

In a saucepan, on medium heat, melt butter. Add cocoa and blend well. Remove from heat. Add milk and blend well. Sift in icing sugar until the mixture reaches a good spreading consistency. Add vanilla. Spread on cakes, cookies or squares.

Chocolate Meringue Frosting

2 cups	butter	500 ml	4	egg whites	4
12 1-oz squares	semisweet chocolate	12x30 g	1 cup	white sugar	250 ml
			1 tsp	vanilla	5 ml

Whip the butter until light and fluffy. In a large bowl, beat the egg whites to soft peaks. Add the sugar gradually to the egg whites, beating constantly. Add the whipped butter and the vanilla. The frosting may clump if the butter is chilled. Beat until smooth. Melt the chocolate in a double boiler or in the microwave. Cool slightly (the chocolate should still be fairly warm), and beat into the butter mixture.

Sachertorte Icing

1 tbsp	butter or margarine, softened	15 ml	6 tbsp	coffee, strongly brewed	90 ml
4 1-oz squares	semisweet chocolate	4x30 g	1½ cups	icing sugar	375 ml
			1 tsp	vanilla	5 ml

Melt butter and chocolate in a double boiler over hot water. Add the coffee and beat well. Sift and add the icing sugar and the vanilla. Spread the warm icing on the top and sides of a torte or cake.

Extra-Special Quick Fudge Frosting

2 oz	unsweetened chocolate	60 g	1 tsp	vanilla	5 ml
			⅛ tsp	salt	0.5 ml
1 10½-oz can	sweetened condensed milk	300 ml			

Melt chocolate with milk in a heavy-bottomed pan, stirring constantly. Remove from heat and beat in vanilla and salt. Add about 1 tbsp (15 ml) of hot water a few drops at a time until frosting is thin enough to spread. This will frost a 2-layer cake.

Quick Caramel Frosting

| ¼ lb | butter | 125 g | ¼ cup | milk | 50 ml |
| ½ cup | brown sugar | 125 ml | 2 cups | icing sugar | 500 ml |

Melt butter and sugar in a heavy-bottomed pan, stirring over moderate heat until sugar is dissolved. Add milk and blend. Cool. Beat in icing sugar until thick enough to spread. If too hard, add a few drops of milk. This will frost an 8- or 9-inch (20-22 cm) 2-layer cake.

Marzipan

2 cups	icing sugar, sifted	500 ml	2	small eggs, slightly beaten (or egg substitute)	2
¼ cup	sugar	50 ml			
2 cups	almonds, ground	500 ml	1 tbsp	brandy or whisky	15 ml

Mix sugars and almonds together and stir in brandy or whisky. Add egg (or egg substitute) to make a firm paste. Roll on board dusted with icing sugar. This recipe makes enough marzipan to cover a 9-inch Christmas cake. It can also be shaped into cake decorations. Food colouring may be added—red and green for Christmas or orange colouring for carrots on a carrot cake—be creative! Cover marzipan balls with melted dark chocolate and roll in chocolate sprinkles to make confections for a party tray.

• SQUARES & COOKIES •

• Best •

• Traditional •

• Trendy •

Carrot Raisin Squares

1 cup	brown sugar, packed	250 ml		½ tsp	baking soda	2 ml
				½ tsp	baking powder	2 ml
½ cup	butter	125 ml		½ cup	raisins, rinsed and drained	125 ml
1 tsp	vanilla	5 ml				
2	eggs	2		1½ cups	carrots, finely grated	375 ml
¼ tsp	nutmeg	1 ml				
1 cup	flour	250 ml		⅓ cup	chopped nuts	75 ml
½ cup	whole wheat flour	125 ml				

Beat together sugar, butter, vanilla and nutmeg. Add eggs one at a time, beating well. Add flours, soda and baking powder. Stir in raisins and carrots. Spread evenly in a greased 9-inch (23 cm) square pan. Sprinkle nuts on top. Bake at 350F (175C) for 10-15 minutes. Cool. Cut into squares.

Mrs. Mahar's Bars

Crust:

1 cup	butter	250 ml
2 cups	brown sugar	500 ml
2	eggs, beaten	2
2 tsp	vanilla	10 ml
2½ cups	flour	625 ml
1 tsp	baking soda	5 ml
1 tsp	salt	5 ml
3 cups	oatmeal	750 ml

Filling:

12 oz	chocolate chips	360 g
1 10½-oz can	condensed milk	300 ml
2 tbsp	butter	30 ml
½ tsp	salt	2 ml
1 tsp	vanilla	5 ml

Crust: Cream butter and sugar; add eggs and vanilla. Mix well. Sift flour, salt, and soda. Add to batter and mix. Add oatmeal and mix all together into a crumbly mixture. Reserve ¼ of mixture for the topping. Pat remaining mixture into an 18x15-inch (46x38 cm) jellyroll pan or two 9x13-inch (23x33 cm) pans. Bars should be ¾ inch (2 cm) thick when cooked.

Filling: Combine ingredients in the top of a double boiler. Heat and stir until melted. Spread filling on crust and sprinkle top with reserved oatmeal mixture. Bake at 350F (175C) for about 20 minutes or until golden brown.

Nanaimo Bars

Bottom layer:

¼ cup	sugar	50 ml
½ cup	butter	125 ml
5 tbsp	cocoa	75 ml
1	egg, beaten	1
1¾ cups	graham wafer crumbs	425 ml
¾ cup	coconut	175 ml
½ cup	walnuts, chopped	125 ml

Middle layer:

½ cup	butter	125 ml
2 tbsp	vanilla custard powder	30 ml
2 cups	icing sugar	500 ml
3 tbsp	milk	45 ml

Top layer:

2 tbsp	butter	30 ml
⅔ cup	semisweet chocolate chips	150 ml

Melt butter and cocoa in a heavy saucepan. Add sugar. Add beaten egg. Stir until thickened. Remove from heat. Stir in crumbs, coconut and nuts. Press firmly into an ungreased 9-inch (23 cm) square pan. For middle layer, cream butter, milk, custard powder and icing sugar together well. Beat until light. Spread over bottom layer. For the top layer, melt chips and butter over low heat. Cool. While still liquid, spread over second layer. Chill. Cut with a sharp knife. These squares freeze well.

Shortbread

1 cup	butter	250 ml	
¾ cup	icing sugar	175 ml	
½ cup	cornstarch	125 ml	

2 cups	pastry flour or 1½ (375 ml) cups flour	500 ml

Cream butter until fluffy. Blend in icing sugar and cornstarch. Knead in flour for at least 8 minutes. Kneading is important for a flaky shortbread. Pack into an 8-inch or 9-inch (20-23 cm) square pan. Prick tiny holes over top with a fork in an attractive design. Decorate, if desired, with tiny pieces of red and/or green cherries. Bake at 325F (165C) until slightly browned, approximately 20 minutes. Cut into small squares while hot. If desired, a little icing may be used to decorate these squares. Ice just before serving. Place cherries on top of icing.

Christmas Shortbread Squares

1 cup	butter	250 ml
¼ cup	sugar	50 ml
2 cups	flour	500 ml
1½ cups	coconut	375 ml
⅔ cup	red and green candied cherries	150 ml

¼ cup	raisins or currants	50 ml
⅓ cup	walnuts or almonds	75 ml
1 10½-oz can	sweetened condensed milk	300 ml

Cream butter and sugar. Blend in flour until mixture resembles coarse crumbs. Pat into a 9x9-inch (23x23 cm) pan. Bake at 350F (175C) for 20 minutes. Combine remaining ingredients. Spread evenly over shortbread base. Bake an additional 35 minutes at 325F (165C) or until golden brown. Cool thoroughly and cut into bars.

Matrimonial Squares (Date Squares)

These are less crumbly than the usual recipes.

½ lb	dates	250 g
½ cup	sugar	125 ml
⅔ cup	water	150 ml
1¼ cups	flour	300 ml
1½ cups	rolled oats	375 ml

1 cup	brown sugar	250 ml
1 tsp	baking soda	5 ml
½ tsp	salt	2 ml
1 cup	butter	250 ml
1 tsp	vanilla	5 ml

Place dates, sugar and water in saucepan. Bring to boil, watching carefully. Reduce heat and simmer until dates are mushy. If dates are too thick to spread easily, add a little water. Add vanilla. Sift flour, soda and salt into mixing bowl. Add rolled oats. Mix together and cut in butter until mixture is crumbly. Press one half crumb mixture into a 9-inch (23 cm) square pan. Spread date mixture evenly over top. Sprinkle remaining crumbs on top. Press down. Bake at 350F (175C) for 30 minutes—until squares are a rich brown colour.

Date Squares

1½ cups	flour	375 ml
½ tsp	baking soda	2 ml
1½ cups	rolled oats	375 ml
1 cup	brown sugar	250 ml
½ cup	butter	125 ml
½ tsp	salt	2 ml

Filling:		
1 cup	hot water	250 ml
1 cup	brown sugar	250 ml
1 lb	dates	500 g
1 tsp	vanilla	5 ml
	salt	

Cream brown sugar and butter. Add flour, soda and salt. Mix together. Add rolled oats and rub mixture together. Press half of the oats mixture into a 9x9-inch (23x23 cm) square pan. Combine filling ingredients in a saucepan and cook over medium heat until soft and mushy. Remove from heat. Add vanilla. Spread on top of first layer. Add remainder of oat mixture and press down firmly. Bake in a 350F (175C) oven until slightly browned, approximately 25-30 minutes. Cut into squares.

Snickerdoodle Squares

1 cup	brown sugar	250 ml
4 tbsp	shortening	60 ml
½ cup	sour milk	125 ml
1 tsp	baking soda	5 ml
¾ cup	dates, finely chopped	175 ml

1 tsp	vanilla	5 ml
1	egg	1
½ tsp	salt	2 ml
1¾ cups	flour	425 ml
	brown sugar, for sprinkling	

Blend brown sugar and shortening. Add egg and beat well. Stir in sour milk and vanilla. Add flour, soda, and salt to the mixture. Add dates last. Pour into a 9x9-inch (23 cm) square pan. Sprinkle generously with brown sugar. Press lightly. Bake at 350F (175C) for 20 minutes until browned and cake springs back when top is touched lightly. Remove from oven. Cool and cut into squares or bars.

Phyllis' Divine Toffee Squares

½ cup	flour	125 ml		⅓ cup	brown sugar, firmly packed	75 ml
¾ cup	Rice Krispies	175 ml		¼ tsp	salt	1 ml
¼ tsp	baking soda	1 ml		⅓ cup	butter	75 ml

Mix all ingredients together and press into an 8x8-inch (20 cm) or a 9x9-inch (23 cm) pan. Bake at 350F (175C) for about 10 minutes or until just starting to brown.

In a heavy saucepan, combine:

1 10½-oz can	condensed milk	300 ml		½ cup	brown sugar, firmly packed	125 ml
½ cup	butter	125 ml				

Bring to a full boil for 5 minutes, stirring continuously. Remove from heat and pour over crust. Melt ½ cup (125 ml) chocolate chips. Stir in 1¼ cup (300 ml) Rice Krispies until well coated. Spread over caramel filling, using two forks. Chill in refrigerator. Remove from refrigerator ½ hour before cutting. Do not overcook the filling or it will become quite hard.

Eat More Bars

1 cup	chocolate chips	250 ml		3 cups	Rice Krispies	750 ml
1 cup	corn syrup	250 ml		¼ cup	peanut butter	50 ml
1 cup	peanuts, crushed	250 ml				

In the top of a double boiler, melt chocolate chips and corn syrup. Add peanut butter; stir to blend. Remove from heat; stir in peanuts and Rice Krispies. Using two forks, mix until cereal is evenly coated. Press warm mixture into a well-buttered wax paper or parchment-lined 8x8-inch (20 cm) pan. Cut into narrow strips about 1 inch wide and 2 inches long (2.5x5 cm). Keep cold.

Sweet Marie Bars

½ cup	peanut butter	125 ml		½ cup	peanuts	125 ml
½ cup	corn syrup	125 ml		2 cups	Rice Krispies	500 ml
½ cup	brown sugar	125 ml		1 tsp	butter	5 ml

Melt peanut butter, corn syrup, brown sugar, and butter. Add peanuts and Rice Krispies. Spread into a 9x9-inch (23x23 cm) pan. Ice with 1 cup (250 ml) chocolate chips and 2 tbsp butter (30 ml) melted together.

Crunch Bars

½ cup	butter	125 ml		¼ tsp	salt	1 ml
¾ cup	sugar	175 ml		¼ tsp	baking powder	1 ml
2	eggs, beaten	2		½ cup	walnuts, chopped	125 ml
2 tsp	vanilla	10 ml		2½ cups	miniature marshmallows	625 ml
¾ cup	flour	175 ml				

Cream butter and sugar. Beat in eggs and vanilla; add flour, baking powder and salt, sifted together. Stir in walnuts. Spread mixture into a greased 9x13x3-inch (23x33x5 cm) cake pan. Bake at 350F (175C) for 15-20 minutes. Remove from oven. Place marshmallows evenly over cake, return pan to oven and bake for 2 more minutes. Allow cake to cool for 1 hour.

Topping:

1 cup	semi-sweet chocolate pieces	250 ml		1 cup	peanut butter	250 ml
				1½ cups	Rice Krispies	375 ml

Melt chocolate pieces over low heat in a saucepan. Remove from heat. Stir in peanut butter and fold in Rice Krispies. Spread evenly over cake. Refrigerate.

Chewy Chews

½ cup	butter	125 ml		¼ tsp	salt	1 ml
1 cup	sugar	250 ml		1 tsp	baking powder	5 ml
2	eggs	2		1 cup	flour	250 ml
⅔ cup	cherries, halved	150 ml		2 tsp	vanilla	10 ml
½ lb	dates, sliced	225 g			granulated sugar, for sprinkling	
⅔ cup	walnuts, coarsely chopped	150 ml				

Cream butter and sugar until fluffy. Add beaten eggs and blend. Add sifted flour, salt, and baking powder. Fold in sliced dates, cherries, walnuts and vanilla. Spread into a 9-inch (23 cm) pan. Bake in a moderate oven for 25-30 minutes. When cool, dust generously with granulated sugar and cut into squares.

Raspberry Almond Bars

1½ cups	flour	375 ml		1	egg	1
½ cup	brown sugar	125 ml		1 tsp	almond extract	5 ml
¼ cup	granulated sugar	50 ml		2 tbsp	flour	30 ml
½ tsp	baking powder	2 ml		¾ cup	raspberry jam	175 ml
½ tsp	salt	2 ml		1	egg yolk	1
½ tsp	cinnamon	2 ml		1 tsp	water	5 ml
½ cup	butter	125 ml				

Combine 1½ cups flour, both sugars, baking powder, salt and cinnamon. Mix well. Cut in butter until mixture resembles coarse meal. Add egg and extract. Mix with fork. Remove ½ cup of mixture and add 2 tbsp flour to the ½ cup of mixture. Press remaining mixture into a lightly greased, 9-inch (23 cm) square cake pan. Spread jam evenly over top. Add water to reserved mixture until it holds together. Roll into 12 pencil strips and weave strips diagonally over jam to form a lattice. Brush lattice with a mixture of egg yolk and water. Bake at 375F (190C) for 25-30 minutes or until golden. Cool, then cut into bars. Makes 30 bars.

Raisin Puffs

1 cup	white sugar	250 ml		**Filling:**		
1 cup	shortening	250 ml		2 cups	raisins	500 ml
2	eggs	2		½ cup	sugar	125 ml
2 cups	flour	500 ml		3 tbsp	cornstarch	45 ml
2 tsp	baking powder	10 ml		1 tsp	vanilla	5 ml
½ tsp	salt	3 ml		pinch	salt	
1 tsp	vanilla	5 ml			water to cover	

Cream sugar and shortening. Beat in eggs and vanilla. Add sifted dry ingredients. Mix well. Make filling by placing raisins in saucepan. Mix salt with cornstarch and add sugar; pour all into saucepan. Stir well, cover with water and cook until sauce is transparent and thickened. Remove from heat and add vanilla. Press half the dough into a 9-inch (23 cm) square pan or 13x9-inch (33x23 cm) pan. Spread all filling on dough. Roll out other half of dough on wax paper, shaping to fit pan. Lay dough over filling (the wax paper helps to hold the dough together and can be peeled off). Prick holes in crust for steam vents. Bake at 325F (165C) for 45-50 minutes or until browned. Cut into squares when cool.

Cherry-Walnut Squares

Cream ⅓ cup (75 ml) butter and add 1 cup (250 ml) brown sugar. Beat in 1 egg and add all to mixture below, beating well.

Sift together:

1 cup	flour	250 ml
1 tsp	baking powder	5 ml
½ tsp	salt	2 ml

Mix well and fold in 1 tsp (5 ml) vanilla, ⅓ cup (75 ml) chopped cherries and ⅓ cup (75 ml) chopped walnuts. Bake in an 8x8-inch (20 cm) pan at 350F (175C) for 20 minutes. When cool, ice with thin butter icing. Sprinkle a few thinly sliced nuts over frosting.

Square Tarts

1⅓ cups	flour	325 ml	1¼ cups	brown sugar	300 ml
2 tbsp	sugar	30 ml	1 cup	raisins	250 ml
½ cup	margarine	125 ml	1 tbsp	vinegar	15 ml
2	eggs	2	1 tsp	vanilla	5 ml
¼ cup	margarine, melted	50 ml	1 tsp	flour	5 ml

Mix flour, sugar, and ½ cup (125 ml) margarine in mixing bowl until mixture is crumbly. Press into a 9-inch (23 cm) square pan. Bake at 350F (175C) for 10-12 minutes or until golden. Whisk eggs and brown sugar until well blended. Stir in remaining ingredients. Mix well. Spread over crust. Bake 25-30 minutes until just set and golden brown. Cut into squares. Underbaking gives a soft, runny filling; longer baking time gives a firmer filling. May be frozen.

Andrea's Peanut-Butter Bars

Melt:

1 cup	peanut butter	250 ml
1 cup	butter	250 ml

Add:

2½ cups	icing sugar	625 ml
1 cup	graham wafer crumbs	250 ml
1 cup	rolled oats	250 ml

Press into a 9x13-inch (23x33 cm) pan.

Melt:

1 cup	chocolate chips	250 ml
¼ cup	butter or margarine	50 ml

Spread over top and refrigerate. Cut into bars and serve.

Hermit Fruit Bars

2 cups	sugar	500 ml	½ tsp	salt	2 ml
¼ cup	shortening	50 ml	¼ tsp	cinnamon	1 ml
½ cup	molasses	125 ml	¼ tsp	nutmeg	1 ml
1	egg	1	¼ tsp	allspice	1 ml
½ cup	water	125 ml	1 cup	raisins	250 ml
4 cups	flour	1 L	½ cup	walnuts	125 ml
1 tsp	baking soda	5 ml			

Cream sugar and shortening. Add molasses and egg. Beat well. Sift together and add to first mixture: flour, soda, salt, cinnamon, nutmeg and allspice. Fold in raisins and walnuts. Mix well. Shape into long rolls of dough (about 1 inch (2.5 cm) in diameter and place on a cookie sheet. Flatten each roll. Bake at 375F (190C) for 25 minutes. While warm, cut diagonally across the strips.

Confetti Squares

¼ cup	margarine	50 ml	¾ cup	peanut butter chips	175 ml
½ cup	peanut butter, crunchy	125 ml	2 cups	miniature marshmallows, coloured	500 ml

Melt the margarine, peanut butter and butterscotch chips in the top of a double boiler over hot (not boiling) water. Cool to lukewarm. Stir in marshmallows. Chill in an 8-inch (20 cm) square pan until firm. Cut into squares.

Chocolate Confetti Squares

¼ cup	butter	50 ml	1 cup	semi-sweet chocolate chips	250 ml
½ cup	peanut butter	125 ml	1 cup	miniature marshmallows	250 ml

Melt butter and peanut butter in a large saucepan. Stir in chocolate chips until melted. Cool slightly and add marshmallows. Stir to coat. Pack into a 9-inch (23 cm) square pan lined with wax paper. Cut into squares. Freezes well. Keep in refrigerator.

Choco-Crunchy Squares

½ cup	margarine	125 ml	2 cups	flaked coconut	500 ml
1 cup	peanut butter	250 ml	2 cups	Rice Krispies	500 ml
1½ cups	chocolate chips	375 ml	1 cup	miniature marshmallows	250 ml
1½ cups	butterscotch chips	375 ml			

Melt first four ingredients in a double boiler. Let cool slightly, then add remaining ingredients. Grease a 9x13-inch (23x33 cm) pan with butter and pour mixture into it. Store in refrigerator. Cut into squares. Can be frozen.

O Henry Slice

¼ cup	margarine or butter	50 ml		2 cups	peanuts, crushed	500 ml
1 cup	brown sugar, lightly packed	250 ml		4 cups	Rice Krispies	1 L
				1½ cups	chocolate chips	375 ml
1 cup	peanut butter	250 ml				
1 cup	corn syrup	250 ml				

Melt margarine in a nonstick pan. Add brown sugar, syrup and peanut butter. Mix well. Remove from heat. Add peanuts and Rice Krispies. Mix well. Grease a 13x9-inch (33x23 cm) pan and spread the mixture evenly, packing lightly. Sprinkle chocolate chips to cover the top, and place under the broiler for approximately 30 seconds or until chocolate chips have melted. Spread smoothly over mixture. Cool and slice.

Cocoa-Walnut Bars

1 cup	butter	250 ml		1 cup	flour	250 ml
2 cups	brown sugar	500 ml		2 tbsp	cocoa	30 ml
2	eggs	2		¾ cup	walnuts	175 ml
2 tsp	vanilla	10 ml				

Butter icing:

1 tbsp	butter	15 ml		2 tbsp	milk	30 ml
2 cups	icing sugar	500 ml		1 tsp	vanilla	5 ml
2 tbsp	cocoa	30 ml				

Cream butter and brown sugar. Add eggs and vanilla and beat. Sift flour and cocoa and mix well with butter mixture. Stir in walnuts. Pour into a 9-inch (23-cm) square pan. Bake at 350F (175C) for 25-30 minutes. To make icing, add milk to icing sugar, cocoa and butter. Flavour with vanilla. Ice while warm. Cut into squares.

Turtle Squares

2 cups	flour	500 ml		1 cup	brown sugar	250 ml
½ cup	butter, softened	125 ml		1 cup	pecans, halved	250 ml
½ cup	brown sugar	125 ml		⅔ cup	butter	150 ml
1 cup	chocolate chips	250 ml				

Combine butter, flour and brown sugar to make fine crumbs. Pat into a 9x13-inch (23x33 cm) pan. Sprinkle pecans evenly over unbaked crust. In a saucepan combine 1 cup (250 ml) brown sugar and ⅔ cup (150 ml) butter. Cook over medium heat, stirring constantly, until entire surface begins to boil. Boil 1 minute, stirring constantly. Pour over pecans and crust. Bake for 18-20 minutes at 350F (175C) until caramel is bubbly; do not overcook. Remove from oven and sprinkle immediately with chips. Allow the chips to melt and swirl over top. Cool a little and cut into squares.

Hello Dollies

4 tbsp	butter	60 ml		1 cup	chocolate chips	250 ml
1 cup	coconut	250 ml		1 cup	walnuts, crushed	250 ml
1 cup	graham wafer crumbs	250 ml		1 10½-oz can	condensed milk	300 ml

Mix butter and crumbs together and pat into an 8-inch (20 cm) square pan. Add remaining ingredients in layers: milk, coconut, walnuts and chips. Press top layers into the milk. Bake at 325F (160C) for 20-25 minutes. Cut into squares.

Rainbow Squares

Base mixture:

2 cups	flour	500 ml		2 tbsp	white sugar	30 ml
1 cup	margarine	250 ml		¼ tsp	salt	1 ml

Mix all, and press into a 9-inch (23 cm) square pan. Bake at 350F (175C) for 15 minutes. Cool and set aside.

Filling:

1 19-oz can	crushed pineapple, with juice	540 ml		3 tbsp	flour	45 ml
				1 cup	cherries, drained	250 ml
½ cup	white sugar	125 ml		1¼ tsp	almond flavouring	6 ml

Topping:

2	egg whites	2
4 tbsp	sugar	60 ml

In a saucepan, combine all filling ingredients and cook until thick. Cool. Pour over base mixture. For topping, beat egg whites while gradually adding sugar. Spread over pineapple mixture and bake at 350F (175C) for 20 minutes.

Frozen Strawberry Yogurt Squares

4 cups	vanilla yogurt, frozen	1 L		18	graham crackers	18
3 cups	fresh strawberries, sliced	750 ml				

Arrange 9 crackers in an 8-inch (20 cm) square pan. Fold sliced berries into softened yogurt. Spread yogurt mix over crackers and cover with remaining crackers. Freeze until firm. Cut into 9 squares.

Honey Squares

Bottom:

½ cup	butter	125 ml
½ cup	sugar	125 ml
2	egg yolks, slightly beaten	2
2 cups	pastry flour	500 ml
2 cups	walnuts, chopped	500 ml
1 cup	unsweetened coconut	250 ml

Filling:

2	egg whites	2
2 cups	brown sugar	500 ml
1 tsp	vanilla	5 ml
	walnut halves	

Cream butter and sugar together, then add egg yolks. Mix in the flour until the mixture reaches a fine, crumbly consistency. Press into a 9-inch (23 cm) square pan. Sprinkle the chopped walnuts and coconut over the bottom layer. For the filling, beat the egg whites until stiff. Gradually fold in the brown sugar and the vanilla. Spread on top. Garnish with walnut halves—one per square. Bake at 325F (160C) for 45 minutes. Cut into squares while still slightly warm.

Yum Yums

½ cup	butter	125 ml	2 tsp	vanilla	10 ml
½ cup	brown sugar	125 ml	½ tsp	salt	2 ml
2	eggs, separated	2	½ cup	walnuts	125 ml
1½ cups	flour	375 ml	1 cup	brown sugar	250 ml
2 tsp	baking powder	10 ml			

Blend together butter and ½ cup (125 ml) brown sugar. Beat in egg yolks. Sift together flour, baking powder, and salt, and add to batter. Mix well. Spread into a 13x9-inch (33x23 cm) pan. Sprinkle with nuts. Beat egg whites until stiff then add 1 cup (250 ml) brown sugar and vanilla. Beat until smooth. Spread over nuts in pan. Bake at 350F (175C) for 30-40 minutes.

Pineapple Squares

2 tbsp	sugar	30 ml		1 14-oz can	crushed pineapple, drained	398 ml
1 tbsp	butter	15 ml		2 cups	coconut, shredded	500 ml
2	eggs	2		1 cup	white sugar	250 ml
1 cup	flour	250 ml		2	eggs, beaten	2
1 tsp	baking powder	5 ml		1 tbsp	butter	15 ml
¼ tsp	salt	1 ml				

Line an 8-inch (20 cm) square pan with wax paper. Mix first 6 ingredients and pour into pan. Bake 10-15 minutes in a 350F (175C) oven. Remove from oven and spread drained pineapple over baked mixture. Mix together remaining ingredients and spread over pineapple. Bake at 350F (175C) for about 30 minutes or until golden brown.

Apple Dream Squares

1 cup	flour	250 ml		2 cups	apples, peeled and diced	500 ml
¼ cup	icing sugar	50 ml		¼ cup	walnuts	50 ml
½ cup	butter	125 ml		½ cup	flour	125 ml
2	eggs	2		1 tsp	baking powder	5 ml
1 cup	brown sugar	250 ml		½ tsp	salt	2 ml
1 tsp	vanilla	5 ml				

Sift together flour and icing sugar, then combine with butter. Press mixture into an 8x8-inch pan. Bake at 350F (175C) for twenty minutes. Meanwhile beat eggs until thick and lemon-coloured. Stir in brown sugar, vanilla, apples, and walnuts. Stir together remaining ingredients, and stir into egg mixture. Spread over baked layer. Bake at 350F (175C) for 35 minutes. Cut into squares. May be topped with whipped cream and served as a dessert.

Chinese Chews

1 cup	dates	250 ml	¾ cup	flour	175 ml
1 cup	walnuts	250 ml	1 tsp	baking powder	5 ml
1 cup	sugar	250 ml	½ tsp	salt	2 ml
2	eggs	2	1 tsp	vanilla	5 ml

Mix dry ingredients. Add dates and nuts. Add well-beaten eggs. Mix well.
Spread mixture thinly on a large, greased baking sheet. Bake at 300F (150C) for
20 minutes. Let cool slightly and cut into squares. Roll into balls and roll in
sugar to coat. Store in tightly covered containers.

Annapolis Valley
Apple Squares

⅓ cup	butter	75 ml	1 cup	flour	250 ml
1 tbsp	brown sugar	15 ml			

Blend together and pack into an 8-inch (20 cm) square pan. Set aside. Prepare
the filling:

½ cup	sugar	125 ml	1	egg	1
1	large apple, thinly sliced	1	1	lemon, juice and rind	1
			2 tsp	butter	10 ml

Mix all together and cook over low heat until soft. Cool and spread on base in
pan. Prepare the topping:

¾ cup	sugar	175 ml	1	egg	1
1 tbsp	butter	15 ml	1¼ cups	coconut	310 ml

Mix sugar and butter. Beat in egg and add coconut. Spread over filling. Bake at
350F (175C) for 30-40 minutes. Remove from oven. Cool and cut into squares.

Butterscotch Squares

So quick and easy. Few dishes to clean up!

¼ cup	butter	50 ml	1 tsp	baking powder	5 ml
1 cup	brown sugar	250 ml	1 tsp	vanilla	5 ml
1	egg	1	½ cup	pecans or walnuts, chopped	125 ml
1 cup	flour, sifted	250 ml			
¼ tsp	salt	1 ml			

Melt butter in a heavy saucepan and blend in sugar. Remove from heat and cool to lukewarm. Add unbeaten egg and mix well. Add flour, salt and baking powder. Beat until smooth. Add nuts and vanilla. Bake in an 8-inch (20 cm) square pan at 350F (175C) until set and lightly browned and fairly soft to the touch. Cool and frost with vanilla butter icing. Sprinkle with a few nuts and cut into squares. Instead of nuts, desiccated coconut may be used. The recipe can be doubled.

Maple Cream Squares

These squares were popular in 1930. They're still popular in 2001.

1 cup	brown sugar	250 ml	Topping:		
¼ cup	butter	50 ml	2	egg whites	2
2	egg yolks	2	1 cup	brown sugar	250 ml
1½ cups	flour	375 ml	1 tsp	vanilla	5 ml
2 tsp	baking powder	10 ml			
½ tsp	salt	2 ml			
1 tsp	vanilla	5 ml			

Cream brown sugar and butter. Beat in egg yolks and vanilla. Add sifted dry ingredients. Press into a buttered, 9x12-inch (23x33 cm) pan.
Topping: Beat egg whites until stiff, but not dry. Beat in brown sugar gradually. Add vanilla. Mix well. Turn out over first layer and spread evenly. Bake at 350F (175C) until meringue crusts over, approximately 15 minutes. (Watch closely for burning, and turn down heat, if necessary.) Cut into squares while warm, using a sharp knife dipped in hot water.

Peanut Butter Munchies

2 tbsp	corn syrup	30 ml		3 1-oz squares	semi-sweet chocolate	3x30 g
¼ cup	brown sugar	50 ml		½ cup	peanut butter	125 ml
¼ cup	peanut butter	50 ml		12	pecan halves	12
2 tbsp	butter, melted	30 ml				
2 cups	Rice Krispies	500 ml				

Combine corn syrup, brown sugar, ¼ cup peanut butter and butter. Stir in Rice Krispies. Press into 12 well-greased muffin cups. Bake at 375F (190C) for 5-8 minutes. Cool for 5 minutes and remove from pan. Melt chocolate over low heat. Blend in remaining ½ cup peanut butter, and stir over low heat until smooth. Spread on top of Rice Krispies cups, spreading almost to the edge. Garnish each with a nut or other decoration. Chill and serve.

Favourite Fudge Brownies

1 cup	butter	250 ml		4	eggs, beaten	4
2 cups	sugar	500 ml		1 cup	flour	250 ml
4 tbsp (heaping)	cocoa	60 ml		1 cup	walnuts, chopped	250 ml
				2 tsp	vanilla	10 ml

Cream butter and sugar, and add cocoa. Mix until well blended. Add beaten eggs and vanilla. Add flour and mix well. Fold in walnuts. Bake in a 9x13-inch (23x33 cm) pan at 350F (175C) for 40-45 minutes. Top will appear underdone and fallen in centre but do not overcook. They should be moist and chewy. Immediately after removing from oven, ice with chocolate icing. The heat from the hot brownies will melt the icing into a shiny glaze.

Brownies

These are cakelike, but very moist.

1 cup	margarine	250 ml	4	eggs	4
4 1-oz squares	unsweetened chocolate	4x30 g	1 tsp	vanilla	5 ml
			1 cup	flour	250 ml
2 cups	sugar	500 ml	1 tsp	salt	5 ml

Melt chocolate and margarine in a double boiler. Let cool. Add sugar. Add eggs one at a time, beating well after each addition. Add remainder of ingredients. Pour into a 9x13-inch (22x33 cm) pan. Bake at 350F (175C) for 35 minutes.

Bangor Brownies

This is a very old brownie recipe given to me by a family friend in Princeport.

¼ cup	shortening, melted	50 ml	1 cup	flour	250 ml
1 cup	molasses	250 ml	1 tsp	baking powder	5 ml
1	egg	1	½ tsp	salt	2 ml
1 tsp	vanilla	5 ml	1 cup	nuts	250 ml
2 1-oz squares	bitter chocolate, melted	2x30 g			

Sift flour, baking powder and salt together. Cream shortening, molasses, egg and vanilla. Beat in melted chocolate. Add sifted dry ingredients. Beat together and add nuts. Bake for about 15 minutes at 325F (165C) in an 8-inch (20 cm) square pan. Cut into squares.

Nut Brownies

These are moist with a light crumb.

½ cup	butter	125 ml		2 tsp	vanilla	10 ml
1 cup	sugar	250 ml		1 cup	pecans or walnuts	250 ml
3	eggs, well beaten	3		½ tsp	salt	2 ml
1 cup	pastry flour	250 ml			crushed nuts	
2 1-oz squares	chocolate, melted and cooled	2x30 g				

Cream butter, and add sugar, blending well. Add eggs and vanilla. Mix in the melted chocolate. Fold in flour and salt sifted together. Fold in nuts. Turn into a 9-inch (23 cm) square pan or, for a thinner brownie, use a 13x9-inch (33x23 cm) pan. Bake at 350F (175C) until done. Frost before completely cooled. Scatter a few crushed nuts on top.

Chocolate Dipped Cherries

2 cups	maraschino cherries, with stems	500 ml		½ cup	pecans, chopped or Rice Krispies, crushed	125 ml
1 cup	peanut butter	250 ml		½ cup	chopped dates	125 ml
1 cup	icing sugar	250 ml		8 oz	semi-sweet chocolate	250 g
1 tbsp	butter	15 ml		1 2-inch square	paraffin wax	1x5 cm

Drain cherries on paper towels for several hours or overnight. Prepare a mixture of peanut butter, icing sugar, pecans, dates and butter. Blend well. Enclose each cherry in a thin layer of the peanut butter mixture. Prepare chocolate for dipping by melting paraffin wax and chocolate in a double boiler over medium heat. Dip cherries in chocolate. Hold in air briefly; place on waxed paper to dry. Refrigerate until ready to serve.

Hilda's Boterkoek:
Dutch Butter Cake Bars

⅔ cup	butter	150 ml
1 cup	sugar	250 ml
1 tsp	almond extract	5 ml
1	egg, beaten	1
1½ cups	flour	375 ml
½ tsp	baking powder	2 ml

Topping:		
1	egg	1
1 tbsp	milk	15 ml
1 tbsp	almonds, sliced	15 ml

In bowl, cream butter and sugar. Add almond extract; blend in egg. Mix flour and baking powder; add to butter mixture. Stir dough with fork until smooth. Spread dough in a greased 8-inch (2 L) square cake pan.

Topping: In a bowl, beat egg and milk; brush over dough. Top with almonds. Bake at 350F (175C) for 30 minutes or until golden brown. Cut into bars.

My Mother's Lemon Slices

Tangy enough to really please.

1 box	graham wafers	1
2	lemons	2
1 10½-oz can	condensed milk	300 ml

Squeeze the juice from 2 lemons into a bowl with sweetened condensed milk. Grate into it the rind of 1 lemon. Mix together. Line an 8-inch (20 cm) square pan with whole graham wafers. Pour half the milk mixture over the wafers. Lay a second layer of graham wafers. Pour the remainder of the milk mixture over this layer. Top with a third layer of wafers, and cover with a lemon-butter icing. Decorate with a light dusting of graham wafer crumbs. Refrigerate overnight before cutting.

Mom's Mocha Cakes

2	eggs	2	½ tsp	salt	2 ml
1 cup	sugar	250 ml	½ cup	milk, heated	125 ml
1 tsp	vanilla	5 ml	2 tbsp	butter	30 ml
1 cup	flour	250 ml	1 lb	peanuts, crushed	500 g
1 tsp	baking powder	5 ml			

Beat eggs and add sugar a little at a time. Add vanilla. Sift in flour, baking powder and salt. Lastly add milk with butter melted into it. Beat well. Pour into a 9-inch (23 cm) square pan; bake at 350F (175C) for 25-30 minutes. Turn out onto rack and cool. When cake is cold, cut into 1-inch (2.5 cm) cubes. Make frosting by combining 2 cups (500 ml) icing sugar, 2 tbsp (30 ml) butter, and 1 tsp (5 ml) vanilla. Add enough milk to make a very thin icing. Dip cubes of cake in frosting, making sure to cover all sides. Roll frosted cubes in crushed peanuts. Place on waxed paper to set. Store in tightly covered containers.

Ruby's Soft Molasses Cookies

They smell so good when you open the oven, you can't resist the urge to sit down and have one—or two.

1¼ cups	shortening	300 ml	4 tsp	baking soda	20 ml
⅓ cup	brown sugar	75 ml	3 tsp	ginger	15 ml
1	egg	1	1¼ tsp	allspice	6 ml
1½ cups	molasses	375 ml	½ tsp	cinnamon	2 ml
½ cup	boiling water	125 ml		salt	
5 cups	flour	1250 ml		raisins, if desired	

Cream shortening and sugar. Beat in egg and molasses. Add 2 cups (500 ml) flour. Mix all spices in the water and add. Add remaining flour and soda. Chill and roll out. Cut with a cookie cutter and place cookies on a sheet. Bake at 350F (175C) for 20 minutes. If not using raisins in the dough, a nice fat raisin, pressed into the centre of each cookie, will please the little ones.

Molasses Crinkles

This old recipe comes from Esther Archibald's kitchen. She must have made thousands of these cookies to satisfy a daughter, four sons, a husband, herself, and many friends.

¾ cup	shortening	175 ml		2 tsp	baking soda	10 ml
1 cup	brown sugar	250 ml		1 tsp	cinnamon	5 ml
1	egg	1		1 tsp	ginger	5 ml
½ cup	molasses	125 ml		½ tsp	cloves	2 ml
2¼ cups	flour, sifted	550 ml			salt, to taste	

Sift dry ingredients. Mix in order given. Shape into walnut-sized balls. Dip in sugar. Place on a cookie sheet and flatten each ball with a fork. Bake for 15 minutes at 350F (175C).

Ginger Snaps

This old recipe came to me from Sarah MacKenzie Creelman, who lived in my home community of Princeport. We all called her "Aunt Sadie." She always took a little lard pail filled with these cookies to every party. They were truly "snaps"—she could roll them thinner than any other cook I know. Before cutting out the cookies, she traced a plaid design in the dough with a fork.

2 cups	molasses	500 ml		¼ cup	boiling water	50 ml
1 cup	shortening	250 ml		½ tsp	salt	2 ml
4 tsp	ginger	20 ml			flour, to mix fairly stiff	
4 tsp	baking soda	20 ml				

Place molasses in a heavy saucepan. Let come to boil. Add shortening, salt, ginger, and soda dissolved in the hot water. Bring to boil again. Cool. Add flour until the mixture is fairly stiff and then "put on ice" to chill. Be careful not to use too much flour as the mixture gets very hard when chilled. This dough is good for gingerbread men at Christmas. Bake at 325F (165C) oven but watch carefully—the cookies burn easily with all that molasses. Last, try the plaid design and think of Aunt Sadie.

Parkins

Nice with a glass of cold milk or a cup of tea.

1 cup	butter	250 ml		2 cups	rolled oats	500 ml
1 cup	molasses	250 ml		3 cups	flour	750 ml
1 cup	brown sugar	250 ml		2 tsp	baking soda	10 ml
2	eggs	2		½ tsp	salt	2 ml

Cream butter and sugar, and add molasses and eggs. Mix well. Add flour, soda and salt sifted together. Mix. Add rolled oats. Bake as drop cookies at 350F (175C) for 20-25 minutes. Cookies will spread in the oven. Watch carefully—they burn quickly.

Peanut Butter Cookies

This was the first recipe I tried when I moved into my home in 1951. My new Enterprise wood range cooked them beautifully.

Cream together:

½ cup	butter	125 ml		½ cup	white sugar	125 ml
½ cup	peanut butter	125 ml		½ cup	brown sugar	125 ml

Beat in 1 egg, then 1 heaping cup (250 ml) flour sifted with 1 tsp (5 ml) baking soda and ¼ tsp (1 ml) salt. Form into balls. Press flat in pan with a fork dampened in cold water. Bake at 350F (175C) for 18-20 minutes.

Fruit Jumbles

1½ cups	raisins	375 ml	¼ tsp	cloves	1 ml
¼ cup	apple juice	50 ml	¼ cup	brown sugar	50 ml
⅔ cup	flour	150 ml	2 tbsp	butter, softened	30 ml
¾ tsp	baking soda	3 ml	1	egg	1
¾ tsp	cinnamon	3 ml	2 cups	pecans or walnuts	500 ml
¼ tsp	nutmeg	1 ml	½ cup	cherries, chopped	125 ml

Soak raisins in apple juice for one hour. In another bowl, cream brown sugar, butter and egg until fluffy. Add dry ingredients. Mix and fold in fruit. Drop on a greased cookie sheet. Bake at 325F (165C) for 20 minutes. Store in an airtight container.

Snack Cookies

½ cup	shortening or butter	125 ml	1½ cups	flour	375 ml
¾ cup	white sugar	175 ml	¾ tsp	baking soda	3 ml
¼ cup	molasses	50 ml	½ tsp	cinnamon	2 ml
1	egg	1	½ tsp	salt	2 ml
			1 cup	dates, cut up	250 ml

Cream shortening and sugar. Add molasses and egg. Beat. Add sifted dry ingredients. Fold in dates. Drop on a cookie sheet, and bake at 325F (165C) for 20 minutes.

Ethel Brenton's Sugar Cookies

These will make for good conversation over a cup of tea.

1 cup	sugar	250 ml		2½ cups	flour	625 ml
1 cup	shortening	250 ml		1 tsp	baking soda	5 ml
2	eggs	2		2 tsp	cream of tartar	10 ml
1-2 tsp	vanilla	5-10 ml		½ tsp	salt	2 ml

Mix ingredients in order. Roll out onto a floured board and cut into rounds. Bake at 350F (175C) until golden, approximately 10 minutes.

1930s Toll House Cookies

Before the easy days of chocolate chips, we cut up bitter chocolate!

Sift together and reserve:

2 cups	flour, sifted	500 ml		½ tsp	baking soda	2 ml
				½ tsp	salt	2 ml

Preheat oven to 375F (190C). Beat together:

⅓ cup	butter	75 ml		½ cup	brown sugar	125 ml
⅓ cup	vegetable shortening	75 ml		1	large egg	1
				1 tsp	vanilla	5 ml
½ cup	white sugar	125 ml				

Stir in flour mixture, then add:

½ cup	nuts, chopped	125 ml
1¼ cups	chocolate pieces	300 ml

Drop from a teaspoon onto a cookie sheet. Bake at 375F for 10-12 minutes.

Maple Walnut Cookies

1 cup	butter	250 ml	⅓ cup	sour cream	75 ml
¾ cup	maple sugar	175 ml	3½ cups	flour	875 ml
¾ cup	brown sugar, firmly packed	175 ml	½ tsp	salt	2 ml
			1 tsp	baking soda	5 ml
¾ cup	maple syrup	175 ml	6 oz	chopped walnuts	180 g
2	eggs	2	1 cup	maple butter	250 ml

Preheat oven to 350F (200C). Cream the butter with the maple sugar, brown sugar and maple syrup. Beat in the eggs and the sour cream, and set aside. Sift the flour, salt, and baking soda together and combine with the egg-butter mixture, beating until smooth. Fold in the walnuts. Drop onto greased cookie sheets by the teaspoonful. Bake for 8-10 minutes and, while still warm, spread with maple butter.

Chewy Peanut Butter and Chocolate Chip Cookies

¾ cup	flour	175 ml	1	egg	1
½ tsp	baking soda	2 ml	1 tsp	vanilla	5 ml
½ cup	butter	125 ml	½ cup	peanuts, cut in chunks	125 ml
½ cup	peanut butter	125 ml			
½ cup	sugar	125 ml	½ cup	chocolate chips	125 ml
½ cup	brown sugar, lightly packed	125 ml			

Combine flour and soda; sift together. Cream butter, peanut butter, sugar, egg, and vanilla. Blend dry ingredients into creamed mixture. Stir in peanuts and chocolate chips. Drop from a teaspoon, 2 inches (5 cm) apart on an ungreased baking sheet. If desired, press down with floured fork to form a pattern. Bake at 350F (175C) for 10-12 minutes or until golden brown. Leave on sheet 1 minute; remove and cool.

Ella's Chocolate Chip Cookies

This recipe was given to me by Diane McRae of Halifax. The recipe—a family favourite—was given to her by her mother, Ella McRae of Bible Hill, who considered it to be the best. I'm sure that you'll agree!

2 cups	shortening	500 ml	4	eggs	4
3 cups	sugar, brown or yellow, firmly packed	750 ml	4 cups	flour	1 L
			2 tsp	salt	10 ml
			2 tsp	baking soda	10 ml
4 tsp	vanilla	20ml	1 pkg	chocolate chips	1

Preheat oven to 350-375F (180C). Cream together shortening and sugar. Add vanilla and eggs and beat until smooth. Sift together the 4 cups flour, salt and soda and add to creamed mixture. Combine well. Mix remaining flour with chocolate chips and add to cookie dough mixture. Using floured hands, roll dough into balls. Place on greased cookie sheets (do not flatten). Bake for 10-12 minutes. Makes approximately 65 cookies.

Judy's Chewy Chocolate Chip Cookies

¾ cup	shortening	175 ml	1½ cups	flour	375 ml
1¼ cups	brown sugar	310 ml	1 tsp	salt	5 ml
1	egg	1	¾ tsp	baking soda	3 ml
1 tbsp	milk	15 ml	1 cup	chocolate chips	250 ml
2 tsp	vanilla	10 ml			

Cream shortening, sugar, and egg. Add milk and vanilla. Sift flour, salt, and soda. Mix well. Fold in chocolate last. Drop onto a cookie sheet. Bake at 350F (175C) for 12-15 minutes. Remove when slightly underdone. Leave on cookie sheet to cool.

Chocolate Chip
Oatmeal Cookies

This recipe came all the way from Lilla Gilroy's kitchen in Cumberland County. She is one of the best—and so are her famous cookies.

2 cups	flour, sifted	500 ml		¾ cup	corn oil	175 ml
½ tsp	salt	2 ml		1 cup	brown sugar, lightly packed	250 ml
2 cups	quick-cooking rolled oats	500 ml		1 tsp	baking soda	5 ml
½ cup	semisweet chocolate chips	125 ml		¼ cup	boiling water	50 ml
				1 tsp	vanilla	5 ml

Preheat oven to 350F (175C). Sift flour and salt. Mix in rolled oats and chocolate chips. Combine oil and brown sugar in a bowl. Dissolve baking soda in boiling water and stir into oil mixture. Add vanilla. Mix well. Make a well in dry ingredients. Add liquid ingredients all at once and mix. Drop by the teaspoonful onto cookie sheets. Flatten with fork. Cook for 12-14 minutes.

Chris' Double-Chocolate
Chip Cookies

⅓ cup	butter	75 ml		2 1-oz squares	unsweetened chocolate, melted	2x30 g
½ cup	sugar	125 ml		1 cup	flour	250 ml
¼ cup	brown sugar, firmly packed	50 ml		½ tsp	baking soda	2 ml
1 tsp	vanilla	5 ml		½ tsp	salt	2 ml
1	egg	1		1 8-oz pkg	white chocolate chips	225 g

Beat butter, sugar, vanilla, egg, and unsweetened chocolate until fluffy. Mix dry ingredients and add to butter mixture. Add white chocolate chips. Drop onto a greased cookie sheet by the teaspoonful. Bake at 350F (175C) for 10-12 minutes.

Helene's Chocolate
Chip Cookies

1 cup	butter, softened	250 ml		2 cups	flour	500 ml
1 cup	peanut butter	250 ml		2 tsp	baking soda	10 ml
1 cup	white sugar	250 ml		1 cup	coconut	250 ml
1 cup	brown sugar	250 ml		1 cup	chocolate chips, or more	250 ml
2	eggs	2				

Mix all together and bake at 350F (175C) for 8-10 minutes.

Low-Fat Chocolate
Chip Apple Cookies

½ cup	white sugar	125 ml		½ tsp	baking soda	2 ml
½ cup	brown sugar	125 ml		1 tsp	ginger	5 ml
½ cup	butter	125 ml		1 cup	apple, peeled and grated	250 ml
1	egg	1				
¾ cup	whole wheat flour	175 ml		¾ cup	dark chocolate chips	175 ml
¾ cup	white flour	175 ml				
½ tsp	salt	2 ml		½ cup	rolled oats	125 ml

In a large mixing bowl, cream butter with sugars. Beat in egg. Add white flour, salt, soda and ginger. Add to egg mixture. Stir in whole wheat flour. Stir in grated apple, chocolate chips and rolled oats. Drop mixture by rounded teaspoon onto a well-greased cookie sheet. Bake at 350F (175C) for 10 minutes.

Whoopie Pies

½ cup	shortening	125 ml	1 tsp	baking soda	5 ml
1 cup	white sugar	250 ml	½ tsp	salt	2 ml
2	egg yolks	2	5 tbsp	cocoa	75 ml
1 cup	milk	250 ml	1 tsp	vanilla	5 ml
2¼ cups	flour	550 ml			

Filling:

¼ cup	shortening	50 ml	1 tsp	vanilla	5 ml
2 cups	icing sugar	500 ml	¼ tsp	salt	1 ml

Cream shortening and sugar. Beat in egg yolks. Stir in vanilla and milk. Add sifted dry ingredients. Drop onto a greased cookie sheet. Bake at 375F (190C) for 10 minutes. Remove from oven. Cool. Filling: Cream shortening and beat in icing sugar until fluffy; add vanilla and salt. Put two cookies together with a layer of filling in the middle.

Jem Jams

Jelly-filled molasses cookies—very traditional.

1 cup	shortening	250 ml	2 tsp	baking soda	10 ml
⅔ cup	brown sugar	150 ml		dissolved in ¼ cup (50 ml) hot water	
½ cup	molasses	125 ml			
1	egg	1	½ tsp	salt	2 ml
1½ tsp	vanilla	7 ml		jelly	
				flour	

Cream shortening and sugar. Add molasses, egg and vanilla. Mix soda in hot water and add to mixture. Add flour and salt, using enough to roll wafer-thin cookies. Bake at 350F (175C) for 10-15 minutes and watch very carefully for burning. Sandwich jelly between two hot cookies. These cookies are delicious and make a great addition to a lunch box.

Molasses Jelly Cookies

¾ cup	brown sugar	175 ml	2 tsp	baking soda	10 ml
¾ cup	margarine	175 ml	2 tsp	vanilla	10 ml
½ cup	molasses	125 ml	1 tsp	salt	5 ml
⅓ cup	hot water	75 ml	4 cups	flour	1 L

Cream sugar and margarine. Add molasses and vanilla. Dissolve soda in hot water and add, alternating with flour and salt. Roll into balls. Make a dent in each cookie and fill dent with jelly or jam. Bake at 350F (175C) for 15-20 minutes.

Butterscotch Cookies

1 cup	shortening or margarine	250 ml	¾ tsp	salt	3 ml
			¾ cup	boiling water	175 ml
1¼ cup	brown sugar	300 ml	1¼ tsp	baking soda	6 ml
1	egg	1	2½ cups	flour	625 ml
2 tsp	vanilla	10 ml	½ cup	walnuts, if desired	125 ml

Cream margarine and brown sugar. Beat in egg and vanilla. Stir in hot water in which soda has been dissolved. Add flour and salt, and walnuts, if desired. Drop from a spoon onto a floured cookie sheet. Bake at 350F (175C) for 15-20 minutes.

Judy's Chocolate
Fudge Cookies

2 cups	sugar	500 ml	2½ cups	rolled oats	375 ml
½ cup	milk	125 ml	½ cup	cocoa	125 ml
½ cup	shortening	125 ml	1 tsp	vanilla	5 ml
1 cup	coconut	250 ml			

Boil sugar, milk and shortening in pot for about 2 minutes. Add vanilla. Mix coconut, oats, and cocoa in a large bowl. Add dry mixture to liquid mixture. Work quickly. Drop from a spoon onto waxed paper. Set aside to cool.

Lorraine's Pumpkin Hermits

A soft and spicy cookie.

¾ cup	butter	175 ml	½ tsp	salt	2 ml
1¼ cups	brown sugar, packed	300 ml	1 tsp	cinnamon	5 ml
			½ tsp	cloves	2 ml
2	eggs	2	½ tsp	allspice	2 ml
2 tsp	vanilla	10 ml	½ tsp	nutmeg	2 ml
1 cup	pumpkin, canned	250 ml	1 cup	raisins	250 ml
2 cups	flour	500 ml	1 cup	dates, chopped	250 ml
1 tsp	baking powder	5 ml	¾ cup	nuts, chopped	175 ml
½ tsp	baking soda	2 ml			

In a large mixing bowl, cream butter and sugar. Beat in eggs and vanilla. Beat in pumpkin. Sift together flour, baking powder, soda, salt and spices. Stir in raisins, dates and nuts. Drop by the tablespoon onto cookie sheets. Bake at 350F (175C) for 20 minutes. Cool completely. Store in an airtight container. Freeze if desired.

Myrtle Kennedy's Fruit Cookies

Mildly spicy, very tasty.

1½ cups	brown sugar	375 ml	1 tsp	baking soda	5 ml
1 cup	margarine	250 ml	½ tsp	baking powder	2 ml
1	egg	1	1 tsp	cinnamon	5 ml
4 tbsp	milk	60 ml	½ tsp	nutmeg	2 ml
1 tsp	vanilla	5 ml		raisins	
2-3 cups	flour, to make a stiff dough	500-750 ml			

Blend sugar and margarine. Add egg, milk, vanilla and nutmeg; beat well. Add flour, soda, baking powder, and cinnamon, sifted together. Work in raisins, as desired. Roll and cut out cookies with a large cookie cutter. Sprinkle with a little sugar. Bake at 350F (175C) until nicely browned, approximately 10 minutes.

Santa's Favourites

Good enough to make Santa blush.

1 cup	butter	250 ml	¾ cup	red cherries, chopped	175 ml
1 cup	sugar	250 ml	½ cup	pecans, chopped	125 ml
2 tbsp	milk	30 ml	¾ cup	coconut, flaked	175 ml
1 tsp	vanilla	5 ml		cherry juice	
2½ cups	flour	625 ml			

In a mixing bowl cream together sugar and butter. Blend in milk and vanilla. Stir in flour, chopped cherries and nuts. Form into two 8-inch rolls. Roll in flaked coconut to coat outside. Wrap in waxed paper. Cut into ½-inch (1.3 cm) slices. Place on cookie sheets. Bake at 350F (175C) for 10-12 minutes. If desired, use a little red cherry juice, in place of milk, to tint cookie dough; you then have blushing Santas.

Christmas Fruit Drops

1 cup	butter	250 ml	3½ cups	flour	875 ml
1½ cups	brown sugar	375 ml	1 tsp	baking soda	5 ml
3	eggs, slightly beaten	3	½ tsp	salt	2 ml
			1 cup	raisins or dates	250 ml
2 tbsp	rum, or 2 tsp (10 ml) vanilla	30ml	1 cup	walnuts	250 ml
			½ cup	cherries	125 ml

Cream butter and brown sugar. Beat in eggs and rum or vanilla. Sift together flour, soda and salt and add to mixture. Beat. Stir in fruit and nuts. Drop from a teaspoon, 1 inch (2.5 cm) apart. Bake at 350F (175C) for 10 minutes.

Robin Hood's Oat Cookies

Quick and inexpensive.

¼ cup	shortening	50 ml	½ tsp	baking soda	2 ml
¼ cup	butter	50 ml	2 tbsp	hot water	30 ml
½ cup	brown sugar	125 ml	1 cup	rolled oats	250 ml
½ tsp	salt	2 ml	1 tsp	vanilla	5 ml
¾ cup	flour	175 ml			

Cream butter and shortening with brown sugar. Add vanilla and mix. Sift flour, soda, and salt and add to mixture. Stir and add hot water, stir again. Mix in rolled oats. Roll into balls. Flatten with a fork. Bake at 350F (175C) for 8-10 minutes. Balls may be rolled in coconut before baking.

Dad's Cookies

This recipe makes a large amount of cookies, but these wholesome treats will soon disappear. Not only will Dad like them, but Mom and the children will also sneak a few!

1½ cups	margarine	375 ml		1 tsp	baking soda	5 ml
2 cups	brown sugar	500 ml		½ tsp	baking powder	2 ml
2 tsp	vanilla	10 ml		½ tsp	salt	2 ml
2	eggs, well beaten	2		2 cups	rolled oats	500 ml
2 cups	flour	500 ml		2 cups	desiccated coconut	500 ml

Cream margarine and sugar. Add eggs and vanilla. Sift flour, baking powder, soda and salt, and mix into sugar mixture. Work in rolled oats and coconut. Chill, if desired. Roll into balls; flatten with floured fork. Bake at 350F (175C) until lightly browned, approximately 10 minutes. Cookies will spread.

Cathy's Whipped Shortbread

Combine:

1 lb	butter, room temperature	500 g		3 cups	flour, sifted	750 ml
				⅛ tsp	salt	0.5 ml
½ cup	cornstarch	125 ml		1 tsp	vanilla	5 ml
1 cup	icing sugar	250 ml				

Whip for 7 minutes with an electric mixer until fluffy. Roll into balls and lightly press with a fork dipped in flour. Chill for 15 minutes if dough is too soft to handle. Use a Tupperware melon baller dipped in flour to make perfect and uniform cookies! Decorate with small pieces of red and green cherries. Bake on greased pans 25 to 30 minutes at 275F (140 C). Watch very carefully, they burn easily.

The Great Nova Scotia Cookbook

Brown Sugar Cookies

This was my mother's favourite cookie recipe, given to her by a friend from Lunenburg County. It became a favourite in my family and brings back happy memories of holiday times when we worked together creating cookie dough.

1½ cups	brown sugar	375 ml		2 tsp	cream of tartar	10 ml
1 cup	butter	250 ml		1 tsp	baking soda	5 ml
2	large eggs	2		1 tsp	salt	5 ml
1 tbsp	milk	15 ml		2-3 cups	flour, enough to make stiff dough	250- 375 ml
2 tsp	vanilla	10 ml				

Cream sugar and butter; add eggs and beat. Mix in milk and vanilla. Sift together flour, cream of tartar, soda, salt, and add to butter mixture. Roll to desired thickness. May be cut in fancy shapes for Christmas, Valentine's Day or Easter. Bake at 350F (175C) until browned, about 10-12 minutes. Nice with icing and coconut. A variation on this recipe, Date-Filled Cookies, follows.

Filling:

1 lb	dates	500 g		pinch	salt
1 cup	brown sugar, or less	250 ml		1-2 tsp	vanilla	5-10 ml

Place dates and sugar in saucepan. Cover with cold water. Stir. Place on medium heat and stir frequently until dates are soft and mushy. When smooth, remove from heat add a pinch of salt and 1-2 tsp (5-10 ml) of vanilla. Using the Brown Sugar Cookie recipe, roll dough and cut into 2½-inch (7.5 cm) rounds. Place cookies on cookie sheet. Mound a heaping teaspoon of date filling in the centre of each cookie. Top with another cookie and press edges firmly together. Bake at 350F (175C) until nicely browned, about 10-12 minutes.

Railroad Cookies

My husband worked for many years for the CNR. These cookies had a special meaning to our children, who were quite intrigued by these little railway tracks.

¾ cup	shortening	175 ml
2 cups	brown sugar	500 ml
2	eggs	2
2 tsp	vanilla	10 ml

3 cups	flour	750 ml
1 tsp	cream of tartar	5 ml
½ tsp	baking soda	2 ml
1 tsp	salt	5 ml

Filling:

1½ cups	dates, chopped	375 ml
½ cup	sugar	125 ml

½ cup	boiling water	125 ml
1 tbsp	lemon juice	15 ml

To make dough, cream shortening and sugar. Beat in eggs and vanilla. Add sifted dry ingredients. Mix well. Chill. To make filling, place dates, sugar, water and lemon juice in a saucepan. Cook until thickened. Cool. Roll out dough and spread with date mixture. Roll up as for a jellyroll. Chill. Slice and bake at 350F (175C) for 10 to 12 minutes.

Glazed Pineapple Cookies

1 cup	brown sugar	250 ml
½ cup	shortening or margarine	125 ml
1	egg	1
¾ cup	pineapple, crushed and drained; save 2 tbsp juice	175 ml

2 tsp	vanilla	10 ml
2 cups	flour	500 ml
1½ tsp	baking powder	7 ml
¼ tsp	baking soda	1 ml
¼ tsp	salt	1 ml
1 cup	icing sugar	250 ml

Cream margarine and add brown sugar. Beat in egg. Add pineapple and vanilla. Combine flour, baking powder, soda and salt. Stir into creamed mixture. Drop from a teaspoon onto a greased cookie sheet. Bake at 350F (175C) for 10-12 minutes. Stir pineapple juice into icing sugar, spread glaze over cooled cookies.

Mocha Cookies

½ cup	unsalted butter, softened	125 ml		½ tsp	salt	2 ml
1 cup	brown sugar	250 ml		1¾ cups	flour	425 ml
3 tbsp	granulated sugar	45 ml		1½ tsp	instant espresso powder, slightly crushed	7 ml
1	egg	1				
2 tbsp	vanilla	30 ml		1 8-oz pkg	semisweet chocolate chips	225 g
½ tsp	baking soda	2 ml				
½ tsp	baking powder	2 ml				

Cream the butter with the sugars until fluffy. Beat in the egg and the vanilla. Combine the dry ingredients and beat into the butter mixture. Stir in the chocolate chips. Drop from a large spoon onto a greased cookie sheet. Bake at 375F (190C) for 8-10 minutes, 10-12 minutes for a crisper cookie.

Macaroons

5⅓ cups	flaked coconut	1.3 L		½ tsp	almond extract	2 ml
1 10½-oz can	condensed milk	300 ml			candied cherries, red or green	
1 tsp	vanilla extract	5 ml				

Combine all ingredients, mixing thoroughly. Drop from a rounded teaspoon onto a parchment-lined baking sheet. Place a piece of cherry on each macaroon. For a round macaroon, mold with fingers into ball shapes. Bake at 325F (165C) until a hint of golden brown appears on the edges and tops, approximately 18-20 minutes. Remove from oven and let cool on sheet before removing. If parchment is not used, grease the sheet and remove macaroons while warm.

Chocolate Macaroons

In a bowl over hot water, melt 1 cup (250 ml) semi-sweet chocolate chips. Remove from heat and add 1 can condensed Milk. Combine well. Add 5⅓ cups (1.3 L) flaked coconut and 1 tsp (5 ml) vanilla. Drop from a rounded teaspoon onto parchment-lined baking sheets. Garnish each with a sliced almond. Bake at 325F (165C) for 10-15 minutes.

Pecan Kisses

1	egg white	1	1 tsp	vanilla	5 ml
¼ tsp	cream of tartar	1 ml	2 cups	pecans, coarsely chopped	500 ml
¼ tsp	salt	1 ml			
1 cup	brown sugar, packed	250 ml			

Beat egg white with cream of tartar and salt until mixture is foamy and begins to hold its shape. Beat in brown sugar gradually. Add vanilla. Beat until mixture is stiff and sugar is dissolved. Grease and flour two cookie sheets. Drop from a teaspoon onto sheets 1½ inches (3.75 cm) apart. Bake at 325F (160C) for 15 minutes or until cookies are puffy and set. Turn off heat. Let cookies dry in oven for two minutes. Remove cookies from cookie sheets while still warm.

Egg White Cookies

This recipe has its origin in Holland. It was given to me by a dear friend, Jean Kolstee, (an excellent cook) who came to Canada as a farmer's wife to start a new life .

3	egg whites	3		2 tsp	vanilla	10 ml
1½ cups	white sugar	375 ml		2 cups	coconut	500 ml

Beat egg whites until stiff but not dry. Add sugar gradually. Place this mixture in a double boiler. Stir while heating until a crust forms on bottom of pan. Remove from heat. Add coconut and vanilla. Blend together. Drop by teaspoons onto a greased or parchment-lined sheet. Bake at 325-350F (165-175C) until puffed and slightly browned, approximately 15 minutes.

Cranberry Hermits

⅓ cup	butter, softened	75 ml		1¾ cups	flour	425 ml
⅔ cup	brown sugar	150 ml		½ tsp	baking powder	2 ml
1	egg	1		½ tsp	baking soda	2 ml
⅓ cup	corn syrup	75 ml		½ tsp	cinnamon	2 ml
1 tsp	vanilla	5 ml		½ tsp	allspice	2 ml
1 tsp	orange rind, grated	5 ml		½ tsp	nutmeg	2 ml
2 tbsp	orange juice	30 ml		2 cups	cranberries, dried	500 ml

Icing:

2 cups	icing sugar	500 ml		3 tbsp	orange juice	45 ml

In a large bowl, cream brown sugar and butter. Beat in egg, corn syrup, vanilla, orange rind and juice until light and fluffy. In a separate bowl, combine flour, baking soda, baking powder and spices. Stir into butter mixture. Mix in cranberries. Drop from a rounded teaspoon about 2 inches (5 cm) apart onto baking sheets. Flatten tops with the back of a spoon. Bake in the centre of a 350F (175C) oven until golden, approximately 15 minutes. Let cool in pans for 2-3 minutes. Transfer to racks and let cool. Whisk icing sugar with orange juice. Drop by teaspoonfuls on centre of each cookie. Sprinkle a little grated orange rind on top, if desired.

Ruby's Lumbies

Plates heaped with these great, stick-to-the-ribs molasses cookies would be waiting for hungry men when they came in for supper at the lumber camps.

½ cup	brown sugar	125 ml		1 tsp	baking soda	5 ml
½ cup	shortening	125 ml		½ tsp	salt	2 ml
2	eggs	2		1 tsp	ginger	5 ml
¾ cup	molasses	175 ml		½ tsp	cloves	2 ml
½ cup	sour milk	125 ml		1 cup	raisins	250 ml
2 cups	flour	500 ml				

Cream sugar and shortening. Beat in eggs and molasses. Add sour milk and mix well. Add sifted dry ingredients. Mix well. Stir in raisins last. Drop onto baking sheets. Bake at 350F (175C) for 12 to 15 minutes.

Fig Thumbprint Cookies

Fig filling:

			Cookies:		
4 oz	figs	125 g	½ cup	butter	125 ml
2 tbsp	sugar	30 ml	⅓ cup	brown sugar	75 ml
2 tsp	orange rind, grated	10 ml	1	egg	1
1 tbsp	orange juice	15 ml	1 tsp	vanilla	5 ml
1 tbsp	brandy, if desired	15 ml	1¼ cups	flour	300 ml
			½ tsp	salt	2 ml
			¾ cup	walnuts, ground	175 ml

Prepare filling by placing all ingredients in saucepan. Bring to a boil, stirring constantly. Lower heat and simmer until thick. Cool. To prepare cookies, cream butter and beat in sugar until light and fluffy. Beat in egg and vanilla. Stir in flour and salt until dough holds together. Chill. Shape dough into 1-inch (2.5 cm) balls. Roll balls in walnuts to coat and place 1 inch apart on cookie sheets. Make an indentation in the centre of each ball. Bake at 350F (175C) until lightly browned (approximately 12 minutes) Remove from oven and cool. Before serving, fill each cookie with fig filling. Filling could be made with dates instead of figs or replaced by jam or jelly.

Jean Taggart's
Ice Box Ribbons

1 cup	butter	250 ml	¼ cup	red cherries, chopped	50 ml
1 cup	sugar	250 ml			
1	egg	1	⅓ cup	chocolate chips, melted	75 ml
1 tsp	vanilla	5 ml			
2½ cups	flour	625 ml	⅓ cup	nuts, chopped	75 ml
1 tsp	baking powder	5 ml	⅓ cup	coconut	75 ml
¼ tsp	salt	1 ml		red food colouring	

Cream butter and sugar. Beat in egg and vanilla. Sift flour, baking powder and salt together and mix in. Divide dough into three equal parts. First layer: To one part of dough add enough red food colouring to make it pink. Add cherries to this part. Second layer: To the second part of dough, add chocolate and nuts. Third layer: To the last part of dough add coconut. Roll each part into a loaf-size brick and stack in a foil-lined loaf pan. Chill overnight. Cut into ¼-inch (0.7 cm) slices, then cut each slice into 3 pieces. Arrange on a cookie sheet. Bake at 350F (175C) for 10-12 minutes. For Christmas, tint the second layer green instead of using chocolate.

Hazelnut Shortbread
Refrigerator Cookies

Keep some dough frozen for quick baking.

1 cup	flour	250 ml	¾ cup	hazelnuts, finely chopped	175 ml
½ cup	cornstarch	125 ml			
⅔ cup	icing sugar	150 ml	¾ cup	butter	175 ml

Combine flour, cornstarch, and icing sugar in a large bowl. Blend in butter until a smooth dough forms. Add hazelnuts. Shape dough into a roll. Wrap with waxed paper and chill until firm. Cut with a sharp knife into slices. Place slices on a baking sheet and bake at 375F (190C) until edges brown (approximately 10-12 minutes). Cranberries or cherries may be added, and pecans or walnuts will do instead of hazelnuts.

Boiled Raisin Cookies

This recipe was given to me by Myrna Kennedy in 1944. These cookies were popular at her home, where I boarded during my teaching days in Pleasant Valley.

1½ cups	raisins	375 ml	1 cup	cold water	250 ml

Boil raisins in water until liquid is gone. Cool.

1 cup	sugar	250 ml	3 cups	flour	750 ml
1 cup	margarine	250 ml	1 tsp	baking powder	5 ml
3	eggs	3	1 tsp	baking soda	5 ml
2 tsp	vanilla	10 ml	½ tsp	salt	2 ml

Cream sugar and margarine. Add eggs and vanilla. Beat well. Add sifted dry ingredients. Add boiled raisins last. Drop onto a cookie sheet. Press down. Bake at 350F (175C) for 12-15 minutes.

Chewy Maple Syrup Cookies

½ cup	shortening	125 ml
1 cup	brown sugar	250 ml
1	egg	1
½ cup	maple syrup	125 ml
½ tsp	vanilla or maple flavouring	2 ml

1½ cups	flour	375 ml
2 tsp	baking powder	10 ml
½ tsp	salt	2 ml
1 cup	flaked coconut	250 ml

Cream shortening and sugar. Beat in egg, syrup and vanilla until well mixed and fluffy. Stir in coconut. Combine flour, baking powder and salt, and add to batter. Drop from a tablespoon, 2 inches (5 cm) apart, onto greased baking sheets. Bake at 375F (190C) until lightly browned for 12-15 minutes.

Honey Nut and Oatmeal Cookies

¾ cup	butter	175 ml
¾ cup	brown sugar	175 ml
1	egg	1
¼ cup	honey	50 ml
1 tsp	vanilla	5 ml
¾ cup	flour	175 ml
½ tsp	baking powder	2 ml

¼ tsp	salt	1 ml
¾ cup	whole wheat flour	175 ml
2 cups	rolled oats	500 ml
1 cup	coconut, flaked	250 ml
1 cup	raisins	250 ml
¾ cup	pecans, chopped	175 ml

In the large bowl of an electric mixer, cream butter and brown sugar until fluffy. Beat in egg, honey and vanilla. Stir in sifted dry ingredients: white flour, baking powder and salt. Mix well. Add whole wheat flour. Stir in oats, coconut, raisins and pecans. Chill dough. Divide dough into 3 parts and roll each part into a 2-inch (5 cm) log. Roll in extra coconut. (Tint coconut red and green for Christmas.) Chill. When ready to bake, slice into ½-inch (1.3 cm) slices. Bake at 375F (190C) for 10 to 12 minutes, until lightly brown. Let cool on racks. Store in tightly covered tins. May be frozen.

Charlie Brown's Peanut Cookies

Good grief, they're full of Peanuts!

1 cup	shortening	250 ml
2 cups	brown sugar	500 ml
2	eggs	2
2 tsp	vanilla	10 ml
½ tsp	baking soda	2 ml
1 tsp	baking powder	5 ml

1½ cups	Spanish peanuts, unsalted, small with brown jackets	375 ml
1 cup	corn flakes, crushed	250 ml
2 cups	rolled oats	500 ml
2 cups	flour	500 ml

Cream shortening and sugar. Add eggs and beat. Add vanilla. Add dry ingredients, leaving peanuts until last. Roll into balls. Flatten with a fork. Bake at 350F (175C) for 10-12 minutes.

Elda's Jumbo Raisin Cookies

Enough to feed a crowd!

1 cup	water	250 ml
2 cups	raisins	500 ml
¾ cup	shortening	175 ml
¼ cup	butter	50 ml
2 cups	brown sugar	500 ml
3	eggs, beaten	3
1 tsp	vanilla	5 ml

1 cup	nuts, chopped	250 ml
4 cups	flour	1 L
1 tsp	baking powder	5 ml
1 tsp	baking soda	5 ml
2 tsp	salt	10 ml
1½ tsp	cinnamon	7 ml
¼ tsp	nutmeg	1 ml

Boil water and raisins gently for 5 minutes, and cool. Cream butter and shortening; add sugar. Cream well. Add eggs and beat well. Add vanilla, nuts and cooled raisins. Sift together dry ingredients and add to shortening mixture. Blend well. Drop from a teaspoon onto a greased cookie sheet. Bake at 350F (175C) for 12-15 minutes.

Ruby's Swedish Pastries

Very pretty on a cookie tray.

¼ cup	brown sugar	50 ml	1 tsp	vanilla	5 ml
½ cup	butter	125 ml	1	egg white, slightly beaten	1
1	egg yolk, beaten	1			
1 cup	flour	250 ml		walnuts, finely chopped	
⅛ tsp	salt	0.5 ml			

Cream butter and brown sugar. Beat in egg yolk and vanilla. Mix in sifted flour and salt. Chill. Roll into small balls, and dip in slightly beaten egg white, then roll in nuts. Place on a greased baking sheet. Make a dent in each. Bake in a 350F (175C) oven for 5 minutes. Remove from oven and make a deeper dent in each cookie. Bake for 10-15 minutes longer. Fill with red jam or jelly if using immediately—if not, store and fill when ready to serve.

Cherry Flips

This recipe came from Mary Kennedy's kitchen—what great cooks lived and still live in Pleasant Valley!

1 cup	butter	250 ml	2 cups	flour	500 ml
½ cup	icing sugar	125 ml	¼ tsp	salt	1 ml
2	egg yolks, slightly beaten	2	1 tsp	almond extract	5 ml
				maraschino cherries	

Cream butter and icing sugar together. Add egg yolks and beat well. Sift flour and salt together and add to mixture. Blend in almond extract. Chill dough. Roll into balls, then flatten each ball. Place a well drained maraschino cherry on each piece of dough and fold dough around cherry. Bake at 325F (175C) for 10-12 minutes. After baking, each ball may be rolled in icing sugar or dipped in icing made with cherry juice, and a small decoration may be placed on top.

Florentine Triangles

1½ cups	flour	375 ml		2 tbsp	whipping cream	30 ml
½ cup	icing sugar, sifted	125 ml		2 tsp	vanilla	10 ml
½ cup	butter	125 ml				

Topping:

¾ cup	butter	175 ml		½ cup	candied green cherries, chopped	125 ml
½ cup	sugar	125 ml				
¼ cup	whipping cream	50 ml		1 cup	sliced almonds, blanched	250 ml
½ cup	candied red cherries, chopped	125 ml				
½ cup	candied pineapple, chopped	125 ml		2 1-oz squares	semisweet chocolate, melted	2x30 g

Combine flour and icing sugar in mixing bowl. Cut in butter until mixture is crumbly. Stir in cream and vanilla, mixing until dough clings together. Press dough evenly into a greased 15x10-inch (2 L) jellyroll pan. Chill. Combine butter, sugar, and cream in a medium-size saucepan. Bring to boil, stirring often, then boil 1-2 minutes, stirring constantly until thickened. Remove from heat. Stir in fruit and nuts. Spread evenly over chilled crust. Bake at 375F (175C) for 15-20 minutes. Cool in pan. Drizzle with melted chocolate. Cut into triangles.

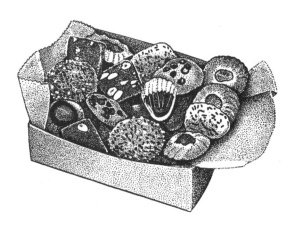

Evelyn's Cookies

A favourite recipe of an old school friend from times past.

½ cup	butter	125 ml	1½ cups	rolled oats	375 ml
½ cup	shortening	125 ml	1½ cups	flour	375 ml
1 cup	brown sugar	250 ml	1 tsp	baking powder	5 ml
½ cup	white sugar	125 ml	1 tsp	baking soda	5 ml
1 tbsp	vanilla	15 ml	½ cup	salt	2 ml
1	egg	1	1 cup	coconut	250 ml

Cream together butter, shortening, sugars and vanilla. Beat in egg. Add sifted flour, baking powder, soda and salt. Mix well. Stir in rolled oats and coconut. Roll into balls and flatten. Bake at 350-375F (175-190C) for 10-12 minutes. Watch carefully, as they burn easily. The extra vanilla is the secret here—it makes for a very delicious cookie.

Peanut Butter Balls

1 cup	peanut butter	250 ml	1 cup	dates, chopped	250 ml
1 cup	icing sugar	250 ml	½ cup	walnuts	125 ml
½ tsp	salt	2 ml	1 tsp	vanilla	5 ml
1 tbsp	cream	15 ml		walnuts, finely crumbled	
¼ cup	butter, softened	50 ml			

Cream peanut butter, butter, icing sugar and salt. Work in cream and vanilla. Add walnuts and dates. Roll into balls and then roll in fine walnut crumbs. Store in tightly covered tins and keep cool.

Chocolate Balls

1 cup	peanut butter	250 ml		½ tsp	salt	2 ml
2 cups	dates, chopped	500 ml		1 tsp	vanilla	5 ml
½ cup	nuts	125 ml		1 tbsp	cream	15 ml
1 cup	icing sugar	250 ml				

Mix in given order. Shape into small balls. Melt:

4 1-oz squares	semisweet chocolate	4x30 g		⅛ square	paraffin wax

Dip balls in chocolate mixture; put on wax paper and refrigerate.

Chocolate-Cherry Balls

1 10½-oz can	condensed milk	300 ml		1 tsp	vanilla	5 ml
					cherries	
2 squares	chocolate, broken into pieces	2		extra wafers for rolling	
21	graham wafers, crushed	21			

Place milk and chocolate in the top of a double boiler. Heat until chocolate melts. Remove from heat and blend together. Stir in crushed wafers and vanilla. Mould crumb mixture around cherries to form balls. Roll balls in the extra wafer crumbs. Refrigerate.

Cherry Surprises

1½ cups	desiccated coconut	375 ml
1½ cups	icing sugar	375 ml
½ cup	butter	125 ml
1 tbsp	cream	15 ml
1 tsp	almond extract	5 ml

	maraschino cherries, well drained
	graham wafer crumbs

Blend together coconut, sugar, butter, cream and extract. Mold mixture around individual cherries, then roll in graham wafer crumbs. Cover tightly and refrigerate.

Snowballs

¾ cup	butter, softened	175 ml
1 tsp	vanilla	5 ml
1 tbsp	water	15 ml
⅛ tsp	salt	0.5 ml
⅓ cup	sugar	75 ml

2 cups	flour, sifted	500 ml
1 cup	chocolate pieces	250 ml
1 cup	pecans, finely chopped	250 ml
	powdered sugar	

Combine first 5 ingredients and blend well. Stir in flour and chocolate pieces. Form into 1-inch balls; roll in chopped pecans. Place balls on an ungreased cookie sheet and flatten slightly. Bake at 350F (175C) for 12-15 minutes. Roll in powdered sugar while warm. Makes 2 dozen.

Peanutty Butterscotch Balls

This was Ester Kennedy's recipe; she was a nurse and a wonderful cook. These little treats surely warmed the heart.

1 10½-oz can	condensed milk	300 ml	1 cup	butterscotch chips	250 ml
			1 cup	flaked coconut	250 ml
⅔ cup	peanut butter	150 ml			
2½ cups	graham wafer crumbs	625 ml			

Combine milk with peanut butter. Stir in crumbs and chips. Mix well. Shape into 1-inch balls. Roll in coconut. Store in a tightly covered container in the refrigerator. Makes about 5 dozen.

Rum Balls

1 cup	cream cheese, softened	250 g	3 cups	graham wafer crumbs	750 ml
¾ cup	chocolate chips	180 ml	1 cup	maraschino cherries, well drained, chopped	250 ml
¾ cup	butterscotch chips	180 ml			
3 tbsp	rum	45 ml		chocolate trimettes	

Beat cream cheese using electric mixer. Melt chocolate and butterscotch chips in the top of a double boiler over hot (not boiling) water. Beat melted mixture into cream cheese. Mix in rum, crumbs and cherries. Chill for 30 minutes. Roll into small balls and dip in trimettes or other decoration. Chill and store in the refrigerator. Makes 85 balls. Place in tiny foil cups before serving.

Ruby's Cherry Dream Cakes

½ cup	butter	125 ml
⅓ cup	sugar	75 ml
1	egg yolk	1
1 tsp	vanilla or almond extract	5 ml

1 cup	flour	250 ml
⅛ tsp	salt	0.5 ml
	cherries	

Cream butter and sugar. Add egg yolk, and extract. Add flour and salt, sifted together. May be chilled. Roll into balls. Place on a greased cookie sheet. Flatten with a fork. Press a whole cherry into each. Bake in a 350F (175C) oven, until very slightly browned, approximately 10-12 minutes.

Rose's Frying Pan Cookies

For many years, Rose Carter was in charge of pastries at Truro's only hospital, where patients looked forward to her desserts.

To a cold frying pan, add:

2	eggs, unbeaten	2
1 cup	sugar	250 ml

1½ cups	dates, sliced	375 ml
	salt	

Cook and stir over low heat for 10 minutes. Remove from heat and stir in:

2 cups	Rice Krispies	500 ml

1 tsp	vanilla	5 ml

Roll into balls, dip in coconut and serve.

No Bake Peanut Chews

⅔ cup	skim milk powder	150 ml		1 cup	chocolate chips	250 ml
⅔ cup	corn syrup	150 ml		¾ cup	peanuts, chopped	175 ml
¼ cup	butter	50 ml		2 cups	icing sugar	500 ml

Mix together skim milk powder and icing sugar. Melt chocolate chips over hot water and add butter and corn syrup. Add this mixture to dry ingredients. Work all together and knead on board until smooth. Add chopped peanuts. Form into rolls and cut with scissors into pieces. Decorate with a small silver dredge. Add more icing sugar, if sticky.

Peanut Raisin Clusters

1 10½-oz condensed milk can		300 ml		1 cup	peanuts	250 ml
				1 cup	raisins	250 ml
1 cup	chocolate chips	250 ml				

Line a cookie sheet with parchment paper. In a saucepan, heat condensed milk and chocolate chips, and stir until mixture is smooth. Bring to a gentle boil, reduce heat to low and simmer for 10 minutes, whisking frequently until mixture is thick and has a pudding-like consistency. Remove from heat and stir in peanuts and raisins. Cool slightly. Drop from a tablespoon onto the prepared sheet. Refrigerate until firm. Store in airtight containers with wax paper between layers.

Chocolate Golf Balls

1 5-oz condensed milk can		150 ml		1 tsp	vanilla	5 ml
1 cup	graham wafer crumbs	250 ml		2 1-oz squares	unsweetened chocolate	2x30 g
⅛ tsp	salt			1½ cups	maraschino cherries	375 ml
					flaked coconut	

Mix milk, wafer crumbs, salt and vanilla. Roll into balls, dip in melted chocolate then roll in flaked coconut. Put whole cherry on top.

· CONFECTIONS ·

• Best •

• Traditional •

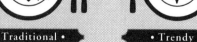
• Trendy •

Magic French Fudge

3 cups	chocolate chips	750 ml		1½ tsp	vanilla	7 ml
1 10½-oz can	condensed milk	300 ml		½ cup	nuts	125 ml
dash	salt					

Melt chocolate in a double boiler. Remove from heat and add remaining ingredients. Spread in an 8-inch (20 cm) parchment-lined square pan. Chill for 2 hours. Pull off paper and cut.

Brown Sugar Fudge

I'm sure I've made a barrelful of this fudge. It was a must at Christmas and for sale at fundraising events. My Sunday school children looked forward to it as a weekly treat too. Follow all of the rules of fudge-making carefully.

2 cups	brown sugar	500 ml		3 tbsp	butter	45 ml
⅔ cup	cream or evaporated milk	150 ml		½ cup	walnuts or coconut	125 ml
2 tbsp	corn syrup	30 ml		1 tsp	vanilla	5 ml

Place sugar, cream, and corn syrup in a heavy saucepan (I prefer fresh cream to evaporated milk). Stir constantly until sugar is dissolved and mixture starts to boil, making sure the candy is stirred away from the sides of the pan. Cook without stirring until a soft ball forms when tested in cold water. Cool. Beat until creamy. Add butter, vanilla and nuts or coconut. Pour into a greased pan, and cut into squares immediately.

Note: Finding the right length of cooking time takes practice; try and try again until you are happy with the results.

Chocolate Fudge

1 cup	white sugar	250 ml		½ cup	walnuts or peanuts, ground	125 ml
1 cup	brown sugar	250 ml				
½ cup	milk or cream	125 ml		1 tsp	vanilla	5 ml
⅓ cup	corn syrup	75 ml		2 tbsp	butter	30 ml
½ cup	cocoa, or 2 1-oz squares (60 g) unsweetened chocolate	125 ml				

Place sugars, cream, syrup and cocoa in a heavy saucepan. Stir over medium heat until mixture starts to boil. Cook to the soft-ball stage. Allow to cool for 20 minutes. Beat until thick and add remaining ingredients. Put in pan, and cut into squares.

Almond Butter Cream Fudge

Light in colour—different, but good.

2 cups	brown sugar, packed	500 ml		¼ cup	milk	50 ml
				¼ cup	corn syrup	50 ml
1 tbsp	cornstarch	15 ml		3 tbsp	butter	45 ml
1 tsp	baking powder	5 ml		⅓ cup	almonds, sliced	75 ml
⅛ tsp	salt	0.5 ml		1 tsp	vanilla	5 ml

Mix dry ingredients; add milk, syrup and butter. Dissolve over low heat and stir constantly. Bring to boil and boil to soft-ball stage: 238F (119C). Remove from heat and cool for 3 minutes. Beat until slightly thickened and add nuts and vanilla. Pour into a greased pan. Cut into squares.

Helene's Peanut Butter Fudge

2 cups	white sugar	500 ml		1½ cups	peanut butter	375 ml
2 cups	brown sugar	500 ml		1 cup	miniature marshmallows	250 ml
¾ cup	milk	175 ml				

In a saucepan, combine sugars and milk, and boil vigorously for 90 seconds, stirring constantly. Remove from heat. Stir in peanut butter and marshmallows. Stir to combine. Pour into a 9-inch (23 cm) square pan and allow to set. Cut into squares.

Peanut Butter Fudge

2 cups	granulated sugar	500 ml		2 tbsp	corn syrup	30 ml
⅛ tsp	salt	0.5 ml		¼ cup	peanut butter	50 ml
¾ cup	cream	175 ml		1 tsp	vanilla	5 ml

Combine sugar, salt, cream and corn syrup in a heavy saucepan; mix well. Stir over medium heat until it boils. Continue to boil without stirring to a soft-ball stage: 234F (112C). Remove from heat and let cool, without stirring, until lukewarm: 110F (43C). Mix in peanut butter and vanilla and beat until mixture begins to thicken. Pour into a buttered pan. When firm, cut into squares.

Divinity Fudge

2⅓ cups	white sugar	575 ml	½ tsp	vanilla or preferred flavouring	2 ml
⅔ cup	corn syrup	150 ml		chopped cherries or coconut, optional	
½ cup	water	125 ml			
¼ tsp	salt	1 ml			
2	egg whites	2			

Measure sugar, corn syrup, water and salt into a saucepan. Cook and stir over low heat until dissolved. Increase heat. Cook, without stirring, to the hard-ball stage. Beat the egg whites stiffly and gradually pour the hot syrup over them. Beat. Mix in vanilla and cherries or coconut, stir to combine. Pour into a greased 8-inch (20 cm) square pan or drop by the teaspoonful onto wax paper.

Light Fudge

2 cups	granulated sugar	500 ml	⅛ tsp	salt	0.5 ml
1 cup	cream	250 ml	1 tsp	vanilla	5 ml

Combine sugar, cream and salt. Stir well. Place over medium heat and stir until mixture comes to a boil. Continue to boil until the syrup reaches the soft-ball stage: 234F (112C). Remove from heat and cool to lukewarm: 110F (43C). Add vanilla; beat until creamy. Pour into buttered tin. Cover with a damp cloth for thirty minutes to keep fudge creamy. Cut into squares when firm. After cutting, store in an airtight container.

Oreo Cookie Crunch

8 1-oz squares	semisweet chocolate, chopped	8x30 g	1 cup	Oreo cookies, coarsely chopped	250 g

Partially melt chocolate in a microwave or on the stovetop. Remove from heat. Stir in cookies. Pour mixture into a pan lined with waxed paper. Tap pan to smooth mixture. Refrigerate until firm (approximately 1 hour). Break into pieces. Store in the refrigerator.

Breton Brittle

28	Dare Breton crackers	28	1 pkg	semisweet chocolate chips	300 g
1 cup	butter	250 ml			
1 cup	brown sugar	250 ml	⅓ cup	pecans, finely chopped	75 ml

Cover the bottom of a 9x13-inch (23x33 cm) baking pan with parchment or foil. Spread crackers so that the bottom of the pan is covered. In a saucepan, stir butter and sugar until boiling. Pour over crackers and bake in a 400F (200C) oven for 5 minutes. Remove from oven and cover with chocolate chips. Spread to cover crackers. Quickly sprinkle with nuts. Cool and break into pieces. Keep refrigerated.

Pecan Brittle

2 cups	granulated sugar	500 ml	2 tbsp	butter	30 ml
1 cup	corn syrup	250 ml	½ tsp	salt	2 ml
½ cup	water	125 ml	½ tsp	baking soda	2 ml
1½ cups	pecans	375 ml	1 tsp	vanilla	5 ml

In a heavy saucepan, combine sugar, corn syrup and water; bring to a boil over medium heat. Cover and cook for 3 minutes; uncover and stir in pecans. Place a candy thermometer in the saucepan and cook, without stirring, for 15 minutes or until the soft-crack stage: 270-290F (132-143C). Test by dropping a little syrup into very cold water. Remove syrup from water and bend; it should be brittle and snap easily. Stir in butter, vanilla and baking soda; immediately pour mixture into a well-greased 17x11-inch (45x29 cm) jellyroll pan. With wooden spoons, spread as thinly as possible; let cool. With rolling pin or mallet, break candy into pieces. Makes about 1¼ lb (625 g).

Peanut Brittle

¼ cup	water	50 ml	2 tsp	baking soda	10 ml
2 cups	sugar	500 ml	1¾ cups	salted peanuts, skinned	425 ml
1 cup	corn syrup	250 ml			
2 tbsp	butter	30 ml			

Oil two cookie sheets and divide peanuts evenly between pans—spreading them out in one layer. Combine water, sugar and corn syrup in a heavy saucepan, stirring well. Stir over moderate heat until mixture reaches boiling. Continue to boil, without stirring, to soft-crack stage: 280F (125C). Remove from heat and add butter in small pieces. Move pan around so that butter melts. Return to heat and heat to hard-crack stage: 295F (143C). Remove from heat and add soda, stirring thoroughly. Pour syrup over peanuts. Spread evenly. When cool enough to handle, pull and stretch candy into as thin a layer as possible. When cool, break into irregular pieces. Store in an airtight container.

White Chocolate Bark

6 1-oz squares	white chocolate, chopped	6

½ cup	sweetened and dried cranberries, or blanched almonds, toasted in oven	125 ml

Melt chocolate. Stir in cranberries or almonds. Pour chocolate on a waxed paper-lined cookie sheet. Smooth surface. Refrigerate until firm. Break into pieces. Note: Other dried fruits such as chopped apricots or raisins may be used. Keep in refrigerator.

For Dark Chocolate Bark, substitute 8 squares of semi-sweet chocolate for 6 squares of white chocolate.

Almond Bark

2 cups	sugar	500 ml	¼ tsp	salt	1 ml
1 tbsp	corn syrup	15 ml	1 tsp	vanilla	5 ml
2 tbsp	butter	30 ml	1 cup	fresh almonds, toasted	250 ml
⅔ cup	milk	150 ml			

Combine sugar, milk, corn syrup and salt. Cook, stirring constantly, until sugar dissolves and comes to a boil. Cook to the soft-ball stage: 234F (112C). Remove from heat and add butter. Do not stir. Let cool to lukewarm. Add vanilla. Beat until mixture is thick and creamy. Add almonds and spread ½ inch (1.3 cm) thick over buttered waxed paper. Do not make on a damp day; it will not set.

Chocolate Butter
Crunch Candy

Preheat oven to 300F (150C). In one pan, toast ¾ cup (175 ml) whole almonds until lightly browned. Turn off oven and leave almonds inside to cool. In another pan, toast 1½ cups (375 ml) finely chopped almonds; reserve. Coarsely chop the whole almonds, and reserve. Warm and butter a baking sheet and butter a spatula. In a heavy saucepan, bring to a boil the following ingredients:

| ⅓ cup | water | 75 ml | ⅓ cup | corn syrup | 75 ml |
| 1¼ cups | sugar | 300 ml | | | |

Cover and simmer over low heat for 2 minutes. Add ½ lb (250 g) unsalted butter. Stir until melted. Bring to a medium boil. Stir frequently until 240F (115C) is reached, then stir continuously until temperature reaches 300F (150C) (but no more). Remove from heat and stir in:

| ½ tsp | salt | 2 ml | ¾ cup | warm, coarsely chopped almonds | 175 ml |
| ¼ tsp | baking soda | 1 ml | | | |

Pour onto the prepared baking sheet. Spread to a ¼-inch (0.7 cm) thickness with the buttered spatula. Let cool until pliable. Cut into 1x2-inch (2.5x5 cm) pieces with a sharp knife. Separate the pieces slightly, and let cool. Push pieces back together. In a double boiler, gently melt the following ingredients:

| 6 oz | dark, sweetened chocolate | 168 g | 4 1-oz squares | unsweetened baking chocolate | 4x30 g |
| | | | 1½ tsp | salad oil | 7 ml |

Stir until well blended, then cool until thick enough to spread but still thin enough to pour. Pour over candy, spreading evenly. Sprinkle the finely chopped almonds evenly over the chocolate and press in gently. Let cool. Break candy pieces apart and store in an air-tight container.

Peanut Chewies

½ cup	peanut butter, crunchy	125 ml		pinch	salt	
				¼ cup	icing sugar	50 ml
3 tbsp	honey	45 ml		½ cup	unsalted peanuts, finely chopped	125 ml
1 tsp	vanilla	5 ml				
¾ cup	instant skim milk powder	175 ml				

Mix the peanut butter, honey, vanilla, milk powder, salt and sugar together in a bowl. Using hands, blend mixture thoroughly, then shape into 1-inch balls and roll in chopped peanuts. If weather is damp or hot, store in the refrigerator.

Coconut Candy

4 cups	granulated sugar	1 L		½ cup	coconut	125 ml
1 cup	milk (part coconut milk, if desired)	250 ml			pink colouring	
					peppermint flavouring, if desired	
3 tbsp	butter	45 ml				

In a heavy saucepan, stir sugar and milk and cook until mixture reaches the hard-ball stage. Add butter; boil for 5 minutes more. Remove from heat and add coconut, pink colouring and flavouring. Beat until thick. Pour into a buttered pan. Cut immediately into squares. Add peppermint flavouring. This candy will have a hard, sugary texture; it is tasty and very pretty.

Caramels

½ lb	butter	250 g	1 10½-oz can	sweetened, condensed milk	300 ml
1 cup	corn syrup	250 ml	3 cups	brown sugar	750 ml

Boil ingredients until mixture forms a very crisp ball when tested in cold water. Beat. Pour into a buttered pan. Cut into squares before mixture has completely cooled. Wrap each square in waxed paper.

Vanilla Nut Caramels

1 cup	brown sugar	250 ml	⅔ cup	milk	150 ml
1 cup	granulated sugar	250 ml	1 cup	nuts	250 ml
1 cup	corn syrup	250 ml	2 tsp	vanilla	10 ml
½ cup	butter	125 ml			

Mix ingredients well. Stirring constantly, cook until hard-ball stage: 246F (118C). Pour into a greased pan. Cut before mixture hardens. Wrap each square in wax paper to store.

Denise's Easter Nests

Every Easter, Denise Mayo makes these nests for her two little girls and their friends.

½ cup	coconut, coloured	125 ml		¼ cup	margarine	50 ml
½ cup	corn syrup	125 ml		2 cups	corn flakes	500 ml
3 tbsp	white sugar	45 ml		½ cup	walnuts, chopped	125 ml

Put corn syrup, sugar, and margarine into a saucepan over medium heat. Bring to a boil, stirring constantly, and boil for 5 minutes. Remove from heat; add coloured coconut, corn flakes and walnuts and mix well. With well buttered hands, shape into 8-10 nests. Make sure that you shape the nests while the mixture is hot for it hardens quickly. Place small coloured Easter eggs or jelly beans in nests.

Pecan Toffee

¾ cup	pecans, chopped	175 ml		1 cup	brown sugar	250 ml
1 cup	butter	250 ml		½ cup	chocolate chips	125 ml

Line a 9x13-inch (23x33 cm) pan with parchment paper. Sprinkle on chopped pecans. In a heavy saucepan, melt the butter. Add brown sugar and, stirring constantly over medium heat, bring mixture to a boil. Maintaining the boil, stir constantly for 6 minutes, then pour the mixture over the pecans. Sprinkle with chocolate chips. Allow chips to melt, then spread to make a chocolate layer. Cool in fridge or freezer until firm, then break into pieces. Makes a great gift.

Molasses Popcorn Balls

½ cup	corn syrup	125 ml	1 tsp	vinegar	5 ml
½ cup	molasses	125 ml	2 tbsp	butter	30 ml
¼ tsp	salt	1 ml	6 cups	popped corn	1.5 L

Combine corn syrup, molasses, salt and vinegar in saucepan and cook until a little syrup forms a hard ball when plunged into cool water. Stir carefully while cooking to prevent burning. Remove from heat and add butter, stirring only enough to mix. Slowly pour the cooked syrup over the popped corn and mix well. With greased hands, shape mixture into balls. Can be wrapped in plastic wrap and tied with ribbons to suit the occasion.

Caramel Popped Corn

16 cups	popped corn	4 L	¾ cup	brown sugar	175 ml
1¼ cups	white sugar	300 ml	1 tsp	vanilla	5 ml
1 cup	boiling water	250 ml			

Heat white sugar in heavy saucepan, stirring continuously, until sugar melts and turns light brown. Gradually add hot water, stirring until sugar is completely melted. Add brown sugar. Stir over slow heat until sugar is melted. Cook and stir until the soft-ball stage. Add vanilla. Place popped corn in two large bowls. Pour syrup over popped corn. Stir well to coat. Turn mixture out onto greased cookie sheets. Break into pieces. May be wrapped with plastic wrap.

Baked Caramel Popcorn

2 cups	brown sugar	500 ml	½ tsp	baking soda	2 ml
1 cup	butter	250 ml	1 tsp	vanilla	5 ml
½ cup	corn syrup	125 ml	1 cup	popcorn kernels	250 ml
1 tsp	salt	5 ml			

Pop corn as directed on package. Melt butter; stir in brown sugar, syrup and salt. Bring to a boil, stirring constantly, then let boil for 5 minutes, without stirring. Remove from heat and stir in baking soda and vanilla. Gradually pour over popcorn, mixing well. Turn into two large shallow pans. Bake at 250F (120C) for 1 hour, stirring every 15 minutes. Remove from oven, cool and break apart.

Basic Fondant

1 cup	water	250 ml	¹⁄₁₆ tsp	cream of tartar	0.25 ml
3 cups	sugar	750 ml			

Place water in a heavy saucepan and bring to a boil. Add sugar and stir until dissolved. Return to heat and shake in cream of tartar. Stir at once. Cover for 2-3 minutes so that the steam washes the crystals from the sides of the saucepan. Uncover and cook, without stirring, to the soft-ball stage. Remove from heat, and pour syrup onto a platter sprinkled with ice-cold water. Do not scrape pan. Let the syrup cool on the platter until it holds a thumbprint for a moment. Work the hardening syrup with a spatula, lifting the edges toward the centre. When the syrup becomes opaque, knead it well with your hands. After kneading fondant, place it in an airtight container to rest for a day or up to a week. To use in other recipes, place as much as you need in the top of a double boiler and heat over hot water until it is soft enough to shape. Fondant can be tinted as desired, rolled into small pieces and dipped in chocolate to make candies.

The Great Nova Scotia Cookbook

Chocolate Fudge Fondant

4 1-oz squares	chocolate	4x30 g		⅔ cup	basic fondant	150 ml
				3 tbsp	butter	45 ml
2 tbsp	corn syrup	30 ml		2 tsp	vanilla	10 ml
¾ cup	milk	175 ml		¼ tsp	salt	1 ml
2 cups	sugar	500 ml				

Finely cut chocolate and put in a saucepan. Add corn syrup, milk and sugar. Mix well. Cook slowly until sugar dissolves. Continue to cook until the soft-ball stage: 238F (114C). Stir occasionally, while cooking. When done, remove from heat. Add butter, and set aside until lukewarm. Add vanilla and fondant. Beat until mixture is no longer glossy and is the right consistency to mold. Press into a pan, and cut into squares or roll into balls. Balls may be filled with dried fruit or small pieces of fondant flavoured with almond, peppermint or coconut.

Sweet Hearts

½ cup	butter or margarine	125 ml		3 cups	desiccated coconut	750 ml
2 cups	icing sugar	500 ml		1 tsp	vanilla	5 ml
3 tbsp	cream	45 ml			pink food colouring	

Melt butter in a saucepan. Remove from heat and stir in cream, icing sugar and vanilla. Add coconut. Mix in food colouring to make a medium pink. Shape into 1-inch balls, flatten, and cut or mold into a heart shape. A silver dredge may be placed in the centre. Keep in the refrigerator, uncovered, to dry. No cooking is required. Use within a few hours.

Penuche

3 cups	brown sugar	750 ml	2 tbsp	butter		30 ml
¼ tsp	salt	1 ml	1 tsp	vanilla		5 ml
1 cup	cream	250 ml	1-1½ cups	nutmeats		250-375 ml

Dissolve first 3 ingredients in a heavy saucepan. Stir well until sugar dissolves. Place over heat and stir until boiling. Continue to boil, without stirring, to the soft-ball stage: 234F (112C). Remove candy from heat and add butter. Cool to 110F (43C). Beat until smooth and creamy. Add vanilla and nutmeats. Pour in buttered pan and cut in squares.

Potato Candy

½ cup	potato, cooked and put through ricer	125 ml	1 lb	icing sugar	500 g
			1 cup	desiccated coconut	250 ml
2 tbsp	butter	30 ml	1 tsp	vanilla	5 ml

Blend potato and butter, vanilla, and coconut, and work in enough icing sugar to make a thick consistency. Press into a pan. Chill and cut into squares. A few well-drained, cut-up cherries or walnuts may be added to the tops.

Blind Dates

⅓ cup	peanuts, whole	75 ml		3 tbsp	granulated sugar	45 ml
30	California dates, slit on one side	30				

Stuff 2 or 3 peanuts into each date or instead of peanuts, try walnut pieces. Stuff in as much as the date will hold. Press dates closed. Roll in sugar or dip in a soft icing flavoured with vanilla. Roll in desiccated coconut. Place on a rack to set, and store in an airtight container, separating each layer of dates with wax paper. If sugar melts, re-roll in sugar just before serving.

Corn Flake Caramels

1 10½-oz can	condensed milk	300 ml		6	large milk chocolate bars	6
1 9-oz box	Corn Flakes	300 g				

Boil an unopened can of milk for 2½ hours the night before making this recipe. Do not open can until the next day. Crush corn flakes. Melt chocolate and pour over crumbs. In small candy cups, layer chocolate crumbs; add a spoonful of caramelized milk and top with more chocolate crumbs. Pat gently. Chill until firm. Baker's semi-sweet chocolate can be substituted for ½ of the chocolate bars.

Molasses Taffy Candy

We used to have great fun at Hallowe'en when all of the neighbour's children came in for a taffy pull. The whole house had to be cleaned the following day. We would always say, "never again!"

½ cup	molasses	125 ml		¼ tsp	cream of tartar	1 ml
1½ cups	sugar	375 ml		4 tbsp	butter	60 ml
½ cup	water	125 ml		⅛ tsp	baking soda	0.5 ml
1½ tbsp	vinegar	22 ml				

In a heavy saucepan, stir molasses, sugar, water and vinegar together over heat until mixture starts to boil, then add cream of tartar. A little vanilla can be added if desired. Return to a boil. When a test piece turns hard in cold water, add butter and soda. Stir, remove from heat and cool; then pull with buttered hands until it turns a light golden colour. Pull into twisted strands and cut into bite-size pieces. Wrap in wax paper, twist ends and store in a covered container.

White Chocolate Truffles

1½ lb	white chocolate, chopped	750 g		1 tbsp	orange liqueur	15 ml
1 10½-oz can	sweetened condensed milk	300 ml			coconut, finely shredded, if desired	

Melt 1 lb (500 g) of the white chocolate with the sweetened condensed milk. Remove from heat and stir in liqueur. Chill 3 hours or until firm. Shape into 1-inch (2.5 cm) balls. Place on waxed paper. Chill until firm. Melt remaining white chocolate. Dip chilled truffles in melted chocolate and roll in coconut, if desired. Chill. Makes approximately 5 dozen truffles.

Christmas Pudding Candy

This is an old recipe that appeared in a Watkins' cookbook back in the 1920s. My mother made the candy every year and stored it in a large crock. It was always made early so that it could "ripen" for two weeks. It is different but really tasty.

1 tbsp	butter, heaping	15 ml		1 lb	figs, chopped coarsely in blender	500 g
3 cups	white sugar	750 ml				
1 cup	light cream	250 ml		1 lb	raisins (may be cut up)	500 g
1 tsp	vanilla	5 ml				
1 lb	dates, pitted and chopped coarsely in blender	500 g		1 lb	coconut, shredded	500 g
				2 cups	nuts, chopped	500 ml

In a saucepan, melt butter. Stir in sugar, cream and corn syrup. Heat to soft-ball stage: 234-240F. Beat until creamy. Stir in vanilla, fruit, nuts and coconut until well mixed. Shape into rolls, and roll in coconut. Wet cotton cloths such as old napkins, cup towels or pieces of old linen about 15-inches (37.5 cm) square. Place rolls of candy on wet cloths and wrap. Wrap rolls in wax paper. Store, preferably in a crock, and leave at least two weeks to ripen. Mom always used walnuts but pecans are good too.

The candy may appear wet after a few days. Don't worry, it will dry out at the end of the ripening time. Keep cold.

Chocolate Almond Crunch

1 cup	butter	250 ml
2 cups	light brown sugar	500 ml
⅓ cup	water	75 ml
½ lb	almonds, unblanched, chopped	250 g

½ lb	semi-sweet chocolate, melted	250 g

Roast almonds at 350F (175C).

Cook butter, sugar and water together to hard-crack stage: 300F (149C). Remove from heat and stir in almonds. Pour onto a buttered 9x14-inch (23x35.5 cm) cookie sheet. When cool, spread with half the melted chocolate. Let chocolate harden and remove the block of candy from the pan. Turn over and spread with the remaining chocolate. Cool and break into pieces. Makes approximately 1½ lb (675 g).

· PRESERVES ·

· Best ·

· Traditional ·

· Trendy ·

Blackberry Jam

Put as many well-washed blackberries as you want in a kettle and cook over low heat until soft; they will release their juices as they get hot. When berries have reached a boil, remove from heat. Place in a strainer and force pulp through so that most of the seeds are separated from the juice. To each cup (250 ml) of strained berries, add ½ cup (125 ml) of sugar. Return to heat and boil for 25 minutes. Remove from heat. Stir frequently to remove skum. Pour into sterilized jars and seal.

Grape Jam

This is a delicious jam.

Wash and stem Concord grapes. Press pulp from skins. Cook pulp for 10 minutes and put through sieve to remove seeds. Place skins in a blender and process just long enough to break up into small pieces. Add skins to sieved pulp. Measure pulp and skins mixture and bring to a boil, uncovered, for about 10 minutes until skins are tender. Measure sugar, using ⅔ cup (150 ml) sugar to each 1 cup (250 ml) pulp. Add sugar and return to a boil. Boil to jam stage, about 20 minutes, stirring frequently. Pour into hot sterilized jars. Seal with paraffin and cover tightly.

Black Currant Jam

5 cups	black currants	1.25 L	½ bottle fruit pectin liquid	½
7½ cups	sugar	1.875 L		

Wash and stem currants. Crush in a blender, mixer, or fruit press. Measure into a saucepan and stir in the sugar. Bring to a boil, stirring occasionally. Boil hard for 1 minute, then remove from heat and stir in pectin. Continue stirring and skimming for 3-4 minutes. Ladle into 10-12 jars and cover with paraffin.

Heavenly Strawberry Jam

2 cups	strawberries, fresh or frozen, crushed	500 ml		2 tbsp	orange rind, finely grated	30 ml
1 19-oz can	crushed pineapple, drained	540 ml		1 box	fruit pectin crystals	57 g
2 tbsp	lemon juice	30 ml		5 cups	sugar	1.25 L

Combine all ingredients except sugar in a large saucepan. Bring mixture to a full rolling boil and add sugar. Bring again to a full rolling boil. Boil hard 1 minute. Remove from heat. Stir and skim for 5 minutes. Ladle into hot, sterilized jars. Seal immediately. Makes 3 pints (1.5 L).

Rhubarb and Pineapple Jam

8 cups	rhubarb	2 L		4 cups sugar	1 L
2 cups	pineapple, chopped into ¼-inch (5 mm) cubes	500 ml			

Combine rhubarb and pineapple. Place over low heat and cook until juice begins to form. Then bring to a boil and boil uncovered for 15 minutes, stirring to prevent sticking. Add sugar; bring back to a boil. Boil uncovered to the jam stage (about 25 minutes), stirring frequently. Pour into hot, sterilized jars. Cool slightly and seal with tight-fitting covers. Makes about 5½ cups (1.375 L).

Gooseberry Jam

4 lb	gooseberries	2 kg	2 cups	water	500 ml
4 lb	sugar	2 kg			

Wash, top and tail gooseberries. Place berries and water in a large, heavy saucepan. Bring to a boil, then turn down heat and simmer gently for 15 minutes. Add sugar; stir and continue to cook gently. When sugar is completely dissolved, bring to a boil. Stir constantly, and boil for 10-15 minutes or until jam reaches setting point. Remove from heat, skim and fill sterilized jars. Cover tightly.

Grape and Pear Jam

8 cups	Concord grapes	2 L	10 cups	pears, chopped	2.5 L
3 cups	water	750 ml	4½ cups	sugar	1.125 L

Wash grapes, separating skins from pulp. Add 1½ cups (375 ml) water to skins and 1½ cups (375 ml) of water to pulp. Simmer skins and pulp separately until tender—about 15 minutes. Press pulp through a sieve to remove seeds. Add cooked grape skins, chopped pears and sugar to the sieved pulp. Bring to boil and boil uncovered until jam stage, about 45 minutes; stir frequently. Pour into hot, sterilized jars. Cool slightly and seal. Makes about 8½ cups (2.25 L).

Note: Grape skins may be ground coarsely before cooking, if desired.

Marion's Zucchini
Apricot Jam

This tastes great!

6 cups	zucchini, peeled and grated	1.5 L	¾ cup	pineapple, crushed, and juice	175 ml
6 cups	white sugar	1.5 L	½ cup	lemon juice	125 ml
			2 3-oz pkg pkg	apricot Jell-O	2 85 g pkg

Cook zucchini and sugar for 15 minutes; add pineapple, pineapple juice and lemon juice; continue cooking for 6 minutes. Remove from heat and add apricot Jell-O. You also may use strawberry, cherry or raspberry Jell-O. Stir well. Seal in sterilized jars. Makes 5 pints.

Black Currant Preserves

4 cups	black currants	1 L	3 cups	sugar	750 ml
¾ cup	water	175 ml	1	lemon, juiced	1

Remove the tops and tails of currants, then wash thoroughly. Combine currants with water in a saucepan and slowly bring to a boil. Cover, reduce heat and simmer gently until soft but not mushy. Add sugar and boil gently for 5-6 minutes until slightly thickened. Add lemon juice and cook for 2 minutes longer. Pour into jars and seal.

Ginger Preserves

Peel green ginger and cover with cold water for 15 minutes. Place on heat and boil until very tender. During this boiling time, change water twice. Remove from heat and drain. Weigh ginger and then place in ice cold water. Allow 1¼ lb (625 g) of sugar for every pound (500 g) of ginger. Place the required amount of sugar in a preserving kettle and wet it with 1 cup (250 ml) of water for every pound of sugar. Bring sugar mixture to a boil. Skim off any scum that rises to the surface. When syrup is free of scum, remove kettle from heat and let syrup become cold. Cut ginger into large pieces and lay them in cold syrup. Let stand for 24 hours. Remove ginger and place syrup on heat. Remove from heat. When syrup is lukewarm, place ginger back in syrup. Let stand for about 2 days. Remove ginger. Let syrup stand for about 2 weeks. Boil syrup again, then drop in ginger again. Distribute ginger and syrup among jars. Let stand for at least one month.

Pumpkin Preserve

There is no reason to discard your Halloween pumpkin.

To prepare a large, ripe pumpkin: Cut up pumpkin, removing pulpy centre and skin. Cut into 1½-inch (3.5 cm) cubes. Weigh. Place in colander and pour boiling water over the cubes. Measure an equal weight of sugar and put into kettle, layering the fruit and the sugar until all is used. Let stand at least 24 hours. The fruit will shrink. Bring slowly to a boil; when half cooked, add about 6 oranges, peeled, quartered and seeded, and the finely sliced rind of one orange. Add fewer oranges if the pumpkin is small. Cook slowly for several hours. It should be amber-coloured when done. Bottle while hot and seal.

Peach Conserve

This is a "jam" conserve, not a pickle.

3	medium oranges	3	9 cups	sugar		2.25 L
1 cup	water	250 ml	8 cups	peaches, peeled and cut into small cubes		2 L
1 6-oz bottle	maraschino cherries	170 g				

Slice oranges very thinly and then cut into quarters. Place in kettle and add water. Cover and simmer until tender, about 20 minutes. Meanwhile, drain cherries, reserving the juice, and cut cherries into quarters. To the cooked oranges, add peaches, sugar and the juice from the cherries and cook, uncovered, until thickened, about 30 minutes. Add cherries and boil for 5 minutes longer. Pour into sterilized jars. Seal with tight-fitting covers. Makes 10 cups (2.5 L).

Ann's Rhubarb Conserve

6 cups	rhubarb, finely chopped	1.5 L	1 cup	brown sugar	250 ml
			1 cup	raisins	250 ml
2 tbsp	water	30 ml	1 cup	dates, finely chopped	250 ml
1 cup	white sugar	250 ml			

Place rhubarb and water in a large saucepan over low heat. Cook until rhubarb is soft. Then add sugars, raisins and dates. Cook, stirring often, until mixture is soft and the ingredients are well combined. This will take about 1 hour. Pour into sterilized jars and seal.

Norma's Pumpkin Marmalade

12 cups	pumpkin,	3 L	3	large oranges (or 5 small ones), sliced thinly, seeds removed	3
8 cups	sugar	2 L			
2	large lemons, sliced thinly, seeds removed	2	2½ tsp	dry ginger	12 ml

Prepare pumpkin by removing peel, pulp and seeds. Cut pumpkin into small pieces. Two small pumpkins should give you 12 cups (3 L). Wash and dry the pumpkin pieces, and place in a large bowl. Add sugar. Cover and let stand overnight. Put orange and lemon slices in another bowl. Mix ginger into fruit, and cover with water. Cover bowl and let stand overnight. In the morning, place both mixtures into one large preserving pot. Cook over medium heat for 1½ to 2 hours, until it reaches desired thickness. While marmalade is still hot, ladle it into hot, sterilized jars. Seal tightly.

Ginger Orange Marmalade

3-5	Seville oranges	3-5	5 cups	sugar	1.25 L
⅛ tsp	baking soda	0.8 ml	½ bottle	fruit pectin liquid	85 ml
1½ cups	water	375 ml	8 oz	preserved ginger, sliced finely	250 g

Cut oranges into quarters. Peel. Slice off any white pith from peel, then finely slice the rind. Put into a saucepan with soda and water. Bring to a boil and simmer for 20 minutes, stirring frequently. Meanwhile, discard all white skin and seeds from orange sections, and chop fruit. Add pulp and juice to the contents of the saucepan, and simmer for 10 minutes.

Measure 3 cups (750 ml) of this mixture into a very large saucepan. Add sugar and mix thoroughly. Bring to a boil over high heat, stirring constantly. Let boil rapidly for 1 minute. Remove from heat; stir in pectin. Skim off foam, then add ginger. Makes about 4½ lb (about 2.25 kg).

Ginger Marmalade I

1-1¼ lb	mature ginger	500-625 g
6 cups	water	1.5 L
½ cup	fresh lemon juice, strained	125 ml

1 pouch	fruit pectin liquid	1
	sugar	

Pare or scrape off the skin of the ginger root, and grate only the tender outer layer. Grate enough to obtain 1⅓-1½ lightly packed cups (325-375 ml). Combine grated ginger with 6 cups (1.5 L) of water. Bring to a boil, and boil for 5 minutes. Drain. Add fresh cold water and repeat the boiling process, draining twice. Measure 3 cups (750 ml) of the ginger and liquid. (Spoon off surplus liquid and reserve as a drink.) In a large preserving kettle, combine the measured 3 cups of ginger with the lemon juice and sugar. Bring to a rolling boil over medium-high heat; boil for exactly 1 minute. Stir in the liquid fruit pectin, and return to another rolling boil. Boil for another minute and remove from heat. Stir marmalade for 5 minutes to cool, then ladle it into sterilized jars with two-piece lids. Follow canning directions, leaving ½ inch (1.3 cm) headspace. Process jars for 15 minutes in a boiling-water bath, again following canning directions. Remove from canner and seal. Cool and store.

Rhubarb Marmalade

3 lb	rhubarb, chopped	1.4 kg
2	large oranges, thinly sliced	2

2	lemons, thinly sliced	2
	sugar	

Chop and slice fruit at night, and add 3 cups (750 ml) water. Let stand over-night. Do not drain. The next morning, weigh the above mixture, and add the same amount in sugar. Place this mixture in a large preserving kettle, and boil until all is soft and thick. Stir frequently over low to medium heat for about 5 minutes. Pour into sterilized jars and seal.

Pear Medley Marmalade

2½ cups	ripe Bartlett pears, peeled, cored and finely chopped	625 ml		½ cup	maraschino cherries, finely chopped	125 ml
1	medium orange, peeled, sectioned, and finely chopped	1		5 cups	sugar	1.25 L
				1 box	fruit pectin crystals	57 g
1 can	crushed pineapple, drained	1				

Measure prepared fruit into a large saucepan. Stir fruit pectin crystals into fruit and mix well. Place saucepan over high heat and stir until mixture comes to a full boil. Stir in sugar. Continue to cook, stirring over high heat until mixture comes to a full, rolling boil. Boil hard for 1 minute, stirring constantly. Remove from heat. Stir and skim foam for 5 minutes to prevent floating fruit. Quickly pour marmalade into warm, sterilized jars, filling jars up to ¼ inch from rim. Seal while hot with new, sterilized two-piece lids. Makes 7 cups (1.75 L).

Pear Marmalade

10 cups	sliced pears	2.5 L		¼ cup	preserved or candied ginger, 2 tbsp (30 ml) grated ginger	50 ml
6 cups	sugar	1.5 L				
2	lemons, juiced with grated rind	2				

Place pears in preserving kettle with layers of sugar, lemon rind and juice. Let stand for 2 to 3 hours. Add ginger and bring to a boil, uncovered; stir frequently until thick and clear—about 45 minutes. Pour into hot sterilized jars. Cool slightly and seal. Yields about 6 cups.

Carrot Marmalade

2 lb	carrots	about 1 kg	7 cups	sugar	1.75 L
2	oranges, medium	2	1 pouch	fruit pectin liquid	1
4	lemons, medium	4		cinnamon or ginger (optional)	

Cook carrots until tender. Grate rind and dice pulp of the oranges. Squeeze juice from the lemons. Drain carrots, and chop finely. Mix chopped carrots with oranges and lemons. Measure 4 cups (1 l) of this mixture into a large saucepan. Add sugar (and cinnamon or ginger, if desired) to fruit in saucepan, and mix well. Cook over high heat, bringing the mixture to a full, rolling boil. Boil hard for 1 minute, stirring constantly. Remove from heat and immediately stir in the liquid pectin. Skim off foam with a metal spoon. Then stir and skim for 5 minutes to cool. Quickly pour into sterilized jars with new, two-piece covers. Makes about ten 8-oz (25 ml) jars.

Ginger-Apple Marmalade

5 oz	ginger root, peeled and sliced	140 g	5 lb	tart apples, cut into medium-size chunks	2.5 kg
2 cups	water	500 ml	5 lb	sugar	2.5 kg
3	lemons, juiced, with grated rind	3			

Let ginger simmer in the water for three hours, adding more water when necessary to keep it at the measure of 2 cups (500 ml). Remove ginger. Add the lemon juice and grated rind to the water. Add sugar, and boil syrup for about 10 minutes, stirring frequently. Add apple chunks, and cook until apples are tender and mixture is clear. Pour into sterilized jars and seal.

Seville Orange Marmalade

3 lb	Seville oranges, well washed	1.5 kg
6 lb	sugar	2.5 kg
2	lemons, well washed	2

| 11 cups | water | 2.75 L |
| 1 tbsp | molasses, if desired | 15ml |

Place 9 cups (2.25L) of water in a preserving kettle with the oranges. Cut lemons in half and squeeze, reserving juice in a covered jar in the refrigerator. Add lemon peels to kettle. Cover and bring to boil, then simmer for at least 1 hour (fruit should be soft when pierced with a tester). Remove from heat and let sit overnight.

In the morning, remove fruit from pan, leaving the liquid. Cut oranges in half, scoop the pulp and seeds from the oranges and lemons, into a saucepan. Add the remaining 2 cups (500ml) of water to the pith and seeds and boil for 10 minutes. Drain the pith through a sieve into preserving kettle. This liquid will provide the pectin for the marmalade to "set."

Cut the orange and lemon peel into slivers, thick or thin as desired. Add the peel to the preserving kettle. Add sugar, stir well and bring to a fast or hard boil, stirring almost constantly and watching closely to prevent scorching. It may take about 30 minutes for the marmalade to set. Remove kettle from heat and test a small portion by removing a spoonful to a saucer and placing it in the refrigerator. If it is ready, a skin will form over the marmalade after 5 minutes in the fridge. If it is ready, return kettle to stove, Add reserved lemon juice along with molasses. Return to a boil and remove from heat. Prevent fruit from floating by cooling marmalade before placing it in hot, sterilized jars.

Rhubarb Jelly

This is excellent on hot, buttered toast.

3½ cups	rhubarb juice	875 ml	2 pouches	fruit pectin liquid	2
7 cups	sugar	1.75 L			

To prepare rhubarb juice, cut about 2 lb (1 kg) rhubarb into 1-inch (2.5 cm) pieces, approximately 8 cups (2 L). Add 3 cups (750 ml) water and simmer until rhubarb is tender. Place fruit and juice in a jelly bag. Let drip until juice is extracted. Do not squeeze the bag or jelly will be cloudy. Measure 3½ cups (875 ml) juice into a large kettle. Add sugar and mix well. Place over heat and bring to a boil, stirring constantly. Stir in fruit pectin. Bring to a full rolling boil and boil hard for 1 minute, stirring constantly. Remove from heat and skim off foam. Pour into sterilized jars. Cover immediately with hot paraffin and tight-fitting lids. Makes 10 small jars.

Rose Hip Jelly

4 cups	rose hips, to make 2 cups (500 ml) juice	1 L	3½ cups	sugar	875 ml
			2	lemons, juiced	2
			1 pouch	fruit pectin liquid	1

Wash rose hips, removing blossom ends and stems. Place in a heavy saucepan and add 3 cups (750 ml) of water or enough to cover berries. Bring to a boil, reduce heat and simmer for 30-40 minutes. Place mixture in jelly bag and strain. You will need 2 cups (500 ml) juice (if there is not quite enough juice, add a little water). Place the juice in a heavy saucepan. Add sugar and lemon juice. Stir well. Place over high heat and bring to a boil, stirring constantly. Add fruit pectin and bring back to a hard boil. Boil 1 minute, stirring constantly. Remove from heat, skim and bottle in sterilized jars. Seal with wax and tight lids.

No-Cook Raspberry Freezer Jam

This recipe can be multiplied; be sure to increase all ingredients precisely.

2 cups	raspberry pulp	500 ml	4 cups	sugar	1 L
2 tbsp	lemon juice	30 ml	1 pouch	liquid fruit pectin	1

Sterilize glass jars with lids by boiling for 15 minutes. The capacity of each jar should be no more than 2 cups. Select well-ripened fruit with no blemishes. Mash, one layer at a time, with a potato masher. Using a liquid measuring cup, measure exactly 2 cups (500 ml) of fruit into a large bowl. Add sugar and let stand for 10 minutes. After 10 minutes stir in lemon juice and fruit pectin. Stir for three minutes to dissolve sugar crystals. Fill jars, leaving ¼ inch at the top to allow for expansion of fruit during freezing. Cover jars and let them stand at room temperature until set. This may take 24 hours. Store in the freezer. No-Cook Strawberry Jam may be made from the same recipe but strawberry jam requires only 1¾ cups (430 ml) of sugar for the 2 cups (500 ml) of fruit. Other ingredients and method remain the same.

No-Cook Raspberry Peach Jam

2 cups	raspberries	500 ml	⅓ cup	lemon juice	75 ml
1½ cups	peaches, fresh, peeled, pitted, and finely chopped	375 ml	7¼ cups	sugar	1.8 L
			2 pouches	fruit pectin liquid	2

Follow instructions and method for raspberry or strawberry no-cook jam, using the above ingredients. This is a delicious combination of fruit. Freeze.

No-Cook Tropical Strawberry Jam

1 cup	strawberries, crushed	250 ml	⅓ cup	lime juice	75 ml
			3 cups	sugar	750 ml
⅔ cup	pineapple juice, unsweetened	150 ml	1 pouch	fruit pectin liquid	1
			¼ cup	orange juice	50 ml

Crush strawberries, one layer at a time. Measure 1 cup (250 ml) into a large bowl. Add pineapple and lime juices. Add sugar and mix well. Let stand for 10 minutes. Stir in fruit pectin and orange juice. Continue to stir for 3 minutes until most of the sugar is dissolved. Pour into sterilized jars. Cover with tight lids and let stand for 24 hours. Store in the freezer. Yields 4 cups (1 L).

No-Cook "Light" Blueberry Rhubarb Jam

2¾ cups	blueberries, crushed	675 ml	3 tbsp	lemon juice	45 ml
			3¼ cups	sugar	800 ml
1¼ cups	rhubarb, finely chopped	300 ml	1 box	light fruit pectin crystals	57 g

Measure prepared fruit and lemon juice into a large bowl. Measure sugar and set aside. Combine fruit pectin crystals with ¼ cup (50 ml) of measured sugar. Gradually add to fruit, stirring well. Let stand for 30 minutes. Add remaining sugar and continue to stir for 3 minutes until most of the sugar is dissolved. Pour into clean jars or plastic containers. Cover with tight lids and let stand at room temperature until set (may take 24 hours). Store in the freezer. Jam may be stored in the refrigerator if used within 3 weeks. Makes 5¼ cups (1.3 L).

Marion's Zucchini Pickle

2 lb	small zucchini, sliced	1 kg	½ tsp	dry mustard	2 ml
2 lb	onions, thinly sliced	1 kg	1 tsp	celery seed	5 ml
¼ cup	coarse salt	50 ml	1 tsp	mustard seed	5 ml
2 cups	white vinegar	500 ml	1 tsp	turmeric	5 ml
1 cup	white sugar	250 ml			

Place onions and zucchini in a bowl and cover with water. Add salt and let stand for 1 hour, then drain and rinse. In a pot, combine remaining ingredients and bring to a boil. Pour over the zucchini and onions. Let stand for 1 hour, then bring to a boil and cook for 3 minutes. Pack in sterilized jars and seal. Makes 3 pints (1.5 L).

Bread and Butter Pickles

4 quarts	cucumber, sliced	4 L	5 cups	white sugar	1.25 L
6	medium onions	6	3 cups	white vinegar	750 ml
1	green pepper	1	1½ tsp	turmeric	8 ml
1	red pepper	1	1½ tsp	celery seed	8 ml
⅓ cup	coarse salt	75 ml	2 tbsp	mustard seed	30 ml

Use small or medium cucumbers. Wash well and slice thinly—do not peel. Slice the onion. Wash the peppers, remove stems and seeds and cut into thin strips. Layer the vegetables in a large crock or bowl. Sprinkle coarse salt over each layer. Mix a tray or two of ice cubes through the vegetables and cover with another tray of ice cubes. Let stand 3 hours. Rinse and drain vegetables well. Combine the sugar, vinegar, turmeric, celery seed and mustard seed and pour over drained pickles. Heat only to the boiling point. Ladle into sterilized jars. Store one month before using. Makes about 10 pints (5 L).

Bread and Butter Pickles II

6 cups	small cucumbers, thinly sliced	1.5 L	¼ tsp	ground cloves	1 ml
			1 tbsp	mustard seed	15 ml
1 lb	onions, sliced	500 g	1 tsp	celery seed	5 ml
¼ cup	coarse salt	50 ml	2 cups	cider vinegar	500 ml
2 cups	brown sugar	500 ml		cracked ice	
½ tsp	turmeric	2 ml			

Mix the cucumbers, onions and salt. Cover with cracked ice and mix well. Let stand 3 hours. Mix the remaining ingredients in a large stainless steel pot. Bring slowly to the boiling point and boil for 5 minutes. Drain the vegetables in a colander and rinse well with cold water. Drain. Add them to the hot syrup and heat to just below the boiling point. Spoon into sterilized jars and seal. Jars may be processed in a boiling water bath for 10 minutes. Follow canning instructions.

Margaret's Mustard Pickles

Margaret's pickles are among the very best.

1 cup	celery, diced	250 ml	4 cups	vinegar	1 L
2 cups	cauliflower, diced	500 ml	4 cups	sugar	1 L
2-3	onions, diced	2-3	4 tbsp	dry mustard	60 ml
12 cups	cucumbers, diced	3 L	1 tbsp	turmeric	15 ml
¾ cup	coarse salt	175 ml	1 cup	flour	250 ml

Peel, seed and dice cucumbers and place in a medium-size enamel roaster. Add salt and stir. Fill roaster ¾ full with water. Let sit overnight. Boil vinegar with 2 cups (500 ml) of sugar. Sift mustard, turmeric, flour and remaining sugar. Take half of the vinegar and add to the mustard mixture to form a smooth paste, then add the paste to the hot vinegar and sugar mixture. Boil until well thickened. Watch carefully to prevent scorching. Drain cucumbers well and add to the vinegar mixture along with the rest of the vegetables. Heat through and bottle in sterilized Mason jars. Makes approximately 9 pints.

Helene's Bread & Butter Pickles

28 cups	cucumbers, sliced	7 L	6 cups	sugar	1.5 kg
4 cups	onions, sliced	1 L	1 tsp	mustard seed	5 ml
1 cup	salt	250 ml	1 tsp	celery seed	5 ml
9 cups	water	2.25 L	1 tsp	turmeric	5 ml
3 pints	vinegar	1.5 L			

You can use any cucumbers you want but I prefer the pickling (dill) ones as they are small and uniform in size. Let cucumbers, onions, salt and water sit for 2 hours. To a large preserving kettle, add last five ingredients and bring to a boil. Add drained vegetables. Bring to the boiling point, but do not boil. Bottle in sterilized jars.

Easy Cucumber Pickles

Use the tiny cucumbers.

Wash cucumbers and pack into a crock. Mix the following ingredients and pour over cucumbers:

1 gallon	vinegar	4.5 L	2 cups	white sugar	500 ml
1 cup	dry mustard	250 ml	1 tsp	powdered alum	5 ml
1 cup	coarse salt	250 ml			

Mix all together and add to cucumbers. Stir well. Neither cooking nor heating is required. Place a cover on the crock and use the pickles as needed. Store in a cold place. Always use coarse salt—sometimes called "pickling salt," for pickling.

Alum may be purchased at a drug store; it is sometimes powdered, but may also be available in large, crystallized pieces. Use a stainless steel or enamel bowl for pickling (aluminum pots will discolour the pickles). Use a spoon when removing seeds from large cucumbers. Turn the "bowl" of the spoon upside down, and scoop downwards to remove seeds and pulp.

Nine Day Pickles

My mother's recipe—very easy.

6 quarts	basket gherkins or large cucumbers, cut into pieces	6 L

⅔ cup	coarse salt	150 ml

Wash and drain cucumbers and cover with boiling water and salt. Let stand overnight. In the morning, drain and dry.

Make syrup of:

½ gallon	cider vinegar	2.27 L
4 tbsp	dry mustard	60 ml
4 tbsp	sugar	60 ml
3 tbsp	coarse salt	45 ml

1 cup	whole mixed pickling spices	250 ml
1 piece	alum, walnut-sized	1

Place syrup ingredients in a large kettle (not aluminum). Heat and bring to boil. Remove from heat and cool. Pack drained, dry cucumbers into a large crock. Add cooled syrup to cucumbers in crock. For the next nine days add 1 scant cup (250 ml) of sugar per day until 3 lb (1.5 kg) of sugar have been used. Stir well. Store in a cool place. No need to seal. Use pickles out of the crock as needed. Keep crock covered.

Mustard Ripe
Cucumber Pickle

10 cups	ripe cucumber, peeled and diced	2.5 L

1½ cups	onion, coarsely chopped	375 ml
2 tbsp	coarse salt	30 ml

Combine the vegetables with the salt and let stand 1 hour. Drain thoroughly. Cook gently in about 2 cups (500 ml) of water until tender—10-15 minutes. Drain thoroughly. Make the following mustard sauce:

3 cups	vinegar	750 ml
2 cups	brown sugar	500 ml
½ cup	flour	125 ml
¼ cup	dry mustard	50 ml

1 tbsp	celery seed	15 ml
1 tsp	turmeric	5 ml
	coarse salt, to taste	

Mix brown sugar, flour, mustard, turmeric and salt. Make a thin paste with some of the vinegar. Heat remaining vinegar and celery seed to the boiling point. Slowly add hot vinegar to the mustard paste, blending well. Return to heat to cook until thickened, about 5 minutes. Add drained, cooked vegetables to the mustard sauce and bring to a boil. Pour into hot, sterilized jars and seal. Makes about 8 cups.

Mustard Pickles

A must for year-round enjoyment.

3 quarts	cucumber, peeled, seeded and cut into chunks	3.42 L		1	sweet green pepper, cut into chunks	1
5 lb	silver skin onions, peeled	2.25 kg		1	sweet red pepper, cut into chunks	1
1	cauliflower, cut into chunks	1		½ cup	coarse salt	125 ml

Layer vegetables in a large pot, sprinkling each layer with coarse salt. Cover with 6 quarts (6 L) of cold water and leave to sit overnight. Drain well in the morning. In a large saucepan, combine:

¾ cup	flour	175 ml		1 tbsp	turmeric	15 ml
4 tbsp	dry mustard	60 ml		4 cups	white sugar	1 L
1 tsp	ginger	5 ml				

Mix well and add:

3½ cups	white vinegar	875 ml

Stir until smooth. Simmer on low heat until thick. Pour over vegetables and mix well. Bring to a slow boil (it will take about 45 minutes to reach this point), then simmer for 20 minutes. Bottle when hot. Makes about 14 pint-size jars. Note: If cucumbers are small and tender, they do not need peeling. Seeds must be removed. If a more tart pickle is desired, use 3 cups (750 ml) sugar; cider vinegar may be used instead of white vinegar.

Polish Dill Pickles

1 quart	vinegar	1 L	2 cups	sugar	500 ml
1 pint	water	500 ml	½ cup	coarse salt	125 ml

Boil vinegar, water, sugar and salt. In each jar place 2 slices onion. Half-fill each jar with cucumber slices. Add 2 more onion slices and a sprig of dill. Fill up jar with cucumber slices. Top the jar with dill. Cover with syrup and seal.

Dill Pickles with Salt

19-20 cups	water, boiled	4.75 -5 L	1 cup	coarse salt	250 ml

Place 2 sprigs of dill, 1 bay leaf and 1 tsp (5 ml) pickling spice in each jar. Fill jar with cucumber. Put more dill on top. Mix water and salt and pour brine over cucumbers and seal. Keep at room temperature for 3 days. Store in refrigerator or cold room.

Dills

20 cups	water, boiled	5 L	1 cup	coarse salt	250 ml
1 cup	vinegar	250 ml			

Prepare jars and place dillweed to taste in each jar. Fill jars with small cucumbers. Mix together water, vinegar and salt to make brine. Fill jars with hot brine. Seal. Place jars in hot water (not boiling) until cucumbers change colour.

Icicle Pickles

30	cucumbers, about 6-inches long	30	9 cups	vinegar	2.25 L
9 cups	sugar	2.25 L	¾ cup	coarse salt	175 ml

Cover the cucumbers with ice water and let stand overnight. Drain and pack upright in sterilized Mason jars. Combine the vinegar and sugar with 3 cups (750 ml) of water in a pot. Boil for 3 minutes, then add the salt. Stir well; pour over cucumbers, leaving ¼ inch (5 mm) headspace. Close the jars according to canning instructions and process in a boiling water bath for 10 minutes.

Dill Pickles I

20 cups	water, boiling	5 L	50	small cucumbers	50
1 cup	pickling salt	250 ml		fresh dill sprigs	

Dissolve salt in boiling water. Place large sprig of dill in bottom of each sterlized jar. Fill jar with cucumbers. Place more dill on top.

Pour brine over cucumbers and seal with glass covers. Keep at room temperature for three days. Then keep in refrigerator.

Dill Pickles II

50	small cucumbers, about 3-inches long	50	¾ cup	coarse salt	175 ml
				fresh dill sprigs	
1 quart	cider vinegar	1 L		garlic cloves, if desired	

Scrub cucumbers and pack into the sink. Cover with cold water and let stand overnight. Drain and pack cucumbers into hot, sterilized jars. Combine vinegar and salt with 2 quarts (2 L) water in a pot and bring to the boiling point. Pour over the cucumbers, leaving ¼ inch (5 mm) headspace. Add a sprig or two of fresh dill to each jar. Close the jars according to canning instructions and process in a boiling water bath for 15 minutes.

Dill Beans

Important: Store in refrigerator no longer than 3 weeks!

2 lb	green beans, fresh	1 kg	2 tbsp	coarse salt	30 ml
4 cloves	garlic	4	4 cups	white vinegar	1 L
4 sprigs	dill, fresh	4	4 cups	water	1 L
1 tsp	red pepper flakes	5 ml			

Trim beans and divide among four 16-oz (500 ml) sterilized jars. To each jar add 1 clove garlic, 1 sprig dill and ¼ tsp (1 ml) red pepper flakes. Bring salt, vinegar, and water to a boil; pour over beans and seal. Store in refrigerator for 2 weeks before using. Use within a week. These are good calorie counters for diabetics.

Pickled Mustard Beans

Cut about 1 peck (12-15 lb) (6-7.5 kg) of yellow beans into small pieces. Place in a stainless steel or an enameled pot, with ⅓ cup (75 ml) coarse salt and enough water to cover. Boil for about ½ hour or until just tender. Remove from heat and drain thoroughly. In a large stainless steel or enameled pot, pour 6 cups (1.8 L) vinegar. Add 3 lb (1.8 kg) sugar. Stir well and let come to a boil.

Mix the following ingredients with a little cold vinegar:

1 cup	flour	250 ml	½ cup	mustard, dry	125 ml
2 tsp	turmeric	10 ml	2 tsp	celery seed	10 ml

Add to the boiling mixture. When sauce has thickened add drained beans and bring to a boil for about 5 minutes. Watch and stir constantly. Bottle and seal in sterilized jars.

Note: Do not use aluminum pots for this recipe.

Pickled Beets

Definitely the best!

Trim and wash young beets. Cover and boil until tender. Cool and peel. Slice and pack in sterilized jars.

For each quart (1 L) jar of sliced beets, prepare the following syrup:

1 cup	vinegar	250 ml	2 cups	brown sugar	500 ml

Bring the above ingredients to a boil and pour over prepared beets. Add 4-6 whole cloves to the top of each jar. Seal tightly.

Note: For approximately 10 lb (5 kg) beets, try 4 cups (1 L) vinegar and 8 cups (2 L) brown sugar for the syrup.

Cabbage Pickle Relish

5 lb	cabbage, finely chopped	2.5 kg
6	medium onions	6
2	green peppers, finely chopped	2
2	red peppers, finely chopped	2

½ cup	coarse salt	125 ml
¾ cup	mustard seeds	175 ml
2 tbsp	celery seeds	30 ml
4 cups	sugar	1 L
	vinegar	

Mix the vegetables in a bowl; add the salt. Stir well and let stand for 24 hours. Rinse and drain well. Add mustard seeds, celery seeds and sugar; mix well. Add enough vinegar to cover. Pack into sterilized jars. Store in a cool place. Makes about 9 pints (4.5 L).

Margaret's Small Green Tomato Relish

This is very tasty.

8 lb	small green tomatoes	4 kg
½ cup	coarse salt	125 ml
1 quart	vinegar	1 L

3 lb	sugar	1.5 kg
1 tbsp	whole cloves	15 ml
3	cinnamon sticks	3

Cut ends off tomatoes and let stand overnight. In the morning, cover with water; add salt and boil until tender, about 20 minutes. Drain. Make a syrup by boiling vinegar and sugar. Put cloves and cinnamon sticks in a spice bag. Add to syrup and boil for 5 minutes. Add tomatoes and boil again for 2-3 minutes. Let stand for 2 days and bring to a boil again. Ladle into sterilized jars and seal. Makes 6-6½ pints.

Chopped Pickle Relish

Well worth the extra chopping.

3 quarts	green tomatoes	3 L		1 tsp	dry mustard	5 ml
1 quart	ripe tomatoes	1 L		1 tsp	pepper	5 ml
3 bunches	celery, small	3 bunches		1 tsp	ground spices, as desired (cloves and cinnamon are good)	5 ml
3	large onions	3				
3	red peppers	3		2 tsp	celery seed	10 ml
3	green peppers	3		1 cup	coarse salt	250 ml
2 lb	brown sugar	1 kg		4 quarts	cold water	4 L
3 quarts	vinegar	3 L				

Put all vegetables, except ripe tomatoes, through a chopper. Remove skin from ripe tomatoes and cut into chunks. Make brine by mixing salt and cold water. Cover vegetables (except tomatoes) with brine and let stand overnight. Drain well. In a large preserving kettle, make syrup by heating vinegar, brown sugar and spices. Stir well and add all vegetables to the hot syrup. Bring to the boiling point and cook for 15-20 minutes, stirring frequently. Seal while hot.

Rhubarb Relish

2 quarts	rhubarb, cut into 1-inch pieces	2 L		2 tsp	coarse salt	10 ml
				1 tsp	allspice	5 ml
2 quarts	onions, chopped	2L		2 tsp	cinnamon	10 ml
4 cups	cider vinegar	1 L		1 tsp	cloves	5 ml
8 cups	brown sugar	2 L		½ tsp	pepper	2 ml

Combine all ingredients and boil gently until fairly thick. Stir often and watch carefully to prevent scorching. Pour into hot, sterilized jars and seal.

Indian Relish

6	large cucumbers	6		3 lb	brown sugar	1.5 kg
15	large green tomatoes	15		2 tsp	black pepper	10 ml
15	large onions	15		2 tsp	dry mustard	10 ml
3	red peppers	3		2 tsp	celery seed	10 ml
1 cup	coarse salt	250 ml			vinegar	

Put cucumbers, green tomatoes, onions and red peppers through a chopper; cover with coarse salt and leave overnight. In the morning, drain and add brown sugar, black pepper, dry mustard and celery seed. Place all in preserving kettle with enough vinegar to cover completely. Cook until onions are soft. Place in sterilized jars and seal.

Corn Pepper Relish

A good use for "older" corn.

18	ears of corn	18		2 tbsp	dry mustard	30 ml
4	onions	4		2 cups	sugar	500 ml
2	green peppers	2		1 cup	flour	250 ml
¼ cup	coarse salt	50 ml		1 tsp	turmeric	5 ml
2 quarts	vinegar	2 L				

Cut corn from cob; chop onions and peppers to the size of corn kernels. Cook vegetables in 1 quart (1 L) of the vinegar for 15 minutes; begin timing when the mixture begins to boil. Mix together salt, mustard, sugar, flour and turmeric. Add gradually to the remaining vinegar and let boil. Add this mixture to the corn mixture, making sure to stir almost constantly to prevent scorching. Heat through and bring to a boil. Remove from heat, pour into sterilized jars and seal.

Corn Relish

18	ears of corn	18
1	medium cabbage	1
4	celery stalks	4
5	large onions	5
2	green peppers	2
1	red pepper	1

2 quarts	vinegar	2 L
4 cups	sugar	1 L
4 tbsp	mustard, more if desired	60 ml
1 tbsp	turmeric	15 ml
½ cup	coarse salt	125 ml

Remove seeds from peppers. Cut corn from cobs. Chop cabbage, celery, onions and peppers (in food chopper, if desired). Place all ingredients, except corn, in a large preserving kettle. Cook together for 30 minutes. Add corn and cook for 15 minutes longer. Stir almost constantly. Pour into sterilized jars and seal while hot.

Elda's Mustard Relish

You could call Elda "the Queen of Pickle-Makers."

After cutting into small pieces, measure the following ingredients:

1½ quarts	cucumbers, peeled and seeded	1.5 L
1 quart	onions	1 L

1 bunch	celery	1
1	red pepper, seeded	1
1	green pepper, seeded	1

Sprinkle with pickling salt and let stand for about 4 hours. Drain well. Pour 1 quart (1 litre) of vinegar into a large preserving kettle, and heat to boiling. Measure the following ingredients, blend together and add to vinegar:

1 tsp	turmeric	5 ml
3 tsp	dry mustard	15 ml
¾ cup	flour	175 ml

1 tbsp	salt	15 ml
3-4 cups	sugar	750 ml-1 L

Stir well and reheat to boiling. Add vegetables. Simmer for a few minutes, stirring frequently. Pour into sterilized jars and seal tightly.

Zucchini Relish

2	medium zucchini	2	5 cups	sugar	1.25 L
1	cauliflower	1	1½ tsp	turmeric	8 ml
4	onions	4	1½ tsp	mustard seeds	8ml
2	green peppers	2	3 cups	vinegar	750 ml
				salt	

Finely chop vegetables. Sprinkle with salt and let stand for 1½ hours. Rinse and drain. Place vegetables and remaining ingredients in a stock pot. Cook until cauliflower is tender. Store in sterilized canning jars.

Hot Dog Relish

Rarely an autumn goes by that I don't make a batch of this relish. The flavour is wonderful with burgers or hot dogs and on sandwiches. Truly, it is one of the best relishes.

8	large cucumbers, seeded but not peeled	8	2 lb	onions	1 kg
			2	red peppers	2

Grind all vegetables and soak overnight in a brine of ½ cup (125 ml) coarse salt and ½ gallon (2 L) hot water. The next day, drain well—mixture must be pressed to remove last trace of brine. Pour 1 quart of white vinegar into a large enamel or stainless steel pot. Place on heat; when hot add:

6 cups	white sugar	1.5 L	2 tbsp	mustard seed	30 ml
1 tbsp	turmeric powder	15 ml	1 tbsp	celery seed	15 ml

Bring to a boil and add vegetables. Let simmer over low heat after mixture has boiled. Watch carefully, it burns easily. Pack into sterilized bottles. Use paraffin to seal and cover tightly.

Onion Sauce Relish

| 7 | medium cucumbers, peeled | 7 | 6 | large onions | 6 |

Grind cucumbers and onions until fine. Sprinkle with salt and let stand for 2 hours. Drain well. Make sauce from the following ingredients:

3 cups	vinegar	750 ml	½ cup	flour, mixed with 1 tsp (5 ml) ginger	125 ml
1 cup	hot water	250 ml			
2½ cups	sugar	625 ml	¾ tsp	turmeric	3 ml

Boil sauce for 10 minutes. Add drained cucumbers and onions. Cook until tender, stirring constantly. Bottle and seal.

Cranberry-Ginger Relish

A variation on cranberry sauce.

| 2½ cups | cranberry sauce | 625 ml | 2 tbsp | candied ginger | 30 ml |
| 2 tbsp | orange rind | 30 ml | | | |

Cut ginger and orange rind into very fine strips. Combine with cranberry sauce. Let stand to allow flavours to blend. Bottle and seal.

Garden Relish

3 cups	corn, cut from cob	750 ml		½ cup	sweet red pepper, chopped	125 ml
2 cups	cucumber, coarsely chopped	500 ml		2 cups	onions, chopped	500 ml
2 cups	ripe tomatoes, coarsely chopped	500 ml		1½ tbsp	coarse salt	22 ml
				1 tbsp	dry mustard	15 ml
2 cups	celery, coarsely chopped	500 ml		1½ tsp	turmeric	8 ml
				2½ cups	vinegar	625 ml
½ cup	green pepper, chopped	125 ml		1¼ cups	brown sugar	300 ml

Mix ingredients in a large preserving kettle. Simmer uncovered until thickened (about 50 minutes), stirring frequently. Pour into hot, sterilized jars and seal. Makes about 8 cups.

Cucumber Relish

7	large cucumbers	7		3 cups	white sugar	750 ml
4	large onions	4		½ cup	flour	125 ml
4 tbsp	coarse salt	60 ml		2 tbsp	turmeric	30 ml
2½ cups	vinegar	625 ml		¼ tsp	cayenne pepper	1 ml
2 cups	boiling water	500 ml				

At night, peel cucumbers and onions. Grind in a food chopper. Sprinkle with coarse salt. Let stand overnight. Drain well in the morning and rinse with cold water to remove salt. Combine other ingredients and boil for 5 minutes to make sauce. Add cucumbers and onions to sauce and boil for 10 minutes. Stir often. Pour into sterilized jars and seal.

Gooseberry Relish

4 quarts	gooseberries	4 L	1½ tbsp	cinnamon	22 ml
4 lb	sugar, more if gooseberries are very tart	2 kg	1 tbsp	cloves	15 ml
			1 tbsp	allspice	15 ml
2 cups	cider vinegar	500 ml			

Wash and drain berries. Place in a large preserving kettle with remaining ingredients. Bring all to a boil. Reduce heat and simmer for 3 hours. Pour into sterilized jars and cover tightly.

Corn Cabbage Relish

20	large ears of fresh corn, cut	20	6 cups	vinegar	1.5 L
			1 cup	water	250 ml
6	medium green peppers	6	4 cups	sugar	1 L
6	medium red peppers	6	2 tbsp	dry mustard	30 ml
4	large onions, coarsely ground	4	2 tbsp	celery seed	30 ml
			2 tbsp	coarse salt	30 ml
1	medium cabbage, coarsely chopped	1	1 tbsp	turmeric	15 ml

In a large kettle, combine all ingredients. Simmer uncovered for 20 minutes, stirring frequently. Ladle hot relish into hot jars, leaving ¼-inch headspace. Adjust caps and follow canning instructions. Process for 15 minutes in a boiling water bath. Makes 16 pints (8 L).

Mustard Beet Relish

12 cups	beets, grated	3 L		2 tsp	white mustard seed	10 ml
1½ cups	sugar	375 ml		2 tbsp	dry mustard	30 ml
2 cups	vinegar	500 ml		3 tsp	salt	15 ml

Wash and cook beets in enough water to cover completely. Cool and remove skins. Grate beets on a coarse grater. Pack into sterilized jars. Mix remaining ingredients thoroughly and add to jars. Store in the refrigerator or a cool place.

Marion's Zucchini Relish

Marion Melanson lives in Greenwich, Kings County—the heart of vegetable country.

12 cups	zucchini, chopped	3 L		4 cups	white sugar	1 L
4	large onions, chopped	4		3 tbsp	cornstarch	45 ml
2	red peppers, chopped	2		2 tsp	celery seed	10 ml
2	green peppers, chopped	2		2 tsp	mustard seed	10 ml
⅓ cup	pickling salt	75 ml		2 tsp	turmeric	10 ml
3 cups	white vinegar	750 ml				

Combine vegetables with pickling salt and leave overnight. Drain and rinse. Combine remaining ingredients with vegetables and boil for 20 minutes. Place in sterilized jars and seal.

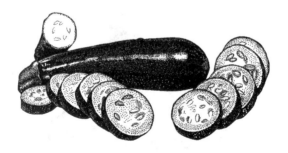

Spiced Crabapples

Serve with pork and ham or have one any time.

7 lb	crabapples	3.5 kg		¼ cup	whole cloves	50 ml
8 lb	sugar	4 kg		1	cinnamon stick	1
4 cups	vinegar	1 L				

Remove the blossom ends from crabapples but leave stems on. Wash and drain. Tie spices in bag (leaving a few whole cloves loose to remain in the syrup). Add to sugar and vinegar in a large boiling pan. Bring to a boil and add "crabs" pricked with a fork. Cook until tender but not broken. Remove spice bag and fill hot jars with hot fruit and syrup. Seal at once.

Spicy Peach Freezer Chutney

3 cups	peaches, prepared	750 ml		½ tsp	ground cloves	2 ml
1 tbsp	onion, grated	15 ml		½ tsp	cinnamon	2 ml
2 tbsp	crystallized ginger, finely sliced	30 ml		2 cups	sugar	500 ml
½ cup	raisins	125 ml		½ cup	brown sugar, firmly packed	125 ml
3 tbsp	vinegar	45 ml		1 box	light fruit pectin crystals	57 g
1 tsp	salt	5 ml				
1 tsp	allspice	5 ml				

Peel and pit peaches. Finely chop and measure 3 cups (750 ml) into bowl. Add onion, ginger, raisins, vinegar, salt and spices. Mix sugars in another bowl. In a small bowl combine pectin with ¼ cup (50 ml) of the sugar. Gradually add fruit pectin to fruit mixture, stirring vigorously. Set aside for 30 minutes, stirring frequently. Gradually stir in remaining sugar until dissolved. Pour into sterilized jars immediately. Cover. Let stand at room temperature until set. This may take 24 hours. Store in the freezer. Makes about five 8-oz (250 ml) jars.

Rhubarb Chutney

Come fall, anything that grows in a garden is apt to get into a pickle.

7 cups	rhubarb, cut into ½-inch pieces	1.75 L	1 tsp	cinnamon	5 ml
			¼ tsp	cloves	1 ml
1	large onion, sliced	1	¼ tsp	allspice	1 ml
			¼ tsp	cayenne pepper	1 ml
1 cup	vinegar	250 ml	1 tsp	whole pickling spices (tied in a cheesecloth bag)	5 ml
1¼ cups	sugar	300 ml			
¾ tsp	salt	3 ml			
1 tsp	ginger, ground	5 ml			

Combine onion, rhubarb and vinegar and cook uncovered for 20 minutes. Add remaining ingredients, and cook uncovered until the consistency is that of jam, about 40 minutes. Stir to prevent sticking. Pour into hot, sterilized jars. Makes about 3½ cups (925 ml).

Berry Red Chutney

2	medium apples, chopped	2	4½ cups	sugar	1.125 L
1	lemon, quartered	1	½ cup	water	125 ml
1 12-oz pkg	cranberries	340 g	¼ cup	brandy	50 ml
			1 box	fruit pectin crystals	57 g
½ cup	pecans, if desired	125 ml			
½ cup	raisins	125 ml			

In a food processor, process fresh fruit, until coarsely chopped. Add nuts and raisins. Thoroughly mix in sugar; let stand for 10 minutes. Mix water, brandy and pectin in a small saucepan. Bring to a boil and boil for 1 minute, stirring constantly. Stir into fruit; continue stirring for 3 minutes (a few crystals will remain). Pour into containers. Cover with lids. Let stand at room temperature until set (24 hours). Store in a refrigerator for up to 3 weeks or freeze.

The Great Nova Scotia Cookbook

Peach Chutney

An unusual and sweet accompaniment to grilled meats and curries, and a delicious spread on toast with cream cheese.

2	peaches, ripe	2
½ cup	sugar	125 ml
¼ cup	red onion, finely chopped	50 ml
2 tbsp	white vinegar	30 ml

2 tbsp	green pepper, finely chopped	30 ml
1 tsp	ginger, grated	5 ml
⅛ tsp	ground cloves	0.5 ml
½ tsp	turmeric	2.5 ml
	black pepper, to taste	

Blanch peaches for 30 seconds in boiling water; remove skins and pits and cut into slices. Combine with all other ingredients in a microwavable jar, leaving at least 1½ inches free above the peaches to prevent boil-over. Microwave on high for 7 minutes, stirring once. Seal tightly with a sterilized lid and refrigerate. Will keep up to 3 months. Makes about 1 cup (250 ml).

Cranberry Chutney

4 cups	cranberries	1 L
2	small oranges	2
1	lemon	1
2	apples, cored	2
1 cup	raisins	250 ml
1 cup	brown sugar	250 ml

½ tsp	ginger	2 ml
2 tbsp	candied ginger	30 ml
2 tbsp	onion, grated	30 ml
6 tbsp	sweet green pepper, chopped	90 ml

Grind cranberries, oranges, lemon, apples and raisins. Add remaining ingredients; mix well. Cover and store in the refrigerator. Will keep for a month. Makes about 3 pint jars (1.7 L).

Chow

Few people ever forget the smell of chow simmering on the kitchen stove. It fills the whole house and lingers for days. It is only a memory now for some of us, but what a great one. Some can even see Mom, near the kitchen table with a huge mound of green tomatoes, the onions and the tears.

15 lb	green tomatoes	7.5 kg	¾ cup	coarse salt	175 ml
5 lb	onions, peeled	2.5 kg	1-2 tsp	dry mustard	5-10 ml
2 quarts	vinegar, or less	2 L	¼ cup	mixed pickling spice, tied in cheescloth	
5 cups	granulated sugar	1.25 L			

Slice tomatoes and onions. Mix in ¾ cup coarse salt. Let stand overnight. In the morning, drain. Rinse and drain again. Place vegetables in a large preserving kettle. Add 2 quarts vinegar and 1 to 2 tsp (5-10 ml) of dry mustard. Cook for about 30 minutes. Meanwhile, make a spice bag by placing ¼ cup (50 ml) mixed pickling spice in piece of cheesecloth, and tying the four corners together. Add spice bag to centre of boiling mixture. Stir in sugar. Bring to boil, stirring frequently. Let simmer for about 2 hours. Fill hot, sterilized jars and seal.

Chow Chow

1 quart	green tomatoes	1 L	3 tbsp	turmeric	45 ml
6	onions	6	1 tbsp	allspice	15 ml
2	red peppers	2	1 tbsp	pepper	15 ml
3 tbsp	coarse salt	45 ml	1 tbsp	cloves, powdered	15 ml
2 quarts	cider vinegar	2 L	¼ cup	pickling spice, in a gauze bag	50 ml
5 cups	sugar	1.25 L			
4 tbsp	mustard seed	60 ml			

Chop the vegetables into small pieces. Cover with cold water and sprinkle with salt. Let stand overnight. Rinse and drain well. Combine vinegar, sugar, mustard seed, turmeric, allspice, pepper and cloves, and bring to a boil. Pour over the vegetables and cook until tender with the pickling spices hanging in the centre of the pot. Stir often. Ladle into sterilized jars. Makes about 8 pints (4 L).

Spiced Plums

Especially good with baked ham or cold beef. Good served over cream cheese or cottage cheese.

3½ lb	prune plums	1.75 kg	1½ tsp	ground cloves	7 ml
6 cups	sugar	1.5 L	½ tsp	salt	2 ml
1 tbsp	cinnamon	15 ml	1½ cups	white vinegar	375 ml

Cut plums in half. Remove stones. Cut each half into at least 8 pieces, so that skin will not appear in big pieces. Place in a large pot. Add remaining ingredients. Stir over medium-high heat until sugar dissolves. Bring to a boil, stirring occasionally, for about 5 minutes or until plums are mushy. Cool. Run through a food processor in batches to finely chop skin. Bring to a boil once more. Pour into hot, sterilized jars to within ¼ inch (6 mm) of top. Seal.

Apple Butter

We had a Wolf River apple tree in our old orchard. The fruit was beautiful, large and crimson in colour, but it was not a good apple for either baking or eating. Mom used them to make apple butter.

4-5 lb	apples, unpeeled, washed and quartered	2-2.5 kg	1 tsp	cloves	5 ml
			½ tsp	nutmeg	2 ml
	brown sugar		½ tsp	ginger	2 ml
2 tsp	cinnamon	10 ml	2 cups	apple cider	500 ml

Choose apples that are not very juicy. Cook apples in a small amount of water. Remove from heat and press through a sieve. Measure pulp into a heavy pot. For each cup of pulp, add ¾ cup (175 ml) brown sugar. Add spices and apple cider. Bring to a boil. Reduce heat and simmer until thick, at least 4 hours. Bottle in hot, sterilized jars and seal.

Peach Butter

4 lb	peaches	2 kg	½ tsp	allspice	2 ml
½ cup	sugar	125 ml		juice and grated	
2 tsp	cinnamon	10 ml		rind of 1 lemon	
1 tsp	cloves	5 ml			

Wash, peel and pit peaches. Place fruit in heavy saucepan. Cook and stir until soft. Remove from heat. Press fruit through a food press or sieve. Measure fruit: to every cup of sieved fruit add ½ cup (125 ml) sugar. Add spices and lemon juice. Cook and stir until mixture falls from a spoon in a sheet. Test it by placing a small amount in a saucer. If cooked, it will jell quickly. Remove from heat and pour into sterilized jars.

Freezing Fruit

Peaches

Choose firm, ripe fruit. Dip in boiling water for 1 minute, then plunge into cold water. Remove skin and pit, and slice in half. To prevent discolouration, add ¼ tsp (1 ml) powdered ascorbic acid (Vitamin C) to 4 cups (1 L) of cold syrup. Make syrup for peaches in the proportion of 1 cup (250 ml) sugar to 1½ cups (375 ml) water. Add sugar to water and stir to dissolve: then chill. Slice fruit directly into syrup in containers. Freeze.

Plums

Choose firm, mature fruit. Wash, halve and pit. Pack in cold, thin syrup to freeze. Make syrup in the proportion of 1 cup (250 ml) sugar to 2 cups (500 ml) water.

Strawberries

Choose firm, fully ripe berries. Berries can be whole, cut in quarters, sliced or mashed. They may be packed in dry sugar, using proportions of ½ cup (250 ml) sugar to 4 cups (1 L) whole berries or ⅔ cup (150 ml) sugar to 4 cups (1 L) crushed or cut-up berries. Strawberries can be frozen without sugar. They can also be frozen whole; place in a single layer on a cookie sheet—taking care to leave space between berries so that they will not clump together when removed from cookie sheet. Place in freezer bags or containers to store.

Blueberries, Gooseberries, Cranberries, Currants & Rhubarb

These berries may be frozen without sugar. It is convenient to divide fruit by measuring exact quantities of 1 cup (250 ml), 2 cups (500 ml), 3 cups (750 ml) etc. into plastic bags. Use these quantities in recipes. Pears do not freeze well.

A Note on Freezing Vegetables

Most vegetables and greens freeze very well. Follow freezing directions provided in freezing guides. For string beans, choose pencil-shaped beans. Do not freeze flat beans. Sliced broad beans freeze well. Asparagus, peas, spinach, whole kernel corn and corn on the cob freeze very well.

Green Tomato Mincemeat I

Orange, lemon and vinegar give this filling its uniqueness.

3 lb	green tomatoes, chopped in meat grinder	1.4 kg	½ cup	lemon juice	125 ml
			1 cup	suet	250 ml
			½ cup	vinegar	125 ml
3 lb	apples, chopped in meat grinder, save juice	1.4 kg	1 tsp	mace	5 ml
			1 tsp	nutmeg	5 ml
1 lb	raisins, washed and drained	500 g	1 tsp	cinnamon	5 ml
			1 tsp	cloves	5 ml
1 lb	currants, washed and drained	500 g	1 tsp	salt	5 ml
			4 cups	brown sugar	1 L
1	orange, chopped in meat grinder, save juice	1			

Chop tomatoes and drain. Cover with cold water and bring to a boil. Scald for 30 minutes. Drain. Chop apples and orange. Save as much juice from apples and orange as possible. Place the above ingredients in a large pot. Add raisins, currants, lemon juice, vinegar, mace, nutmeg, cinnamon, cloves, salt and brown sugar. Stir all well. Bring to a boil and simmer for 2-3 hours, until thick. During the last ½ hour, add suet. Keep in sterilized jars, sealed tightly. May be frozen. Use in pies or tarts.

Mincemeat

Who could imagine Christmas festivities without mincemeat pie? And there is really no better mincemeat than that made from venison.

8 cups	beef or venison, prepared	2 L		7 cups	brown sugar	1.75 l
1 tbsp	salt	15 ml		4 cups	apple juice (some may be saved from grinding apples)	1 L
12 cups	ground apples, unpeeled, cored and seeded	3 L		4 tsp	cinnamon	20 ml
				4 tsp	ground cloves	20 ml
4 cups	ground suet	1 L		2 tsp	nutmeg	10 ml
3 cups	seedless raisins	750 ml		2 tsp	allspice	10 ml
3 cups	currants	750 ml		2 cups	brandy, if desired	500 ml
4 cups	venison stock	1 L				

Prepare raw meat by cleaning and washing it carefully. Remove all traces of fat and skin. Place in a pot. Add salt and water to almost cover meat. Cook until meat is tender. Remove from pot and place in a pan to cool. Chill stock and discard fat. Strain stock and reserve to use in mincemeat. Meanwhile, remove meat from bones. Discard bones, fat and gristle. Break meat into pieces and place in a meat grinder. Do not grind too finely—it can become powdery. In the same grinder, grind the apples and collect the juice. Mix meat and apples in a large pot. Strain meat stock and apple juice through a fine sieve and add to meat-apple mixture. Add cleaned raisins and currants. Add cinnamon, cloves, nutmeg and allspice to brown sugar and mix well. Add this sugar-spice mixture to the meat and fruit and mix very well. Place pot on heat. Bring to boil, stirring constantly. Turn heat down and let simmer for an hour. Test the ingredients and add salt as desired. Finally, add suet, taking care that it is well distributed throughout the mincemeat. Simmer for 10-15 minutes. Remove from heat; add brandy if desired. Fill jars and seal. Keep cold or freeze. The mincemeat may appear too syrupy; when baked in a piecrust, however, the juice will give it a special flavour. When making pies, make pastry for double crusts. Avoid over-stuffing the pie plate with mincemeat; the pie should be slightly under-filled. A good mincemeat pie has just the right balance of pie crust and mincemeat.

Green Tomato Mincemeat II

5 lb	green tomatoes	2.5 kg	½ cup	butter	125 ml
2 lb	brown sugar	1 kg	1 tsp	cinnamon	5 ml
1 lb	raisins	500 g	1 tsp	cloves	5 ml
1 lb	currants	500 g	1 tsp	nutmeg	5 ml
2 cups	apples, unpeeled and ground	500 ml	½ tsp	ginger	2 ml
			1 tsp	mace	5 ml
1	orange, unpeeled	1	1 tsp	salt	5 ml

Wash fruit. Chop tomatoes in a grinder and drain. Cover with cold water and bring to a boil. Let simmer for 30 minutes on low heat. Remove from heat and drain. Add sugar, raisins, currants, apples, orange and butter. Stir well and boil. Simmer for about 2 hours. After about an hour of cooking, add spices and stir well. Pack into sterile jars, cover with wax and seal.

Rhubarb Mincemeat

2 cups	apples. diced	500 ml	1 cup	raisins	250 ml
4 cups	rhubarb, chopped	1 L	1 cup	citron peel	250 ml
1	orange, grated peel, and juice	1	½ cup	apple juice	125 ml
1	lemon, grated peel, and juice	1	½ tsp	each salt, allspice, cloves, nutmeg and cinnamon	2 ml
2 cups	brown sugar	500 ml	½ cup	butter	125 ml

Combine all ingredients in a large kettle and simmer slowly for 1 hour until a nice rich colour is achieved. Bottle and seal with paraffin until ready for use in pies or tarts.

• BEVERAGES •

• Best •

• Traditional •

• Trendy •

Bog Punch

2 cups	cranberries	500 ml	1 cup	pineapple chunks, in juice	250 ml
2 cups	water	500 ml	½ cup	lemon juice	125 ml
2 cups	apple juice	500 ml	1 quart	ginger ale	1 L
1 cup	cranberry juice	250 ml			
1 cup	sugar	250 ml			

Bring the cranberries, sugar and water to a boil, then let simmer until the cranberries are soft and the sugar has dissolved. Strain and let the juice cool. Mix the juice with the remaining ingredients and chill. Serve in punch cups and garnish with lemon slices. Serves 12.

Golden Punch

2 cups	sugar	500 ml	1 cup	boiling water	250 ml
1½ cups	orange juice	375 ml	½ cup	pineapple juice	125 ml
1½ cups	lemon juice	375 ml	1 quart	ginger ale	1 L

Dissolve the sugar in the water and allow to cool. Pour into a punch bowl and stir in the fruit juices plus 2 cups (500 ml) of water. Mix well. Add the ginger ale and sprinkle with ice cubes. Serve in punch cups and garnish with fruit slices. Serves 10.

Sherbet Punch

	water		2 cups	cranberry cocktail, chilled	500 ml
1 6-oz can	orange juice, frozen concentrate	1	2 cups	lemon sherbet	500 ml
1 6-oz can	pineapple juice, frozen concentrate	1	2 cups	ginger ale, chilled	500 ml

In a punch bowl, add water to orange and pineapple concentrate according to directions on cans. Add cocktail. Add sherbet in small scoops. Add ginger ale and serve. Makes 40 servings.

Ginger Punch

1 cup	ginger root, sliced	250 ml	½ cup	orange juice	125 ml
1 cup	sugar	250 ml	½ cup	lemon juice	125 ml
1 cup	water	250 ml	1 quart	club soda	1 L

Bring first 3 ingredients to a boil and cook for 15 minutes. Strain. Let cool. When cooled, pour in a punch bowl and stir in the fruit juices. Add the club soda and ice cubes and serve in punch cups. Serves 4.

Ginger Peach Punch

1 cup	peach nectar	250 ml	2 cups	ginger ale, chilled	500 ml
1 cup	orange juice	250 ml		ginger, cut into small pieces	
½ cup	lemon juice	125 ml			

Stir the first 3 ingredients and chill. Just before serving, pour into a pitcher and add the ginger ale. Serve in cocktail glasses and garnish with a piece of ginger. Serves 4.

Angel Punch

2 quarts	white grape juice	2 L	8 oz	sugar syrup	250 ml
1 quart	green tea	1 L	4 quarts	club soda	4 L
1 pint	lemon juice	500 ml			

Stir first 4 ingredients and chill. Pour into a punch bowl over a large block of ice and add the soda. Serve in punch cups with a slice of lemon. Serves 24.

Tropical Punch

1 10½-oz can	sweetened condensed milk	300 ml	1 6-oz can	pineapple juice, frozen concentrate	1
1 6-oz can	orange juice, frozen concentrate	1	2 quarts	club soda	2 L

Thaw concentrates. Mix the milk and the concentrates in a large punch bowl. Add the club soda and stir gently. Add ice cubes or a large block of ice and garnish with orange slices. Serve in punch cups. Makes 22 servings.

Christmas Juice Punch

2 quarts	apple juice	2 L		1 cup	sugar	250 ml
2 quarts	cranberry juice	2 L		1 gallon	ginger ale	4 L
1 cup	lemon juice	250 ml				

Mix all ingredients except ginger ale in a punch bowl. Add ice cubes and the ginger ale, and serve in punch cups. Serves 12.

Tea Punch

4 tbsp	aromatic tea, brewed and chilled	60 ml		4 tbsp	apple juice	60 ml
				2 tbsp	pineapple juice	30 ml

Combine ingredients and serve with ice. Serves 1. To make larger servings, keep the same proportions.

Ruby-Red Cran-Raspberry Punch

2 6-oz cans	cranberry cocktail concentrate, partially thawed	2		1 bottle	cranberry cocktail, chilled	1.89 L
1 6-oz can	raspberry juice concentrate, partially thawed	1		1 gallon	raspberry ginger ale, chilled	4 L
				2 pkg	frozen raspberries, in light syrup, thawed	2

Mix the frozen cranberry coctail and raspberry juice concentrate in a punch bowl. Add chilled cranberry cocktail. Just before serving, add raspberry ginger ale. Stir in frozen raspberries, taking care not to crush the berries. Serves 12.

Rhubarb Cocktail

8 cups	rhubarb, finely chopped	2 L		12 oz	water	350 ml
				⅔ cup	sugar	150 ml
4 cups	boiling water	1 L		9 cups	ginger ale	2.25 L
½ 6-oz can	lemonade concentrate, frozen	½				

Place rhubarb in a saucepan. Add boiling water. Place on low heat and let warm for about 1 hour. Remove from heat and strain into a pitcher. Chill or freeze. When ready to use, add lemonade, water and sugar. Stir to dissolve. Add ginger ale and ice cubes. Serves 24.

Double Berry Punch

8 cups	cranberry juice, chilled	2 L		1½ cups	raspberries, fresh or thawed	375 ml
3 cups	raspberry soda, chilled	750 ml		4 cups	raspberry sherbet	1 L

Gently stir the cranberry juice and the soda in a large, chilled punch bowl. Pour into individual punch cups, over small scoops of sherbet. Garnish with raspberries. Serves 28.

The Great Nova Scotia Cookbook

Apple Cider Punch

4 quarts	apple cider	4 L	6	cloves, whole	6
1 cup	brown sugar, packed	250 ml	6	allspice, whole	6
			1 tsp	nutmeg	5 ml
¾ cup	lemonade, frozen	175 ml	3	cinnamon sticks	3
¾ cup	orange juice, frozen	175 ml			

Tie the cloves and allspice in a cheesecloth bag. Combine all remaining ingredients and heat in a large saucepan. Add the spice bag. Stir occasionally. Serves 16.

Beach Blanket Bingo

6 tbsp	cranberry juice	90 ml		club soda, to taste	
6 tbsp	grape juice	90 ml			

Mix juices and serve over ice in a highball glass. Top up with soda. Garnish with a lime wedge. Serves 1.

Cape Breton Sunrise

⅓ cup	cranberry juice	75 ml		crushed ice	
2 tbsp	lime juice, fresh	30 ml			

Shake juices with crushed ice and strain into a wine glass. Garnish with a slice of lime and a fresh mint sprig. Serves 1.

Raspberry Lemonade

| 2 tbsp | raspberry syrup | 30 ml | 1 | lemon, juiced | 1 |
| 2 tsp | powdered sugar | 10 ml | | | |

Stir with ice cubes into a collins glass. Garnish with fruit slices. Serves 1.

Black and Blue Berries

| 1 cup | blueberries blackberries, mixed | 250 ml | 2 tbsp | honey or sugar | 30 ml |
| 1 cup | soda water | 250 ml | 2 tsp | lemon juice | 10 ml |

Blend until smooth and pour into a highball glass. Serves 1.

Boston Cream

2½ lb	sugar	1.25 kg	6 cups	boiling, water	1.5 L
2 oz	citric acid	55 g		baking soda	
1 tbsp	lemon juice, concentrate	15 ml			

Mix the citric acid, sugar and boiling water until the sugar has dissolved, then let cool. Stir in the lemon juice. Chill, bottle and store. Use as a tonic, mixing a pinch of baking soda and a teaspoon of the mixture for every glass of water.

The Great Nova Scotia Cookbook

Rickey

2 tbsp	lime juice	15 ml	dash	bitters	
dash	grenadine			club soda, to taste	

Stir with ice cubes into an old-fashioned glass. Garnish with a twist of lime. Serves 1.

Mulled Apple Drink

4 cups	apple juice	1 L	6	allspice berries	6
½ cup	brown sugar	125 ml		cinnamon sticks, if desired	
¼ tsp	salt	1 ml			
6	cloves, whole	6			

Place all ingredients into a large saucepan. Heat to boiling, stirring occasionally. Simmer for 10-12 minutes. Strain. Serves 4.

Mulled Cranberry Juice

4 cups	cranberry cocktail	1 L	¼ cup	sugar	50 ml
1 tbsp	lemon juice	15 ml	½ tsp	ground allspice	2 ml

Place all ingredients in a large saucepan. Heat to boiling. Simmer for 10 minutes. Pour into a pitcher. Serve in punch cups with cinnamon sticks. Serves 4.

Sunrise Splash

6 tbsp	pineapple juice	90 ml		2 tbsp	sour mix (pre-made drink mix)	30 ml
6 tbsp	orange juice	90 ml				
4 tbsp	lemon-lime soda	60 ml		1 tbsp	grenadine	15 ml

Stir with ice into a parfait glass. Garnish with a pineapple slice. Serves 1.

Strawberry Lemonade

1	lemon, juiced	1		10	strawberries	10
1 tbsp	sugar	15 ml		1 cup	water	250 ml

Toss everything into a blender and mix until fairly smooth. Serve over ice. Serves 1.

Summertime Barbarian

½ cup	grapefruit juice	125 ml		½ cup	strawberries	125 ml
½ cup	pineapple	125 ml		1 cup	crushed ice	250 ml

Blend until smooth and pour into two glasses. Garnish each glass with a kiwi wheel. Serves 2.

Strawberry Shivers

1½ cups	strawberries	375 ml		½ cup	water	125 ml
4 tsp	honey	20 ml				

Blend together at medium speed until smooth. Serves 2.

Apple Juice Cocktail

2	baking apples	2		6 tbsp	lemon juice	90 ml
½ cup	pineapple, sliced	125 ml			sugar, to taste	
½ cup	orange juice	125 ml				

Slice the apples. Mix the fruit juices with the sugar until sugar is dissolved. Add the slices of apple and pineapple and chill. Serve in tall glasses, and garnish with a cherry.

Honey Lemonade

Mix together:				½ cup	lemon juice	125 ml
2 cups	soda water	500 ml		2 tbsp	honey	30 ml

Blend together until smooth. Serves 4.

Hot Lemonade

1	lemon, juiced	1	dash	cayenne pepper	
2 tbsp	maple syrup	30 ml		ice water	

Pour the lemon juice into a 10-oz glass. Add maple syrup and cayenne pepper. Fill with ice water. Stir. Serves 1.

Jungle Juice

1	banana	1	dash	ginger	
2 cups	orange juice	500 ml			

Blend together at medium speed until smooth. Serves 2.

Grapple

1 cup	grape juice	250 ml	1 tsp	lemon juice	5 ml
1 cup	apple juice	250 ml	¼ tsp	cinnamon	1 ml

Mix all. Serves 2.

The Great Nova Scotia Cookbook

Hot, Mulled Pineapple Juice

¼ cup	sugar	50 ml		1 48-oz can	pineapple juice	1.5 L
1 cup	water	250 ml				
1 tbsp	lemon rind, grated	15 ml			cinnamon stick	
10	cloves	10			muddlers	
3 tbsp	lemon juice	45 ml				

Simmer sugar, water, lemon rind and cloves together for 15 minutes. Strain. Add lemon and pineapple juices. Heat until piping hot. Serve with a stick of cinnamon. Serves 4.

Tomato Tang

2 cups	tomato juice	500 ml		dash	celery salt
splash	lemon juice				

Blend together at medium speed until smooth. Serves 2.

Runner's Mark

1 cup	V8 Juice	125 ml		ice cubes
2 drops	lemon juice			celery stalks,
2 drops	Tabasco sauce			for garnish
dash	Worcestershire sauce			

Stir ingredients with ice cubes, into an old-fashioned glass. Garnish with a celery stick. Serves 1.

Tomato Cooler

1 cup	tomato juice	250 ml		tonic water, to taste	
2 tbsp	lemon or lime juice	30 ml		ice	

Stir with ice into a highball glass. Garnish with a wedge of lime and a cucumber slice. Serves 1.

Mocha Shake

1½ cups	coffee, cold	375 ml		salt	
¾ cup	milk	175 ml	3 cups	vanilla ice cream	750 ml
4 tbsp	sugar	60 ml	3 tbsp	chocolate syrup	45 ml

Combine the coffee, milk, sugar and salt in a blender and mix on medium speed for 15 seconds to dissolve sugar. Add ice cream and chocolate syrup. Blend on high speed until smooth and creamy. If necessary, stop blender and stir mixture with a spoon to help blend ingredients. Pour into glasses. Serves 8.

Sweet Bananas

2 cups	milk	500 ml	1 tbsp	honey	15 ml
1	banana	1			

Blend together at medium speed until smooth. Serves 2.

Dutch Treat

2 cups	milk	500 ml	2 tbsp	honey	30 ml
2 tbsp	cocoa	30 ml	½ tsp	cinnamon	2 ml
½ tsp	vanilla extract	2 ml			

Blend all ingredients at medium speed until smooth. Serves 2.

Iced Mocha

2 cups	milk	500 ml	whipped cream
⅓ cup	chocolate syrup	75 ml	crushed ice
1 tbsp	instant coffee	15 ml	chocolate shavings

Mix first 4 ingredients and pour over crushed ice into a collins glass. Top with whipped cream and chocolate shavings. Serves 4.

Berry Berry

1 cup	berries (your choice)	250 ml	1 tbsp	honey	15 ml
1 cup	milk	250 ml			

Blend until smooth and pour into a tall glass. Serves 1.

Brazilian Chocolate

1½ cups	coffee, hot and strong	375 ml		1 oz	unsweetened chocolate, solid	30 g
1 cup	cream	250 ml		1 tsp	vanilla extract	5 ml
1 cup	water, boiling	250 ml		½ tsp	cinnamon	2 ml
¼ cup	sugar	50 ml		dash	salt	

In a double boiler, melt the chocolate, sugar and salt. Stir in boiling water and continue to heat until the mixture is well blended and hot. Add coffee and cream, and stir well. Add the vanilla and the cinnamon, and pour into mugs. Serves 4.

Banana Milkshake

1	banana, sliced	1		1 tbsp	honey	15 ml
1 cup	milk	250 ml		4 drops	almond extract	
3 tbsp	orange juice	45 ml			whipped cream	

Blend all ingredients and garnish with whipped cream. Serves 1.

Energy Shake

1 cup	skim milk	250 ml		2 tbsp	wheat germ	30 ml
1	banana, ripe, or 1 cup (250 ml) fresh or frozen unsweetened berries, peaches or similarly juicy fruit			1 tbsp	honey	15 ml
				4	ice cubes	

Place all ingredients in a blender or food processor and blend until thick and smooth. Serves 1.

Coffee Nog

3 tbsp	instant coffee granules	45 ml		1 cup	whipping cream	250 ml
				1 tbsp	sugar	15 ml
3 tbsp	water, boiling	45 ml		few drops	vanilla	
8 cups	egg nog, pasteurized	2 L		sprinkle	nutmeg	
¼ cup	brown sugar	50 ml		½ tsp	cinnamon	2.5 ml
1 cup	Tia Maria liqueur (optional)	250 ml				

In a large bowl, stir instant coffee granules into boiling water. Cool. Add eggnog, brown sugar and cinnamon. Stir in Tia Maria. Pour into a punch bowl. Beat cream, sugar and vanilla until thick. Spoon over top. Sprinkle whipped cream with nutmeg. Serves 10.

Strawberry Pineapple Milkshake

1 pint	strawberries	500 ml		2 cups	milk	500 ml
½ 14-oz can	pineapple chunks	200 ml				

Blend until smooth and pour into a parfait glass. Serves 2.

Strawberry Shake

1 cup	milk	250 ml		1 tbsp	sugar	15 ml
½ cup	strawberries, fresh	125 ml			cracked ice	

Blend milk, strawberries and sugar with cracked ice until smooth and pour into a tall glass. Garnish with fresh strawberries.

Honey Milk Shake

1 cup	milk	250 ml		1 tbsp	honey	15 ml
3 tbsp	vanilla ice cream	45 g				

Blend ingredients until smooth and serve in a highball glass with a straw. Serves 1.

Blueberry Shake

1 cup	milk	250 ml		1 tbsp	sugar	15 ml
½ cup	blueberries, fresh	125 ml			cracked ice	

Blend ingredients until smooth and pour into a tall glass. Garnish with fresh blueberries. Serves 1.

Banana Strawberry Shake

½ lb	strawberries, frozen	250 g		2 cups	apple juice	500 ml
1	banana, frozen	1				

Blend together until smooth. Serves 2.

Earth Shake

1½ cups	pineapple juice	375 ml		1	carrot, peeled and chopped	1
½ cup	pineapple, crushed	125 ml				

Blend all on medium speed until smooth. Serves 2.

Kidsicle

1 cup	milk	250 ml	dash	grenadine	
4 tbsp	orange juice	60 ml		whipped cream	
2 tbsp	lemon-lime soda	30 ml	2	cherries, for garnish	2
½ scoop	vanilla ice cream				

Blend the milk, ice cream and orange juice until smooth and pour into a parfait glass. Add soda and top with whipped cream. Drizzle grenadine over the whipped cream and garnish with a cherry. Serves 1-2.

Yellowjacket

2 tbsp	pineapple juice	30 ml	cracked ice	
2 tbsp	orange juice	30 ml	lemon slice, for garnish	
1 tbsp	lemon juice	15 ml		

Shake all. Strain over ice cubes into an old-fashioned glass. Garnish with a lemon slice. Serves 1.

Black and White Milk Shake

1 pint	milk	500 ml	2 tbsp	chocolate ice cream	30 ml
4 tbsp	vanilla ice cream	60 ml			

Blend all until smooth and serve in a tall glass. Serves 1.

Banana Strawberry Smoothie

½ lb	strawberries, frozen	250 g		1 cup	milk	250 ml
1	banana, frozen	1			honey	
1 cup	plain yogurt	250 ml				

Blend all until smooth. Add honey to taste. Serves 2.

Coffee Almond Float

4 cups	milk	1 L		2 tbsp	brown sugar	30 ml
¼ cup	instant coffee	50 ml		¼ tsp	almond extract	1 ml
2 tbsp	water	30 ml			chocolate ice cream	

Dissolve the coffee in the water. Add all other ingredients, except the ice cream. Stir well and pour over ice cubes in parfait glasses. Top each glass with a scoop of ice cream. Serves 4-5.

Ice Cold Coffee Cream

2 cups	ice cold water	500 ml		2 cups	vanilla ice cream	500 ml
3 tsp	instant coffee	15 ml		pinch	cinnamon	

Place all ingredients in a blender. Blend for 15 seconds. Use larger amounts of ice cream for a thicker drink. Serves 4.

Icy Rhubarb Shrub

2 lb	fresh rhubarb	1 kg	⅔ cup	sugar	150 ml
3 cups	water	750 ml	1 pint	lime sherbet	500 ml

Wash rhubarb and cut into 1-inch (2.5 cm) pieces. Cook in water until tender. Strain through a sieve. Add sugar to juice; stir until sugar is dissolved. Chill. Serve in tall glasses, topping each with a small scoop of sherbet. Serves 4.

Apple Berry Smoothie

1 cup	strawberries, raspberries or any berry you wish	250 ml	2	apples, cut into wedges	2

Blend until smooth. Serves 2.

Kill-the-Cold Smoothie

1 slice	ginger		1 cup	hot water	250 ml
¼	lemon, with peel	¼		cardamom, to taste	

Mix ginger and lemon and add it to hot water. Place in blender and blend until smooth. Add cardamom. Serves 1.

Kiwi Papaya Smoothie

| 3 | kiwi fruit | 3 | ½ | papaya, seeded and sliced | ½ |

Toss fruit into a blender and purée. Serves 1.

Grape Lemon
Pineapple Smoothie

| 1 cup | grapes | 250 ml | ½ cup | pineapple, diced and peeled | 125 ml |
| ¼ | lemon, peeled | ¼ | | | |

Peel lemon and pineapple and cut into chunks. Blend until smooth. Serves 2.

• BREAKFASTS •

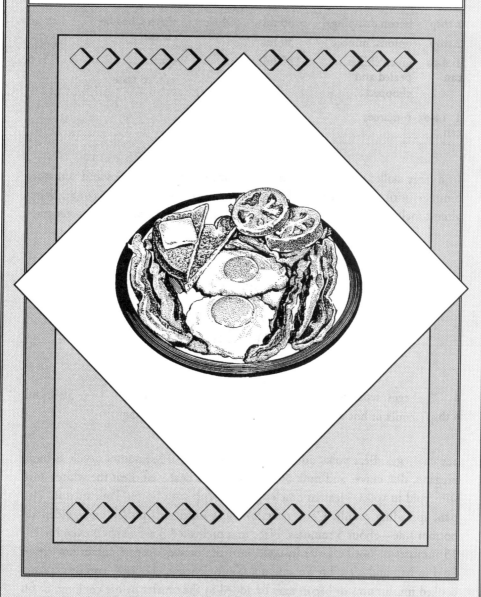

• Best •

• Traditional •

• Trendy •

Ranch Eggs

2 tbsp	bacon drippings	30 ml		4 oz	sharp Cheddar cheese	125 ml
2 tbsp	onions, minced	30 ml				
1 4-oz can	green chilies, peeled and chopped	125 ml		6	eggs	6
					salt, to taste	
1 14-oz can	tomatoes	398 ml				

In a large skillet, sauté onions in bacon drippings. Add chilies and tomatoes. Simmer until almost dry. Add cheese, cut into ¾-inch (2 cm) cubes. When almost melted, drop in whole eggs one at a time. Cook to desired consistency.

Foamy Omelet

4	eggs, separated	4		2-3 tbsp butter	30-45 ml
4 tbsp	milk or hot water	60 ml		seasonings	

Separate eggs. Beat yolks until light and creamy. Add seasonings such as basil, oregano, dill, chives and milk or hot water, and beat well. Beat the whites until stiff. Fold in yolks. Heat an omelet pan and rub with butter. Pour mixture into pan, spreading evenly. Cook over low heat until well puffed and golden on bottom side—about 5 minutes. Place in a preheated 350F (175C) oven for 10-15 minutes or until a knife inserted into the omelet's centre comes out clean. Fold in half and serve brown side up. Grated cheese, chopped ham or chicken, cooked mushrooms or bacon may be added to the omelet before cooking, or fill with mushroom sauce, creamed chicken or ham, jelly or grated cheese.

Overnight Breakfast

6	eggs	6	1 lb	sausage, browned	500 g
2 cups	milk	500 ml	1 cup	Cheddar cheese, grated	250 ml
½ tsp	salt	2 ml			
1 tsp	mustard	5 ml	½ cup	green pepper, chopped (optional)	125 ml
3 slices	white bread, cubed	3			

Beat eggs with milk. Add salt and mustard. In a 9x13-inch (23x33 cm) baking dish, layer bread, sausage and cheese. Pour egg mixture on top and sprinkle with green pepper. Refrigerate overnight. Bake at 350F (175C) for about 45 minutes.

Scrambled Eggs over Potato and Bacon

2½ lb	potatoes	1.25 kg	16	eggs, beaten	16
1 lb	bacon, thickly sliced	500 g	1⅓ cups	Parmesan cheese	325 ml
			¼ cup	chives chopped	50 ml
¾ cup	butter	175 ml	1 tsp	pepper	5 ml

In a saucepan of boiling, salted water, cook potatoes for 10 minutes; drain and cool. Grate into a bowl; set aside. Chop bacon into 1-inch (2.5 cm) pieces. In a large skillet, cook bacon over medium heat for about 7 minutes or until crisp. Drain on a paper towel. Stir into grated potatoes. Using two small skillets, melt 1 tbsp (15 ml) of butter into each. Pat ½ cup (125 ml) of the potato mixture into each. Cook over medium heat for about 8 minutes until golden on the bottom. Turn and cook for about 5 minutes, or until golden and crisp. Transfer to a large baking sheet. Repeat with the remaining potato and bacon mixture to make about 6 more patties.

Scrambled Eggs: In a large, clean skillet, melt remaining butter (about 2 tablespoons) over medium heat. Pour in eggs and cook until starting to set. Stir in cheese, chives and pepper; cook, stirring until eggs are creamy. Meanwhile, in a 400F (200C) oven, reheat potato patties. Transfer each one to a serving plate and top with a ½ cup (125 ml) scrambled eggs. Serves 8.

French Toast

3	eggs	3	½ tsp	cinnamon	2 ml
1 cup	light cream	250 ml	4 tbsp	butter	60 ml
½ cup	milk	125 ml	12 slices	cinnamon bread (thick slices)	slices 12
1 tsp	vanilla	5 ml			

In a shallow bowl, beat the eggs, cream, milk, vanilla and cinnamon. In a heavy skillet, melt 1-2 tbsp clarified butter. Soak both sides of the bread in the egg mixture and fry in butter over medium heat until both sides are brown and crisp. Add butter as needed. Serve immediately with butter and hot syrup. Serves 6.

Baked Apple French Toast

1 cup	brown sugar, firmly packed	250 ml	3 cups	apples, thinly sliced, or frozen blueberries	750 ml
½ cup	butter	125 ml	1 cup	sugar	250 ml
2 tbsp	light corn syrup	30 ml	1 tsp	cinnamon	5 ml
1 cup	pecans, chopped	250 ml	½ tsp	nutmeg, grated	2 ml
8-10 cups	Italian bread, cubed (10 slices)	2-2 ½ L	6	large eggs	6
			2 cups	milk	500 ml
2 oz	cream cheese (light, if preferred)	60 g	1 tsp	vanilla	5 ml
			½ tsp	salt	2 ml

Combine brown sugar, butter and corn syrup in a small saucepan and cook over medium heat until thickened, stirring constantly. Pour into a 9x13-inch (23x33 cm) baking dish, and sprinkle the pecans over the syrup. Top with 4 heaping cups of bread. Slice the cream cheese into 4 thin slices. Cut each one in half lengthwise, then cut into small cubes. Arrange cheese cubes evenly over the cubed bread. Next, place the fruit over all. Mix the sugar, cinnamon and nutmeg together and pour over the fruit. Use the remaining bread cubes to form a layer over the fruit and sugar. Beat the eggs, add the milk, vanilla and salt, and pour evenly over the whole dish, making sure the bread is moistened. Cover the dish and refrigerate for 8 hours or overnight. Remove from fridge 30 minutes before baking. Bake uncovered in a pre-heated 350F (175C) oven for 1 hour or until lightly browned. Let stand for 15-20 minutes to firm up. Turn upside down onto a serving platter and cut into pieces. Serves 8.

Waffles

Have lots of warm maple syrup waiting.

3	eggs	3		2 cups	flour	500 ml
1 cup	milk	250 ml		½ tsp	salt	2 ml
½ cup	butter or margarine, melted	125 ml		1 tbsp	baking powder	15 ml
1 tbsp	vanilla	15 ml		2 tsp	sugar	10 ml

Beat eggs in a bowl until thick. Beat milk, melted butter and vanilla into eggs. In a separate bowl, combine remaining ingredients. Sift into egg mixture and mix well. Pour batter into a hot waffle iron. Bake until golden. For apple cinnamon waffles, add 1 cup shredded apple and ½ tsp cinnamon. Serves 4.

Apple Pancake Pie

¼ cup	butter or hard margarine	50 ml		3	large eggs	3
⅓ cup	brown sugar, packed	75 ml		¾ cup	milk	175 ml
dash	cinnamon			½ tsp	salt	2 ml
2-3	apples	2-3		¾ cup	flour	175 ml

Peel and core apples. Cut into ¼-inch (5mm) slices. Melt butter in a 9-inch (22 cm) pie plate in a 425F (220C) oven. Stir in brown sugar. Sprinkle cinnamon over top. Spread apples in a single layer over top and cook in oven for 10 minutes. Beat eggs. Add milk, salt and flour. Stir to moisten. Batter will be lumpy. Pour over apples. Return to oven. Bake for 20-25 minutes. Cut into wedges. Serves 4.

Spiced Pumpkin Pancakes

A great improvement on the ordinary pancake.

1½ cups	flour	375 ml		2	eggs, lightly beaten	2
½ tsp	baking powder	2 ml		1⅓ cups	buttermilk	325 ml
½ tsp	baking soda	2 ml		¼ cup	butter, melted	50 ml
¼ tsp	cinnamon	1 ml		3 tbsp	pumpkin, canned	45 ml
¼ tsp	allspice	1 ml		¼ cup	sugar	50 ml
¼ tsp	salt	1 ml				

Sift together flour, baking powder, soda, cinnamon, allspice and salt. In the large bowl of a mixer, blend eggs, buttermilk, butter, pumpkin and sugar until smooth. Add dry ingredients to wet ingredients and blend with mixer just until smooth. Do not overmix. Heat skillet over medium heat. Coat pan with cooking spray. Pour ¼-cup (50 ml) portions in hot skillet. When bubbles appear on surface and edges begin to harden, turn pancakes over and cook until browned. Serve with butter and maple syrup or molasses. Serves 4.

Standard Recipe for Pancakes

1½ cups	flour	375 ml		2	eggs, at room temperature	2
2½ tsp	baking powder	12 ml				
½ tsp	salt	2 ml		3 tbsp	melted butter, or oil	45 ml
3 tbsp	sugar	45 ml		1 cup	milk, at room temperature	250 ml

Mix and sift dry ingredients. Beat eggs and add milk and melted butter. Slowly add egg mixture to dry ingredients. Mix only enough to blend. Fry. This makes a thick pancake. Serves 4.

Suggested toppings: fruit, icing sugar, whipped cream, chopped nuts, molasses or syrups.

The Great Nova Scotia Cookbook

Popovers

Youngsters love these for breakfast.

⅞ cup	flour (1 cup, less 2 tbsp)	220 ml	2	eggs	2
			1 cup	milk	250 ml
¼ tsp	salt	1 ml	1 tbsp	butter, melted	15 ml

Preheat oven to 450F (230C). Grease muffin pans, using butter for flavour. Sift flour and salt into a mixing bowl. In a separate bowl beat eggs until thick; combine with milk. Make a hollow in the centre of flour and gradually stir in milk and egg mixture. Add melted butter. Beat hard for 1 minute. Put pans in oven until sizzling hot. Pour batter into sizzling hot muffin tins and bake for 15 minutes at 450F (230C). Decrease oven temperature to 350F (175C) to finish baking. Remove from pans immediately. Serve at once. If centre is moist or if popovers collapse on cooling, they have not been baked long enough. Serve with maple syrup, strawberries and whipped cream or other suitable toppings. Using beef drippings instead of butter for greasing pans, this batter can be used for Yorkshire pudding. Makes 1 dozen.

Cornmeal Pancakes

1	egg	1	1 tbsp	sugar	15 ml
1 cup	buttermilk	250 ml	1 tsp	baking powder	5 ml
2 tbsp	olive oil	30 ml	½ tsp	salt	2 ml
1 cup	cornmeal	250 ml	½ tsp	baking soda	2 ml

Beat egg in a medium-size bowl. Add buttermilk and oil; mix well. Combine dry ingredients and add all at once to liquid. Mix well. Heat an oiled skillet over medium heat. Make small pancakes, as they are delicate and difficult to turn if they are too large. Watch carefully, as they brown quickly. Cooked pancakes can be held in a warm oven. Serves 4.

Yogurt Pancakes

2 cups	flour	500 ml		1 cup	plain yogurt	250 ml
2 tbsp	sugar	30 ml		½ cup	milk	125 ml
2 tsp	baking powder	10 ml		2	eggs	2
½ tsp	baking soda	2 ml		2 tbsp	melted butter or vegetable oil	30 ml
½ tsp	salt	2 ml				

In a large bowl mix the flour, sugar, baking powder, baking soda, and salt. In a blender mix the yogurt, milk, eggs, and melted butter or oil. Rub a skillet or electric frying pan with a little butter, then heat until a drop of water sizzles on the pan. Combine liquid and dry ingredients very gently until dry ingredients are absorbed. Ignore the lumps. Ladle mixture into the frying pan and cook pancakes until golden brown on both sides. Serve with butter and maple syrup. Serves 4.

Wild Blueberry Whole Wheat Pancakes

1½ cups	whole wheat flour	375 ml		1½ cups	milk	375 ml
½ cup	toasted wheat germ	125 ml		½ cup	plain yogurt	125 ml
2 tsp	baking powder	10 ml		3 tbsp	butter, melted	45 ml
¼ tsp	salt	1 ml		2	egg whites, beaten stiffly	2
2	egg yolks	2		1½ cups	blueberries	375 ml
3 tbsp	maple syrup	45 ml				

In large mixing bowl, combine the flour, wheat germ, baking powder, and salt. In a medium-size bowl, beat the egg yolks, maple syrup, milk, yogurt and butter until well blended. Add the wet ingredients to the dry, mixing enough to blend. Fold in egg whites and blueberries. Cook on a moderately hot, buttered griddle; turn gently when bubbles appear. Serve with blueberry sauce or maple syrup. Makes ten to twelve 5-inch pancakes.

The Great Nova Scotia Cookbook

Dutch Babies and
Baby Apple Dumplings

1 tbsp	margarine	15 ml		½ tsp	salt	2 ml
3	eggs	3		½ cup	flour	125 ml
½ cup	milk	125 ml				

Dutch Babies: Preheat oven to 425F (218C). Melt margarine in a skillet in the oven. Beat eggs gradually, adding flour. Mix in milk and salt. Pour batter into the heated skillet. Bake for 20 minutes, then lower the temperature to 300F (150C) and bake for 5 minutes longer.

Baby Apple Dumplings: Follow recipe for batter as above. Add 1 apple—cut in wedges and slice thinly into the batter. Pour into skillet. Bake for 20 minutes and sprinkle with brown sugar and cinnamon. Bake for 5 minutes longer at 300F (150C). Serves 4.

Oatmeal Pancakes

2 cups	rolled oats	500 ml		2 tbsp	brown sugar	30 ml
2 cups	buttermilk	500 ml		1 tsp	baking soda	5 ml
2	eggs	2		1 tsp	baking powder	5 ml
¼ cup	melted butter	50 ml		½ tsp	cinnamon	2 ml
½ cup	currants	125 ml		1 tsp	vanilla	5 ml
½ cup	flour	125 ml		¼ tsp	salt (optional)	1 ml

Combine oats and buttermilk. Refrigerate for a ½ hour or overnight. Add all other ingredients and stir until smooth. Fry on a griddle over medium-low heat. Serves 4.

Corn Pancakes

1	egg	1		1 tsp	salt	5 ml
1 cup	milk	250 ml			flour (enough to achieve desired consistency)	
1 cup	creamed corn	250 ml				
1 tsp	cream of tartar	5 ml		⅓ cup	butter, melted	75 ml
½ tsp	baking soda	2 ml				

Combine all ingredients. Drop small amounts on a hot fry pan. Flip when bubbles appear. Serve with maple syrup. Serves 4.

Potato Pancakes

3	medium potatoes, scrubbed and unpeeled	3		1 tbsp	milk	15 ml
				1	egg, beaten	1
				½ tsp	salt	2 ml
1 tbsp	flour	15 ml				

Grate potatoes. Place on a paper towel and press out most of the moisture. Put the potatoes in a bowl and add flour, milk, egg and salt. Toss until mixed. Heat oil in a fry pan. Measure about 2 tbsp of batter for a 3- or 4-inch circle. Drop in as many as pan will hold without crowding. Cook until bottoms brown, then turn. (They will be crisp.) Keep warm in an oven until all the pancakes are cooked. These are wonderful served with roast pork and applesauce. Work quickly with raw grated potatoes or they will discolour. Serves 4.

The Great Nova Scotia Cookbook

Honey Bran Banana Pancakes

1¾ cups	Five Roses flour with wheat bran	425 ml		1½ cups	buttermilk	375 ml
				¼ cup	vegetable oil	50 ml
1 cup	Nabisco 100% Bran cereal	250 ml		2 tbsp	liquid honey	30 ml
				1	banana	1
2 tsp	baking powder	10 ml		1	egg, slightly beaten	1
1 tsp	baking soda	5 ml		1 tsp	vanilla	5 ml
¼ tsp	salt	1 ml				

Combine flour, cereal, baking powder, soda and salt in a medium-size bowl. In a blender, process buttermilk, oil, honey, banana, egg and vanilla until smooth. Add liquids to dry ingredients, stir just until moistened. For each pancake, scoop about ¼ cup (50 ml) of batter and pour onto a lightly greased or nonstick skillet or griddle. Cook 1½-2 minutes until golden brown; turn when bubbles break on surface. Cook for about 2 minutes more. Makes 16 pancakes.

Cheddar Baked
Bagels and Eggs

4	bagels, halved	4	½ tsp	pepper	3 ml
2 tbsp	butter	30 ml	½ cup	Cheddar cheese, shredded	125 ml
8	eggs	8			
½ tsp	salt	3 ml		bacon slices (optional)	

Butter bagels on cut sides. Place bagels, buttered side down, in a heavy skilled over medium heat, and cook until golden brown. Work in batches. Transfer bagels to a baking sheet. Break an egg in the centre of each bagel, sprinkle with salt and pepper, and sprinkle cheese over all. Bake at 400F (200C) until eggs are set. Remove from oven and top with crisp bacon slices, if desired. Makes 4 servings.

• RECIPES FOR KIDS •

• Best •

• Traditional •

• Trendy •

Learning to Cook &
Making Your First Cake

Ask mom or dad to help you when measuring ingredients. They can also explain words like blend, cream, beat, fold, batter, dough and other words used in cooking. You need to learn how to safely use electric mixers or blenders and how to use the stove (turning on the top electric elements and the oven). You also need to know how to read temperatures and how to tell time. There are lots of things to learn.

Be very careful with sharp knives, electricity, hot stoves and boiling water. Always ask for help when removing hot pans from the oven. Start with easy recipes and you will soon be able to make more difficult ones.

If your hair is long, tie it back, and roll up your sleeves or, better still, wear short sleeves. Scrub your hands and fingernails right up to your elbows, even if it is unlikely that you will be putting them in a mixing bowl!

Make sure you wash vegetables and fruit thoroughly and check that all dishes and utensils are very clean. Wash and wipe off counters. Find the ingredients you will need for your recipe and set them on the counter. Also have ready measuring cups, spoons, a flour sifter and baking pans.

Try some easy recipes at first, like French toast, pancakes or scrambled eggs. When you feel confident, try a white cake—maybe someone special is having a birthday. Decide on the shape of the cake and prepare your pans. You can grease them with cooking spray or line them with paper. Parchment paper is an excellent choice. Set your oven at the required temperature. Most white cakes bake at 350F (175C). It is important to know exactly how to turn on your oven.

Your oven is heating, your pan is prepared, and you are ready to make the cake. Here is an easy-to-follow cake recipe. Good luck!

Miracle White Cake

Use two 8-inch (20 cm) round cake pans. Preheat oven to 350F (175C). Baking time is about 25 minutes. Ask mom or dad to show you how to test the cake to see if it's done.

2 cups	cake flour, sifted before measuring	500 ml		½ cup	shortening	125 ml
				2	eggs	2
2½ tsp	baking powder	12 ml		¾ cup	milk	175 ml
¾ tsp	salt	3 ml		2 tsp	vanilla	10 ml
1 cup	granulated sugar	250 ml				

Sift flour first, then measure 2 cups (500 ml) back into sifter. Measure baking powder and salt into sifter and sift again. Place shortening in a mixing bowl and cream until soft. Add sugar gradually and beat well to combine. It will take about 4 minutes. Add unbeaten eggs, one at a time, and continue to beat until the mixture looks like yellow whipped cream. Add vanilla to milk. Add about ¼ of the sifted dry ingredients to the sugar mixture and about ⅓ of the milk to the sugar mixture. Blend well. Continue until all of the flour has been added and all of the milk is gone. Blend together at low speed. Divide the batter between the two pans. Place pans in oven and bake until done. Turn cakes out onto racks to cool. When cold, place one cake on a pretty plate. Spread with frosting and place other cake on top. Spread frosting over top and sides. You may tint frosting to any colour you like. A nice frosting recipe follows, along with an idea for birthday cake decorations.

Frosting:

½ cup	butter, softened	125 ml		¼ tsp	cream of tartar	1 ml
1 lb	icing sugar	500 ml		1 tsp	vanilla	5 ml
5 tbsp	milk powder	75 ml		¼ cup	warm water or enough to make a spreading consistency	50 ml
½ tsp	salt	2 ml				

Cream butter and add all remaining ingredients. Beat very hard until smooth. Spread on cake.

Gumdrop Flower
Cake Decorations

Choose a colour for your gumdrop flowers—red ones are pretty. Place a sheet of wax paper on a breadboard. Sprinkle paper generously with icing sugar. Place a gumdrop on paper. Place more icing sugar on top of gumdrop. Cover with another sheet of wax paper. Using a rolling pin, press very hard on the gumdrop. Keep rolling until gumdrop is very flat. Add more icing sugar if it becomes sticky.

When gumdrop is flattened very thin, shape into dime-size portions. Fold one portion to resemble the centre of a rose and place other portions around the centre, forming the petals of the flower. Add as many petals as you wish. Place the finished roses around the cake. Follow the same procedure with green gumdrops to make leaves. Add a few silver beads and candles and you'll have a very pretty birthday cake.

Dabba-Doo Squares

¼ cup	margarine	50 ml	3 cups	Post Cocoa Pebbles cereal	750 ml
⅓ cup	smooth peanut butter	75 ml			
3 cups	miniature marshmallows	750 ml			

Melt margarine, peanut butter and half of the marshmallows in a saucepan, stirring frequently. Remove from heat. Add remaining marshmallows and cereal. Stir to coat with peanut butter mixture. Press mixture into a greased 8-inch (20 cm) square pan. Chill for 1 hour. Cut into squares. Wrap individually. Recipe may be doubled.

Peanut Butter Balls

3 cups	Rice Krispies	750 ml
½ cup	butter, softened	125 ml
2 cups	icing sugar	500 ml

2 cups	peanut butter	500 ml
	graham wafer crumbs, finely grated coconut or finely crushed peanuts	

Mix together the butter, icing sugar and peanut butter. Add Rice Krispies. Shape into balls with hands. Place on a cookie sheet lined with wax paper. Roll in crumbs, coconut or nuts. Store in refrigerator until firm or freeze. Makes 80 small balls.

Peanut Butter Popcorn Balls

8 cups	popped corn	2 L
3 cups	Shreddies	750 ml
¼ cup	butter	50 ml

¾ cup	smooth peanut butter	175 ml
1 8-oz pkg	miniature marshmallows	250 g

Toss popped corn and shreddies in a large bowl. Set aside. In a large microwavable bowl, melt butter and peanut butter on medium for 1 minute. Add marshmallows; microwave on medium for 1 more minute. Marshmallows will puff. Add cereal mixture to peanut butter mixture and mix well. Form into small balls. Use clean rubber gloves to make forming the balls much easier.

Rocky Road Brownies

Easy to make and you don't use many dishes!

4 1-oz squares	unsweetened chocolate	4 x 30 g	¾ cup	flour	175 ml
			½ cup	pecans, chopped and toasted	125 ml
¾ cup	butter	175 ml			
1½ cups	sugar	375 ml	1 tsp	vanilla	5 ml
3	eggs	3			

Melt chocolate and butter in a large bowl over (not in) boiling water until melted. Stir until smooth. Stir sugar into chocolate mixture until blended; stir in eggs until mixed. Add vanilla and stir. Blend in flour and nuts. Spread into a greased 9-inch (23 cm) square pan. Bake at 350F (175C) for 40 minutes or until a wooden pick inserted comes out clean. Cool in pan. Cut into squares. These hot brownies may be topped with mini marshmallows and placed under the broiler to brown slightly.

School House Cookies

½ cup	vegetable oil	125 ml	1½ tsp	baking powder	7 ml
1 cup	brown sugar, lightly packed	250 ml	½ tsp	salt	2 ml
			1 cup	yogurt, plain or fruit	250 ml
1 tbsp	orange rind, grated	15 ml			
1 tsp	vanilla	5 ml	½ cup	dried fruit: raisins, apricots, prunes, dates or a mixture of each	125 ml
2	eggs	2			
3 cups	dark rye flour	750 ml			

Combine oil, brown sugar, rind and vanilla and beat until light. Add eggs, one at a time, beating until light. Combine dry ingredients and stir into oil mixture, alternating with yogurt. Stir in dried fruit. Drop from a spoon onto greased cookie sheets and bake at 350F (175C) for approximatley 20 minutes. If you wish, drizzle a little orange glaze over tops of cookies. To make glaze: Use 1 cup (250 ml) icing sugar, 2 tsp (10 ml) orange rind and 2 tbsp (30 ml) orange juice. Stir all together.

Breakfast Cookies

Who says you can't have a cookie for breakfast?

4	medium bananas, ripe	4	1½ cups	mixed dried fruits: raisins, prunes, dates	375 ml
⅓ cup	canola oil	75 ml	¾ cup	whole wheat flour	175 ml
1 tsp	vanilla	5 ml	½ cup	almonds, chopped	125 ml
1	orange rind, grated	1			
1½ cups	rolled oats	375 ml			

Mash bananas in a large bowl. Stir in oil, vanilla, and rind. Combine oats, fruit, flour and almonds. Stir into banana mixture until well blended. Drop from a spoon onto a greased cookie sheet. Flatten with a fork. Bake at 350F (175C) for 10-12 minutes. Cool on a rack. Store in the refrigerator.

Brown Sugar Squares

Base:

½ cup	margarine	125 ml	1 cup	flour	250 ml
1 cup	brown sugar	250 ml			

Mix flour and sugar, then cut in margarine until mixture is crumbly. Press dough into a 9-inch (23 cm) square pan. Bake in a 350F (175C) oven for 15 minutes. Remove from oven and cool.

Topping:

2 tbsp	flour	30 ml	1 cup	brown sugar	250 ml
¼ tsp	salt	1 ml	1 tsp	vanilla	5 ml
2	eggs	2	½ cup	walnuts (optional)	125 ml

Beat eggs until frothy. Add sugar and beat until fluffy. Add vanilla and mix. Sift in flour and salt and blend well. Spread topping over cooked base. Bake at 350F (175C) for about 30 minutes. Let cool in pan. Cut into squares.

Oatmeal-Cinnamon Raisin Cookies

Good with a glass of cold milk!

¾ cup	butter, softened	175 ml	¼ tsp	cloves, ground	1 ml
½ cup	white sugar	125 ml	½ tsp	cinnamon, ground	2 ml
1 cup	brown sugar	250 ml	1 tsp	baking soda	5 ml
1 tsp	vanilla	5 ml	2 cups	rolled oats	500 ml
1	egg	1	1 cup	raisins	250 ml
1¾ cups	flour	425 ml			

Cream butter. Blend in sugars until fluffy. Add vanilla and egg and beat well. In another bowl, sift together flour, cloves, cinnamon and soda. Add gradually to butter mixture. Stir in oats and raisins. Drop by rounded teaspoons onto a cookie sheet. Bake for 10-12 minutes at 350F (175C).

Cinnamon-Sugar-Butter Slices

Sugar and spice make all things nice.

1 cup	butter or margarine, softened	250 ml	2½ cups	flour	625 ml
			1 tsp	cinnamon	5 ml
			½ tsp	baking soda	2 ml
½ cup	brown sugar	125 ml			
½ cup	white sugar	125 ml	Topping:		
1	egg	1	⅓ cup	sugar	75 ml
1 tsp	vanilla	5 ml	2 tsp	cinnamon	10 ml

Cream butter or margarine. Add sugars and beat. Add egg and vanilla and beat again. Add flour, cinnamon and soda sifted together. Mix well. Form dough into log shapes. Wrap in wax paper and chill. Cut into ¼-inch (5 mm) slices. Place on a cookie sheet. Combine topping ingredients and sprinkle over slices. Bake at 350F (175C) for 10 minutes.

Chewy Choco Cookies

1 cup	butter, softened	250 ml		¾ cup	sifted cocoa	175 ml
1 cup	white sugar	250 ml		2 tsp	baking powder	10 ml
1 cup	brown sugar	250 ml		½ tsp	salt	2 ml
2	eggs	2		¾ cup	unsweetened chocolate chips	175 ml
2 tsp	vanilla	10 ml				
2 cups	flour	500 ml				

Beat butter and sugars together. Add eggs and vanilla and beat. Sift together flour, cocoa, baking powder and salt, and add to butter mixture. Blend well. Add chocolate chips and mix well. Drop onto cookie sheets and bake in a 325F (160C) for 12-15 minutes.

Button Cookies

Buttons you can eat!

1 cup	margarine or butter	250 ml		1	egg	1
1 cup	brown sugar	250 ml		2½ cups	flour	625 ml
1 tsp	vanilla	5 ml		½ tsp	salt	2 ml

Cream butter or margarine. Blend in brown sugar. Beat in egg and vanilla. Sift flour and salt and fold into butter mixture. Chill dough. Roll into a log shape and chill again. Slice into ¼-inch (5mm) slices. Place on parchment-lined cookie sheets. Use a toothpick and press four holes (fairly large) into each cookie. Bake at 350F (175C) until golden brown, approximately 10 minutes.

Chocolate Chip Macaroons

So chewy!

⅔ cup	condensed milk, sweetened	150 ml		2½ cups	flaked coconut	625 ml
				¾ cup	mini chocolate chips	175 ml
1 tsp	vanilla	5 ml				

Combine all ingredients. Drop from a teaspoon onto parchment-lined cookie sheets. Bake at 350F (175C) until light brown. for about 10-15 minutes or until slightly browned.

Peanut Butter Granola Bars

These are good and good for you!

1 cup	peanut butter, light	250 ml		2 cups	rolled oats	500 ml
				½ cup	wheat germ	125 ml
¼ cup	oil	50 ml		½ cup	raisins	125 ml
½ cup	honey	125 ml		½ cup	apricots, chopped	125 ml

Mix peanut butter, oil and honey. Stir in dry ingredients and fruit. Spread into a greased 9-inch (23 cm) square pan. Bake at 350F (175C) for 25 minutes. Cut into bars and cool.

Banana and Peanut Butter Pinwheels

Cut unsliced whole grain bread into lengthwise slices, and remove crusts. (Save crusts for breadcrumbs.) Spread bread with butter and peanut butter. Peel one banana for each bread slice. Dip bananas in lemon juice, and place across bread. Roll up like a jelly roll. Wrap and chill. When ready to use, simply slice across rolls.

Spicy Banana Cookies

½ cup	butter	125 ml
1 cup	sugar	250 ml
2	eggs	2
1 tsp	vanilla	5 ml
2¼ cups	flour	550 ml
½ tsp	cinnamon	2 ml

¼ tsp	baking soda	1 ml
pinch	cloves	
¼ tsp	salt	1 ml
3	bananas, mashed	3
½ cup	walnuts, finely chopped	125 ml

Cream butter. Blend in sugar. Beat in eggs and vanilla. Sift together flour, cinnamon, soda, cloves and salt, and add to butter mixture. Add bananas and nuts and mix very well. Drop by rounded teaspoons onto greased cookie sheets. Bake in a 350F (175C) oven for 10-12 minutes until lightly browned. Dust with powdered sugar if desired or frost with cream cheese icing.

Chocolate Haystacks

Work fast!

2 cups	white sugar	500 ml
⅓ cup	cocoa	75 ml
½ cup	milk	125 ml
½ cup	butter	125 ml
3½ cups	rolled oats, quick cooking	875 ml

1 cup	coconut, flaked	250 ml
½ cup	walnuts, flaked	125 ml
½ tsp	vanilla	2 ml
dash	salt	

In a saucepan, bring first 4 ingredients to a boil. Remove from heat and stir in remaining ingredients. Drop quickly from a teaspoon onto parchment paper. Cool. Makes about 48 "haystacks."

Scary Spider Cookies

2 cups	semi-sweet chocolate chips, divided	500 ml		¼ cup	shredded coconut	50 ml
½ cup	Rice Krispies, cereal	125 ml		1½ cups	chow mein noodles	375 ml

To make the spiders' bodies: Melt 1 cup of chocolate chips in a saucepan over low heat. Add the cereal and the coconut. Drop the mixture by rounded teaspoon onto a cookie sheet lined with wax paper.

To make the spiders' legs: Melt the second cup of chocolate chips. Very gently stir in chow mein noodles. Remove the mixture from heat and let cool. Pick noodles out one by one and attach them to the spider bodies (8 to a spider). Makes 36 cookies.

Molasses Sparkle Balls

These cookies smell great!

¾ cup	butter, softened	175 ml		½ tsp	baking soda	2 ml
1 cup	sugar	250 ml		½ tsp	cloves	2 ml
⅓ cup	molasses	75 ml		1 tsp	ginger	5 ml
1	egg	1		½ tsp	cinnamon	2 ml
3 tbsp	milk	45 ml		½ tsp	salt	2 ml
2 cups	flour	500 ml			sugar, for rolling	

Beat butter and sugar. Add egg, molasses and milk, mixing well. Add sifted dry ingredients. Chill. Shape into 1-inch (2.5 cm) balls. Roll in sugar. Bake on cookie sheets at 350F (175C) for 10-12 minutes. Watch carefully so they don't burn.

Mud Cakes

These are really great—just like candy, but we eat them like cookies.

½ cup	butter	125 ml	½ cup	coconut, medium ground	125 ml
2 cups	sugar	500 ml	1 tsp	vanilla	5 ml
½ cup	milk	125 ml	pinch	salt	
6 tbsp	cocoa	90 ml		ground nuts, if desired	
3 cups	rolled oats	750 ml			

Put butter, sugar and milk into a large saucepan. Heat over medium heat until it reaches the boiling point. Remove from heat. Add remaining ingredients. Stir well. Drop from a spoon onto parchment paper or a cookie sheet. Work quickly—these get hard in a hurry. Do not bake. Store in a tightly covered container and use wax paper between layers.

Chocolate Snowflake Cookies

A real cookie snowstorm!

⅓ cup	shortening	75 ml	1 tsp	baking powder	5 ml
¾ cup	sugar	175 ml	½ tsp	salt	2 ml
1	egg	1	2½ tbsp	milk	37 ml
1 tsp	vanilla	5 ml	¼ cup	nuts, chopped	50 ml
1 cup	flour	250 ml		icing sugar, for dipping	
3 tbsp	cocoa	45 ml			

Cream shortening. Add sugar, egg, and vanilla. Beat until light and smooth. Sift together flour, cocoa, baking powder and salt. Add sifted ingredients to shortening mixture. Stir well. Add milk, and stir until all is smooth and blended. Refrigerate for an hour. Form into 1-inch (2.5 cm) balls, then roll in icing sugar. Place on a greased or parchment-lined cookie sheet and bake at 350F (175C) for 12-15 minutes. Allow to cool on the cookie sheet before removing to a rack.

Chocolate Diamonds

⅓ cup	butter or margarine	75 ml		¼ cup	flour	50 ml
2 tbsp	cocoa	30 ml		1 tsp	vanilla	5 ml
½ cup	sugar	125 ml		⅓ cup	nuts, chopped (peanuts are good)	75 ml
1	egg	1				

Melt butter or margarine in a saucepan. Add cocoa, mixing until smooth. Remove from heat and add remaining ingredients, except nuts. Beat until well blended. Spread in a 9-inch (23 cm), well-greased square pan. Sprinkle nuts over batter. Bake at 375F (190C) for 10-12 minutes. Cool slightly and cut into diamonds. Cool completely before removing from pan.

Chocolate-Yogurt Dip

A delicious dip for scrumptious, ripe strawberries.

½ cup	chocolate fudge sauce	125 ml		5 tsp	orange juice concentrate	25 ml
½ cup	no-fat yogurt	125 ml				

Blend all ingredients together and serve in a wide-mouthed bowl. Arrange whole perfect berries (with caps attached), in a pretty bowl or on a platter. Invite your guests to help themselves.

Baked Apples

Select 1 apple per serving. Wash well and remove cores. Place in a glass baking dish. Fill centres of apples with brown sugar. Sprinkle apples with lemon juice and a dash of cinnamon and dot each apple with butter. Add enough water to cover the bottom of the dish. Cover with aluminum foil. Bake at 350F (175C) until tender. Remove from oven. Spoon cooking juices in bottom of dish over apples. Serve warm with ice cream or whipped cream.

Fruit Salad

1 14-oz can	pineapple chunks	398 ml	¼ cup	unsweetened coconut	50 ml
1 14-oz can	mandarin oranges	398 ml	¼ cup	maraschino cherries	50 ml
1	banana, peeled and sliced	1			

Drain pineapple chunks and mandarin oranges into a large cup. Place pineapple and oranges in a salad bowl. Add banana. Sprinkle with coconut and cherries. Drizzle with 2 tbsp juice (drained from fruit). Stir together very gently. Serve.

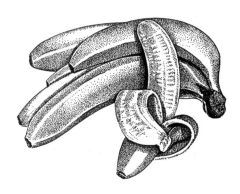

Cherry Refrigerator Dessert

Really pretty!

1⅓ cups	graham wafer crumbs	325 ml		1 19-oz can	cherry pie filling	540 ml
¼ cup	butter, melted	50 ml		½ pint	whipping cream, whipped,	250 ml
¼ cup	brown sugar	50 ml				
1 10½-oz pkg	miniature marshmallows	250 g		1 tbsp	sugar	15 ml
				1 tsp	vanilla	5 ml

Mix graham wafers, butter and sugar. Set aside 3 tbsp (45 ml) of mixture for topping. Press remaining mixture into an 8-inch (20 cm) square pan. Bake crust at 375F (190C) for 8 minutes. Cool. On top of graham wafer crust, layer ½ the package of marshmallows. Carefully add the cherry pie filling, then another layer of marshmallows. Whip the cream, add sugar and vanilla, beating until light and fluffy. Spread cream over marshmallows. Refrigerate before serving. Serves 12-16.

Apple Surprise Pudding

1 cup	flour, sifted	250 ml		Sauce:		
2 tsp	baking powder	10 ml		1 cup	brown sugar	250 ml
2 tbsp	sugar	30 ml		1 tbsp	lemon juice	15 ml
⅛ tsp	salt	0.5 ml		1½ cups	boiling water	375 ml
1 cup	apple, peeled and chopped	250 ml		2 tbsp	butter	30 ml
				½ tsp	cinnamon	2 ml
½ cup	milk	125 ml				

Sift dry ingredients. Add milk and chopped apple. Stir just enough to mix. Mixture will be stiff. Spread into a greased, deep baking dish. Mix ingredients for sauce and pour over top. Bake at 375F (190C) for 20-25 minutes. You will have to wait until the pudding is cooked to get your surprise. Makes about 6 servings.

One Apple Pudding

Only one apple left in the fridge? That apple may be made into a very nice dessert for about 6 people. Amazing!

2	eggs	2	½ tsp	baking powder	2 ml
¾ cup	sugar	175 ml	1	apple	1
⅓ cup	flour	75 ml	½ cup	walnuts, if desired	125 ml
¼ tsp	salt	1 ml	1 tsp	vanilla	5 ml

Beat eggs. Gradually add sugar, and vanilla and beat until light. Sift and measure flour. Sift flour, salt and baking powder over egg-sugar mixture; mix lightly. Core but do not peel apple. Dice finely. Fold apple and nuts into batter. Bake at 350F (175C) for about 30 minutes in an 8x8-inch (20x20 cm) pan. Serve warm with a whipped topping. Serves 6.

Fruit Crumble Dessert

Whatever fruit you have on hand will be great for this recipe—you can even mix them up.

1 cup	flour	250 ml		or:	
½ cup	whole wheat flour	125 ml	4 cups	apple, chopped	1 L
⅓ cup	sugar	75 ml	¾ cup	sugar	175 ml
½ cup	margarine	125 ml		or:	
½ tsp	salt	2 ml	3 cups	rhubarb, chopped	750 ml
½ tsp	baking powder	2 ml	1 cup	strawberries, raspberries, or blueberries	250 ml
Fruit Combinations:					
4 cups	rhubarb, chopped	1 L			
1 cup	sugar	250 ml	¾ cup	sugar	175 ml

Mix dry ingredients. Rub in margarine until mixture resembles fine bread-crumbs. Place half the mixture in a deep, 8x8-inch (20 cm) baking dish. Choose one of the fruit/sugar combinations and add. Cover with remaining half of the crumbs. Bake 30-45 minutes in a 350F (175C) oven. Serve with ice cream, whipped cream or a prepared light topping.

Fruit Salad Supreme

So tasty any time. Use whatever fruits you like best. Try a variety of colours.

apple, diced, cored but not peeled	peach, diced and peeled
pear, diced, cored but not peeled	

Dip the above fruit in lemon juice to prevent it from turning brown.

kiwi slices	orange segments, cut in half
watermelon chunks	strawberries
melon chunks	seedless grapes, red and green
cantaloupe chunks	raspberries, blueberries and cherries

Arrange in a deep glass bowl. Add a little sugar to release flavours. Let set in the fridge.

Jell-O Funny Faces

Dissolve 1 3-oz pkg (90 g) Jell-O powder, any flavour, in 1 cup (250 ml) boiling water. Cool to room temperature. Slowly pour cooled jelly into 1½ cups (375 ml) of 2% milk at room temperature. Stir constantly. Pour into serving dishes. Chill until set. Decorate to make funny faces with assorted fruits, candies and marshmallows, etc. Make hair from butterscotch chips, coconut, cut-up licorice strings, All Bran, ground nuts, etc. Make ears from peanut halves, strawberry slices, gumdrops, dates, prunes, etc. Make eyes from licorice "Allsorts" candies, Life Savers, chocolate pieces, blueberries, almonds, etc. Make mouths from kiwi pieces, orange slices, apple slices, raspberries, cranberries, celery etc.

Have fun!

The Great Nova Scotia Cookbook

No-Drip Pops

1 4½-oz pouch	Kool-Aid sugar-sweetened drink mix	135 g		1 3-oz pkg	Jell-O powder	85 g
				2 cups	boiling water	500 ml
				1½ cups	cold water	375 ml

Be careful with boiling water. Dissolve drink mix and jelly powder in boiling water. Add cold water. Pour into moulds, ice cube trays or paper cups. Freeze until partially set, about 3 hours. Insert popsicle sticks. Freeze until firm. Makes about 16 pops.

Jell-O Jubes

Lightly brush the inside of ice cube trays with vegetable oil. Mix a 3-oz (85 g) pkg of Jell-O powder with 2 tsp (10 ml) of cornstarch. Stir in ½ cup (125 ml) cold water. Boil and stir in a small saucepan. Remove from heat. Stir 1 minute. Spoon jelly into prepared trays. Cool 5 minutes, then refrigerate for 20 minutes to set. To remove, use fingertips to pull away from sides of moulds. Store in the refrigerator.

Fancy Fruit Kabobs

Use your favourite fruit—bananas, apples, grapes, pineapple, peaches, pears, strawberries and kiwi.
A couple of wooden kabob sticks
Your favourite flavour of yogurt
2 handfuls of granola

Wash fruit and cut into bite-size pieces. Pour yogurt on a plate. Put granola on another plate. Slide pieces of fruit on each stick until it is full. Roll the kabobs in the yogurt so that all fruit is covered. Then dip in granola. Enjoy!

Vegetable Dip

¼ cup	sour cream	50 ml	½ tsp	onion flakes	2 ml
½ tsp	beef bouillon powder	2 ml			

Put all ingredients into a small bowl. Mix well. Prepare carrot sticks, pepper strips, celery sticks, broccoli and cauliflower florets. Serve raw vegetables with dip.

Yogurt Honey Dip

1 cup	vanilla or strawberry yogurt	250 ml	2 tbsp	honey	30 ml
			½ tsp	almond flavouring	2 ml
1 tbsp	lemon juice	15 ml			

Combine ingredients and blend until smooth. Refrigerate until ready to serve. Serve with luscious red strawberries, which should be nicely arranged and wearing their little green hats.

Celery Caterpillars

celery	raisins
Cheese Whiz	

Wash and halve celery stalks. Fill with Cheez Whiz. Place raisins in a line on the filling in each stalk.

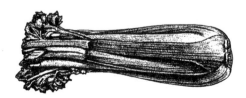

Barbecue Sauce

½ cup	soft butter	125 ml	1 tsp	dill	5 ml
2 tbsp	lemon juice	30 ml	½ tsp	salt	2 ml
½ tsp	basil	2 ml	¼ tsp	cayenne	1 ml

Combine all ingredients. Brush on burgers or hot dogs.

Easter Egg Treats

Placed in little baskets, these treats make nice gifts.

1 pkg	Jell-O instant pudding	1	⅓ cup	butter	75 ml
⅓ cup	boiling water	75 ml	3 cups	icing sugar, sifted	750 ml
			6 1-oz squares	semi-sweet chocolate	6 x 30 g

Stir pudding, water and butter in a large bowl until smooth. Mix in sugar by the cupful, stirring until mixture forms a ball. Form into 1½-inch (3 cm) egg shapes. Refrigerate until firm. Partially melt chocolate in a separate bowl over hot water. Remove from heat and continue stirring until all chocolate is melted and smooth. Dip egg shapes into chocolate; decorate with coloured sprinkles or icing. For multi-coloured eggs, make two fillings using two pudding flavours. Roll small centres from one flavour; surround by a second flavour. Makes 24 eggs.

Peanut Butter Candy

natural peanut butter, no sugar added	chocolate, melted
liquid honey	coconut, grated
skim milk powder	nuts, crushed

Mix honey and peanut butter in equal amounts. Add half the amount of skim milk powder. Roll into balls and refrigerate. Dip balls in any combination of chocolate, coconut and nuts.

Hot Chocolate

3 cups	powdered milk	750 ml	½ cup	sugar (more, if desired)	125 ml
¾ cup	cocoa	175 ml			
			pinch	salt	

Combine sugar and cocoa; add powdered milk and a dash of salt. Store in a bottle with a tight cover. For 1 serving, place ⅓ cup dry mixture in a cup, add boiling water and stir. Serves 8.

Strawberry Fruit Sparkle

First, ask a parent if you may use the blender.

4 cups	strawberries, frozen	1 L	4 cups	apple juice, unsweetened	1 L
½ cup	sugar	125 ml			
1 cup	water	250 ml	8 cups	raspberry ginger ale	2 L
¼ cup	lemon juice	50 ml			

Combine strawberries, sugar, water and lemon juice in a blender. Blend on high until smooth. Empty blended mixture into a punch bowl. Add apple juice and ginger ale; stir and serve. Whole frozen strawberries may be floated on top. Makes about 4 quarts (4 L).

Tomato Cocktail

½ tsp	Worcestershire sauce	2 ml		½ cup	tomato juice	125 ml
1 tsp	lemon juice	5 ml		dash	pepper	

Mix all together in a glass. Add an ice cube.

Lemonade Soda

juice	of 1 lemon			club soda
2 tsp	powdered sugar	10 ml		

Dissolve sugar in lemon juice. Add an ice cube and fill glass with club soda. Garnish with a cherry and a slice of lemon or orange. Serve with a straw.

Moonmint Drink

2 cups	cold milk	500 ml		¼ tsp	mint extract	1 ml
	chocolate syrup, as desired					

Blend together at medium speed or stir with a spoon until smooth.

Zippy Ginger Ale

2 tsp	corn syrup or honey	10 ml		ginger ale, chilled
2 tsp	lemon juice	10 ml		

Mix syrup and lemon juice in a tall glass. Fill with ginger ale.

Vanilla Milk Shake

Ask if you may use the blender; you may need help.

vanilla ice cream	vanilla extract
cold milk	

Place ice cream, vanilla and milk in a blender. Blend until smooth and frothy. Serve in a glass with a straw. You may make different flavours by adding different ingredients. Here are some ideas:

For a chocolate milkshake, add chocolate syrup to the milk and ice cream. For fruit varieties, add cut-up pieces of banana, blueberries, strawberries, or raspberries.

Chocolate Syrup

1 cup	corn syrup	250 ml	4 tbsp	melted butter or soft margarine	60 ml
2 tbsp	water	30 ml			
1 pkg	instant chocolate pudding	1			

Put corn syrup and water in a medium-size bowl. Empty contents of pudding package into syrup mixture. Add butter. Beat until thoroughly mixed. Use as a topping for ice cream or use 2 tbsp (30 ml) to one cup of milk for a chocolate drink.

Speedy Chocolate Syrup

Have it on hand for special treats.

½ cup	cocoa	125 ml	⅛ tsp	salt	0.5 ml
1¼ cups	sugar	300 ml	1¼ cups	boiling water	300 ml
½ tsp	vanilla	2 ml			

Measure cocoa, sugar and salt into a saucepan. Stir in boiling water. Boil 1 minute over low heat; stir constantly. Remove from heat; add vanilla. Cool. Store in the refrigerator. Use to make chocolate milkshake recipe. Makes about 2 cups.

Orange Julius

1 cup	water	250 ml
1 cup	milk	250 ml
½ cup	sugar	125 ml
6-8	ice cubes	6-8

6 oz	orange juice concentrate, frozen	180 ml
1 tsp	vanilla	5 ml

Combine all ingredients in blender and mix until ice is crushed. Serve immediately. Serves 4.

Honey-Berry Float

4 cups	milk, chilled	1 L
3 tbsp	honey	45 ml
2 cups	strawberries, fresh and crushed	500 ml

½ tsp	almond extract	2 ml
2 cups	vanilla ice cream	500 ml

Combine milk, honey, strawberries, almond extract and ice cream in a blender. Whirl until smooth. Pour into glasses and garnish with a scoop of ice cream. Serves 6-8.

Pink Lassies

1 cup	cranberry juice	250 ml
¼ cup	orange juice	50 ml

2 cups	vanilla ice cream, softened	500 ml

Place all ingredients in blender. Process on medium until smooth. Serve in cocktail glasses with straws.

Peach Cooler

1 cup	milk	250 ml		¼ tsp	almond extract	1 ml
1½ cups	peaches, sliced	375 ml		1 cup	vanilla ice cream, softened	250 ml

Place all ingredients in a blender. Process on medium until smooth. Serve in cocktail glasses with straws.

Root Beer Float

vanilla ice cream		cold root beer

You will need a tall glass, a long-handled spoon and a drinking straw for each person you are serving.

Use an ice cream scoop or a heavy spoon to scoop the ice cream. Place two scoops of ice cream into each glass. Fill each glass with root beer. Place a spoon and a straw in each glass. Serve a nice cold float along with a paper napkin to each guest. Change soda flavour for variety; try orange, cream soda, and cola.

Pools of Floaties

1	apple	1			any other fruit	
1	peach	1		¼ cup	orange juice	50 ml
	a few strawberries			¼ cup	apple juice	50 ml
1	banana	1				

Cut up fruit into bite-size pieces. Put in a bowl. Pour juice over fruit. Refrigerate for a little while. Enjoy!

Fruit Pizza

Be really creative and make a pretty arrangement.

To make the crust:

5 cups	Rice Krispies	1.25 L	32	large marshmallows	32
¼ cup	margarine	50 ml			

Melt margarine in a large saucepan over low heat. Add marshmallows; stir until melted and well blended. Remove from heat. Add Rice Krispies, stirring until cereal is coated. Grease pizza pan. Press cereal mixture into pan. Cool.

To prepare the topping:

1 8-oz pkg	cream cheese	250 g	⅓ cup	cocoa	75 ml
2 cups	icing sugar	500 ml			

Place cream cheese, icing sugar and cocoa in the small bowl of a mixer. Beat on low speed until all is blended. On medium speed, beat until smooth. Spread over the cooled pizza base.

To prepare the fruit:

15	medium strawberries, halved and hulled	15	2	kiwi fruit, peeled and sliced	2
1	banana, peeled and sliced	1			

Arrange fruit around pizza in circles, paying attention to colour, size and texture.

To prepare a glaze:

3 tbsp	apricot jam	45 ml	2 tsp	water	10 ml

Mix jam and water in a small bowl. With a pastry brush, dab the fruit with glaze to prevent fruit from turning brown.

Now garnish:
Beat 1 cup (250 ml) whipping cream and add 2 tsp (10 ml) sugar and a little vanilla. Place whipped cream in decorating tube and make little flowers around the fruit arrangement. Cut pizza into wedges and serve.

Bunny Hop Salad

1	medium pear, cored and halved	1	2	large almonds, split	2
	lemon juice		12	carrot sticks, thin	12
4	raisins	4	2	miniature marshmallows	2

Dip the cut sides of the pear in lemon juice. Place pear halves on plate, cut side down. Decorate top end of each half with two raisins for eyes, almonds for ears, 6 carrot strips for whiskers and marshmallows for nose and tail.

Super Peanut Butter Sandwich

On one slice of whole wheat bread, sprinkle grated carrot, then place one cheese slice and one heaping tbsp (15 ml) of raisins. Top with another slice of bread that has been spread with peanut butter. Cover this piece of bread with bananas sliced lengthwise. Over this sprinkle alfalfa sprouts. Top with another slice of bread. Press together and slice as you wish. Now, open your mouth very politely and enjoy this super lunch.

Waldorf Club Sandwich

Mix together:

1 6½-oz can	tuna	184 g	¼ cup	celery, chopped	50 ml
			¼ cup	red onion	50 ml
¼ cup	Kraft Sour Cream and Onion Ranch Dressing	50 ml	¼ cup	pecans, chopped	50 ml
				curry powder, as desired	

Mix ingredients and layer this mixture with Cheddar cheese slices and sliced green apple (lightly brushed with dressing) between three slices of brown bread. Cut sandwiches into triangles or fingers. Makes 2 sandwiches.

Wiener Roll-Ups

12	wieners	12		Heinz sandwich spread
12 slices	bread	12		mustard

Boil wieners until cooked. Remove from water and drain. Trim crusts from bread if desired. Spread each slice with sandwich spread. Add a little mustard. Place a wiener diagonally on each slice of bread, roll up diagonally and secure with toothpicks. Place on a greased cookie sheet and bake at 425F (220C) for 5 minutes or until golden and crisp.

Pizza Melts

1½ cups	Mozzarella cheese, shredded	375 ml		½ cup	mayonnaise	125 ml
½ cup	Cheddar cheese, shredded	125 ml		2 tbsp	green onions, chopped	30 ml
½ cup	pepperoni, finely chopped	125 ml		1 tbsp	Parmesan cheese, grated	15 ml
				4	English muffins, split and toasted	4

In a medium-size bowl, combine Mozzarella cheese, Cheddar cheese, pepperoni, mayonnaise, onion and Parmesan cheese. Place 4 toasted English muffin halves on a plate lined with paper towel. Spread ¼ cup (50 ml) of cheese mixture on each half. Microwave at medium for 2-2½ minutes or at high for 1-1½ minutes until cheese melts. Repeat with remaining 4 muffin halves and cheese mixture. Makes 8 small pizzas.

Peanut Butter and Banana on Crackers

1	banana, ripe	1	crackers, unsalted
	peanut butter		

Spread peanut butter on crackers. Slice bananas and place one round on each cracker. This is a great after-school snack.

Poached Eggs

Grease the bottom of a 6-8 inch (15-20 cm) pot. Add about 4 inches (10 cm) of water and a little salt. Let water come to a boil. Break an egg into a small bowl. Use a wooden spoon to swirl the water in the pot into a circle and, while it swirls, slide the egg from the bowl into the water. This swirling will help the egg to keep a round form and not spread out. Boil egg gently until firm.

Lift out egg and place on hot, buttered toast. Serve immediately with a little pepper and paprika sprinkled over top.

Grilled Cheese Sandwich

For each sandwich, you will need two slices of bread, white or whole wheat, about 1 tbsp (15 ml) butter or soft margarine and one yellow cheese slice. Heat a frying pan over medium heat. Butter both slices of bread on one side. Put remaining butter or margarine in a frying pan. Place one slice of bread, buttered side down, in the frying pan. Put the cheese slice on top. Cover with other slice, buttered side up. When the bottom-side browns, flip the sandwich over with a pancake lifter. Brown the other side. Use the lifter to remove the sandwich to a plate. Cut in half.

Scrambled Egg Sandwich

Scrambled eggs are usually lighter and fluffier if done over hot water in a double boiler. If you are in a hurry, use a fry pan. For two servings, melt 1 or 2 tbsp (15-30 ml) butter in a heated fry pan. Turn burner to a low heat.

Beat together:

3	eggs	3	⅛ tsp	paprika	0.5 ml
¼ tsp	salt	1 ml	2 tbsp	milk	30 ml
⅛ tsp	pepper	0.5 ml			

Pour mixture into a heated skillet. Increase heat a little and move the eggs about gently with a spatula. As eggs begin to cook, turn over and under until they are set and thickened. For a scrambled egg sandwich, divide eggs between four slices of buttered bread. You may also serve them with hot, buttered toast and sausage, sausage rounds or bacon. Someone might like maple syrup or ketchup. Don't forget the fruit juice and a pitcher of cold milk.

Crunchy Salad Snack

2	small chunks iceberg lettuce	2	4	cucumber, bite-size chunks	4
1	large Romaine lettuce leaf, broken into bite-size pieces	1	2	small celery sticks	2
			3	small carrot sticks	3
1	small tomato, cut into 8 bite-size pieces	1		Cheddar cheese, cubed (as desired)	

Wash all vegetables carefully and drain. Serve in a salad bowl with your favourite dressing. This may be packed in a covered container and taken to school for lunch. Keep cool but do not freeze.

Tasty Vegetable Dip

Nice for raw vegetables or a variety of crackers.

½ cup	sour cream	125 ml	¼-½ tsp	chicken or beef bouillon powder	1-2 ml
1 tsp	onion soup mix	5 ml			

Mix together and keep cold until serving time.

The Great Nova Scotia Cookbook

Sloppy Joes with Ketchup and Soup

1 lb	lean ground beef	500 g	1 tbsp	sugar		15 ml
¼ cup	barbecue sauce	50 ml	1 10-oz can	chicken gumbo soup		284 ml
¼ cup	ketchup	50 ml				

In a large skillet, cook beef until it loses its pink colour; add remaining ingredients and cook until thick. Serve over toasted hamburger buns. After working with ground meat, take great care to scrub your hands, dishes and countertops!

Mexicano Sloppy Joes

1 lb	lean ground beef, crumbled	500 g	¼ tsp	pepper	1 ml
			⅓ cup	vinegar	75 ml
1 tbsp	chili powder	15 ml	1 14-oz can	stewed tomatoes with Mexican seasoning	398 ml
1	green bell pepper, finely chopped	1			
½ tsp	salt	2 ml	4	hamburger buns	4

Heat fry pan over medium heat. Add beef, chili powder, green pepper, salt and pepper. Brown beef and drain off any fat. Stir in vinegar. Add tomatoes. Cook until thickened. Spoon mixture onto buns and serve immediately.

Kraft Dinner Lasagna

Who doesn't like Kraft dinner? I have never heard anyone say no to this recipe either.

1 6½-oz pkg	Kraft Dinner (cheese and tomato)	200 g	2 cups	Mozzarella cheese	500 ml
			2 tbsp	Parmesan cheese, grated	30 ml
1½ cups	pasta sauce	375 ml			
½ lb	lean ground beef, cooked and drained	250 g			

Prepare Kraft Dinner according to directions on package. Place half of the macaroni and cheese in an 8x11-inch (2 L) baking dish. Layer with half of the pasta sauce, beef and Mozzarella cheese. Repeat layers, ending with Mozzarella. Sprinkle with Parmesan. Bake at 350F (175C) for 20 minutes. Serves 8.

Tuna Cheese Melts

1 6½-oz can	tuna	184 g	¼ cup	mayonnaise	50 ml
			4	tomato slices	4
¼ cup	celery, finely chopped	50 ml	4	cheese slices	4
			4	hamburger buns, split	4
¼ cup	onion, finely chopped	50 ml			

Mix tuna, celery, onion and mayonnaise together. Spread tuna mix on each bun. Cover with a slice each of tomato and cheese. Bake for 15 minutes in a 350F (175C) oven.

At-Home Lunch

Fry bologna slices in a little butter until edges curl to form a cup. Fill each cup with baked beans and sprinkle with shredded cheese.

Chicken Fingers

1 lb	chicken breasts boneless	500 g		Shake and Bake coating mix	
1	egg, beaten	1			

Cut breasts into 1-inch (2.5 cm) fingers. Moisten with egg. Shake off excess. Coat chicken with coating mix. Bake on an ungreased baking sheet at 400F (200C) for 15 minutes or until tender. Serve with a favourite dip and assorted raw vegetable sticks. Always wash your hands, utensils and dishes with lots of soap and hot water after handling raw chicken.

Hearty Salmon Sandwich

Enough for two.

1 7-oz can	salmon	220 g	1	green onion, chopped	1
2 tbsp	Miracle Whip (light) salad dressing	30 ml	4 slices	whole wheat bread, toasted	4

Mix the above ingredients together. Spread toasted whole wheat bread slices with Cheese Whiz and salsa dip. Place layers of salmon, a spinach leaf and tomato slice on toast. This will make two nice sandwiches.

The Perfect Hard-Boiled Egg

Good for breakfast and good for sandwiches.

Place eggs in cold water in a medium-size saucepan. Turn heat to medium and bring to a boil. Remove from heat and let sit in hot water for 20 minutes. Cool under running water to stop the cooking and to prevent dark circles from developing around the yolks. When eggs boil they become tough. To make delicious egg sandwiches, peel off shells and chop eggs. Add finely chopped onion—enough to add lots of flavour to the eggs. Add mayonnaise to moisten. Add a little salt and pepper. Mix in parsley flakes. Spread mayonnaise on whole wheat bread slices. Add generous amounts of egg filling, a piece of crispy lettuce and another slice of buttered bread. These may be wrapped and chilled. Slice into small sandwiches, and serve.

Stir-Fried Cauliflower and Red Pepper

Needs little cooking and is best tender-crisp. You can whip this up in no time at all.

1	medium cauliflower, cut into florets	1	⅓ cup	classic herb dressing (Kraft is good)	75 ml
1	red pepper, cut into julienne strips	1	2	green onions, sliced diagonally	2

Heat dressing in a wok or large frying pan; add cauliflower and pepper. Stir fry for 2-3 minutes; reduce heat. Cover and let steam for 5-7 minutes. Just before serving, sprinkle with green onion.

Nutty Cheese Ball

2 cups	medium Cheddar cheese, shredded	500 ml	2 tsp	Worcestershire sauce	10 ml
			½ tsp	garlic powder	2 ml
1 8-oz pkg	cream cheese, softened	250 g	½ cup	milk	125 ml
			¾ cup	pecans, finely chopped	175 ml
⅓ cup	old Cheddar cheese, shredded	75 ml			

Mix the cheeses, milk, sauce and garlic powder in a large bowl. Chill if necessary before shaping into a ball. Roll in pecans. Chill for 2-3 hours. Serve with crackers.

"Chicken-Little" Puffs

1½ cups	cooked chicken, finely chopped	375 ml	1 tbsp	parsley flakes, dried	15 ml
			1 tsp	salt	5 ml
½ cup	almonds, chopped	125 ml	1 tsp	celery seed	5 ml
1 cup	chicken broth	250 ml	⅛ tsp	cayenne pepper	0.5 ml
½ cup	vegetable oil	125 ml	1 cup	flour	250 ml
2 tsp	Worcestershire sauce	10 ml	4	eggs	4

Combine chicken and almonds, and set aside. In a large saucepan, combine the next seven ingredients; bring to a boil. Add flour all at once; stir until a ball of dough forms. Remove from heat, and let stand about 5 minutes. Drop in eggs one at a time, beating well after each addition. Beat until smooth. Add chicken and almonds. Drop from a heaping teaspoon onto greased baking sheets. Bake until golden brown, about 12 minutes. Serve warm as appetizers. Makes about 6 dozen puffs.

Creamed Peas

2 cups	frozen peas	500 g		salt and pepper, to taste	
½ cup	water	125 ml	¼ cup	sour cream	50 ml
1 tsp	chicken-flavoured bouillon powder (optional)	5 ml			

Dissolve bouillon in water and heat to boiling. Add salt and pepper. Add peas and boil for about 3 minutes. Drain. Add sour cream and stir to coat. Return to heat just long enough to heat through.

Pizza for One

Alone? Here is a quick snack.

3 slices	bacon	3	1	English muffin	1
2 tbsp	tomato ketchup	30 ml	1	Cheddar cheese slice	1
½ tsp	onion powder	2 ml	1	Mozzarella cheese slice	1
pinch	oregano				

Cut bacon into small pieces and fry over medium-low heat. Drain on a paper towel. Stir together ketchup, oregano, and onion powder in a small bowl. Split the English muffin in two and place on a broiler pan. Spread ketchup mixture over the two halves. Over that, lay the Cheddar cheese, then the Mozzarella cheese slice. Divide the bacon pieces between the 2 muffin halves. Put the broiler pan on the top rack of the oven. Broil pizzas for 1-2 minutes to melt the cheese. Watch carefully so they don't burn. Remove from pan and transfer your pizzas to a plate. Enjoy!

Quick and Easy Corn Chowder

2 tbsp	butter	30 ml	1 12-oz can	corn kernels, drained	341 ml
2 tbsp	flour	30 ml			
1 tsp	salt, less if desired	5 ml	1 tbsp	green pepper	15 ml
⅛ tsp	pepper	0.5 ml	1-2 tbsp	red pepper	15-30 ml
2 cups	milk, or more	500 ml			

Melt butter in a saucepan. Stir in flour until smooth. Gradually add milk and seasonings. Stir until mixture boils and thickens. Add remaining ingredients. You can adjust the ingredients, adding a little more milk and corn, as needed. The recipe can easily be doubled.

Quick Chicken Soup

Place the first 7 ingredients in a large saucepan:

5 cups	water	1.25 L	½ cup	rice, uncooked	125 ml
2	chicken bouillon cubes	2	1 14-oz can	tomatoes, with juice	398 ml
½ cup	carrots, diced	125 ml	1 6½-oz can	chicken or turkey flakes, broken apart	184 g
½ cup	potatoes, diced	125 ml			
¾ cup	onion, sliced	175 ml			

Cover and place on medium heat. Let come to a boil. Stir often to prevent soup from sticking to the bottom of the pot. Reduce heat and simmer for about an hour. When it's almost time to serve the soup, add the chicken or turkey. Heat again. Serve with crackers or rolls.

Vegetable Beef Soup

You want your friends to stay for lunch but you have only a small amount of ground beef and some vegetables in the fridge. Here's something you can make.

½ lb	ground beef, more or less	250 g		1 cup	onions, diced and peeled	250 ml
	vegetable oil			1 tbsp	beef bouillon powder	15 ml
1 14-oz can	tomatoes, with juice	398 ml		4 cups	water	1L
1-2 cups	frozen mixed vegetables	250-500 ml		¼ tsp	pepper	1 ml
				¼ tsp	thyme	1 ml

Place oil in a large frying pan and heat. Add meat and fry until browned and crumbled. Add the remaining ingredients. Stir well. Bring to a boil and cover. After four or five minutes, reduce heat and simmer until vegetables are tender and flavours have blended. Serve with crackers or rolls.

Easy Scalloped Potatoes

Use a covered casserole. Preheat oven to 375F (190C).

4-5	medium-size potatoes	4-5		1 10-oz can	mushroom soup	284 ml
1 tsp	salt	5 ml				
½ tsp	pepper	2 ml		2 tbsp	butter	30 ml

Wash and peel potatoes. Remove all blemishes or spots. Rinse. Slice about one-half of the potatoes into the casserole, taking care to slice them thinly—no thicker than ⅛ inch (0.3 cm). Sprinkle salt and pepper over potatoes. Spoon half of the can of mushroom soup over sliced potatoes. Slice remaining potatoes over first layer and add remaining soup. Dot with butter. Cover casserole. Bake for 1½ hours at 350F (175C). Remove cover during last twenty minutes of cooking.

Hamburg and Spaghetti

A hearty supper for four.

1 tbsp	oil	15 ml	¼ tsp	dried basil	1 ml
1 lb	lean ground beef	500 ml	¼ tsp	dried oregano	1 ml
1 cup	onion, chopped	250 ml	1 tsp	parsley flakes	5 ml
1 14-oz can	tomatoes, cut in pieces, with juice	398 ml	1 tsp	sugar	5 ml
			¼ cup	Parmesan cheese	50 ml
1 10-oz can	mushrooms, sliced	284 ml	1 tsp	salt	5 ml
			¼ tsp	pepper	1 ml
1 5½-oz can	tomato paste	156 ml	1	bay leaf	1
			½ lb	spaghetti, broken	250 g
1½ cups	water	375 ml		Parmesan cheese, grated	
¼ tsp	garlic powder	1 ml			

Heat oil in a large saucepan. Add ground beef and onion. Stir and cook until browned and crumbled. Add tomatoes, mushrooms, tomato paste, water, spices and sugar. Stir. Add spaghetti and cover pot with lid. Boil until spaghetti is tender. Remove from heat. Remove bay leaf from pan. Sprinkle mixture with Parmesan cheese.

Quick Tuna Casserole

1 7-oz can	tuna	220 g	½ cup	milk	125 ml
			¾ cup	potato chips, crushed	175 ml
1 10-oz can	cream of mushroom soup	284 ml			

Place tuna in a casserole. Blend soup and milk together. Pour over tuna and mix together. Sprinkle crushed potato chips over top. Bake at 375F (190C) for 30 minutes or until heated through.

Plain Hamburgers

1 lb	lean ground beef	500 g		¼ cup	milk	50 ml
1 tsp	salt	5 ml		2 tbsp	rolled oats, uncooked	30 ml
½ tsp	pepper	2 ml				
¼ cup	onions, grated or finely chopped	50 ml		1	egg	1

Place all ingredients in a bowl and mix well together. Shape into 4 or 5 patties. Do not press into firm patties; they are better if gently molded. Fry or broil patties until they are fully cooked and no longer pink inside. Serve on buns with ketchup, cheese, relish, pickle or sauces, chopped lettuce, slices of tomato and peppers.

Grilled Pizza Sandwiches

⅔ cup	pizza sauce, canned	150 ml		4	thick cheese slices	4
8 slices	Italian bread	8		1 tsp	garlic powder	5 ml
	salami			1 tbsp	butter or margarine	15 ml

For each slice of bread, butter one side and spread pizza sauce on the other side. Top sauce with salami, then with cheese slice. Sprinkle with garlic powder. Top with second slice of bread, sauce side down, butter side up. Grill. Makes 4 sandwiches.

Powerful Pita Pizza

2	pita breads	2
1 pkg	sliced meat: ham, pepperoni, salami, etc.	1
1 can	pizza sauce	1

1 10-oz can	pineapple tidbits	1
1 small pkg	Mozzarella cheese, shredded	1

Spread sauce on pita. Put toppings on it and heat in the microwave.

Cream Cheese Mold

1 3-oz pkg	lime Jell-O	90 g
19 oz can	crushed pineapple	540 ml
8 oz pkg	cream cheese	250 g

½ cup	Cheddar cheese, shredded	125 ml
1 cup	hot water	250 ml

Grease mold pan. Mix Jell-O with hot water and add the juice from the crushed pineapple. Pour about ¼ inch (0.7 cm) to ½ inch (1.3 cm) of this mixture into the mold pan to set. In a blender beat cream cheese and remainder of Jell-O mixture until fluffy. Put in refrigerator to thicken. When fairly thick, fold in crushed pineapple and shredded cheese. Pour into mold to set. Return to refrigerator.

Orange Jelly Mold

2 3-oz pkg	orange Jell-O	2x85 g	1 10-oz can	mandarin oranges	284 ml
1 cup	boiling water	250 ml	1 cup	fruit juice	250 ml
1 small can	pineapple, crushed	1	1 cup	carrots, grated	250 ml

Stir Jell-O and boiling water together until dissolved. Drain pineapple and oranges and save liquid. Substitute saved liquid for the 1 cup (250 ml) cold water called for in the Jell-O package instructions—you may have to add a little extra water to make up the cup. Pour the Jell-O into a Jell-O mold and set in refrigerator to partially set. When fairly thick, stir in pineapple, oranges and carrot. Mix together and return to refrigerator to finish setting.

School Bus Scones

You can eat these anywhere!

1¼ cups	all-purpose flour	300 ml	¼ tsp	salt	1 ml
1¼ cups	rolled oats	300 ml	⅓ cup	milk	75 ml
⅓ cup	raisins	75 ml	¼ cup	butter, melted	50 ml
3 tbsp	sugar	45 ml	1	egg, beaten	1
1 tbsp	baking powder	15 ml		cinnamon sugar	

In a large bowl, combine flour, oats, raisins, sugar, baking powder and salt. In another bowl, stir milk, melted butter and beaten egg together. Stir liquid ingredients into dry ingredients, just until moistened. Turn dough onto a floured board. Knead lightly 4-5 times. Ask mom or dad to show you how. Pat dough into an 8-inch (20 cm) circle. Sprinkle lightly with cinnamon sugar. Score into 8 wedges and place on an ungreased cookie sheet. Bake at 375F (190C) for 12-15 minutes.

Sweet and Sour Meatballs

Taste the zing!

¾-1 cup	brown sugar	175-250 ml	1	onion, finely chopped	1
¾ cup	water	175 ml			
1 cup	ketchup	250 ml	2 lb	hamburg	1 kg
¾ cup	vinegar	175 ml		salt and pepper, to taste	
1 tbsp	dry mustard	15 ml			

To make the sweet and sour sauce, stir the first 5 ingredients in a saucepan until sugar is dissolved. Crumble hamburg in a bowl. Mix in chopped onions. Season with salt and pepper. Mix together with a fork and form into small balls. Place meatballs on a cookie sheet. Bake at 350F (175C) until lightly browned. Remove from oven. Place in a casserole dish and cover with sweet and sour sauce. Return to oven to set flavour. If a thicker sauce is desired you may add a little thickening by mixing 1 tbsp flour in a little cold water. Add to sauce and bring to a boil.

Hamburg Casserole

2 cups	macaroni	500 ml	1 cup	carrots or peas, diced (optional)	250 ml
½ lb	hamburg	250 g			
2	onions, chopped	2	2 tbsp	butter	30 ml
1 14-oz can	tomatoes	398 ml	½ cup	cracker crumbs, ground	125 ml
				salt and pepper	

To cook macaroni, follow directions on the package. You will need about 1 cup (250 ml) of dry macaroni. Place butter in fry pan and heat. Add onions and stir until slightly browned. Add meat and fry until slightly browned and crumbly. Add macaroni, tomatoes and vegetable. Add seasoning. Turn mixture into a casserole. Top with cracker crumbs. Add a little extra butter on top.

Whirly Wigs

Delicious served with a little butter and a glass of milk.

2 tbsp	butter, melted	30 ml	½ tsp	cream of tartar	2 ml
2 cups	flour	500 ml	½ tsp	salt	2 ml
3 tbsp	sugar	45 ml	¼ cup	butter or shortening	50 ml
4 tsp	baking powder	20 ml	¾ cup	milk	175 ml

Melt 2 tablespoons (30 ml) butter on a dinner plate. Measure dry ingredients into a flour sifter. Sift dry ingredients into a mixing bowl. Cut ¼ cup (50 ml) butter into flour mixture with a pastry blender until the mixture is crumbly. Add the milk and stir until the mixture is wet and forms a ball. Knead on a floured surface about 8 times. Divide the dough into about 12 pieces. Roll each piece into a long rope about 12 inches (30 cm) long. Do not handle too much. Make a coating of ½ cup (125 ml) brown sugar and 2 tsp (10 ml) cinnamon, and place in a long pan with low sides. Roll one rope at a time in melted butter and then dip in cinnamon-sugar mixture. Place ropes on cookie sheet and roll up like a snake when it coils itself up. Tuck the end in under the bun. Repeat until all 12 are done. Bake at 400F (200C) for 10-12 minutes. Cool on a rack.

Corn Bread

2 tbsp	shortening, melted	30 ml	¾ tsp	salt	3 ml
1 cup	flour	250 ml	3 tsp	baking powder	15 ml
¾ cup	cornmeal	175 ml	1	egg	1
2-5 tbsp	sugar	30-75 ml	1 cup	milk	250 ml

Prepare a 13x9-inch (33x23 cm) pan by melting shortening in pan. Preheat oven to 425F (220C). Beat the egg in a small bowl. Add the milk to the egg and stir until they are well mixed. Pour melted shortening into the egg and milk mixture and add cornmeal. Stir. Sift flour, sugar, salt and baking powder and add to the milk mixture. Stir until thoroughly mixed. Do not beat. Grease your baking pan again. Pour batter into the pan. Bake for 25-30 minutes or until done. Cut into squares and serve hot with butter, molasses or corn syrup. Wonderful with baked beans, chili or bacon and eggs.

Pancakes

Thick and fluffy.

3 tbsp	shortening, melted	45 ml	3 tbsp	sugar	45 ml
1½ cups	flour	375 ml	1	egg	1
3½ tsp	baking powder	17 ml	1¼ cups	milk	300 ml
½ tsp	salt	2 ml			

Break the egg in a small bowl. Beat until bubbly. Add milk and melted shortening to the egg. Stir. Sift flour, baking powder, salt and sugar. Combine milk mixture with sifted ingredients. Stir until smooth. Do not beat. Meanwhile, heat the fry pan. Grease well. Add small spoonfuls of batter to the pan. Small pancakes are much easier to turn. Cook on one side until the pancake is puffed and bubbles form. Flip over with a pancake turner and cook briefly. Serve hot with butter and syrup.

Craft Ideas For Kids

Play Dough with Alum

Just for play—not to be eaten!

2 cups	flour	500 ml
2 tbsp	powdered alum	30 ml
½ cup	salt	125 ml
1½ cups	water	375 ml

1 tbsp	vegetable oil	15 ml
	red, yellow, green and blue food colouring	

Mix salt and oil into the water and heat to just boiling. Pour into the flour and alum, which have been mixed together. Knead and divide into four parts. Add a different colour to each part. Knead well.

Stove Top Play Dough

Just for play—not to be eaten!

Combine:

1 cup	white flour	250 ml
¼ cup	salt	50 ml

2 tbsp	cream of tartar	30 ml

Mix together and add to the above:

1 cup	water	250 ml
2 tsp	food colouring	10 ml

1 tbsp	vegetable oil	15 ml

Transfer all to a pot and cook over medium heat for 3-5 minutes. Stir constantly. The mixture will form a ball. Turn out and knead on a floured board. Store in an airtight container or plastic bag.

Uncooked Play Dough

Just for play—not to be eaten!

2 cups	flour	500 ml	food colouring,	as desired
⅓ cup	salt	75 ml		
2 tbsp	cooking oil	30 ml	boiling water	

Measure flour and salt into a bowl. Mix food colouring into the oil. Use as much colouring as you wish—you only need a few drops for light-coloured dough. Add more if you wish a to have a deeper colour. Add and mix in boiling water, starting with 1 cup (250 ml); add more as needed until the dough forms into a ball that you can squeeze. If too soft, add a little more flour. Keep dough stored in plastic bags or in a tightly covered jar. It should stay soft for several months.

Ask permission to use the rolling pin, cookie cutters, cookie sheets and oven. Roll out play dough with a rolling pin and cut out any design you wish. Make a small hole in the top, if you are making hanging ornaments. Lay designs on a cookie sheet. These may be left on the counter to dry or placed in the oven on the centre rack at 300F (150C) for about 1 hour. Remove from oven and cool. Paint with watercolours or acrylic paint. When dry, varnish or shellac both sides.

White Play Clay
for Ornaments

Just for play—not to be eaten!

2 cups	baking soda	500 ml	1¼ cups cold water		300 ml
1 cup	corn starch	250 ml			

Mix ingredients together in saucepan. Cook over medium heat, stirring constantly, until the consistency is that of hot, moist, mashed potatoes. Turn out onto a plate and cover with a damp cloth until cool enough to handle. Roll to a ¼-inch (0.6 cm) thickness. Cut out shapes with a small cookie cutter or by tracing around a cardboard shape or simply creating one on the spot. Press a hole in the top with a toothpick for hanging later. Allow to dry flat and harden overnight. After hardening, ornaments may be painted or decorated. They may be glazed, if desired. These will last for years and will become treasured mementoes. Make them for Valentine's Day, Easter, Christmas or any other occasion when you want to create a memory. Great for home, parties, Sunday school and school. Don't forget to sign and date them.

Homemade Soap Bubbles

Just for play—not to be eaten!

Dissolve some fine soap powder in about 2½ cups (625 ml) of warm water. Add 4 tbsp olive oil or vegetable oil and a little food colouring. Shake the solution until the colour is distributed. (Take care to not use ink or any poisonous colouring, which small children may swallow.) Liquid detergents make good bubble solutions for older children.

Soap Bubbles

Just for play—not to be eaten!

¼ cup	dishwashing liquid	50 ml		1 tsp	glycerin	5 ml
1¼ cups	water	300 ml		1 drop	food colouring, any colour	1

Place ingredients in a jar with a tight cover. Stir well or shake slightly. Find a small piece of wire. (Ask your mom or dad for help.) Make a ring with a handle, from which to blow some pretty bubbles.

Finger Paint I

Just for play—not to be eaten!

¼ cup	powdered laundry starch	50 ml		1 cup	water	250 ml

Cook the mixture until clear; then thin with water if necessary. Colour it with bluing, watercolour, tempera or food colouring. Store, covered, in the refrigerator.

Finger Paint II

Just for play—not to be eaten!

1 cup	liquid laundry starch	250 ml		1 tsp	vinegar	5 ml
				1 tbsp	talcum powder	15 ml
1 cup	soap flakes	250 ml				

Place starch over low heat. Add other ingredients and stir until thick. Add colouring. Place in a covered jar. You can buy special paper for finger painting but you may also use wrapping paper. Make sure the piece is quite large, preferably 10x15 inches (23x37.5 cm). Place a blob of paint in the centre of the paper and spread out over the entire surface. Wear an old shirt or apron to protect your clothes. Create your own masterpiece. Put your name and the date on the back of your paintings. Someday, each one will be a treasure.

Cookie Bones: For Dogs Only!

2 cups	whole wheat flour	500 ml		1 tbsp	vegetable oil	15 ml
1 cup	corn meal	250 ml		¾ cup	hot water	175 ml
¼ cup	wheat germ	50 ml		¼ cup	beef or chicken stock	50 ml
½ tsp	garlic	2 ml				
1	egg	1				

Mix together flour, cornmeal, wheat germ and garlic. Add egg, oil, hot water and stock. Stir well. Dust counter or a large cutting board with flour. Roll the dough out to about ½-inch (1 cm) thickness. Cut into shapes—bones, mice, birds, circles or any shape you think your dog would like most. Arrange on a cookie sheet. Bake in the centre of a 275F (140C) oven for about 2 hours. Let cool and stand to dry for about 2 hours. Your dog will love you for your home-cooked treat!

Conversion Tables

About Measurement Conversions

Most cooks are aware of the different systems of measurement that are used in different countries such as: Imperial, U.S. standard, Australian and metric.

However, many may not realize that different methods of measuring ingredients are also used. The most significant difference is whether ingredients are measured by weight (e.g. ounces, pounds, grams, kilograms) or volume (e.g. tablespoons, cups, millilitres, liters). In Canada and the United States cooks usually measure dry and liquid ingredients by volume, while in Europe it is customary to measure dry ingredients by weight and liquid ingredients by volume. To complicate matters even more, many countries use measuring devices with similar or identical names that are in fact different in actual size. For example 1 cup has the following equivalents: U.S. standard = 227.3 millilitres, Imperial = 284 millilitres, and Australian = 250 millilitres.

For the purpose of simplification and the fact that Canadians most commonly use American-made measuring utensils—for example, Pyrex measuring cups—Canadian cookbooks have generally adopted a standard that conforms to the American-made measuring devices using standard increments of measure.

To compensate for the differences between the systems and possible awkward numbers, all metric measurements in this book have been rounded. These rounded numbers conform to standard metric units and measuring utensils. In the case of fluid (liquid) and dry measures, mathematically correct fractional divisions of the standard metric units have not been used in this book. It is important to recognize that the metric measurements have been simplified. Exact metric conversions have been presented in the conversion tables for comparative purposes, and for instances where a cook chooses to use scientific measuring devices.

It is very important to select one system when preparing a recipe. Mixing metric units with standard units within the same recipe could achieve less than perfect results. Similarly, cooks should check their measuring devices to make sure that they are not using both U.S. standard and Imperial measuring devices. Choosing one system or the other should in most cases produce successful results. Selecting one brand name of measuring utensils would be another way to ensure accuracy. Most of the recipes in this cookbook have not been developed or tested using metric measures. When converting recipes to metric, some variation in quality may be noted.

All the recipes in *The Great Nova Scotia Cookbook* use volume measurement for both dry and liquid ingredients. This means that the dry ingredients in this book are not weight measurements. Tables containing volume to weight conversions are not presented in this book because of space limitations.

Metric Conversions from Conventional Measure

Volume Measurement Conversions

Spoons/fluid oz/qt	Standard Metric	Exact Metric
⅛ teaspoon	0.5 millilitre	0.6 millilitres
¼ teaspoon	1 millilitre	1.2 millilitres
½ teaspoon	2 millilitres	2.4 millilitres
¾ teaspoon	3 millilitres	3.5 millilitres
1 teaspoon	5 millilitres	4.7 millilitres
2 teaspoons	10 millilitres	9.4 millilitres
2½ teaspoons	12 millilitres	11.8 millilitres
4½ teaspoons	22 millilitres	21.2 millilitres
1 tablespoon	15 millilitres	14.2 millilitres
1 fl oz (2 tbsp)	30 millilitres	28.4 millilitres
1 quart (32 fl oz)	1 litre (1000 ml)	1136 millilitres

Cups

	Standard Metric	Exact Metric
¼ cup	50 millilitres	56.8 millilitres
⅓ cup	75 millilitres	75.6 millilitres
½ cup	125 millilitres	113.7 millilitres
⅔ cup	150 millilitres	151.2 millilitres
¾ cup	175 millilitres	170.1 millilitres
1 cup	250 millilitres	227.3 millilitres
4 cups (32 fl oz)	1000 millilitres (1 litre)	1136 millilitres

Weight Measurement Conversions

Ounces	Standard Metric	Exact Metric
1 ounce	30 grams	28.3 grams
2 ounces	55 grams	56.7 grams
3 ounces	85 grams	85.0 grams
4 ounces	112 grams	113.4 grams
5 ounces	140 grams	141.7 grams
6 ounces	170 grams	170.1 grams
7 ounces	200 grams	198.4 grams
8 ounces	250 grams	226.8 grams
16 ounces (1 lb)	500 grams (.5 kilogram)	453.6 grams
32 ounces	1000 grams (1 kilogram)	917.2 grams

Pans and Casseroles

8 x 8 inch	=	20 x 20 cm, 2 L	8 x 2 inch round	=	20 x 5 cm, 2 L
9 x 9 inch	=	22 x 22 cm, 2 L	9 x 2 inch round	=	22 x 5 cm, 2.5 L
9 x 13 inch	=	22 x 33 cm, 2 L	10 x 4½ inch tube	=	25 x 11 cm, 5 L
10 x 15 inch	=	25 x 38 cm, 2 L	8 x 4 x 3 inch loaf	=	20 x 10 x 7 cm, 1.5 L
11 x 17 inch	=	28 x 43 cm, 2 L	9 x 5 x 3 inch loaf	=	23 x 12 x 7 cm, 2 L

Temperature Conversions

Fahrenheit	Celsius	Fahrenheit	Celsius	Fahrenheit	Celsius
32 F	0 C	275 F	135 C	400 F	205 C
175 F	80 C	300 F	150 C	425 F	220 C
200 F	100 C	325 F	165 C	450 F	230 C
225 F	110 C	350 F	175 C	475 F	245 C
250 F	120 C	375 F	190 C	500 F	260 C

• INDEX •

RECIPES FOR KIDS 581